The Collected Letters

of Joanna Baillie

The
Collected Letters of
Joanna Baillie

Volume 1

Edited by
JUDITH BAILEY SLAGLE

Madison • Teaneck
Fairleigh Dickinson University Press
London: Associated University Presses

Associated University Presses
440 Forsgate Drive
Cranbury, NJ 08512

Associated University Presses
16 Barter Street
London WC1A 2AH, England

Associated University Presses
P.O. Box 338, Port Credit
Mississauga, Ontario
Canada L5G 4L8

The paper used in this publication meets the requirements of the American National Standard for Permanence of Paper for Printed Library Materials Z39.48-1984.

Library of Congress Cataloging-in-Publication Data

Baillie, Joanna, 1762-1851.
　　[Correspondence. Selections]
　　The collected letters of Joanna Baillie/edited by Judith Bailey Slagle.
　　　　p.　cm.
　　Includes index.
　　ISBN 0-8386-3812-0 (alk. paper)
　　1. Baillie, Joanna, 1762-1851–Correspondence.　2. Women dramatists, Scottish–19th century–Correspondence.　3. Scotland–Intellectual life–19th century.　I. Slagle, Judith Bailey.　II. Title.
PR4056.A83　1999
822'.7–dc21　　　　　　　　　　　　　　　　　　　　　　　　98–36605
　[B]　　　　　　　　　　　　　　　　　　　　　　　　　　　　　　CIP

For

Alice, Beulah, Bonnie, Exie, Frances, Louise, Nancy, Paula, and Sharon

CONTENTS

Volume 1

Volume 2

(Forthcoming from Fairleigh Dickinson University Press)

PREFACE

At a time when scholars have begun to take a new critical look at Scottish playwright Joanna Baillie (1762-1851), it is important that the theoretical studies not dominate to the exclusion of her life story. Baillie's unpublished letters record the development of a remarkable thinker and writer who knew from the beginning of her creative span that writing had become gendered.[1] In an effort to circumvent prejudice, Baillie felt the need to publish her first volume of plays and its introductory theory anonymously in 1798. In the midst of her productive and active life, her letters reveal her struggle as an artist.

As Ellen Donkin records in *Getting into the Act: Women Playwrights in London, 1776-1829*, Joanna Baillie was the victim of the reviewers' double standard, and Lord Byron reflected the dominant ideology of his generation in two of his letters about Baillie. In 1815 he speculated that "Women (saving Joanna Baillie) cannot write tragedy. They haven't the experience of life for it"; and in 1817 he concluded, "When Voltaire was asked why no woman has ever written even a tolerable tragedy, 'Ah (said the Patriarch) the composition of a tragedy requires testicles.' If this be true, Lord knows what Joanna Baillie does--I suppose she borrows them."[2] But Baillie's genius and tenacity came from a much more intellectual source, an imagination cultivated from her youth by caring friends and family and her own curiosity and ambition; and Anne Mellor asserts that Baillie, Barbauld and others upheld a coherent aesthetic theory opposed to theories advanced by their male contemporaries.[3] Surely, tragedy touched Baillie's personal life as it did any man's; she lost two people she cared for deeply long before she was prepared to, her brother Matthew and her closest friend Walter Scott; and she lived to see the demise of almost all of her women companions before her own. And while she contested gender bias in a theatre of intellectuals, she was often unheard. Baillie *did* have the experience of life to know tragedy but displaced it so

---

1. Marjean D. Purinton argues that Baillie critiques gender as a cultural practice rather than as a biological function (see *Romantic Ideology Unmasked: The Mentally Constructed Tyrannies in Dramas of William Wordsworth, Lord Byron, Percy Shelley, and Joanna Baillie* [Newark: University of Delaware Press, 1994]).

2. Qtd. in Ellen Donkin's "Joanna Baillie Vs. The Termites Bellicosus" in *Getting into the Act: Women Playwrights in London, 1776-1829* (London and New York: Routledge, 1995), 178. These letters appear in *Byron's Letters and Journals*, ed. Leslie A. Marchand (Cambridge: Harvard University Press, 1976).

3. Anne K. Mellor, "A Criticism of Their Own: Romantic Women Literary Critics." In *Questioning Romanticism*, ed. John Beer (Baltimore and London: Johns Hopkins University Press, 1995), 29-48.

that her life and work could positively affect generations of friends and writers. Baillie's theoretical writing, explains Catherine Burroughs, was "keenly concerned with the problems the Licensing Act had created" and provides us "with ways of looking critically at the trope and concept of 'the closet' in Romantic theatrical criticism."[4] Jeffrey Cox believes that Baillie is central to a discussion of the Gothic.[5] And as other critics are just beginning to give credence to her significance as a writer, the letters in these two volumes provide their own argument for her relevance.

Methods of Research

I began work on Joanna Baillie in summer 1994 in a National Endowment for the Humanities summer seminar for college teachers held at the London Public Record Office, directed by Professor Paula Backscheider and entitled "Biography and the Use of Biographical Evidence." My proposal for the seminar on biography was to complete research for and write *The Life of Joanna Baillie,* a plan which seemed fairly uncomplicated until my research at various archives began to uncover hundreds of unpublished letters from Baillie to family, literary figures, scientists, religious leaders, artists and friends in England, Scotland and the United States. These letters are a biography in themselves, documenting problems with publishers, soliciting other writers for poems for collections, describing encounters with Wordsworth, Byron and other literary figures, outlining a long relationship with Scott and Berry, consulting with Lady Byron on her marriage and generally placing an active literary woman in the historical and social setting of early to mid-nineteenth-century Britain. My former plan to write a biography became, instead, a project to collect the letters, annotating and explaining what was necessary to make them useful to both eighteenth- and nineteenth-century scholars of British, Scottish and American studies and of women's studies. I returned to England in summer 1995 through an American Philosophical Society grant to collect the letters archived in English repositories and followed with trips to the Houghton Library, the Harry Ransom Humanities Research Center and the Huntington Library for letters there. Finally, I collected the Scottish letters in 1996 through a summer research grant from Middle Tennessee State University and an

---

4. Catherine B. Burroughs, *Closet Stages: Joanna Baillie and the Theater Theory of British Romantic Women Writers* (Philadelphia: University of Pennsylvania Press, 1997), 12.

5. Jeffrey N. Cox, ed., *Seven Gothic Dramas, 1789-1825* (Athens: Ohio University Press 1992), 51.

honorary research fellowship at The University of Edinburgh Institute for Advanced Studies in the Humanities.

This two-volume collection of more than 800 letters represents certainly the vast majority of Baillie's correspondence, although private collectors surely hold some additional letters. It is possible there could be more single letters scattered at various libraries in the U.K. whose holdings are not always catalogued or recorded in London's National Registry of Archives, but I have made my best effort to include *all* the letters in American, British and Scottish repositories and believe this is, in fact, a complete collection. But Baillie herself sometimes makes reference (in a letter to one friend, for example) to a letter she has written to another person; often that letter does not exist in any repository. With the possibility that some letters are missing, I still hold to my title of *The Collected Letters of Joanna Baillie* rather than *Selected Letters*.

The Hunters (Joanna's mother's family) and the Baillies were copious letter writers, and there are literally hundreds of family letters preserved in the libraries of the Royal College of Surgeons of England and the Wellcome Institute for the History of Medicine in London; there are also Hunterian museums attached to both the Royal College of Surgeons of England and the University of Glasgow. Books could be, and have been, written on many members of the Hunter or Baillie family as it existed between 1700 and the mid-1800s. Because of this massive correspondence, I have had to focus *only* on Joanna Baillie's letters, reading letters from the Hunters and other relatives in the process. A never-ending project could evolve in attempting to link the letters from *all* branches of the family, albeit a fascinating one.

The Text

I have made *no* editorial changes to Baillie's letters; spelling is corrected in brackets beside a word only where there might be some confusion for modern readers, or [*sic*] is added beside obvious misspellings. English spellings are not Americanized, and consistently misspelled names and other words are not always noted since they occur so frequently (e.g., discription, Welch, etc.); Baillie uses "i" and "e" interchangeably, and double "l" (e.g., traveller) appears often where American writers most often use a single letter.

Neither have I made punctuation changes, even if the punctuation seems to be incorrect. Baillie often leaves out periods and apostrophes, especially for contractions, and I have not amended her practice. If I have had to guess at a word because of smeared ink, holes in the paper, or simply illegible handwriting, I have made a note to that effect. If she has repeated a word, usually because of a page turn (a catchword), I have repeated the same word in parentheses. A few annotations, especially identifying people, are questionable, but I have also made notes to that effect; friends and neighbors who are not particularly famous for any reason have sometimes been impossible to trace even through county records or census reports. I have used an early unpublished dissertation by Chester Lee Lambertson as a cross reference for my own collection, though Lambertson's collection ends in 1832 and includes letters from only five repositories;[6] this collection contains letters from over 30 repositories and continues to Baillie's death in 1851. If Lambertson's reading of a word[s] is different from mine, I make a note to that effect; for Baillie's handwriting is often *very* difficult to read. Capital letters are not always obvious, but she usually begins days of the week in lower case as she sometimes does months. Lower case and upper case "S" look much the same; and capital "I" and "J" look the same, as do capital "M, "B," and "R." She uses dashes for transitions, almost like paragraph breaks; and spaces in compound words occur fairly consistently. Finally, her use of superscripts is consistent for dates and forms of address (e.g., Jany 4th and M^{rs}); what is not consistent is her use of a line, or sometimes simply a dot, under these superscripts. I have done my best to reproduce what is on the letter with a line under the superscript when indicated in her writing, for I believe her short lines or dots to be meant for underlining, given the trend in letters from others written during this era which adopt the same practice. An interesting note is that, as with most letters punctuated by a quill or other pen's dips into the inkwell, there is often a rhythm similar to the rhythm of speech in these letters, connecting the writing more closely to speaking. The pauses and ebb and flow of ink from dark to light to dark again give the writing a very personal quality not found in the mechanical text of typewriters and computers.

A word about notes–identifications are made for people, literary works, etc., at their first occurrence in the chapter of letters and not repeated at every occurrence within the chapter. This is inconvenient for someone who is reading only particular letters and not the entire chapter, but the notes have become so unwieldy that repetition is not feasible, and the index should provide a more thorough list of citations. A list of friends or people to whom Baillie often refers appears in the introduction of this collection ("Circle of Friends and Acquaintances"), and a chronology appears at the end of the "Introduction." My procedure of putting the letters in chapters to particular correspondents rather than simply

---

6. See "The Letters of Joanna Baillie (1801-1832)." (Ph.D. diss., Harvard University, 1956).

aligning them all chronologically, the custom for editing most letters, might also be inconvenient for some readers; but my purpose is to establish a circle of Baillie's friends, some of whom are women writers about whom we know very little. In reading other published collections of letters, I found it often very disruptive to interrupt correspondence to one person with letters to another, and I believe that in this particular collection continuity often verifies a depth of friendship and mutual interests, especially in the letters to Scott.

I have worked from the original manuscript letters and not from copies and have done my best to be accurate, but having spent three summers and several research grants in the U.K. transcribing into a lap-top computer, I could not justify return trips to reread all the letters; and I realized too late that this was a project deserving more than a single researcher. I have, however, reread as I transcribed each letter, noted words I absolutely could not decipher, and consulted with as many Romanticists, archivists, and Baillie scholars as possible.

The Introduction

The first obstacle in writing about Joanna Baillie, even for a brief introduction to these letters, appears in beginning with her illustrious uncles, her mother Dorothea's brothers, physician William Hunter and surgeon John Hunter. The Hunterian Museum of the Royal College of Surgeons of England holds part of John Hunter's anatomy collection and the library his letters and papers, the Hunterian Museum of the University of Glasgow William Hunter's, while the Wellcome Institute for the History of Medicine in London contains a substantial collection of a variety of Hunter papers (along with a lock of Joanna Baillie's hair); and, of course, there is Hunter Square in the midst of Edinburgh. Among all these fascinating manuscripts and other items are many of Joanna Baillie's letters to family members and friends. Since there are numerous biographies of the Drs. Hunter and a very recent one on Dr. Matthew Baillie, I have noted these and leave the reader to use the detailed information in them at his or her discretion. It is, however, with the Hunters and with her father the Rev. James Baillie that this biographical information must begin. My sources for information on the life of Joanna Baillie herself are limited to Baillie's manuscript letters and to autobiographical papers rather than to published sources or undocumented hearsay; even recent biographical accounts whose authors have not had access to Baillie's letters are not always accurate or documented. Thus this "Introduction" does not aim to be a literary biography but, instead, a brief account of Baillie's life and acquaintances through her unpublished letters. Considerable critical attention is currently being given to Baillie's works, and that, along with these letters, will provide the groundwork for a separate, detailed biography to follow. In the meantime, I hope that the character of this perceptive literary architect and theatre theorist shines through her correspondence herein, a character that has been missing in previous biographical portraits of Joanna Baillie.

ACKNOWLEDGMENTS

I have many people to thank for support of this long research project, not the least of whom are my family and friends. I am grateful to Dr. Nancy Goslee, The University of Tennessee, for initially sparking my interest in Joanna Baillie. I thank the National Endowment for the Humanities (1994 summer seminar award), the American Philosophical Society (1995 summer research grant), and Middle Tennessee State University (1996 summer research grant) for funding, and the University of Edinburgh Institute for Advanced Studies in the Humanities for providing an honorary research fellowship (1996 summer) and a pleasant and creative atmosphere in which to work. I thank Dr. David Lavery, former English department chair at Middle Tennessee State University, for originally suggesting that I submit the project for the NEH summer seminar. I thank research assistant Michael Burgin for his work on annotations to the William Beattie and Andrews Norton letters and, especially, research assistant Patsy Fowler for tedious proofreading and for the introduction and annotations to the Samuel Rogers letters, many of the annotations to the Margaret Holford Hodson letters, and for assistance with archival research in London in summer 1996. I thank Dr. Michael Neth, associate professor at Middle Tennessee State University, for suggestions on many annotations and for scrupulous copy editing and Dr. Theodore Sherman, also at Middle Tennessee State University, for aid with a multitude of questions. My gratitude for outside assistance goes to Professor Amanda Gilroy, coeditor (with Keith Hanley) of *Joanna Baillie: A Selection of Poems and Plays* (Pickering and Chatto, 1998), for answering many questions about Baillie's plays and to Professor Catherine Burroughs (*Closet Stages: Joanna Baillie and the Theater Theory of British Romantic Women Writers*, University of Pennsylvania Press, 1997) for her review and perceptive editorial suggestions. But, particularly, I thank Dr. Paula Backscheider, Pepperell-Philpott Eminent Scholar at Auburn University, for direction and for sharing her knowledge of British repositories from the onset; without her the project would never have begun.

Finally, I owe a great debt to all the archivists and libraries that allowed me to work in their repositories and to publish holdings with permission as follows:

Bodleian Library, University of Oxford
British Library
Brotherton Collection, Leeds University Library
Cambridge University Library

Camden Local Studies and Archives Centre
Courtney Library, Royal Institution of Cornwall
Dartmouth College, Baker Library
Edinburgh University Library
Fitzwilliam Museum, University of Cambridge
Folger Shakespeare Library
Harrowby Mss Trust
Hornby Library, Liverpool City Libraries
Houghton Library, Harvard University
Huntington Library
Keele University Library
Lilly Library, Indiana University
Mitchell Library, Glasgow City Libraries
National Library of Scotland
New York Public Library, Berg and Pforzheimer Collections
Pierpont Morgan Library
Laurence Pollinger Limited, Author's Agent for the Earl of
    Lytton[1]
Harry Ransom Humanities Research Center, University of
    Texas
Robinson Library, University of Newcastle upon Tyne, and Mr.
    Robin Dower
Royal Academy of Art
Royal College of Surgeons of England
Royal Society
John Rylands Research Institute, University of Manchester
Scottish Record Office
Trinity College Cambridge, Master and Fellows
University of Birmingham
University College London
University of Glasgow
University of Nottingham, Hallward Library
University of Reading
Victoria and Albert Museum
Wellcome Institute for the History of Medicine
Dr. Williams's Library
Wisbech & Fenland Museum
Wordsworth Trust, Dove Cottage

---

1. Permission rights for letters in the Lovelace-Byron collection owned by the Earl of Lytton had to be purchased by this editor at an extreme price. Permission rights for letters held by all of the libraries listed here, however, were granted without or with minimal fees.

In addition, I thank The University of Tennessee Hodges Library and many of the English department faculty, the London Public Record Office, the Royal Commission on Historical Manuscripts, the Corporation of London Records Office, Guildhall Library, the Greater London Record Office and History Library, the National Maritime Museum and the University of London Library for allowing me access to their records, information and services.

ABBREVIATIONS

Literary Sources

BMGC	*British Museum General Catalogue of Printed Books to 1955*
DAB	*Dictionary of American Biography*
DLB	*Dictionary of Literary Biography*
DNB	*Dictionary of National Biography*
DPW	*The Dramatic and Poetical Works of Joanna Baillie (1851)*
NUC	*National Union Catalogue Pre 1956 Imprints*
OCEL	*Oxford Companion to English Literature*
OED	*Oxford English Dictionary*
SND	*Scottish National Dictionary*

Archives

BL	British Library
CLS	Camden Local Studies and Archives Centre
EU	Edinburgh University
HL	Huntington Library
HRH	Harry Ransom Humanities Research Center
HU	Harvard University, Houghton Library
ML	Mitchell Library
NLS	National Library of Scotland
NYPL	New York Public Library
OU	Oxford University, Bodleian Library
RA	Royal Academy of Art
RCS	Royal College of Surgeons of England
RS	Royal Society
UCL	University College London
UG	University of Glasgow
UN	University of Nottingham
W I	Wellcome Institute for the History of Medicine

The Collected Letters

of Joanna Baillie

In 1757 Joanna Baillie's father, the Reverend James Baillie (1722-78), married Dorothea Hunter (1721-1806), sister of the famous Hunter physicians of Edinburgh.[1] Their first child, James Baillie, died an infant. Their second child was Agnes Baillie (1760-1861), the next Matthew Baillie (1761-1823) and the last Joanna Baillie (1762-1851), the sister of a twin who died a few hours after their premature delivery on 11 September 1762.[2] The parents had recently moved to the manse of Bothwell in Lanarkshire, Scotland, after the Rev. Baillie had chosen to leave a less desirable position in the parish of Shotts. In a letter dated 22 February 1838 to her nephew William Hunter Baillie (1797-1894), Joanna answers some of his questions about the Baillie descent as it was partially traced by her friend John Richardson:[3]

> General Baillie seems to point out our descent as being from his family and probably by a Brother of Principal Baillie.[4] Your best

---

1. Some important Hunter/Baillie biographies are as follows:
    Franco Crainz, *The Life and Works of Matthew Baillie* (Santa Palomba: PelitiAssociati, 1995).
    J. Dobson, *John Hunter* (Edinburgh and London: Livingstone, 1969).
    J. Kobler, *The Reluctant Surgeon: A Biography of John Hunter* (New York: Doubleday, 1960).
    G. R. Mather, *Two Great Scotsmen, The Brothers William and John Hunter* (Glasgow: James Maclehose & Sons, 1894).
    G. C. Peachey, *A Memoir of William and John Hunter* (Plymouth: William Brendon & Son, 1924).
  2. Although this is commonly recorded genealogical information, I have verified dates, etc., through the genealogical data bank maintained by the Church of Jesus Christ of Latter-Day Saints in their London Public Record Office location during summer 1994.
  3. John Richardson (1780-1864) was a parliamentary solicitor and for 30 years discharged the duties of crown agent for Scotland, reputed as the most learned peerage lawyer of his time. He had literary tastes and in 1821 was introduced to George Crabbe in Joanna Baillie's house; he regularly corresponded with Walter Scott, whose deathbed he attended shortly before Scott's demise. He married Elizabeth Hill, a close friend of Thomas Campbell, in 1811 (*DNB*, XVI:1118-19). Richardson submitted "Song - Her features speak the warmest heart" for Baillie's 1823 *Collection* and in a letter dated 18 January 1842 tells Baillie that "It is, as it has long been, a great pride and gratification to me to have enjoyed your friendship; a few circumstances of my life have afforded me more real pleasure" (NLS Ms 3990, f.41).
  4. Robert Baillie, DD, Principal (i.e., President) of the University of Glasgow (1599-1662) and much connected with public affairs, is identified as Baillie of Jerviston (see *DNB*).

way will be to get the life of Principal Baillie which is published at the beginning of his letters, a work still extant, for he was much connected with public affairs in his days, and see what account is given there of his Father's family. Mr Richardson has ascertained that the first School master of our name in the Parish of Chrighton [Crichton] was called Andrew Baillie, and if there be a Brother Principal Baillie mention'd as bearing the name of Andrew, he is <u>more</u> than probably the man who fled to Holland and on his return became Schoolmaster of Chrighton. Your Grand Father's only Brother was named Andrew. I can think of nothing else to be done and this will not make the descent a certain thing, but, with other corroborating circumstances, pretty near it. —— Our ancestor fled to Holland no doubt on account of his religion and of having been connected with Baillie of Jerviswood, and it is possible that his opinions might not agree in many points with those of his Brother and the Principal & he have little intercourse with one another which may account for my Father never mentioning, as far as I know, any thing of his family or their consanguinity to Principal Baillie. ——— As to making out a genealogy for your little Matthew, you need give yourself little concern, for he will be very well off with the immediate descent that undoubtedly belongs to him, though it would make but a poor figure in a Welch Pedigree. His Father a Gloucester S h^r Squire, Lord of the Manor of Duntisbourn; his Grand father an eminent Court Physician and his Great Grand father a distinguished Scotch Clergyman & Professor of Divinity in the University of Glasgow. Surely this is very respectable, and more than this, though you could trace his direct line to Baliol king of Scotland[5] would do him little good.[6]

Certainly, during the 1830s both Baillie's family and her friend Mary Berry (1763-1852)[7] were encouraging Baillie, already seventy, to leave

---

Jerviston (see *DNB*).

5. There is much confusion about the pedigree of the Baliol family, but at least two were kings of Scotland, namely, John de Baliol (d. 1315) and his son Edward Baliol (d. 1363). Another, John de Baliol (d. 1269), was founder of Balliol College, Oxford (*DNB*, I:981-90).

6. See complete letter MS 5613/60 from the Wellcome Institute for the History of Medicine in chapter "To Family" herein.

7. Mary Berry was probably one of Baillie's earliest friends in London, for Baillie wrote the prologue and epilogue for her *Fashionable Friends*, produced at Drury Lane in 1802. See letters to Mary Berry herein.

them with some type of memoir, along with information about her ancestors. In such an autobiographical manuscript (1831) written at the request of her friend and writer Mary Berry, Joanna relates her earliest memories of childhood,

> The farthest back thing that I can remember is sitting with my Sister on the steps of the s[t]air in Bothwell Manse, repeating after her as loud as I could roar the letters of the Alphabet while she held in her hand a paper on which (on which) was marked in large letters the A B C &c. I was then about 3 years old, and this was, I suppose the very beginning of my education. . . . not being able to read but in a very imperfect manner at the age of eight or nine. . . . I was sent to day-school at Hamilton where my Father was then settled as Clergyman, but even the sight of a book was hateful to me. . . . I was an active stirring child, quick in apprehending & learning any thing else.[8]

In the manuscript "Memoirs Written to please my Nephew William Baillie," Joanna further elaborates,

> My first faint recollections are of Bothwell where I was born and passed the first four years of my life. They are chiefly out of door recollections –– running in the garden and looking at the flowers and seeing pigeons flying in the air or gathered on the round roof of a pigeon house that belonged to the manse and above all an occasional walk to the Clyde with my Sister, when our Nurse-maid put us both into the water to be <u>douket</u>[9] and dance & splash about as we pleased. It is curious enough that remembering these little circumstances pretty vividly, almost every thing that passed within doors are almost entirely lost; and that the important change of going to a new residence – Hamilton is in my mind a blanc altogether. My being sent to the reading-school I dont remember, but well do I remember sitting there on a weary bench day after day working on letters & stories which I did not understand and had no desire to know – the worst or one of the worst scholars in the School. My only bright time was when playing out of doors with other Children –– playing at make-believe grown people or Gentlemen & Ladies, generally in some open cart or wagon that served us for a house. It is such a common

---

8. See RCS manuscript HB.ii.56c.
9. douk or douke: to dive or dip forcibly under water (*SND*).

pastime with Children that it would scarcely be worth while to mention it only that I was so particularly fond of it and my Sister who could read and amused herself with books never entered into it at all. But there was one occupation which we both joined in with equal avidity ––– listening to Ghost stories told us by the sexton of parish who, frequently came to the house of a winter evening and sat by the Kitchen fire. We always, I dont know how, contrived to escape from the parlor when we heard that <u>John Leipen</u>, so he was called, was in the house. His stories excited us much, and as the house we lived in was said to be haunted by the ghost of a man who had in former years hanged himself in the Garret, we became so frighten'd that we durst not go up stairs alone even in broad day light.[10]

Baillie confirms to Berry that ghost stories had a great deal to do with arousing her and Agnes' imaginations, making them fear the dark as children: "My Father & Mother were never aware of the state of our minds in this respect," she explains, "for we durst not acknowledge it lest we should be obliged to be alone & in the dark to get the better of our timidity."[11]

Baillie also recalls one of her first "play-fellows," the only daughter (unidentified) of a nearby farmer, whose house she often visited on winter days; it was in this house that the two girls engaged in make believe and spent many pleasant hours together. Both Joanna and Agnes Baillie were obviously well liked by neighbors and others who knew of the family, for Joanna reports that "when visitors from a distance" came to her father's house and asked that the sisters be allowed to accompany them to local sites and gardens, "it was also a delightful thing," the pictures in nearby palaces opening their imaginations. These visits, along with excursions into the old forest, writes Baillie,

> ... did my fanciful untaught mind much good. ... but into the Town itself I never looked to go except in a Fair-day when the streets were crowded with country people & Lads & Lasses, dressed in

---

10. This comes from the WI MS 5613/68/1-6 which has no address but a note from William Baillie as follows: "This version must not be published or allowed to be read out of the family, May 25, 1860." There does not appear to me any reason for William Baillie's secrecy, for the brief and incomplete memoirs, clearly written in Joanna's hand, only reinforce her powers of imagination even in childhood; I will, however, honor his request and only summarize and provide excerpts from the manuscript.

11. RCS HB.ii.56c.

their holiday gear . . . where the sound of fiddles & dancing gave notice of the merry-making within, to say nothing of the booths with all their tempting treasure. . . .[12]

Joanna and Agnes went away to boarding school in Glasgow in 1772, where, Joanna concedes, she finally developed an interest in books, learning to read before she began school there in order to avoid embarrassment but finding that even though she could read she had no real pleasure in books. It happened, however, that shortly before her venture to boarding school she stumbled on some broken bottles one day, cut her ankle and was required by the doctor to lie upon the sofa for some weeks:

> Agnes, like a kind Sister came to me with books in her hand and coaxed me to try reading some story . . . in this way Oceans [Ossian's] Poems became the first book I ever read of my own good will without being obliged to do it. . . . I then read of my own accord various poetical works & afterwards prose, though I had not pleasure enough in the occupation to sit at it long at a time. What first induced me to read history was the pleasure of reading by my Brother, sitting by his side & doing as he did, my love for him was beyond all the affection I felt for any body else. . . . When the summer was ended, he went to College and I was put to a boarding school at Glasgow. This great change of scene and mingling with so many new companions, quickened my mind & opened my ideas & notions in many respects.[13]

To her surprise, at boarding school Joanna found herself as good a reader as the other young girls, resolving her insecurity somewhat, but her spelling was still imperfect. "This defect has made me all my life an uneasy bad writer of letters," she later wrote in her memoir for Berry, also citing her difficulties in setting verses to memory.

The Baillie family had moved to Glasgow after the Reverend James Baillie's appointment as professor of divinity at the University of Glasgow in December 1775, and he died in Glasgow on 28 April 1778.[14]

---

12. WI MS 5613/68/1-6.

13. WI MS 5613/68/1-6; Matthew Baillie matriculated Glasgow University in 1774 (Crainz, 173).

14. Lucy Aikin writes that Agnes remembered the Rev. James Baillie as an excellent parent; once when Joanna was bitten by a dog thought to be rabid, he sucked the wound at the hazard of his own life. But Aikin also reports that he never gave Joanna a kiss, though she yearned to be caressed as a child (see *Memoirs, Miscellanies*

Being left with only a small inheritance, Dorothea Hunter Baillie and her three children were now supported by the generosity of Dorothea's brother Dr. William Hunter, who provided them a home at Long Calderwood in Scotland; but Matthew Baillie had received a fellowship in Balliol College, Oxford (matriculated 1779), so he left the family home for England and soon became a lecturer in anatomy at William Hunter's medical school in Great Windmill Street, London. Dr. John Hunter was also a prominent London surgeon, but the brothers were reportedly at odds, having had professional differences earlier. A famous argument between the two Hunters over William's supposedly using a discovery of John's without giving proper credit has been made much of, but representatives at the Hunterian Museum, Royal College of Surgeons, believe it has been much exaggerated, for the brothers were still corresponding frequently after this alleged argument around 1751.[15] In a letter to Dr. Andrews Norton, however, Joanna explains that she knew only her uncle John Hunter, never having met her uncle William.[16] That seems accurate, since William was dead when Joanna moved to London around 1784, where both he and John had been since before her birth. There she maintained a close relationship with John Hunter and his wife the poet Anne Home Hunter, as well as with their daughter Agnes, later Lady Campbell.

Shortly after William Hunter died in 1783, Joanna, Agnes and their mother Dorothea moved to London to be with and keep house for Dr. Matthew Baillie. Some time after his marriage in 1791 to Sophia Denman (1771-1845), daughter of Thomas Denman and Elizabeth Brodie, Joanna, Agnes and their mother reportedly moved to Red Lion Hill; the two sisters finally settled together in Hampstead on Dorothea Baillie's death.[17] It

and Letters of the Late Lucy Aikin, ed. Philip Hemery Le Breton [London: Longman, Green, Longman, Roberts, and Green, 1864], 8). Baillie, however, does not mention anything like this in any of her letters.

15. The brothers' correspondence is housed in the Royal College of Surgeons and in the Wellcome Institute for the History of Medicine.

16. See Houghton Library MS Eng 944 (8) to Norton.

17. Discrepancies appear in addresses recorded for Agnes and Joanna after their move from Dr. Baillie's. A December 1801 letter to Anne Millar shows a return address of Hampstead (NLS 9236 ff.3-7). But Guildhall Pamphlet FO 3155 reports they moved to Red Lion Hill with their mother in 1802 and after her death in 1806 settled at Bolton House, Windmill Hill, Hampstead, where they remained the rest of their lives. Letters 11 and 12 to Margaret Holford, however, dispute this: "But it seems to be a season of change - with us, for Agnes & I also are about to quit the house in which we spent 21 years, and my Brother has at last been released from his long attendance at Windsor" (#11, 12 February 1820). The letter following provides a more specific address: "If I were as strong as I have been I would walk to Hendon to see you, for our new house is nearer you than the old one, being on what is called Holly Bush hill & very near the heath, but besides old age a cold & fatigue from

was at her initial move to London around 1784 that Joanna Baillie, then twenty-two, seems to have begun to write seriously; but in an account of her earliest writing inspiration, she tells Mary Berry,

> My Father had a man-servant who was very vain & particular about his dress though at the same time very uncouth . . . . My first verses were composed in ridicule of him and sung by myself & others to a ballad tune to his great mortification & annoyance. . . . he came privately to me, beseeching me not to sing it, and promising in return to give me a ride behind him every time he took my Father's horse to be watered. I consented: he kept his promise; and this was the first reward I received for what might be termed literary labours. . . . my Brother came one day from the Grammar school, some what disturbed by the Master's having enjoined him & some of his boys of his class to compose a few couplets on the seasons, –– My Father saying to him, "tut man! Jack (the name I then went by) could do that.["] I was set to it forthwith and composed a few common-place lines upon the subject, the copy of which has happily been long since lost. . . . However my Mother very sensibly knocked that on the head, by saying to me when I had completed my tenth year, "Remember you are no longer a child and must give up making verses."[18]

After this suggestion, "I followed her advice," says Baillie, "and thought no more at that time & long after, of writing verse." During the years of her teens, however, Baillie began to read plays; "a love for the Drama took hold of me," she writes, "and I began to borrow Play books and to read them with great avidity. . . . The only Dramatic books which my Father's library afforded — a copy of Shakespear with no pictures in it was sadly overlooked & neglected."[19] Joanna relates in her brief autobiography for William Baillie that after her father's election to the Divinity Chair in Glasgow, a gentleman of the town often stayed at the house of her friend Miss Graham and had in his possession a copy of *Bell's Theatre*, with engravings of actors and actresses in stage costumes; this work, certainly more intriguing for a young girl than the unilluminated Shakespeare edition, enhanced her interest in tragedy and comedy.[20]

---

moving &c has made me a very poor creature at present" (#12, 29 March 1820).

18. RCS HB.ii.56c.

19. RCS HB.ii.56c. As was the general practice in the 18th and 19th centuries, Baillie often uses two variant spellings of Shakespeare (Shakespear and Shakespere).

20. *Bell's Edition of Shakespeare's Plays, As they are now performed at the Theatres Royal in London* was published by John Bell in 1774. Each play was

The move to London and Joanna's ability to see "Mrs Siddons and other good Actors in Theatres" increased her love for drama,[21] and one day, Joanna explains,

> . . . seeing a quantity of white paper lying on the floor which from a circumstance needless to mention had been left there . . . it came into my head that one might write something upon it . . . that the <u>something</u> might be a play. The play was written or rather composed while my fingers were employed in sprigging muslin for an apron and afterwards transferred to the paper, and though my Brother did not much like such a bent given to my mind, he bestowed upon it so much hearty & manly praise, that my favorite propensity was fixed for ever. I was just two & twenty when we first came to London and this took place I believe the following summer about 9 months afterwards.[22]

Baillie demonstrates in her memoir to William that it was a great transition from her somewhat retired country home in Scotland to the dark, narrow streets of London, and the move did little to awaken her imagination. She kept her curiosity alive to see places she had read of

---

prefaced by a picture of actors in full costume from a specific scene of the play that followed. Baillie explains further, "I have mentioned Bell's Theatre & Shakespere, but nothing in a dramatic form ever charmed me so much as Milton's Comus which I read (I forget exactly when) a year or two before we left Scotland" (WI MS 5613/68/1-6). She confirms to Berry that when she was about 15,
> . . . having heard a great deal about Milton I thought I must read Paradise Lost, but after going through the two first books, I could not proceed; it was beyond the level of my mind at that time. But when I was about 3 years older I fortunately met with Comus, and read it with so much delight that I took courage and began again to try Paradise; then indeed I did perceive the grandeur, sublimity & beauty of the Poem, and read through it with great admiration & interest, though the many learned allusions & the Theology did often make it heavy, and I could not help wishing that the great Poet had been a less learned man. (RCS HB.ii.56c)

21. About a girlhood theatrical experience in Glasgow, Baillie writes,
    I now beheld a lighted up Theatre with fine painted scenes and gay dressed Gentlemen & Ladies acting a story on the stage, like busy agitated people in their own dwellings and my attention was riveted with delight. It very naturally touched upon my old passion for make-believe, and took possession of me entirely. The play was a singing sentimental comedy not very interesting in itself but the after-piece was one of Foott's Farces. . . . I with my young companions went home with our heads full of it; each repeating all the scraps from it she could possibly remember. (WI MS 5613/68/1-6)
22. RCS HB.ii.56c.

and had seen in pictures, but genuine inspiration came from her aunt by marriage, Anne Home Hunter, the daughter of surgeon Sir Everard Home, who had written several beautiful and popular songs and began to read to Joanna "every new composition as it came from her pen":

> To write as she did was far beyond any attempt of mine, but it turned my thoughts to poetical composition. . . . One dark morning of a dull winter day, standing on the hearth in Windmill Street and looking at the mean dirty houses on the opposite side of the street, the contrast of my situation from the winter scenes of my own country came powerfully to my mind. . . . and with little further deliberation I forthwith set myself to write the "Winter day" in blank verse.[23]

From the British Library, Joanna began to borrow the dramatic works of French poets Corneille, Racine, Voltaire and Molière, later adding the plays of Beaumont and Fletcher and older English dramatists: "However," she elucidates, "I did not find much in our old plays to interest me . . . I proceeded in my work, following simply my own notions of real nature, I began to feel imaginary scenes & Theatrical representation."[24] About this time Baillie published her first work, a volume of *Poems* (1790) which included works later to appear in *Fugitive Verses*, but the volume evidently garnered no attention.[25] Undaunted, she continued to expand her talent, at the same time increasing her circle of literary acquaintances. One was the poet Samuel Rogers, who wrote in his journal in 1791 that Joanna Baillie was "a very pretty woman with a broad Scotch accent" much admired in Hampstead,[26] while her neighborhood friend and writer

---

23. WI MS 5613/68/1-6. "A Winter's Day," later published in Baillie's *Fugitive Verses* (1840, dedicated to Samuel Rogers), begins with,
> The cock, warm roosting 'mid his feather'd mates,
> Now lifts his beak and snuffs the morning air,
> Stretches his neck and claps his heavy wings,
> Gives three hoarse crows, and glad his task is done,
> Low chuckling turns himself upon the roost,
> Then nestles down again into his place.

(*The Dramatic and Poetical Works of Joanna Baillie* [London: Longman, Brown, Green, and Longmans, 1851), 772)

24. WI MS 5613/68/1-6.

25. *Fugitive Verses* was later published by Moxon in 1840 (see Margaret S. Carhart's *The Life and Work of Joanna Baillie* [New Haven: Yale University Press, 1923], 11, though she mistakenly titles this 1790 volume *Fugitive Verses*).

26. Carhart speculates that Rogers and other literary men and women met Baillie in connection with Mrs. John Hunter in the 1790s. It is to Rogers that Joanna's

Lucy Aikin said that "the first thing which drew upon Joanna the admiring notice of Hampstead society was the devoted assiduity of her attention to her mother, then blind as well as aged, whom she attended day and night."[27] Baillie says that once when she was about 27, she occupied her mind with a very singular task:

> . . . I heard a friend of ours, a mathematician, talking one day about squaring the circle as a discovery which had been often attempted but never found out . . . I very simply set my wits to find it out. . . . "But surely" thought I "it will be found in Euclid," so I borrowed from my friend Miss Fordyce, now Lady Bentham, an old copy of Euclid. . . . I went through it by myself as well as I could, though in no very plodding way, being only intent on this one purpose. . . . But my disappointment & mortification may easily be guessed, when on arriving at the apendix [sic] of the book, in a small collection of particular discoveries. . . I found my own discovery . . . proved in a different manner. "So I have mistaken what is meant by squaring the circle" said I very bitterly to myself, and thus ended my mathematical pursuits. I had by this time written Basil & De Monfort and very soon consoled myself for such a wild goose chase. . . .[28]

These dramas were, of course, to appear in volume one of Baillie's three-volume work *A Series of Plays: in which it is attempted to delineate the stronger passions of the mind, each passion being the subject of a tragedy and a comedy*, published anonymously in London in 1798 and including her famous introductory discourse on drama along with the plays *Count Basil*, *The Trial* and *De Monfort*. Subsequent word of her authorship made her company arguably the most sought after in London. Thereafter Baillie's was not the sheltered life some critics have suggested,[29] and Lucy Aikin remembers her, excepting Mrs. Barbauld, as making "by far the deepest impression" on her when they finally met:

---

nephew William sends the first poignant word of her death 23 February 1851 (13).

27. See Guildhall Library Pamphlet FO 2218. Dorothea Hunter Baillie died on 30 September 1806, not 1808 as Carhart states, and was blind for three years before her death (see letter 212c to Lady Davy).

28. RCS HB.ii.56c.

29. For unaccountable reasons, such is suggested both in Carhart's brief biography and P. M. Zall's "The Cool World of Samuel Taylor Coleridge: The Question of Joanna Baillie," *The Wordsworth Circle* XIII:1 (1982): 17-20.

I was a young girl when I first met her at Mrs. Barbauld's, to whom she had become known through her residence at Hampstead, her attendance on Mr. B.'s ministry, and her connection with the Denman family. Her genius had shrouded itself under so thick a veil of silent reserve, that its existence seems scarcely to have been even suspected beyond the domestic circle, when the 'Plays on the Passions' burst on the world. The dedication to Dr. Baillie gave a hint in what quarter the author was to be sought; but the person chiefly suspected was the accomplished widow of his uncle John Hunter. Of Joanna no one dreamt, on the occasion.[30]

Baillie later revealed to her nephew William the sexism she encountered on ultimately confessing authorship:

The first vol of Plays lay for some months at the Booksellers, who had refused to publish them at his own risk and cared very little about its success, without being called for or noticed, notwithstanding a review of them full of the highest & most liberal praise, published in the first Review for reputation in those days, the writer of it being equally ignorant of the Author. . . . None of those literary persons, as far as I know, took any notice of it but Miss Berry, who saw much company at her house and spoke in the highest terms of it to every body. To her zeal in the cause I have always felt myself to be a debtor. Thus, after a time, it got into circulation, became a subject of conversation in the upper circles, and John Kemble through the medium of my book sellers, asked leave to bring out De Monfort at Drury lane.[31] . . .Thus envigorated, without being intoxicated, I began to write Ethwald . . . so passed away the earlier & brightest part of my career, till the feeble success of de Monfort on the stage, and the discovery of the hitherto conceald [sic] Dramatist being not a man of letters but a private Gentlewoman of no mark or likelihood, turned the tide of publing [public] favour, and then influential critics and

---

30. Le Breton, 7.

31. *De Monfort* appeared for eight nights, beginning 29 April 1800, at Drury Lane. Jeffrey N. Cox states that four other Baillie plays were performed without success (*Seven Gothic Dramas, 1789-1825* [Athens: Ohio University Press, 1992], 231); Baillie's *The Family Legend*, however, was a huge success in Edinburgh. Though Scott's insistence put *The Family Legend* on stage, on 29 January 1810 the curtain rose to a packed house in Edinburgh, and the highland play scored a tremendous success for three weeks, followed by a revival of *De Monfort* (see Edgar Johnson's *Sir Walter Scott: The Great Unknown*, 2 vols. [New York: Macmillan, 1970], 223-24).

Reviewers from all quarters North & South, attacked the intention of the work as delineating in each of the Dramas only one passion, and therefore quite unnatural & absurd. . . . the inferences drawn from their <u>own</u> remarks was all that they deigned to lay before their Readers. . . .[32]

Two more volumes, this time bearing the author's name, followed between 1802 and 1812, Volume 2 containing *The Election, Ethwald* (parts 1 and 2) and *The Second Marriage*; Volume 3, *Orra, The Dream, The Siege* and *The Beacon*.[33] Baillie had met Walter Scott in 1806, and in a letter relating to her friend Fanny Head's translation of Klopstock's *Messiah*, Baillie would later disclose (1826) that a woman writer's gravest mistake was in revealing her identity:

She [Miss Head] would fain have kept her name & sex unknown, i f her friends would have allowed it, and they were not very wise friends who thwarted her on this point. I speak feelingly on this subject like a burnt child. John <u>any-body</u> would have stood higher with the critics than Joanna Baillie. I too was unwisely thwarted on this point.[34]

Nevertheless, Baillie continued in a flourish of creative activity during this period, engaging in a long correspondence with music publisher/historian George Thomson in 1804 and contributing literally dozens of lyrics for his Scottish, Welsh and Irish collections (in all, eleven volumes, culminated by a royal octavo edition of six volumes in 1822) which appeared over two decades. In 1804 Baillie's volume of *Miscellaneous Plays* (London: Longman, Hurst, Rees, and Orme) also appeared, containing *Rayner, The Country Inn* and *Constantine Paleologus*, followed by historical verses entitled *Metrical Legends of Exalted Characters* (1821), a work greatly influenced by her friendship with Scott and admiration of his historical romances:[35]

---

32. WI MS 5613/68/1-6. One such attack came from the *Edinburgh Review*'s Francis Jeffrey. See both William D. Brewer's "Joanna Baillie and Lord Byron," *KSJ* XLIV (1995): 165-81) and Ellen Donkin's "Joanna Baillie *vs.* the Termites Bellicosus" in *Getting Into the Act* (London and New York: Routledge) for details on Byron's help with reviving *De Monfort* and suppositions about Baillie's failure on the stage.

33. Many of the plays contained in the 3-volume work were also published as single edition copies.

34. See NLS letter 3903 ff.131-33 to Scott (13 October 1826).

35. The admiration was mutual, and they remained friends until his death. Much of Scott's voluminous correspondence is to Baillie, and he also sent her several gifts,

In the great & deserved sensation of admiration excited by the Poems of Walter Scott, a few years later, I had my share, and the generous encouragement I always received from him was certainly of great use in keeping me to my work. The fascination of his heroic Ballads made the drama less interesting for a time and then an idea of Metrical Legends of exalted Characters, in which there should be no mixter [sic] of fiction in the events . . . first came into my head. . . . You know that I have been in Switzerland and have seen objects there which you would naturally expect me to notice but during the short time I was in that sublime region, my mind was occupied with anxious thoughts, and . . . I carried nothing home with me to add to the indwelling treasures of my heart. . . . I did not carry home with me what I might have done under different circumstances. The clouds seen in my youthful days floating across Benlomon[d] . . . as seen from the high lands of Longcalderwood, were my chief store of mountain-Ideas and continued so through life.[36]

Certainly, her close collaborative relationship with Scott, to whom she was introduced in 1806 by writer and friend William Sotheby, touched her life and work in various ways. Their exchange of criticism and gifts, along with the unaffected tone in which the two correspond, imparts an intimacy neither shared with other correspondents. Baillie also met the Benthams some time before 1810,[37] William Wordsworth in 1808 and Lord Byron between 1813 and 1815, having become friends with Annabella Milbanke, later Lady Byron, in March 1812.[38] While her relationship

---

including a brooch set with a sacred green pebble from Iona. The brooch appears in the earliest portrait of Baillie, catching the scarf at her neck. She knitted Scott a purse in return and enclosed a lock of hair from the head of Charles I, with the words "Remember" surrounding it (see Guildhall Library Pamphlet FO 2218 and letters to Scott herein).

36. WI MS 5613/68/1-6.

37. Baillie mentions Samuel Bentham, younger brother of Jeremy Bentham, often in her letters. Jeremy Bentham writes on 20 November 1810 that he "dined at the Miss. B.'s who had been to see their brother the Dr at Windsor"; Samuel encourages his uncle on 2 January 1813 that "If you will be so good to come you shall lead down the first dance with Miss Joanna Baillie" (see Stephen Conway, ed., *The Correspondence of Jeremy Bentham* [Oxford: Clarendon, 1994], 8:83 and 300).

38. Baillie describes meeting Wordsworth and Southey in the Lake District in 1808. Wordsworth provided two sonnets, "Not love nor war" and "A volant tribe of bards," for Baillie's 1823 *Collection of Poems*. She writes to Scott in October 1808 about meeting Wordsworth (and Southey) on her visit to the Lakes: "He is a man with

with Wordsworth over the years seems indifferent, her early professional relationship with Byron was quite intense, ended only by his abuse of her friend Annabella. Even afterwards, it is primarily Byron's poetry that Baillie reads and criticizes in her letters to Scott, *not* Wordsworth's poetry.[39]

While Baillie's fascination with Scott's historical romances and with the sublime in nature influenced her dramatic works, much of her later creativity was also directed toward poetry and "charitable" editing.[40] In 1822, soliciting unpublished works from her author friends, she proposed to edit a volume of poetry for the benefit of a needy friend, Mrs. James Stirling, and to call it *A Collection of Poems, Chiefly Manuscript, and from Living Authors* (London: Longman, Hurst, Rees, Orme, and Brown, 1823). Most of her letters from 1822-23 refer to this edition, which contained poems by Walter Scott, Thomas Campbell, Agnes Hunter, Robert Southey, William Wordsworth, George Crabbe, Anna Laetitia Barbauld, Samuel Rogers, Felicia Hemans, Anna Maria Porter, Anne Grant of Laggan, Baillie and many others, earning well over £2,000 with its subscription. Baillie's letters throughout this task reveal her good business sense, tenacity, critical perceptiveness and tactful editing, for she had no compunction about sending bad poetry back for revision. This enthusiastic period was dampened, however, by the unexpected death of her brother Matthew on 23 September 1823, from which her spirits never seem to have recovered entirely. And because of her longevity, she witnessed the deaths of most of her closest friends and many family members; a major blow also came with the death of Sir Walter Scott in 1832. In one of Scott's last visits to London (1828), he recorded a meeting with his old friend:

> Breakfasted with Joanna Baillie and found that gifted person extremely well and in the display of all her native knowledge of character and benevolence. She looks much more aged however. I would give as much to have a capital picture of her as for any

good strong abilities and a great power of words, but I fear there is that soreness in regard to the world & severity in his notions of mankind growing upon him that will prevent him from being so happy as he deserves to be, for he is I understand a very worthy man" (NLS Scott letter 3877, f. 158-61).

39. See Brewer's (165-181) excellent account of this relationship and its effect on Byron.

40. Meanwhile, *Constantine Paleologus* had been performed in Edinburgh in 1820, and *De Monfort* had been brought out by Kean at Drury Lane in November 1821 (see letters 14 and 20 to Margaret Holford Hodson, Volume 2).

portrait in the world. She gave me a Manuscript play to read upon Witchcraft.[41]

Nevertheless, her interest in religious dogma (*A View of the General Tenour of the New Testament Regarding the Nature and Dignity of Jesus Christ*, 1831) and literary enterprises continued, including major British and American editions of *Dramas* (3 vols.) in 1836, *Fugitive Verses* in 1840, *Ahalya Baee: A Poem* in 1849, and *The Dramatic and Poetical Works of Joanna Baillie* in 1851, the last volume (composed specifically for her heirs) over which she had control.

While Joanna Baillie was realistic about the plight of a single woman in nineteenth-century Britain, she chose to remain unmarried. When in 1806 her friend Mary Berry was pursued by a certain "Gentleman of Yorkshire," Baillie advised,

> You wish for employment, and you wish to be useful in the world: as the Wife of a man of fortune you will have this much more in your power than you are ever likely to have by remaining single. . . . This is enough in the mean time to set you thinking upon it seriously which is all I want. — Now in what I am saying to you I am most disinterested, for every single woman, who is to remain so, has great pride in seeing such a woman as you of her Sister hood, and cannot possibly see you quitting the ranks but with considerable regret.[42]

For the single Joanna Baillie a constant source of pleasure came not only from friends, writers and frequent visitors to Hampstead, but from her immediate family. Joanna's brother Dr. Matthew Baillie had become a prominent London physician and one of the court physicians to George III, attending him during many years of illness; he was well paid for his services, his accounts showing that from 1813-1820 he received £23,327 from His Majesty.[43] Matthew was requested to be present for the birth of Princess Charlotte's child, George IV's grandson and heir to the throne; and as he arrived reluctantly, he spent the day in the library, reportedly not responsible for the bungling that caused the death of both mother and son. Before his stay in Gloucestershire, convenient to Windsor, the Baillies

---

41. See Scott's 18 April 1828 entry in W. E. K. Anderson, ed., *The Journal of Sir Walter Scott* (Oxford: Clarendon, 1972), 460. Baillie's play was entitled *Witchcraft: a Tragedy in Prose*. Scott and Baillie met for the last time in the autumn of 1831.

42. See WI MS 5616/64 to Mary Berry dated 25 December 1806.

43. Crainz, 143 (from Mrs. Baillie's account book 1792-1844, property of P. H. Jobson, Esq.).

purchased Duntisbourne House in 1806, first used as a country retreat but later becoming a permanent home which William Baillie would inherit.[44] Matthew Baillie was at Duntisbourne as Queen Caroline lay dying and was implored to go at once to London to attend her. As he had always sympathized with the queen, he set out, later writing his granddaughter that there was nothing he could do for the poor queen, "who died in poverty and unbefriended. 'Nothing Royal about this deathbed except the doctors' was the other doctor's comment."[45] This series of events and illnesses at court is outlined mostly in Joanna Baillie's letters to Walter Scott, in which she exhibits nothing but sympathy and affection for George III during the difficult years of his reign.

Dr. Matthew and Sophia Baillie were the parents of three children, of whom only one, James Baillie (1792-93), did not survive them. Their daughter Elizabeth Margaret Baillie Milligan (1794-1876) and son William Hunter Baillie (1797-1894) are continuous topics of Joanna Baillie's letters, and they appear a very devoted family. Baillie's niece Elizabeth Margaret was from the beginning a favorite of both Joanna and Agnes and was reportedly fond of both music and poetry. She became a companion of Sir Walter Scott's oldest daughter Sophia (later Mrs. John Lockhart) whenever Sophia accompanied him to London. That the Baillie family was at first devastated in 1816 at her desire to marry Capt. Robert Milligan, a mere soldier, is evident in Joanna's letter to Scott in July of that year:

> I know you are truly interested in what concerns my happiness, and I am going to tell you of an event in our family which deeply concerns us all and has one way or another agitated our minds very much for these some months past. My Niece is going to be married; and tho' she has chosen a very worthy young man, whose family we have long known & highly respect, yet our anxiety for her happiness has been very great, perhaps unreasonably so, and I would not live the last April & May over again for a great hire. She is a very clever woman, fond of books and with a mind & taste well cultivated; he is a plain honest Soldier, whose education has been quite neglected and who, dogs & horses & military matter excepted, has little information on any subject. This being the case, you may believe we had all of us many discouraging thoughts in regard to her future happiness, and her poor Mother above all

---

44. Anne Carver, *The Story of Duntisbourne Abbots* (Gloucester: Albert E. Smith, 1966), 27.

45. Carver, 32.

has been very anxious; but the young man himself has behaved under some very trying circumstances and throughout the whole of the affair, with so much sense & delicacy & sweetness of temper & forbearance, that we now, thank God! begin to hope with some confidence that she will really be happy. You will wish them all good I know, when I tell you that he was one of our brave Dragoons at Waterloo, where he was what was called severely wounded. He is to remain in the army, and hopes soon to get into the guards which are never ordered abroad but on actual service. He has a good moderate fortune, and being admirably fitted both in mind & body for a Soldier, it is the best plan. His name is Milligan, and it was a Sister of his, who sat next you when you last dined with us at Hampstead. You may have forgotten her indeed, but she will never forget having sat by you. I believe this same wedding will take place next week. And a thing is to follow this marriage (at least is intended to do so) which I think you will rather be pleased with; a most unlooked for thing I am sure to me. I am going abroad with the new married pair and my Nephew William to spend some weeks & see part of Switzerland & Geneva. . . .[46]

The family's anxiety was understandable, but the couple appear to have been compatible, living most of their lives with their only daughter Sophia Milligan (1817-82) near the coast at Ryde where all the Baillies often visited.

Joanna's nephew William became the Squire of Duntisbourne Abbots in 1823. He had been provided an expensive education at Westminster School and at Oxford and was later called to the Bar. William was clearly attached to his aunts Joanna and Agnes, visiting them frequently (almost every day in their last years) and keeping his own family close to them. He knew a variety of engaging people, many of them friends of Joanna, such as Maria Edgeworth and Sarah Siddons. That he was interested in genealogy is indicated in Joanna's letters to him, and he was responsible for having his great-uncle John Hunter's body moved from the vaults of St. Martin's in the Fields to Westminster Abbey. He was present at the trial of Queen Caroline, whom his uncle Thomas Denman defended, and later acted as Judge's Marshal to him when he advanced to the bench; but apparently William never practiced law, mostly traveling and managing his estates. He married Henrietta Duff, the daughter of a Scottish Minister, in 1835, shortly after being introduced to her at the house of Dr.

---

46. See NLS letter 3887 ff.83-85 to Scott dated 2 July 1816.

Baron in Margaretta Terrace, Cheltenham;[47] Dr. Baron later willed his house to the young couple. William and Henrietta had eight children, but only three outlived their father (William Hunter, Helen Mary Henrietta and Agnes Elizabeth); and when Henrietta died in 1857 at the age of 49, William never remarried.[48]

It is disappointing that no early letters survive in Joanna Baillie's hand (at least I have found none) to afford a clearer picture of her young adult life, but from 1804 to her death the letters transcribed herein provide a clear picture of her life, friends and passions. Consequently, I submit in this introduction more limited biographical information from 1804 on because the letters *are* the life and should be read as such.

Joanna Baillie died in Hampstead on 23 February 1851 at the age of 88. As a fitting end to this brief introduction, I offer the following letter from Joanna's nephew William Baillie to her old friend Samuel Rogers:

> Tuesday Feb.y 23 [1851]
> 4 Upper Harley Street
> My dear Sir
> I cannot bear that you so old a friend of our family & so much attached to my dear Aunts, should hear an event from the newspapers which I am sure will afflict you very much — My dear Aunt Joanna drew her last breath this day. She was much the same yesterday as she has been for sometime, but after being in bed complained of a pain in her back & chest, & sank till this afternoon about four o'clock when all was over. The pain & weariness she suffered were slight & a more placid termination of life could not be. She only ceased to breathe.
> My Aunt Agnes behaved with the utmost firmness & seemed afterwards pretty well. She was in some degree confused, but I trust this was only the consequence of agitation, & a perfectly sleepless night. She took some dinner, & afterwards slept, & I left her sleeping. She was to be conveyed to bed as soon as possible, & D.r Evans was to see her the first thing in the morning.

---

47. John Baron, MD (1789-1851), was a physician who spent much of his life in Cheltenham and a friend of Dr. Matthew Baillie (*DNB*, I:1189).

48. See both Crainz and Carver 34-35, though Carver states incorrectly that only two children survived their father William.

I am sure you will be interested in all these particulars &
remain
>   Dear Sir
>   yrs very truly
>   WHBaillie[49]

Various obituaries followed; below is an excerpt from the newspaper
reprint of *The Living and the Dead*, this copy owned by Dr. Williams's
Library in London (Ms. 8.27) and reprinted on Joanna's death:

> There is something exceedingly striking in the appearance of
> Joanna Baillie. Though she is no longer young, and her features
> have lost the glow and freshness of youth, the rays of beauty still
> linger about her countenance, and over its expression the tyrant has
> had no power. Her face is decidedly tragic, not altogether unlike
> that of Mrs. Siddons -- and capable of pourtraying the strongest
> and deepest emotion. Her air is lofty and reserved; and if there be
> a dash of hauteur in her manner, amounting, at times, almost to
> sternness, there is, on the other hand, something delightfully
> winning in the tone of her deep fine voice. Her eye -- I hesitated
> long before I could decide its hue, and, after all, I am not quite
> certain whether it be dark blue or hazel — has a most melancholy
> expression; though time has not quenched its fire, or bent, in the
> slightest, her erect but attenuated form. She appeared about 50;
> thin, pale, and dressed with a Quakerlike simplicity; and though
> some might be inclined to say she is too conscious of her powers,
> and to quarrel with the precision of her manner, there is much of
> the majesty of a genius about her, and, in person altogether, she is
> one, who once seen, is not easily to be forgotten.

The following obituary from an unidentified newspaper is attached to
a note from Baillie to Sir John Sinclair (Dc.4.101-3) in Edinburgh
University's Special Collections:

> DEATH OF JOANNA BAILLIE. -- We have to announce the
> decease of Joanna Baillie. She was born in 1762, in the manse of
> Bothwell, near Glasgow, of which place her father was minister.
> The works of Joanna Baillie, which appeared anonymously at the
> end of the last century, when a brilliant phalanx of names had

---

49. Ms. 14/55, University College London's Sharpe Collection ("Letters from
Well-Known People").

begun to excite general attention, created as great a sensation as any production of the period, and the impression which was the result of their first appearance was much heightened when, contrary to all expectation, they were found to be the writings of a woman. This impression was still further increased when it was discovered that the authoress was still young, and always led a secluded life. Several of her dramas have been acted. John Kemble and his sister sustained the chief characters of "de Montfort" [*sic*] upon several occasions, and the elder Kean selected the same tragedy for one of his benefit nights. The "Family Legend" obtained a considerable run in Edinburgh, where Sir Walter Scott, the warm friend and great admirer of Joanna Baillie, wrote a prologue to this tragedy, while the author of the "Man of Feeling" contributed the epilogue. The "Separation" and "Henriquez" have in more modern times been acted, but the writings of Joanna Baillie are rather adapted for reading than the stage. Though her fame tended greatly to draw her into society, her life was passed in retirement. It was pure and moral in the highest degree, and was characterised by the most consummate integrity, kindness, and active benevolence. Gentle and unassuming to all, with an unchangeable simplicity of manner and of character, she counted many of the men most celebrated for talent and genius among her friends, nor were those who resorted to her modest home confined to the natives of this country, but many from various parts of Europe, and especially from America, sought introductions to her.

And, also from the Edinburgh University's Special Collections, are excerpts from the 1 March 1851 account of her death in the *London News*:

JOANNA BAILLIE, one of the most eminent female writers and poets that these countries have produced, was a native of Scotland. Her father was the Rev. James Baillie, a clergyman of the Kirk, and, at the time of Joanna's birth, minister of Bothwell parish, near Glasgow; his wife, Joanna's mother, was Dorothea Hunter, sister of the celebrated anatomists William and John Hunter. Joanna Baillie was born in Bothwell Manse, in 1762. Her brother was George the Third's favourite medical adviser, Matthew Baillie, a physician whose name ranks high among those of the distinguished men that have adorned the British annals of medicine: he died in 1823, and his monument is in Westminster Abbey.

Miss Baillie commenced early in life that literary career which was to extend over more than half a century. The first production that stamped her fame was her "Plays on the Passions," one volume of which appeared in 1798; the second volume was published in 1802. Sir Walter Scott was among the ardent admirers of this work. Mentioning in a letter at that time his own "House of Aspen," he says, "the 'Plays of the Passions' have put me entirely out of conceit with my Germanized brat." His esteem of the talents of the author led, in Miss Baillie's case, as in that of Miss Edgeworth and others, to Scott's acquaintance and friendship with the woman. The cordial and agreeable intimacy between Miss Baillie and Scott, which ceased but with the life of the latter, dates from his introduction to her at Hampstead, in 1806, by the translator and poet, Sotheby. . . .

Though Miss Baillie's fame tended greatly to draw her into society, her life was passed in retirement. It was pure and moral in the highest degree, and was characterized by the most consummate integrity, kindness, and active benevolence. . . . Gentle and unassuming to all, with an unchangeable simplicity of manner and of character, she counted many of the most celebrated for talent and genius among her friends; nor were those who resorted to her modest home at Hampstead confined to the natives of this country, but many from various parts of Europe, and especially from America, sought introductions to one whose fame is commensurate with a knowledge of English literature.

To the inexpressible grief of all who knew her, this great poet and excellent woman departed this life on the 23rd ult., at Hampstead, being at the time close on her ninetieth year. In her death passed away, we believe, the last of those maiden authors whose brilliant list includes the names of Edgeworth, Porter, and Moore. . . .

While these eulogies demonstrate praise of a woman who spent much of her active life in the public sphere, a letter written to her friend Miss Anne Millar from a niece provides a look at the private:

NLS 9235 ff.154-154 (No address or postmark)
[1851]
My dear Aunt Millar
    I went over yesterday to enquire after Mrs Agnes. M^{r} & Mrs W. Baillie were with her & they were engaged in reading Mrs Joanna's will written by herself on a folio sheet. M^{rs} WB is

anxious to write herself to tell you in what way you are remembered therefore I will not say more than that with the exception of several legacies, chiefly books, & small articles of jewelry, gifts from distinguished people, she leaves <u>every thing</u> to M<u>rs</u> Agnes.

M<u>r</u> & M<u>rs</u> W.B think it best to make no change in her existence or mode of living, but to leave her at Hampstead with her 3 maids, one of them, they say a superior woman, who manages her mistress judiciously — Her temper, they say, would not allow of her having a lady companion, & they intend to watch over her themselves, & pay her bills once every fortnight or 3 weeks —

I found M<u>rs</u> Agnes in bed, where they say, she is now most comfortable, & where she misses her Sister less than when down in the Drawing Room – She is quite lively & merry occasionally – then sometimes her mind wanders very much & she asks where her Sister is, & why she does not come to look at her the first thing in a morning – & she cries & is very low — Indeed the changes in her spirits, indicate her extreme feebleness & the slenderness of the thread that still holds her life – I cannot believe any one so aged & so worn can live long[50] — She requires either whiskey or brandy & water in small quantities to be administered at short intervals, but suffers very little, or not at all, from any sort of bodily pain —

When I was with her she talked much of Milheugh, & its beauty & dwelt upon the garden, & she took both my hands & said most earnestly "do tell dear Ann Millar that when I can hold my pen steady I shall write her a few lines" — She had been reading the newspaper herself – & all the reading she does, she manages for herself, as she says she does not like to be read to.

M<u>r</u> W. B is intending to write a short life of his Aunt, & keeps himself the key of the cabinet that contains her papers & correspondence – M<u>rs</u> Agnes has a will of her own, but M<u>r</u> W. B is too delicate to speak to her about it, tho' both M<u>rs</u> W. B & I think that considering M<u>rs</u> Agnes present condition, & the servants by whom she is constantly surrounded, it ought to be placed at Coutts' – & not left exposed, or liable to be tampered with — When James comes home I will ask him to advise about it for M<u>r</u> W. B seems to be almost morbidly afraid of the slightest interference, even as to its safe custody —

I hope my dear Aunt Millar these particulars for which you asked will not tend to make you less cheerful – for my part I cannot

---

50. Agnes, in fact, lived much longer, dying 27 April 1861 at the age of 100.

look upon Mrs Joanna's death with any pain – she suffered so little at the last & was spared all the fretfulness & irritation that are frequently the accompaniments of advanced age, that I look upon her departure as a calm & dignified withdrawal from the world which she had enjoyed so much & when the full time was come for her to complete the absolute condition upon which we all hold life. James is not likely to be home for a week but writes word he keeps free from cold – The children are well, & I have reason to be thankful – With best wishes for your ancle [sic] & hoping to hear soon, I remain
> yr affecJ __[51]

Here ends this brief chronicle of playwright and theatre theorist Joanna Baillie, a vibrant woman born into a patriarchal world; her life spanned the second half of the eighteenth century and the first half of the nineteenth. Aside from her twenty-seven plays, seven metrical legends and dozens of poems, her greatest legacy lies in the hundreds of eloquent letters she left from which historians and literary scholars can formulate a sense of the intellectual society emerging with early Romanticism. Hers was a time of social, political and intellectual change, prompted not only by two major revolutions, but also by major shifts in literary style and focus of the imagination on the sublime.[52] Joanna Baillie was a participant in her era, commenting on the salient issues of her time, and not simply a spectator. To conclude as some writers have done that her life was uneventful and her later years pitiable is both uninformed and critically naive; for even Baillie's later letters reveal a tenacious and ambitious woman, receiving visits from friends and family, publishing *Ahalya Baee: a poem* in 1849, and editing her complete works nearly to the time of her death in 1851 at the age of 88.[53] What is pitiable, however, is Baillie's lack of genuine acceptance in a male-dominated literary society which, while it may have accepted her as an accomplished "gentlewoman," marginalized her critical intelligence and afforded her visibility mostly through her relationships with famous men, from her uncles and brother to Sir Walter Scott and onward.

---

51. Signature is unreadable but probably Janet Millar.
52. Jeffrey N. Cox believes Baillie is also central to the Gothic tradition, "because her plays offer a self-conscious examination of some of the fundamental conventions of the Gothic and of their implications for the construction of the feminine" (51).
53. For whatever reason, Carhart states that Baillie's closing years were "pathetic" (66).

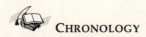 **CHRONOLOGY**

The following chronological table extends from the birth of Joanna Baillie's parents (1721-22) to the death of her nephew William Hunter Baillie (1894) and includes important birth, death and marriage dates along with Baillie's publication dates (in bold) and recorded first meetings with significant writers and friends.[1] The many songs that Baillie wrote for George Thomson are not included individually below (see letters to Thomson).

(Key: JB = Joanna Baillie; b = birth, d = death, m = marriage, p = publication)

1721	26 January	Dorothea Hunter, JB's mother, b
1722	5 August	James Baillie, JB's father, b
1757	7 December	James Baillie m Dorothea Hunter
1759	?	James Baillie, Jr., JB's brother, b
1760	?	James Baillie, Jr., d
1760	24 September	Agnes Baillie, JB's sister, b
1761	27 October	Matthew Baillie, JB's brother, b
1761	2 September	The Rev. James Baillie becomes Minister at Bothwell
1762	**11 September**	**Joanna Baillie b**, her twin dies
1766	23 October	The Rev. James Baillie becomes Minister at Hamilton
1771	9 July	Margaret and Sophia Denman b
1772		JB and Agnes sent to boarding school in Glasgow
1775	19 December	The Rev. James Baillie becomes Prof. of Divinity, Glasgow University
1778	28 April	Prof. James Baillie d
1779	9 April	Matthew Baillie matriculates Balliol College, Oxford
1783	15 March	William Hunter, JB's uncle, d

---

1. In addition to public birth and death records, I have used Crainz's *Life* of Matthew Baillie as a source, though Crainz provides much more detail for events in the life of Matthew (publications, great grand children, etc.) which I exclude here. I have recorded first meetings with significant writers when Baillie records them; but most often I do not have specific dates with which to identify these.

1784		JB, Agnes and their mother move to London to live with Matthew Baillie
1787	?	Robert Milligan, Matthew Baillie's son-in-law, b
1789	3 November	Margaret Denman m Richard Croft
1790		Anonymous *Poems* p in London
1791	5 May	Sophia Denman m Matthew Baillie
1791		JB, Agnes and their mother move to Hampstead
1792	26 September	James Baillie, Matthew Baillie's first child, b
1793	11 January	James Baillie d
		1st ed. of Matthew Baillie's *The Morbid Anatomy* p
1793	16 October	John Hunter, JB's uncle, d
1794	12 February	Elizabeth Margaret Baillie, Matthew Baillie's daughter and JB's niece, b
1797	14 September	William Hunter Baillie, Matthew Baillie's son and JB's nephew, b
1798		Vol. 1 of *A Series of Plays: in which it is attempted to delineate the stronger passions of the mind-- each passion being the subject of a tragedy and a comedy* p anonymously by Cadell & Davies (incl. *Count Basil, The Tryal, De Monfort*)
1799		2nd ed. of Vol. 1 of *A Series of Plays*, etc., p by Cadell & Davies
1798-1800		JB meets Mrs. Siddons and John Kemble
1800	April	*De Monfort* produced at Drury Lane
1800	November	"Epilogue to the Theatrical Representation at Strawberry Hill" p (no imprint)
1802		Vol. 2 of *A Series of Plays: in which it is attempted to delineate the stronger passions*, etc., p by Cadell & Davies (incl. *The*

		Election, Ethwald, pts. 1 & 2, *The Second Marriage*)
1804		*Miscellaneous Plays* p by Longman (incl. *Rayner, The Country Inn, Constantine Paleologus*)
		JB begins to write lyrics for Thomson's Welsh airs
1805		2nd ed. of *Miscellaneous Plays* p by Longman (adding *The Family Legend*)
1806		*Die Leidenschaften* (*A Series of Plays*) p in Amsterdam & Leipzig (also in 1807)
		JB introduced to Walter Scott by Sotheby
1806	30 September	Dorothea Baillie, JB's mother, d
1807		*Ethwald, ein Trauerspiel in fünf Acten* p in Amsterdam
1808	?	Henrietta Duff, Matthew Baillie's daughter-in-law, b
		JB meets Wordsworth
		De Monfort; a tragedy p by Longman
1810	27 October	Matthew Baillie appointed Physician Extraordinary to George III
1810		*The Family Legend* p in Edinburgh (2 editions by Ballantyne) and in New York by Longworths
1810	January	*The Family Legend* produced in Edinburgh
1810-13		JB meets Margaret Holford
1811		*Basil* p in Philadelphia by Carey (again in 1823)
		The Election p in Philadelphia by Carey
		The Tyral p in Philadelphia by Carey
1812		Vol. 3 of *A Series of Plays: in which it is attempted to delineate the stronger passions*, etc., p by Longman (incl. *Orra, The Dream, The Siege, The Beacon*)
		The Beacon p in New York by Longworths

		The Dream p in New York by Longworths
		Orra p in New York by Longworths
		The Siege p in New York by Longworths
		JB meets Anne Isabella Milbanke (later Lady Byron)
		JB sits for Masquerier (portrait hangs in University of Glasgow Special Collections)
1813		JB meets Maria Edgeworth
1813-15		JB meets Lord Byron
1816	11 July	Elizabeth Margaret Baillie m Robert Milligan
1816	22 July	Matthew Baillie appointed Physician in Ordinary to Princess Charlotte Augusta (d November 1817)
1817	4 July	Sophia Milligan b to Elizabeth and Robert Milligan
1818-20		JB meets John Gibson Lockhart
1820		*Constantine Paleologus* performed in Edinburgh
1821		*Metrical Legends of Exalted Characters* p by Longman (2 ed. in 1821)
		New edition of *A Series of Plays* p by Longman
		De Monfort performed at Drury Lane
1823		*A Collection of Poems, Chiefly Manuscript, and from Living Authors* p by Longman
1823	23 September	Matthew Baillie, JB's only brother, d
1826		"A Lesson Intended for the Use of the Hampstead School" p by Miller, Camden Town
		The Martyr p by Longman
1828		*The Bride* p in London by Colburn & Philadelphia by Neal
1830		*Un Mariage du grand monde. Tradiut de l'anglais de Miss Baillie* [or rather the Hon. Caroline Lucy, Lady Scholl], *par*

		Madame***traducteur d'Elisa Rivers, etc., p in Paris
1831		*A View of the General Tenour of the New Testament Regarding the Nature and Dignity of Jesus Christ* p
1832		*The Complete Poetical Works of Joanna Baillie* p in Philadelphia by Carey & Lea, 1st American ed.
		2nd ed. of *A Collection of Poems, Chiefly Manuscript, and from Living Authors* p
		"Lines on the Death of Sir Walter Scott" p
1835	23 June	William Hunter Baillie m Henrietta Duff
1836		*Dramas* p in 3 vols. by Longman
		"Epistles to Literati" p in *Fraser's Magazine*
1836	18 April	Sophia Joanna Baillie b to William & Henrietta Baillie
1837	7 July	Matthew John Baillie b to William & Henrietta Baillie
1838	12 November	William Hunter Baillie, Jr., b to William & Henrietta Baillie
		2nd ed. of *A View of the General Tenour of the New Testament Regarding the Nature and Dignity of Jesus Christ* p
1840		*Fugitive Verses* p by Moxon
1841	21 February	John Baron Baillie b to William & Henrietta Baillie
1842		2nd ed. of *Fugitive Verses* p by Moxon
1843	26 May	Helen Mary Henrietta Baillie b to William & Henrietta Baillie
1845	5 August	Sophia Denman Baillie, JB's sister-in-law, d
1846	23 April	Agnes Elizabeth Baillie b to William & Henrietta Baillie
1847	24 September	Margaret Denman Croft, Sophia Baillie's twin sister, d

1849		*Ahalya Baee: A Poem* p by Spottiswoods & Shaw
1850	27 February	Robert Denman Baillie b to William & Henrietta Baillie
1851		1st ed. of *The Dramatic and Poetical Works of Joanna Baillie* p by Longman, last publication JB oversees (2 more editions follow in late 1851 and 1853)
1851	**23 February**	**Joanna Baillie dies**
1853	25 August	Henrietta Clara Marion Baillie b to William & Heniretta Baillie
1857	3 February	Henrietta Duff Baillie, William Baillie's wife, d
1861	27 April	Agnes Baillie, JB's only sister, d
1875	21 December	Robert Milligan, Matthew Baillie's son-in-law, d
1876	25 June	Margaret Elizabeth Baillie Milligan, JB's niece, d
1894	24 December	William Hunter Baillie, JB's nephew, d

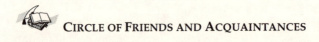

The following people appear in Joanna Baillie's letters more than once. Some people who are only mentioned once, usually with not much significance, are not listed below but do appear in the notes and index to the letters. Biographical entries are shortened here for those friends for whom introductions and entire chapters of letters are included in this collection.

Aikin, Lucy, (1781-1864) daughter of Martha and John Aikin, MD, and niece of Anna Laetitia Aikin Barbauld, was a translator and a writer, an early fictional work being *Lorimer; a Tale* (1814). Her first historical work, *Memoirs of the Court of Queen Elizabeth* (1819), was followed, among other works, by *The Life of Joseph Addison* (1843), written during her residence in Hampstead. She and Joanna became close friends, and her "Recollections of Joanna Baillie" provides an enticing look both at Baillie and at their circle of friends. See *Memoirs, Miscellanies and Letters of the late Lucy Aikin*, ed. Philip Hemery Le Breton (London: Longman, 1864).

Alexander, Chief Baron Sir W., (1767-1816) artist and first keeper of prints and drawings in the British Museum, became a student at the Royal Academy in 1784 and in 1792 proceeded with Lord Macartney's embassy to China as a junior draftsman. Some of his illustrations were published as Sir George Staunton's account of the embassy in 1797, and Alexander himself published *Views of the Headlands, Islands, &c., taken during the voyage to China* in 1798. In 1805 he published a volume of engravings of the Egyptian antiquities in the BM, along with many other sketches throughout his tenure there (*DNB*, I:281).

Alison, Archibald, (1757-1839) was a writer on "taste" and became minister of the Episcopal chapel, Cowgate, Edinburgh, in 1800, where he remained the rest of his life. His sermons were much admired, and two volumes published in 1814-15 went through several editions, and Sir Francis Jeffrey gave an admiring exposition of Alison's theories in the *Edinburgh Review* for May 1811. Alison was married to Dorothea Gregory, daughter of Dr. John Gregory, author of *A Father's Legacy to his Daughters* (*DNB*, I:186-87).

Andre, Major John, (1751-80) was in charge of the secret negotiations with Benedict Arnold concerning the intended betrayal of West Point. He was captured and hanged as a spy, leaving three sisters: Mary Hannah, Anne Marguerite, and Louisa Catherine (see Robert McConnell Hatch, *Major Andre: a Gallant in Spy's Clothing* [Boston: Houghton Mifflin, 1986]).

Baillie, Agnes, (1760-1861) was Joanna Baillie's only sister and constant companion. Dr. Matthew Baillie writes that Agnes Baillie, born in the Manse of Shotts on 24 September 1760, had "a quick ready Understanding, with a good deal of various knowle[d]ge, so as to be much beyond the common level of Women in these respects" (qtd. in Franco Crainz, *The Life and Works of Matthew Baillie* [Santa Polomba: PelitiAssociati, 1995], 10).

Baillie, Lady Grisell, (1665-1746) was the daughter of Sir Patrick Hume of Polworth and Grisell Kerr. She reportedly saved her father's life (under suspicion for participating in the Rye House Plot) by hiding him in the family vault near Redbraes Castle; her father's friend Robert Baillie was hanged, drawn and quartered on the same charge in 1685. The family fled to Utrecht, exiled with other Scottish Presbyterians, and Grisell made a secret voyage back to Scotland to rescue her sister and the family's fortune. At the 1688 revolution she and her mother returned to Britain in the company of the Princess of Orange. She married George Baillie, son of the executed Robert, in 1692, and helped manage his and her father's estates. Her works include *Orpheus Caledonius or a Collection of the Best Scotch Songs set to Music by W. Thomson* (1726) and *The Household Book of Lady Griselle Baillie* (1692-1733) (Janet Todd, ed., *British Women Writers* [New York: Continuum, 1989], 28-29).

Baillie, Dr. James, (1722-78) professor of divinity at the University of Glasgow, married Dorothea Hunter (1721-1806) on 7 December 1757. These were the parents of James Baillie (1759-1760), Agnes Baillie (1760-1861), Dr. Matthew Baillie (1761-1823) and Joanna Baillie (1762-1851).

Baillie, Dr. Matthew, (1761-1823) was the only brother of Joanna and Agnes Baillie. Dr. Baillie had been trained by and had taken over the medical school of his uncle Dr. William Hunter and was a respected physician to George III. He married Sophia Denman, daughter of Dr. Thomas Denman and sister of Lord chief-justice Denman, in 1791 who became one of Joanna's closest friends; their two children were William and Elizabeth. Sophia continued to live at Cavendish Square in London after Matthew's death on 23 September 1823 (see Crainz). To attest to Dr. Baillie's medical prominence, a biography by James Wardrop, Esq., appeared in 1825, just two years after Matthew's death.

Baillie, Sophia Denman, (1771-1845) daughter of Dr. Thomas Denman (1733-1815) and Elizabeth Brodie Denman (1746-1833) and sister of Lord chief-justice Thomas Denman (1779-1854) and Margaret Denman Croft (1771-1838), married Joanna's only brother Dr. Matthew Baillie in 1791 and became one of Joanna's closest friends; Sophia and Matthew's two children were William Hunter Baillie (1797-1894) and Elizabeth Margaret Baillie Milligan (1794-1876) (see Crainz).

Baillie, William Hunter, (1797-1894) the only son of Matthew and Sophia Baillie, graduated from Oxford, married Henrietta Duff in 1835, lived many years in Hampstead, moved to Richmond and later back to Upper Harley Street in Joanna's last years. They were the parents of 8 children: Sophia Joanna (1836-1882), Matthew John (1837-1866), William Hunter (1838-1895), John Baron (1841-1868), Hellen Mary Henrietta (1843-1929), Agnes Elizabeth (1846-1925), Robert Denman (1850-1870) and Henrietta Clara Marion (1853-78).

Baird, George Husband, DD, (1761-1840) was principal of the university of Edinburgh and considered an evangelical rather than a moderate, but family ties put him often into cultivated circles. In 1799 Principal Baird was translated to the new North parish church and in 1801, on the death of Dr. Blair, was appointed his successor in the high parish church where he remained until his death. He was married to the eldest daughter of Thomas Elder, lord provost of Edinburgh. Towards the close of his life, Baird, supported by the General Assembly, gave all his efforts to a project to educate the poor in the highlands and islands of Scotland (*DNB*, I:917-18).

Ballantyne, John, (1774-1821) publisher, was the younger brother of James Ballantyne, printer of Scott's novels. He became a clerk in his brother's printing establishment in 1806. In 1808 Scott, on the apparent ground of a misunderstanding with Constable and Hunter, established the firm of John Ballantyne & Co. with John as manager. In this firm Scott held one half share, while each of the Ballantyne brothers retained one quarter each. When the company failed and almost ruined Scott financially in 1825, Lockhart placed the blame on the Ballantynes but Scott did not (*DNB*, I:1002-3; also see Eric Quayle, *The Ruin of Sir Walter Scott* [London: Rupert Hart-Davis, 1968]).

Barbauld, Anna Laetitia, (1743-1825) was the only daughter of classicist and Nonconformist minister John Aikin and became one of the teachers at the new Dissenting academy in Warrington. In 1774 she married **Rochemont Barbauld**, also a Nonconformist cleric, who took over a congregation in Plasgrave, Suffolk, where ALB took charge of a school for young boys. The Barbaulds traveled in Europe for a while and settled in Hampstead where Barbauld ministered to a congregation and ALB took pupils. Mr. Barbauld was never very stable and died insane in 1808. In 1782-6 ALB, in conjunction with her brother, wrote *Evenings at Home* for her adopted son and in 1804 edited *The Correspondence of Samuel Richardson* in six volumes and *The British Novelists*, in 50 volumes, in 1810, along with *The Female Speaker* (1811), selections of the best British prose and poetry long used in the education of girls (Todd, 37-40). Barbauld contributed "On the King's Illness" and "On Returning a Plant after the Bloom was over" to Baillie's *A Collection of Poems, Chiefly Manuscript* in 1823.

Bartley, George, (1782?-1858) was a comedian born in Bath whose father was box-keeper at the Bath theatre. George acquired stage experience as a youth, appearing at Cheltenham in 1800 as Orlando in *As You Like It*. His London debut was in 1802, though for some time he was apparently employed as an understudy. In 1809-11 he unsuccessfully managed the Glasgow theatre, subsequently acting with increasing reputation as a comedian in Manchester, Liverpool and other locations. In 1814 he married his second wife, Sarah Smith, a successful tragic actress who appeared that same year as Ophelia at Drury Lane while George appeared as Falstaff, thereafter his favorite character. In 1818 the Bartleys made a successful trip to America, and on their return Bartley accepted a winter engagement at Covent Garden. In 1829 when Covent Garden's management collapsed, Bartley headed the actors who came forward with a proposal to furnish funds and recommence performances. The loss of his son at Oxford led to Bartley's retirement from the stage. His only remaining child, a daughter, died shortly afterwards and Mrs. Bartley in 1850. Bartley then appeared as Falstaff at Windsor Castle in a performance arranged by Charles Kean, taking his farewell performance on 18 December 1852 (*DNB*, I:1255-56).

Beattie, William, MD, (1793-1875) distinguished himself at the University of Edinburgh by undertaking the mastership of the parochial school at Cleish, Kinross-shire, taking his MD in 1818. He remained for two years at Edinburgh after taking his degree, teaching, lecturing and translating. During this time he wrote *The Lay of a Graduate, Rosalie,* and *The Swiss Relic*. After moving to London in 1822, he married

Elizabeth Limmer, a lady of some fortune. In 1827 Beattie was admitted as licentiate of the Royal College of Physicians and established himself at "Rose Villa" in Hampstead, where he enjoyed an extensive practice for 18 years. He was a frequent contributor to periodicals, edited the *Scenic Annual*, for which Campbell was to have been responsible, *Beckett's Dramatic Works*, *Lives of Eminent Conservative Statesmen*, *Scotland Illustrated* and later *The Life and Letters of Thomas Campbell* (1849). In 1842 Campbell's *Pilgrim of Glencoe* was dedicated to Beattie in remembrance of a long friendship. Beattie was a friend of Countess of Blessington, Samuel Rogers, and Lady Byron, who reportedly told him the true reason of her separation from the poet (*DNB*, I:25-27). See introduction and letters.

Beaumont, Sir George Howland, (1753-1827) patron of art and a landscape painter himself, married Margaret Willes with whom he cultivated the society of poets and painters. Sir George entered Parliament in 1790 and in 1800 began to rebuild Coleorton Hall where, according to Wordsworth's dedication to his 1815 edition, several of Wordsworth's best pieces were composed. Beaumont knew Dr. Johnson, was a close friend of Sir Joshua Reynolds and helped Coleridge procure his pension. He also befriended Sir Humphrey Davy, Samuel Rogers, Lord Byron and Sir Walter Scott (*DNB*, II:56; also see Felicity Owen and David Blayney Brown, *Collector of Genius: A Life of Sir George Beaumont* [New Haven: Yale University Press, 1988]). Beaumont contributed "Additional Lines to Retaliation" to Baillie's 1823 *A Collection of Poems, Chiefly Manuscript*.

Bell, Sir Charles, (1774-1842) was elected a fellow of the College of Surgeons of Edinburgh in 1799 and moved to London in 1804 where he met Dr. Matthew Baillie. Bell's *Anatomy of Expression* appeared in 1806 and *The Nervous System of the Human Body* in 1830, in addition to many other works on the nervous system. He received the medal of the Royal Society in 1829 for his discoveries and returned to Scotland in 1836 as chair of surgery at the University of Edinburgh (*DNB*, II:154-57).

Bentham, Lady, Sophia Fordyce, married Sir Samuel Bentham (1757-1831) in 1796 but survived him many years. Sir Samuel was a naval architect, engineer and inventor of mechanical contrivances. He was knighted and died in 1831, a year before the death of his brother of Jeremy Bentham (*DNB*, II:281-84). Children Baillie mentions include Sarah (1804-1864) and Mary Sophia (1797-1865).

Berry, Mary, (1763-1852) was a long-time friend of Baillie and one of the first to praise her *A Series of Plays: in which it is attempted to delineate the stronger passions*, etc., in 1799. Berry was also a writer and asked Baillie to provide the prologue to her *Fashionable Friends* in 1801. See introduction and letters

Bigelow, Dr. Jacob, (1787-1879) was an eminent Boston physician and medical writer. He was president of the Massachusetts Medical Society and the American Academy of Arts and Sciences and a member of the Royal Society. Among other medical works, he published *American Medical Botany* (1820), *Nature in Desease* (1854) and a volume of humorous poems entitled *Eolopoesis, American Rejected Addresses* (1855) (see *Appleton's Cyclopaedia of American Biography*, ed. Grant Wilson and John Fiske [New York: Appleton, 1902], 1:260).

Boott, Dr. Francis, MD, (1792-1863) was born in Boston and traveled a great deal between the United States and England. He decided to pursue a doctor's degree at age 28, receiving it in 1824. After practicing successfully for seven years in London, Boott retired and spent the last 35 years of his life in various literary, scientific and classical pursuits (*DNB*, II:854).

Bowles, Rev. William Lisle, (1762-1850) poet and antiquary, is probably best known for his controversial ten volumes on Pope (1806) which drew attacks from Lord Byron (*DNB*, II:977). Included in Baillie's 1823 *Collection* is his poem "The Greenwich Pensioners."

Bowdler, Henrietta Maria, (1754-1830) was author of *Poems and Essays* (1786), *Sermons on the Doctrines and Duties of Christianity*, which appeared anonymously, and *Pen Tamar, or the History of an Old Maid* (posthumously, 1830) (see the unpublished dissertation of Chester Lee Lambertson, "The Letters of Joanna Baillie [1801-1832]" [Ph.D. diss., Harvard University, 1956], cxxv-cc).

de Bruce, Robert, (1274-1329) was crowned king of Scotland after William Wallace's death. Amidst controversy about former ties with England's Edward I, Bruce was finally successful in routing Edward from Scotland (see Agnes Mure Mackenzie, *Robert Bruce, King of Scots* [Edinburgh: Oliver & Boyd, 1956] and G. W. S. Barrow, *Robert Bruce: and the Community of the Realm of Scotland* [Edinburgh: Edinburgh University Press, 1988]).

Brunton, Mary Balfour, (1778-1818) published her first novel *Self-Control* in 1810 and dedicated it to Joanna Baillie, following with *Discipline* in 1814. She died in 1818 after giving birth to a stillborn son, and her husband published her memoirs along with an unfinished story "Emmeline" in 1819 (*DNB*, III:148).

Bulwer, Earle William Henry Lytton, (1801-72) diplomatist and writer, published, in addition to other social and political works, *The Monarchy of the Middle Classes*, to which he prefixed in a Paris edition of 1835 a sympathetic *Life of Lord Byron* (*DNB*, III:263-65).

Bunbury, Sir Henry Edward, (1778-1860) married first (1807) the daughter of General Fox and second (1830) a sister of Sir Charles Napier of Scinde. Henry Bunbury, seventh baronet of Mildenhall and Barton Hall, Suffolk, was a lieutenant-general and author of several historical works, including *Correspondence of Sir Thomas Hanmer, Bart., Speaker of the House of Commons* (1838) and *Narrative of the Campaign in North Holland in 1799* (1849) (*DNB*, III:265-66).

Burns, Robert, (1759-96) was born to tenant farmers and came to know firsthand the ballads, legends and songs of the Scottish peasantry. An apt pupil, Burns read everything he could, his favorite writers being Sterne, Mackenzie and Macpherson. Heavy farm labor in his yearly years instigated the rheumatic heart disease which eventually killed him, but in his short life he contributed some of the most significant Scottish poetry, including, *Poems Chiefly in the Scottish Dialect* (1786), *Tam O'Shanter* (1791) and *Poems* (2 vols., 1793). Using the language of common people, Burns anticipated Wordsworth by nearly 15 years (see Thomas Crawford's *Burns: A*

Study of the Poems and Songs [Stanford: Stanford University Press, 1960]). Baillie clearly reveres Burns and mentions him in several letters.

Byron, Lady, Anne Isabella Milbanke, (1792-1860) married Lord Byron in 1815 and shared a long correspondence with Baillie; see introduction and letters to Lady Byron.

Campbell, Lady, Agnes Hunter, surviving daughter of Dr. John Hunter and Anne Home Hunter and cousin to Baillie, married Sir James Campbell first; after his death, she married Col. Benjamin Charlewood, retaining her title. She had no children.

Campbell, Thomas, (1777-1844) born in Glasgow and educated at Glasgow University, was a friend of Byron, a poet and editor of the *New Monthly Magazine.* Campbell contributed "To the Rainbow" to Baillie's *A Collection of Poems* in 1823. He helped found London University, which he called, "the only important event in his life" (*DNB*, III:844-48).

Carey, Henry Charles, (1793-1879) was an economist and publisher born in Philadelphia. He published for Thomas Carlyle, Washington Irving, and Sir Walter Scott and, before the period of international copyright, insisted on making adequate payment to foreign authors. In the 1830s he turned his attention to the economic writing for which he earned his reputation, publishing his *Essay on the Rate of Wages* in 1835 and *Principles of Political Economy*, 3 vols., in 1837-40 (*DAB*, III:487-89).

Carr, Frances, was the daughter of Thomas Carr, sister-in-law of Dr. Stephen Lushington and Lady Byron's amiable friend and traveling companion.

Carr, Thomas William, and Mrs. Carr of Frognal, Hampstead, were the parents of Thomas, William, Frances, Isabella (Lady Smith), Anna, Laura (Lady Cranworth) and of Sarah Grace (Mrs. Stephen Lushington). Thomas Carr was solicitor to the excise and a close friend of the Benthams.

Chaloner, Louisa, was the daughter of one of Judith Milbanke's oldest friends and was a friend of both Lady Byron and Mary Montgomery.

Channing, William Ellery, (1780-1842) was ordained to the ministry in 1803, pastored the Federal Street Church in Boston from 1805-42, and became a leader in the Unitarian movement by his argument against Calvinism. He organized the Berry Street conference of liberal ministers in 1820 and the American Unitarian Association in 1825. Interested in Jeffersonian politics and in literature, he influenced Emerson and Thoreau, supported abolition, temperance and peace. He authored such works as *Remarks on the Character and Writings of John Milton* (1826), *Analysis of the Life and Character of Napoleon Bonaparte* (1828), *The Importance and Means of a National Literature*, and his *Works* went through 20 editions in England and America. Channing was an intimate friend of Baillie, who kept him up with literary happenings in Britain and reported on the success of his work there. She informed him of Byron's death and later questioned him about "that 'rake' Tom Moore" (see Arthur R. Brown, *A Biography of William Ellery Channing: Always Young for Liberty* [Syracuse, N. Y.: Syracuse University Press, 1956], 161-62). Baillie was particularly impressed with Channing's Dudleian lecture of 1821 on "The Evidences of Christianity" (David P.

Edgell, *William Ellery Channing, An Intellectual Portrait* [Boston: Beacon Press, 1955], 202).

Channing, William Henry, (1810-84) strongly influenced by his uncle William Ellery Channing, spent his life as a reformer and champion of the common man. A Unitarian minister, Channing held posts in Boston, New York City and Rochester, finally replacing James Martineau in Liverpool. Channing was commemorated in Emerson's "Ode, Inscribed to W. H. Channing" (*DLB*, I:24).

Chantrey, Sir Francis Legatt, (1781-1841) sculptor, began earning his reputation with a bust of Dr. John Brown and a statue of George III for Guildhall. He received commissions at once and began to rise steadily to the head of his profession. A long list of credits includes busts of Scott, Wordsworth, James Watt, etc. He actually executed two of Scott, one in 1820 and one in 1828; the earlier one was made a present to Scott with a copy sent to the National Gallery (*DNB*, IV:44-7).

Coleridge, Sara, (1802-52) editor, children's writer and daughter of Samuel Taylor Coleridge and Sara Fricker, married her cousin Henry Nelson Coleridge in 1829 and with him edited her father's unpublished work. For her two children, Edith and Herbert, she developed elaborate games and tales, including *Phantasmion* (1837).

Constable, Archibald, (1774-1827) Scottish publisher, set up his own shop on the north side of High Street, Edinburgh, in 1795 after several years of apprenticeship. His tendency to take risks and accept varied publications enabled him to transform the business of publishing. In 1802 the start of the *Edinburgh Review* saw his connection with Walter Scott, and he had a share with Longman & Co. in the publication of *Lay of the Last Minstrel* (1805). In 1814 the first chapters of *Waverley* were shown to Constable, who detected the author and arranged to publish it by dividing the profits with Scott. On the advice of John Ballantyne, Scott afterwards sometimes deserted Constable for other publishers, but they remained friends. On the failure in 1826 of Hurst, Robinson, & Co., the London agents for Constable & Co., the latter firm became insolvent along with James Ballantyne & Co., consuming the investments of Scott along with them (*DNB*, IV:957-58).

Corbett, Misses, sisters, first published *The Odd Volume* in 1826, following with the novel *The Busy-bodies* in 1827. In 1831 they edited a 2-volume collection entitled *The Sisters' Budget* with works by various authors, including Margaret Hodson's "The Conspirator." The Corbetts' other works included *Tales and Legends* (1828), *Elucidations of Interesting Passages in the Sacred Volume* (1835) and *The oriental Key to the Sacred Scriptures* (1837). Their first names are never mentioned (see *National Union Catalog Pre 1956 Imprints* 122:429 and *British Museum General Catalogue of Printed Books to 1955*, 6:268).

Coxe, Edward, (1784-1814?) a minor poet and friend of Scott, contributed "The Last Leaf" and "On Reading Marmion" to Baillie's 1823 *A Collection of Poems.*

Crabbe, George, (1754-1832) was a parish doctor before deciding to travel to London and pursue a career in writing. He took orders, becoming a curate in 1781, and established himself as a poet with *The Village* and its grim picture of rural poverty. Crabbe met and became friends with Sir Walter Scott. Throughout the

Romantic movement, Crabbe persisted in presenting a precise, realistic vision of rural life and landscape. Byron called him "Nature's sternest painter yet the best," while Scott referred to him as "the English Juvenal" (*OCEL*, 237).

Croft, Elizabeth, was the sister of Sir Richard Croft and a close friend of Sir Thomas Lawrence (*DNB*, V:113).

Croft, Dr. Sir Richard, (1762-1818) married to Sophia Denman Baillie's sister Margaret, was one of the court physicians in attendance at the death of Princess Charlotte and her still-born son in November 1817 (*DNB*, V:113). He committed suicide shortly after.

Cunningham, Allan, (1784-1842) born in Dumfriesshire and married to Jean Walker, was a miscellaneous writer and friend of Scott, producing several works, including, *Remains of Nithsdale and Galloway Song* (1810), drama *Sir Marmaduke Maxwell* (1820), *Traditional Tales of the English and Scottish Peasantry* (1822), and four volumes entitled *The Songs of Scotland, Ancient and Modern* (1825) (*DNB*, V:308-10).

Dacre, Lady, Barbarina Brand, (1768-1854) was a poet, dramatist, translator and sculptor. The third daughter of Admiral Sir Chaloner Ogle, Bart., and Hester, she married Valentine Henry Wilmot in 1789, an officer in the Guards. After Wilmot's death she married Thomas Brand, 21st lord of Dacre, in 1819. Her published works include *Pedarias* (1811), *Ina* (1815), *Translations from the Italian* (1836), etc. (*DNB*, II:1120). Lady Dacre contributed "Stanzas suggested by a Canzone of Petrarch" to Baillie's 1823 *Collection of Poems*. Lord Dacre was appointed arbitrator for Lady Byron on the death of her mother in 1822.

Damer, Anne Seymour, (1749-1828) sculptor, was the only child of Field-marshall Henry Seymour Conway and his wife Lady Caroline Campbell, daughter of the 4th duke of Argyll and widow of Lord Aylesbury. She was a favorite of Horace Walpole and adored by her father. She studied anatomy under Cruikshank and took lessons from Ceracchi. In 1767 she married John Damer, heir to his father Lord Milton's fortune. She was a staunch Whig, met Josephine and Napoleon, and presented the latter with a bust of Fox; he presented her with a diamond snuff-box with his portrait (now in the British Museum). She was a friend of Mary Berry and produced her *Fashionable Friends* at Drury Lane in 1802 to ill reviews. In 1818 she moved to Twickenham, where she brought together a collection of her own busts and terra cottas and her mother's worsted work (*DNB*, V:450-51).

Dana, Richard Henry, Sr., (1787-1879) was a poet and essayist who was born in Cambridge and worked extensively with the *North American Review* (*DAB*, V:59-60).

Davy, Sir Humphrey, (1778-1829) was a natural philosopher with significant discoveries to his credit and a minor poet who became president of the Royal Society in 1820 (*DNB*, V:637-43). On 11 April 1812 he married Mrs. Apreece, the widow of Shuckburgh Ashby Apreece and daughter and heiress of Charles Kerr, the Lady Davy to and about whom Baillie writes.

De Morgan, Sophia Elizabeth, friend of Lady Byron, married mathematics professor Augustus De Morgan (1806-71) in 1837. Professor De Morgan wrote to Lady Byron in 1844 about Ada's mathematical genius (see Mayne's *Life of Lady Byron*).

Denman, Francis, (1812-90) was the niece of Baillie's sister-in-law Sophia Denman Baillie and the daughter of Lord Chief Justice Thomas Denman. In 1846 she married Sir Robert Lambert Baynes (1796-1869), an admiral in the Royal Navy; she is best known for her diaries which are housed in the Wigan Central Public Library (see Cynthia Huff, *British Women's Diaries* [New York: AMS, 1985], 15, and *Dictionary of Canadian Biography* [Toronto: University of Toronto Press, 1976], 9:35).

Denman, Sir George, (1819-96) was the fourth son of Lord Chief Justice Denman and nephew of Sophia Denman Baillie. He was a popular man better known as a scholar than as a lawyer (though he was named to the Queen's Bench), privately publishing several Greek and Latin translations (*DNB Supplement*, I:554).

Denman, Dr. Thomas, (1733-1815) a physician and son of an apothecary, began practicing as a physician at Winchester in 1764. Denman married Elizabeth Brodie (d.1833) and they had a son, Thomas, and twin daughters; Sophia married Matthew Baillie, and the elder Margaret married Dr. Richard Croft (1762-1818), one of the physicians present when Princess Charlotte gave birth to a still-born child (*DNB*, V:808).

Denman, Lord Chief Justice Thomas, (1779-1854) Sophia Denman Baillie's only brother, came to London to study law in 1800 and began his own practice in 1803. He married Theodosia Vevers in 1804, moving to Russell Square, the most fashionable region for leading lawyers. He was an advocate of legal reform, abolition of slavery and was connected with several important trials. Thomas and Theodosia had 5 sons and 6 daughters (*DNB*, V:809).

Dirom, Alexander, (d. 1830) of Dumfriesshire first appears on the Army List as a Lieutenant of the 88th Foot Guards and by 1813 had made lieutenant-general. He was author of *A Narrative of the Campaign in India Which Terminated the War with Tipoo Sultan* (1793) and minor works such as *An Inquiry into the Corn Laws and Corn Trade of Great Britain* (1796) and *Account of the Improvement on the Estate of Mount Annan* (1811) (Lambertson, cxxv-cc, and *DNB*, V:1001). Dirom contributed "Annan Water" to Baillie's 1823 *A Collection of Poems*.

Doyle, Selina, was a friend to both Judith and Annabella Milbanke; she consulted with Annabella on and strongly supported her separation from Byron.

Edgeworth, Maria, (1768-1849) first focused her writing on educational topics, translating Madame de Genlis's *Adèle et Théodore*. She experimented with various teaching methods, publishing a series including *The Parents Assistant* (1796) and *Early Lessons* (1801); but she became well known for her novels *Castle Rackrent* (1800), *Belinda* (1801), *Popular Tales* (1804), *The Modern Griselda* (1805), *Leonora* (1806), the six volume *Tales of Fashionable Life* (1809-12), *Ormond* (1817), *Helen* (1834), etc., many of which document Irish society. Edgeworth is one of the first women novelists "to apply an insight articulated by Wollstonecraft, that women have their own language" (see Todd 204-7). Baillie and Edgeworth met in 1813 (see Scott letter 3884 ff.184-187), forming a close friendship thereafter. Her sisters were Mrs. Beaufort and Mrs. Lestock Wilson.

Ellis, George, (1753-1815) was an author and friend of Scott whose works include *Poetical Tales by Sir Gregory Gander* (1778), *Specimens of Early English Romances in Metre* (1805), some translations and contributions to the *Anti-Jacobin*. Scott often stayed with Ellis at his home at Sunninghill near Ascot (*DNB*, VI:694-95).

Elliott, Anne, of Honiton, Devonshire, visited Baillie often when she was visiting relatives at Fenchurch Street in London, and Baillie often traveled to Devon to see Anne.

Ellison, Mr. and Mrs. Cuthbert, were friends of Lady Byron; Mr. Ellison was one of the trustees of the Byron's marriage settlement.

Elliston, William, (1774-1831) an actor who made his debut at Drury Lane in 1804, became lessee and manager of the theatre from 1819-26, retiring in debt in 1826.

Englefield, Sir Henry Charles, (1752-1822) was an antiquary and scientific writer who was elected a fellow of the Royal Society in 1778 and president of the Society of Antiquaries from 1811-12. He was a friend of William Sotheby and was painted by Lawrence (*DNB*, VI:792-93).

Erskine, William, Lord Kinneder, (1769-1822) became an intimate friend of Scott when the two young men began to study German together in the 1790s. It was Erskine who negotiated for Scott's translation of Bürger's ballad "Lenore" in 1796, helping launch Scott's literary career; and Scott dedicated the 3rd Canto of *Marmion* to Erskine in 1808. Erskine became sheriff depute of Orkney in 1809, and in 1814 Scott accompanied him and other friends on a voyage to the Orkney Islands. Lockhart credits Erskine with the critical estimate of the Waverley novels. In 1822 Erskine was promoted to the bench as Lord Kinneder but died shortly afterward under the stress of having been unjustly accused of "improper liaisons" (see *DNB*, VI:864-65 and Edgar Johnson's *Sir Walter Scott: The Great Unknown*, 2 vols. [New York: Macmillan, 1970]).

Fanshawe, Catharine Maria, (1765-1834) the second of three daughters of John Fanshawe, Esq., Clerk of the Board of green cloth in the household of George III, suffered from ill health, lived with her sisters in Berkley Square for many years and contributed "Epistle to the Earl of Harcourt" and others (anonymously) to Baillie's *Collection of Poems, Chiefly Manuscript, and from Living Authors* in 1823 (see Reading University Library's Longman Collection for Baillie's epitaph, excerpted in note to Montgomery letter 93, ff.187-189).

de Fellenberg, Emanuel, (d. 1844) was responsible for setting up for Switzerland a system of popular education for the working classes founded in the requirements of the nation and capable of independent development; motivated by the idea of training by action, he advanced theory into practice for industrial schools. See Lady Byron's "A History of Industrial Schools" (Mayne, 479-92).

Ferrier, Susan Edmonstone, (1782-1854) Scottish novelist known for satirical sketches on society, published her first novel *Marriage* in 1818 (anonymously), followed by *The Inheritance* in 1824 and *Destiny,* dedicated to Scott, in 1831 (see *DNB*, VI:1255 and *Feminist Companion to Literature,* ed. V. Blain, P. Clements, and I. Grundy [New Haven, CT: Yale University Press, 1990], 368).

Fletcher, Angus, (1799-1862) son of Mrs. Elizabeth Fletcher, gave up a law practice to attend the Royal Academy Schools in 1825, exhibiting at the Academy from 1831 to 1839. His best busts are of the Duke of Argyll (1831), J. B. S. Morritt of Rokeby (1834) and author Charles Dickens (1839), to whom Fletcher reportedly endeared himself. He also exhibited two busts of Felicia Hemans in 1830 and 1832 (Lambertson, cxxv-cc).

Fletcher, Mrs. Elizabeth, (1770-1858) was the wife of Archibald Fletcher and mother of sculptor Angus Fletcher of Edinburgh. Fletcher and Baillie had a great many friends in common, including Susan Ferrier, Sotheby, L. Barbauld and Scott (Lambertson, cxxv-cc).

Fox, Caroline, (1819-71) was a prolific diarist who began keeping a journal at age 16 and continued for more than 30 years. She was a member of the Society of Friends, and her father was a member of the Royal Society. Her journals mention friendships with John Stuart Mill, John Sterling and Thomas Carlyle; acquaintances also included Wordsworth, Tennyson and Hartley Coleridge (see D. L. Hobman, "A Victorian Diarist," *Contemporary Review* 189 [1956]: 41-45, and *The Feminist Companion to Literature in English,* 390).

Freeling, Sir Frances, (1764-1836) was a postal reformer and book collector, elected fellow of the Society of Antiquaries in 1801 (*DNB*, VII:679).

Fry, Elizabeth Gurney, (1780-1845) early feminist and prison reformer, was the sister of Louisa Gurney, who was married to Sir Samuel Hoare (see June Rose, *Elizabeth Fry* [New York: St. Martin's Press, 1980]).

Gilly, William Stephen, (1789-1855) divine, author and canon residentiary of Durham, published works for the betterment of the poor along with *Valdenses, Valdo and Vigilantius; being the articles under these heads in the seventh edition of the Encylopædia Britannica,* 8vo, Edinburgh (1841), the third article reprinted separately in 1844 (*DNB*, VII:1256).

Grahame, James, (1765-1811) was a Scottish poet born in Glasgow. He studied for the church and was admitted to the Society of Writers to the Signet in 1791. In 1809 he was ordained by the Bishop of Norwich and appointed curate of Shipton Moyne, Gloucestershire, but left to attend to family matters in 1810. He was an unsuccessful candidate for St. George's Chapel, Edinburgh, but was later appointed sub-curate of St. Margaret's, Durham, transferring to the curacy of Sedgefield in the same diocese. His poems were admired by Scott and attacked by Byron; works include *The Sabbath* (1804), *Birds of Scotland* (1806), *British Georgics* (1808) and *Poems on the Abolition of the Slave Trade* (1810) (*DNB*, VIII:366).

Grant, Anne, (1755-1838), known as Mrs. Grant of Laggan, was born in Glasgow to Highlander and military careerist Duncan Macvicar and was educated in various countries where her father was stationed. She married Rev. James Grant in 1779, and the couple moved to Laggan in Inverness-shire where Anne ran a farm and integrated herself into the Highland community, learning Gaelic and becoming an authority on folklore. The sudden death of her husband in 1801 left her without income to raise her large family, and she was persuaded by friends to publish a subscription volume entitled *Poems* (1803) for financial means. This was followed by *Letters from the Mountains* (1807), an instant success for its picture of Highland life and Scottish rural traditions. She became a friend of Frances Jeffrey and Scott, who secured her a civil-list pension in 1826. Many works followed: *Memoirs of an American Lady: With Sketches of Manners and Scenery in America* (1808), *Essays on the Superstitions of the Highlanders of Scotland* (1811), *Letters* and *Memoirs*, etc. (Joanne Shattock, *The Oxford Guide to British Women Writers* [Oxford: Oxford University Press, 1993], 188-89). Baillie mentions Mrs. Grant's work in several letters, and both were submitting verses to George Thomson for his songs around 1808.

Hall, Louisa Jane Park, (1802-92) wrote two verse plays, among other works, entitled *Miriam* (1837) and *Hannah, the Mother of Samuel the Prophet and Judge of Israel* (1839) to show that religion is the chief motivating force in life, and both illustrate the importance of women as teachers and examples of faith. *Miriam* is about the love between a Roman governor and a Christian girl ready to die for her faith (see *American Women Writers*, ed. Lina Mainiero, 4 vols. [New York: Ungar, 1980], II:222-23).

Harness, William, (1790-1869) writer and Anglican minister, is best known for his eight volumes *The Dramatic Works of William Shakespeare* (1825), followed by *Literary Remains of Catharine Maria Fanshawe, Life of Mary Russell Mitford*, etc. Intimate friends included Baillie, Lord Byron, Crabbe, Southey, Wordsworth and others of the same circle (*DNB*, VIII:1300 and Lambertson).

Head, Fanny, translated poet Friedrich Gottlieb Klopstock's (1724-1803) *Messiah* (see NLS letter 3903 ff.131-33 to Scott).

Hedge, Mary Ann, has twelve volumes listed in the *British Museum General Catalogue of Printed Books* (Vol. 100), including several children's books published in Colchester between 1819 and 1824: *Samboe: or the African boy* (1823), *Juvenile Poems* (1823) and *The Orphan Sailor-Boy; or Young Arctic voyager* (1824).

Hemans, Felicia, (1795-1835) poet, hymn writer and essayist, published many works, among them, *Poems* (1808), *The Restoration of Works of Art in Italy* (1816), *Modern Greece* (1817), *Hymns for Childhood* (1827), *Records of Women* (1828), *National Lyrics and Songs for Music* (1834), etc. Educated by her mother and tutored by friends, she published her first book of poetry when she was only 15. She married Captain Alfred Hemans, an Irishman serving in the Royal Welsh Fusiliers with her brother, and bore five sons. Her marriage ended after the birth of her fifth son (~1818), possibly because of financial difficulties, and her husband departed for Rome. Hemans continued to publish and tried playwrighting with *Vespers of Palermo*, performed with some success at Covent Garden and Edinburgh, but two other plays were never performed. After the death of her mother in 1827 she moved near Liverpool and then to Dublin in 1831, where she published four books; she met Sir Walter Scott in 1829. Hemans often contributed to the *Edinburgh Monthly Magazine* and *Blackwood's* and is said to owe more to the 18th century for her style than to her contemporaries (see Todd, 327-28). Though Baillie writes to and about Felicia Hemans, they apparently never met (Harvard letter No. 12 dated 1835 to Dr. Andrews Norton); Hemans, however, contributed "Belshazzar's Feast" to Baillie's 1823 *A Collection of Poems.*

Herschel, Caroline Lucretia, (1750-1848) was an astronomer who, though trained as a musician, consistently aided her brother William in his astronomical studies until his death and between 1786 and 1797 discovered eight comets herself. After William's death, Caroline took great interest in her nephew John's career but spent her later years with the German side of the family in Hanover. The Newtonian 7-foot reflector, through which many of her discoveries had been made, was presented to the Royal Astronomical Society in 1840 by Caroline and Sir John. Minor planet No. 281 was named "Lucretia" in her honor in 1889 (*DNB*, IX:711-14).

Herschel, Sir John, (1792-1871) was a friend of Baillie though it is unclear when or where Herschel first met her; it is probable they met through her brother Dr. Matthew Baillie. Herschel must have admired her work, for his journal entry for January 1, 1837, states that he has just "Read Miss Baillie's Martyr" (*Herschel at the Cape: Diaries and Correspondence of Sir John Herschel, 1834-1838*, ed. David S. Evans, *et al* [Austin: University of Texas Press, 1969], 273). It appears from some of the other letters in the Royal Society collection, however, that Herschel might have had a more familiar relationship with Agnes (see *Dictionary of Scientific Biography*, ed. Charles Coulston Gillispie [New York: Charles Scribner's Sons, 1972], VI:323-28).

Herschel, Dr. William, (1738-1822) was an astronomer whose reputation was second to none. Of "fundamental importance to him was his lifelong attempt to provide a third dimension to the stars, in which failure of the double-star method restricted him to inferring distance from brightness," a photometric problem which he solved near the end of his life (Michael A. Hoskin, *William Herschel and the Construction of the Heavens* [New York: W. W. Norton, 1963], 188-89).

Hoare, Samuel, who married Louisa Gurney, was Lady Byron's banker, and Baillie was a close friend of his family. He purchased Hampstead Heath House in 1790 near the Baillies. Children JB mentions include Jane, Joseph and several others.

Hobhouse, John Cam, Baron Broughton, (1786-1869) was a statesman, writer and intimate friend of Lord Byron. His works include *Essay on the Origin and Intention of Sacrifices* (1809), *Imitations and Translations from the Ancient and Modern Classics* (1809), *A Journey through Albania, and other Provinces of Turkey in Europe and Asia* (1813), *A Defence of the People, in reply to Lord Erskine's "Two Defences of the Whigs"* (1819) and *Italy: remarks made in several visits from the year 1816 to 1854* (1859), in which the notes to the 4th canto of *Childe Harold* are "recast and greatly enlarged" (*DNB*, IX:941-42).

Hodson, Margaret Holford, (1778-1852) was the daughter of Allen Holford and writer Margaret Wrench Holford and wife of Rev. Septimus Hodson (m. 1826). Margaret Holford published *Wallace, or the Fight of Falkirk* (1809), *Margaret of Anjou* (1816), *Warbeck of Wolfstein* (1820) and other works. She probably met Baillie between 1810 and 1813 and was a close friend of Robert Southey (see *DNB*, IX:968 and *The Feminist Companion to Literature in English*). See letters in Volume 2.

Hogg, James, (1770-1835) the Ettrick Shepherd, was born at Ettrick, Selkirkshire, becoming a shepherd to Mr. Laidlaw from 1790-1800, whose son William became a friend of Scott. Hogg began to write poetry in 1796, aspiring to be Burns's successor, and through Scott's intervention was published by Constable. Hogg also formed friendships with Wordsworth and Southey and sent a copy of his *The Queen's Wake* to Byron, who recommended it to John Murray. In 1810 he started *The Spy*, a weekly critical journal that was short lived; works include poems *Pilgrims of the Sun* (1815) and *Madoc of the Moor* (1816) and fiction *The Brownie of Bobsbeck and Other Tales* (1817), *Confessions of a Fanatic* (1824), *Queen Hynde* (1826) and others (*DNB*, IX:992-95).

Home, Sir Everard, (1756-1832) was a surgeon, much influenced by Dr. John Hunter, who later became a professor at the College of Surgeons. A blot on his record is that he destroyed many of the Hunter manuscripts on anatomy after having used, some critics argue, some of the information as his own. He was the father of Anne Hunter.

Hope, Charlotte Harriet Jane Lockhart, daughter of John Gibson Lockhart and Sophia Scott, married James Robert Hope on 19 August 1847 and later inherited Abbotsford. Hope was the son of Lady Hope and General the Hon. Sir Alexander Hope of Rankeillour and Lufness.

Howison, William, (*fl.* 1823) was a poet and philosopher who lived in Edinburgh and was a friend of Scott. Publications include *The Robber Polydore, Europe's Likeness to the Human Spirit*, etc. (*DNB*, X:122).

Howitt, Mary, (1799-1888), novelist, nature writer, writer for children, editor and translator, was the second of four children born to strict Quaker parents Samuel and Ann Botham. She married Quaker William Howitt in 1821, and they collaborated on several works. Some of her own publications include *The Seven Temptations* (1834), *Sketches of Natural History* (1834), *Wood Lighten, or a Year in the Country* (1836), *The Heir of West Waylay* (1847) and many others (Todd, 335-37).

Hunter, Anne Home, (1742-1821) writer and oldest daughter of surgeon Everard Home, married Baillie's uncle Dr. John Hunter in 1771. Of her four children, two survived her, son John and daughter Agnes who married Sir James Campbell. Anne Hunter published *Sports of the Genii* (1797) and miscellaneous poems throughout her life, several of which appear in Baillie's 1823 *A Collection of Poems*.

Jameson, Anna, (1794-1860) was an essayist, travel writer and art historian who married lawyer Robert Jameson in 1825 but separated from him in 1837. Seldom living with her husband during the marriage, Anna accompanied her father and friends on many tours through Canada, the Low Countries and Germany. Her circle of friends included Baillie, Lady Byron, Fanny Kemble, Elizabeth Gaskell, and the Brownings; and her many published works include *The Diary of an Ennuyée* (1826), *Memoirs of the Beauties of the Court of Charles II* (1831), *Memoirs of Early Italian Painters* (1845), and the voluminous *Sacred and Legendary Art* (1848-52) (Todd, 351-53).

Jeffrey, Francis, (1773-1850) was a critic-journalist for his generation, producing some 200 review articles on literature and public issues of the day; no journalist was so influential. He was notorious for injuries to Wordsworth, Baillie and their contemporaries but is said to have invented the review article and to have made criticism a profession (see Philip Flynn's *Francis Jeffrey* [Newark, Delaware: University of Delaware Press, 1978]).

Johns, Rev. J., is possibly William Johns (1771-1845), Unitarian minister and author who also proved himself an able teacher. He held church positions mostly in Cheshire and Manchester, where he also opened a school, became a member of the Manchester Literary and Philosophical Society and was joint secretary for many years with John Dalton, a professor of mathematics and natural philosophy at Manchester New College. Johns contributed many papers to the *Monthly Repository* and the *Christian Reformer* (*DNB*, X:892).

Jones, Henry Bence, MD, (1814-73) physician and chemist, received numerous degrees from Cambridge and studied medicine at St. George's Hospital, London. A licentiate of the Royal College of Physicians, he became a fellow of the Royal Society in 1846 and was secretary from 1860 until almost the end of his life. In 1842 he married his cousin Lady Millicent Acheson, daughter of the 2nd Earl of Gosford and produced a large family. Jones published several works on medicine and chemistry, including *Gravel, Calculus, and Gout, the application of Liebig's Physiology to these Diseases* (1842), *The Chemistry of Urine* (1857), *Lectures on Animal Chemistry* (1860) and many others (*DNB*, X:998-99).

Kean, Edmund, (1781-1833) was an actor born into the theatre, where as a young child he reportedly represented Cupid in a ballet of Noverre. In 1795 he ran away from home and shipped as a cabin boy to Madeira but soon returned to London, where he received gratuitous lessons in acting, fencing, etc., from an uncle, an actress at Drury Lane (Miss Tidswell) and D'Egvile. At Drury Lane he played Prince Arthur to Kemble's King John, and it was presumably in 1806 that Kean made his first appearance at Haymarket. Mrs. Siddons found him disagreeable; his roving nature made him somewhat irresponsible, and he feuded with the public and the press. In 1814 he appeared in his memorable role as Shylock, followed by Richard III. Philip Kemble's retirement in 1817 left Kean the undisputed master of the stage. He appeared in several more productions at Drury Lane before his departure to America, some of them adaptations of Scott novels, and was in an "altered" production of *De Monfort* on 27 November 1821. He died at Covent Garden playing Othello on 25 March 1833 (*DNB*, X:1146-53).

Kemble, Fanny, (1809-93) was the daughter of actor Charles Kemble and niece of Sarah Siddons and John Kemble. She debuted as Juliet in *Romeo and Juliet* in Covent Garden in 1829, an immediate success. She later toured both England and America and is known as a writer of *Journal of a Residence on a Georgian Plantation, 1838-39* (see both Margaret Armstrong, *Fanny Kemble, A Passionate Victorian* [New York: Macmillan, 1938] and *Fanny Kemble, Journal of a Young Actress*, ed. Monica Gough [New York: Columbia University Press, 1990]). In his last years Sir Thomas Lawrence took a special interest in the career of Fanny Kemble, for he had supposedly once been in love with her sister Sally Kemble.

Kemble, John Philip, (1757-1823) one of England's most famous actors, began playing parts in his father's company in early childhood. His sister, Sarah Kemble Siddons, first recommended him to the Chamberlain's company as Theodosius in Lee's tragedy in 1776, with dozens of parts to follow. Kemble was a scholar, a man of breeding and a fine actor with a larger range of characters in which he excelled than any English tragedian. He wrote prologues for charitable institutions in York and Leeds, where he appeared for the first time in *Hamlet*--he is said to have written out the part over 40 times. He managed the Edinburgh Theatre for a while in 1781, and his first appearance in London was at Drury Lane as Hamlet in 1783. He remained at Drury Lane for 19 years, presenting over 120 characters himself; and on 25 January 1800 Kemble played De Monfort in Baillie's play. In 1802 he acquired a share of Covent Garden, but in 1808 when the house burned, taking 20 lives, Kemble and other investors were nearly ruined for lack of insurance. A loan of £10,000 from Lord Percy helped him reopen the new Covent Garden Theatre. Portraits of John Kemble abound, several of which are by Sir Thomas Lawrence, notably Kemble as Cato, as Hamlet and as Rolla (*DNB*, X:1260-66).

Lamb, Lady Caroline, (1785-1828) was the daughter of Viscount Duncannon and married the Hon. William Lamb, later Lord Melbourne, in 1805. She had a brief affair with Lord Byron in 1812 which she made the most of publicly with her novel *Glenarvon* in 1816. She separated from her husband briefly in 1813 and finally in 1825 (Doris Langley Moore, *Ada, Countess of Lovelace, Byron's Legitimate Daughter* [London: Murray, 1977], 522).

Lamb, Hon. Mrs. George, lived near Annabella Byron at Esher and was one of the few girlhood friends who survived her (D. Moore, 427-28).

Landseer, Charles, (1799-1879) historical painter, sent his first picture to the Royal Academy, "Dorothea" from *Don Quixote* in 1828. In 1833 he exhibited "Clarissa Harlowe in the Spunging House," now in the National Gallery, and was elected an associate of the Royal Academy in 1837 and keeper of the Royal Academy in 1851 (*DNB*, XI:504-5). His painting of Baillie's De Monfort was commissioned by Lady Byron ca. 1841.

Landor, Walter Savage, (1776-1864) has been described as a "classic writing in a romantic age." He inherited his father's fortune, living independently after 1807, married Julia Thuillier (19 years his junior), and deserted his family to live in Italy between 1815-35, later returning to Bath. His works include *Poems* (1802), *The Citation and Examination of William Shakespeare* (1834), *Pericles and Aspasia* (1836), *The Hellenics* (1847), etc. (see Douglas Bush's *Mythology and the Romantic Tradition in English Poetry* [1937; reprint, New York: W. W. Norton, 1963], 229-64).

Lawrence, Rose, was a writer whose works included *The Last Autumn at a Favourite Residence and other Poems: and recollections of Mrs Hemans* (1836) (see the *British Museum General Catalogue of Printed Books*).

Lee, Hannah Farnham, (1780-1865) married George Lee and published *The Log-cabin, or, The World Before You* in 1844.

Lee, Henry, (1782-1867) and his wife Mary resided in Boston where Henry was a successful merchant and publicist, producing, among other works concerned with trade, *Report of a Committee of the Citizens of Boston and Vicinity, Opposed to a Further Increase of Duties on Importations* (*DAB*, XI:108-9).

Lockhart, John Gibson, (1794-1854) was a satirist and the Tory biographer of Sir Walter Scott. A good classical scholar, his strong literary tastes led him to study German; and he translated F. Schlegel's lectures on the history of literature for Blackwood in 1838, becoming a regular contributor to *Blackwood's Magazine* and attacking the *Edinburgh Review*, the "cockney school of poets," and Coleridge's *Biographia Literaria*. In 1820 Lockhart married Scott's eldest daughter Sophia, and they lived on the Scott estate as intimate members of his domestic circle. In 1825 Murray offered him the editorship of the *Quarterly Review*, and he settled in London's Regent's Park for the remainder of his life. While editing the *Review*, Lockhart wrote his life of Burns, a life of Napoleon, and *The Life of Scott*, a biography surpassed only by Boswell's *Life of Johnson*, in seven volumes (*DNB*, XI:47-49).

Lockier, Misses, were three sisters (two later married as Mrs. Gee and Mrs. Price) who conducted a school for young ladies at Hendon in the 1820s; they were daughters of John and Elizabeth Lockier of Bristol (Lambertson, cxxv-cc).

Longfellow, Henry W., (1807-82) spent much of 1842 traveling abroad, lodging in London for about two weeks with Charles Dickens (see Hilen's *The Letters of Henry Wadsworth Longfellow* [Cambridge: Harvard University Press, 1966]). Longfellow called on Baillie while she was away from home, and, apparently, they never met.

Longman III, Thomas, (1771-1842) published such authors as Wordsworth, Coleridge, Sir Walter Scott and Baillie, carrying on in the publishing tradition of Thomas Longman (1699-1755), who founded the publishing firm which still exists today. After the collapse of Archibald Constable in 1826, the firm became the sole proprietors of the *Edinburgh Review*, of which they had previously owned one half; but by this time the firm had become Longman, Hurst, Rees, Orme, Brown, & Green. Thomas Longman died at Hampstead 29 August 1842 (*OCEL*, 585).

Lovelace, Ada Byron King, Lady Byron's daughter married William, the 8th Lord King, later created Earl of Lovelace, at Fordhook on 8 July 1835. The couple later had three children: Byron Noel (Lord Ockham, b. 1836), Anne Isabella Noel (Baroness Wentworth, b. 1837), and Ralph Gordon Noel (Baron Wentworth, b. 1839).

Lushington, Sarah Grace Carr, (d. 1837) the daughter of Mr. and Mrs. Thomas William Carr, married Stephen Lushington in 1821. **Stephen Lushington** (1782-1873) was one of the attorneys involved in the Byron separation settlement. He was also retained as counsel for Queen Caroline before the House of Lords and made a masterly speech in her defense in October 1820. He was an ardent reformer, supporting the abolition of capital punishment, and an able advocate. The Lushingtons had 5 sons and 5 daughters (*DNB*, XII:291-93).

Macaulay, Thomas Babington, (1800-59) historian and writer, was brought up with his 8 sisters and brothers (one of whom married Lord Chief Justice Thomas Denman's daughter) in an intellectual and political atmosphere which led him to public life in his agitation against slavery. He was a young favorite of writer Hannah More and could recite Scott's *Marmion* by heart when he was 8. He attended Trinity College, Cambridge, making friends with Derwent and Henry Nelson Coleridge, W. M. Praed and Charles Austin; his first article (on Milton) appeared in 1825, and he entered Parliament in 1830. Works include "Pompeii" (1819), *Lays of Ancient Rome* (1842), *Critical and Historical Essays contributed to the Edinburgh Review* (1843) and *The History of England from the Accession of James II*, 5 vols. (1849-61) (*DNB*, XII:410-18).

Mackenzie, Henry, (1745-1831) miscellaneous writer and novelist, was born in Edinburgh. His first sentimental novel entitled *The Man of Feeling* (1771), influenced by Sterne, appeared anonymously and was mistakenly attributed for a while to a Mr. Eccles, a clergyman of Bath. One of the earliest members of the Royal Society of Edinburgh, Mackenzie was a friend of Hume, Dr. Home, Davy and Scott (*DNB*, XII:594-96).

Mallet, Louis/Lewis, descended from a French Huguenot family who had settled in Geneva, was the son of Mallet du Pan, a famous journalist who was forced to flee Paris for England at the start of the French Revolution. Louis was well known to Pitt and through his influence became a clerk in the audit office after 1800. Mallet's wife Frances was the daughter of John Merivale, a respected scholar (*DNB*, XII:871).

Marryat, Frederick, (1792-1848) navy captain and novelist, was elected a fellow of the Royal Society in 1819 and gained his literary reputation for his 3-volume novel *The Naval Officer, or Scenes and Adventures in the Life of Frank Mildmay* (1829), a realistic narrative of naval adventure followed by *Peter Simple* (1834), *The Phantom Ship* (1839) and many others. Marryat spent 1837-38 in Canada and the US, producing *A Diary in America, with remarks on its Institutions*, 3 vols. (1839). His works were quite popular, and Lockhart stated that "in the quiet effectiveness of circumstantial narrative he sometimes approaches old Defoe" (*DNB*, XII:1086-88).

Martineau, Harriet, (1802-76) was a journalist, historian, novelist, autobiographer, travel writer, children's writer and called the "national instructor" for her zeal in popularizing information for the improvement of her compatriots. She began growing deaf in her teens, adopting her famous "ear-trumpet" in 1830. Martineau produced more than 50 books and over 1,600 leaders in the *Daily News* (1851-66), but made her reputation by illustrating the principles of political economy in a series of stories (nine volumes) entitled *Illustrations of Political Economy* (1832-4) (Todd, 452-56).

Masquerier, John James, (1778-1855) was the son of French parents and student of the Royal Academy, joining the studio of John Hoffner around 1796 and painting his friends as well as the famous. He retired to Brighton a wealthy man in 1823 (*DNB*, XIII:1-2). Masquerier's portrait of Joanna Baillie hangs in Special Collections at the University of Glasgow.

Merivale, John Herman, (1779-1844) was a scholar and minor poet, accomplished in classical and romantic literature. He was a friend of Byron, who praised his translations and poetry, and published such works as *Orlando in Roncesvalles* (1814), a 2-volume collection of poems in 1838, and translations of the minor poems of

Schiller. Merivale married Louisa Heath Drury with whom he had 6 children (*DNB*, XIII:281-2).

Milbanke, Sir Ralph, and Judith Noel Milbanke, the parents of Anne Isabella Milbanke (Lady Byron), took the surname Noel by royal license in accordance with terms of his wife's inheritance from her brother, the 2nd Viscount Wentworth.

Millar, Anne, a childhood friend of Joanna and Agnes, was the daughter of John Millar, a professor at the University of Glasgow and colleague of Joanna's father James. John Millar had three daughters; one married Professor James Mylne and the other, probably Helen, Dr. John Thomson (*DNB*, XIII:403).

Milligan, Elizabeth Margaret Baillie, (1794-1876) the only daughter of Matthew and Sophia Denman Baillie, married Capt. Robert Milligan (1781-1875) on 11 July 1816, and the couple, with one daughter Sophia (1817-1882), lived at Ryde on the Isle of Wight for most of Joanna's life.

Milman, Henry Hart, (1796-1868) Dean of St. Paul's and Oxford Professor of Poetry, was the most distinguished ecclesiastical historian of his day and a close friend of Lockhart who said, however, that his friend "ought never to have been a poet." Scott praised his *The Fall of Jerusalem* (1820), but Byron attacked him in *Don Juan*. He married Mary Anne Cockell in 1824, with whom he had 4 sons. Milman contributed regularly to the *Quarterly Review* and produced many literary and historical works, including, *The Martyr of Antioch* (1822), *Belshazzar* (1822), *History of the Jews* (1829) and translations of Horace (*DLB*, 96:236-42).

Mitford, Mary Russell, (1787-1855) essayist, playwright, novelist and poet, is best remembered for *Our Village* (1824-32). Her easy conversational style won her the praise of Charles Lamb; and her most successful play, *Rienzi* (1828), was presented at Drury Lane to considerable public acclaim. Her later years were spent nursing an aged father who had gambled most of the family fortune away, and she suffered from crippling rheumatism but retained a "calmness of mind and clearness of intellect" (Todd, 470-71).

Montgomery, Mary Millicent, grew up under the guardianship of Lady Gosford, a friend of Judith Milbanke, and later became Annabella's (Lady Byron) closest friend, spending a great deal of time at Seaham. Though she spent much of her life as an invalid, Montgomery outlived Annabella.

Moore, Thomas, (1779-1852) Irish poet, is remembered today mostly for his Irish songs and for his friendship with Lord Byron. Works include *A Selection of Irish Melodies* (1808-34), set to music by Sir John Sevenson, and *History of Ireland* (1835-46). Moore and Francis Jeffrey almost engaged in a duel in 1806, but no shots were fired, and the two later became close friends (*DNB*, XIII:828). Baillie mentions Moore several times but does not seem to have been a friend.

Morgan, Lady, neé Sydney Owenson, (ca. 1778-1859) was a prolific writer of novels, poetry, biography and memoirs. She managed never to reveal her true age and at her death was receiving a Civil List pension of £300 (*OCEL*, 668; also see D. J. O'Donaghue, *The Poets of Ireland* [New York: Johnson Reprint Corporation, 1976]).

Morritt, John Bacon Sawrey, (1772?-1843), traveler and classical scholar, visited Scott in 1808, 1816 and 1829. Their friendship was never broken. Returning from London in 1809, Scott spent a fortnight at Rokeby, Morritt's estate, and described it as one of the most enviable places he had seen; in 1811 he discussed with Morritt his intention to make it the setting of his poem of the same name. Morritt was an occasional contributor to the *Quarterly Review* and produced such works as *The Curse of Moy, A Highland Tale* (a poem), "History and Principles of Antient Sculpture" (essay), and *Miscellaneous Translations and Imitations of the Minor Greek Poets* (volume) (*DNB*, XIII:1009-10).

Norton, Dr. Andrews, (1786-1853) was a literary and Biblical scholar and Harvard divinity professor, who carried on a long correspondence with Baillie and was instrumental in promoting interest in her works in America. See introduction and letters.

O'Neill, Elizabeth, (1791-1872) later Lady Elizabeth Becher, played Ellen in a Dublin version of *Lady of the Lake* and debuted as Shakespeare's Juliet in Covent Garden in 1814; though she took some comic roles, she excelled at tragedy but left the stage in 1819 when she married an Irish MP (*DNB*, II:74-5).

Paley, William, (1743-1805) was a principal proponent of theological utilitarianism. In his *Natural Theology* (1802) he attempts to show proof of the existence of God in natural phenomena, particularly in the mechanisms of the human body. In this work he introduced the celebrated analogy of an abandoned watch found upon a heath. Just as "the watch must have had a maker," so must the natural world (*OCEL*, 731).

Park, John Ranicar, (1778-1847) theologian and surgeon and only son of surgeon Henry Park, was born in Liverpool and later educated at Jesus College, Cambridge, receiving an MD in 1818. He was made a fellow of The Royal College of Surgeons in 1819 and was also a fellow of the Linnean Society. His professional works include *Inquiry into the Laws of Animal Life* (1812) and *The Pathology of Fever* (1822). But his subsequent works, the ones Baillie alludes to in the letters to Dr. Norton, were theological and included *Views of Prophecy and the Millennium* and *Concise Exposition of the Apocalypse* in 1823, *The Apocalypse Explained* in 1832, *An Amicable Controversy with a Jewish Rabbi on the Messiah's Coming* in 1832, and *An Answer to Anti-Supernaturalism* in 1844 (*DNB*, XV:218).

Porter, Jane, (1776-1850) was a childhood friend of Walter Scott in Edinburgh but moved to London in 1803 where she met Hannah More and Mrs. Barbauld. Her works include romance *Thaddeus of Warsaw* (4 vols., 1804), the successful novel *The Scottish Chiefs* (5 vols., 1810), drama *Switzerland*, acted at Drury Lane in 1819, *Sir Edward Seaward's Narrative of his Shipwreck and consequent Discovery of certain Islands in the Caribbean Sea* (3 vols., 1831), etc. Baillie acknowledged her indebtedness to Porter's *Scottish Chiefs* when writing her *Wallace* for *Metrical Legends*, and Scott, given credit for developing the historical novel, might surely be indebted to Porter as well (*DNB*, XVI:182-84).

Quillinan, Dora Wordsworth, (1804-47) William Wordsworth's oldest daughter, became the wife of widower **Edward Quillinan** at the home of Isabella Fenwick on 11 May 1841 against her father's wishes. All were later reconciled, and Dora died of tuberculosis in July 1847, an insupportable loss for her father (see Stephen Gill, *William Wordsworth: A Life* [Oxford: Clarendon, 1989]).

Richardson, John, (1780-1864) was a parliamentary solicitor and for 30 years discharged the duties of crown agent for Scotland, reputed as the most learned peerage lawyer of his time. He had literary tastes and in 1821 was introduced to George Crabbe in Joanna Baillie's house; he regularly corresponded with Walter Scott, whose deathbed he attended shortly before Scott's demise. He married Elizabeth Hill, a close friend of Thomas Campbell, in 1811 and had several children (*DNB*, XVI:1118-19). Richardson submitted "Song - Her features speak the warmest heart" for Baillie's 1823 *Collection*; and in a letter dated 18 January 1842, tells Baillie that "It is, as it has long been, a great pride and gratification to me to have enjoyed your friendship; a few circumstances of my life have afforded me more real pleasure" (NLS Ms 3990, f.41).

Rogers, Henry, (?1775-1832) took over the banking business around 1802, allowing his brother Samuel to follow literary pursuits (*DNB*, XVII:140).

Rogers, Samuel, (1763-1855) was a banker and well-known art collector who became a highly successful poet in his lifetime. Between 1822-28 he published a collection of verse tales entitled *Italy*. See introduction and letters.

Rogers, Sarah, (?1772-1854) was Samuel Rogers's sister, lifelong confidant and traveling companion. She never married and was a part of his social circle. Rogers had another sister, Maria, who married Sutton Sharpe (see P. W. Clayden, *Rogers and His Contemporaries*, 2 vols. [London: Smith, Elder & Co., 1889]).

Schiller, Johann Christoph Freidrich, (1759-1805) was a German poet, dramatist, historian and philosopher who gained access to the newest literature of the time (Klopstock, Goethe, Rousseau, etc.) in Stuttgart and completed his first drama, *Die Räuber*, in 1780, followed by several historical and romantic tragedies. His trilogy *Wallenstein* appeared in 1799, and his ballads are said to be unsurpassed in German literature (*European Authors, 1000-1900: A Biographical Dictionary of European Literature*, ed. Stanley J. Kunitz and Vineta Colby [New York: H. W. Wilson, 1967], 842-44).

Scott, Thomas, (d.1823) Sir Walter Scott's brother, was made paymaster of the 70th regiment in 1811, accompanied it to Canada in 1813, and died there in April 1823 (*DNB*, XVII:1019).

Sedgwick, Catharine Maria, (1789-1867) was one of the first authors to draw from American life for material for fiction. Many of her works possessed a strong moral purpose, endeavoring to render wholesome living and unaffected goodness attractive. *Redwood* (1824), while conventionally romantic in plot, relied on a simple home life for backdrop. She was among the most popular writers of her time, and Hawthorne called her "our most truthful novelist" (*DAB*, VIII:547-48).

Sharpe, Maria Rogers, wife of Sutton Sharpe and sister of Samuel Rogers, had four sons: Samuel Sharpe (1799-1881), a noted Egyptologist who worked on a translation of the Bible and published over 37 scientific volumes; William Sharpe, who published a volume of Rogers's memoirs and letters in 1806; Henry Sharpe (1803-?); and Daniel Sharpe (1806-1856), a geologist, member of the Royal Society and president of the Geological Society in 1856 (see *DNB*, XVII:1363 and Clayden, who also lists an elder son, Sutton Sharpe [1797-1843]).

Siddons, Cecilia, daughter of actress Sarah Siddons and granddaughter of Sarah Kemble, married in 1833 George Combe, writer to the signet, Edinburgh (*DNB*, VIII:200).

Siddons, Harriet Murray, (1783-1844) was married to actress Sarah Siddons's eldest son **Henry Siddons**. Her London stage debut was as Perdita (*Winter's Tale*) in 1798, and she later moved to Edinburgh with her husband to manage the Edinburgh Theatre. Usually suffering monetary losses, the turning point for the theatre came with its popular production in February 1819 of Scott's *Rob Roy*, with Mackay as the Bailie (*DNB*, VIII:194).

Siddons, Sarah, (1755-1831) actress and eldest child of Roger Kemble, received much attention as a young beauty. As a young girl, she was sent to be lady's maid to Mrs. Greatheed, where she often recited Shakespeare before aristocratic company. Her parents reluctantly consented to her marriage to William Siddons in 1773. Hearing of her talent shortly thereafter, Garrick sent one of his men to see her in *The Fair Penitent* and hired her at £5/week for Drury Lane, where she became the foremost tragic actress of the day. A friend of Baillie and the Milbankes, Siddons achieved celebrity under Garrick's management, giving her farewell performance as Lady Macbeth at Covent Garden in 1812 but continued to give private readings. Siddons played the role of Jane in Baillie's *De Monfort* in 1800 (*DNB*, VIII:195-202; many biographies are available).

Sinclair, Sir John, (1754-1835) lawyer and M.P. for Caithness, Scotland, often took up lost causes. He tried to form a third political party after the impeachment of Warren Hastings in order to overthrow Pitt, presided over the Gaelic versions of *Ossian* which Macpherson refused to produce and attempted to advise both Baillie and Scott in literary endeavors (Lambertson, cxxv-cc). Also see *The Correspondence of the Right Honourable Sir John Sinclair, Bart.*, 2 vols. (London: Henry Colburn and Richard Bentley, 1831).

Smyth, Professor William, (1765-1849) was a modern history professor at Cambridge. Smyth tutored the elder son of Richard Brinsley Sheridan (1751-1816) for 13 years. But his relationship with Sheridan was hardly smooth, as his pay was often in arrears and Sheridan himself less than sympathetic. Appointed regius professor of modern history in 1807, he held the position till his death (*DNB*, XVIII:599-600).

Somerville, Dr. William and Mary, resided for some years in the Chelsea section of London. Mary Somerville was a prominent scientist, whose *Connection of the Physical Sciences* was published in the 1830s and who became a friend and "tutor" to Ada Byron. The couple had two daughters, Martha and Mary, and a son from Mrs.

Somerville's first marriage, Woronzow Greig (see Betty A. Toole, *Ada, The Enchantress of Numbers* [Mill Valley, California: Strawberry Press, 1992], 55).

Sotheby, William, (1757-1833) was a prodigious poet, playwright, and translator and the consummate man of letters in the Romantic Era. Though Byron disliked him, satirizing him as Mr. Botherby in *Beppo* (1818), Sotheby provided a societal focal point for many of the brightest literary minds of his time. Baillie, Scott, Wordsworth, Coleridge, Southey were his friends (*DLB*, XCIII:160-170).

Southey, Robert, (1774-1843) a college friend of Coleridge and one of the "Lake Poets," was Poet Laureate from 1813-43, having accepted a pension five years earlier. Given the pronounced Jacobinism of his youth, several of Southey's contemporaries, especially Byron and Hazlitt, felt he had betrayed the principles of his youth in such acceptance (*OCEL*, 923). Southey was first married to Edith Fricker, the sister of S. T. Coleridge's wife, and second to writer Caroline Anne Bowles. His "Lines in the Album, at Lowther Castle" and "The Cataract of Lodore" appeared in Baillie's 1823 *A Collection of Poems*.

Sparks, Jared, (1789-1866) biographer and historian, was editor of the *North American Review* until 1830 and also played a valuable role in the collection and preservation of Revolutionary War manuscripts. His biography of Benjamin Franklin (1836-40), of George Washington (1834-36), and his 25-volume *The Library of American Biography* (1834-48) are among his greatest works (*DLB*, XXX:298-309).

Stables, Miss., is probably the daughter of a Mrs. Stables of London who is also mentioned as a friend of the Carrs.

Staël, Mme. de, (1766-1817) Anne Louise Germaine Necker, Baronne de Staël-Holstein, was a French writer who admired Rousseau and dedicated her first serious essay to him in 1788. She met Goethe, Schiller and Weimar in Germany in 1803-04 and was much disliked by Napoleon. Her novel *Delphine* appeared in 1802, followed by *Corinne* in 1807 (*The New Century Cyclopedia of Names*, 3:3683).

Staunton, Sir George Leonard, (1737-1801) a diplomat and MD educated in France and elected to the Royal Society, spent much of his life in the West Indies. His first important service was performed in India in 1782 where he was sent to confer with Warren Hastings. Lord Macartney's appreciation of his services culminated in their mission to China in 1792; and in 1797 Staunton published *An authentic account of the Earl of Macartney's Embassy from the King of Great Britain to the Emperor of China*. Staunton's son, Sir George Thomas Staunton, who spent much of his early education in China, also published *Miscellaneous Notices relating to China and our Commercial Intercourse with that Country* (1822) and several other works on his and his father's China experience (*DNB*, XVIII:1000-1).

Stirling, Lady, Caroline Elizabeth Sarah Maxwell, (1808-87) was a poet and novelist (*DNB*, XIII:115).

Stirling, Mrs. James, was the long-time friend for whose benefit Baillie's *A Collection of Poems, Chiefly Manuscript, and from Living Authors* (London: Longman,

Hurst, Rees, Orme, and Brown, 1823) was produced. The successful volume earned over £2,000 for her friend.

Stuart, Lady Louisa, was daughter of Lord Vere Bertie and wife of Sir Charles Stuart (1753-1801) (*DNB*, XIX:74).

Struthers, John, (1776-1853) Scottish poet, was born in Lanarkshire while Baillie's family were residents of Long Calderwood, and they read to him and played with him while he was a child. Struthers became a shoemaker in Glasgow but, reading widely and writing considerably, began to earn some literary reputation. He gave up his trade to become an editor for two different publishing firms, finally becoming librarian of Stirling's public library in Glasgow. His most popular publication was *The Poor Man's Sabbath* (1804) which went into 4 editions, followed by *The Peasant's Death* (1806), *The Winter Day* (1811) and *Poems, Moral and Religious* (1814) (*DNB*, XIX:63).

Talma, Francois Joseph, (1763-1826) was a French tragic actor educated in England. A friend of Napoleon, he made his debut in Paris in 1787 in Voltaire's *Brutus* and first introduced on the French stage the custom of wearing costumes of the period represented in the play. His dramatic roles were numerous (*The New Century Cyclopedia of Names*, 3:3788).

Terry, Daniel, (1780?-1829) actor and playwright born at Bath and respected in London and Edinburgh alike, idolized Scott and imitated him in manner and style. Terry, who performed dozens of roles opposite such greats as Mrs. Siddons and Kean, played Argyle in Baillie's 29 January 1810 production of *The Family Legend* and on 12 March 1816 produced a musical adaptation of Scott's *Guy Mannering*. Terry's second wife Elizabeth Nasmyth was known for her taste in design and reportedly shared in decorating Abbotsford. After Terry's death she married lexicographer Charles Richardson (*DNB*, XIX:563-66).

Ticknor, George, (1791-1871) graduated from Dartmouth at the age of 16, and his later attempts to revise the curriculum at Harvard proved the beginning of a reform movement that would lead to the departmental system prevalent today. His *History of Spanish Literature* (1849) was the first truly comprehensive study of its subject. Actively involved in philanthropic works, Ticknor was one of the founders of the Boston Public Library, contributing over 3,000 volumes by his death (*DAB*, IX:526-28). Baillie spells the name several different ways.

Tuckerman, Dr. Joseph, (1778-1840) was born in Boston, graduated from Harvard in 1798 with Channing, and became one of the original members of the Anthology Society, publishers of the *Monthly Anthology and Boston Review*. Author of tracts and sermons, he visited England from 1833-34 to establish missionaries in London and Liverpool (*DAB*, XIX:46).

Walker, Mrs. Joshua, of Hendon, Middlesex, is Margaret Holford Hodson's sister.

Wallace, William, (1272?-1305) Scottish general and patriot famed for his skill and almost superhuman strength, led a successful Scottish uprising against Edward I for which he was executed in 1305. In both English and Scottish records, Wallace stands as the chief champion of the Scottish nation in its struggle for independence and the chief enemy of Edward in his premature attempt to unite Britain under one sceptre. It has been said that Wallace's natural hatred of the English and their king was the measure of the natural affection of his own people (see *DNB*, XX:563-72, and James A. Mackay's *William Wallace: brave heart* [Edinburgh and London: Mainstream, 1995].

Ware, Dr. Henry, (1764-1845) was a Unitarian minister and professor of divinity at Harvard. He had three sons: Henry (1794-1843), also a Unitarian minister and Harvard theology professor; John (1795-1864), a physician; and William (1797-1852), a Unitarian minister (*DAB*, XIX:447-52).

Wilkie, Sir David, (1785-1841) says he began drawing before he could read. He entered the Trustees' Academy and made some progress in portrait painting but in 1804 left Edinburgh and returned to his home of Cults to paint on his own. In 1805 he left for London, carrying a small picture entitled "Bounty Money; or, the Village Recruit," and established himself at Portland Road, shortly after beginning attendance at the Academy and finally earning true fame in 1810 with "The Village Festival" now in the National Gallery. He became ill around this time and was attended by Dr. Matthew Baillie, migrating for his convalescence to the house of Joanna Baillie. Scott invited him to Abbotsford in 1817, and while there he painted the Scott family in the garb of south-country peasants, put on exhibit in 1818. By 1830 Wilkie was made painter in ordinary at the death of Sir Thomas Lawrence, retaining this office under Queen Victoria. He was knighted in 1836 (*DNB*, XXI:253-58).

Wordsworth, William, (1770-1850) is mentioned by Baillie several times in various letters. Margaret Carhart writes that Baillie probably did not meet him until around 1812 (23); but, in fact, Baillie describes meeting Wordsworth and Southey in the Lake District in 1808. Wordsworth provided two sonnets, "Not love nor war" and "A volant tribe of bards," for Baillie's 1823 *Collection of Poems*. Baillie writes to Scott in October 1808 about meeting Wordsworth (and Southey) on her visit to the Lakes: "He is a man with good strong abilities and a great power of words, but I fear there is that soreness in regard to the world & severity in his notions of mankind growing upon him that will prevent him from being so happy as he deserves to be, for he is I understand a very worthy man" (NLS letter 3877, f. 158-61).

Wrangham, Francis, (1769-1842) a classical scholar and miscellaneous writer, became archdeacon of Cleveland in 1820, later acquiring the prebendal stall of Ampleforth in York Cathedral (*DNB*, XXI:980-83).

Wright, Ichabod Charles, (1795-1871) translator of Dante, was educated at Eaton and Oxford and became the joint manager of the bank at Nottingham in 1825. He married Theodosia Denman, daughter of Sophia Denman Baillie's brother Thomas Denman, first lord Denman. Between 1830-1840 he gave his leisure to the study of Italian literature, producing a metrical translation of the *Divina Commedia* in three installments (*DNB*, XXI:1020-21).

1

 To *Family*

(?1821-1851)

Following are miscellaneous letters from Joanna Baillie to members of her family. In comparison to the vast number of letters she wrote to friends, the meager store of Baillie's letters to her family is perplexing. Since she was very close to her family, especially to her brother Matthew, it is reasonable that she would have had occasion to send numerous notes and letters even though she lived only a short distance away and saw family members often. If more family letters existed, they should surely have been part of the Hunter-Baillie papers at the Royal College of Surgeons of England or at the Wellcome Institute for the History of Medicine. These family letters, however, would have been passed down through generations of Baillies, and since her nephew William alone had eight children, it is probable that most have not survived or that many are in the hands of private collectors.[1]

See the "Introduction" in this volume for more detailed accounts of Baillie's family and Franco Crainz's 1995 biography entitled *The Life and Works of Matthew Baillie, MD, FRS, L&E, FRCP, etc. (1761-1823)*. When dating is positive, these letters have been arranged chronologically rather than by collection or recipient.

---

1. Biographer Margaret Carhart quotes from one long published letter dated 19 October 1805 from Joanna to Dr. Matthew Baillie in which she politely explains why she is rejecting Sir John Sinclair's (1754-1835) advice on writing tragedies adapted for stage effect (he offers her *On the Fall of Darius* to consider). She does, however, accept Sinclair's suggestion to write a play for charitable reasons and later produces *The Family Legend* in Edinburgh to such end. This letter to Matthew is probably extant because Matthew forwarded it to Sinclair with his own attached note (dated 20 November 1805), and Sinclair retained it for his own collection of ms. letters. I do not include the letter here because I have not found the manuscript letter and because it is reprinted both in Carhart's *The Life and Work of Joanna Baillie* (New Haven: Yale University Press, 1923) and in *The Correspondence of the Right Honourable Sir John Sinclair, Bart.*, 2 vols. (London: Henry Colburn and Richard Bentley, 1831).

University of Glasgow
MS Gen 1587 p.77 (No address or postmark, UG identifies recipient as Lady Campbell, 1821) [2]

[1821?]

My dear Cousin

We have received by last night's post a letter from M[rs] Baillie,[3] conveying information in which we are much interested since it so deeply concerns your happiness, and we thank you for this mark of friendship towards us that it is at your desire we have received it. We both unite in sending you our kindest wishes. May the very important step you are about to take turn out in every respect for your future comfort & happiness. I earnestly hope & will gladly believe that you have chosen a man, who will prove a kind & pleasant companion to you thro' life; and thankful & happy I shall be, should i live long enough, to have this hope & this belief turned into certainty.

God bless & keep you then, my dear Cousin! in whatever state you may be placed! and with all kindness & affection (the united feeling of my Sister & myself)[4] I remain

most truly yours
J Baillie

---

2. Lady Campbell, Agnes Margaretta Hunter (1776-1838), surviving daughter of Dr. John Hunter and Anne Home Hunter and cousin to Baillie, married Sir James Campbell first; after his death, she married Col. Benjamin Charlewood, retaining her title. She had no children. Baillie often misspells Charlewood as Charliwood.

3. Sophia Denman Baillie (1771-1845), daughter of Dr. Thomas Denman (1733-1815) and Elizabeth Brodie Denman (1746-1833) and sister of Lord chief-justice Thomas Denman (1779-1854) and Margaret Denman Croft (1771-1838), married Joanna's only brother Dr. Matthew Baillie (1761-1823) in 1791 and became one of Joanna's closest friends; Sophia's two children were William Hunter Baillie (1797-1894) and Elizabeth Margaret Baillie Milligan (1794-1876); she continued to live at Cavendish Square in London after Matthew's death on 23 September 1823. See Franco Crainz, "Genealogical Table," *The Life and Works of Matthew Baillie* (Santa Palomba, Italy: PelitiAssociati, 1995).

4. Agnes Baillie (1760-1861) was Joanna Baillie's only sister and constant companion. Dr. Matthew Baillie writes that Agnes Baillie, born in the Manse of Shotts on 24 September 1760, had "a quick ready Understanding, with a good deal of various knowle[d]ge, so as to be much beyond the common level of Women in these respects" (qtd. in Crainz, 10).

University of Glasgow
MS Gen 1587 p.79 (No address or postmark, UG dates 1822)

[1822?]

My dear Lady Campbell,

I return the Manuscripts with thanks for having been entrusted with them so long. I have little more to say regarding them than what I told you before, when we last met. Some of the smaller pieces which have not yet been published, are worthy of the Author, and the Heir of Newton Buzzard is a very well told story with all the graces of easy verse & happy expression. Miss Edgeworth is with us at present and I have read it to her. She has been much pleased with it; and has taken a small extract from it, of about six lines, which she means to make the motto to a short work of her's [sic] just forth coming. It is to be set down as lines "from the Heir of Newton Buzzard a Ms poem," not mentioning by whom.[5] If the tale should never be published this will do it no harm, and if it should, will be of service to it. I therefore took upon me to give her leave to do so, as there was no time to wait for your consent without stopping the press which could not be done. The other tale I am to read to her this evening. The work in question is the confirmation of a story already published which she calls little Frank.

Agnes & I are to be in Town next week, and it will go hard with us indeed if we dont get to see you in your new abode. With best regards to

---

5. Maria Edgeworth (1768-1849) first focused her writing on educational topics, translating Madame de Genlis's *Adèle et Théodore*. She experimented with various teaching methods, publishing a series including *The Parents Assistant* (1796) and *Early Lessons* (1801); but she became well known for her novels *Castle Rackrent* (1800), *Belinda* (1801), *Popular Tales* (1804), *The Modern Griselda* (1805), *Leonora* (1806), the six-volume *Tales of Fashionable Life* (1809-12), *Ormond* (1817), *Helen* (1834), etc., many of which document Irish society. Edgeworth is one of the first women novelists "to apply an insight articulated by Wollstonecraft, that women have their own language" (Janet Todd, ed., *British Women Writers: A Critical Reference Guide* [New York: Continuum, 1989], 204-7). Baillie and Edgeworth met in 1813 (see NLS Scott letter 3884 ff.184-187). At this time Edgeworth was staying with Joanna and Agnes and writes on 14 January 1822: "I part with Agnes and Joanna Baillie, confirmed in my opinion that the one is the most amiable literary woman I ever beheld, and the other one of the best informed and most useful" (Augustus J. C. Hare, ed., *The Life and Letters of Maria Edgeworth*, 2 vols. [Boston: Houghton, Mifflin, 1895], 2:396). I have found no mention of Lady Campbell's story of Newton Buzzard in Edgeworth's works.

Col: Charliwood [*sic*] & kind love to yourself, I remain
    my dear Lady Campbell
        your Affc^te Cousin
            J Baillie
Hampstead Jany 11th

Huntington Library HM41082 (No address or postmark)

[1822]

My dear Lady Campbell,
    I have undertaken to edit a vol. of collected poems to be published by
subscription for the benefit of a friend of mine who is left with her family
in very distressing circumstances, and I wish to have the book as creditable
as I can and chiefly filled with MS. poetry; will you permit me to have a
few of your Mother's smaller pieces? both her name & her writing will be
of great use to it, and I shall feel myself very much obliged. You shall
know who this friend is and all about it when we meet.[6] In the mean time I
remain with all kind wishes to yourself & Col. Charliwood [*sic*]
    Your affectionate Cousin,
        J Baillie
Hampstead
tuesday Jan^r 29th
    1822

University of Glasgow
MS Gen 1587 p.5 (Address: Lady Campbell)

Duntisbourne Septr 24th [1823]

My dear Cousin,
    You will see by this paper that our heaviest affliction has at length
come upon us and that all our nursing & hope & anxiety are now at an end.
My excellent Brother expired yesterday about one o'clock after suffering a
great deal from the restlessness & wanderings of fever for better than 8
days.[7] This return of fever came upon him at the end of that lingering

---

6. Baillie's *A Collection of Poems, Chiefly Manuscript, and from Living Authors*
(London: Longman, Hurst, Rees, Orme, and Brown, 1823) was a subscription
publication for the benefit of her friend Mrs. James Stirling. Lady Campbell submitted
7 of her mother's (Anne Home Hunter) poems : "The Lot of Thousands," "Oh Power
Supreme, that fill'st the whole," "The Evening Primrose," "A Simile--I saw the wild
rose," "Tomorrow," "To the Nymph of the Mountain" and "Song--When hollow bursts
the rushing winds." Anne Home Hunter published *Sports of the Genii* (1797) and
miscellaneous poems throughout her life.

7. Dr. Matthew Baillie (1761-1823) had been trained by and had taken over the
medical school of his uncle Dr. William Hunter and was a respected physician to

illness, from which he appeared just to be beginning in a small degree to amend, and he had not strength to contend with it. Sir H. Halford was sent for and came here on sunday evening & stayed till yesterday morning and behaved with the greatest kindness; Dr Warren came accidentally – I should rather say providentially on monday evening and stayed till all was over which proved to be of the greatest use at the end, as Dr Baron his most friendly & regular Physician from Gloucester did not arrive till too late in the day.[8] These are things to mention because tho' unavailing to save what we have lost, they give satisfaction to those who remain particularly poor Mrs Baillie who has gone thro' all her most painful & fatiguing duties with a strength which seemed to be lent to her by a merciful God for the trying occasion. When we meet if you desire it, I will tell you more about this about the last awful scene,[9] but now I cannot, nor would it be fitting. — She has had some sleep but the waking again this morning was very wretched; however, her health does not suffer, and time, if it may not cure, soothes every affliction. Elizabeth & her husband[10] are with us & our dear William[11] & my Sister, who are all as well as can be expected. — I hope we shall see you soon in Town where we expect to be in about a fortnight[.]

George III. Biographer Crainz cites Dr. Baillie's last letter to Sir Henry Halford, written three days before his death: "I have within these few days become so very much worse, that, if not very inconvenient to you, I should be glad to see you at my house." To this letter son William added: "There is swelling of the left foot and hand, and at times considerable confusion of intellect. The pulse is seldom under 100, frequently more. . . . The foregoing detail will sufficiently show how urgent the case is, and how needful it is to afford any relief that may be administered as speedily as possible" (55). To attest to Dr. Baillie's medical prominence, a biography by James Wardrop, Esq., appeared in 1825, just two years after Matthew's death.

8. Sir Henry Halford, MD, (1766-1844) changed his surname from Vaughan to Halford by Act of Parliament in 1809; he was Physician to the Middlesex Hospital from 1793-1844, Physician Extraordinary to George III in 1793, Physician in Ordinary in 1812, and Physician in Ordinary to George IV, William IV and Victoria. John Baron, MD, (1786-1851) was Physician to the General Infirmary and Consulting Physician to the Lunatic Asylum at Gloucester until his retirement in 1832. Pelham Warren, BM & MD, (1778-1835) was Physician to St. George's Hospital from 1803-1816 (see Crainz, 27, 30 & 66, and NLS letter 3897 ff.84-86 to Scott).

9. Wording is awkward here.

10. Elizabeth Margaret Baillie Milligan (1794-1876), the only daughter of Matthew and Sophia Denman Baillie, married Capt. Robert Milligan (1781-1875) on 11 July 1816, and the couple, with one daughter Sophia (1817-1882), lived at Ryde on the Isle of Wight for most of Joanna's life.

11. William Hunter Baillie (1797-1894), the only son of Matthew and Sophia Baillie, graduated from Oxford, married Henrietta Duff in 1835, lived many years in Hampstead, moved to Richmond and later back to Upper Harley Street in Joanna's last years. William and Henrietta were the parents of 8 children.

Yours, my dear Cousin, very affectionately
    J Baillie
PS. The funeral is to take place some time next week[.] He is to be buried in Duntisbourne[.][12]

Wellcome Institute for the History of Medicine

MS 5617/85 (No address or postmark)

[1823 or 1824]

My dear dear Sophia it goes to my heart to see your gowns lying here on the bed and to think that I am never again to behold you but in the dress of sorrow. But be it so; every thing that has belonged to you is precious to your affectionate Sister
    J Baillie

University of Glasgow

MS Gen 1587 p.67 (No address or postmark, UG identifies recipient as Lady Campbell)

Hampstead Jan[ry] 20th [1824]

My Dear Cousin

It is by M[rs] Baillie's special desire that I write, for she longs to know how you do, and I obey her very willingly. You are, I suppose, in quiet again at Fleurs, enjoying your Husband's society after all the bustle of your Newcastle quarters. And I hope he returned to you well and had as pleasant a journey from London as the season of the year will admit. We were quite mortified that he should have called twice in Cavendish Sq[r] before he went and that both Agnes & I being out, should have missed the pleasure of seeing him, while poor Sophia was in her room unable to speak. William called on Col. Charliwood [*sic*] to express all our regrets, but he in his turn was out. Pray offer him our thanks & best regards and tell him that we were all very sorry. — I have not a very got [good] report to give you of our dear friend, but one with which, perhaps we ought to be satisfied. Her chest is easier and she now & then is able to speak for a short time in her natural voice; and as the frost is gone & the air mild, I trust the windpipe will get sound by degrees. She is still confined to her own room & the drawing room, and excludes all company which might oblige her from courtesy to speak.[13] William, who has hitherto appeared

---

12. Dr. Matthew Baillie was buried on 30 September 1823 in Duntisbourne Abbots Church, his marble tablet, designed by Sir Francis Legatt Chantrey, inscribed as follows: "Sacred to the memory/ of Matthew Baillie, MD/ who terminated his useful and honourable life/ September 23rd, 1823, aged 62" (Crainz, 56). Also see Anne Carver, *The Story of Duntisbourne Abbots* (Gloucester: Albert E. Smith, 1966).

13. After an attempt to nurse him back to health, Sophia Baillie took the death of

very averse to it, is beginning to go more into society and this pleases her, for she was distressed with his constantly staying at home with her and feared he would become a habitual recluse, a bad habit which a shy man is too apt to fall into.

Agnes & I have been much in Cavendish Sq^r but these last eight days we were at home, and getting over the dark part of the Winter together as well as we may. Dark indeed it is to me, and I feel as if no coming time would ever be brighter: I feel it more strongly than I did at [the] beginning of our calamity. But it is a perverse unreasonable feeling and it is my duty to strive against it. Agnes does all she can to bear me up & herself also, and her debtor I am for her sisterly exertions. -- Our most remarkable event for these some weeks past has been going to the Caledonian Chapel to hear Mr Irving.[14] With some difficulty we procured tickets, and made part of a very full congregation. He gave us an able discourse of an hour & a half which did not seem too long, delivered well & impressively, as far as voice is concerned, but the action of his arms did not seem to me natural and was far wide of what I should deem graceful. He is much attended by Lawers [sic] & members of Parliament. I begin to suspect that they are, tho' not word-bound, extremely arm-bound, so that a man who is bold enough in public to stretch out his arms in any manner, is to them an object of admiration. But let us hold our tongue; whatever takes them to church is good, and must not be spoken against. — Farewell, my Dear Cousin! let us -- I mean particularly Mrs Baillie, hear from you presently. I hope we shall learn that you are well and beginning to think of the time for returning to us again.

    Yours affectionately

    J Baillie

---

her husband Matthew very hard, becoming ill herself afterwards. See NLS letters 3897 ff.84-86 and 3898 ff.56-57 to Scott.

    14. Edward Irving (1792-1834) was educated at Edinburgh University and became a friend of Thomas Carlyle. As a preacher his oratory was pronounced, his voice resonant and his assumptions in the pulpit extravagant. When he came to London in 1822, a great revival of enthusiastic religious feeling was beginning; and the "unknown tongues" heard to come from the mouth of one of his congregation in 1830 provided the crowning development of his ministries. The "Irvingite" or "Holy Catholic Apostolic Church" still survives in a fine Gothic structure in Gordon Square (*DNB*, X:489-93).

University of Glasgow
MS Gen 1587 p. 51 (No address or postmark, UG identifies recipient as Col. Benjamin Charlewood, 1825?)

Hampstead saturday morning [1825?]

My dear Colonel

I have made a mistake of a week in my counting the days of this month; it is for next saturday the 20th that my Sister & I request the pleasure of seeing you at dinner to meet William. We hope you are disengaged for that day, and will be kind enough to come to us. —

most truly yours

J Baillie

New York Public Library, Berg Collection
Scott Letter Books, V.1, No. 49 (No address or postmark)

[1833]

My dear Sophy[15]

Tell your Mama that I did not write to her again because your Grandmama intended writing to her which she did last night. Give my love to her, however & say that, if your Grandmama has given a favorable report of her health, as I suppose she has, your Mama may trust to it. Indeed she looks well and has got rid of her headachs [*sic*] and is altogether in a state for which we have cause to be very thankful. —

You will find inclosed, two copies of my lines on the Death of Sir Walter Scott, one is for yourself, my dear Child, and the other you will present with my love to your Mama.[16] Give my kind love to your Papa & Aunt Mary. —

Your affectionate Grand Aunt

— J Baillie

Cavendish Sq[r]
Jan[y] 26th, 1833

---

15. Sophia Milligan (1817-1882) was the daughter of JB's niece Elizabeth Margaret Baillie Milligan.

16. After the death of Scott on 21 September 1832, Baillie composed her "Lines on the Death of Sir Walter Scott" (Hampstead, n.p., 1832) which appears in her 1851 *Dramatic and Poetical Works of Joanna Baillie*.

Wellcome Institute for the History of Medicine

MS 5616/48 (Address: Mrs W. Baillie / Suffolk Square / Cheltenham--postmarked 1837)[17]

Hampstead June 25 1837

My dear Henrietta

You will receive a letter from your Aunt Agnes by Mrs Baillie very soon, but in the mean time I flatter myself that a few lines of love & affection from me, conveyed in an ordinary way, will not be unwelcome. Neither William nor you are very long absent from my thoughts, and now that the summer is so far advanced and your time of expectation at hand, I naturally think of you the oftener.[18] May God bless you & strengthen you, and make all you have to pass through prosperous in every respect! We shall then have great cause for thankfulness and will, I trust, be humbly & truly thankful. The heat of the weather, should it continue, is I believe very favorable for a good <u>time</u> to women in your condition, but then it is not quite so favorable for recovering strength afterwards; but you will have your kind Mother-in-law, dear William & your excellent Aunt Baron to attend to all your comforts & cheer your chamber (I will not say sick-chamber) and you will be very well off, though the state of the thermometer should (should) be somewhat oppressive.[19] My good Sister Sophia has, I hope, much satisfaction abiding her, yet I envy her most of all that she will see again so soon that lovely Child our sweet Sophy whom we left in the perfection of Infant beauty so many months ago, and who has suffered so much in the interval. I dont think I can ever love any child you may have so much as her.[20] A little Matthew will be very acceptable and a little Henrietta we shall by no means despise, but I feel as if they could never entirely touch my heart as this dear Child does & has done. ——— I hope you will find Mrs Baillie looking pretty well after the severe winter & the sufferings arising from it, and probably the change of air at Mortimer may have removed the cough before you see her, and then every thing will be well. When we (my Sister & I) see her again a t

---

17. Henrietta Duff (1808-57) married William Baillie in 1835, and the couple had 8 children.

18. Henrietta and William Baillie's second child, Matthew John Baillie (1837-66), was born at this time. See letter following.

19. Dr. and Miss Baron are also mentioned at the close of this letter and may refer to John Baron, MD (1789-1851), a physician who spent much of his life in Cheltenham and a friend of Dr. Matthew Baillie (*DNB*, I:1189). I have not, however, established a genealogical link to Henrietta Duff Baillie.

20. Henrietta and William Baillie's first child was Sophia Joanna Baillie (1836-82), easily confused with William's sister Elizabeth's daughter Sophia Milligan (1817-82).

the end of the summer, I hope we shall find her renovated in every respect, and the happiness she will have enjoyed with her children in Cheltenham & Ryde, visible in her countenance & form. —— My Sister & I are both pretty well again, and we have been at church this morning and have heard prayers offered up for the first time in behalf of our young Queen — prayers which I hope will be heard. But our Clergyman, who is a very high Church Tory, made no allusion at all to the good king we have lost, only exhorting us under every calamity to put our trust in God; not even hinting that our present calamity is of a public nature though the pulpit in which he stood was hung with black and the congregation clothed in sables.[21] I trust the ministers will retain their power and things go on peaceably, but no body can say what kind of Parliament this coming dissolution will produce and what will be the result. The circumstances of the times & the nearly equal balancing of parties throws a great deal of power into the hands of a very young woman. However, we should not be better off, perhaps not so well, were it in the hands of a very young man. —— A good Providence has been very merciful to this country in former perilous times, and we must trust to that high Protection which hath hitherto saved us. ——— Our late but abundant hay-harvest (we have no other in this neighbourhood) is begun & Irish women with swarms of children begging in every Lane. The good things of the garden are all come at last & good of their kind. —— Our neighbour M^rs & Miss Hoare[22] & Mrs Greaves are returned to us, so we are better off for society than we were a short time since. They frequently enquire for you & William[.] I had a letter from Miss Milligan some time ago;[23] every thing is sunshine & prosperity at Creetown. — Agnes unites with me in kindest love to Wil^m & you & your baby. God bless you all! Rember [*sic*] me kindly to D^r & Miss Barron [*sic?*]

your affectionate Aunt   J Baillie

PS. Monday morning, My Sister is going out this morning to make two distant visits, wheel'd in a Bath Chair, the first time in her life that she ever visited in this fashion: the progress of old age. ——

---

21. Eighteen-year-old Victoria became queen in June 1837 after the death of her uncle King George IV and married her first cousin Albert, Prince of Saxe-Coburg-Gotha, in 1840.

22. Samuel Hoare, Lady Byron's banker, was married to Louisa Gurney, and Baillie was a close friend of their family. Children she mentions include Jane, Joseph and several others. I have not identified Mrs. Greaves.

23. Miss Milligan is probably the sister-in-law of Baillie's niece Elizabeth Margaret Milligan.

Wellcome Institute for the History of Medicine

MS 5615/96 (Address: William H. Baillie Esqr / Suffolk Square / Cheltenham--postmarked July 10, 1837)[24]

[1837]

My dear William

With joy & thankfulness did we receive the news of your yesterday's letter; and may the blessing of God rest upon your little Boy — upon the dear Mother & her <u>Children</u>.[25] -- upon you & yours! We indeed rejoice with you and humbly hope that your Matthew Baillie will do credit to his name which is an honoured one, and will by & by be repeated by many a yearning heart in rembrance [sic] of him who first gave it its value. But for this, I should have been as well pleased with a Girl, and dear Sophy, be she fat or thin, rosy or pale, will still be my darling. I hope I shall live to see them both tottling about, hand in hand and Henrietta & you & dear Grand Mama looking with affection on the tiny pair. Though the report you give is so favorable, we shall be anxious for further [word] every two or three days for some time to come; every post's knock at the door will make our thoughts on the instant fly to Cheltenham. Give my kindest love to the young Mother with thanks for my share of the happiness she has conferred upon us; and I am very glad that the weather is not so oppressively hot to day as it was yesterday for her sake. -- Give my kind love & congratulations to your Mother; she has got a nice little Grandson without waiting very long for him, and she will have time to see him thrive & get bigger before she leaves you. I am mighty glad to hear that the young Gentleman has good sized feet & hands; this is a thing of favorable promise. You may tell her besides that her literary property is encreased by the present of a Tragedy from Peter Stirling, sent to my care yesterday. I fear from the preface it is published at his own risk, a very perilous thing for such a Poet in such times as these.[26] She is also encreased in worldly goods, by a pot of bright scarlet geraniums from the seed-beds of Miss Mitford.[27] We are taking care of it in the mean time. It has a

---

24. Joanna Baillie's note is actually the second part of a letter begun and signed by Agnes Baillie.

25. The new baby was Matthew John Baillie (1837-66), following Sophia Joanna (1836-82).

26. I have not identified this tragedy, so it is possible that Mr. Sterling did publish at his own risk.

27. This is probably Baillie's friend Mary Russell Mitford (1787-1855), essayist, playwright, novelist and poet, best remembered for *Our Village* (1824-32). Her easy conversational style won her the praise of Charles Lamb; and her most successful play, *Rienzi* (1828), was presented at Drury Lane to considerable public acclaim. Her later years were spent nursing an aged father who had gambled most of the family fortune away, and she suffered from crippling rheumatism but retained a "calmness of

companion along with it which bears the illustrious name of Joanna Baillie, but what kind of a thing it will prove to be when it . . .[28] told you about Miss Napier[29] & our drinking your son's health and our intended visit to Sunbury &c. so I shall say no more, but that I am happy & thankful & congratulate you most affectionately

Joanna Baillie

University of Glasgow
MS Gen 542/8 (Address: Miss Hunter / Maison de Madame le Sage Capecure / Boulogne sur Mer / France--postmarked 1837)

Hampstead August 30th 1837

My dear Miss Hunter,[30]

I am much obliged to you for remembering your kind promise to write to us, and my Sister & I are glad to hear that you have upon the whole found your abode in France agreeable. If you could have given us a more favorable account of your own health for the latter part of the time, we should have been quite satisfied. But since the advice & medicine of your Countryman has already done you so much good, I hope the time for your being quite restored to health is not far distant. Your encreasing facility too in speaking french with your Landlady who knows no English is a great advantage and one that you will enjoy more & more every day. I wish that in the early part of my life I had been placed in the same predicament -- it would have been very impotant [sic] and useful to me ever after. To be forced to speak is the best way to get on. What an agreeable picture you give of the common people in your discription of the Fisherman's Ball! it is indeed a mortifying reproof to our own countrymen; and should particularly put Glasgow to shame where so much has been done by Temperance Societies &c to reclaim them from bad habits. You tell us nothing of your future plans therefore we may suppose you intend

---

mind and clearness of intellect" (Todd, 470-71).

28. The method of binding has covered this line of the letter.

29. Baillie mentions Col. Napier in other letters, and this may be a daughter or sister. There were several distinguished military men by this name, including Col. the Hon. George Napier (1752-1804), Gen. Sir Charles Napier (1786-1860) and Gen. Sir William Napier (b 1786). The Napier family was connected through marriage to Louisa Fox and Caroline Fox, also friends of Baillie (see Priscilla Napier's *I have Sind: Charles Napier in India, 1841-1844* [Great Britain: Michael Russell, 1990]). In a journal entry, Scott mentions reading Col. William Napier's *War in the Peninsula* in 1828. The NYPL also owns a very brief Misc. Ms 3200 from JB to "My dear Friend" which the archivist suggests may be addressed to one of the Napiers.

30. Miss Hunter and her brother mentioned at the end of the letter are probably relatives of William or John and Anne Home Hunter, but I cannot provide a positive identification.

remaining where you are for some time. But we shall hear more about you by & by, I hope when your Brother comes to London.

We are much obliged by your friendly enquiries after us, and I am thankful to say I have a pretty good report to give in return. My Sister suffered occasionally from rheumatism & siatica [*sic*] even during the warm weather but it has not continued long with her at a time nor been very severe. I have been very well. ––– We received a very satisfactory letter from M͞r͞s Baillie the other day, who is now with her Daughter in the Isle of Wight, after having spent a considerable time with William & his Wife at Cheltenham. A Granson [*sic*] was added to her treasures while she was with them, Mother & Child did quite well, and she prolonged her visit to see him Christened, Matthew being his name, and a dear name to her & to us all. I hope it will please God to spare him to his Parents and make him a comfort & credit to them. She will pass some weeks, happily I trust, with the Milligans and then return to Cavendish Sq͞r revived & strenthened [*sic*] for the following winter. We miss her sadly when she is away, but we willingly give up her society for a time when it is so much for her own good & happiness. We have had a bright warm summer without being oppressively warm till lately when rainy broken weather has prevailed with some thunder storms. We hear a good account of the harvest all over England and I hope it also extends to Scotland & Ireland, so that our young Queen may begin her reign with peace & plenty.[31] I am not a sufficient Politician to guess how things may turn out in other respects, for parties, (as you will see by your English newspaper) in the house of Commons are very nearly balanced. She is very affable, selfpossessed & graceful, as we hear say, and is exeedingly [*sic*] popular, or seemingly so, with both Whigs & Tories; never saw her in my life, though she has been frequently since her accession in an open carriage upon our heath. –– My Sister unites with me in kind regards to your Sister & yourself; and we hope ere long to hear of you from your Brother. We shall be glad to see him again, for it is a long time since we had that pleasure. Believe me, my dear Miss Hunter with many thanks for your friendly letter,

   your sincerely obliged friend
   J Baillie

---

31. Queen Victoria--see note 21 above.

Wellcome Institute for the History of Medicine
MS 5613/55 (Address: For William Baillie--no postmark)

[1838?]

Copy of the account of our Family given to Mr Richardson Decr 17$^{\underline{th}}$ 1837

My Father was one of the Guardians appointed by the Will of the Old Laird of Carnbroe to his Son Matthew Baillie (afterwards General Baillie) and was considered as a distant relation of the family, but I do not recollect my Father ever saying one word about it. The late Gen. Baillie says, in a letter to my Brother, that we are descended from his family, and that our ancester [sic] branching off from them, was the Brother of Principal Baillie. Gen. Baillie was the direct representative of Principal Baillie, and on this account he proposed, some time before he died, to bequeath to my Nephew William a picture that was in Carnbroe house, among the other family pictures, as the portrait of our ancester. When he died, however, there was no mention in his Will of this Picture; and, as his affairs were much embarrassed, the effects were all sold and who bought this picture we dont know. — So far Gen. Baillie's story goes. —

I have heard my Aunt M$^{\underline{rs}}$ Allen, (my Father's only surviving Sister) say that her Grand father, consequently my Father's Grand father, was a distant relation & friend of Baillie of Jerviswood, and that when Jerviswood was apprehended & imprisoned he fled to Holland, where he remained till after the revolution, when he returned, having lost or spent all that he had possessed (probably not much) in company with Mr Primrose (we think his name was Primrose) the former Minister of Crighton, and that having no better prospect before him, he was glad to become the Schoolmaster of the Parish under his friend. His son & my Father's Father was educated for the Church, but an early marriage & some other difficulties disappointed that (that) intention, and he became the Successor of his Father in the School. He left two Sons, both Scotch Clergymen, the eldest of whom was my Father, the other died early and unmarried. So far goes my Aunt's account of our family, according to my recollection: I never heard her mention Principal Baillie, but she always said that we were originally descended from the Baillies of Lamington. If we could ascertain that the man who fled to Holland, and returned again after the Revolution, was the Brother of Principal Baillie,[32] then there would be no difficulty in reconciling the two accounts. --- I have no distinct dates to give, but, from circumstances which I remember myself the second School master whose name was Matthew died somewhere about the

---

32. William Baillie's note: "He could not have been the brother but he might have been the nephew or great nephew of the Principal & descended from the brother of the Principal." A note from William also appears at the end of the letter.

1770s and his grave-stone & likewise that of his Father may be still to be found in the Church yard of Crighton

The above was written by Mrs Joanna Baillie ——
WHB

Wellcome Institute for the History of Medicine
MS 5613/60 (Address: William Baillie Esqr--no postmark)
Hampstead Feby 22^d^ 1838

My dear William
    In your last letter to your Mother concerning Mr Richardson['s] enquiries as to our descent,[33] you desire her to ask your Aunts for further particulars, and I am sorry to say we have no information to add to that which I set down on paper and which he carried with him to Scotland. The way of tracing descents is by examining the title deeds of landed property or of houses that have been transferred from one family to another or of Testaments disposing of property of any kind, but our Ancestor who returned from Holland had no property and had possessed no lands, so any search after him in Scotch Registers &c would be to no purpose. No sum therefore that you might be willing to spend upon it would be of any avail. General Baillie seems to point out our descent as being from his family and probably by a Brother of Principal Baillie.[34] Your best way will be to get the life of Principal Baillie which is published at the beginning of his letters, a work still extant, for he was much connected with public affairs in his days, and see what account is given there of his Father's family. Mr Richardson has ascertained that the first School master of our name in the Parish of Chrighton [Crichton] was called Andrew Baillie, and if there be a Brother Principal Baillie mention'd as bearing the name of Andrew, he is more than probably the man who fled to

---

33. John Richardson (1780-1864) was a parliamentary solicitor and for 30 years discharged the duties of crown agent for Scotland, reputed as the most learned peerage lawyer of his time. He had literary tastes and in 1821 was introduced to George Crabbe in Joanna Baillie's house, and he regularly corresponded with Walter Scott, whose deathbed he attended shortly before Scott's demise. He married Elizabeth Hill, a close friend of Thomas Campbell, in 1811 and had several children (*DNB*, XVI:1118-19). Richardson submitted "Song - Her features speak the warmest heart" for Baillie's 1823 collection; and in a letter dated 18 January 1842, tells Baillie, "It is, as it has long been, a great pride and gratification to me to have enjoyed your friendship; a few circumstances of my life have afforded me more real pleasure" (NLS Ms 3990, f.41).
    34. Robert Baillie, DD, Principal of the University of Glasgow (1599-1662) and much connected with public affairs, is identified as Baillie of Jerviston (see *DNB* entry).

Holland and on his return became Schoolmaster of Chrighton. Your Grand
Father's only Brother was named Andrew. I can think of nothing else to be
done and this will not make the descent a certain thing, but, with other
corroborating circumstances, pretty near it. ⸺ Our ancestor fled to
Holland no doubt on account of his religion and of having been connected
with Baillie of Jerviswood, and it is possible that his opinions might not
agree in many points with those of his Brother and the Principal & he
have [sic] little intercourse with one another which may account for my
Father never mentioning, as far as I know, any thing of his family or their
consanguinity to Principal Baillie. ⸺ As to making out a genealogy for
your little Matthew, you need give yourself little concern, for he will be
very well off with the immediate descent that undoubtedly belongs to
him, though it would make but a poor figure in a Welch Pedigree. His
Father a Gloucester Sh^r Squire, Lord of the Manor of Duntisbourn; his
Grand father an eminent Court Physician and his Great Grand father a
distinguished Scotch Clergyman & Professor of Divinity in the University
of Glasgow. Surely this is very respectable, and more than this, though
you could trace his direct line to Baliol king of Scotland would do him
little good. — You say in your letter "We have a picture of him (viz your
Por[trait?])[35] in our possession, School masters do not often have their
pictures taken[.]" This is a mistake, for the picture in question is the
portrait of Dr Hunter's Father, and was originally painted in Crayons by
his son James Hunter, who had a turn for drawing, and was afterwards
copied by Remsdike or Pine for Dr Hunter.[36] Your Aunt Agnes & I have a
copy from <u>that</u> copy done by Lady Montgomery.[37] ⸺ I do not think from
the tenor of your letter that you have seen the statement which I wrote to
guide Mr Richardson in his enquiries. I wish you had seen it, and I will
write out a copy of that statement whenever you please. ⸺

We are very glad to hear such good accounts of you & Henrietta & your
Children. I hope dear little Sophy, since she has not yet shewn signs of

---

35. Baillie has inserted this illegible word.

36. Drs. William and John Hunters' father was John Hunter, Sr. The James Hunter
mentioned here must be his third son who died young (see Norton letter 8, Volume 2),
though no mention is made of James in recent Hunter/Baillie biographies. John
Remsdyke was a natural history draftsman born in Holland who settled at Bristol
and worked for Dr. Hunter; assisted by his son, in 1778 he published a collection of
natural history illustrations taken from the British Museum (*Bryan's Dictionary of
Painters and Engravers*, 4 vols. [London: G. Bell & Sons, 1921], 4:209). Robert Pine (d.
1790) was an historic painter whose collection also included portraits and theatrical
scenes; his brother Simon Pine (d. 1772) was an English miniature painter (*Bryan's*,
4:121).

37. Lady Montgomery could be one of several Montgomery/Montgomerys of
Scottish peerage. I have not identified her.

the measles, will escape till she has more strength to encounter it. Give our united love to Henrietta, and pray offer our kind regards to <u>Col. Charlewood</u>: I hope you will be able to cheer him up a little, and that the change of air will be of service to his health. ——— Your Aunt Agnes has a bad <u>common</u> cold and I am very well; this is all the report I have to give from Hampstead hill. Not a very bad report all things considered.

    Yours, my dear William very affectionately

      J Baillie

Wellcome Institute for the History of Medicine

MS 5613/58 (Address: William H. Baillie Esqr / Suffolk Square / Cheltenham--postmarked 1838)

Hampstead August 8<u>th</u> 1838

My dear William,

    I have just been overlooking your last letter which has lien [*sic*] in my packet of unanswered letters a shameful time. Why I have been so long of making any reply I know not and I shall not occupy my pen & my paper any more about it. You will not be very angry with Aunt Jo. for being lazy & forgetful, at least you will be a foolish man if you be. We had some conversation about our descent with Mr Richardson a good while ago, who thinks and I have no doubt of it, that our Ancestor, Andrew Baillie the exile, was not the Brother but the Nephew of the Principal, for in one of his letters which Richardson read, he thanks a friend in Holand [*sic*] for being kind to his Nephew. He did not, however name him, for if he had and the name were Andrew, this would make the thing certain. He had fled the country as being connected with Baillie of Jerviswood, but being the son of a younger son, he might lose a little money but would have no property that could be confiscated. Principal Baillie was the son of Baillie of Jervis<u>ton</u> and probably a near relation of Baillie of Jervis<u>woods</u>', both of them descended from the Baillies of Lamington which, by tradition at least, is <u>our</u> descent. My Father's name <u>was</u> James, and his younger Brother's name was Andrew, agreeing exactly with the Parish Register of Chrighton. There can be little doubt, I think, that Principal Baillie had a Brother, for how else could we be connected with the Carnbroe Baillies, and the picture mentioned by Genl Baillie as the picture of our Ancester which he intended to bequeath to you must have been the portrait of the Laird of Jerviston, Principal B's Father and our Exile's Grand Father. Richardson will probably dine with us before he leaves Town for the season, and then we shall have a further talk upon the subject. I shall be sure to make a fair copy for you of the statement regarding our family that you desire, and it shall be ready for you when you come to Town whenever that may be, so our <u>Forebears</u> (as the Scotch call them) may rest for the present. —— I received a note from Mr Picquot a few days ago, inclosing some papers of proposal for publishing by subscription a history of the Caliphate of Bagdad in 2 vol at thirty shillings.[38] I have written to him in reply that my Sister would subscribe for one copy & myself for another, but that my interest for subscription among my other friends is quite exhausted and I could not promise to do more. A History of Bagdad if pretty well written may be useful for young people, for I dont know of any in a <u>Come stable</u> shape.[39] I wish he may make something of it. He has of course written to you.

And now for a more agreeable subject — Wife & Bairns! I think of you & them every day, and were we nearer, should I think, be among you every day without the least fear of being a troublesome visitor. Indeed you & Henrietta & the little ones are all as my Children, and I have nothing in this world so agreeable to think of. I long to hear what your Mother will say of Sophy & Matthew when she sees them. And how complete her satisfaction is now in her Children & Grand Children, being all united in good will & affection with one another. She is to return from Mortimer to day, and we shall have a visit from her (not a long one I fear) before she sets out for Ryde. All our friends in Town are scattering off for the season, and we are receiving fare well calls every day. Amongst such visitors we received the other morning M^r & Mrs Denman,[40] previous to their leaving Town for Gloucester Sh^r. And what a grand Place Duntisbourn is to become! Window curtains in the Drawing room! They are both very happy at the prospect before them, and when you go to visit them, I hope these same curtains will put you in concert with your own house. There is a kind of originality about that Pair which I like, they shape their own way through the every-day matters of the world according to their own fashion, and nothing comes amiss to them. Our everyday matters at present are confused enough, chimney's sweeping, carpets lifting, walls cleaning & pictures taken down &c. Yesterday in the midst of all this hurly burly two Ladies with their school-Girl niece & a maid sev^t came &

---

38. Whether Mr. Picquot is the author, editor or proposed publisher of this proposed work is not clear here, but I find no published work on Bagdad by an author of this name.

39. come stable: edible, fit for food; in this case, probably fit for consumption (*SND*).

40. This is probably Lord Chief Justice Thomas Denman (1779-1854), Sophia Denman Baillie's only brother, who came to London to study law in 1800 and began his own practice in 1803. He married Theodosia Vevers in 1804 and moved to Russell Square, the most fashionable region for leading lawyers. He was an advocate of legal reform, abolition of slavery and was connected with several important trials. Thomas and Theodosia had 5 sons and 6 daughters (*DNB*, V:809). Because of the late date, this could also be a son of the Denmans and his wife.

had luncheon with us, then followed Dr Park before they left us,[41] then came Miss Beaufort (Miss Edgeworth's friend) & her Niece,[42] and last of all Lady Davy,[43] full of chat & good humour, and our little parlour became quite a gay place. To day our hurly burly has some what subsided, so probably we shall have fewer visits. Your Aunt Agnes creeps about very slowly & is soon fatigued, but does not suffer much either from rheumatism or stomach. To night we are to be rather gay – we are to go to Lady Alderson, who is our neighbour for a while, to hear her Niece Miss Giffard sing. We are told she sings very sweetly and we expect some Scotch songs as they (there are two Sisters) have lived with their Mother in Edin^r for some years. All this little gossip if you should not care for it, will be received with more sympathy by Henrietta. Aunt Agnes sends her kind love united with mine to you both. May God bless you & yours! Your affectionate Aunt

    J Baillie

Wellcome Institute for the History of Medicine

MS 5615/84 (Address: Mrs William Baillie / Suffolk Square / Cheltenham--postmarked 1838)

                         Hampstead tuesday Augst 21 1838

My dear Henrietta

It always gives us great pleasure to hear favorable accounts of yourself and the dear Children, and the last we had were as good as could well be, thank God for it! I hope this will find you & them in as good condition as you were then in. Now that we have lost our Sister of Cavendish Sq^r for a season, we shall hear seldomer of you, William & you therefore must take this into consideration and let us hear the oftener from you. We shall miss her sadly, but she is going to those with whom she will be happy, who

---

41. Baillie's friend John Ranicar Park (1778-1847), theologian and surgeon and only son of surgeon Henry Park, was born in Liverpool and later educated at Jesus College, Cambridge, receiving an MD in 1818. He was made a fellow of The Royal College of Surgeons in 1819 and also a fellow of the Linnean Society. His professional works include *Inquiry into the Laws of Animal Life* (1812) and *The Pathology of Fever* (1822). But his subsequent works were theological and included *Views of Prophecy and the Millennium* and *Concise Exposition of the Apocalypse* in 1823, *The Apocalypse Explained* in 1832, *An Amicable Controversy with a Jewish Rabbi on the Messiah's Coming* in 1832, and *An Answer to Anti-Supernaturalism* in 1844 (*DNB*, XV:218).

42. Maria Edgeworth's sisters were Mrs. Beaufort and Mrs. Wilson. Miss Beaufort may be a future in-law.

43. Lady Davy, the widow of Shuckburgh Ashby Apreece and daughter and heiress of Charles Kerr, married natural philosopher and poet Sir Humphrey Davy (1778-1829) on 11 April 1812. See letters to Lady Davy herein.

have the nearest claims to her affection, and we must not repine but rejoice in it. Our immediate neighbours have all gone away or are about to do so, and by & by we shall be left to the charity of more distant ones on down shire hill & other outstanding places and I daresay we shant be entirely deserted. M<u>rs</u> & Miss Hoare are going to celebrate another wedding in their family and will afterwards take up their abode for a time at Brighton. Yesterday we had a very interesting visit from D<u>r</u> Lushington whom we had not seen since he lost his wife.[44] It was a great effort for him to come & see us & M<u>rs</u> Hoare, but he commanded his feelings as well as he could, though tears at one time, when he talked of his little dumb Girl, would not be repressed. This poor Child was with him & Miss Carr who lives with him and takes care of them all at present. I hope indeed she will remain altogether for what could they do without her. This last sad year has brought more lines upon his face, has quenched in some degree the fire of his keen eye & whitened his head with many more grey hairs than should naturally have come in the course of eleven months. But this is a melancholy subject and you were but slightly acquainted with our dear Sarah Lushington. I will turn to one full of brightness & hope, your little Sophy & Matt playing on the floor with all their own peculiar ways of shewing intelligence & affection. It would indeed give your old Aunts here great delight to see it. We must enjoy the next best thing, thinking of it, and picturing it often in our imagination. How often we shall think of you dear Henrietta as your time draws near.[45] May God bless & prosper you and, if it be <u>his</u> will spare you from great suffering! We shall all (old Aunties & all) think ourselves the richer for another healthy Baby added to the stock whether it be Boy or Girl. — I am very glad to hear that your Uncle & Aunt, to whom we beg to be kindly remembered, found your Mother & Grand Mother & all your near relations in the north so well. My Sister unites with me in kindest love to you & William & the little folks, having something particular to say to William and not wishing to send a double letter, ignorant likewise of the craft & mystery of cross writing,[46] I must

---

44. Stephen Lushington (1782-1873) was one of the attorneys involved in the Byron separation settlement, and he married Sarah Grace Carr (d. 1837), the daughter of Mr. and Mrs. Thomas William Carr, in 1821. He was also retained as counsel for Queen Caroline before the House of Lords and made a masterly speech in her defense in October 1820. He was an ardent reformer, supporting the abolition of capital punishment, and an able advocate. The Lushingtons had 5 sons and 5 daughters (*DNB*, XII:291-93).

45. William and Henrietta Baillie's son William Hunter Baillie was born in 1838 (d. 1895).

46. Many letter-writers from this period employed cross-writing as a method of saving paper. The writing appeared in the usual horizontal lines on the page and was then overwritten vertically or at an angle; the reading of such letters is often very

now take my leave of you, remaining always my dear Niece yours very affectionately

J Baillie

My dear William,

Richardson & part of his family came to us on sunday se'nnight and he brought a packet of papers regarding the descent which will be put into your hands very soon after you receive this, your Mother having offered to inclose it in a parcel to be sent to Cheltenham in a few days. I have looked over them and see, as you will do, that though Mr Hill has been very diligent in his researches, we are no further advanced as to our main purpose than when I wrote to you last. The exile[d] Andrew Baillie may still be presumed to have been the Nephew of Principal Baillie, and Richardson says he has no doubt of it, but till we can find some mention of a Nephew of his named <u>Andrew</u> there is no certainty. Mr Hill is still to be on the watch for further information, and, as you will see, has desired him to send the statement of expences incurred to him (Richardson) We may or rather <u>he</u> may pass upon the information we desire in looking over title deeds of lands connected with the Carnbroe or Principal's family, and should there be no success you will at least have the satisfaction of having done all that could be done. Richardson is a great man for Pedigrees himself, so he enters into your views con amore. He & his eldest Daughter, the bright-eyed Hope and his Son Roland set off for Scotland last thursday and expect to dine in his own house in Selkirk sh^r on the following saturday. Last sunday we had Dr Allen Thomson & your old acquaintance Angus Fletcher to dine with us.[47] Fletcher was just recovered from a severe attack of English Cholera which however had left no marks of sickness on his countenance,[48] and he was as cheerful and made as good a

---

difficult!

47. This may be biologist Allen Thomson (1809-1884), educated in Edinburgh and later representing the University of Edinburgh and the University of Glasgow through a distinguished career (*DNB*, XIX:713). Angus Fletcher (1799-1862), son of Mrs. Elizabeth Fletcher, gave up a law practice to attend the Royal Academy Schools in 1825, exhibiting at the Academy from 1831 to 1839. His finest busts are of the Duke of Argyll (1831), J. B. S. Morritt of Rokeby (1834) and author Charles Dickens (1839), to whom Fletcher reportedly endeared himself. He also exhibited two busts of Felicia Hemans in 1830 and 1832 (Chester Lee Lambertson, "The Letters of Joanna Baillie [1801-1832]" [Ph.D. diss., Harvard University, 1956], cxxv-cc).

48. The first world-wide epidemic of cholera, with its vibrio attacking the intestines through contaminated food or water, began in 1817 in India and spread to Russia and western Europe. England was invaded in 1831 with approximately 50,000 deaths resulting throughout the British Isles. Four other pandemics during the 19th century showed similar characteristics (see Sir Macfarlane Burnet, *Natural History of Infectious Disease*, 3rd ed. [Cambridge: Cambridge University Press, 1962],

dinner as we could desire. I believe his new business in casts & in modelling, carried on in Dean St: Soho, is doing very well and that will keep him in good heart. Your Aunt & I are going to be very enterprising this week we are absolutely to drive as far as Totridge [Totteridge] . . .[49] us to do so, and she is the Daughter of an old friend whom with the good man her husband it is pleasant to see prosperous in the world. — Good by to you, my dear William! I have now said my say.

University of Glasgow
MS Gen 542/3 fragment (Address: William H. Baillie Esqr / The Hermitage / Richmond / Surrey--postmarked 22 July 1842)

[1842]

. . . a visit from . . .[50] who has been ill, and indeed his looks told us so, for he is very thin & yellow. If he has any thoughts of matrimony in his head, he must not go a courting at this bout. ——— Your Aunt Agnes unites with me in kindest love to your Mother & Henrietta; we trust you are all enjoying Richmond hill together as this showery weather will permit. The damp gives your poor Aunt a good deal of pain in her limbs, but I hope it will not long continue. —

We had Miss Campbell from Stoke Newington to dine with us day before yesterday, and she has got pretty well <u>on</u> with subscriptions for her book and will soon, I hope have it in the press.[51] She was Candidate for a situation belonging to one of our new institutions that would, I think have suited her well, and out of twenty Candidates, or more, three were selected as most proper by the Committee and she was one of the three. The friend who recommended her had then great hopes that she would be successful, but unluckily upon examination before the Committee on theological matters, she did not answer some knotty point about predestination to their mind and she failed, disappointment took place a few days ago. I hope, however, she will find some suitable solution by & by. ——— We are to have Mr Richardson & his Daughter Helen to dine with us next Sunday, and come early that they may hear Mr Ainger preach.[52] Having given you

---

331-32).

49. An entire line here is illegible because of the letter's binding.

50. The introductory words and name have been thoroughly marked out in ink on this letter.

51. I have not identified Miss Campbell or this work. There was a Miss Harriett Campbell publishing in London around this time, but with no more information from Baillie, I cannot verify.

52. Thomas Ainger (1799-1863) became curate of St. Giles, Reading, in 1822 and in 1841 was presented by Sir Thomas Wilson to the perpetual curacy of Hampstead which he held until his death (*DNB*, I:188).

such a minute account of ourselves I take my leave.

Your affectionate Aunt

J Baillie

Cowie Collection, Mitchell Library, Glasgow
218c (No address or postmark, ML dates Nov. 14, 1844)

Hampstead Thursday [1844?]

My dear Sophia,

We were sorry to leave you yesterday without saying some words of parting kindness, but we did not like to disturb you with your visitor so we went silently away, though our hearts were full of grateful thoughts after all the enjoyment we had had so quietly & comfortably in your society. Always kind & considerate & affectionate to us! much cause we have to bless God that our lots have been so connected for many years. — Agnes came home very well, had her chocolate & toast [at] six o'clock and went to bed at eight. She has not however had a good night, but it turns out to be bile and is working it self [*sic*] off, so that I trust she will be well to morrow. Lady Bentham is sitting with her now in her room, but she means to be down stairs to Dinner.[53] I heard from William this morning: he knows nothing of the stray book, but will search for it, and gives a good account of Henrietta & the Children. —— I have made a good many visits this fine morning; I have been at Mrs Hoare's, Mrs Stoner, Mrs Mallet's[54] & poor Mrs Greave. The day was so fine it would have been both sin & folly not to have used it.

Your cheese went to Mrs Jones, and the Page who came to fetch it brought a note informing us that the Queen has given Mr P. Tyller a pension of £200 a year which he well deserves. I know you will be glad of this too. When I called for Mrs Mallet I found that she was gone out and that Mrs H. Merivale left us yesterday.[55] —— Farewell, I will write again to morrow, if Agnes does not, and in the mean time I must return to Lady B.

---

53. Lady Bentham, Sophia Fordyce, married Sir Samuel Bentham (1757-1831) in 1796 but survived him many years. Samuel was a naval architect and engineer and brother of Jeremy Bentham (*DNB*, II:281-84).

54. Louis/Lewis Mallet descended from a French Huguenot family who had settled in Geneva, was the son of Mallet du Pan, a famous journalist who was forced to flee Paris for England at the start of the French Revolution. Louis was well known to Pitt and through his influence became a clerk in the audit office after 1800. Mallet's wife Frances was the daughter of John Merivale (*DNB*, XII:871).

55. John Herman Merivale (1779-1844) was a scholar and minor poet, accomplished in classical and romantic literature. He was a friend of Byron, who praised his translations and poetry, and published such works as *Orlando in Roncesvalles* (1814), a 2-volume collection of poems in 1838, and translations of the minor poems of Schiller. Merivale married Louisa Heath Drury with whom he had 6

affectionately yours
        J Baillie
PS. I forgot to say that I met Mrs M. Pryor to day on the street, who wished to know if you could do without her votes for your candidate, and I ventured to say that you could. I hope I have not done wrong. —

National Library of Scotland
2522 f.1-2 (No address or postmark)

                                    Hampstead monday morning [~1844]
My dear Sophia,
        Agnes says you kindly wished to have some report of my health this morning, and I am thankful to have a pretty good one to give. I lay in bed the whole day yesterday as I should have done no good by keeping out of it, but this morning I have been up at breakfast, and have settled all the last weeks accounts as usual. I wish I had as good a report to give of poor Agnes herself. She is in bed with a cold that goes over her head & down one side of her throat and is, with the addition of rhuematism [*sic*], to say the least of it, very uncomfortable. She was very busy taking care of me yesterday, and I must be as good as I can to her to day[.] If the weather would be come milder and the frost really go away, we should soon be better, at present we are very poor bodies indeed. — She cheered me on Saturday evening by giving a better account of your looks and also an improved report of poor Mary Milligan[,] for Mrs Hoare on Saturday forenoon had read me a very desponding letter from one of the Freston's on the state of her disease. I hope she will yet be spared to enjoy her health and do good to others. Dear Mary! how kind & benevolent she has always been! We could very ill spare her though we are blessed with more kind affectionate friends than most people are at our advanced age. — You may be sure, my dear Sophia, it was a great disappointment to us not to go to you on Saturday as we had fixed to do; some days of your society would have cheered & revived us. But we hope this pleasure will not be very long postponed, and you shall hear from us again very soon.
        Our kind Neighbour Mrs Jones has supplied us with a new book, (new to us at least) Conningsby [*sic*], but some how or other I dont take very kindly to it, and I question much if I shall get through it.[56] Satyrs on the world are not very attractive reading for those who must expect so soon to leave it. ――― I had a kind note from William the other day which I shall

children (*DNB*, XIII:281-2).
        56. Benjamin Disraeli's *Coningsby: or, The New Generation* (1844) was part of a trilogy focusing on the condition of the working class and associating its author with the Tory "Young England" group.

answer this morning. I need not tell you the good report he gives of them all at Belgrave house.

Agnes sends you her kind love with mine. She had a visit yesterday from Sir John Herchell [sic],[57] and I was glad she had something to rouse & interest her while I was in bed. Always most affectionately your

    J Baillie

Wellcome Institute for the History of Medicine

MS 5617/87 (No address of postmark)

                                Hampstead thursday Jany 3$^{\underline{d}}$ 1851

My dear Elizabeth, my dear Aunt Mary, my own dear Sophy — all very dear to us:[58] the account you give of your Xmas & new year festivities & gambols is quite delightful, and it makes our hearts glad to hear it. Your gifts both for finery & feasting are excellent & beautiful: receive our hearty thanks. I have very good reports to give you of Aunt Agnes to day. She has made a good Luchion [sic] and that is a great point for the evening dinner often is of less importance. She thinks that she sleeps very little but she has more sleep than she is aware of, for she sees people coming into her room and they roam about and she is not affraid [sic] of them. William is one of her nightly visitors though it is a vision not a dream. We may have more returns of this kind but probably it will do her no harm. Since I sat down to write this we have received a very kind & courteous visit from Lord Cranworth & the Peeress resting on his arm, both very happy and, as I well know, deserving to be so.[59] It is really a pleasant thing to look on them.

---

57. Sir John Herschel (1792-1871) was a friend of Baillie though it is unclear when or where Herschel first met her; it is probable they met through her brother Matthew. Herschel must have admired her work, for his journal entry for 1 January 1837, states that he has just "Read Miss Baillie's Martyr" (Evans, 273). It appears from some of the other letters in the Royal Society collection, however, that Herschel had a more familiar relationship with Agnes. See *Dictionary of Scientific Biography,* ed. Charles Coulston Gillispie (New York: Charles Scribner's Sons, 1972), VI:323-28. There are many useful works on John Herschel, among them *Herschel at the Cape: Diaries and Correspondence of Sir John Herschel, 1834-1838,* ed. David S. Evans, *et al* (Austin: University of Texas Press, 1969). See letters to Herschel, Volume 2.

58. This letter, one of Joanna's last, is probably to her niece Elizabeth Margaret Milligan and daughter Sophia Milligan. Aunt Mary [Milligan] must be Elizabeth's aunt by marriage, but I have been unable to verify.

59. Lord Cranworth, Robert Rolfe (1790-1868), was Lord Chancellor and reportedly a man of high character. He married Laura Carr, daughter of Thomas Carr of Hampstead, on 9 October 1845 (*DNB,* XVII:158-61).

I must now lay down the pen. You will probably hear more of us and our nightly visions soon.

very affectionately yours
     Joanna Baillie
We shall think of Henrietta & her great party as the evening comes on and wish her well through it

The following letters are undated and have no passages which make dating positive. These are arranged by collection.

Cowie Collection, Mitchell Library, Glasgow
222c (Address: M<u>rs</u> Baillie, no postmark)

Hampstead Saturday [after 1835]
We thank you dear Henrietta, for your kind note, received this morning, and wish you a happy meeting with our friends on Monday. I hope they will come to you not the worse for their journey and bring you good tidings of your dear Mother. ――― In regard to engagements, do for us what suits William & yourself & your dear Guests best, and let us know; we shall make it all good as well as we are able. ―――

I am going to Bays water this morning to see Miss Jane Porter and I am glad I go to day,[60] for it will not come in way of any plans for next week. Poor Miss P. has been confined with illness all the winter and wished to see me and it is very kind in Miss Longman to take me in her warm close carriage.[61] ―――

Your Aunt sends her love & thanks. She has just left her room and suffers a good deal to day.

     Yours affectionately
          J Baillie

---

60. Jane Porter (1776-1850) was a childhood friend of Walter Scott in Edinburgh but moved to London in 1803 where she met Baillie, Hannah More and Laetitia Barbauld. Her works include romance *Thaddeus of Warsaw* (4 vols., 1804), the successful novel *The Scottish Chiefs* (5 vols., 1810), drama *Switzerland*, acted at Drury Lane in 1819, *Sir Edward Seaward's Narrative of his Shipwreck and consequent Discovery of certain Islands in the Caribbean Sea* (3 vols., 1831), etc. Baillie acknowledged her indebtedness to Porter's *Scottish Chiefs* when writing her *Wallace* in *Metrical Legends*, and Scott, given credit for developing the historical novel, might surely be indebted to Porter as well (*DNB*, XVI:182-84).

61. This is probably the daughter of Baillie's neighbor and friend Thomas Longman III (1771-1842), who published such authors as Wordsworth, Coleridge, Scott and Baillie, carrying on in the publishing tradition of Thomas Longman (1699-1755) who founded the publishing firm which still exists today (*OCEL*, 585).

University of Glasgow
MS Gen 1587 p.69 (Address: Lady Campbell--no postmark)

Cavendish Sq^r
Wednesday [after 1833]

My Dear Cousin,

It gives my Sister & me very great pleasure to hear that you go on recovering so well, making advances to <u>more</u> than your usual health which has of late been weak & uncertain, and I am glad to take the opportunity of Mrs Baillie's cover to inclose a few lines of cheering of which as you will easily believe come from the heart. To think that we shall see you so restored in health & strength to enjoy life again and to give comfort & gladness to your friends, does us good, and God bless you in your convalescent state! which is often with affectionate friends around one, a happier condition than that of perfect health. — Before you can receive this, I hope Col. Charliwood's [sic] influenza-cold will be entirely gone. We begrudged very much that his visit to Town should have been so much disturbed by it, when a little change of scene & amusement would have been desirable. But he submitted to his fate with a good grace, and is rewarded now by seeing you so well. — Agnes & I came to Town last monday on a very gay errand, to carry a young Scotch friend of ours to Mr Bartley's benefit, where we saw Mad^{lle} Grisi & all the wonders of the Opera house at no great cost & much at our ease, though the Theatre was as full as it could cram.[62] The actors in the play were all dressed in court suits as in former days, why or wherefore we could not tell, as the Piece was a new one & the scene laid in modern times. — I have been twice with the Sotheby's since we came, and was sorry to find the family still in some distress on poor Harriet's account.[63] She is again under Dr Holland's care,

---

62. Italian operatic soprano Giulia Grisi (1811-69) made her debut at seventeen in Rossini's *Zelmira*. From 1829 she sang in Milan, moving to Paris in 1832 as a leading singer at the Italiens until 1849. She made her London debut in 1834 and sang there with much success until 1861, returning after her retirement to sing again in 1866. She continued to give concerts and made her home in London (Oscar Thompson, ed., *The International Cyclopedia of Music and Musicians* [New York: Dodd, Mead, 1985], 875).

63. William Sotheby (1757-1833) was a prodigious poet, playwright, and translator and the consummate man of letters in the Romantic Era. Though Byron disliked him, satirizing him as Mr. Botherby in *Beppo* (1818), Sotheby provided a societal focal point for many of the brightest literary minds of his time. Scott, Wordsworth, Coleridge and Southey were his friends (*DLB*, XCIII:160-70 and see letters to Sotheby). The Sothebys had 5 sons and 2 daughters, and Harriet is probably a family member, but I have not been able to identify her.

suffering under a rheumatic fever, M<u>rs</u> Sotheby looking very shrunk in the face & very helpless and Miss Sotheby is sad & anxious & thin. —

We return home to morrow, and next week, when every body will be occupied with the grand festivals in the Abbey, M<u>rs</u> Baillie will pass quietly on Hampstead hill with us. I wish you were to be near us tho: it would be a pleasant thing for us to have you for a neighbor next door, and to run in & out of your apartment four or five times in the day. I readily admit, however, that you are much better where you are, and that my wish is a very selfish one. — I suppose you read the quarterly <u>Review</u> and have (and have) been interested with that article which gives an account of M<u>r</u> Henry Taylor's Dramatic Romance.[64] The extracts justify the praise bestowed upon it, and I mean to read the work itself when I can do so without spending any money, for I am too poor to buy books, be they ever so tempting. Whatever comes in a Dramatic form, I have some curiosity to read, though a Dramatic Romance in these parts is rather a formidable thing to encounter. But there is another Dramatic Novelty which I have read with great avidity — The Seven Temptations by Mary Hewit [sic] of Nottingham, a Quaker Lady.[65] There is real genius both in the design & execution of the plan, and the work is only one small volume, so you will not find it tedious in any respect. For authors now are like American authors who, when they have got occupation of the floor, hold out for some six or seven hours at a stretch. Pray give me one short novel instead of two long ones! is a prayer I should often make; but who would attend to it when their Highnesses the Booksellers say that long works pay them best. — — Agnes writes with me in kindest wishes to yourself & to Col. Charliwood.

Yours affectionately My Dear Lady Campbell! how my heart warmed to that part of your letter to M<u>rs</u> Baillie which mentions the kind attentions shown to you by the medical profession as the Daughter of John Hunter! it gratified very much your aged cousin

　　J Baillie

---

64. This is probably playwright Sir Henry Taylor (1800-86), born at Durham and earning a knighthood for service in the colonial office. Without a date it is difficult to pinpoint which play and which *Review*, but his dramas, never produced, included *Philip van Artevelde* (1834), *Edwin the Fair* (1842), *The Virgin Widow* (1850) and others (Ian Ousby, ed., *The Cambridge Guide to Literature in English* [Cambridge & New York: Cambridge University Press, 1993], 928).

65. Mary Howitt (1799-1888), novelist, nature writer, writer for children, editor and translator, was the second of four children born to strict Quaker parents Samuel and Ann Botham. She married Quaker William Howitt in 1821, and they collaborated on several works. Some of her own publications include *The Seven Temptations* (1834), *Sketches of Natural History* (1834), *Wood Lighten, or a Year in the Country* (1836), *The Heir of West Waylay* (1847) and many others (Todd, 335-37).

Wellcome Institute for the History of Medicine[66]
MS 5608/42 (No address or postmark)

My dear Sophia

I just write to say that we cannot have our carriage to morrow as it happens to be the Coach man's yearly club day and must not be disturbed, but we shall be at your door on tuesday morning and if you will go with us to the Exhibition, it will most surely be an additional pleasure to us, provided it be perfectly convenient to yourself.

Your kind invitation I am sorry to say we must decline and return here before dinner, for the Miss Hunters are to dine with us next thursday and we are to dine with Mrs Hoare on friday, so we have as much to do in one week as we have strength for. With all kind love from us both, believe me affectionately yours my dear kind Sister

J Baillie
Sunday afternoon
June 27th
(We shall be at your door on tuesday before eleven)

Wellcome Institute for the History of Medicine
MS 5614/38 fragment (No address or postmark)

Hampstead Wednesday Novr 22 [after 1843]

My dear Henrietta,

I am not naturally given to write letters or notes, but I must needs Congratulate you & William for the great honour paid to your youngest Daughter. To have her beauty Celebrated in verse and latin verse too, by one of the distinguished classical schollars [sic] of Eaton in former days![67] Truly she is an honoured Chit, and will not be spoilt by it. Let (let) Mama bear the implied compliment made to herself as meekly, and then there will be no harm done of any kind. Dear little Helen! Grand mama Duff will I am very sure be pleased with the honour done to her namesake, and probably at her age was as worthy of the Poet's praise. I am told that all the classical Scholars of Portland place are vying with one another in making translations of it, and the aged Poet himself will almost become young again in having caused such a pleasant commotion. I hope all the

---

66. Wellcome Institute MS 5613/77/1-3 are mistakenly listed as being from Joanna Baillie to Miss Berry.

67. WI suggests this poet is Mr. Blount. Henrietta and William Baillie's daughter Helen Mary Henrietta was born in 1843 (d.1929), dating the letter after that time.

other young companions of this celebrated Lady are well, and enjoying her distinction, as far as they can understand it. ——

Your Aunt Agnes has suffered a good deal with cold in her head & face, but is now almost well; she was in misery with the pain at first. We are now all dislodged from the Church and are put in possession for the time being, of places in Wellwalk Chapel. But that is at too great a distance for Agnes, and must take a Fly or a chair when she goes. It is said the church will be ready to receive us by the new year, but that I doubt. Your friend Mr Collins has his mind occupied at present with other things than pews & pulpits, he is going to be married. The Lady he has chosen has good commendations of all who know her. She is the Daughter of a wealthy Book . . . .[68]

Wellcome Institute for the History of Medicine
MS 5616/46 (No address or postmark)

Hampstead Decr 28th

My dear William

I hope this will not be very long of reaching you and with it a copy of Fraser's Magazine, for your Mother contrives to have things conveyed very cleverly and seldom lets an opportunity escape. In this, as in many other things, she has greatly the advantage over me, for I let many opportunities escape from stupidity & want of readiness and so it has been with me through the whole of my life. — I hope Henrietta & you though in an indirect way, have received our thanks for your very bountiful present of Xmas provisions. Finer fowls & turkey I never saw; they might have done honour to the Larder of an Alderman and indeed it would have required the stomachs of Aldermen to have mastered them, had they been served up on one table. Many thanks to you then for <u>four</u> excellent dinners on our own little parlor and one in the house of a very kind neighbour where more & younger mouths were set to work in subduing the gallant Turkey. Many many thanks! ——— Your Aunt & I have been almost constantly at home since we returned from Cavendish Sq^r and when we did go out it was more a matter of duty than of pleasure, for "wind & <u>weet</u> and snow & sleet" have made our own chimney corner the only desirable place to be in. Happily for us some of our kind neighbours, stronger & more enterprising than ourselves, have now & then dropt in upon us of a morning and told us somewhat of the sayings & doings of the world round us, and we have not been left in perfect solitude & ignorance. — we were quite pleased to hear of Baby's two coming teeth which perhaps are actually <u>come</u> by this time, but rather more surprised than pleased at her new

---

68. The remainder of the letter is missing.

accomplishment of whistling. What kind of noise is it that you call whistling? Crowing hens & whistling Lasses, says the old proverb, are <u>no</u> canny.[69] I must own, however, that if she has aught of the witch in her, she is a very bewitching witch and will I trust prove to be of the white kind. We had a note from James Mylne the other day to announce the birth of a fine Boy, a present as he calls it, from his wife to him on Xmas morning.[70] But you have heard of this no doubt already and sympathize with his joy on the happy occasion. I hope all will go on well with the Mother & child. James is not always agreeable, but he is always friendly and seems always to consider himself as allied & connected with you which goes a good way in really making him so. Did your Mother tell you that when we were in Town we went with her to drink tea with M<u>rs</u> Mylne on a Saturday evening and met with Barry Cornwall, that double worthy belonging to law & poesy, the man of two professions as well as two names, and other men of law & merchandise who had dined with them.[71] Procter or Cornwall had much to say and kept by the side of my chair murmuring in a low dull voice all his opinions, some of them as far, as I could hear them, sensible ones of modern writers, theatres & actors &c till I was right glad when a good plain Merchant, with less refinement & a louder voice came up to me on the other side and sent him away. ———— We have this morning heard of the Brighton Mail that has been lost amongst the snow with its four passengers, and once or twice Col. Charlewood has glanced painfully across my thoughts. But as he would probably travel in company with his Nieces to this great wedding, there is surely very little chance of his being one of the four. — Your Aunt Agnes, who is sitting by me, desires you to accept her love, and unites with me in wishing you, Henrietta & Baby a happy new year: happy and many may the years be that lie before you!

We have all much reason to be thankful for the kindness of Providence

---

69. "A whistling woman and a crowing hen are neither fit for God nor men" or "A crooning Cow, a crowing Hen and a whistling Maid broded never luck to a House" (J. A. Simpson, ed., *The Concise Oxford Dictionary of Proverbs* [Oxford & New York: Oxford University Press, 1982], 245).

70. John Millar was a professor at the University of Glasgow and colleague of Joanna's father James (*DNB*, XIII:403).

71. Barry Cornwall (Procter, Bryan Waller [1787-1874]) was a poet born at Leeds and educated at Harrow. A successful barrister, he began to contribute to the *Literary Gazette* in 1815 and thereafter produced several volumes of poetry, including, *Dramatic Scenes* (1819) and *English Songs* (1832) and a tragedy *Mirandola* (1821). His daughter was the poet Adelaide Anne Procter (Ousby, 210).

hitherto, and may well trust that what is best for us will be given to us.
——

    Believe me always, my dear William
        Your affectionate Aunt
          J Baillie

Wellcome Institute for the History of Medicine
MS 5616/62 (No address or postmark)

                         Hampstead tuesday March 3$\underline{d}$
My dear Sophia
    We were indeed well pleased to hear that Robert is gone into Lincolnsh^r with his friend though it will remove the pleasure of seeing you here for some days farther. Next week then we shall be most happy to see you at dinner, and may I venture to say tuesday, as monday is not a convenient day here for marketing &c? By putting the visit off till then, we shall have a chance of milder weather; and if it be convenient for Sophy to make a longer visit to us at that time, we shall have her bed & her room in such good condition, that we shant be afraid of her being the worse for it. Give our love to her and to <u>Mama</u>, and say how happy old Aunties will be to have such a kind Inmate for as long a time as her other engagements will allow her to spare. Our Damsels too will make comfortable quarters for her maid. When we have your answer, we shall bespeak <u>Mrs & Miss Hoare</u> to meet you in the evening. This is on the whole a bright day for the wedding in that family; we have not as yet heard any thing about it but that there were 13 carriages of the Bridal train went to church. — Our kind Mrs Greaves came home last friday, dined with us on saturday, and we have met some time or other every day since. But I am sorry to say she is to leave us again next friday, I fear for a good while. She is interested just now for a poor blind Boy which a friend of her wants to get into the Asylum: can you give her any help? Agnes also desires me to say that the button woman is in Town and will probably call soon for her money. — I sympathize very much with the happiness of Caroline & Annie in the prospect of going to Rhyde [*sic*]. Never to have seen the sea and the first sight of it so near at hand! how much delight is included in all this! and I trust they will not be disappointed.
    Looking forward then to next tuesday with pleasure, I remain, my dear Sister
        affectionately yours
          J Baillie
Agnes sends her kindest love to you & your dear Circle.
If next tuesday should not suit you, any day afterwards that you please to name will suit us. ——

Royal College of Surgeons
    HB.ii-45 (No address or postmark)

[after 1843]

    Niece Henrietta with poor skill
    I've tried your biding [bidding?] to fulfill
    But in an Old, unready Muse
    Set thus a rhyming, Willy, Nilly
    Failures you kindly must excuse.
    What think ye of your Matt and your Wee Willy?

My dear Henrietta I send you the inclosed verses on your two Sons and pray be as well pleased with them as you can for I can write no better.[72] As we say in the west of Scotland "I dow do no mair." — I am ashamed to send a copy of them with a blotted outline in it, but I could not make up my mind nor my fingers to write another.
    your affectionate Aunt
      J Baillie

City of Liverpool, Leisure Services Directorate, Central Library
Boaden Vol. 2 p.254 (No address or postmark)

Hampstead friday evening [after 1835]

My dear Henrietta,
    Poor Ryand [?] has made a bad business of it in coming up to Hampstead to find Lodgings in such a day as this. However, had the day been fair, I dont think even with Mary's assistance, she would have made any thing of it; for she had no clear idea of what she wanted. I should think you had better do nothing more in this business till you are settled in your house and can look about the neighbourhood yourself. If she is to have a furnish'd room with the use of a Copper for washing &c. the rent will be five shillings a week, and if she wishes for an unfurnished room into which she can bring her own things, they will not let her have it for so short a time, as your term in Mr Cameron's house. ——— I hope your dear

---

72. Enclosed are two ms. poems entitled "Two Brothers" (HB.ii-47) and "To James Baillie, an Infant" (HB.ii-48). Henrietta and William Baillie's first three sons were Matthew John (1837-66), William Hunter (1838-95) and John Baron (1841-68), followed later by Robert Denman (1850-70); Helen Mary Henrietta was born in 1843. The poem to James Baillie must have been written for Joanna's sister-in-law Sophia on the birth of son James Baillie (1792), who died in 1793 (Crainz, "Genealogical Table"). "Two Brothers" appeared in Baillie's *Fugitive Verses* in 1840 (with alterations); "To James B. Baillie, an Infant" appeared in *The Dramatic and Poetical Works of Joanna Baillie* in 1851.

Mother has not felt this wet day very uncomfortably. Longing for next thursday very much, I rest dear Henrietta, affectionately your

J Baillie

Fitzwilliam Museum, Cambridge
Holland, ALS 29/2 (No address or postmark)

My dear M[r] Denman,[73]

Perhaps M[r] Holland, the young Gentleman who was so kind as to call upon ~~you~~ us yesterday, might like to accompany you next sunday, if no better engagement should come in his way. It would add to our pleasure in seeing you. Pray tell him so, if it suits <u>your</u> convenience to have a companion; if not say nothing at all about it. ——

Truly yours

J Baillie

New York Public Library, Berg Collection (No address or postmark)

My dear Henrietta

We had a very kind & confidential visit from Lady Beaufort this morning and one by the evening's post from Helen Richardson mentioning Lady Bell & other visitors at Kirklands, very comfortable . . . and you shall have particulars to morrow. We spoke to Lady Beaufort of Miss Carnaigey's kindness, and all went off well. You have done very right in taking rest to yourself to day. You will find the benefit of it I trust. Good night!

Your affectionate Aunt

JB.

Saturday evening

Aunt A is very <u>very</u> tired & gone to bed.

The following early letter from Dr. Matthew Baillie on behalf of his sister Joanna is included in miscellaneous letters in the University of Glasgow's Special Collections:

---

73. If an early letter, this might be to Sophia Denman's brother, but most likely it is to one of several of her nephews.

MS Gen 542/21 (Address: Messrs Cadell & Davies / Booksellers--no postmark)

[1799]

Dr Baillie presents his compliments to Messrs Cadell & Davies — The Author of the Series of Plays does not mean to give away any copies of the second Edition, and therefore it will be unnecessary to send her any — If any Person should occur to whom she may think it right to send a copy, she presumes that Messrs Cadell & Davies will readily permit her to have one, free of expence ——

Gt Windmill Street

Friday June 21 – 1799[74]

In addition to letters, the Royal College of Surgeons of England owns other Joanna Baillie items of interest, including poems, plays in manuscript, etc. Item HB.ix-27 is a theatrical magazine entitled *The Dramatic Censor; or, Weekly Theatrical Report. Comprising, in the Form of a Journal, A Complete History of the Stage* (No. XVIII) and includes an account, actually a plot summary of the play rather than a critical account, of the 29 April 1800 performance of De Montfort [*sic*] at Drury-Lane, excerpted as follows:

The literary reader scarcely need to be informed that the *printed* Tragedy, on which Mr. Kemble[75] has employed his practical skill in

---

74. Written at the bottom of the leaf in another hand is the following note: "Ans^d the 22^d that C. & D. would with Pleasure furnish the Author with as many Copies for Presents as she would do them the Favour to accept –".

75. John Philip Kemble (1757-1823), one of England's most famous actors, began playing parts in his father's company in early childhood. His sister, Sarah Kemble Siddons, first recommended him to the Chamberlain's company as Theodosius in Lee's tragedy in 1776 with dozens of parts to follow. Kemble was a scholar, a man of breeding and a fine actor with a larger range of characters in which he excelled than any English tragedian. He wrote prologues for charitable institutions in York and Leeds, where he appeared for the first time in *Hamlet*--he is said to have written out the part over 40 times. He managed the Edinburgh Theatre for a while in 1781, and his first appearance in London was at Drury Lane as Hamlet in 1783. He remained at Drury Lane for 19 years, presenting over 120 characters himself; and on 25 January 1800 Kemble played De Monfort in Baillie's play. In 1802 he acquired a share of Covent Garden, but in 1808 when the house burned, taking 20 lives, Kemble and other investors were nearly ruined for lack of insurance. A loan of £10,000 from Lord Percy helped him reopen the new Covent Garden Theatre. Portraits of John Kemble abound, several of which are by Lawrence, notably Kemble as Cato, as Hamlet and as Rolla (*DNB*, X:1260-66).

scenic representation, is one of a series of Plays, illustrative of the passions, published without the name of the author, but tacitly acknowledged to be the production of a female writer, and generally attributed to the pen of Mrs. Hunter,[76] the widow of the late celebrated anatomist. This report has recently been contradicted, and the Play in question is now referred to Miss Bailey [*sic*], sister to the physician of that name. . . . Hence it appears, that to appreciate the merits of the new Tragedy, as a dramatic composition . . . it is essentially necessary to compare the Play, as now *acted* (with Mr Kemble's alterations) at Drury-Lane, with the original, as *written* by Miss Bailey.

---

76. Anne Home Hunter (1742-1821), writer and oldest daughter of surgeon Everard Home, married Baillie's uncle Dr. John Hunter in 1771. Of her four children two survived her, son John and daughter Agnes who married Sir James Campbell. See Huntington letter HM41082 herein.

 To *George Thomson*

(1804-1842)

George Thomson (1757-1851), son of schoolmaster Robert Thomson and Anne Stirling Thomson, was a collector of Scottish music and one of the directors of the first Edinburgh musical festival in 1815.[1] He played the violin and took an active role in Edinburgh's St. Celia concerts of his day. Hearing Tenducci's rendering of Scottish songs at these concerts, he conceived the idea of collecting songs for the national arts, ultimately issuing three folio collections: the Scottish in six volumes (1793-1841), the Welsh in three volumes (1809-14), and the Irish in two volumes (1814-16). A royal octavo edition in six volumes made up from all these appeared in 1822.

Because there were no introductory or concluding symphonies to the airs he collected, he determined to supply them, calling on Pleyel, Kozeluch, Haydn, Beethoven, Weber, Hummel and Bishop to provide the accompaniments; and it was Bishop who suggested he set Burns's "Jolly Beggers" to music. Because Thomson found some of the original words to the old airs objectionable, he solicited the talents of Burns, Scott, Hogg, Moore, Byron, Campbell and Baillie for revisions. In addition to his collections of airs, he edited the poems of Mrs. Anne Grant of Laggan in 1802 and published under a pseudonym (1807) a *Statement and Review of a recent Decision of the Judge of Police in Edinburgh, authorizing his Officers to make Domiciliary Visits in Private to stop Dancing.* In 1840 Thomson moved to London but returned to Edinburgh in 1845, and in 1847 his friends presented him with an honorary silver vase when his work was praised by Lord Cockburn. His only daughter Georgina married George Hogarth; their daughter Catherine later became the wife of Charles Dickens.

Hadden explains in *George Thomson, The Friend of Burns* that if Thomson had taken Joanna Baillie's word for her inability to write songs she would not have enriched his collection so extensively. She argues repeatedly that she has no talent for writing songs, but repeatedly she produces exactly what he appears to want. When Thomson began the

---

1. General biographical information comes from J. Cuthbert Hadden's *George Thomson, The Friend of Burns: His Life & Correspondence* (London: John C. Nimmo, 1898), and the *DNB*, XIX:722. Hadden uses excerpts from 35 Baillie letters for his biography but edits spelling, punctuation, etc.

following correspondence with Baillie in 1804, he was working on his volumes of Welsh airs, and their correspondence continued almost to the end of their lives (both died in 1851). Hadden appraises the 35 letters he used from Joanna Baillie as the best in the Thomson collection; there are 38 letters and additional verses included in this chapter to Thomson.

The following letters are transcribed through permission of The British Library and are addressed to George Thomson, York Place, Edinburgh (any letters from other repositories are specifically identified). Walter Scott was also writing Thomson at the time, as were Amelia Opie, Beethoven, and many others. Because early published editions of the songs and ballads that Baillie includes in many of these letters are rare, I am using my own copy of the 1851 *Dramatic and Poetical Works of Joanna Baillie* as a control copy; this is the last edition over which Baillie had direction, but the verses there could be altered somewhat from their first appearance in Thomson's original volumes. Interestingly, Thomson annotates many of these letters from Baillie himself, providing dates, etc.; these I have usually added as notes. Also of interest are the following Baillie manuscripts housed in the British Library:

Add. Ms. 35,118, f. 252: The Prologue to *De Monfort*
Add. Ms. 42,934, ff.770-816: *The Separation. A Tragedy in 5 Acts*:
This manuscript is dated 16th Feb^r 1836 and initialed G.C. (Geo. Colman Esq.), but the handwriting does not appear to be Baillie's. A note preceding the play dated 11 February 1836 asks the Lord Chamberlain's permission that this tragedy be performed at the Theatre Royal Covent Garden, signed M: Rophine Lacy, acting manager.
Add. Ms. 42,935, ff.274-314b: *Henriquez, a Tragedy In 5 Acts*:
This manuscript is dated 18th March 1836 and initialed G.C., but, again, the handwriting does not appear to be Baillie's.

Add. Ms. 35,263:
f. 217 (Address: George Thomson / York Place / Edinburgh)
Hampstead Feb^{ry} 18th 1804
Sir,

I received your polite letter about a week ago, along with that from my friend Miss Millar.[2] I am always ready to agree to whatever she wishes; but independently of this, to the Friend of Burns and my own countryman, it is impossible to refuse, in such a work as you are engaged in, any little assistance that I am able to give. I have lost no time in writing to Mrs Hunter, and have the pleasure to inform you that she cheerfully

---

2. Anne Millar, a childhood friend of Joanna and Agnes, was the daughter of John Millar, professor of law at the University of Glasgow and colleague of Joanna's father James (see Chester Lee Lambertson, "The Letters of Joanna Baillie [1801-1832]" [Ph.D. diss., Harvard University, 1956], cxxv-cc). Her sister is Helen Millar.

grants your request.[3] I sent to her the music with your paper of directions, desiring her to take her choice of the airs in the first place, and she has already this morning sent me her contribution to the work. This consists of three songs with which I flatter myself you will be perfectly satisfied. If your people of taste in Edin.^r are disposed to find fault with them, I must really be permitted to say, they are very difficult, or rather, in good plain Scotch, they are very <u>misleart</u>.[4] — I have written today to another friend of mine, who writes verses with elegance & feeling, to beg she will let me have two songs to make up our number, and I hope she will not refuse me. In regard to my own part of the task, I shall do it as well as I can; but as I have really neither the elegance nor the skill in musical numbers that are required for this kind of writing, and should never in my life have written a single song if I had not sometimes wanted one for my own particular purposes, you must not be surprised if those I send you should not prove exactly what you could wish. If they should not, I beg you will make no ceremony in setting them aside. — I shall take the first opportunity of sending you my packet when it is compleated, and, with all good wishes to the work in which you are engaged, remain,
Sir
     your obedient humble ser.
          J Baillie
P.S. May I take the liberty to beg you will present my best remembrances to Mrs Fletcher?[5]

f. 219 (Address: George Thomson / York Place / Edinburgh)

Hampstead March 21st [1804]

Sir,
     I have now the honour to send you the promised packet with your songs, and if they are of any use to your collection, I shall be glad. I beg leave to remind you of what, I think at least, I have already mentioned to you, that none of them must be received into your work to the exclusion of

---

3. Anne Home Hunter (1742-1821), writer and oldest daughter of surgeon Everard Home, married Baillie's uncle Dr. John Hunter in 1771. Of her four children, two survived her, son John and daughter Agnes who married Sir James Campbell. Anne Hunter published *Sports of the Genii* (1797) and other miscellaneous poems throughout her life, and several appeared in Baillie's *A Collection of Poems, Chiefly Manuscript* (1823).

4. misleart: misguided (*SND*).

5. This is probably Mrs. Elizabeth Fletcher (1770-1858), wife of Archibald Fletcher and mother of sculptor Angus Fletcher of Edinburgh. Fletcher and Baillie had a great many friends in common, including Susan Ferrier, Sotheby, Laetitia Barbauld and Scott (Lambertson, cxxv-cc).

other words which may perhaps fall into your hands better suited to the same airs, I shall, at least in regard to those I have written myself, not a t all take it amiss if they should be laid aside. —— Mrs Hunter has sent you hers set to music, and an additional air & words, which I believe her note will inform you of. I have likewise the promise of a Welch air, with words written for it by a Gentleman of my acquaintance which will probably be put into the packet before it is seal'd up, tho' of this I cant be certain. To the 3 first airs I have written words myself, and to the 4th & 6th airs the friend whom I mentioned to you has had the goodness to write. — The inclosed note from Mrs Hunter I have had by me a long time, for she sent it when she sent me her songs, but as I know it is merely a note of anality [?],[6] I did not think it worth while to send it to you by post. —— With all good wishes to you & your work, believe me, Sir,
      your obedient humble ser^t
         J Baillie

ff. 221-24[7]

No 2^d The inspired Bard
      Now, bar the door, shut out the gale
      And fill the horn with foaming ale;
      A cheerful cup, and rousing fire,
      And thrilling harp, my soul inspire

      Dark rusted arms of ancient proof
      Hang clanging in the greezy roof,
      And tell of many a Welchman bold
      And long remember'd deeds of old.

      Come, Mountain Maid, in Sunday gown,
      With freckled cheek of rosy brown,
      There sit thou gayly by the while
      And nod thy head and sweetly smile.

      Draw closer friends the table round
      And cheerly greet the rising sound:

---

6. This word is unclear and puzzling. Baillie may be using a form of "analier," an obsolete term for one who gives up possession of something (*OED*), which fits the context here.
7. The following four verses are included as part of the preceding letter.

Love, Arms and Ale & rousing fire
And thrilling harp may soul inspire

No 1st The pursuit of Love — [8]
    O Welcome Bat & owlet gray,
    Thus winging low your airy way!
    And welcome moth & drowsy fly
    That to mine ear come humming by!
    And welcome shadows long[9] & deep,
    And stars that from[10] the pale sky peep!
    O welcome all! to me ye say,
    My woodland Love is on her way.

    Upon the soft wind floats her hair;
    Her breath is in the dewy air;
    Her steps are in the whisper'd sound
    That steals along the stilly ground.
    O dawn of day, in rosy bower!
    What art thou to this witching hour?
    O noon of day, in sunshine bright!
    What art thou to the fall of night?

No 3[d] Multracth [Muirtack?] - The Maid of Lanvilling[11]
    I've no goats[12] on the mountain nor boat on the lake;
    Nor coin in my coffer to keep me awake,
    Nor corn in my garner, nor fruit on my tree,
    Yet the Maid of Lanvilling smiles sweetly on me.

    Softly tapping at eve to her window I came,
    And loud barked[13] the watch-Dog, loud scolded the Dame

---

8. This poem appears as "Song, Written for a Welsh Air, Called 'The Pursuit of Love'" in the final *Dramatic and Poetical Works of Joanna Baillie* (hereafter abbreviated as *DPW*) (London: Longman, Brown, Green, and Longmans, 1851), 831. I am using my own copy of the 1851 first edition collection as the authoritative version since that was the last publication in which Baillie had a hand. Since I am not attempting a variorum edition of Baillie's poems here, only substantive changes are noted.

9. "Long" is changed to "dim" *DPW* (831). See changes to this poem appearing in ff. 229-30.

10. "From" is "through" in *DPW*.

11. See "Song, Written for a Welsh Melody" (*DPW*, 831). JB spells Llanwellyn as Lanvilling in this manuscript.

12. "Goats" to "sheep" in *DPW*.

For shame, silly Lightfoot! What is it to thee
Tho/ the Maid of Lanvilling smile sweetly on me?

The neighbours lament that I'm clownish & shy,[14]
And my limbs are too long and my nose is awry.
I thank you, good neighbours, but so let me be,
Since the Maid of Lanvilling smiles sweetly on me.

[No heading here but apparently the title is No. 4 below.][15]

Forc'd to leave my only treasure,
    Gently she my grief beguil'd;
Still my beating heart felt pleasure,
    Sweetly through her tears she smil'd;

Bid me live, and live to bless her,
    Live again in Towry's plain;
Distant far, I still possess her,
    still I hear that voice again.

Still my fancy sees the mountain
    Where together we have stray'd;
Oft in day dreams hear the fountain
    Where our vows of love were made.

When dark clouds of fate are near me,
    Oft I see her lovely form;
That last smile still live to cheer me,
    Sunshine in the darkest storm.

---

13. "Barked" is "bay'd" in *DPW*.

14. These last two quatrains are replaced in *DPW* as shown below and appear to be Baillie's changes (see ff.229-30 following):

    The farmer rides proudly to market or fair,
    The clerk at the alehouse still claims the great chair,
    But, of all our proud fellows, the proudest I'll be,
    While the Maid of Llanwellyn smiles sweetly on
      me.
    For blythe as the urchin at holiday play,
    And meek as a matron in mantle of gray,
    And trim as a lady of gentle degree,
    Is the Maid of Llanwellyn, who smiles upon me.

15. "The Flowers of London" is the song of an unidentified friend (see f. 227 following).

N°. 4   The Flowers of London

PS. I have sent my friend's 2^d song first as you sent it to me, and she begs
you will alter it to the measure in any way you please, as neither she nor I
understand how many feet the last line but one of each verse ought to have
as you have marked it, and she is afraid of again making some blunder. --
I have just received words for one of your airs, that were written some time
ago by a Gentleman, a friend of mine, who has been kind enough to let me
have them, in case they should be of any use to you, as I find in your Scotch
music you have often two sets of words for the same air —

f. 227[16] (Address: George Thomson / York Place / Edinburgh)

Hampstead April 11th 1804

Dear Sir,
    I have I fear delayed writing to you too long in hopes every day of
receiving the song of the Marshes of Rudlan [?] from the Author with the
alterations you wish, but still I hope this will reach you before you leave
London. When he does send it to me I can enclose it to Miss Millar when I
shall be writing in a trunk to Sealand and she will get it conveyed to you.
My friend who writes the other two songs has sent me a still farther
improved copy of her first song, and I inclose it to you. If you really think
it is improved, she desires you to adopt it. As for the "day dreams" instead
of dreams which you prefer, she is still inclined to preserve it as the line
in the copy. -- She desires me also to tell you that she begs leave to
conceal her name, and I believe the author of Rudlan will be inclined to
follow her example. --- I come now to my own little matters regarding
this same perverse Maid of Lanvilling, whom I cannot get properly trick'd
out as she should be, let me take ever so much pains upon her. It is not that
I canna be pushed, but that really & truly I dough do me mair.[17] As for the
last stanza which you think inferior to the rest, I must e'en in the sturdy
spirit of an author say that I think it is rather the best of them all tho' I
am willing enough to admit there is not one of them very good. Perhaps it
would be better to say "meek as the Palmer all hooded in gray" instead of
"good as the Palmer";[18] and for this Lake, Where a Lake should not be,
which is still a stumbling block in the way, I would have you to scratch it

---

16. This letter is very difficult to read, the ink faded and smeared in several
places. The enclosure Baillie mentions is no longer with this letter.
    17. I dough do me mair: I am unable to do greater (*SND*).
    18. This line finally appears as "And meek as a matron in mantle of gray" in *DPW*
(831).

out altogether, and make the first lines run thus, "I've no goats on the mountain nor trout in my stream - Nor coins in my coffer nor ox in my team."[19] However dont take this assessment unless you really like, for I am not very fond of it myself. ——— I hope you will have fine weather for your journey to Edin[r] and a pleasant meeting with all your friends there, and with best wishes remain, dear Sir,

 your obliged humble sert.

  J Baillie

PS. I should like if you wish to put my name to my songs that it were put simply "Joanna Baillie" without adding to it the title of either Miss or Mistress, which has a formality in it that I dislike.

ff. 229-30:

Forc'd to leavy my only treasure,
 Gently she my grief beguil'd;
Still my beating heart felt pleasure,
 Sweetly through her tears she smil'd.

Bade me live, and live to bless her,
 Still those soothing words remain;
In my heart I still possess her,
 Distant far removed from Towry's plains.

In fancy see the mountain
 Where together we have stray'd;
Oft in day dreams hear the fountain
 Where our vows of love were made.

When dark clouds of fate are near me
 Still I see her lovely form;
That last smile still lives to cheer me
 Sunshine in the darkest storm.

---

19. See revision in ff. 229-30, but these lines appear as follows in *DPW* (831), with spelling also changed to "Llanwellyn":
 I've no sheep on the mountain, nor boat on the
  lake,
 Nor coin in my coffer to keep me awake . . .

The Maid of Llanvilling[20]
with additives & amendments

I've no sheep on the mountain nor boat on the lake
Nor coin in my coffer to keep me awake,
Nor corn in my garner, nor fruit on my tree,
Yet the Maid of Llanvilling smiles sweetly on me.

Softly tapping, at eve to her window I came,
And loud bay'd the watch-cur,[21] loud scolded the Dame
For shame, silly Lightfoot! What is it to thee
Tho' the Maid of Llanvilling smile sweetly on me?

Rich Owen will tell you with eyes full of scorn[22]
Thread-bare is my coat & my hoses are torn:
Scoff on, my rich Owen! for faint is thy glee
When the Maid of Llanvilling smiles sweetly on me.

The farmer rides proudly to market &[23] fair
And the Clark at our Alehouse still claims the great thing,[24]
But of all our proud fellows the proudest I'll be
While the Maid of Llanvilling &c.

For sly[25] as the Urchin at holy-day play,
And good as the Palmer all hooded in gray,[26]
And trim as the Lady of noble[27] degree
Is the Maid of Llanvilling who smiles upon me.
(for Welsh work. Vol 2. 58)

---

20. These lines apparently have been sent to Thomson apart from a letter, or the letter is missing.
21. "Watch-cur" is "watch-dog" in *DPW*.
22. This 4-line stanza does not appear in *DPW*.
23. "&" is "or" in *DPW*.
24. "Thing" is "chair" in *DPW*.
25. "Sly" is "blythe" in *DPW*.
26. See note 18 above.
27. "Noble" is "gentle" in *DPW*.

f. 231 (Address: George Thomson / York Place / Edinburgh)

Hampstead April 27 [1804]

Dear Sir,

I send you inclosed my friends two songs, altered for the proper measure of the music; the first song enlarged and I hope you will think improved also.

As for my Maid of Lanvilling, I could wish for her sake that there were lakes in Wales; however, as lakes will not rise out of the earth for our convenience, and I am unwilling to alter the line, we must just hope that a good proportion of our readers will be as ignorant or thoughtless as I was when I wrote it, and that those, who are not so, will have the good nature to suppose that this Lover of hers, tho' in love with a Welch Woman, might be himself a Cumberland man, and that will set every thing right. The line that has a foot too much had better be put "Threadbare is my coat and my hoses are torn" leaving out the that which can very well be spared without injuring the sense.[28] –– I am sure you are more partial to the verses I have sent you than you ought to be, if, after all the trouble I have given you with my ignorance of music & measure, you can still wish to have two more of your Welch airs saddled with words of mine. I hope you will believe I have every inclination in the world to be as useful to you as I can, and if you do send me the two airs from Edin.[r] I shall certainly do as well for them as I can, but having, as I have mentioned to you before, little turn for writing pieces of this kind, and having no pleasure in it, I must be allowed to beg that you will only send me two, and that you will excuse me if I should not exactly do them all the justice that could be wished.

I hope you have not suffered from walking home in the rain last Sunday. — My Mother & Sister join me in offering our best compliment;[29] and wishing you a pleasant journey to Scotland and every other good thing, I remain, dear Sir,

your obliged humble sert.

J Baillie

---

28. This part of the stanza does not appear in *DPW*.

29. Agnes Baillie (1760-1861) was Joanna Baillie's only sister and constant companion. Brother Dr. Matthew Baillie writes that Agnes Baillie, born in the Manse of Shotts on 24 September 1760, had "a quick ready Understanding, with a good deal of various knowle[d]ge, so as to be much beyond the common level of Women in these respects" (qtd. in Franco Crainz, *The Life and Works of Matthew Baillie* [Santa Polomba: PelitiAssociati, 1995], 10). Their mother Dorothea Hunter (1721-1806) married Dr. James Baillie (1722-78), professor of divinity at the University of Glasgow, on 7 December 1757.

PS. My friend desires me to say that if you dont like the name of Towry's vale in her song, you may alter to any other you think will do better, and suit the measure. — Since I wrote the above, it comes into my head that if you are really scrupulous about this Lake of mine, you may alter the lines thus, "I've no goats on the mountain, nor sheep on the hill - nor well hoarded treasure my coffer to fill." However, I like the first way better. — I gave you no addition to what you call my good humour'd Bard; it was the additional verses to the Maid of Lanvilling that I mentioned when I gave you the manuscript. It seems to me to be a Whole as it stands now, giving all the natural circumstances that might be supposed to raise him into the humour for singing; I would not well add more to it unless I gave you his song, which would be too great an undertaking.

f. 239 (Address: George Thomson / York Place / Edinburgh)

Hampstead June 21st 1804

Dear Sir,

I send you inclosed the Marshes of Rhuddlan [?], which has been alter'd as much as the Author will condescend to alter it; and if, as it is, it can be of any use to you I shall be glad. The Author does not chuse his name to be known. — I hope your work goes on thrivingly, and that you find that an agreeable amusement in these long summer days to yourself which will give pleasure to so many others. I hope you have been perfectly well since your return to Edin^r and look forward to visiting London again before it be very long. —— Pray forgive my writing to you in this half sheet of paper, which I was obliged to do lest I should too much increase the weight of a trunk in which I am to inclose it to Miss Millar, and believe me.

> Dear Sir
> > your obliged humble ser't.
> > > J. Baillie

f. 247 (Address: George Thomson / York Place / Edinburgh)

Hampstead Novr 25th 1804

Dear Sir

You were so obliging as to allow me to take my leisure in providing words for the music you sent me, yet I should not quite so far have taken advantage of it if family distress, on account of my Mother's illness, who is now recovering very slowly from an alarming complaint, had not made me unfit to attend to any thing of the kind. I now send you two songs of my own writing & two written by a friend which fills up your demand; and if nothing better suited to the music should happen to fall in your way, I hope they will be useful to you. The two first, viz. my juvenile days & my spinning wheel are written by the same friend who assisted me before in making up my last contribution; and as she does not chuse her name to be known, I should be glad for my satisfaction if you would mark her songs with the letter S that one may know in the work where to find them. The Black cock & the New Year's gift are my own;[30] and I assure you you are under very great obligation to me for the last, which is in the vilest of all measures - dump-i-ty dump-i-ty dump- so that I had to count my fingers again & again to put the same numbers of sylables [*sic*] in each line, my ear being of no manner of use to me. I hope they are now all right, and much good may they do you! I have put the word catening [?][31] into the last line but one, supposing that it may be so put, but if it won't be correctly applied so, you must scratch it out & put offering[32] in its place. I could lay my hands upon no town thru Wales but that of Gilpin in South Wales up the Wye, and therefore if our localities don't please you, alter the names of rivers & mountains as you please.[33] Snowdon sounds well enough, but it is perhaps too high a mountain for the Black cock to breed in. Mrs Hunter has prepared a very bountiful packet for you which she means to send about the same time with this; if this should come to your hands first, you will be pleased to hear that its companion follows not far behind. —— I hope you have been perfectly well since I had the pleasure of hearing from you, and have enjoy'd the respite from . . . [34] you then looked forward to. Your friend Mrs Fletcher I hope is well; and if you should see her soon, have the goodness to present my best compliments & remembrances   Believe me, dear Sir,

Your very obedient sert
J Baillie

---

30. Both "The Black Cock, Written for a Welsh Air, Called 'The Note of the Black Cock'" and "Song, Written for a Welsh Air, Called 'The New Year's Gift'" appear in *DPW* (831).

31. This word is unclear and also puzzling, and Baillie repeats it in the following letter. I do not find "catening" or a close derivative in either the *OED* or the *SND*.

32. The word is "offering" in *DPW*.

33. Gilpin is actually a river that rises southeast of Windermere, Cumbria, and flows south into the River Kent, southwest of Levens. If there is also a town by this name, I have been unable to find a reference.

34. Word is rubbed out here.

f. 257 (Address: George Thomson / York Place / Edinburgh)

Hampstead Feb^{ry} 18th 1805

Dear Sir,

I certainly did not think to be so long of answering your last obliging letter when I received it; but intending to send it by Mrs Hunter's last packet, which has it seems, without my knowing of it, been gone some time, I have been prevented from writing till now. This, however, as you are in no hurry is of no consequence if you will have the goodness to believe I have not been willingly negligent. —— My friend & I are both pleased that you have found our verses so well adapted to the music; and if they pass decently & respectably amongst your other songs, our ambitions upon this score will be satisfied. —— Now for those things that you object to in my songs. — The appellation of help-mate in Catenig [?] is first to be considered.[35] I intended those verses as an address from a husband and not from a Lover; and when I make him say "Last year of earth's treasures I gave thee my part," it is as much to say, "I endowed thee with all my worldly goods" which will, I should think, in this country at least, where similar words are used in the marriage ceremony, be perfectly understood; and as the music is Welch & not Scotch, I think if you please, it had better remain as it is. The next thing is the "crimson moon" in the heath-cock.[36] I meant <u>this</u> to express the kind of arched spot of deep red that is over each of the eyes of this bird; but as I never really saw the bird but once a long time ago, and take my account at him from a book, it may probably not be sufficiently discriptive. If you are not acquainted with the heath-cock yourself, you had better refer the matter, if you think it is worth while to be at so much trouble, to some of your friends who are acquainted with him. If the present expression is not approved of, you may change it into "Thy crimson moon'd and azure eye" or "Thy crimson-arched azure eye" best if it is admissible.[37] The last thing to be noticed is that other part of the same song which you think is obscure, viz. "The rarest things to light of day - Look shortly forth & shrink away."[38] This I don't think I could well alter and make more plain without taking entirely away all the ease & delicasy [*sic*] of the lines; and as a degree of obscurity is allowed in poetry, I will, with your permission shelter myself under this privilege.

I am very much obliged to you for your kind intention of sending me the 1st vol. of your Scotch Songs; but indeed you are too liberal, and as I am not muscial, and you have a great many people to send to, I feel as if I did

---

35. See "Song . . . 'New Year's Gift'" (*DPW*, 831).
36. See "The Black Cock" (*DPW*, 831).
37. The line remains, "Thy crimson moon and azure eye" in *DPW*.
38. Line remains as suggested here in *DPW*.

worry to occupy what would be made better . . .[39] in other hands. Do not therefore, send it. I shall get a sight of the copy you will probably send Mrs Hunter whenever I wish for it, and that will do for me. —— I have been very much delighted lately in reading Walter Scott's Lay of the last Minstrel.[40] I hope you have some assistance from him, if he condescends to write songs. He has the true spirit of a poet in him and long may he flourish! --

I am glad to hear you are well, and have, some time back at least, been so pleasantly employed. My Mother whom you are kind enough to enquire after is just in the same state she has been in for some months, entirely confined to her bed, but free from pain. -- I beg to be remembered to Mrs. Fletcher when you see her, who is very good to allow me still to occupy a little nook in her memory. — With best wishes, I remain

    dear Sir your obliged & obedient ser^t

      J Baillie

f. 299 (Address: George Thomson / York Place / Edinburgh--postmarked 1808)

Dear Sir,

My Sister & I are much obliged to you for your kind remembrance of us in Mrs Hunter's letter, and are glad of the opportunity of her writing to you again to send our compliments & best wishes to you & Mrs Thomson & the young Ladies, who, we hope, have been all well since we had the pleasure of seeing you in Edin^r. --- In regard to the alterations you propose in my song, I think the word <u>blithe</u> instead of sly is indeed an improvement;[41] tho' you have in some degree mistaken my meaning, as the slyness of an Urchin, in my idea, implies arch playfullness rather than cunning. The line of "Meek as a Nun in her vestments of grey," I don't like; <u>vestments</u> being too artificial a word, and besides not sounding well to my ear. If you please then, we will alter the line thus "and meek as a Matron in mantle of grey"[42] which both Mrs Hunter & myself like better.-- I am glad to

---

39. Word is rubbed out here.

40. *The Lay of the Last Minstrel* was published early in January 1805, making Scott famous overnight (see Edgar Johnson, *Sir Walter Scott, The Great Unknown*, 2 vols. [New York: Macmillan, 1970], 225).

41. This is clearly Thomson's change.

42. See note 18 above.

hear your work is coming out so soon, and wishing it all the success you can desire, remain Dear Sir,

truly yours &
J Baillie
Hampstead
October 3ᵈ [1808]

f. 304 (Address: George Thomson / York Place / Edinburgh)

Hampstead 17 Janʳʸ 1809

Dear Sir,

I received your obliging letter two days ago, and have considered of the line in the song you mention. I should be very glad to make the alteration you wish, but the moth along with the drowsy fly seems to me so characteristic of twilight, that I am unwilling to leave it out; and besides the substitute you propose of "every drowsy fly" is too much a loose indetermined expression that savours of common place, at least it strikes me so, and therefore, if you please, we will let the line stand as it was originally written, viz.

And Welcome Moth & drowsy fly.[43]

I am really sorry not to alter the line to your taste, as I am sure, from your writing expresly [sic] about this line there must be something in the word Moth really disagreeable to your ear. If this be so, I have no objection to your altering the line as you propose; but then you must have the goodness in a note at the bottom of the page where it is printed to mention that you have so altered it, and to give the line there as I originally wrote it. In this way your readers, or rather your singers will choose for themselves; and, if your line should become more popular than mine, I shall not at all be offended. —

My Sister & I are much obliged to Mrs Thomson & your young Ladies for their obliging remembrance of us, and both join in sending to them & yourself our best wishes;[44] and many happy returns of this season may you all see!

Believe me, dear Sir
sincerely yours
J Baillie

---

43. This is from "Song, Written for a Welsh Air, Called 'The Pursuit of Love'" and appears as she suggests (*DPW*, 831).

44. Thomson married the daughter of a Lieutenant Miller and had 2 sons and 6 daughters, two of whom died as children.

f. 306 (Address: George Thomson / York Place / Edinburgh)

Hampstead July 27th 1809

Dear Sir,

I am very much obliged to you for the 1st vol: of Welsh Airs which you had the goodness to send to me some time ago, and am afraid you will think me somewhat tardy in acknowledging it. I hope, however, you will not suppose this has been the case from any want of respect from your kind present, for which I beg you to accept my best thanks. At first when I received it, I was very much engaged, and tempted to delay it; and after having so delayed it, I was unwilling to write till I should have had some opportunity of hearing the airs sung with their words. I have at last heard a good many of them sung and played, tho' not to much advantage, from being performed by young people unaccustomed to that stile of music, and who had never seen them before, and cannot therefore judge of the effect they might have under more favourable circumstances. Some of the tunes seemed to me very pretty and to go very well with the words, particularly those which have any resemblance to tunes I had heard before; and I suppose many of the others will please me afterwards when my ear becomes familiar to what we call the lilt of them. I have been very much pleased indeed with many of the words of the songs, Mrs Grant's rising of the lark,[45] Mr Lewis' Widdow's lament,[46] and above all the shoeing of the war horse by Walter Scott[47] & Mr Roger's sleeping beauty

---

45. Anne Grant (1755-1838), known as Mrs. Grant of Laggan, was born in Glasgow to a Highlander and was educated in various countries where her father was stationed. She married the Rev. James Grant in 1779, and the couple moved to Laggan in Inverness-shire where Anne ran a farm and integrated herself into the Highland community, learning Gaelic and becoming an authority on folklore. The sudden death of her husband in 1801 left her without income to raise her large family, and she was persuaded by friends to publish a subscription volume entitled *Poems* (1803) (the *DNB* cites Thomson as editor for this collection) for financial means. This was followed by *Letters from the Mountains* (1807), an instant success for its picture of Highland life and Scottish rural traditions. She became a friend of Francis Jeffrey and Scott, who secured her a civil-list pension in 1826. Many works followed: *Memoirs of an American Lady: With Sketches of Manners and Scenery in America* (1808), *Essays on the Superstitions of the Highlanders of Scotland* (1811), *Letters and Memoirs*, etc. (Joanne Shattock, *The Oxford Guide to British Women Writers* [Oxford: Oxford University Press, 1993], 188-89).

46. Hadden identifies as Matthew Gregory Lewis (1775-1818), citing a letter from Thomson to "Monk" Lewis dated 4 February 1804, advising him about two airs for which he needs words (286). Lewis's masterpiece *The Monk* and other works exercised some influence on Scott and Byron.

47. Sir Walter Scott submitted *many* verses for Thomson's song collection, for Baillie had suggested him to Thomson as a songwriter. In 1806 he provided the words

delighted me.[48] Mrs Hunter's I knew before and therefore do not mention. Indeed I was proud to see my Black Cock &c in such good company, and i f he is thought deserving of the company he keeps, I shall be satisfied. ---
I hope the work will please the public, and reward you for all the pains you have taken with it. ---

My Sister joins me in best compliments to Mrs Thomson & the young Ladies, who with yourself, I hope, have all been well since we heard of you last. —— I remain

Dear Sir

Your obliged & etc.

J Baillie

PS. The Incognitto [sic] to whom you have sent a copy of the songs, thinks you by far too generous to her, and is quite distressed about it. ——

f. 312 (Address: George Thomson / York Place / Edinburgh)

London Grosvenor St: Jan^r 6th 1810

Dear Sir,

I received your obliging letter & the beautiful shawl two days ago; They did not come to my hand sooner, as Mrs Baillie,[49] who expected me in Town, did not send them out to Hampstead. The shawl is indeed beautiful, and an excellent imitation of the Indian and I shall have great pride in shewing it as the manufacture of Scotland. Many thanks to you for your very handsome gift: there is only one thing that diminises [sic] my pleasure in receiving it, that is, that I don't think I deserve it; having considered myself as before more than repaid for my songs by the Scotch & Welch music you so obligingly sent me. I saw Mrs Hunter, who may wear hers with less compunction, last night; she wore it about her shoulers, for she has at present a bad cold, and a Lady who was near her with an Indian shawl, did not look so handsomely equipped.

I have also received your two Irish airs which I shall some time hence try to find words for; tho it is a work I dont at all find myself at home in,

---

for "When the heathen trumpets clang" and "On Ettrick Forest's mountains dun"; others followed (Hadden, 157).

48. Samuel Rogers (1763-1855) was a banker and well-known art collector who became a highly successful poet in his lifetime. Between 1822-28 he published a collection of verse tales entitled *Italy*, and he consented to write "Sleeping Beauty" in 1805 but declined further attempts at songwriting (Hadden, 157).

49. Sophia Denman Baillie (1771-1845), daughter of Dr. Thomas Denman (1733-1815) and Elizabeth Brodie Denman (1746-1833) and sister of Lord chief-justice Thomas Denman (1779-1854) and Margaret Denman Croft (1771-1838), married Joanna's only brother Dr. Matthew Baillie in 1791 and became one of Joanna's closest friends; Sophia's two children were William Hunter Baillie (1797-1894) and Elizabeth Margaret Baillie Milligan (1794-1876) (see Crainz).

being, whatever kind of a poet you may be pleased to reckon me, a very unready & indifferent rhymester. I never wrote a song in my life from inclination, therefore I certainly am not naturally a song writer. My Niece has played the music to me,[50] and I think the first air very pretty, but surely the second resembles it very much, and has more the character of a country dance than a song.

You are very kind to express your satisfaction at learning I have a play coming out at Edin.[r] I trust you will have the goodness with other friends there to give it your good countenance, and speak as favourably of it as your conscience will possibly allow you.[51] —— I hope M[rs] Thomson and all your young Ladies are well; they are very good to remember us. My sister and I beg to offer them our best wishes. I met the other evening your old acquaintance M[rs] Popkin [?], who spoke of you & your family with great interest & kindness. She sings I believe as well as ever, but M[rs] Hunter does not think her well. I hope, however this is M[rs] Hunter's apprehention [sic] with no good foundation. —— Believe me

Dear Sir,
    Your obliged & sincere
        J Baillie

f. 318 (Address: George Thomson / York Place / Edinburgh)

Hampstead May 8th 1810

Dear Sir,

I send you inclosed two songs which I wrote some time ago for your Irish airs, keeping them by me till now that I might give them the advantage of correction &c. after I should have nearly forgotten their contents. Tho' they are not so good as I could wish, I fear I should not be able to do any thing much better for you, so I have only to hope you will not find them entirely unworthy of a place in your work. The river Shannon, in the first song, I have treated as a broad navagable [sic] river, as I suppose it is near its junction with the sea: if I am wrong in this, you may turn it into the Liffy.[52] ——— And now there is a very great favour I must ask of you. M[r]

---

50. Elizabeth Margaret Baillie [Milligan] (1794-1876), the only daughter of Matthew and Sophia Denman Baillie, later married Capt. Robert Milligan (1781-1875) on 11 July 1816, and the couple, with only daughter Sophia (1817-82), lived at Ryde on the Isle of Wight for most of Joanna's life.

51. Walter Scott's persistence had put Baillie's *The Family Legend* on the Edinburgh stage in January 1810, and it was a tremendous success. A revival of *De Monfort* followed. See 1810 letters to Scott herein.

52. Reference is to "A Song, Written for an Irish Melody" which follows in this letter with these changes in *DPW* (829):

His boat comes on the sunny tide,

James Graham[e] Author of the Sabbath,[53] with whom you are probably acquainted, and who is now a Clergyman of the English Church, is a t present a Candidate for the Lectureship of St: Georges Chapel in Edinburgh, and the nomination belongs to the vestry consisting of the following Gentlemen viz. Lord Elibank, Mr Erskine of Mar, Mr Ker of Blackshiels, Mr Drummond of Stragouth, Admiral Sir Edward Neagle, Mr Scott of Seabank, Mr Dallas writer to the signet, Mr Manderson Apothecary, Mr David George Extractor, Mr Charles Stewart writer to the signet, Mr Hume of Carrolside, & Mr Laing Architect: if amongst those names you would have the goodness to exert your interest to procure us some votes for Mr Graham, I should think myself excedingly [sic] endebted to you. I have never heard Mr Graham preach; but he did preach to a polite Congregation in London some time ago, and a Lady who heard him and is I should think qualified to judge, told me his manner of preaching & his sermon were both very good and seemed to make a very favourable

---

And briskly moves the flashing oar,
The boatmen carol by his side,
And blithely near the welcome shore.

How softly Shannon's currents flow,
His shadow in the stream I see;
The very waters seem to know,
Dear is the freight they bear to me.

His eager bound, his hasty tread,
His well-known voice I'll shortly hear;
And oh, those arms so kindly spread!
That greeting smile! that manly tear!

In other lands, when far away,
My love and hope were never twain;
I saw him thus, both night and day,
To Shannon's banks return'd again.

53. James Grahame (1765-1811), Scottish poet born in Glasgow, studied for the church and was admitted to the Society of Writers to the Signet in 1791. In 1809 he was ordained by the Bishop of Norwich and appointed curate of Shipton Moyne, Gloucestershire, but left to attend to family matters in 1810. He was an unsuccessful candidate for St. George's Chapel, Edinburgh, but was later appointed sub-curate of St. Margaret's, Durham, transferring to the curacy of Sedgefield in the same diocese. His poems were admired by Scott and attacked by Byron; works include *The Sabbath* (1804), *Birds of Scotland* (1806), *British Georgics* (1808) and *Poems on the Abolition of the Slave Trade* (1810) (*DNB*, VIII:366).

impression on his audience. This favour of course I can only beg as far as
your other connections or engagements may permit you to act. —

    My Sister sends along with mine her best compliments to Mrs Thomson
& the young Ladies who are, I hope, with yourself, all well. Believe me,

    Dear Sir,
        Yours sincerely
           J Baillie

    Song

His boat comes on the sunny tide
And brightly gleams the flashing oar;
The Boatmen carol by his side
And blythely near the welcome shore.

How softly Shannon's currents flow!
His shadow in the stream I see:
The very waters seem to know
Dear is the freight they bear to me.

His eager bound, his hasty tread,
His well-known voice I'll shortly hear:
And O those arms so kindly spread!
That greeting smile! that manly tear!

In other lands when far away,
My love with hope did never twain;
It saw him thus, both night & day,
To Shannon's banks return'd again.

Song[54]

Come draw we round a cheerful ring
And broach the foaming ale,
And let the merry Maiden sing,
The Beldame tell her tale.

And let the sightless Harper sit
The blazing faggot by:
And let the Jester vent his wit,
His tricks the Urchin try.

Who shakes the door with angry din,
And would admitted be?
No, Gossips Winter! snug within,
We have no room for thee.

---

54. "Song, For An Irish Air," appears with changes as follows in *DPW* (823-24):

Come, form we round a cheerful ring,
    And broach the foaming ale,
And let the merry maiden sing,
    The beldame tell her tale.

And let the sightless harper sit
    The blazing fagot near;
And let the jester vent his wit,
    The nurse her bantling cheer.

Who shakes the door with angry din,
    And would admitted be?
No, Gossip Winter! snug within,
    We have no room for thee.

Go send it o'er Killarney's lake,
    And shake the willows bare,
Where water-elves their pastime take,
    Thou'lt find thy comrades there.

Will-o'-the-wisp skips in the dell,
    The owl hoots on the tree,
They hold their nightly vigil well,
    And so the while will we.

Then strike we up the rousing glee,
    And pass the beaker round,
Till every head, right merrily,
    Is moving to the sound!

Go send it o'er Killarney's lake,
And shake the Willows bare;
The water Elf his sport doth take,
Thou'lt find a comrade there.

Will o' the Wisp shifts in the dell,
The Owl hoots on the tree;
They hold their nightly vigil well,
And so the while will we.

Add. Ms. 35,264:
f. 3 (Address: To George Thomson / Trustee's Office / Edinburgh--
postmarked 1811)

Hampstead April 2 1811

Dear Sir,

I have either not received some letter that you have sent me or I have forgotten part of the contents of your last. I have no recollection whatever of the song you mention "Fly not yet" and did not know that you expected any words from me to suit its melody. However, you shall have a song in its place, as you desire; and if I have been lucky enough to write such a one as you wished for, I shall be glad. The idea of St. Cecilia & an ode frightened me; and if this is what you intended, I have not at all obeyed you, and feel very sincerely that it is not in my power; having never written any thing the least like an Ode in my life, and being perfectly convinced that if I did, it would be a very bad one. I have therefore done what, from some other expression in your letter, seems to be more your idea viz. written a simple song of the same measure with "His boat comes on the sunny tide" in which, as you desire, I have praised the power of music or rather song from the heart, and have alluded to the three countries of these kingdoms who have national music & whose airs you have published. You will find this same song inclosed. You do me great honour in wishing to make it the introductory song of your last volume; but as I have managed it (for the reasons above mentioned) I doubt it will not be thought dignified enough for this; and if you can find some of your friends, which you may easily do, to write something of a musical ode on your subject, I shall think my song very handsomely treated if you give it the second place or any other place in the vol. that you please. ——— I am sure those who are fond of national songs (I believe a very numerous class of people) are much obliged to you; and I hope this forthcoming vol. will be received by them as it deserves.

My Sister joins me in offering our best compliments to Mrs Thomson & the young Ladies. I hope you have all kept your health during the winter, which has been in this part of the world a very mild one.

　　　Believe me, dear Sir
　　　　　yours sincerely
　　　　　　J Baillie

Sweet Power of Song! that canst impart
To Lowland Swain or Mountaineer,
A gladness, thrilling thro' the heart,
A joy so tender & so dear:

Sweet Power! that on a foreign strand
Canst the rough soldier's bosom move
With feelings of his native land
As gentle as an Infant's love:

Sweet Power! that makest youthful heads
With thistle, leek, or shamrock crown'd,
Nod proudly as the carol sheds
Its spirit thru' the social round.

Power,[55] that canst cheer the daily toil
Of Cottage Maid or Beldame poor,
The Ploughman on the furrow'd soil
Or herd-boy on the lonely moor:

Or he, by Bards the Shepherd hight
Who mourns his Maiden's broken tye,
Till the sweet plaint, in woe's despite,
Hath made a bliss of agony:

Sweet Power of Song! thanks flow to thee
From every kind & gentle breast!
Let Erin's, Cambria's Minstrels be
With Burnses tuneful spirit blest!

---

55. With the exception of changes in punctuation and capitalization, "Song, Written at Mr. Thomson's Request, as a Kind of Introduction to His Irish Melodies" appears the same in *DPW*. This line, however, reads: "Sweet Power! that cheer'st the daily toil" (830).

The following letter to Thomson is the property of the National Library of Scotland, included by their permission:

786 ff.43-44 (Address: George Thomson Esq[r] / Trustee's / Edinburgh-- postmarked 1811)

Hampstead April 8th [1811]

Dear Sir,

I received your letter containing the music of "Fly not yet" along with the drawing, about 5 or 6 hours after I had put my last letter to you into the post; and should have acknowledged it sooner, but for having company in the house and other engagements which have kept me fully occupied till to day. In regard to the song I have nothing to say since I have already done, or have at least attempted to do, what you desired. As for the drawing, it is very beautiful;[56] I shall value it much; and I return you a great many thanks for it. I must, however, be permitted to say, without being accused of ingratitude, that I was distressed at receiving it; and I hope you will never give me any more pain of this kind. If the few things I have written for you have been of any service to your work, I have been more than sufficiently rewarded by the copies of your work which you have given me; and the shawl you sent me last summer & this drawing, are acknowledgements which I cannot help regretting, tho' I must value them as marks of your good will. ---- My sister sends her best compliments to yourself & M[rs] Thomson along with mine. —— I remain,

Dear Sir,
your sincere obliged &c
J Baillie

The following letter to Thomson is the property of the University of Glasgow, Special Collections, included by permission:

---

56. A note on the letter in the recipient's hand states that Baillie "has received the Drawing of Rome, but begs I will not send her any farther presents, as she thinks herself compensated for the Songs she has written for me."

Ms Gen 501/8 (Address: For George Thomson Esqr / Trustee's Office / Edinburgh--postmarked 1811)[57]

Sunning Hill Sep^t 18th 1811

Dear Sir,

I ought sooner to have acknowledged your obliging letter and thanked you for your last volume of Welch airs, had I not delayed doing so till I had actually seen the Vol. which I did not receive from Mrs Hunter till last week, when I passed thro' Town on my way hither. This did not proceed from want of attention on her part or curiosity on mine, but because I was too much occupied in various ways at Hampstead to enjoy it, and desired it to be kept for me till I should have the leisure of this quiet place at my command.[58] The Music I am still unacquainted with; for tho' my Niece, who reads music very readily, has played them over to me, we have no body to sing them; but the words of the songs are in general good, and will, I should think, go smoothly to the airs they are joined to. Some of Mrs Grant's & Mrs Opie's,[59] not to mention our friend Mrs Hunter's, are very pleasing; but the sweetest thing to my fancy in the whole collection is Mr Roscoe's verses on the Vale of the Cross.[60] Many thanks to you for the pleasure I have received from it: I am now by your means very rich in song books which I make my young friends, who are musical, sing to me whenever I have an opportunity.

The song you wish me to write I shall certainly attempt since you so earnestly desire it; tho' I did not recollect that there was any second song that you expected from me; and you may be sure I shant object to exchanging a Welch air for a Scotch one. I hope, however, you are in no hurry for it, as I feel myself strangely disinclined to the business at present, and would

---

57. Thomson's note: "Miss Joanna Baillie, Sunning hill, has rece^d the 2^d Welsh volume, and will write a Song for the Shepherd's son."

58. At this time Joanna's brother Dr. Matthew Baillie, one of George III's court physicians, had taken a house near Windsor to be closer his patient, and she was spending time there in addition to finalizing her third volume of *A Series of Plays: in which it is attempted to delineate the stronger passions*, etc. (published in 1812).

59. Amelia Opie (1769-1853) married historical painter John Opie (1761-1807) in 1798, after he divorced his first wife, and began to write seriously such works as *The Father and Daughter* (1801), *Simple Tales* (1806), *Valentine's Eve* (1816), *Lays for the Dead* (1834), etc. She became a Quaker in 1825 (Shattock, 325-26).

60. This is most likely the work of historian and writer William Roscoe (1753-1831), whose works included translations of Italian literature and history and a collection of hymns for the congregation of Protestant dissenters at Renshaw St., Liverpool (1818). Felicia Hemans spoke of him in his later years as a delightful old man surrounded by busts, books, and flowers (Henry Roscoe, *The Life of William Roscoe, by His Son*, 2 vols [London: T. Cadell, 1833]).

fain wait till I am more in the humour. If I hear nothing to the contrary from you, I shall take it for granted that I need not hurry myself.

My Sister & I are now with my Brother's family in a neat pretty Cottage on the skirts of Windsor Forest, — a beautiful country round us on every side, where we enjoy ourselves very much. Mrs Hunter has got a Cottage for a few weeks near us which she takes possession of to day, so we shall make a snug circle of friends in these autumnal evenings which now begin to close in at an early hour. ——— I hope you & your family are well, and beg to offer my best compliments to M^r [sic] Thomson & the young Ladies. I am, Dear Sir,

your truly obliged

J Baillie

PS. My fair unknown friend, as you call her, has received her copy of the Welch airs, and returns you many thanks. —

[BL] Add. Ms. 35,264:

f. 58 (Address: To George Thomson Esq. / Trustees Office / Edinburgh)

Hampstead Decr 16th 1811

Dear Sir,

I have at last found time & spirit to write a song for you & you will find it inclosed. On making a Friend play the air to me, I remembered it as an old tune which some of the common people, spinning on their wheels, used to sing long ago, the burthen of which was O no! Merry no! O my love come follow me! and the music, as I remember it, is suited to the measure as I have written it, and to the lines in your first letter viz.

"There was an Ettrick shepherd's sone" &c. This measure, however, does not suit the tune as you have it set in the music you sent me, where the verses run thus,

There was a shepherd's son

Kept sheep upon a hill &c

which has only 6 syllables in the first line as well as in the second, and having to my taste a very bad effect. I have therefore taken it for granted that the music is ill set, and have followed in my song the former verses in prerence [sic] to those that accompany the music. The old & best set of the tune indeed, if I may venture to say so to you, is nothing better than what one calls a good old <u>drunt</u>,[61] but as such I have a good will to it. Being Scotch music I have written Scotch words for it; not the old Scotch, but such Scotch as is still spoken in the country. I hope you will not think it very

---

61. drunt: drone, usually referring to the bagpipe (*SND*).

bad; and as I dont very well know how to spell the Scotch words, I shall be obliged to you if you will have the goodness to correct spelling. Know which I mean for a hillock or knoll,[62] I have spelt like the verb which I daresay is wrong: Luckey, which I mean for Grand Mother,[63] is probably wrong too, & so on. I have varied the burthen to every verse which makes the song lighter, and gives you leave to print it in full to every verse & thereby make a long song which I trust you like better than a short. —— I have at last published a 3[d] vol. of the series of plays and some copies which I intend for my friends in Scotland will be received by them very soon.[64] The books are sent to M[r] Ballantyne[65] with a list of the names, but there is one name which has been omitted: This is M[rs] Fletcher North Castle St. If you are acquainted with Mr. Ballantyne, I should be very much obliged to you to have the goodness to mention this omission to him; and to say that I request he will be so good as to send a copy of the book to M[rs] Fletcher, from the Author, and have it done up like the others that are sent to my Friends. I hope you will excuse this trouble: it will save me writing to Ballantyne; and I know you will have some kind consideration for one who hates writing a letter most perfectly.

I hope yourself & M[rs] Thomson & all the family are well, and beg with my Sister to be remembered. We have had a very fine winter here, as far as weather is concerned; but I fear you have not, from what I have heard, been so well off in the North. —— Farewell, and believe me, Dear Sir,

　　　　your sincere & obedient
　　　　J Baillie

The gowan glitters on the sward,
The Lavrock's in the sky,
And Colley on my plaid keeps ward,

---

62. know: hillock (*SND*).

63. luckie or lucky: familiar address to an elderly woman (*SND*).

64. Baillie's 3rd volume of *A Series of Plays: in which it is attempted to delineate the stronger passions of the individual*, etc. appeared from Longman, Hurst, Rees, Orme and Brown in 1812 and contained *Orra, The Dream, The Siege,* and *The Beacon*.

65. Publisher John Ballantyne (1774-1821) was the younger brother of James Ballantyne, printer of Scott's novels. He became a clerk in his brother's printing establishment in 1806. In 1808 Scott, on the apparent ground of a misunderstanding with Constable and Hunter, established the firm of John Ballantyne & Co. with John as manager. In this firm Scott held one half share, while each of the Ballantyne brothers retained one quarter each. When the company failed and almost ruined Scott financially in 1825, Lockhart placed the blame on the Ballantynes, but Scott did not (*DNB*, I:1002-3; also see Eric Quayle, *The Ruin of Sir Walter Scott* [London: Rupert Hart-Davis, 1968]).

And time is passing by.
　　　Oh no! sad & slow!
I hear nae welcome sound:[66]
The shadow of our tristing bush
It wears so slowly round!

My sheep bell tinkles fra' the west
My lambs are bleating near
But still the sound that I lov' best
Alac I canna' hear.
　　　Oh no! sad & slow
The shadow lingers still
And like a lanely ghaist I stand
And croon upon the hill.

I hear below the water roar,
The Mill wi' clacking din;
And Luckey scolding fra' her door
To bring the Bairnies in
　　　Oh no! sad & slow!
These are nae sounds for me:
The shadow of our tristing bush,
It creeps sae drearily!

I crosst ye streem, from Chapman Tam,
A snood of bonny blue,
And promised when our tristing cam
To tye it round her brow.
　　　Oh no! sad & slow
The time it winna' pass
The shadow of that weary thorn
Is tether'd on the grass.

O now I see her on the way
She's past the Witches know:
She's climbing up the Browny's brae:
My heart is in a low.
　　　Oh no! 'tis nae so!
'Tis glamrie I ha' seen:

---

66. This line of "A Scotch Song" appears as follows in *DPW*: "And lengthen'd on the ground" (824). No other substantive changes appear in that published version.

The shadow of that hawthorn bush
Will move nae more till e'en.

My book o'grace I'll try to read,
Tho' conn'd wi' little skill;
When Colley barks I'll raise my head,
And find her on the Hill.
   Oh no! sad & slow!
The time will ne'er be gone;
The shadow of the tristing bush
Is fix'd like ony stain.

f. 80 (Address: George Thomson / Trustees Office / Edinburgh)

Hampstead Feb^ry 1st 1813

Dear Sir,

I received your letter a few days ago, and would have answered it without loss of time had I not then been confined to bed with a bad cold. I at the same time received the books which as I cannot possible [*sic*] accept, I shall send to morrow to your Brother in London,[67] who will have the goodness to give them house-room till you can give directions how you would wish them to be disposed of. I suppose your Bookseller here will very readily take them. I have always said to you that a copy of your work when published, was a sufficient reward for any little assistance I might give to the work; and when I accepted of the drawing & the shawl, it was with some struggle against my own feelings that I did so, and I had flattered myself that I had so expressed myself on this subject that nothing of this kind would on your part have been repeated. I am sorry you have not done me the honour to suppose that I did really speak it in sincerity; and I must be allowed to say, you ought to have spared me this pain.

I am glad to hear you are so near the close of your work, and must give you great credit for the unwearied zeal with which you have pursued it. I have frequently told you that I have no pleasure in writing songs, and I am certainly not much in the mood for it at present; and more-over I do not believe the work will be one bit better received by the public for having a greater or less proportion of the songs written by one person rather than another, yet that we may part in charity with one another at the end of it, if you will send me two of your airs I shall find words for them as well as I can. —— My Sister joins me in compliments & kind wishes to Mrs Thomson

---

67. George Thomson's brother was David Thomson (d. 1815), landscape painter and amateur musician.

& the young Ladies, and I beg to offer my best remembrances to your Son in law Mr Stark when you see him.

I am, Dear Sir,
>   your sincere & obedient,
>>   J Baillie

f. 98 (Address: To George Thomson / Edinburgh)

Hampstead April 19th 1813

Dear Sir

I was pleased to receive your obliging letter, for, as it was longer than usual of coming, I was afraid I might have expressed my feelings in my last more strongly than I ought: and if I could willingly give any thing more than a very temporary sensation of uneasiness to any of my friends, I'm sure I should not deserve to have friends. —— I inclose two songs for your two airs which I hope may suit them tolerably. The first air is a very pretty thing indeed, but I could make no sense at all of the second. However, I only heard them played once, and might have liked the 2^d better on hearing it often repeated. I hoped to have sent them to you sooner, but it was not till the other morning that I could find quiet leisure to write any thing, and I always like to let such things lie by me a day or two after they are written before I write out the clear copy, so that I could not well send them sooner to you than I have done.

I saw Mrs Hunter about a week ago, looking very well after a winter in which she has had a good deal of confinement from colds & petty ailments. Her Daughter Mrs Campbell[68] is just arrived from Sicily, and she is looking about for some place in the country where they may spend the summer together.

I thank you for your kind enquiries after my health: I am quite well, and we are all enjoying here the finest April - I might almost say June - weather imaginable. It has continued with us almost a fortnight.

My Sister joins me in best compliments to yourself & Mrs Thomson. ———
I remain,

Dear Sir
>   very truly yours
>>   J Baillie

---

68. Agnes Hunter, Lady Campbell, surviving daughter of Dr. John Hunter and Anne Home Hunter and cousin to Baillie, married Sir James Campbell; after his death, she married Col. Benjamin Charlewood (Baillie often spells as Charliwood), retaining her title. She had no children.

The morning air plays on my face
And thro' the grey mist peering
The soften'd silvery sun I trace[69]
Wood wild & mountain cheering.
       Larks aloft are singing
       Hares from covert springing
And o'er the fen the wild-duck's brood[70]
Their early way are winging.

Bright every dewy hawthorn shines,
Sweet every herb is growing
To him whose willing heart inclines
The way that he is going.
       In fancy I see now[71]
       The thing that will be now;
I'm patting at her door poor Tray,
.Who's fawning upon me now

How slowly moves the rising latch!
How quick my heart is beating!
That worldly Dame is on the watch
To frown upon our meeting.
       Yet why should I mind her[72]
       Since one stands behind her
Whose eye doth on her Trav'ller look
The sweeter & the kinder

O every bounding step I take,
Each hour the clock is telling,
Bears me o'er mountain bourne & lake[73]
Still nearer to her dwelling:

---

69. This and the next line of "Song, Written for an Irish Air" appears in *DPW* as, "The soften'd sun I sweetly trace,/ Wood, moor, and mountain cheering" (823).

70. The line is "And o'er the fen the wild-duck brood" in *DPW*.

71. The following lines are as follows in *DPW*:
    Clearly do I see now
    What will shortly be now;
I'm patting at her door poor Tray,
Who fawns and welcomes me now.

72. See these three lines in DPW: "Fy! why should I mind her,/ See who stands behind her,/ Whose eye upon her traveller looks. . . ."

73. See *DPW*: "lake" becomes "brake."

The Day shining brighter,
    And limbs moving lighter[74]
While every thought to Nora's love
But binds my faith[75] the tighter.

————————————

The stroke on the smithy, the click of the mill,[76]
The hum of the school, & the ditty so shrill,
The housewife's loud thrift, & the children at play
And the crowing of Cocks at the noon of the day:

Ah! this was the music delighted my ear,
And to think of it now is so sad & so dear!
Ah! to listen at ease[77] by mine own cottage door
To the sound of mine own native village once more!

I knew ev'ry Dame in her holiday airs,
I knew ev'ry Maiden that danced at our fairs;
I knew ev'ry Farmer to market who came,
And the dog, that ran after him, call'd by its name

And who know I now in this far-foreign land[78]
But the stiff-collar'd sergeant, the trim-coated Band?
No kinsman to comfort his own flesh & blood,
Nor merry ey'd Damsel to do my heart good.

To my sight or my ear no gay cheering doth come[79]
But the flare of our colours, the tuck of our drum;
The fierce flashing steel of our long muster'd file
And the sharp dinning piper that playeth the while[80]

At night as I keep on the wearisome watch,
The sound of the west wind I greedily catch;

---

74. "Limbs are moving lighter," in *DPW*.
75. The word is "love" in *DPW*.
76. See "Song, for an Irish Melody" in *DPW* (830) and extensive changes to stanza 1 appearing in letter f. 219 following.
77. In *DPW* "at ease" becomes "again."
78. This and the following line are "And whom know I now in this far distant land,/ But the stiff collar'd sergeant, and red-coated band" in *DPW*.
79. Line is "To mine eye or mine ear no gay cheering e'er comes" in *DPW*.
80. Line is "And the sharp shrilly fifers a-playing the while" in *DPW*.

And the shores of dear Ireland the[y][81] rise to my sight
And mine own native valley that spot of delight

Divided so far by a wide stormy main
Shall I ever return to our valley again?
Ah! to listen at ease by mine own cottage door
To the sound of mine own native village once more!

f. 102 (Address: To George Thomson / Edinburgh)

Hampstead May 3[d] 1813

Dear Sir,

I am glad that my songs have so far pleased you, and should be very glad if I could make the first song entirely to your mind. I have tried to alter the four last lines of the 2[d] stanza [words marked out here] which you think so much inferior to the rest; I am sure I have bestowed more thought upon it than upon the whole of the song originally; yet I have not been able to alter it any now to please me, and am fain to keep it very little, tho' somewhat changed, from what it was. I am really sorry I can do no more for it, but I think it is a little better. I flatter myself that you will now find all the short lines in all the stanzas as they should be to suit the air. It was a stupid oversight in me not to make them so at first. You will guess from this that I am unwilling to comply with your request to suit the lines by an aditional [sic] syllable to another air. The truth is that I like this air, and as I have not often been lucky enough to write a song for an air that really pleased my own unlearned ear, I do not like to give it up. I make you very welcome to change the word smithy for anvil in the other song. I thought of it at first but rejected it, because I considered the other as a simpler & more rustic term. However, I find on looking the dictionary that I have mistaken the word which should have been stithy,[82] a word that certainly cannot well be sung; had I been wise enough to have looked the dictionary at first it had been better. —

I hope you will soon get comfortably to the end of your labours in your long under-taking, and that it will have a good reception from the public when you do bring it forth. It is perhaps rather unfortunate that Stevenson has lately published Irish airs with songs by Moore, and this may in some degree injure the circulating of the work.[83] But I hope it will not do so

---

81. Word is "will" in *DPW*.
82. stithy: stiff, rigid, firm (*SND*).
83. Composer Sir John Andrew Stevenson (1760?-1833) was born in Dublin, son of John Stevenson, a native of Glasgow and violinist. John Andrew was a chorister at St. Patrick's Cathedral from 1775-80, becoming the vicar-choral there in 1783 and moving to Christ Church in 1800. He was created Mus. Doc. of Trinity College and

materially; and those who have already your Scotch & Welch airs will
surely wish to have your works compleat.

My best compliments to Mrs Thomson & your Daughters. I remain
> Dear Sir,
>> Yours sincerely
>>> J Baillie

The morning air plays on my face,[84]
And thro' the grey mist peering,
The soften'd sv'ry sun I trace,
Wood wild & mountain cheering.
>> Larks aloft are singing,
>> Hares from covert springing,
And o'er the fen the Wild-duck's brood
Their early way are winging.

Bright ev'ry dewy hawthorn shines
Sweet ev'ry herb is growing,
To him whose willing heart inclines
The way that he is going.
>> Fancy shews to me now,
>> What will shortly be now,
I'm patting at her door poor Tray,
Who fawns and welcomes me now.

How slowly moves the rising latch!
How quick my heart is beating!
That worldly Dame is on the watch
To frown upon our meeting.
>> Fy! why should I mind her?
>> See who stands behind her,
Whose eye doth on her Trav'ller look
The sweeter & the kinder.

O! ev'ry bounding step I take,
Each hour the clock is telling,
Bears me o'er mountain bourne & brake

---

knighted in 1803. Stevenson wrote some works for the stage but is best known for his
symphonies and accompaniments to a collection of Irish melodies, the words for
which were written by Irish poet Thomas Moore (1779-1852) (*DNB*, XVIII:1125).

84. "Song, Written for an Irish Air"--see notes to letter f. 98 preceding.

Still nearer to her dwelling!
  Day is shining brighter,
  Limbs are moving lighter,
While ev'ry thought to Nora's love
But binds my faith the tighter

f. 219 (Address: To George Thomson / Edinburgh)

          Hampstead June 17th 1815
Dear Sir,

  I hope you will not accuse me of neglect tho' I have been too long of answering your letter. It came to me when I was very much engaged with friends at home, and I have since been much in Town where it is impossible to write or to think of any thing: I am now returned and have taken my first hour of leisure to read your letter & consider your song again. I have altered the first verse which you had good reason to say, was not suited to a plaintive air, because the <u>second</u> verse could not, I think, be made the <u>first</u> without a bareness or want being felt very sensibly. I hope, as I have altered it, that it may be less objectionable. ——

  My Sister & I are much obliged to you for your kind enquiries. We are both very well. We have had a delightful spring here after a mild winter, and the country looks still beautifully green & fresh. We have our friend Miss Craig from Glasgow with us at present, who has been by no means well since she came here, but is getting better again, and exerting herself as much as she can to see the sights of the great City. —— I saw M[rs] Hunter a few days ago, who is wonderfully revived after having been very much an invalid all the winter. — My Sister joins me in best respects to yourself & M[rs] Thomson. We have truly sympathized with you on the loss of a Brother so justly endeared to you by his worth & his various Talents; I wish we had been better entitled to your thanks for kindness shewn to him. He was fitted to be a very pleasing & valuable member to any society; and we have now to regret that we saw him so seldom. —— Believe me
  Dear Sir
    Sincerely yours
    J Baillie

[85]The Piper, who sat on his low mossy seat,
And piped to the youngsters so loud & so sweet;

---

  85. She begins the lines of "Song," marks them out, and starts again as printed here. These first lines are as follows in *DPW*: "The harper who sat on his green mossy seat,/ And harp'd to the youngsters so loud and so sweet" (830). Thomson obviously follows Baillie's suggestion in the postscript. See letter f. 98 preceding.

The far-distant hum of the children at play
And the Maiden's soft carrol at close of the day

Ah! this was the music delighted my ear
&c. &c.
PS. If there are Harpers who still play to the common people in Ireland as
in Wales, you had better change Piper in to Harper viz.

 The Harper, who sat on his low mossy seat
 And harp'd to the youngsters so loud & so sweet &c.

f. 305 (Address: To George Thomson / Edinburgh)
Hampstead July 20th 1817
Dear Sir,

 Allow me to thank you for the concluding Vol. of Welsh airs which
you had the goodness to send me some time ago; tho', owing it much more to
your goodness than my own deserts, I feel that I thank with a bad grace.
There are in it I make no doubt many beautiful airs which my young friends
perhaps will sing to me by[e] & bye, and your Poets have enriched it with
many sweet & elegant songs. — The receipt of these airs immediately
brought to my mind with some pain, that I had too long neglected to
answer a letter of yours which I received a long time ago; containing a
request which, tho' an unexpected one, yet being a last, I did not mean to
refuse. Various engagements & occupations have since prevented me from
fulfilling my intention, but this morning I have at last found leisure for it,
and inclose a boat song which I have tried to make something like what I
suppose you desired. I hope it will in some degree please you, and that it
does not reach you too late to be of use. I have followed the measure of the
pattern verses, for I dont recollect the air nor have I any body near me to
play it to me. I flatter myself, however, that the verses I have written are
of a character not unsuited to music. —

 I saw M<u>rs</u> Hunter the other day in good looks & spirits. Both her body
and mind wear wonderfully well. M<u>rs</u> Campbell, I hope will soon return to
her at least for some time as she is about to dispose of her cottage in the
country. I believe she intends to settle in or near Town which will be a
comfort to her Mother. —— I beg my best compliments to M<u>rs</u> Thomson, and
hope that all your Family are well.

 I am Dear Sir, Your sincerely obliged
  J Baillie
PS. If nets cannot be said with propriety to float as they are dragged down
by the lead while the pieces of cork only are seen upon the water, let the
second line of the Chorus run thus

"Our nets are <u>circled</u> wide"[86]

Swiftly glides the bonny boat,
      Just parted from the shore,
To the Fisher's chorus note
      Soft moves the dipping oar.
Light is toil with happy cheer,
      And ever may it speed!
That doth weak age & help-mate dear
      And tender Bairnies feed!

Chorus
We cast our lines in Largo Bay
      Our nets are <u>floating</u> wide
Our bonny Boat with yielding sway
      Rocks lightly on the tide.
And happy prove our daily lot
      Upon the summer sea!
And blest on land our kindly cot,
      Where all our treasures be!

Mermaid on her rock may sing
      The Witch may weave her charm.
Water-sprite nor elrich thing
      The bonny boat can harm.
It safely bears its scaly store
      Thro' many a stormy gale
While joyful shouts rise from the shore
      Its homeward prow to hail.

Chorus
We cast our lines in Largo Bay &c &c.[87]

---

86. The first stanza of "Song, for a Scotch Air" is substantially changed in *DPW*:
    O swiftly glides the bonny boat
      Just parted from the shore,
    And, to the fisher's chorus note,
      Soft moves the dipping oar!
    His toils are borne with lightsome cheer,
      And ever may they speed,
    Who feeble age, and helpmates dear,
      And tender bairnies feed. (825)
There are no substantive changes in the chorus.

f. 308 (Address: To George Thomson / Edinburgh)

Hampstead August 10th [1817]

Dear Sir,

I entirely approve of the additional syllables marked with the blue Ink which restore the lines to what they were exactly to what they were when I first composed them; and it was with great unwillingness I altered them when on counting over the syllables of the pattern measure you had sent me, I found they had a syllable too much. But it is not to clear myself on this point that I give you the trouble of a letter, but to beg you will have the goodness to alter two lines which I think are stiff & awkward. Viz.[88]

> "O light is toil with happy cheer,
>   And ever may it speed
> That doth weak age & help-mate dear
>   And tender Bairnies feed.

I would have them run thus,

>   His toils are borne with lightsome cheer,
>   And ever may they speed,
>   That feeble age and Help-mate dear
>   And tender Bairnes feed.

I believe - I am almost sure Mrs Hunter has enjoyed the Opera of Don Giovanni, which has been greatly and I suppose deservedly admired. I wish poor Mrs Campbell had been in a state to have done so too. Her complaint in the knee which has made her unable to walk for several months, has become worse; and after having given up her country cottage she is now come to Town to her Mother, who by Sir E. Home's advice is going to take her to Buxton.[89] She is sadly worse with her confinement, and has borne it, I believe with great patience, ——— Again, with compliments

---

87. Thomson's note: "The above beautiful Song by Mrs Baillie transmitted to me in her letter of the 20 July 1817 – Wrote to her on the 2^d Augt suggesting some slight alterations to render the Song more suitable to the Melody."

88. See preceding letter f. 305.

89. Sir Everard Home (1756-1813) was a surgeon, much influenced by Dr. John Hunter, who later became a professor at the College of Surgeons. A blot on his record is the allegation that he destroyed many of the Hunter manuscripts on anatomy after having used some of the information as his own.

to all your Family, I remain
>   Dear Sir,
>   Yours sincerely
>   J Baillie

Add. Ms. 35,265:
f. 69 (Address: To George Thomson Esqr / Trustee's Office / Edinburgh--
postmarked 1819)
Dear Sir,

You are heartily welcome to join the words you mention, viz. "__[90] quit thy bower &c." with your Scottish air, and I am proud that you think they deserve to be so matched. —— My Sister & I beg to offer our best respects & wishes to yourself & Mrs Thomson. I shall see Mrs Hunter in a few days and shall not forget to let her know that you remember her. She droops sadly this winter which we regret exceedingly, tho' we still hope she may rally again in the spring. I remain
>   Dear Sir,
>   your sincerely obliged &c,
>   J Baillie

Hampstead
Novr 26th [1819]

f. 79 (Address: To George Thomson Esqr / Trustees Office / Edinburgh--
postmarked 1820)[91]

>   Hampstead Decr 22^d 1820

My Dear Sir,

I am very sorry to find you are likely to have some trouble about your Songs, but I trust it will not be much seeing that you have right so plainly on your side.[92] I have followed the wording of your conveyance closely but with the addition of a small parenthesis to save trouble afterwards, not that I am likely soon to publish any Collection of small poems. However, such a publication either on my part or Mrs Hunter's heirs would be no

---

90. The first word is illegible here.

91. Thomson has written the following on the back of the letter: "Certificate by Mrs. Joanna Baillie declaring the twelve Songs written by her for my national collection, to have been presented to me as my sole property for ever. GThomson".

92. At this time Thomson was engaged in the octavo edition (1822) of his collection, a less expensive version of the original, and was concerned about the appearance of musicseller Robert Purdie's *Scottish Minstrel* (vol. 1 appeared in 1821) as a rival publication which edited "objectionable" words and left out "drinking songs" altogether. Thomson later proposed to sell his own collection to Purdie (Hadden, 69).

injury to your musical work, and I doubt not that, if you had thought of it, you would have inserted this clause of your own accord. ——— You will be very sorry to find that Mrs Hunter is too ill to set her name to any thing.[93] I sent your letter to Lady Campbell as soon as I received it and she returned it to me again to draw out the paper for her, and somehow or other she has been prevented from returning it to me till to day. I stupidly forgot to look at that part of your letter which regarded the number of her songs & the works for which they were written which has occasioned the blotting of the lines as you will see, but I suppose this is of no real consequence. ——— I am glad to be able to tell you that Mrs Hunter suffers no pain, tho' she is often very restless & uneasy. Her Daughter waits upon her constantly with great tenderness; and affection for her Daughter is now the only sentiment which she seems to retain. There is no relief to be looked for but one, and we have only to hope, when it does take place, it may be (God grant it may!) without suffering. Pray offer my best wishes to Mrs Thomson & all your family.

I rest dear Sir,

sincerely yours &. J Baillie

I do hereby certify & declare that twelve of the songs published by Mr George Thomson of Edinburgh viz two in the fifth volume of his Scottish Songs, two in the first volume of his Welch Songs; three in the second volume of that work; four in the first volume of his Irish Songs and one in the second volume of that work, each bearing my name, were written by me for those works; and were presented by me to him, as his sole & exclusive property for ever (reserving nevertheless to myself & my heirs the right to insert them in any collection of my poems which may hereafter be published) which I here declare them to be; and I authorize him to prosecute any person or persons, who shall publish or rend any of those Songs without his consent. In testimony whereof I have written & subscribed these presents at Hampstead in the County of Middlesex this nineteenth day of December one thousand eight hundred & twenty

Joanna Baillie

---

93. Baillie's aunt Anne Home Hunter died in 1821.

f. 81[94]

I do hereby certify & declare that seventeen of the songs published by M[r] George Thomson of Edinburgh viz. five in the first volume of his Welch Songs, seven in the second volume of that work & five in the third volume thereof, each bearing my name, were written by me for those works; and were presented by me to him, as his sole & exclusive property for ever, (reserving nevertheless for myself or my heirs the right to insert them in any collection of my poems which may, hereafter, be published) which I here declare them to be; and I authorize him to prosecute any person or persons, who shall publish or rend any of those songs without his consent. In testimony whereof, I have authorized my Daughter to subscribe these presents in my stead, (my hand from weakness being too unsteady to hold the pen) at London this 20th of December 1820.

signed by her for

Mrs John Hunter.   Agnes Campbell

f. 106 (Address: To George Thomson Esq[r] / Trustee's Office / Edinburgh-- postmarked 1822)

Hampstead Wednesday Feb[y] 27th 1822

My dear Sir,

I thank you for the book of Songs which you have sent me and doubt not I shall have great pleasure in perusing it when I can find time, but I am terribly pressed at present, and cant do that I wish. I have taken M[r] Richardson's[95] copy to his house and sent that which you so kindly bestow upon my Niece to Town this morning to be forwarded for her at Windsor where her husband is at present stationed.[96] I am sure she will feel herself

---

94. The following appears to be included in the preceding letter. Thomson notes: "20 Dec 1820 Certificate signed by M[rs] General Campbell for her mother M[rs] John Hunter (whose illness prevents her from writing) declaring the Seventeen Songs which she wrote for my Collection of Welsh Melodies to be my sole & exclusive property for ever. GThomson".

95. John Richardson (1780-1864) was a parliamentary solicitor and for 30 years discharged the duties of crown agent for Scotland, reputed as the most learned peerage lawyer of his time. He had literary tastes and in 1821 was introduced to George Crabbe in Joanna Baillie's house; he regularly corresponded with Walter Scott, whose deathbed he attended shortly before Scott's demise. He married Elizabeth Hill, a close friend of Thomas Campbell, in 1811 and had several children (*DNB*, XVI:1118-19). Richardson submitted "Song - Her features speak the warmest heart" for Baillie's 1823 collection; and in a letter dated 18 January 1842, he tells Baillie, "It is, as it has long been, a great pride and gratification to me to have enjoyed your friendship; a few circumstances of my life have afforded me more real pleasure" (NLS Ms 3990, f.41).

96. Against her family's wishes Elizabeth Margaret Baillie (1794-1876), the only daughter of Matthew and Sophia Denman Baillie, had married Capt. Robert Milligan

much gratified by your present. I should have thanked you sooner, but I did not receive the books nor your letter till last saturday night, having been from home for some time. I have looked at my own Song in it and the observation, with which you have prefaced it; tho' I am obliged to you for your friendly intention, yet I earnestly wish the Song had been inserted simply without any praise or observations at all. Whenever the vol: comes to another edition, I beg you will oblige me by leaving them out. --- I guess this may be about the 13th time that you have promised to me that the song you asked me to write should be the last. You must now in good & honest faith fulfil that promise, for I am heartily tired of song-writing which I never at any time did like. I should have stood out sturdily against this last request but for two reasons: first, that I was unwilling that your engraving should not have something written to correspond with it, and secondly that I wish you to help me a little in a subscription which I am carrying on for the benefit of a friend.[97] I am going to Edit a volume of collected poems, and I wish you to set down your name for one single copy and to forward the subscription amongst your friend[s], as much as you can without doing any thing irksome or unpleasant to yourself. Call on my friend Mrs Thomson in George Street,[98] and she will tell you all about it, and give you a subscription paper. Now remember that you are not to put down your name for more than one copy, for that would hurt me exceedingly. --- I hope to make it a very good collection chiefly composed of Ms poems, some of them by the first writers of this country. There will be a few of my own in it but [letter continues after song]

Woo'd & married & a'[99]

———

The Bride she is winsome & bonny
    Her hair it is snooded so sleek,
And faithfu' & kind is her Johny,
    Yet fast fa' the tears on her cheek.

(1781-1875) on 11 July 1816, "a plain honest Soldier," Baillie relates to Scott (NLS 3887 ff.83-85).

97. This was Baillie's *A Collection of Poems, Chiefly Manuscript, and from Living Authors* (London: Longman, Hurst, Rees, Orme, and Brown, 1823), a subscription collection for the benefit of her friend Mrs. James Stirling.

98. Hadden identifies Mrs. Thomson as the wife of Dr. Andrew Thomson.

99. See "Song, Woo'd and Married And A' (Version Taken from an Old Song of That Name)" in *DPW* (817); few substantive changes occur. Thomson declared this would be "one of our most popular songs, for a more natural and pleasing group never was painted" (Hadden, 241).

New pearling are cause o' her sorrow,
        New pearlings & plennishing too,
The Bride that has a' to borrow,
        Has e'en right mickle a'do
Woo'd & married & a', woo'd & married & a'
        Is na' she very weel off to be woo'd & married & a'

Her Mither then hastily spak,'
        "The Lassy is glaket wi' pride;
In my pouches I had na' a plack
        The day I was a Bride.
E'en tak' to your wheel and be clever,
        And draw out your thread i' the sun;
The geer that is gifted, it never
        Will last like the geer that is won.
Woo'd & married & a'! 'tocher & 'havens so sma'![100]
I think ye are very weel off to be woo'd & married & a'."

"Toot, toot!" quo' the grey-headed Father,
        "She's less o' a Bride than a Bairn,
She's ta'en like a Coult fro' the heather,
        Wi' sense & discretion to learn.
Half husband, I trow! and half Daddy,
        As humour inconstantly leans,
A Child mau be patient & steady,
        That yokes wi' a mate in her teens.
Her chief cuiring* sa neat, locks the wind used blow![101]
I'm bothe like to laugh & to greet when I think of her married at a'"

*Covering if I have not spelt the Scotch for it properly pray correct it

Then out spak' the wily Bridegroom
        Weel wal'd were his wordies, I ween!
"I'm rich, tho' my coffer be toom,
        Wi' the blinks o' your bonny blue eyen.
I'm prouder o' thee by my side,
        Tho' thy ruffles or ribbons be few,
Than Kate o' the Croft were my Bride,

---

    100. Line appears as "Wi' havins and toucher sae sma'!" in *DPW*.
    101. This is "A kerchief sae dounce and sae neat,/ O'er her locks that the winds used to blaw!" in *DPW*.

Wi' purfles & pearlins enew.
Dear & dearest of ony! Ye're woo'd & buiket & a',
And do ye think scorn o' your Johny, and grieve to be married at a'?"

She turn'd & she blush'd & she smiled,
    And she looket so bashfully down;
The pride o' her heart was beguiled,
    And she play'd wi' the sleeve o' her gown;
She twirled the tagg o' her lace,
    And she nippet her boddice so blue,
Sine blinket so sweet in his face,
    And all[102] like a mawkin she flew.
Woo'd & married awa', wi' Johny to ruse her & a'!
She thinks hersel' very weel off to be woo'd & married & a'.

(but) no Songs of mine, one (perhaps) excepted which has never been printed at all. I have with Lady Campbell's permission picked out some very pretty things from the Mss. which M[rs] Hunter left behind her and those I know you will like to see. —— In the engraving you have sent to me I am much pleased with the beauty of the Bride, but her figure would be more natural and much improved if a little breadth could be added to her arm which is too small. If the copies are not printed off, I should think this might easily be done by graving another outline on the plate & erasing the old. ––– With kind remembrances to M[rs] Thomson & all your family

    I remain, my dear Sir, very sincerely yours
        J Baillie

PS. Will you have the goodness to give my love to M[rs] Thomson of George St: and tell her that Sir Walter Scott will inform her what Bank in Edin[r] all the money gathered there for the subscription is to be paid into that it may in the end be remitted to Coutts in London. The Partners of that Banking house having very kindly taken charge of the whole. It must be a branch of the Royal Bank of Scotland, and I have begged of Sir Walter to fix on one for me. ——

---

102. In *DPW* "all" becomes "aff."

f.108 (Address: To George Thomson Esq[r] / Trustee Office / Edinburgh--
postmarked 1822)

Hampstead March 12th 1822

My dear Sir,

I begin first of all by answering the Poscript [*sic*] of your letter. I cannot
possibly accept of your intended present of Flaxman's illustration of the
Iliad,[103] nor of any other present, your own publications always excepted.
My Songs are always sufficiently repaid by receiving a copy of the work in
which you insert any of them and by your approbation. It gives me great
pain that you should propose any other recompense, let me entreat you to
do so no more. ——

As you so solemnly protest that this is the last Song you will ever ask
from me, I wish that we should part friends, and have already written
words to Hooly & fairly which is a tune I used formerly to sing along with
the Guitar;[104] but I will not send it till you have promised me faithfully
that neither Flaxman's Iliad nor any thing whatever shall be sent to me.
When you have done this to my satisfaction, you shall have the song
which I hope will please you as much as those which have preceded it. ——

I did not like the line of the Kerchief very much myself, but, having
so far forgot my old Scotch, I mistook it for the Courche[105] which the
highland women use to put upon their heads as soon as they were married.
I thank you for giving me all the Scotch <u>head-geer</u> to chuse upon, and I
should gladly adopt the cap as you seem to like it best, but a cap is very
modern, and is not in good keeping with the pearlens[106] & other things
mentioned in the song. It shall therefore stand, if you please, thus.

> Toys sa douce & sa neat
> On Locks that the wind used blow![107]

I thank you for subscribing to my book, and for doing me all the good in your
power; I know well how unpleasant it is to ask for subscriptions. I wish I

---

103. Sculptor John Flaxman (1755-1826) was employed early in his career by the
Wedgwoods and became a friend of William Blake. After his marriage to Ann
Denman, the couple went to Rome where he studied design. Returning to England in
1794 as an acknowledged artist, Flaxman became a professor of sculpture at the
Royal Academy in 1810. Works are numerous, including his illustrations to
Alexander Pope's translation of Homer's *Iliad*, and he is said to have been "habitually
armed with a sketch-book" (*DNB*, VII:254-60).

104. Thomson declared "Hooly and fairly" his favorite air (Hadden, 242).

105. curch, curtch or curtsch: covering for the head, kerchief (*SND*).

106. pearlin: lace used as trim (*SND*).

107. These lines are "A kerchief sae dounce and sae neat,/ O'er her locks that the
winds used to blaw!" in *DPW* (817). See preceding letter and notes.

had had it in my power to serve my friend in some other way, and it was with a heavy heart that I first set about it. —— I shall inform Lady Campbell when I see her of your kind intention. Her husband is Col. Charliwood [*sic*] of the Guards, but she still keeps the title of Lady Campbell, and her house is in Hertford St: May Fair no. 29. — I remain

> my dear Sir,
>> yours most sincerely
>>> J Baillie

PS. If you should see Mrs Grant, will you have the goodness to say to her, that I have enquired at Mr Longman himself,[108] some time ago, for the letter & the papers which she is so very kind as to send to me, and they were not arrived, but Mr L. promised to send them to me as soon as they should arrive. When I have received them, I will write to her; and in the mean time thank her for her note of a few lines, received so long since. ——

f.110 (Address: To George Thomson / Trustee Office / Edinburgh-- postmarked 1822)

My dear Sir,

I send you your Song which I am better pleased with myself than with most of those that have gone before it, but that is no proof of its being good. However, if you sing it yourself with some of that glee which you give to Muirland Willy, nobody will find fault with it. —— I must at present send very brief letters to my friends, having more writing on my hands than I well know how to get through. With all kind wishes to you & your family,

> I remain, my dear Sir,
>> yours most sincerely
>>> J Baillie

Hampstead
March 20th 1822

> Hooly & fairly

Oh, Neighbours! What had I a do for to marry!
My wife she drinks possets and wine o' canary,
And ca's me a niggardly, thraw-gabbit Cairly,
O gin my wife wad drink hooly & fairly!
> Hooly & fairly &c &c.

---

108. Thomas Longman (1699-1755) founded a publishing firm which still exists today. Longman helped publish Johnson's *Dictionary*, while Baillie's neighbor Thomas Longman III (1771-1842) published such authors as Wordsworth, Coleridge, Sir Walter Scott and herself (*OCEL*, 585).

She sups wi' her Kimmers on dainties enew,
Aye bowing & smirking & wiping her mou,
While I sit aside and am helpet but sparely,
O gin my wife wad feast hooly & fairly!
         Hooly & fairly &c. &c.

To fairs & to Bridals & preachings & a'
She gangs sa light headed and busket sa braw,
Its ribbons & mantuas that gar me ga barely,
O gin my wife wad spend hooly & fairly!
         Hooly & fairly &c &c

I' the kirk sic commotion last sabbath she made
Wi' Babs o' red roses and breast-knots o'er laid,
The Dominie sticket his psalm very nearly,
O gin my wife wad dress hooly & fairly!
         Hooly & fairly &c. &c.

She's warring & flyting fra' morning till e'en
And if ye gain-say her, her eye glows sa keen!
Then tongue, kneeve & cudgel she'll lay on you sarely,
O gin my wife wad strike hooly & fairly!
         Hooly & fairly &c &c.

When tir'd wi' her cantrips, she lies in her bed,
The wark a' neglected, the chaumer unred,
When a' our good Neighbours are stirring right early,[109]
O gin my wife wad sleep timely & fairly!
         Timely & fairly &c &c.

A word o' good counsel or grace she'll hear none,
She bandies the Elders & mocks at Mess John,
And[110] back in his teeth his own text she flings rarely,
O gin my wife wad speak hooly & fairly!
         Hooly & fairly &c &c

---

109. Except for changes in punctuation and spelling, "Hooly and Fairly. (Founded on an Old Scotch Song.)" appears much the same in *DPW*. This and the next line, however, read: "While a' our guid neighbours are stirring sae early:/ O, gin my wife wad wurk timely and fairly!" (819).

110. "And" is "While" in *DPW*.

I wish I were single, I wish I were freed,
I wish I were doited, I wish I were dead,
Or she i' the mouls, to dement me no mare, lay,
      What does it vail to cry hooly & fairly!
          Hooly & fairly, hooly & fairly,
      Wasting my breath to cry hooly & fairly!

f.173 (Address: To Thomson--no postmark)

Hampstead July 24th [1826?]

My dear Sir,

In looking over my letters <u>not</u> answered I am quite ashamed to find that I have made no acknowledgment to you for your kind present of the sixth volume of your new work and that it is more than a year since I received it & the obliging note with which it was accompanied. Pray forgive me! I have behaved very ill; but I am sure it is neither ingratitude nor want of respect which has occasioned it. You [have] done me honour in having one of my Songs from the Beacon harmonized, and I beg you to believe that I so feel it. I make no doubt that it is done as you say in a delightful manner, but I have so few opportunities of hearing any thing but Italien [*sic*] music that I am not likely soon to be indulged as I could wish.

——

My Sister & I were obliged by your kind enquiries, the answer to which must now regard the health of another year, and may be favourably given, for we have upon the while been reasonably well, tho' our late hot weather made us very heavy & listless. Lady Campbell, who for her Mother's sake you are interested for, has had a great deal of illness the last winter & lately, and is now going with her husband to Scotland & Harrowgate [Harrogate] for her health which I hope will be restored by it. ———

I hope you received my little Drama called the Martyr as other copies sent to my friends in Edin^r were safely delivered.[111] If I hear nothing to the contrary I shall conclude that it is the case. —— I hope that you & Mrs Thomson & the family are well. I have heard of you some times by friends from Edin' but not very lately. My Sister joins me in best wishes & remembrances. —— Pray forgive me, my dear Sir,

and believe me very truly
    your obliged & faithful &c
        J Baillie

---

111. *The Martyr* was published by Longman, Rees, Orme, Brown, and Green in 1826.

PS. This goes by favour of Mr Angus Fletcher,[112] and the date may be somewhat old ere you receive it.

f. 180 (Address: To George Thomson--postmarked 1827)[113]

Hampstead Jany 23^d 1827

My dear Sir,

When I read your obliging & very flattering letter, I at first felt somewhat angry that you should wish to disturb our old popular ballad of "Fy let us a' to the Wedding," and thought that nothing put in its place would have any chance of pleasing my Northern countrymen; but some time afterwards it came suddenly into my head that it might be managed without giving them offence and I set about it forthwith. I have let the rough copy lie by me these ten days, and now send you the fair one with a very few corrections; and if it should be lucky enough to please you, you are welcome to it. The character of the old song is preserved, for I could not think of altering that, yet I question whether the admirers of the old rigamorole [*sic*] with all its pithy nicknames, will give me any thanks for what I have done, or you either for what you have set me upon doing. --- I am very much obliged to you for the musical volume you have had the goodness to send me. and have put it into the hands of some young Neighbours of ours who sing very charmingly, but I have not yet had the opportunity of hearing any part of it. I hope it will be as successful as any of your former publications. --- I am happy to tell you, that Lady Campbell, whom you enquire after, returned from the south of Scotland about two months ago with her health quite recovered and is looking remarkably well. —— We have now got winter in good earnest, tho' it has been late of coming, but have as yet escaped any bad effects from it; I hope you & Mrs Thomson have been as well off. With kind regards to you both, I remain, my dear Sir yours truly

J Baillie

PS. Pray excuse my sending you such a cramped letter. I was afraid of making the packet too heavy.

Fy let us a' to the Wedding
an auld song new busket

---

112. Angus Fletcher (1799-1862), son of Mrs. Elizabeth Fletcher, gave up a law practice to attend the Royal Academy Schools in 1825, exhibiting at the Academy from 1831 to 1839. His best busts are of the Duke of Argyll (1831), J. B. S. Morritt of Rokeby (1834) and author Charles Dickens (1839), to whom Fletcher reportedly endeared himself. He also exhibited two busts of Felicia Hemans in 1830 and 1832.

113. Hadden dates this letter 1827, but Baillie's 4s and 7s look very much alike.

Fy let us a' to the Wedding,
　　For they will be lilting there,
For Jock's to be married to Maggy,
　　The Lass wi' the golden[114] hair.

And there will be jibing & jeering
　　And glancing o' bonny glegg eyen,[115]
Lond laughing & smooth-gabbet speering
　　O' questions baith pawkey & keen.

For there will be Bessy the beauty,
　　Wha raises her cockass[116] sae hie,
And gigles at preachings & duty,
　　Guid grant that she gang na' ajee.

And there will be auld Geordie Tanner,
　　Wha coft a young Wife wi' his gowd;
She'll flaunt wi' a silk-gown upon her,
　　But wow! he looks dowie & cow'd.

And brown Tibby Fouler the heiress
　　Will perk at the tap o' the ha';
Encirled wi' suitors whose care is
　　To catch up her gloves whan they fa';

Repeat a' her jokes as they're cleckit,
　　And haver & glower in her pace,
While tocherless Mays are negleckit, --
　　A crying & scandalous case.

And Mysie wha's clavering Aunty
　　Wad match her wi' Laurie the laird,
And learns the young fuel to be vaunty,
　　But neither to spin nor to card.

---

114. [G]olden is changed to "gowden" in Baillie's "Fy, Let Usa A' To The Wedding. (An Auld Sang, New Buskit.)" (*DPW*, 818). Spelling and punctuation changes also appear throughout.
115. In *DPW* "glegg eyen" is changed to "dark een" (818).
116. Word is "cockup" in *DPW*.

And there will be blate Johny Beaton[117]
    That's dying for impudent Nell;
And Will, wha the brae tak's his seat on
    To keek at himself i' the well.

And Andrew whose Granny is yearning
    To see him a Clerical Blade,
Was sent to the College for learning,
    And cam back a Coof as he gaid.

And Angus, the seer o' fairlies,[118]
    Wha sits on the stone at his door,
And tells ye o' Bogles and mair lies
    Than tongue ever utter'd before

And Eppy the sewster sae genty,
    A pattern for havens & sense,
Will streik on her mittens sae dainty,
    And crack wi' Miss John i' the spence.

And there will be auld widow Martin,[119]
    That ca's herself thrity & two,
And thraw-gabbet Madge, who for certain
    Was gilted by Hab o' the shaw.

And there will be Bawley the boaster,
    Sae ready wi' han's & wi' tongue,
Proud Paty, silly Sam Foster,
    That quarrel wi' auld & wi' young.

And Tom[120] the Town Writer, I'm thinking,
    That trades in his lawyerly skill,
Will egg on the fighting & drinking,
    To bring after grist to his mill.

And Maggy —— na, na! we'll be civil,
    And let the wee Bridie abe,

---

117. This entire stanza does not appear in *DPW*.
118. This stanza appears after the next one here ("And Eppy . . .") in *DPW*.
119. This stanza appears before "And Eppy the sewster . . ." in *DPW*.
120. "Tom" is "Hugh" in *DPW*.

A vilepend tongue is the Deevil,
    And ne'er was encouraged by me.

Then fy let us a' to the Wedding,
    For they will be lilting there,
Fra' mony a far distant ha'ding
    The fun and the feasting to share.

For they will get sheep's head & haggis,
    And browst o' the barley mow;
E'en he that comes latest and lag is,
    May feast upon dainties enow.

Veal Florentines i' the o'en baken,
    Weel plennish'd wi' raisins & fat;
Beef, mutton & chuckies a' taken,
    Het-reeking fra' spit and fra' pat.

And glasses weel fill'd ('tis na said ill)[121]
    To drink the young couple guid luck,[122]
Dealt round wi' a guid beechen ladle,
    Fra' punch-bowl as big as Dumbuck.

And then will come dancing & daffing,
    And reeling & crossing o' han's,
Till even auld Lucky is laughing,
    As back by the aumrey she stan'd.

Sic bobbing & flinging & whirling,
    While Fiddlers are making their din,
And Pipers are dronning & skirling,
    As loud as the roar o' the Lin!

Then fy let us a' to the Wedding,
    For they will be lilting there,
For Jock's to be married to Maggy,
    The Lass wi' the gowden hair

---

121. Changed to "(I trow 'tis na' said ill)" in *DPW*.
122. The line is "Well fill'd wi' a braw beechen ladle" in *DPW*.

f.249 (Address: To Thomson--postmarked 1836)

Hampstead Decr 21^t 1836

My dear Sir,

I see by the date of your last letter that it must have come here during our absence or on the very eve of our departure for the Isle of Wight in Septr which must plead my excuse for having put it by with other letters that, like itself, ought to have been acknowledged sooner. It gave me much pleasure to learn that you had been amongst the western Isles and had enjoyed your excurtion [*sic*]. For that you did enjoy it to the best, is well seen by your sublime & poetical discription of Staffa & its wonderful cave. In truth you write with the fancy & vigour of a young Poet, and this encourages me to think that, if the mind is young, the body must be in good health. Long may you be in this state! And how very kind you have been in sending me the two sketches to give me a more perfect idea of the scenes! Some five or six & twenty years ago, I received a similar discription of the cave in a letter from Sir W. Scott, who visited it before the time of steam boats, when the navigation was more difficult & dangerous.[123] He did not indeed send me a real pencil sketch of its wonders, but he sent me some pebbles picked up by himself on the shores of Iona which are among my precious things to this day. Many thanks for your friendly remembrance of me!

I must thank you too for the cheering things you say on the subject of my Late-published Dramas.[124] I am truly glad that you think I shall lose no credit by them; for it was altogether rather perilous to venture before the public again so late in the day and after such a lapse of time. This which may be called my last offering, has been received with great friendliness & indulgence, and I retire contented & gratified. I dont know whether you are amongst those who dislike & condemn the character of my jealous man, however; if you are, pray for my sake look at the last number of Fraser's Magazine and see what I have there said in defense of it.[125] —— My Sister & I have kept pretty well during what has passed of this wet foggy winter — the very wettest we remember in this country. We have had nothing but heavy clouds over-head, fog or rain for a long time and we are tired of

---

123. In July 1810 Scott and his family took a trip to the Hebrides as guests of Ranald Macdonald, the Laird of Staffa. From Oban, they passed close to the Lady's Rock in the Sound of Mull, the very rock Baillie mentions in her *Family Legend*. See NLS letter 3879 ff.156-158 to Scott.

124. *Dramas* (London: Longman, Rees, Orme, Brown, Green, & Longman, 1836) appeared in 3 volumes.

125. An essay entitled "On the Character of Romiero" appeared in Vol. 14 of *Fraser's Magazine* in 1836 and is, as Baillie says, a vindication of the hero and summary rather than a critical analysis of the play.

picking our steps through the dirt day after day on the summit of our Hill. Xmas, which I hope will be a merry one with you & Mrs Thomson & those belonging to you, and now so near at hand, will draw families together and make them think of the social comforts of a Town. We expect by & by to see your friends M^rs & Miss Fletcher in Town at least I was told so not long ago. She Mrs F. is a person one is always glad to meet and her residence beyond Chatham is quite out of our reach. They enjoyed their summer visit at the Rhine, I understand, very much. Who indeed does not? and that noble River will by & by be as familiar to the Scotch people as the Clyde or the Tay. I hope, however, we shall continue to love what is our own. -- I am sorry to find that you think our taste for our national music is at present obscured. I am sure they will get nothing to supply its taste half so beautiful. However, that it is at present out of fashion is a fact I have no opportunity of knowing fairly. For the partiality of my Sister & I for our own country melodies is so well known amongst our friends that wherever we go some young Lady or other is desired to sing Scotch songs with an accompaniment and every body says O how beautiful! That you, my dear Sir, have done so much to raise the character of our music must be a great satisfaction to you always. --- We are much obliged to Mrs Thomson for her kind remembrances, and both my Sister & I unite in best regards to her & to yourself.

> Believe me, my dear Sir.
>> Your truly obliged & faithful &c
>> J Baillie

f.261 (Address: To Thomson--no postmark)

> Hampstead Jany 11th 1838

My dear Sir

You are heartily welcome to make use of the Songs from the Phantom & the Bride, mentioned in your letter & received by me two days ago, in the way proposed;[126] and I am very glad that the Dramas have afforded any pleasure to you & Mrs Thomson in these long winter evenings. It is well you did not write to Mess^m Longman for the permission required, for I have not disposed of the copy-right of my last Dramas, and they would have had no power either to grant or decline your request. I am glad too that you keep up your enthusiasm for music & song which will still brighten your old age as it has done your youth. ———

---

126. Baillie's musical drama *The Phantom* contains many songs; *The Bride* contains two.

We had the pleasure of seeing your daughter Mrs Hogarth[127] the other day who was kind enough to come with her friend Miss Thomson and see her safely housed under our roof. She is now with us and we are endeavouring to keep her as warm & comfortable as may be, in this very severe weather, while the snow is lying pretty thick on the ground and the water frozen in our bedrooms, though fires burn in them till near the middle of the night. ――― This is very trying for the poor, but it will be good for the Farmer and the community at large. ―― Miss Thomson speaks very gratefully of Mrs Hogarth's great kindness & constant attention to her, and I doubt not she has been Nursed with every friendly tenderness by her. She seems pretty well in health and the poor wretched ankle gaining strength by degrees, but I fear it will be a long time before she is able to walk again without a stick. We hope that this complete change of air from London closeness will be of service to her general health. ――

We have like yourself been very much occupied with the 6th vol. of Sir W Scott's life, particularly the very interesting diary has touched us pleasingly & painfully.[128] I cannot answer your question as to who was the munificent friend who offered the £30,000 on the failure of his affairs, but it has been supposed to be the Late Lord Dudley and it probably was him.[129] ―――

My Sister & self beg to offer our kind regards & the wishes of the season and Miss Thomson also, who is just come from her room desires to be kindly remembered to you & the family

Believe me, my dear Sir,
    very faithfully yours
        J Baillie

f. 284 (Address: To George Thomson Esqr, no street address or year--
Thomson dates it February 1841)

Hampstead Saturday [1841]

My dear Sir

I feel flattered by your wishing to have another of my Songs for your next volume, but the Song you propose I gave away to Dr Clerk[130] of

---

127. George Thomson's daughter Georgina married George Hogarth; the Hogarths' daughter Catherine later became the wife of Charles Dickens.

128. See John Gibson Lockhart's *Memoirs of the Life of Sir Walter Scott* (1838).

129. Lockhart's statement is that a generous offer of £30,000 was conveyed to Scott through an undisclosed, distinguished channel revealed only on Scott's deathbed, but he does not identify (see Hadden, 247).

130. Thomson notes this is Clark. This is possibly Richard Clark (1780-1856), musician and gentleman of the Chapel Royal, Vicar Choral of St. Paul's, etc., who

Cambridge a great many years ago, and I could not in justice wish that it should be joined to any other music than he has set for it which is I believe very good. --- The meaning of the line "And motioned love the measure keep" I intended to be understood as Love expressed by motion, as joy or any other feeling is expressed by motion, a thing that is to be seen every day.

I am glad to hear that M[rs] Thomson is getting better and remain
very sincerely yours
J Baillie

f. 286 (No address--Thomson dates 1 May 1841)

Hampstead saturday
May 1st [1841]

My dear Sir,

I am very glad to hear you have received any pleasure from my volume of Fugitive Verses and thank you truly for the kind & friendly interest you have taken in the two pieces you particularly mention. ── its to my three amended Scotch Songs, "Willy was a Wanton Wag," "Fee him Father fee him" and "Wi' long-legged Tom the Bruise I tryed," you are heartily welcome to put them into your next publication of Scotch music.[131] I shall be pleased to see them there; and you have no leave to ask of any Bookseller, for they are entirely my own property. "Fee him &c" I wrote for Miss Head of Ashfield Devon Shire, who has a delightful voice & taste in music and gave her the first Ms copy many years ago, and it has been sung I believe by no one else.[132]

M[rs] Thomson & yourself are I hope enjoying this delightful weather at Brampton. You will feel most comfortably warm there. Even on our hill we can wander about with our winter wraps laid aside and sit a little in the open air. Your walk, I presume is Hyde Park or Kensington Garden: ours is Hampstead heath, though we scarcely feel strong enough to take the whole length of its long Terrace.

I remain, my dear Sir,
very truly yours
J Baillie

---

published some poetry based on songs. In the still disputed argument, he attributed "God Save the Queen" to John Bull (*DNB*, IV:404-5).

131. Baillie's *Fugitive Verses* first appeared from Moxon in 1840, followed by editions in 1842 and 1844. Included were the poems "The Merry Bachelor" (Willy was a wanton wag) and "Song, To the Scotch Air of 'My Nanny O'" (Wi' lang-legg'd Tam the broose I tried).

132. This may be the Miss Fanny Head who translated composer Friedrich Gottlieb Klopstock's (1724-1803) *Messiah* (see NLS letter 3903 ff.131-33 to Scott).

f.290 (Address: George Thomson--no postmark)

Hampstead monday
May 10th [1841]

My dear Sir,

    I am glad you think my two first mentioned songs will do no discredit to your forth-coming volume, and thank you for the pains you are willing to take in favour of Long-legg'd Tom; but I should not like to have him joined to any other music than the old air of my Nanny O. It is one of those Scotch airs that may be made either plaintive or joyous as you chuse to sing or play them: my song was intended for it in the last character, and Burns[133] or Percy[134] having written words for it, suited to the former, is a matter of no importance in itself; though I readily agree that there would be a confusion & awkwardness in its appearing in its joyous mood in your last volume when it has been melancholy & sentimental in the first. We shall, therefore, if you please think no more about it. I hope the volume you are now preparing for the public may do you as much credit as its predecessors, and have indeed no doubt of it.

    I am sorry you have not yet enjoyed the advantage of being so near Hyde Park, but more favorable weather will I trust by & by enable both Mrs Thomson & yourself to go out & walk or ride as you are inclined. It is very kind of you to think of Hampstead. I need scarcely say we should be glad to see you, but you must make no effort that may stand any chance of hurting you. With all kind wishes,

    I remain, my dear Sir
        very sincerely yours
          J Baillie

---

    133. Scottish poet Robert Burns (1759-96) was born to tenant farmers and came to know firsthand the ballads, legends and songs of the Scottish peasantry. An apt pupil, Burns read everything he could, his favorite writers being Sterne, Mackenzie and Macpherson. Heavy farm labor in his early years instigated the rheumatic heart disease which eventually killed him, but in his short life he contributed some of the most significant Scottish poetry, including, *Poems Chiefly in the Scottish Dialect* (1786), *Tam O'Shanter* (1791) and *Poems* (2 vols., 1793) (see Thomas Crawford's *Burns: A Study of the Poems and Songs* [Stanford: Stanford University Press, 1960]).

    134. Thomas Percy (1729-1811) began his literary life by translating a Chinese novel (*Hau Kiou Choaun* or *The Pleasing History*) from a Portuguese manuscript in 1761, followed by *Miscellaneous Pieces relating to the Chinese* in 1762 and his most famous *Reliques of Ancient English Poetry*, 3 vols. (1765), a collection of English and Scottish ballads which greatly influenced the early Romantics. He became interested in Macpherson's studies in Gaelic and Erse poetry and in 1763 published *Five Pieces of Runic Poetry* from the Icelandic. In 1801 he contributed to an edition of Goldsmith's *Miscellaneous Works* but began losing his eyesight in 1804. In 1840 the Percy Society for the Publication of Ballad Poetry was formed in his honor (*DNB*, XV:882-84).

f.320 (Address: George Thomson / Bedford Place / Kensington--
postmarked 1842)

Hampstead March 30th [1842]

My dear Sir,

Your book came safely to hand the day after I received your friendly
letter, and I thank you for both very sincerely. It gave me pleasure to think
that you had been occupied again in your own way, and I hope this new &
last volume of the melodies will be very successful. I have given a
comission [sic] to a friend to get another copy for me at Soho Square which I
mean to send to a musical family at some distance, as yet I have had no
opportunity of hearing any of the songs sung, going no where of an evening;
but my G^d Niece with her guitar will be with us for a few-days soon, and
then we shall get acquainted, with some of them, at least.[135] It is a very
great advantage to the work that it has come out at this time when M^r
Wilson has delighted the Public so much by singing with his fine voice &
good taste our old Scotch airs,[136] so much neglected of late years. The
aplauses [sic] of crowded audiences in London will no doubt make them
more popular in Edin^r, and our Country will no longer be foolish enough (I
mean our Scotch Ladies) to dispise what belongs to itself. I am very much
flattered to hear that Mr Wilson approves of my modified versions of the
old songs. They are at least more fitted for his polite & more refined
hearers than they were. ---

I am pleased that you should still suppose I have spirit enough to deal
with your Auld Wife & her wee pickle tow, but I do not feel that I have;
the air is an excellent one, but who could give the proper alterations of the
words better than Sir Adam himself?[137] let him take it in hand; and if he
will not, let the same skilful pen that modified Johny Cope so well of late,
be employed on the wee pickle tow, and it will do admirably well.[138]

—— I ought not to have been so long of acknowledging your kind present,
but I have been occupied in various ways and too listless to get on well

---

135. This grand niece would be Elizabeth Baillie Milligan's daughter Sophia
Milligan (1817-82).

136. Scottish vocalist John Wilson (1800-49) worked for the Ballantynes in
Edinburgh for a time and helped set up the *Waverley Novels*. He became interested in
music, studied with John Mather and Benjamin Gleadhill in Edinburgh and appeared
in some of the musical adaptations of Scott novels. His Scottish song entertainments
were an immense success in both England and America. Wilson published an edition
of *The Songs of Scotland* in 1842 and died in Canada of cholera in 1849 (*DNB*).

137. Hadden identifies this as Sir Adam Ferguson, Scott's friend and companion
(248). Sir Adam Ferguson (1771-1855) was keeper of the regalia in Scotland and the
oldest son of Professor Adam Ferguson. See letter following.

138. Thomson did make the alterations himself, his "Jonnie Cope" inscribed to Sir
Adam Ferguson (Hadden, 248).

with any of my occupation. —— I see by the dating of your letter that you must by this time be settled in a new abode. I hope it will agree with your health, and when you are disposed for taking exercise, no walks can be more agreeable than Kensington Gardens. ——— My Sister begs to offer her best remembrances

 Believe me, my dear Sir
  your obliged & faithful &c
   J Baillie

The following two letters to Thomson are housed in The National Library of Scotland:

786 ff.45-46 (No address or postmark--NLS identifies recipient as George Thomson.)

Hampstead Friday April 16th

My dear Sir,

 It is with great pleasure that I take up my pen to thank you for your spirited, improved version of Johnie Cope which I think will still be sung with glee by the present descendants of the Clan's men. I once heard it sung by Sir Adam Ferguson with as much exultation as if the Battle had been fought yesterday, and it was a very great treat. The very pretty little song at the end too, I like much; and if the music be worthy of the words, it cannot fail to meet with favour. I shall give a copy of it to my Niece, who sings and lives among musical people in the Isle of Wight, and hope to hear a good report of it from thence very soon. ——— I fear I must have appeared to you very ungrateful & negligent in not making my acknowledgments sooner, but we were from home when it came, and found it last tuesday evening lying on the table when we returned: yesterday I had no time to write. — My sister & I are also much gratified by your kind & friendly lines to us written on the blank page at the beginning, and thank you sincerely.

 We both unite in kind regards to yourself and Mrs Thomson. I hope you will soon shake off your enemy entirely, and am sorry to hear you have not escaped this dreadful influenza from which so many, old & young have suffered. I am thankful to say, in return to your kind enquiries, that my sister & I have suffered much less than might have been expected from the great severity of the winter.

 Believe me, my dear Sir,
  your truly obliged & faithful &c
   J Baillie

786 ff.47-48 (No address or postmark--NLS identifies recipient as
Thomson)

My dear Sir,
    I thank you for your kind New year's wishes on behalf of my Sister &
myself, and we both beg of you to accept ours in return. I attempt to say no
more, for she is entirely confined to her bed and in a state to make us very
anxious.
    Your Maggy Lauder &c gives me pleasure as a sign that your mind still
retains its former vigour and can take pleasure in poetry & in music. I am
very glad to think so, and thank you for the songs which I shall keep
carefully and may read with proper effect when my mind is more
disengaged. —— You wiil, I am sure, excuse the shortness of this note, and
believe me
    very truly yours — very gratefully yours
               J Baillie
Hampstead
Wednesday January 25th 1849

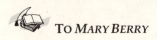 To *Mary Berry*

(1804-1833?)

Writer Mary Berry (1763-1852) was born in Kirkbridge, Yorkshire, to Elizabeth Seton and merchant Robert Berry, who was disinherited by his wealthy uncle Robert Ferguson because of the unprofitable match.[1] After their mother's early death at the birth of her third child in 1767 (the child did not survive either), Mary and her sister Agnes were brought up by their grandmother in Yorkshire and later Chiswick and were largely self educated but extremely well read; much like Joanna and Agnes Baillie, the two sisters remained together for more than 80 years. After uncle William Berry began providing the family an income of £1,000 per year, Berry had the opportunity to travel to the continent and in Florence in 1783 began the first of several journals, later edited with letters by Lady Theresa Lewis in 1865. Mary was sought in marriage by an unsuccessful Mr. Bowman in 1779 and in 1796 broke an engagement to Gerald O'Hara, governor of Gibraltar, not wishing to live so distantly from her family. Berry never married but was to declare near the end of her life that the six months of friendship and correspondence with O'Hara had been her happiest days.

Horace Walpole met the Berry sisters in 1788 when he was over 70 and was so fond of them that he called them his "wives," dedicating several works to them and prevailing upon them in 1791 to take a house he called "Little Strawberry Hill." Walpole's letters record his distress at the sisters' travels to the continent and Paris in 1791 in the midst of the French Revolution, and in 1797 he provided each one the interest from £4,000, ultimately relieving them of any financial strain. Mary Berry, however, spent more time in London than in Twickenham, writing plays, historical works, etc., and attracting such visitors as Joanna Baillie, Anne Damer, Harriet Martineau, Byron, Francis Jeffrey, Samuel Rogers, Malthus,

---

1. Biographical information on Berry comes from *The Feminist Companion to Literature in English: Women Writers from the Middle Ages to the Present*, ed. Virginia Blain, Patricia Clements and Isobel Grundy (London: B. T. Batsford, 1990), 88, and Paul Schlueter and June Schlueter, *An Encyclopedia of British Women Writers* (New York: Garland, 1988), 36-38. Also see Lewis Melville's *The Berry Papers: Being the Correspondence Hitherto Unpublished of Mary and Agnes Berry (1763-1852)* (London: John Lane, n.d.).

Dickens and Fanny Kemble; Madame de Staël is said to have declared her the cleverest woman in England.

Berry looked on novels somewhat disapprovingly; but, ironically, her comedy *Fashionable Friends*, produced at Drury Lane in 1802, was attacked unjustly for its "loose principles." Baillie wrote the prologue and epilogue for *Fashionable Friends*, the latter, "Epilogue to the Theatrical Representation at Strawberry Hill," included in *The Dramatic and Poetical Works of Joanna Baillie* (1851).[2] Berry also edited *The Works of Horatio Walpole, Earl of Orford* in 1798; and her anti-revolutionary, pro-Malthusian principles were expressed strongly in *A Comparative View of the Social Life of England and France from the Restoration of Charles II to the French Revolution* (1828-31), later retitled in her *Works* (1844) which also reprinted her annotated editions of letters by Mme. du Deffand (1810) and *The Life of Rachel, Lady Russell* (1819).[3]

The correspondence in this chapter verifies the close friendship between Baillie and Berry; and manuscript HB.ii-56c, owned by the Royal College of Surgeons of England and entitled "Recollections Written at the request of Miss Berry" (1831), testifies to Berry's interest in establishing a partial biography of her literary companion.

---

2. In *The Life and Work of Joanna Baillie* (New Haven: Yale University Press, 1923), Margaret Carhart cites a letter from Baillie dated 14 October 1801 in which she sends "a plain, simple Prologue of no pretentions, but such I hope as you will not dislike; if you do, throw it aside, and I shall not be at all offended" (15). I have not located this manuscript letter.

3. Schlueter and Schlueter report that Baillie described *Lady Russell* as an "edifying example to the young women of the day, who consider religion too exclusively connected with mystery" (37).

Except for one letter from the Folger Shakespeare Library, the following letters to Mary Berry are part of the Hunter-Baillie collection at the Royal College of Surgeons of England and the Hunter-Baillie collection of the Wellcome Institute for the History of Medicine, transcribed through their permission. The Royal College of Surgeons of England also own two manuscript poems in Baillie's hand, HB.ii-44 "Lines to Agnes Baillie on her birth day" and HB.ii-45 "Recollections of a dear & steady Friend" (written for Lady Byron).

RCS HB.ix-15 (Address: For Miss Berry / Little Strawberry Hill / Twickenham / Middlesex--postmarked 1804)

Hampstead Novr 29th 1804

Tales of Wonder, at least such as I write, unless they be meant at the same time (as one of our reviewers said) for tales of plunder, are good for nothing else but amusing ones friends of a winter evening in the country by the fireside, and so I very willingly send you my two <u>things</u> to get as much amusement out of as you can. This will depend very much upon yourselves. If you read them pretty late at night by a good fire & all the house still, they may do pretty well, but if you read them in day light with servants' feet clattering up & down stairs and Busy barking, they will be good for nothing. I have sent them to Town this morning to be left at Mrs Damer's[4] upper Brook St: till call'd for, and you may return them to me again when it is convenient, only dont lose them. I would have mention'd them in my last letter, as you had said you should like to see them, but I completely forgot it. —— My Mother I think is rather better since I wrote to you last.[5] — Have you heard any thing of the Greatheads [*sic*] since you learnt their grievous loss?[6] They have received one of the most severe strokes that i t

---

4. Sculptor Anne Seymour Damer (1749-1828) was the only child of Field-marshall Henry Seymour Conway and his wife Lady Caroline Campbell, daughter of the 4th duke of Argyll and widow of Lord Aylesbury. She was a favorite of Horace Walpole and adored by her father. She studied anatomy under Cruikshank and took lessons from Ceracchi. In 1767 she married John Damer, heir to his father Lord Milton's fortune. She was a staunch Whig, met Josephine and Napoleon, and presented the latter with a bust of Fox; he presented her with a diamond snuff-box with his portrait (now in the British Museum). She was a friend of Mary Berry and produced her *Fashionable Friends* at Drury Lane in 1802 to ill reviews. In 1818 she moved to Twickenham, where she brought together a collection of her own busts and terra cottas and her mother's worsted work (*DNB*, V:450-51).

5. Baillie's mother, Dorothea Hunter Baillie, died in 1806 after a long illness.

6. Dramatist Bertie Greatheed (1759-1826), who lived in Florence much of his life, published collections of poems and brought out a tragedy called *The Regent* in April 1788. Though supported by John Kemble and Mrs. Siddons with an epilogue by Mrs. Piozzi, the play was not very successful and was withdrawn after a few nights.

is possible for death – simple death – to give. I have not heard of any loss of the kind happening to people with whom I am not acquainted that has affected me more. —— My Love to Agnes:[7] I met Mrs Dundas in Town a few days ago, and had a very favourable account of her looks indeed.[8] Remember me kindly to Mrs Damer & your good Father, and believe me truly & affectionately yours

    J Baillie

WI MS 5616/70 (Address: Miss Berry North Audley Street / Grosvenor Square / London--postmark unclear)

Hampstead July 12th 1805

My dear Friend,

I hope this will find you return'd from strawberry hill, after having enjoy'd, at least, <u>some</u> pleasure during the week with Mrs D. & your friend Lady Douglass;[9] and picking a little pleasure amongst pain is what we are all set to do in this world, tho' the quantity of the pickings, I grant, that falls into each persons lot is some times very different. — I long very much to know what this new plan or determination of yours is.[10] God grant it may be some thing practicable & successful! that you will have firmness & perseverance enough to follow it out and give it a fair trial, I have not the least doubt; and that it will be form'd with as true a regard to the interest of her who drives you to it as to your own I am fully persuaded.

We shall be truly glad to see you any day next week that is most agreeable to you, receiving due notice before-hand by penny post note that I may take care to be in the way when you come, and also, as I have told you before that we may have time to prepare the <u>great feast</u> that is to be given upon the occasion. I hope it will prove a fine day that Miss Seaton, who with your Sister, I hope, is to be of the party, may have a walk upon the heath which will do her good. If Mr Berry is not better engaged, and will take his usual ride by Kilburn or Highgate that day, and drop in upon us at four o'clock, we shall be glad. ——— With every kind wish for

---

The Greatheeds' only son, Bertie, an amateur artist, died in Italy on 8 October 1804 at the age of 23 (*DNB*, VIII:475).

    7. This is Mary Berry's sister Agnes Berry (1764-1852).

    8. This could be the second wife (Lady Jane Hope) of Home Secretary Henry Dundas (1742-1811), for almost 30 years one of the most powerful political men in Scotland. There were at that time, however, several prominent figures of that name.

    9. Baillie refers to Mrs. Damer (see note 4 above), but I am unable to identify which Lady Douglas this could be.

    10. At this particular time Berry could have been planning the edition of *Letters of the Marquise de Deffand* (1810) or her later biography of Lady Russell (1819).

the success of (of) all your views & intention, I remain always affectionately yours

J Baillie

P.S. Do you know of any body who would like to take a good furnish'd house in Hampstead from next Michaelmass till Mich^{ss} followin[g], that is to say for a compleat year? The house in question which belongs to a friend of ours, is delightfully situated with large garden pleasure ground and two acres of field, and has offices & every thing for the accommodation of a pretty large family. If you should hear of any body who want such a thing, I shall thank you to mention this. ——

WI MS 5616/64 (Address: Miss Berry North Audley Street / Grosvenor Square / London--postmarked 1805)

Hampstead Decr 25th 1805

A merry Christmas to you, and many good things beside! I think with satisfaction that few if any of my friends will spend this day in so lonely & mellancholly a way as I and my poor Sister shall, and it pleases me to think so.[11] Give my kindest wishes to your Sister & to Mr Berry: I hope you are well & comfortable whether you are at your own fire side or that of a friend. — I was sorry to leave Town last thursday without seeing you again, but M^{rs} B's carriage which was to fetch my Nephew from school that morning was order'd sooner than I expected, and this prevented me.[12]

Do you know that I having [sic] been thinking of you a great deal since I saw you last? and whether my thoughts be foolish or wise ones I think you ought to know what they are. You have said to a certain Gentleman of Yorkshire, who has long been attach'd to you, that you would marry him to morrow, were it not that the different habits of life you have each acquired are not suited to make you live comfortably together.[13] Perhaps I dont express myself exactly in your words, but if my ears have not play'd me a trick when I listen'd to you, I have at least caught the sense of what you said. Now if you have spoke sincerely to this good man, and have not said so only to make your refusal less painful, let me ask you as a friend warmly interested therein, if you have really & seriously consider'd

---

11. At this time Joanna and Agnes were taking care of their mother Dorothea, who was blind and confined to bed. See letter WI MS 5616/65 following, which tells of another paralytic attack.

12. Mrs B is Sophia Denman Baillie (1771-1845), daughter of Dr. Thomas Denman (1733-1815) and Elizabeth Brodie Denman (1746-1833), who married Joanna's only brother Dr. Matthew Baillie in 1791 and became one of Joanna's closest friends; Sophia's two children were William Hunter Baillie (1797-1894), the nephew mentioned here, and Elizabeth Margaret Baillie Milligan (1794-1876).

13. I have not identified this Yorkshire suitor.

w[h]ether these same habits be actually as weighty an objection as you have represented them. You are not I should think of a very unaccommodating disposition; you have not been accustom'd to have every thing your own way; you have been accustomed to give up to others and to consider them more than yourself; and a man who has so long been attach'd, and who offers to give up the turf, will surely be willing, if he is a good temper'd man, to give up many things. Such a man as you would marry to morrow but for such objections, must have many good qualities, and should not be lightly given up. You wish for employment, and you wish to be useful in the world: as the Wife of a man of fortune you will have this much more in your power than you are ever likely to have by remaining single. He is a widower, and if he has children not too much grown up, so far from being an objection, it is a powerful call upon such a mind as yours. I could say many more things upon this subject – and so I will (if you do not forbid me) when we meet. This is enough in the mean time to set you thinking upon it seriously which is all I want. -- Now in what I am saying to you I am most disinterested, for every single woman, who is to remain so, has great pride in seeing such a woman as you of her Sister hood, and cannot possibly see you quitting the ranks but with considerable regret.

What does Mrs Damer think of this? Is she of my opinion? I am really anxious about it; so either let me see you or hear from you soon. I will make no apology for offering my advice where it [h]as not been ask'd. The worst that can come of it is that you may perhaps call me a goose; and I will run the risk of being so call'd at any time to have the slightest chance of doing you any good.

Farewell affectionately!

J Baillie

PS. How does your cold do? I hope you get well enough to go to Strawberry hill, as you proposed. ---

WI MS 5616/68 (Address: Miss Berry North Audley Street / Grosvenor Square / London--postmark unclear)

[1806?]

I am sorry to find, my dear Friend, that this Gentleman my friend here had in his eye as a Tenant for Little Strawberry, does not turn out, according to your ideas, a good one, for unluckily he has children. Of course this wont do; but I hope you will not be long of finding a good Tenant for it, & one who will take it by the year. I shall let no opportunity pass of mentioning it wherever I think it will be of any use so to do. Your terms I think, as things go, very reasonable.

I am sorry to find you have been so unwell since I saw you: I hope you will soon get rid of your cold; for the walk & wet feet you got here rest a little on my conscience, and I think I managed very badly for you that morning. — I am sorry to hear there is a time fix'd for your Sister's return from Bay's Cliff; I hoped she would have stay'd -- would have been tempted to stay there some time longer, (for I knew she did not intend it when she set out) and it would have been good for both of you. --- I have been reading this morning the account of the taking of the Cape by Sir D. Baird, and I congratulate you on the distinguish'd part your Cousin Gen: Ferguson has had in that action.[14] His services are mentioned as the most conspicuous of any performed in the enterprise; and he has now, at least amongst military men, made himself a mark'd man for life; and how pleasant that is for a man's self & all his connections I need not say to you. I believe you do not rate a little honest earn'd reputation beneath its value. --- I have spent three lonely days in my Mother's bedroom with not a creature to keep me company but now & then pussy; and she comes for the sake of a mouse that has got a hole not far from the chimney corner rather than any regard that she has for me. However, let her motives be what they will, as I have more need of her company at present than she has of mine, I am very civil to her. I expect my Sister home to morrow.[15] With all kind wishes,

    affectionately yours
      J Baillie
Hampstead March 2d

WI MS 5616/65 (Address: Miss Berry / North Audley Street / Grosvenor Square / London--postmarked 1806)
My dear Friend,
    Mrs Damer tells me in her note which came to my hand yesterday that there are some corrections you have to make on the last acts of my Family

---

14. Sir David Baird (1757-1829) was captain of the 71st Highland light infantry which embarked for India in 1779. Baird returned to England after 24 years of nearly continuous absence in the East and was knighted by the king. In 1805 he was ordered to command the army which was to capture the Cape of Good Hope from the Dutch in the following January 1806. His successful military career continued until his death in 1829 (*DNB*, I:914-17). Agnes Berry had been engaged to her cousin Colonel Ferguson some time in 1803, but the engagement was broken off; see note 17 following.

15. Agnes Baillie (1760-1861) was Joanna Baillie's only sister and constant companion. Their brother Dr. Matthew Baillie writes that Agnes Baillie, born in the Manse of Shotts on 24 September 1760, had "a quick ready Understanding, with a good deal of various knowle[d]ge, so as to be much beyond the common level of Women in these respects" (qtd. in Franco Crainz, *The Life and Works of Matthew Baillie* [Santa Polomba: PelitiAssociati, 1995], 10).

Legend, and I should be glad to know what they are as soon as may be.[16] I hope you have noted them down or at least have them so in your head that you can note them down & send them to me in the course of this week, as I am busy writing out the new copy which is to be sent off without loss of time to its destination. They [sic] two last acts I sent to Mrs D. without having even looked over them after they were written, and Mrs Baillie told me there were many inaccuracies which she had found out and should mark on the Margin before the manuscript was return'd; and I suppose this has been done, as I see a good many pencil marks upon it; but besides Mrs Damer's corrections & hers, I should like to have yours too, if you can find time enough to bestow upon me[.]

Since I saw you, (indeed sunday se'nnight) my Mother had another paralitic attack which alarmed us a good deal; but she has recover'd gradually from it; and I hope that in the course of another week she will be nearly in the same state she was in before; at least it does not appear from the progress she has already made that we shall lose much ground by this last shock. — Let me know how you do yourself, and how your Sister has been since she return'd. Mrs D. says nothing about your health, and I hope it has been tolerable. With all kind wishes, affectionately yours

    J Baillie
Hampstead
Tuesday morning [1806]
PS. Pray when you see Mrs Damer, give her my love & many thanks for her kind note and friendly corrections. I have profited less or more by every one of them in the 3 first acts, and I expect to be equally benefitted in the two last. I should have written to her when I sent her the last acts, but my Mother was so unwell at the time, I could not think of writing about it. ——

WI MS 5616/66 (Address: Miss Berry / North Audley Street / Grosvenor Square / London--postmarked 1806)

Hampstead Wednesday
morning [1806]

    I thank you, my dear Friend, for letting me know how your scene (as you call it) with your Cousin Mr F. ended,[17] and I am very glad it has

---

16. Baillie's *The Family Legend* was published in Edinburgh by Ballantyne in 1810. Though Scott's insistence put Baillie's *The Family Legend* on stage, on 29 January 1810 the curtain rose to a packed house, and the highland play scored a tremendous success for three weeks, followed by a revival of *De Monfort* (Edgar Johnson, *Sir Walter Scott: The Great Unknown*, 2 vols. [New York: Macmillan, 1970], 223-24).

17. WI identifies Mr. F. as Col. Ferguson. Agnes Berry had been engaged to her cousin Colonel Ferguson some time in 1803, but the engagement was broken off.

ended so. I hope indeed you will be better friends for having had this little difference so made up. Nothing draws a person nearer your heart than finding them ready frankly to own & make up for an offence: it has the nature of charity in it, and covers &c. — I will trust to you too, for not giving many occasions after this for similar explanations with him: lovers may quarrel every day, but friends must only quarrel now & then — a few times in the course of their lives. I will do what I can, since you invite me to it, to keep you well behaved; and I hope to see you by & by, mild & meek on all occasions, as gentle dame[s] should be.

On Sunday morning, you spoke to me about Miss Seaton's work that has been put into Mr Longman's hand,[18] and wished if I should meet with Mr L. that I should ask him about it: but Mr Ferguson's coming I believe, prevented me from asking you more decidedly what I should really do in regard to it, for ready & willing I am to do any thing. I never see Mr Longman but when we have some business together, and he is always very ready to call for me when I send for him. If I send for him, however, I must learn from you particularly what I ought to say to him, for I cannot send for him to enquire about it, as it were, by the bye. Think of this, and lay your commands upon me when you please. — Hoping to see you soon, some fine morning to take our walk upon the heath, I remain with kind love to your Sister, affectionately — really & truly <u>affectionately</u> yours

J Baillie

WI MS 5616/67 (Address: Miss Berry / North Audley Street / Grosvenor Square / London--postmarked 1806)

Hampstead May 27th [1806]

My dear Friend,

Have you got a guinea to spare, in the midst of all the various expences which a London life in spring necessarily occasions? If you have, I want mightily to put my had [*sic*] in your pocket and pluck it forth, for a subscription which I think you'll approve of, greatly as people are beset with subscriptions in these days. The person who is about to publish is a

---

18. Thomas Longman III (1771-1842) published such authors as Wordsworth, Coleridge, Scott and Baillie, carrying on in the publishing tradition of Thomas Longman (1699-1755), who founded the publishing firm which still exists today. After the collapse of Archibald Constable in 1826, the firm became the sole proprietors of the *Edinburgh Review*, of which they had previously owned one half; but by this time the firm had become Longman, Hurst, Rees, Orme, Brown, & Green. Thomas Longman died at Hampstead 29 August 1842. The elder Longman had helped publish Johnson's *Dictionary* (*OCEL*, 585). I have not identified Miss Seaton or her work.

Miss Warner of Bath, and her situation is this.[19] She lives with her Mother & a Widow Sister, all three great invalids. Her Mother, now an old Woman, had an annuity depending upon the life of another person who is lately dead, so that now the income is so small that the old woman cannot have the little comforts she was accustomed to, altho' those must have been very moderate, as at least, I believe, they had difficulty enough in making things do. In this distress the Daughter has been advised to publish the work, proposals for which I inclose to you, tho' she is, I understand, of a shy, retired character, which makes such an exertion peculiarly hard upon her. Her own story has some thing in it that particularly claims sympathy. In her youth, for she is not now a young woman, she was engaged to be married to a young man to whom she was attached, when her Father discovered that the Lover had an unlucky propensity to gaming. Upon this he made the Daughter give him up, and write a letter to the young man herself, as if it had been entirely her own act, telling him so. The young man, upon receiving it, went & destroyed himself; and since this sad event Miss W. has led a very retired life, and refused many good offers for settling herself in the world. — She is Sister to a M'r Warner who has publish'd Walks over England & Wales &c. I am told by the Lady who recommended her to me, that she is really a very clever woman, and is even on that score entitled to encouragement.

I saw my friend Mr Longman last . . .[20] week who came upon some other business, and I asked him about Miss Seaton's work. He told me that he very much liked the part of it that had been put into his hands, and had begged to have the remainder that he might judge of the whole. He added it was a work, which if it did take, would, he thought, have a great sale. I found he did not know the name of the Lady, and therefore, tho' he made a kind of fetch to get at it, I would not name her neither. I expect to be in Town this week, but shall be too much hurried to make any attempts to see you. We are all here as usual: how goes it with you? My love to your Sister

affectionately yours

    J Baillie

19. Miss Warner is probably Rebecca Warner, sister of Richard Warner mentioned in this letter. Rebecca published *Original Letters* (1817) and *Epistolary Curiosities* (1818). Richard Warner (1763-1857), a divine and antiquary born in Marylebone, was a prolific writer whose works include *Walk through Wales* (1798), *Second Walk through Wales* (1799), *Walk through some of the Western Countries of England* (1800), *Excursions from Bath* (1801), etc. (*DNB*, XX:856-59). I cannot identify the subscription.

20. There is a hole in the leaf here.

WI MS 5616/72 (Address: Miss Berry--no postmark)

Hampstead August 17th [1806]

How fares it with you now, my dear Friend, after all the sultry weather we have had, and all the thunder storms & dark clouds that have passed over our heads since I heard from you? Your last letter to me was a great exertion of good will, (for which I ought to have thanked you sooner) judging of you by myself; for tho' I dont reckon myself very cowardly in regard to thunder, I could not sit down to write to any body on the approach of a very threatening storm, or if I did, woe be to the poor friend who should have the letter to decipher! for I am sure neither the writing nor the spelling of it would be easily made out. I would fain hope we shall have no more of these grand visitations for this season: the air for two days past feels cool & Autumnal, and I hope we shall now have some pleasant settled weather in which we may enjoy ourselves a little. I do say, altho' I am writing to you, "Enjoy ourselves a little" for tho' I know the many drawbacks you have upon your happiness, and how sensible you are to them all, yet the natural buoyancy & sociableness of your disposition enables you in the midst of great discomfort to pick out hours & minutes of apparently great enjoyment, and I trust they are not altogether false appearances.

This, I suppose will find you at Strawberry hill; and you will let me hear from you again before you take your departure for the sea coast or any other place, if you have such a thing in view. I hope to take a little journey myself this week, if nothing come across to prevent it. My Brother & his Family are going to set out to morrow morning for Gloucester sh: to take possession for some weeks of a place he has purchased there, and I am going along with them just to take a look of it & return again.[21] I think altogether I shall be from home a week. I shall come trundling back by myself in the stage coach from Cirencester, and I trust my kind stars will provide for me some little amusement by the way. At any rate, travelling any where in the world thro' a part of the country I have never seen before, is a great matter to me, tho old Nick himself were seated by the side of me. —— I thank you for the names you have sent me for Miss Warner's book, and I paid in the money for them last week to M[rs] Hoare.[22] You shall

---

21. Dr. Matthew Baillie (1761-1823), the only brother of Joanna and Agnes Baillie, had been trained by and had taken over the medical school of his uncle Dr. William Hunter and was a respected physician to George III. The Baillies purchased Duntisbourne House in 1806 (see Anne Carver, *The Story of Duntisbourne Abbots* [Gloucester: Albert E. Smith, 1966], 27).

22. Mrs. Samuel Hoare (Louisa Gurney) was married to Lady Byron's banker, and Baillie was a close friend of the family. Children Baillie mentions include Jane, Joseph and several others.

pay me again at any time that is convenient after you have collected it. I have only set down your name in my list, for I did not know whether I ought to read in your list, Miss Berry, or Miss Berrys; but if I have done wrong it is easily corrected. You have done very handsomely for us already, but if you can easily get us a name or two more, you may be sure we shall be glad. --- What do you think of your friend Mr Moores intended duel with that tremendous man Mr Jeffrys [sic]?[23] Poor man! it is a terrible attack that is made upon him in the Edin^r Review with what justice I know not, as I have never read any of his works, but I hope with little. Talking of Reviews puts me in mind that I have got some proposals to distribute for a new Monthly Magazine, which is expected to be a very good one, so I will take the liberty of inclosing one for you that it may lie upon your table for the information of any of your friends who may be in want of such a publication. -- Remember me kindly to your Sister & Mrs Damer. I hope Agnes was not the worse of the rain she got that day when she made us the kind but short visit in her open carriage &c, and I hope you did not envy her the p^r of garters she had for her pains. Fare well!

J Baillie

This letter, I see will not fold prettily all that I can do, so I must put a cover over it, but as it goes by the peny [sic] post it will cost you no more, I hope.

RCS HB.ii-70 (No address or postmark)

[ca.1810]

My dear Friend,

Here is the Family Legend for you which is just come to hand. I send, for wise reasons, no copies of it to my friends as I have done of my other works, but seeing how much interest you have taken in it from the beginning, there would have been a real want of grace in not sending one to you. — If I do not interfere with the rights of any Mrs Browns or Thomsons that you may have to visit in this part of the world, may we hope for the pleasure of seeing you here soon? Mrs Damer & you with your Sister, may if you are inclined to be very good to us, arrange it together, and spend a day with us wandering on the Heath as much as you please. I hope also

---

23. Irish poet Thomas Moore (1779-1852) published *Odes and Epistles* in 1806, containing criticism of America. Francis Jeffrey, reportedly making this innocuous book pay for the sins of the late Thomas Little (Moore's pseudonym), indicted a savage attack in *The Edinburgh Review* that the volume was "immoral," which led in July to a hostile meeting between author and critic. A duel almost ensued, but no shots were fired, and the two later became friends. Moore procured a considerable income from his Irish Melodies between 1807 and 1834, set to music by Sir John Stevenson (*DNB*, XIII:828).

Mrs Berry will favour us. After next thursday we shall be free from engagements. —

My Sister joins me in kind wishes,
affectionately yours
J Baillie

Hampstead
thursday May 10th

RCS HB.ii-39 (Address: To Miss Berry / North Audley Street / Grosvenor Square--postmarked 1812)
My dear Friend

Has Mrs Baillie given you any notice that she would be glad to have the music-book she sent to you returned, as it is a borrowed book and she does not like to keep it so long from the owner?? Last time I saw her she mentioned this, and I cant tell whether she meant to write a note to you herself or desired me to mention it: and I can more easily write to you at once than ask her at this distance the question. — I thank you for recommending Child Harold to me.[24] On your recommendation & that of My Friend Walter Scott, from whom I received a letter mentioning it the very day I had your note, I read it as soon as I could get it to read, and I liked it so well that I did what I dont often do, read it twice over attentively with very little interval between. I think it a work of real genious [sic]: there are many striking thoughts in it very happily expressed; sometimes good discription, (tho' he is not always happy in this) with some tenderness: and tho' the sentiments I am sorry to say are too often those of a lost & perverted mind, yet, considering them as such, they are natural and well expressed. The versification too is harmonious & very pleasing, and he has, generally speaking, executed a very difficult measure with great skill. He denies in the preface having any intention of giving his own character under that of Child Harold, and as charity believeth all things, I ought to believe what Ld Byron says; but even taking it as entirely an imagined character, he has shewn very great want of taste (not to say worse of it) in threading his pearls together with such a filthy string. — However, having said all this I cannot by any means agree with you in considering him as the best poet that has appeared for many years. If a lofty & vigorous imagination with strong power of invention are two of the chief characteristicks of genius, Ld B. will have a good deal to do before he can raise himself to the same rank with Southey or Campbell, and you know there is another poet in the world whom I

---

24. Lord Byron's *Childe Harold's Pilgrimage* appeared in March 1812.

prefer to both Southey & Campbell.[25] ––– Farewell! I shall be in Town the beginning of the next week, but I doubt I shant get to see you, I only mention it lest you should think of taking an airing this way and I should miss you. — My love to your Sister

yours affectionately

J Baillie

Hampstead

Wednesday [1812]

PS. I liked Ld B.' smaller pieces, and the second particularly is most beautiful[.]

The following letter to Mary Berry is the property of the Folger Shakespeare Library:

(Address: Miss Berry / Audley Street / Grosvenor Square)[26]

Hampstead Feb 7th 1814

My Dear Friend

A Lady, who is much interested about a near connexion of hers, a Boy of fifteen, whose Father wishes to place him with a Clergyman under whose care both his manners & morals may be improved as well as his learning, enquired at me yesterday for such a situation, and I immediately thought of your friend Mr Bannister. Will you have the goodness to let me know whether there is a place in his house to spare at present for such a pupil & what are his terms & regulations. He is a Boy who will have a good fortune, & I dont suppose terms will be any considerable object, but still I should wish to be able to mention them. His Father is particularly anxious to place his son where the Mistress of the house is a sensible and wellbred woman. ——

---

25. Robert Southey (1774-1843), a college friend of Coleridge and one of the "Lake Poets," was Poet Laureate from 1813-43, having accepted a pension five years earlier; he was married to Edith Fricker, the sister of Coleridge's wife. Given the pronounced Jacobinism of his youth, several of Southey's contemporaries, especially Byron and Hazlitt, felt he had betrayed the principles of his youth in such acceptance (*OCEL*, 923). Thomas Campbell, born in Glasgow in 1777, was a friend of Byron, a poet and editor of the *New Monthly Magazine*. The poet JB "prefers," of course, is Walter Scott.

26. My thanks go to the Folger Shakespeare Library and to Donelle Ruwe, who, while at Notre Dame, transcribed this letter at the Folger and sent it to me. The Folger also owns a badly decayed short note from Baillie to Miss Reid (1826) about returning something borrowed.

When you write tell me how you have been lately & what you have been doing. We have been much confined to the house for a long time, tho' both very well; but now with the return of fine weather we have become more active. I was at the play on Monday night to see Kean in Richard,[27] and as far as I could see his countenance looking now & then thru' a glass, he seems to have great power of expression & promises to be a very valuable actor. Sometimes he seemed to me to act admirably well & sometimes with too much effort & labour. Perhaps the largeness of the house may be partly to blame for this last effect. ——

Can you tell me anything of Mrs Wilmot's play?[28] I heard the other day that it is to be really out soon, and I have written to Mr Sotheby to procure a box for the first night, for certain worthies in this place who wish to see it, myself included.[29] —— Have you seen Mrs Baillie lately? and has she told you of my <u>lately</u> assumed dignity? Namely that I take upon me now the grave title of <u>Mistress</u> as I have long threatened to do. My

---

27. Edmund Kean (1781-1833) was an actor born into the theatre, where as a young child he reportedly represented Cupid in a ballet of Noverre. In 1795 he ran away from home and shipped as a cabin boy to Madeira but soon returned to London, where he received gratuitous lessons in acting, fencing, etc., from an uncle, an actress at Drury Lane (Miss Tidswell) and D'Egvile. At Drury Lane he played Prince Arthur to Kemble's King John, and it was presumably in 1806 that Kean made his first appearance at Haymarket. Mrs. Siddons found him disagreeable; his roving nature made him somewhat irresponsible, and he feuded with the public and the press. In 1814 he appeared in his memorable role as Shylock, followed by Richard III. Philip Kemble's retirement in 1817 left Kean the undisputed master of the stage. He appeared in several more productions at Drury Lane before his departure to America, some of them adaptations of Scott novels, and was in an "altered" production of *De Monfort* on 27 November 1821. He died at Covent Garden playing Othello on 25 March 1833 (*DNB*, X:1146-53).

28. Lady Dacre, Barbarina Brand, (1768-1854) was a poet, dramatist, translator and sculptor. The third daughter of Admiral Sir Chaloner Ogle, Bart., and Hester, she married Valentine Henry Wilmot in 1789, an officer in the Guards. After Wilmot's death Barbarina married Thomas Brand, 21st lord of Dacre, in 1819. Her published works include a tragic drama *Pedarias* (1811), *Ina* (1815), *Translations from the Italian* (1836), etc. (*DNB*, II:1120). Lady Dacre contributed "Stanzas suggested by a Canzone of Petrarch" to Baillie's 1823 *Collection of Poems, Chiefly Manuscript*, etc. Lord Dacre was appointed arbitrator for Lady Byron on the death of her mother in 1822. Mrs. Wilmot's verse drama *Ina*, set in Anglo-Saxon England, was produced unsuccessfully at Drury Lane on 22 April 1815 (see Joanne Shattock, *The Oxford Guide to British Women Writers* [Oxford: Oxford University Press, 1993], 125).

29. William Sotheby (1757-1833) was a prodigious poet, playwright, and translator and the consummate man of letters in the Romantic Era. Though Byron disliked him, satirizing him as Mr. Botherby in *Beppo* (1818), Sotheby provided a societal focal point for many of the brightest literary minds of his time. Scott, Wordsworth, Coleridge, Southey were his friends (*DLB*, XCIII:160-70). See introduction and letters to Sotheby herein.

name of ceremony now is <u>Mrs. Joanna Baillie</u> I have always thought that when single women are advanced in years and Mistress of a house with neither Father nor Mother over their heads, they might assume this with propriety. Some of my friends did not much like it at first, but they are beginning to be reconciled to it. My sister, who as Mistress of the house is (in Hampstead at least) <u>Mrs. Baillie,</u> has gone into the change very handsomely tho' it was my idea not hers. — Give my love to your sister & to M<u>rs</u> Damer. I hope to see you before long.

    Sincerely & affectionately yours,

      J Baillie

RCS HB.ix-34 (Address: Mad^{lle} Berry / Dame Anglios / Post Restante / Genes--postmarked 1817)

Hampstead August 9<u>th</u> 1817

I thank you, my dear Friend for your kind letter and I hope this will reach you before you leave your present habitation. Had I known that you wished to hear from me, I should have written to you long ago and M<u>rs</u> Damer would have sent it to you properly directed. But as you altered your plans and were moving about, I expected to hear from you, and was, if not <u>sore</u>, rather discontented that I did not. If you had few Friends here & few Correspondents, I should not have minded this, but you are so rich in both that I feared to add to your burden rather than your pleasure. —

I hope you will have no return of inflammation on your lungs and am very sorry to think you have had this new enemy to contend with. Whether you pass next winter in Rome or Paris, may you & your good affectionate Sister (whose distress & exertions I think of [with] sympathy & interest) return to us again in good condition both of body & mind to find comfort with those who love you in your own country! —

You kindly enquire what I am about, and I will tell you the little that there is to tell. I am (am) just beginning the concluding Drama of the Series, a Musical piece like the Beacon in 3 acts, the subject Religious devotion, the most noble & elevating of all our passions.[30] It is an attempt I have often thought of and always feared to begin; and I should still have delayed it; but my time of life will not now admit of delay; what is to be done must be done; I cannot expect my faculties to improve, and how long God will be pleased to lend me the use of them or life itself I know not. I am endeavouring to put it into a form that may be popular yet as little unworthy of itself as I can make it. I shall write with humble boldness, regarding God & not man, and I hope I shall say nothing that can give just

---

30. Baillie must refer to *The Martyr.*

offence to any sincere Christian. An ancient Christian Martyr is my Hero.

I spent a few weeks last winter in writing what I call a metrical Legend of the Lady Grizald [*sic*] Baillie: a character as given in the notes to Mr Rose['s] answer to Fox['s] history of James 2^d which I admire beyond any Female Character I ever knew or read of.[31] But it will require to be written over again & much improved before it is good for any thing. A few songs excepted, I have written nothing else since I saw you. To speak still of my own things I do not disdain to inform you that my Constantine, was produced as a Melo Drama at the Surry Theatre this summer, and had a run to good houses of 34 nights.[32] I went to see it the last night but one. The Manager had presented the greater part of the dialogue unaltered and tho' it was viley [*sic*] recited and badly acted, yet by dint of shew & magnificence and the story being clearly made out, it had a very good effect. Perhaps Mrs Damer has told you that Mr Arnold at the Lyceum Theatre brought out a good while ago my comedy of the Election changed into an Opera.[33] He altered it, I think, with considerable skill, and it was admirably acted and very well received, yet it did not bring good houses. The Winter Theatres were open at the time; Kemble was acting all his characters over for the last time; Miss O'Neal was acting under an impression that she might not be spared another year; and Talma, during

---

31. Lady Grisell Baillie (1665-1746) was the daughter of Sir Patrick Hume of Polworth and Grisell Kerr. She reportedly saved her father's life (under suspicion for participating in the Rye House Plot) by hiding him in the family vault near Redbraes Castle; her father's friend Robert Baillie was hanged, drawn and quartered on the same charge in 1685. The family fled to Utrecht, exiled with other Scottish Presbyterians, and Grisell made a secret voyage back to Scotland to rescue her sister and the family's fortune. At the 1688 revolution she and her mother returned to Britain in the company of the Princess of Orange. She married George Baillie, son of the executed Robert, in 1692 and helped manage his and her father's estates. Her works include *Orpheus Caledonius or a Collection of the Best Scotch Songs set to Music by W. Thomson* (1726) and *The Household Book of Lady Griselle Baillie* (1692-1733) (Janet Todd, ed., *British Women Writers* [New York: Continuum, 1989], 28-9). Statesman Charles James Fox's (1749-1806) *History of the Early Part of the Reign of James II* was published by Lord Holland in 1808, to which statesman George Rose (1744-1818) responded with *Observations on the Historical Work of the late C. J. Fox* in 1809.

32. Baillie's tragedy *Constantine Paleologus; or the Last of the Caesars* was published as part of *Miscellaneous Plays* by Longman in 1804.

33. Dramatist and theatre manager Samuel James Arnold (1774-1852) had several plays represented at Drury Lane and in 1809 obtained a license to open the Lyceum in the Strand as an English opera house, remodeled and enlarged by architect Samuel Beazley in 1816 (*DNB*, I:584-85). *The Election* had appeared in Volume 2 of *A Series of Plays: in which it is attempted to delineate the stronger passions*, etc.

part of the time, was reciting in the Opera house.[34] I believe it has been acted about 12 times and I dont know whether they have done with it yet or not. M͟r͟s͟ Damer was kind enough at my desire to patronize it one night by her presence. — Along with these high honours I have become, since I wrote you last, a Great Aunt. My Niece brought a little Girl into the land of the living better than a month ago.[35] She has recovered well, and the child tho' small is thriving. She & it are gone for a few weeks to her Father's near Windsor, for the benefit to themselves of the country air & for the pleasure & amusement of the new-made Grand Father & Mother. M͟r͟s͟ Baillie is pretty well and has recovered her spirits considerably. This event I hope will reconcile her more than ever to her own loss. Your old Tenant M͟r͟ Henry Milligan, after spending the summer in Cornwall is about to prepare for wintering in the West Indeas, tho' he is much better than he was. He prefers this to living in London confined to the house. — Give my kind love to your Sister. My Sister joins me in all good wishes to both you & her, so would our Friends in Grosvenor St: were they present. — Yours affectionately

J Baillie

---

34. John Philip Kemble (1757-1823), one of England's most famous actors, began playing parts in his father's company in early childhood. His sister, Sarah Kemble Siddons, first recommended him to the Chamberlain's company as Theodosius in Lee's tragedy in 1776; dozens of parts followed. Kemble was a scholar, a man of breeding and a fine actor with a larger range of characters in which he excelled than any English tragedian. He wrote prologues for charitable institutions in York and Leeds, where he appeared for the first time in *Hamlet*--he is said to have written out the part over 40 times. He managed the Edinburgh Theatre for a while in 1781, and his first appearance in London was at Drury Lane as Hamlet in 1783. He remained at Drury Lane for 19 years, representing over 120 characters himself; on 25 January 1800 Kemble played De Monfort in Baillie's play (*DNB*, X:1260-66).

Baillie's reference is probably to actress Elizabeth O'Neill (1791-1872), later Lady Elizabeth Becher, who played Ellen in a Dublin version of *Lady of the Lake* and debuted as Shakespeare's Juliet in Covent Garden in 1814; though she took some comic roles, she excelled at tragedy but left the stage in 1819 when she married an Irish MP (*DNB*, II:74-5).

Francois Joseph Talma (1763-1826) was a French tragic actor educated in England. A friend of Napoleon, he made his debut in Paris in 1787 in Voltaire's *Brutus* and first introduced on the French stage the custom of wearing costumes of the period represented in the play. His dramatic roles were numerous (*The New Century Cyclopedia of Names*, ed. Clarence L. Barnhart, 3 vols. [New York: Appleton-Century-Crofts, 1954], 3:3788).

35. Elizabeth Margaret, the only daughter of Matthew and Sophia Denman Baillie, married Capt. Robert Milligan on 11 July 1816, and the couple, with only daughter Sophia, lived at Ryde for most of Joanna's life. The Baillie family had not been particularly happy about Elizabeth marrying a soldier (see letters to Scott dated 1817).

RCS HB.ix-17 (Address: Miss Berry--no postmark)

Hampstead Octr 7$^{\underline{th}}$ 1821

So you have been in your own country, my dear friend, these two months, and were for a fortnight in London some time ago, and I, living all the while at Hampstead, new [sic] nothing of the matter. I wish you had written me a line by the 3^d post that I might have run down to North Audley St: and seen you & your Sister, had it only been for an hour. --- I received your letter from almost a year since. It was put into my hands at Abbotsford, just before our return from Scotland, (where my Sister & I spent the summer right pleasantly with several kind friends) and I was very glad to receive it, for I was longing to hear from you and beginning to think you had forgot me all together.[36] Mrs Damer would tell you (at least I hope she did) that I did not care to send a letter to you to Italy, but waited till I should hear of your return to Paris, when I proposed writing to you, and if I could find an opportunity, sending you my last publication. I wrote about a fortnight ago to Twickenham to enquire whether you were yet come to Paris, and wondered that Mrs Damer sent me no answer; but my wonder took another direction when I learnt the other day from your friend Miss Doyle,[37] that she is in Paris & you in Scotland. I hope both your Sister & yourself are well and that I shall have the pleasure of seeing you so in spring when I understand from Miss D. you intend passing some time before you go abroad again. But oh this going abroad! is there to be no end to it? has it sent away your vile headachs [sic] or done any good to you which your own country might not have done? The only thing that could put me in tolerable humour with it is, that you may write your intended work on female manners better there than in London.[38] If this be the case I shall say nothing, but encourage you to go on with your undertaking as fast as you can. I suppose you have seen my Metrical Legends, tho' you have not yet got a copy from the Author, and I shall be glad if they have pleased you in any degree.[39] I am told they are pretty well received in Scotland, but I dont think they are much liked in this southern part of the kingdom. I kept a copy for you a great while, but <u>some how or other</u> it was sent out of

36. Baillie was in Scotland, spending considerable time at Abbotsford, during late summer and fall 1820 (see NLS letters 3891 ff.136-137 and 867 ff.80-82 to Scott); but the time to which she refers here does not seem to confirm those dates.

37. Selina Doyle was a friend of both Judith and Annabella Milbanke; she consulted with Annabella on and strongly supported her separation from Byron.

38. Berry was probably working on *A Comparative View of Social Life in England and France* (2 parts, 1828 & 1831).

39. *Metrical Legends of Exalted Characters* was first published by Longman, Rees, Orme, and Brown in 1821.

the house to <u>some body or other</u>, and now I'm keeping one for you of the 2^d edition (which is better than the first by one or two little corrections) and no body shall take it out of my hands till I put it into your[s]. —

My Sister & I have passed a summer of some enjoyment in our New house which is much more pleasantly situated than our old, but with many drawbacks on our pleasure from the confusion & inconvenience occasioned by <u>dry rot</u>, an evil which we discovered soon after we took possession of it.[40] After having laid the walls bare & renewing beams & wainscotting in various parts of the house, and flattering ourselves that we had got rid of the enemy entirely, we discovered a new inroad two days ago and now we have Brick layers & carpenters knocking & hammering about us again, and dont know when we shall be in any comfortable order. However, if we can keep our heads above water as to expence, we are so pleased with our situation, very near the heath where we can wander at will thro' all its wild paths at any time in perfect security, that we shall not repent having taken the lease of this house. As people grow old it becomes of more importance to have a home pleasantly situated. —— Will you let me hear from you when you have time & are in the mood for it? I put in no claim of desert, but that you owe me something, for not having let me see you when you were in London. ——— Give my love to your Sister. Fare ye well! and much good may the pure air of Scotland do you both! Affectionately yours
    J Baillie

RCS HB.ix-59 (Address: Miss Berry / Tunbridge Wells--unclearly postmarked 1833)

Hampstead July 8th 1833

My dear Friend,

    I would have called upon you again before you left Town if I could have done so without great inconvenience, but I could not, and I gave up my wish to do so the more readily because I thought a long visit would not at that time suit you, and a very short one would not, perhaps, have been satisfactory to either party. I was very sorry to miss seeing you & your Sister when you were so kind as to call in Cavendish Sq^r and was glad to receive your friendly message which, as you see, I am not long of obeying. This indeed is the very first day in which I have had any leisure since we returned home, last thursday —— "Desire her to write to me and tell me

---

40. In a note to JB dated 22 November 1819, Matthew Baillie writes, "I cannot be satisfied without bearing a share at least in the expence of your new Lease – Agnes and you must allow me to pay one Hundred Pounds towards it, and I can not take a refusal without being hurt" (RCS HB.ii-35c).

what she thinks of Dr Channing's last volume of Discourses"[41] —— this I think is your message or the main purport of, and I could not well write to you about any thing that has taken more possession of my own mind. He sent me the book which I received with a letter from himself better than two months ago, and I have read it again & again with great interest & admiration, though there are peculiar ideas of his own upon one point in i t which I wish had not been in it, because I think they may with a great proportion of Readers prevent the work from being so useful as it would otherwise have been. — Of that by & by. — His views of our Saviour's character as the strongest proof of the faithfulness of his revelation and the History of him contained in the Gospels, is beautiful, noble, and powerful in moving the heart and convincing the understanding; and few unprejudiced minds, I should think could withstand it. His discourses too on self-denyal, so powerfully supporting the rights of natural reason as that thing belonging to us, God's best gift, which is <u>not</u> to be denied; and the excellent purposes stated by him, for which those that ought to be denied are brought into the world, evil passions, bodily pain &c; are most ably & eloquently shewn. And can there be any thing more persuasive & powerfully applied to our feelings & conduct than the two last discourses on that verse from St: Paul. "Grace be with all them that love our Lord Jesus Christ in Sincerity."?[42] The 8th discourse on "Fools make a mock a t sin,"[43] makes one tremble like Felix before the Apostle. In short I have found it to be a book that deals more powerfully with head & heart than any book I ever read. – Nothing elaborate, perplexing, or weak is to be found any where; and those whose poor heads would have a world of trouble in following the arguments of some – many of our best divines,

---

41. William Ellery Channing (1780-1842) was ordained to the ministry in 1803, pastored the Federal Street Church in Boston from 1805-42, and became a leader in the Unitarian movement by his argument against Calvinism. He organized the Berry Street conference of liberal ministers in 1820 and the American Unitarian association in 1825. Interested in Jeffersonian politics and in literature, he influenced Emerson and Thoreau, supported abolition, temperance and peace. He authored such works as *Remarks on the Character and Writings of John Milton* (1826), *Analysis of the Life and Character of Napoleon Bonaparte* (1828), *The Importance and Means of a National Literature*, and his *Works* went through 20 editions in England and America. Channing was an intimate friend of Baillie, who kept him up with literary happenings in Britain and reported on the success of his work there (see Arthur R. Brown, *A Biography of William Ellery Channing: Always Young for Liberty* [Syracuse, N. Y.: Syracuse University Press, 1956], 161-62). Baillie was particularly impressed with Channing's Dudleian lecture of 1821 on "The Evidences of Christianity (see David P. Edgell, *William Ellery Channing, An Intellectual Portrait* [Boston: Beacon Press, 1955], 202).

42. See Eph. 6.24.

43. See Prov. 14.9.

would have no difficulty with Dr Channing. ––– I do not like, – his notions concerning the unlimited improvement of mankind hereafter, both as to faculties & knowledge. "I am persuaded" he says "that there is not a glory, a virtue, a power, a joy possed [sic] by Jesus Christ to which his disciples will not successively rise" –– and elsewhere he says that a repented Sinner may Equal the highest order of Angels and be improving through all eternity. –– He builds those hopes upon this argument, that all intelligent minds are of one family. We indeed, from what we feel within ourselves, climb in our thoughts to the attributes of God; but this will not warrant such lofty hopes. Indeed they do not appear to me to be warranted either by analogy or Scripture; and his arguments regarding Newton &c do not possess his usual acuteness. We see the faculties of a man improving from Infancy till five & twenty or thirty, but beyond that, tho' his knowledge may increase every day, his faculties do not grow. Tho' we may improve for ever in knowledge, it does not follow that we shall improve also in faculties. We are told also that the righteous shall shine in the Kingdom of their Father, not all alike, but as one star differeth from another star in Glory, and that "In my Father's house are many Mansions."[44] There is indeed a grandeur in the idea which has, I imagine, captivated Channing's very ardent imagination, but it will make him be regarded by many as extravagant & enthusiastic, therefore I regret very much that it is to be found in a work so calculated otherwise to be very eminently useful: — I have occasionally received letters from him for two or three years past and I heard from him with an old date, however, last saturday. His letter was conveyed to me by a D^r & Mrs Bidgelow [sic],[45] an American Traveller lately returned from Italy & bright intelligent people. They have heard that Dr Channing is coming to England by the end of summer, to pass the next winter in Devonshire; I may hope then to see him before I die. I naturally take more interest in all who come from America, because I think they take interest in me. As a proof of this I received not long since a present from Dr Andrews Norton of Boston of all my works printed in one thick volume like a dictionary with the pages

---

44. See John 14.2.

45. This is probably Dr. Jacob Bigelow (1787-1879), an eminent Boston physician and medical writer, and his wife. He was president of the Massachusetts Medical Society and the American Academy of Arts and Sciences and a member of the Royal Society. Among other medical works, he published *American Medical Botany* (1820), *Nature in Desease* (1854) and a volume of humorous poems entitled *Eolopoesis, American Rejected Addresses* (1855) (*Appleton's Cyclopaedia of American Biography*, ed. Grant Wilson and John Fiske [New York: Appleton, 1902], 1:260). See Rogers letter 14/53, Volume 2.

divided into columns.[46] This surely looks as if I were popular in that country, and I am right proud of my book, tho' it is as ugly a thing to look at on the outside as ever lay upon a table.

I hope you & your Sister are enjoying yourselves at Tunbridge and that your health will profit by it, tho' I am told by those who have seen you lately, that you are both looking remarkably well and seem to want no improvement. My good Agnes here is not so well as I could wish her. She has suffered a great deal from bile & acidity of stomach, and is at present under Dᴿ Maton's directions, living by rule.[47] I hope she will by & by be much better; there is not yet time for any considerable change. ––– We are both deeply engaged with Miss Aikin's new work, the Court of Charles the 1ˢᵗ which is very entertaining & interesting.[48] I suppose you have seen it. — With kindest regards to your Sister & self, I remain your faithful & attached friend

J Baillie

WI MS 5616/69 (Address: Miss Berry North Audley Street / Grosvenor Square / London--no postmark)

Hampstead March 22ᵈ

My dear Friend,

I have been truly affected with your letter. It grieves me to think that with such moderate & rational desires, you are so beset on every side you are not permitted to enjoy the quiet possession of your own mind; an enjoyment at all times; but more particularly at what you call your sober time of life, so favourable for that improvement of character which it is my firm belief we were all sent into this world to make. But I will dwell no more upon this: tho' I look round on every side to find out some path for

---

46. See Baillie letters to Dr. Andrews Norton (Volume 2). The American edition of *The Complete Poetical Works of Joanna Baillie* appeared in Philadelphia from Carey & Lea in 1832.

47. William George Maton, MD (1774-1835), fellow at the Royal College of Physicians, took over much of Dr. Matthew Baillie's practice after Baillie's death in 1823 (see William Munk, MD, FSA, *The Roll of the Royal College of Physicians of London*).

48. Lucy Aikin (1781-1864), daughter of Martha and John Aikin, MD, and niece of Mrs. Barbauld, was a translator and a writer, an early fictional work being *Lorimer; a Tale* (1814). Her first historical work, *Memoirs of the Court of Queen Elizabeth* (1819), was followed, among other works, by *The Life of Joseph Addison* (1843), written during her residence in Hampstead. She and Joanna became close friends, and her "Recollections of Joanna Baillie" provides an enticing look both at Baillie and at their circle of friends. Lucy Aikin published *Memoirs of the Court of Charles I* in 1833. See *Memoirs, Miscellanies and Letters of the late Lucy Aikin*, ed. Philip Hemery Le Breton (London: Longman, 1864).

your enlargement, and still to no purpose, yet I will rest in hope that it will at last be found, and I am sure my heart prays that it may be speedily. —— You will see by what I send you inclosed, that I am willing to lose no time in setting you to some employment, tho' it may not perhaps be an employment so favourable for the peace of mind you pine after as could be wish'd. Still however it is occupation which you certainly have talents for, and if you can set about it <u>reasonably</u> without letting yourself be too anxious for the result, it will do you good, and do good, or at least give pleasure to others also. —— You will look over the story I have given you, which I think might be turn'd into both an amusing & interesting piece, for I mean both Mrs B. — & the Baron to be characters, tho' in some degree perverted by bad example & unlucky circumstances in their youth, and therefore still returning when necessity calls for it the artifice & readiness in resource of people train'd in the adventurous world, still natively good and at the time of the play opens heartily greaved [*sic*] for the errors of their early life.[49] If you think it can be made such a thing as you would like to write upon let me know what alterations you would wish to have made upon it, for I dont flatter my self that it will just at first be all that you could wish, and I shall alter it & <u>re-alter</u> it twenty times over till I get it to suit you. But if you should not fancy it at all, tell me so frankly and then I will try to rake something else out of my noddle that will do better; only in this case you will be so good as to give me an idea of what kind of a story you would like. As to devisions [*sic*] of scenes and sketching of character, we shall say nothing of that at present: it will be time enough to talk of it when the story or outline of the plot is fix'd upon. You will be a day or two of receiving this, as I shall send it to Town by my Sister in-law in preference to the penny post – or rather – alac a day! that it should be so, the <u>three</u> penny post. ——

Remember me kindly to your Sister. All goes on here as usual.

Very affectionately yours   J Baillie

(turn over)

My Sister liked little Roscius in Hamlet very much, at least many parts of his acting she admired, tho' she saw him from a high box to great disadvantage.[50] ———

---

49. The untitled manuscript Baillie mentions is not with her letters in the WI, but there is one included in the Berry letters in the RCS Library: HB.ix-69a-c, a story of M^{rs} B, catalogued as part of the ms. of Baillie's *Ethwald*.

50. Roscius, the name of Quintus Roscius Gallus, designated an actor of outstanding ability or fame, often referring to David Garrick (*OED*). Baillie could refer to Edmund Kean or John Philip Kemble here, but this seems to be a young contemporary actor instead. A Master Betty was also known by the name of Young Roscius (see Montgomery letter 93, ff.217-218, Volume 2).

4

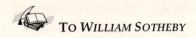 To *William Sotheby*

(1804-1831)

William Sotheby, author and translator, was born in London on 9 November 1757 to Elizabeth Sloan, daughter of William Sloan, esq., and William Sotheby, colonel in the Coldstream guards. When William's father died in 1766, his guardians were Charles Philip Yorke, fourth earl of Hardwicke, and his maternal uncle Hans Sloane; William later succeeded to the estate of Sewardstone, Epping Forest. Sotheby was educated at Harrow but at 17 purchased a commission as ensign in the dragoons and proceeded to study at the military academy of Angers. He was then stationed in Edinburgh, meeting Walter Scott for the first time. In July 1780 he married Mary, youngest daughter of Ambrose Isted of Ecton and Anne, heiress to the fortune of Sir Charles Buck, which enabled him to retire from the army and settle at his residence of Bevis Mount to take up a literary life. The Sothebys had five sons and two daughters, three of whom it was their misfortune to lose; William was killed in the foot-guards in 1815, Hans died in 1827 and George was killed defending the residency of the East India Company at Nagpoore during the Mahratta war in 1817.[1]

William Sotheby devoted himself to studying the classics, and his own first publication was a volume in the Romantic tradition entitled *Poems* (1790; reissued in 1794), derived primarily from a walking tour he and his brother Thomas had made through Wales. In 1791 Sotheby moved to London where he occupied Fair Mead Lodge and acted as a master-keeper of the adjoining Epping Forest. He soon became a prominent figure in London literary society, joining the Dilettante Society in 1792 and the Society of Antiquaries and the Royal Society in 1794. He entertained literary figures regularly, including Scott, Wordsworth, Coleridge, Rogers, Beaumont, Edgeworth, Byron, Southey and Joanna Baillie. It was Sotheby who took Walter Scott to Hampstead to meet Baillie in 1806, and in 1807 it was Sotheby and Sir George Beaumont who encouraged Coleridge to publish *The Friend*.[2]

---

1. This general information comes from the *DNB*, XVIII:673-76, and from Donald Reiman's introduction to Sotheby's *Saul and Constance de Castille*.

2. See Donald H. Reiman's introduction to William Sotheby's *Saul and Constance de Castille. Romantic Context: Poetry* (New York and London: Garland, 1978), vi.

Sotheby gained a sound reputation as a translator by publishing Wieland's German poem *Oberon* (a second edition illustrated by Fuseli in 1805), later basing on it a masque in five acts; and his verse translation of Virgil's *Georgics* (1800) was applauded even by the severe Edinburgh critic Francis Jeffrey.[3] In 1799 Sotheby published an ode entitled *The Battle of the Nile*, dedicated to Lord Spencer, and followed it with *A Poetical Epistle to Sir George Beaumont, Bart., on the Encouragement of the British School of Painting* (1801). An epic called *Saul* appeared in 1807 and *Constance de Castille* in 1810. In 1823 he contributed "Fair Mead Lodge" and "The Lay of the Bell" to Baillie's *A Collection of Poems, Chiefly Manuscript, and from Living Authors*.

Though Sotheby began as a poet, he had a strong affinity for drama, his tragedy *Bertram and Matilda* being acted privately by himself and his friends in 1790. He published several other five-act historical tragedies in blank verse, including *The Cambrian Hero, or Llewelyn the Great* (no date), *The Siege of Cuzco* (1800), *Julian and Agnes, or the Monks of the Great St. Bernard* (1801), *Orestes* (1802) and *Ellen, or the Confession* (1816). Three previously unpublished tragedies, *Ivan*, *The Death of Darnley* and *Zamorin and Zama*, appeared as part of his 1814 collection entitled *Five Tragedies*. There is convincing evidence in some of the following letters, however, that Baillie supplied Sotheby with the plots for some of his plays.

Apparently, only one of Sotheby's tragedies was ever staged professionally, *Julian and Agnes* being acted at Drury Lane in April 1800 by Mrs. Siddons and Kemble. In many letters Baillie discusses Sotheby's difficulties in getting his plays represented, often in the context of her own disappointments with the London theaters; and while Lord Byron, a member of the Drury Lane management committee, was actively supporting Baillie's plays, he may have been obstructing Sotheby's. Byron wrote Hobhouse in 1811 that "Sotheby, whom I abused in my last [letter], improves, his face is rather against him, & his manner abrupt & dogmatic, but I believe him to be much more amiable than I thought"; and even though he praised Sotheby in *English Bards and Scotch Reviewers* and

---

Reiman states that Sotheby often lent books to Coleridge and in 1804 gave him £100 against Wordsworth's promissory note. In 1803, while on their way to France to meet Annette Vallon and Caroline, William and Dorothy Wordsworth were guests at Sotheby's London home (Reiman, vi).

3. Reiman writes that because there were so many translations of Virgil and so many literary figures who read the original in Latin, Sotheby's greatest effort had little impact; however, his translation of Wieland's German, claims Professor Werner William Beyer, had a strong influence on Keats, Coleridge, Wordsworth, Southey and others (Reiman, x).

generally kept on friendly terms with him, Byron, after his exile, attacked the writer in *Beppo*, the first canto of *Don Juan*, and *The Blues: A Literary Eclogue*.[4] In a later letter to John Murray, Byron claimed that he "endeavoured to advance his [Sotheby's] petty attempts at Celibrity; —— I moved the Sub Committee & Kinnaird — & Kean & all the Aristocracy of Drury Lane — to bring out his play — whose insufferable Mediocrity gave it a great chance of success – I bore with him – the Bore — . . . ."[5] Byron justified his attacks on Sotheby by the incident of an anonymous critical letter, but the more likely reason surfaces in a comment to Samuel Rogers about Sotheby's "airs of patronage — which he affects with young writers — & affected both to me and *of* me — many a good year."[6] After his exile, Byron simply had no use for the English aristocracy.

Disappointed at his lack of success in having his drama *Ivan* represented at Drury Lane and distressed by the death of his son William, Sotheby left England in May 1816 to spend a year on the continent; when he returned, he published his impressions in *Farewell to Italy and occasional Poems* (1818; reissued as *Poems* in 1825) and began a verse translation of Homer. The result was the whole of the *Iliad* (in heroics) in 1831 and the *Odyssey* in 1834.

Sotheby was painted by Sir Thomas Lawrence and was both revered and criticized as a writer. On 30 December 1833 Wordsworth wrote to Samuel Rogers about his true grief at the death of Sotheby, Coleridge referred to him always as a "Brother Poet," and Byron declared that Sotheby had only "imitated everybody, and occasionally surpassed his models."[7] Sotheby's wife Mary died shortly after him on 14 October 1834.

---

4. Reiman, vii.

5. Qtd. in Reiman, viii. Byron refers to his attempt to convince the management to produce Sotheby's *Ivan* in 1816, which was withdrawn after only a few rehearsals.

6. Qtd. in Reiman, ix.

7. *DNB*, XVIII:676.

Except for a single letter from the Huntington Library, the following letters to William Sotheby and members of his family are transcribed by permission of The Royal College of Surgeons of England. Because these letters have been renumbered in the library's restored bound version, the numbers do not correspond with those in the old card catalogue; the new numbers are not, however, according to chronological order and have been reorganized here. Undatable letters appear at the end.

There is a wealth of information in this pleasant library about Drs. William and John Hunter and Dr. Matthew Baillie, and the Hunterian museum there provides an incredible study of the English medical profession of the late eighteenth and early nineteenth centuries. The Royal College of Surgeons of England also own the following manuscripts:

HB.ix-63: Baillie's last contract with Longman, Brown, Green, and Longmans, for *The Works of Joanna Baillie in One Volume*, dated 13 April 1850 and signed by Joanna Baillie.

HB.ix-69a-c: This story of a M^{rs} B is card catalogued as part of the ms. of her tragedy *Ethwald*. Also included are several Ms. "Songs for Mr Thomson's Irish Airs."

HB.ii-75: Ms. verses, untitled, beginning "Sweet bud of promise, fresh & fair/ Just moving in the morning air/ The morn of life but just begun/ The sands of time just set to run!"

HB.ix-20 (Address: William Sotheby Esqr / Lodge Loughton / Essex-- postmarked 1804)

Hampstead Decr 12th [1804]

My dear Sir,

Thanks to you for your encouraging praise which, whether I deserve it or not, it is always pleasant to receive. And indeed it is well that I have something of the kind from you, that I may treasure it up and strengthen myself with it when I shall be call[ed] upon, by & by, to abide the rubs – I ought rather to say clapper-clawing of pens which will convey to me a very different kind of greeting.[8] — But why do you say, out upon me for my inflexibility in persevering to attempt acting Plays? A play certainly is more perfect for being fitted for the stage as well as the closet, and why should not I aim with all my strength to make my things as perfect as possible, however short I may fall of the mark? Dont be afraid that I shall injure them as reading plays on this account. It is endeavouring to

---

8. Baillie probably refers either to her 1804 edition of *Miscellaneous Plays* (Longman) or to the upcoming 1805 edition which would add *The Family Legend* to its previous contents.

suit pieces to the temporary circumstances of particular theatres, and not to the stage in general that injure them in this way. One who never expects as long as she lives to see a play of her own acted, and who never intends to offer a play to any of our Theatres under their present management, is not very likely to do her works much harm by keeping the stage in her eye. Dont you therefore find fault with me, or encrease the number of those who are for quietly setting me aside as a closet writer. I will still go on, having my drums & my trumpets, & my striking situations, & my side scenes & my back scenes, & all the rest of it in my mind, whilst I write, notwithstanding all that you can say to the contrary.[9]

I hope you are employing your time well in your leafless groves, and with all the four elements – all the materials of creation under your control, are putting together a fabric that will stand the shock of time. If you go on with the vigour you have begun as I hope you do, it is a task that will keep your mind to its bent, and that, I believe, is a state which you like to be in.

You are very kind in wishing to see me in Town, but my Mother's state of health confines me at present entirely at home, and is likely so to do for many months to come.[10] Mahomet must then come to the Mountain; and tho' we do not at present encourage many visitors, you shall be made an exception and received most cordially whenever you are kind enough to take the trouble of coming to us here. It is better than two months ago that my Mother was sieged with a second paralitic attack which has confined her entirely to her bed ever since, and from which we do not flatter ourselves that she will ever recover but in a very imperfect degree. She is perfectly unruffled & gentle, & free from all pain, and this is a very great comfort to us, and makes the task of nursing comparatively a light one. —— I am happy to hear M[rs] & Miss Sotheby are well, and beg to send by [my?] best remembrances to them in which my Sister[11] begs leave to join me. Believe me always,

    my dear Sir
        Sincerely yours
          J Baillie

---

9. See letter HB.ix-23 following.

10. Baillie's mother, Dorothea Hunter Baillie, was an invalid the last few years of her life, finally losing her sight as well; she died in 1806.

11. Agnes Baillie (1760-1861) was Joanna Baillie's only sister and constant companion. Dr. Matthew Baillie writes that Agnes Baillie, born in the Manse of Shotts on 24 September 1760, had "a quick ready Understanding, with a good deal of various knowle[d]ge, so as to be much beyond the common level of Women in these respects" (qtd. in Franco Crainz, *The Life and Works of Matthew Baillie* [Santa Polomba: PelitiAssociati, 1995], 10).

HB.ix-8 (Address: For William Sotheby Esqr / Upper Seymour Street / Portman Square / London--postmarked 1804)

Hampstead Decr 26th 1804

My dear Sir,

 I have got a favour to ask of you; and tho' you have given me some hopes of seeing you soon, in this bad weather (when indeed I should almost be sorry to see you), I will not trust to that, but prefer my request in this way which is not so good as face to face yet I trust will do. I have a friend in Scotland who is studying German with great eagerness, and wishes much to translate some light amusing german novel, which she (for it is a Lady) might afterwards if she has a mind dispose of to a Bookseller. I have already spoken to my Bookseller about it: what I want you to do for us is to take in to consideration all the german novels of this discription that have not yet been translated into English, particularly those that are lately publish'd and chuse out one for us that you think will not greatly fatigue the Translator and at the same time be likely to have some little success with the public. About two volumes is as long, I think, as it ought to be. Pray have the goodness to give this a thought! I depend entirely upon your taste & judgment, and shall send down to my friend with confidence whatever you shall recommend; and I hope it will not be as irksome [a] task to you to turn over this matter in your noddle by the fireside at night or in the morning while your tea is smoking, and the weather not tempting enough to make you hasten your breakfast. When you have fix'd upon a book, I must also beg of you to have the goodness to inform me where I am most likely to meet with it, for I suppose german books are not to be met with in every bookseller's shop. ––– I beg to offer my best compliments to M^{rs} & Miss Sotheby if they are with you, and to your self & all your family the kind wishes that we send at this season to all those we regard. I cannot say merry Christmas, for there seems to me now no such thing as merry Christmas, at least it is a long time since I have had any thing to do with it. –– My Mother has had another alarming attack since I wrote to you, and is now so far recover'd as to be nearly in the same state that she was in then. Believe me my dear Sir, whether I am in the sunshine or the shade, always sincerely yours

 J Baillie

PS. I find in looking over this letter that I have not once had the grace to make any apology to you for all the trouble I am giving. Will you forgive this omission? I believe you will.

HB.ix-54 (No address or postmark)

Hampstead April 1ˢᵗ 1807

My dear Sir,

After having read your very interesting poem of Saul,[12] I hasten to thank you for the pleasure I have had in reading it, and for the great satisfaction I have felt in receiving from you a gift upon which I set a great value, enriched too with a token of your regard so very flattering & gratifying for me. I should have done this sooner, had I followed my own inclination; but being from home when I received the work, I could only read it in a broken interrupted way – a very unfair way of reading such a work; and this I would not do, doing by you as I should wish myself to be done by. Your sonnet or dedication to Mʳˢ Sotheby & that to your sons, not to mention the one written in the first leaf of the book, more precious in my eyes than a dozen of printed ones, I read in the first place to myself & the Family at my Brother's where I was, and had the pleasure to find them very much admired by Mʳˢ Baillie, who has really a true taste for poetry, and all the other sitters by his fireside.[13] The lines to Mʳˢ Sotheby are particularly tender & touching, and had of course the greater share of praise given to them; as for those in manuscript, so generously & handsomely bestowed upon an unworthy friend of yours, they filled my eyes with tears and put me out of condition to say what merit they profess, but I am told they are very beautiful, and I am very willing – more than <u>willing</u> to believe it. Indeed, indeed! you have made me very proud.

Having said so much of the introductory . . .[14] of the Poem, I must now speak of the poem . . . Many passages of it, which particularly . . . me, I have marked with my pencil . . . I may light upon them again when I list; and perhaps you will not be ill pleased, some time or other, to turn over the book yourself to see where those pencil-marks are. Amongst the discriptive passages, those of Saul going down into the Cave of Endor, – the Temple of . . . & the fearful rites there, – the first meeting of David & Michal, – and that at the beginning which represents Saul in his shepherd's state, have taken strongest hold of my memory; but there are many others of great merit, which I shall be better acquainted with hereafter. In some of the images also you have been very happy: I shall only mention one as an instance; that where Goliah [*sic*] is compared to "some head-land, promontory huge, –– That, nigh the dangerous strait, a sea-mark towers! –– Far-seen and wide o'er ocean darkness casts," –– a

---

12. Sotheby's blank-verse epic poem in two parts entitled *Saul* appeared in 1807.
13. Baillie's brother, Dr. Matthew Baillie, was married to Sophia Denman Baillie, whom she refers to as Mrs. Baillie after the death of her mother in 1806.
14. This and the following ellipses indicate holes in the leaf.

very noble simile . . . regard to the general management of the . . . I will not pretend to say any thing; for I am such a warm admirer – perhaps a bigotted one; . . . two books of Samuel, that I should not have been satisfied with anything that Milton himself with his best powers could have done to improve it. There are many of your readers, however, who have not read these books so often, and do not . . . them to the degree that I do, and those readers will judge of this part of the work more impartially. –– Let me once more return you my grateful thanks.

Mrs Sotheby has kindly permitted me to come & breakfast with you some morning when I am in Town, and I mean to avail myself of it the first opportunity. I beg to present my best respects to her & yourself, and to Miss Sotheby if she be now with you, and remain,

    my dear Sir,
        your sincere & obliged
          J Baillie

HB.ix-9 (Address: For William Sotheby Esqr / Upper Seymour Street / Portman Square--no postmark)
My dear Sir,

    I send you the promised story from the Chronicle,[15] which you will find I hope one that will admit of a great deal of shew & effect on a large theatre. If you dont like it as it is, of course you will alter it to your own fancy, or tell me how you would like to have it altered and I will do it for you. I shall really be proud if I can set you to work on my story. I have made the two principal characters not very young people lest you should have any wish to have them represented by Kemble & Mrs Siddons.[16]

---

15. The manuscript "An Old Story" (not transcribed herein) follows this letter in 8 leaves numbered 10a-b and begins: "The old chronicle or\ legend of the noble Family of Mondega. . . ."

16. John Philip Kemble (1757-1823), one of England's most famous actors, began playing parts in his father's company in early childhood. His sister, Sarah Kemble Siddons, first recommended him to the Chamberlain's company as Theodosius in Lee's tragedy in 1776; dozens of parts followed. Kemble was a scholar, a man of breeding and a fine actor with a larger range of characters in which he excelled than any English tragedian. He wrote prologues for charitable institutions in York and Leeds, where he appeared for the first time in *Hamlet*--he is said to have written out the part over 40 times. He managed the Edinburgh Theatre for a while in 1781, and his first appearance in London was at Drury Lane as Hamlet in 1783. He remained at Drury Lane for 19 years, representing over 120 characters himself; on 25 January 1800 Kemble played De Monfort in Baillie's play. In 1802 he acquired a share of Covent Garden, but in 1808 when the house burned, taking 20 lives, Kemble and other investors were nearly ruined for lack of insurance. A loan of £10,000 from Lord Percy helped him reopen the new Covent Garden Theatre. Portraits of John Kemble abound, several of which are by Lawrence, notably Kemble as Cato, as Hamlet and as

I came with my Sister to Town last night, and we are to remain for a fortnight or three weeks, so I hope we shall have opportunities of talking over this subject. We shall call in Seymour St: soon, but at present I have some remains of a bad cold & must go out catiously [*sic*]. — My best regards to Mrs Sotheby

    Sincerely yours

      J Baillie

L: Grosvenor St: No 72

Thursday morning Feby 20 [1810 or 1811]

HB.ix-18 (Address: William Sotheby Esqr / Upper Seymour Street / Portman Square--postmarked 1810)

Hampstead May 4th [1810]

My dear Sir,

    It is now high time I should thank you for the pleasure my Sister & I have received from reading your Constance of Castile;[17] but I hope you do not suppose I was stupid enough to wait quietly till now for its coming to me from Grosvenor Street. I lost no time in sending for it, and read it forthwith; tho' many petty occupations & cares have delayed my acknowledgments. The opening of the Poem is very happily imagined; and the discription of the Vessel coming into port in the storm by beacon or torch light &c. &c., struck me very much indeed. The sea, with one great swell of waters, bearing a solitary Bark[18] to the shore, for this is all that the partial light presents to you, is a new discription (to me at least) and gives you a stronger idea of the horrours of the tempest than a fuller or more general discription would have done. The first appearance of your Heroine, deviding [*sic*] the darkness like a gleam of light, is very beautiful; and afterwards in the course of the poem, her clothing herself in the veil like the moon in a cloud, is equally or perhaps still more so. The first appearance of Julien at the banquet where the Black Prince & his

---

Rolla (*DNB*, X:1260-66).

    Sarah Siddons (1755-1831), foremost tragedian of her time and friend of Baillie and the Milbankes, achieved celebrity under Garrick's management at Drury Lane, giving her farewell performance as Lady Macbeth at Covent Garden in 1812. Siddons had played the role of Jane in Baillie's *De Monfort* in 1800 and after her retirement continued to give private readings (*DNB*, VIII:195-202; many biographies are available).

    17. The poem *Constance de Castille*, an imitation of Scott's *Lady of the Lake*, was published in 1810. The poem focuses on the crimes of Pedro, King of Castile, his private marriage to Maria de Padilla prior to his public marriage to Blanche of Bourbon, his illegitimate brother Henry Count of Trastamere, etc.

    18. JB has written another letter over the first letter of this word, making the word look like "Mark," though it is probably "Bark."

Peers were assembled, pleased me very much; and indeed the whole of his character is generous gentle & beautiful: the story of his birth also is interesting & pathetic. In short I have much to thank you for, but will not pretend by any particulal [particular?] examination of the work to say how much. — The general opinion runs so strongly against the character of Don Pedro, that I fear he will be an obstacle to the popularity of the Poem which its other merits may not over come so easily as we could wish; but in this I may be deceived, and shall have great pleasure in seeing it as well as your other works occupying a high place in the favour of the public.

My Sister joins me in good wishes, and with best respects to M^{rs} & Miss Sotheby, believe me,
    My dear Sir,
        Truly your much obliged
         J Baillie

HB.ix-11 (Address: For William Sotheby Esqr / Upper Seymour Street / Portman Square--postmarked 1811)

                      Hampstead thursday
                      March 11th 1811

My dear Sir,
    I have kept my word with you, and have employed – not indeed my first sleepless night for I have had none such to employ – but forenoon passed in bed from a feverish cold that has taken hold of me since I returned home, to compose for you a story, whereon to found a splendid & interesting Play. If you should like it, and it can be of any use to you, I shall be glad. I do not mean that you should hamper your genius by writing servily [sic] for any particular actors, yet I have had Mrs Siddons & Kemble in my mind in imagining the principal characters of the story. Tho' I can write nothing for them myself, it would give me great pleasure to see, before they quit the stage, their powers call'd forth in new characters worthy of them, while the piece to which they belong shall be sufficiently striking & splendid for a large Theatre. I need scarcely say, that if you are the Author who shall procure me this gratification, it will be an addition to my pleasure.

    The Husband & Wife in this story, which I send you inclosed, are intended, as you will perceive, for Kemble & Mrs Siddons, and the Brother will do for C. Kemble.[19] — If you think well of it, set about it while you are in the mind, and all good success attend you!

---

19. Actor Charles Kemble was the brother of John Philip Kemble and Mrs. Siddons and the father of Fanny Kemble.

I hope to see you soon here, in the way you so kindly mentioned; and then we can talk further of this matter; tho' I would not advise you to make any other use of me in it than you would really do of an Old Chronicle. If you dont like my story dont let that damp your intention; you will soon find a better one some where else. ――― Offer my best regards to M^rs & Miss Sotheby in which my Sister begs leave to join me; and believe me, Dear Sir,

    Sincerely yours
      J Baillie

HB.ix-11a (No address or postmark)

                                                     [1811?]

My dear Sir,
    Since I saw you I [have] been thinking that the story from the Old Chronicle might have more action put into it by adding a very natural & simple circumstance; and this is the first moment I have had to spare to tell you so. When the Husband gets the letter into his hand which convinces him of his wife's infidelity, let him question the servant from whom it is got more particularly; and gathering from his answers that the person to whom the letter was wrote is probably in the vaults under the castle, let him go there at the time when the Lady is there. Upon his steps being heard, let the Brother conceal himself, till hearing loud & angry upbraidings from the husband & fearing that he may injure his wife, he comes out to defend her; let the Lady upon this hastily put out the torch or lamp, that his face may not be known to her husband, the feeble light of a distant lamp only remaining; let them fight, and the Brother disarm the husband, who having his life spared tho' in the power of his adversary, makes no attempt to hinder his escape, but being now more than ever enraged at his wife, accuses her publicly without delay. This would add to it one very active scene; and another might be added by introducing the children to plead for their Mother, during any part of the play you might see proper.
    I trouble you with these hints because you seemed, notwithstanding the deficiencies of the story, unwilling to give it up; but at the same time, I would by no means advise you to begin writing upon it unless it should

entirely satisfy your better judgment, and take hold of your imagination.[20]
My best wishes to M^rs & Miss Sotheby
Sincerely yours
J Baillie
Hampstead
wednesday morning

HB.ix-42 (Address: For William Sotheby Esqr / Lodge Loughton / Essex--
postmarked 1811)

Sunning Hill Friday
Septr 20th [1811]

My dear Sir,

I received your very friendly letter last night, by my Brother, who
brought it from Windsor to this place;[21] and being sent to me from
Hampstead in this round-about way, I have not got it till the day is past
which you so kindly appointed for your visit to one, who would have been
most happy to see you & your Tragedy both. I am indeed very unlucky to be
out of the way at the time; and (and) shall fret exceedingly if I learn that
you had the trouble of going to Hampstead; but I hope that, finding no
note from me in Seymour St:, you did not go. —

Well; you have been very expeditious with your Tragedy, and from
most poets that I am acquainted with, I should be suspicious of it; but
knowing the happy facility of your pen, I shall not on this account check
my hopes of finding it, what I heartily wish it to be, an interesting &
good acting play.[22] – You ask of me, however what I cannot promise,
because it is not possible that it should be consistent with truth, to
criticize it with unqualified severity. It must be very unlike all your other
works if such a mode of criticism will suit it. I perceive by this that you
have become exceedingly proud; and unless the piece can be pronounced
compleatly excellent, you disdain all inferior praise. I must not tell you
after I have read it, that your principal characters are well drawn, and
the dialogue enriched with many touching & beautiful passages, tho' the
general management of the story is not favourable for stage effect, nor for
being readily understood by an audience in a large Theatre, where it will
be imperfectly heard. No; this is unworthy of your fiery spirit, and yet it
is what in simple truth I may be obliged to say. — But we need not wrangle

---

20. Letter HB.ix-53 following implies that Sotheby does not use Baillie's *Old
Chronicle*.
21. Dr. Matthew Baillie, one of George III's court physicians, had taken a house
near Windsor to be closer his patient.
22. She refers to his *Ivan*; see following letter HB.ix-51.

about this at present, when I should rather be considering when & how I am to get the work into my hands and assure the stern importance of a Northern Critic.[23] I am to remain here about 10 days or a fortnight longer, and in passing thro' London on my way home, I would gladly call in Seymour St: and take possession of the MS. left there for me. I assure you I feel very much gratified with the confidence you place in me, and shall do all that I can to deserve it. ———

Sunning Hill, on the Skirts of Windsor Forrest, where my Brother has taken a small house for his family during the summer, is a cheerful beautiful part of the country; and we are delighted with the rides in the great park, where the forest scenery is very fine, and almost every old oak that you pass might be a noble subject for the pencil. Mrs Hunter has got a cottage near us which she took possession of yesterday, and is to spend the greater part of every day with us;[24] which is an acquisition to our family circle, and will I hope do her good. — I beg my best regards to M^{rs} & Miss Sotheby. — Your much obliged   J Baillie

HB.ix-53 (Address: For William Sotheby Esqr / Upper Seymour Street / Portman Square--postmarked 1811)

Hampstead Octr 7th [1811]

My dear Sir,

I am just come home from Sunning hill, where from circumstances, tedeous [*sic*] to mention, we staid better than a week beyond the time we expected to stay. On our way thro' Town to day, I called at your house and enquired if any packet was lying there for me, but your Housekeeper told me there was none. I begged her to go up stairs & look, but she returned, still saying there was none. This was a disappointment to me, I own; yet I likewise own I had no right to be disappointed; for it was not reasonable to expect that you should let a M.S. of such consequence lie there so long to be picked up at my good pleasure, forsooth! I am very sensible of this; and only write now to ask what is your good pleasure. I shant go from home

---

23. More specifically, the northern critic Francis Jeffrey (1773-1850), critic-journalist for his generation--no journalist was so influential. He was notorious for injuries to Wordsworth and his contemporaries, but he is said to have invented the review article and to have made criticism a profession (see Russell Noyes, ed., *English Romantic Poetry and Prose* [New York: Oxford University Press, 1956], 568-69, and Philip Flynn's *Francis Jeffrey* [Newark, Delaware: University of Delaware Press, 1978]).

24. Anne Home Hunter, (1742-1821) writer and oldest daughter of surgeon Everard Home, married Baillie's uncle Dr. John Hunter in 1771. Two of her four children survived her, son John and daughter Agnes, who married Sir James Campbell. Anne Hunter published *Sports of the Genii* (1797) and other miscellaneous poems throughout her life.

again for a great while; and whenever you chuse to convey the M.S. to me, or to tell me where I can send for it in Town I shall be happy to be indulged with the perusal of it. In the mean time I trust you have put it into better hands, and have got all the criticism upon it that you desire; and that I shall have nothing to do when it comes to me but to enjoy the beauties of it, in return for having turned over a few pages of the Old Chronicle for your behoof, altho' unsuccessfully. Indeed I doubt whether the circumstance of my writing plays myself does not in some [way?] disqualify me from judging clearly & without bias on such matters. I have the will to do every thing you desire me, but more than the will is necessary.

I have now sent my 3d vol: of the series of plays to the press, and have already corrected, after my fashion (that is to say not very correctly) the first proof sheet.[25] A good ending may it have! and then I shall have little more to do with Printers or Booksellers, tho' I cannot say that I have ever been much teased with either of them.

I hope you are all well at Leighton Lodge: give my best regards to Mrs Sotheby & your Daughter. My Sister begs to join me. I remain, my dear Sir,
your sincere & obliged
J Baillie

HB.ix-51 (Address: For William Sotheby Esqr / Lodge Loughton / Essex-- postmarked 1811)

Hampstead Thursday Octr 17th [1811]

My dear Sir,

This is to announce to you the first reading of Ivan.[26] I took a quiet time yesterday after breakfast when my head was clear and the bustle of the day (for even our Hampstead days have a bustle in them) not begun, and the general impression it has left in my mind is much in its favour as a pleasing & interesting Play. The tender connection between Ivan & Petronia with her controul over his irritated & disordered mind, is affecting & finely imagined; and the characters of Petronia & her husband are both noble & natural. To my ear also, the verse is very sweet. -- Now this is my first impression, disencumbering my mind from all ideas of its being acted or not acted; but I shall read it again more in the spirit of a Critic and find as many faults with it as I think I fairly can, both for your satisfaction, and to keep up my own reputation for discernment. I shall then also take my opportunity of mentioning particularly some passages

---

25. The third volume of *A Series of Plays: in which it is attempted to delineate the stronger passions*, etc., appeared from Longman, Hurst, Rees, Orme, and Brown in 1812 and included *Orra*, *The Dream*, *The Siege* and *The Beacon*.

26. Sotheby's tragedy *Ivan* appeared as one of *Five Tragedies* in 1814.

that struck me as having much poetic beauty, tho' I did not allow myself to stop and read them twice over. I wished to have read it with my Sister that I might have seen how it struck her too, but she was too unwell, and obliged to keep her bed. She is to day, however much better. ——

This will find you I hope on your return to your Forest Lodge after having made a very pleasant excurtion. The weather at least is so much in your favour, that unless you have broken your shins, or quarrelled with Mrs Sotheby, or some other unlikely, untoward circumstance has happened, it must be so. I hope above all that nothing ill befell you on your way from Hampstead to London, that your goodness to me at least may not be blamed. Indeed the short sight we had of you was very pleasant and did me some good tho' short. ——— I beg to offer my best respects & wishes, in which my Sister joins me, to M^rs & Miss Sotheby ——— Be not offended if you should not receive this same critical letter from me for some little time, as I may possibly be prevented from writing it, or rather from qualifying myself for writing it, so soon as I could wish. In the mean time farewell.

> your truly obliged
> J Baillie

HB.ix-44 (Address: For William Sotheby Esqr / Upper Seymour Street / Portman Square--postmarked 1812)

I thank you, my dear Sir, for the kind words & kind promises contained in your letter, both of which I value much. I am sorry to say the little book with the specimens of psalms sent to me by the Convener,[27] is no where to be found tho' I have been looking every where for it. I fear some body has run off with it; however, I shall look again, and if it is found, you shall have it. I begin, since my attempt of last Sunday, to hold Hopkins & Sternhold in some consideration.[28] ———

You are very kind to ask me to drop in upon you on friday evening, but I am going on that day to spend some days with a friend who is in very deep distress, and must not be disappointed. —— My best regards to M^rs & Miss Sotheby. I am, my dear Sir

> your truly obliged
> J Baillie

Hampstead
Jany 9th [1812]

---

27. convener: usually a committee chair (*OED*).
28. John Hopkins (d. 1570) was a joint versifier of psalms with Thomas Sternhold (d. 1549).

HB.ix-45 (Address: For William Sotheby Esqr / Upper Seymour Street / Portman Square--no postmark)

My dear Sir,

I have at last found the little book of psalmody. It will give you some idea of what is wanted, and I am sure either of the Psalms you have by you or rather both of them will make a desirable addition to the collection.

Many thanks to you for your kindness in saying you will look them out for the use of the kirk to please me rather than the Convener and many thanks to you for many other proofs of your friendly regard. ——

I have been either with a distressed friend or as head Nurse in a sick chamber since I last heard from you; and tho' I am in Town I cannot get to Seymour St: else I should have taken this book to you myself.

My best regards to Mrs Sotheby.

yours sincerely

J Baillie

Grosvenor St:

Sunday Jany 18th [1812]

HB.ix-49 (Address: For William Sotheby Esqr / Fair mead Lodge / near Loughton / Essex--postmarked 1812)

Tilnest Cottage Sunning hill
Septr 29th [1812]

My dear Sir,

Be it known unto you, that the good company summoned to compear before you and to join in the good fellowship of you & your compeers,[29] have their nightcaps at present not in their pockets but upon their heads, and are therefore fitter for going to bed than appearing in society so brilliant, albeit their inclination would greatly comove them to obey the aforesaid summons. What the two invited by you, who have no bodies to encumber them, may do, I wot not; they may d'off their caps & go to you, very naturally preferring indifferent quarters for better, (and should either yourself or Mrs Wilmot[30] feel any commotion in your heads to

---

29. compear: to appear in court; compeers: associates (*OED*).

30. Mrs. Barbarina Wilmot, later Lady Dacre, (1768-1854) was a poet, dramatist, translator and sculptor. The third daughter of Admiral Sir Chaloner Ogle, Bart., and Hester, she married Valentine Henry Wilmot in 1789, an officer in the Guards. After Wilmot's death Barbarina married Thomas Brand, 21st lord of Dacre, in 1819. Her published works include *Pedarias* (1811), *Ina* (1815), *Translations from the Italian* (1836), etc. (*DNB*, II:1120). Lady Dacre contributed "Stanzas suggested by a Canzone of Petrarch" to Baillie's 1823 *Collection of Poems, Chiefly Manuscript*, etc.

morrow morning you will know the cause of it), but for the third, who h a t h a poor crazy, aged body, sadly oppressed with a bad cold to take about with her, she must per-force give up all thoughts of the very great pleasure proposed to her. —

Indeed my dear Sir, I feel the kindess [*sic*] of yourself & Mrs Sotheby in this invitation very Sensibly, and should have had great pleasure in spending a day or two under your hospitable roof, but I am here at my Brother's confined to the house with a bad cold, and I fear it will oppress me for some time. I hope you will not suppose me so very inattentive — I should say ungrateful, as to be so long of answering your kind letter: I h a v e but this moment received it; for being from home, our letters have been sent to us in a packet which has laid some time in Town.

My Sister & I & a Scotch Lady, who has spent the best part of the summer with us have been here for some time, and Mrs Hunter has a little cottage near and dines with us every day, so we make a pretty large family circle; one day follows another very pleasantly & rapidly. We shall remain a week longer & then return to Hampstead. This is a delightful country, and I delight in it; but, sad to tell! they are going to inclose the greater part of Windsor Park which will then be private property and of course soon lose the appearance of a royal Forest.[31] These are very <u>unroyal</u> doings, and I cannot hold my tongue tho' I be in the family of a court physician. Mrs Wilmot will tell you how good she has been to me in indulging me with a sight of Pedarias,[32] and <u>I</u> will tell you that I h a v e read it with great pleasure, both from the interest I have taken in the story, and the poetical beauty that adorns it. I should like to see it succeed upon the stage, not merely for her sake but my own, for it would w o o the hearts of the public to dramatic writing of different kind from that which has engrossed them so long, and I might hereafter profit by the renewal of this good disposition, not to mention another friend whom you wot of. You see we folks from the north are always thinking of our own interest.

Lord Dacre was appointed arbitrator for Lady Byron on the death of her mother in 1822.

31. The Terrace in Windsor Forest had generally been used for a promenade for citizens and spectators, and George IV, seeking privacy, ordered it closed except for Sundays, causing a great deal of resentment. Local newspapers regarded the closure of the Terrace as necessary for the king's privacy, but the Canons of Windsor were outraged, claiming they had had legal right to walk upon the Terrace since the time of Charles II (Christopher Hibbert, *George IV, Regent and King*, 1811-1830 [New York: Harper and Row, 1973], 169).

32. Mrs. Wilmot's *Pedarias* was a tragic drama written in 1811, its story derived from *Les Incas' of Marmontel*.

Pray offer my kind regards to M^rs & Miss Sotheby, and may I beg you will present my best compliments to Mrs Wilmot.

I am, my dear Sir,
  very truly your obliged
   J Baillie

HB.ix-29 (Address: William Sotheby Esqr--no postmark)
          Hampstead tuesday morning
            April 11th [1814?]

I have, my dear Sir, been exceedingly pleased with your manuscript & delighted with some parts of it and think that it will be a very acceptable & admired addition to the poetical recollections of your travels which have already given so much pleasure to your friends & your friends's friends. I have ventured to mark a passage which tho' good in itself might, I think, be left out with advantage as to general effect. It is well for you to mention the cause of the particular interest you took in the Hospice of St: Bernard as the scene of your Tragedy, and allusions to it are graceful & natural; but when those allusions are too much detailed & lengthened, they take the form of recapitulation which seldom pleases. And I have been bolder still, for I have (for I have) made a cross mark thus X with a pencil where I think some thing might with advantage be added. The mention you make of the youth of the Monks and the reasons for their being so happy in their toilsome & dangerous duties, is interesting & affecting; but they also generously take upon them those duties in their youth which they know for a certainty will make a few years do the work of many on the mortal frame and bring upon them a premature old age & death.[33] Let your dear Monks have this credit added to them (and you know well & feelingly how to do it) and your Hospice to my fancy will be complete. The Dogs Epitaph is quite touching, and indeed throughout the whole the heart is as much refreshed as the fancy. ——— I need not again repeat how kind your yesterday's visit was to me. It brought relief & it brought cheering, and I have already bespoke a frank to send the interesting part of the Literary Gazette to its proper destination, when it will be gladly received; and the more so that I shall add your opinion, that the Translator may now without fear of disappointment go on with the work. —— You will receive along with this, your own manuscript and my copy of the Translation of Klopstock,[34] and if you will read it & let it

---

33. This appears to be a reference to Sotheby's *Julian and Agnes, or the Monks of the Great St. Bernard* (1801), revised and reprinted as *The Confession* in 1814.

34. Miss Fanny Head, Baillie explains in NLS letters 3902 & 3903 to Scott, translated poet Friedrich Gottlieb Klopstock's (1724-1803) *Messiah*.

ly [*sic*] on your drawing room table an[d] speak a good word for it when occasion serves, I shall be very much obliged to you. You may also by way of making a <u>stir</u> enquire at the Circulating Library for it. You need be in no hurry returning the book; it will be of more use to let it ly on your table than to have it here among frugal & cautious neighbours who dont care one rush for Klopstock & the whole generation of German Poets. --- I hope you have told M<u>rs</u> Hanse [*sic*] Sotheby how much I am obliged to her for her Gazette, and have also informed your own kind Lady that I will gladly dine with her on tuesday the 25<u>th</u> and that my Sister hopes to wait upon her in the evening.

    Yours affectionately & gratefully

      J Baillie

PS. My Sister has read your Ms. and has been delighted with it —— I know now who the friendly critic of the Lit. Gazette is but I will not tell you till we meet. It is a person known to the public but whom I never saw, and who has no connection whatever with my friend the translator[.]

HB.ix-22 (Address: William Sotheby Esqr / Upper Seymour Street / Portman Square / London--no postmark)

                    Barmouth July 8th 1814

My dear Sir,

    Mrs Baillie wrote to me not long ago that there is a parcel which she believes to be a book with some papers, sent from you, now lying in Grosvenor St: for me, and proposing to forward them to me by the coach. Now we are, as you will see by the date of this, <u>far a' field</u> and there is no Mail Coach or stage of any kind as far as I know that passes within forty miles of us. The book which I take to be your Ms. volume of plays would indeed be a great treat to us here,[35] and I beg you to accept my hearty thanks for bestowing on me this valued token of your regard; but as I have read them all once (I mean the plays) and have not curiosity to gratify, I am content to wait till our return home for the pleasure of perusing them again; I would not therefore run the risk of losing my book by my impatience. For the papers, the risk of losing them still more to be dreaded as they could not perhaps be replaced. Have the goodness then at your leisure to write to me and direct in this case as seemeth good in your own eyes. My Sister & I will not return to Hampstead till the end of Octr or beginning of Novr. You would wish, perhaps to recall your papers again & send them to me then. In the mean time, like a true Daughter of Eve, I have a great curiosity to know what they are. I hope when you write to learn that Mrs Sotheby & yourself & all the Family are well, and shall be

---

35. Sotheby's *Five Tragedies* appeared in 1814.

glad to know how the summer passes on with you in Epping Forest. Direct for me Mrs J. Baillie Post Office Barmouth Merioneath Sh: ⸺

And now I take for granted you will not be ill pleased to hear how the summer passes with us, and something about our travels. From consideration more shame to us! of cold-hearted prudence & cowardly despair of having our curiosity gratified, we left London just before the Emperor & great people enter'd it,[36] and held our route very prosperously by Buckingham Warwick, Stratford on Avon, Ludlow, Montgomery & Dolgethly [Dolgellau] to Caernarfon, where we rested ourselves a fortnight, and then, turning our faces eastward again, came on to this place, where we mean to remain till the beginning of September – no longer. It is a clean, cheerful Town or Village, a good seacoast for bathing & very quiet & private. The country round is wild & mountainous & rocky as one could desire; and in our morning rambles we scramble about like the sheep, sitting down to rest where we list and gazing at the ocean & the clouds & the mountains as long as we please – no company – no engagements no dressing for dinner – no nothing (as the children say) to interrupt us. . .[37] This is our life at present. As we pass . . . we saw Stowe which delighted us and . . . Ludlow Castles, each in their peculiar charact[er] . . . much. We stopped at Stratford some time . . . much interested & gratified there. It is . . . [Shakes]pear's own Town, for his image is every where and stable Boys at the Inns can repeat his verses. Beside going to Church to his grave, we went to the house & into the room where he was born, all written over with names of Princes & peers & foreigners from every land & people of all conditions, who had been there to pay their devotions. I suppose I might have found out yours too, if I had had time to unravel a perfect tissue of pencil-scrawls which like an immense cobweb covered the whole chamber, roof & all. The good woman of the house, a colateral descendant from Shakespear's family, shew'd us many things that had belonged to him; and then she took from a shelf a china bowl in which were some letters & verses written by her own son, who had died at 9 years old, who would have been, she said, a second Shakespear if he had lived, for he was the greatest genius that had

---

36. On 7 June 1814 an "illuminated London received Alexander I of All the Russias, and Frederick William III, King of Prussia." Alexander took up residence at the Imperial Hotel in Piccadilly, while Frederick William stayed at Clarence House. The Prince Regent, recognizing that the visit must be commemorated, commissioned Thomas Lawrence to paint the portraits of Alexander and Frederick William, along with many of their entourage. After visiting many public sites, they departed at the end of June (Joanna Richardson, *George the Magnificent, A Portrait of King George IV* [New York: Harcourt, Brace & World, 1966], 135).

37. This and following ellipses indicate part of the leaf is missing.

appeared since the days of Shakespear, for it did not signify what came into his head, he could <u>poet</u> any thing. With this affecting ending to our solemn reflections we left the house & pursued our journey. -- Fare well, I have (I have) just left myself paper enough to send (send) kind regards to M^rs & Miss Sotheby, & to subscribe my name. Your obliged & sincere friend
    J Baillie

HB.ix-23 (Address: William Sotheby Esqr / Lodge Loughton / Essex-- postmarked 1814)

                              Barmouth August 4th 1814
My dear Sir
    I received your welcome letter yesterday and lose as little time as our Barmouth Post will allow to thank you for the very great honour you have done me in dedicating your Plays to me, for so your letter surely tells me you have done. This honour has come upon me so unexpectedly, that not being always a very correct reader of written hand, I have been spelling over your words again & again to see if I could make any other sense out of it, and after all this caution, I must still read & believe that you have e'en in good earnest dedicated them to me. I can only say that if putting the highest value on every mark of (of) your regard & feeling it very gratefully could make me deserving of this distinction, you have not unworthily bestowed it. I might add that if being very proud of it & even vain-glorious into the bargain could add any propriety to your favour, I am abundantly gratified to receive it. Yourself & Walter Scott are the two Poets, who, above all my contemporaries, have taken a pleasure in encouraging me with a true, hearty, brotherly, affection -- (I must call it so) and I assure you your genrous [*sic*] pains is not thrown away; I <u>am</u> cheered & encouraged. --- You are very good in being so much concerned about my keeping the remainder of my Plays from the press: my motives for doing so are simply & honestly given in the preface to my last vol:[38]

---

38. Baillie explains as follows:
    The Series of Plays was originally published in the hope that some of the pieces it contains, although first given to the Public from the press, might in time make their way to the stage, and there be received and supported with some degree of public favour. But the present situation of dramatic affairs is greatly against every hope of this kind; and should they ever become more favourable, I have now good reason to believe, that the circumstance of these plays having been already published, would operate strongly against their being received upon the stage. I am therefore strongly of opinion that I ought to reserve the remainder of the work in manuscript, if I would not run the risk of entirely frustrating my original design. Did I believe that their having been already published would not afterwards obstruct their way to the stage, the untowardness of present circumstances should not prevent me from

there is no <u>dessous de cartes</u> in the matter.[39] I had gone on for a long time publishing under the rebuke of the Edin[r] Reviewer and when I publish'd last, at the time I announced my intention of publishing no more, I believed that he would for the future (tho' it did not prove so) be less rather than more severe upon me; fear of him therefore could not and most certainly did not influence me in the slightest degree.[40] —— So you are engaged in preparing a new edition of your Georgics:[41] it is always a pleasant employment when undertaken for a work that has been compleatly successful, tho' otherwise minute corrections are not interesting. To have been the most successful in an undertaking so difficult with so many competitors & Dryden's self amongst the number, is no small distinction. Well may you get thro' it! You have my good wishes in whatever you undertake. — Leading so quiet a life here with time entirely at command, I have been busy with my papers too. But instead of correcting, I have been I fear creating great cause for correction. I have been amusing myself in a new path altogether, and have been really & truly writing in rhyme, a kind legend of our great hero Wallace.[42] No fiction or story, but a <u>true</u> legend with no love matters or lies of any kind. It is not very long and I finished it yesterday, but whether I shall think it worthy to be corrected & written out in fair paper some months hence I know not. I shall take to other papers very soon & make the most of the good opportunity. ——— We lead the same kind of life — when I wrote last, only that we bathe in the sea now which is a great pleasure & refreshment. The sea shore is amusing & delightful. We stood about half an hour night before last, admiring a group of seven Welch Girls who were sporting together amongst the foamy waves of a rough sea like so many Mermaids. They were handsome enough to have been sea Nymphs but as they wore dark drugget & their coats which gave the under part of the figure the appearance at some distance

---

continuing to publish.
(A Series of Plays: in which it is attempted to delineate the stronger passions of the mind, vol. 3 [1812; New York and London: Garland, 1977], xv-xvi)

39. The French is actually *dessous des cartes*, translated as "to be in the know," but that does not work clearly in the sentence. Perhaps JB means more literally that there is no dishonesty in her explanation.

40. On the publication of Baillie's 3rd volume of plays in 1812, Francis Jeffrey wrote in the *Edinburgh Review*: "Miss Baillie, we think, has set the example of plays as poor in incident and character, and as sluggish in their pace, as any that languish on the Continental stage, without their grandeur, their elegance, or their interest" (*Edinburgh Review*, February 1812, vol. 19: 265-66).

41. The second edition of Sotheby's translation of Virgil's *Georgics* appeared in 1815. Even Francis Jeffrey, the reviewer to whom Baillie refers above, called it a perfect translation (see *DNB*).

42. *Wallace* would appear in *Metrical Legends of Exalted Characters* in 1821.

of being roughen'd into a fish, they were to the eye real mermaids. --
Give my love to Mrs Sotheby & the young Ladies. – Fair well! with all
kind regard, your truly honoured & obliged
    J Baillie

HB.ix-16 (Address: William Sotheby Esqr / Upper Seymour Street /
Portman Square--no postmark)

Hampstead Feby 20th [1815]

My dear Sir,
    I hear that Mrs Wilmot's Play is really coming out, (I suppose soon) a t
Drury Lane,[43] and there is a large party of us here, who have a great
desire to go the first night, if we could get a box. But to get a good box for
that night will, I suppose, require some interest with the Author, as
probably they will be reserved for her friends. Now who has more interest
with the Author than yourself, if you be willing (if you be willing) to use
it for a party of obscure Hampsteaders? We shall be much obliged to you i f
you will do us this favour. The box must be set down in Mrs Carr's name,[44]
who will take care to fill it with those who will not hiss. If a good box
cannot be had for this party, I have another favour to ask for my
individual self, namely that you & Mrs Sotheby will have the goodness to
give me a place in your box, if you do not shrink from receiving into your
party such an antiquated person as Mrs Joanna Baillie, the grave title,
becoming my years, which I have now taken up. Mrs Joanna tho' I be, I
shall put on a smart cap and look as well as I can. -- I am really set on
seeing how it is received the first night and shall be truly happy to see i t
crowned with compleat success. ——
    Perhaps you are not yet come to Town; but in this case the person who
keeps your house in Seymour St: will forward this to you. Tell me when you
write how you have passed this severe winter, and what you have been
doing with your pen. I hope Mrs Sotheby & the young Ladies have escaped
bad colds. We were shut up here for a long time by the snow and went no
where nor had a visitor almost of any kind to cross our threshold. -- Do
you know that we are to have Walter Scott soon in Town? I had a letter
from him not long since in which he talks of it as a thing determined. He

---

43. With no year date on the letter it is difficult to determine which of Mrs.
Wilmot's plays this might be. Her third drama *Ina*, a tragedy set in Saxon times, was
produced at Drury Lane on 22 April 1815 and printed that same year (*DNB*, II:1120).
I would guess this is the play Baillie mentions.

44. Thomas William Carr and Mrs. Carr of Frognal, Hampstead, were the parents
of Thomas, William, Frances, Isabella (Lady Smith), Anna, Laura (Lady Cranworth)
and of Sarah Grace (Mrs. Stephen Lushington). They were close friends of Baillie,
who talks about them often in letters to most correspondents.

has thoughts of proceeding to join the Allied army to see the pomp & circumstance of war. —— My Sister joins me in kind regards to M^{rs} & Miss . . .^{45}

  Believe me, my dear Sir,
    very sincerely yours
      J Baillie

HB.ix-64 (Address: William Sotheby Esqr / Grosvenor Street--no postmark)

Hampstead May 9$\underline{th}$ [1815]

My dear Sir,
  Even amongst those who have not the pleasure of knowing you every one sympathizes with you in your present deep affliction – the death of your brave Son;^{46} how much more then must your friends feel for you, who know the tenderness of your heart and strength of your affection to those who are so nearly related & justly dear to you! It was with great concern we learnt by the news-paper the sad event and heard it afterwards confirmed by a friend from Town. We have heard thro' Mrs Baillie, who sent to your house, the usual answer to such enquiries, yet we shall be anxious to hear further how your Family do after this severe stroke, particularly Mrs Sotheby & yourself. But I cannot wish you to write to me, unless your grief is in that softened state when it becomes an ease & gratification to speak & write of what we have loved & lost. In this case you can scarcely write to one who will take part more sincerely in your sorrow —— I mean of those not immediately connected with your Family. But if this should not yet be the mood of your mind, let me have a few lines from any friendly hand that may be near you, to tell me how you do. —— I say nothing of consolation, tho' to lose a Child esteemed & lamented, dying an honourable death, has much in it, at least, to soothe & gratify the mind; and to a higher source of consolation your own pious disposition will naturally lead you. —— My Sister & I beg, if you think fit, to offer our kindest wishes & condolence to Mrs Sotheby. I fear this will be a sad check to her returning health. ——
  I inclose a letter which we received from Mrs Barbauld yesterday to transmit to you,^{47} but I was prevented from doing so by yesterday's post,

---

45. Part of the leaf is torn away.
46. It is likely this is a reference to Sotheby's' son William, who died in 1815 while a lieutenant-colonel in the foot-guards. Another son, George, was killed defending the residency of the East India Company at Nagpoore during the Mahratta war in November 1817, but the May date on this letter would not coincide with this incident (see *DNB*).
47. Anna Laetitia Barbauld (1743-1825) was the only daughter of classicist and

and so I keep it till this evening when Mrs Baillie will carry it to Grosvenor Street. — Believe me, my dear Sir,

>with all regard & esteem,
>>yours sincerely
>>>J Baillie

HB.ix-12 (Address: William Sotheby Esqr / Lodge Loughton / near Epping Essex--postmarked 1815)

>Hampstead Decr 3^{d} 1815

My dear Sir,

When I heard from you a great while ago, you made me hope that I should have the pleasure of seeing you soon; but I mean not to complain of my disappointment as I am confident it did not arise from any want of good-will on your part; I heard by common friends that you were well and your Family enjoying again the society of their Friends, and this I had great satisfaction in hearing. However, I am, now that Mrs Crawford & Mrs Hibbert are out of Town, entirely cut off from knowing any thing about you, so pray write to me soon after you receive this. Is Ivan to be brought out in Drury L: in February as I was once informed? or the Confession in Covent Garden? Tell me about this, and I will pay you for your trouble before hand, by telling you how I am myself circumstanced in regard to these matters which I think you will have some curiosity to know. My story is soon Told. Lord Byron, after inviting me in the most gratifying manner last spring to prepare some of my plays for Drury Lane, and after having pushed the matter very earnestly with his Colleagues & the managers there, has at last been obliged to give up the point.[48] I indeed wished him to give it up much sooner, but his Friendly zeal made him persist longer than I wished. So now I have nothing on my own account to

---

Nonconformist minister John Aikin and became one of the teachers at the new Dissenting academy in Warrington. In 1774 she married Rochemont Barbauld, also a Nonconformist cleric, who took over a congregation in Plasgrave, Suffolk, where ALB took charge of a school for young boys. The Barbaulds traveled in Europe for a while and settled in Hampstead where Barbauld ministered to a congregation and ALB took pupils. Mr. Barbauld was never very stable and died insane in 1808. In 1782-6 ALB, in conjunction with her brother, wrote *Evenings at Home* for her adopted son and in 1804 edited *The Correspondence of Samuel Richardson* in six volumes and in 1810 *The British Novelists* in 50 volumes, along with *The Female Speaker* (1811), selections of the best British prose and poetry long used in the education of girls (Todd, 37-40). Barbauld contributed "On the King's Illness" and "On Returning a Plant after the Bloom was over" to Baillie's *A Collection of Poems, Chiefly Manuscript* in 1823.

48. See introduction to these letters for details on Byron's involvement with Baillie's and Sotheby's plays.

look for; but as I have a strong natural hankering after these matters, I would still gladly have an interest in them on my Friend's account.

I had a very pleasant letter about 8 days ago from Walter Scott, who was at the time of its date busy planting groves of evergreens at Abbot's ford and rejoycing over the dexterity of his son (a lad of 14) who had for the first time shot a black Cock.[49] He has made a new purchase of land which more than doubles his possessions in that quarter. His Waterloo is written with feeling and has fine passages in it, but in grand discription (that in which he is so eminently master) it disappointed me.[50] I wish he had written it at home. A hasty sketch does not suit such a subject and a sketch written in the distraction of seeing all the new sights & new people at Brussels & Paris, who would have attempted but himself? However I liked it for its feeling, and must receive it as he offers it, viz as a Sketch. –– You have perhaps seen by the papers that my Sister in law has lost her worthy Father Dr Denman.[51] It is a great affliction to all his children, and he is much regretted by all his friends & by the poor to whom he was always a liberal benefactor. He had a blessed end without suffering or a moments illness. Give my kindest regards to Mrs Sotheby & your Daughters. I hope to hear from you good accounts of them all. Believe me, my dear Friend very sincerely yours   J Baillie

HB.ix-60 (Address: For William Sotheby Esqr / Lodge Loughton / Essex–
postmarked 1816)

Hampstead March 23^d 1816

My dear Friend,

I doubt I must appear to you as one of the ungrateful in having so long delayed my acknowledgements for the two Plays Ivan & the Confession, as prepared for the stage which you have so kindly sent me. But indeed I am not so. I delayed thanking you till I should have read the Confession, and not being very well or in very good spirits, I could not read it in the way I wished till night before last, & yesterday I was too much engaged with friends to write. Had I been aware that the last mentioned play has so much of new matter in it and is so much altered, curiosity would have got

---

49. This would be Sir Walter Scott's son Walter (b. 1801).

50. See Scott letters of similar dates to this one for more details. Baillie refers to Scott's *Paul's Letters to his Kinsfolk* which would follow in 1816 after his return from the continent.

51. Dr. Thomas Denman (1733-1815), a physician and son of an apothecary, began practicing as a physician at Winchester in 1764. Denman married Elizabeth Brodie (d.1833) and they had a son, Thomas, and twin daughters; Sophia married Matthew Baillie, and the elder Margaret married Dr. Richard Croft (1762-1818) (*DNB*, V:808).

the better of my invalid's listlessness and I should have read it sooner.[52] It
is certainly now better fitted for the Theatre, and the character of Ellen
affords much more occasion for the powers of an Actress to desplay [*sic*]
themselves. That scene between her & the countess, when the latter
discovers who she is, would act I should think particularly well. I should
like to see Miss Oneal act it:[53] but I have given up all hopes both for
myself & my Friends. — Accept of my best thanks this & many other
marks of your friendship & kindness to me. Remember me kindly to M^{rs}
Sotheby & your Daughters. I depend upon your promise to let me know
before the time of your departure, that we may meet again. My Sister
offers her best regards.

    Yours, my dear Sir,
      very sincerely
        J Baillie

HB.ix-62 (Address: William Sotheby Esqr / L: Grosvenor Street--no
postmark)

                    Hampstead tuesday evening
                           August 3^{d} [~ 1816?]

My dear Sir,

    I received your welcome letter this morning and lost no time in
communicating to Lady Byron its contents. Whatever may be the result,
she and myself are most thankful to you & Capt: Sotheby for your ready &
hearty good will. Your Son (as becomes your Son) behaves himself like the
king's & the country's faithful & consciencious Officer, and we anticipated
in some degree the distinction which he would make between the claims of
a Garrisoned officer's Wife & family and those of any other applicants.
Indeed had it not been for this distinction, I should have considered the
request which I ventured to make to you & to him as impudent &
unreasonable. We shall live in hopes that the destination intended for L^{d}
Byron will be transferred to him, and I for my part do so more readily from
supposing that it will be agreeable to himself as well as advantageous for
Mrs Davidson.[54] Lady Byron, whom we must now call Lady <u>Noel</u> Byron, is
anxious that you should not suppose she took up the Idea of Capt: & M^{rs}

---

52. *Ellen, or the Confession* was published in 1816.

53. This is probably Elizabeth O'Neill (1791-1872), later Lady Elizabeth
Becher, who played Ellen in a Dublin version of *Lady of the Lake* and debuted as
Shakespeare's Juliet in Covent Garden in 1814; though she took some comic roles, she
excelled at tragedy, leaving the stage in 1819 when she married an Irish MP (*DNB*,
II:74-5).

54. I have been unable to find anything to clarify this "destination" in Marchand
or other Byron biographies.

Fox's going out in Capt: Sotheby's ship upon slight grounds tho' it appears that no application has yet been made to the Captain on the subject. L$^{\underline{d}}$ Byron was expressly told that this was the case by a man in office who ought to have known and whose name I will tell you when I next write tho' it has at present slipped from my memory. L$^{\underline{d}}$ Byron & his Lady & 3 of their children are now at Hampstead living with Lady Byron where they will remain till he sails for the Sandwich Islands and it is beautiful to see the interest she takes in him & all that concerns him. A friendly heart & a liberal mind she joins to many other good qualities, and excepting a little shy coldness of manner, I dont know one bad quality she has that can tint them with any alloy. You ought to love a person like this and if you dont do so already you will do so in the long run. Let me beg again that you & Capt: Sotheby will accept my best acknowledgments. ——

I please myself with imagining how much M$^{\underline{rs}}$ Sotheby & you with your house full of friends must enjoy this delightful weather in the Forest. You are very kind in wishing to give a corner of your hospitable house to my Sister & I when that shall become vacant. I am sure we have been too happy & too kindly treated there, not to wish to be there again. We expect to go the 20th to Brighton to spend a few weeks with M$^{\underline{rs}}$ Baillie who has need of sea air to revive her and the satisfaction of being near her Daughter & grand child, who are settled there for a considerable time. I fear, however, that we shall have left the place before your autumnal visit to it begins, if you mean to visit it this year. It would be a glad sight to us, wandering along the cliffs, to meet you on your morning walk. ———
But there is a weight hangs on my mind in leaving home at this time; our poor friend at Hendon.[55] Yet I cannot help thinking that I shall still see her alive when we return. She looked better when I saw her last friday than she had done a fortnight before, and the progress of her disease is apparently so slow that one cannot say how long she may last. She is a noble & a blessed spirit, fitted for the state she is in, in which she gives an excellent & cheering lesson to all who approach her, and fitted for that into which she is passing with so much composure & cheerful exaltation of mind. There is a poem called Elgiva [?] or the monks just published & dedicated to her; have you seen it? It is a piece of respect paid to her at a happy moment. Whoever the Author may be I wish the work success with all my heart. —— With all kind regards to you & those belonging to you &

---

55. This is probably Margaret Holford Hodson; see introduction and letters in Volume 2.

thanks to Miss Sotheby for making the extract from her Brother's letter, I remain,

> Your truly obliged & aff$^{\underline{t}}$ friend
> J Baillie

HB.ix-24 (Address: William Sotheby Esq$^{\underline{r}}$ / Pavilion Parade / Brighton--postmarked 1820)

Hampstead Feb$^{\underline{y}}$ 2$^{\rm d}$ 1820

My dear Friend

Your letter is so full of kind affections with some gleams of the poetical spirit passing slyly between, and therefore so characteristic of the writer, that I have read it with peculiar satisfaction. Your fair flower <u>which has been rudely shaken</u> will, I hope, ere long bloom firmly & freshly on its stalk with its little bud by its side more lovely than ever. You really deserve the blessings which you know so well how to value & to possess with such cheerful thankfulness. They open your heart to every other virtuous tie, and make you grateful to God & charitable to man. Even so good a Wife as yours (and I believe her to be very good & amiable) and as good children also, are sometimes bestowed, for ends which we may not presume to search, on the discontented & unhappy. Long may you & M$^{\underline{rs}}$ Sotheby retain all your domestic blessings along with the blessed spirit that enhances them! —— I thank you also for your real & professed poetry, as well as that which you sent me, in the warmth of your heart, unwittingly. The character of the man is justly & feelingly given & the poetical images which are raised in the first part of the poem are very beautiful. But when you desire me to correct them, I think you must be mocking me. You are a Scholar & write correctly which I do not, and your ear for versifycation is more delicate than mine, how then should I pretend to correct? But if to please you I must e'en do something in that way, I will find fault with a thing which probably after all you will not alter.

—— "On where

> Fleet as an arrow thro' the void of air
> The Rhone along the Leman lake amain
> Darts its blue stream with unpoluted flow."

Dont you know that all this is false, and being addressed to a Philosopher its poetical elegance will not be a sufficient plea for retaining it. The rhone which I saw a short way before it enter'd the lake, is not blue at all nor particularly pure, and it is using Lake Leman exceedingly ill, to which it is endebted for all its beauty, to say that it runs thro' it with <u>unpolluted flow</u>, thereby insinuating that the said Lake is muddy. —— I like the ending of the Poem very much which is solemn & touching. Has it ever yet been in print?[56] If it has not, have you any objection to suffer it to be inserted in the Edin[r] Literary Magazine which is edited by a very respectable man, whom perhaps you know by reputation, M[r] Moorehead, the Colleague of Alison?[57] I am sure it would gratify many Friends of the Deceased in that part of the world where he was so thoroughly known & so much beloved. If you give me leave, I will copy it & send it to Moorehead, not else of course.

What a solemn & impressive event has taken place since you wrote to me, in the death of our good old King! alike insensible to his domestic misfortunes & his public triumphs (for Whig as I am I must admit the termination of the war to have been such) he has passed away, while we seem to behold one of the great land-marks of time erected before our eyes in the termination of a reign so long & so eventful.[58] — When you write let me hear more good accounts of M[rs] Charles & her Baby,[59] for I take it for granted you will answer this as there is a request in it. With all kind wishes to you & M[rs] Sotheby & those most dear to you, I remain affectionately yours

J Baillie

HB.ix-56 (Address: William Sotheby Esq[r] / Lodge Loughton / Essex-- postmarked 1821)

My dear Friend,

I received your gratifying note when I came to Town yesterday and read that also which you sent to M[rs] Baillie. I know well all the warm interest you take in the fate of De Monfort or any of my writings, and I should not have been backward in letting you know of Kean's intention of

---

56. I do not find these lines printed in Sotheby's *Poems, The Battle of the Nile, A Song of Triumph*, or *Farewell to Italy*, but it could have certainly appeared in one of the literary magazines, persumably as an elegy.

57. Though I have not been able to identify Mr. Moorehead, Archibald Alison (1757-1839) was a writer on "taste" and became minister of the Episcopal chapel, Cowgate, Edinburgh, in 1800, where he remained the rest of his life. His sermons were much admired, and two volumes published in 1814-15 went through several editions; Sir Francis Jeffrey gave an admiring exposition of Alison's theories in the *Edinburgh Review* for May 1811. Alison was married to Dorothea Gregory, daughter of Dr. John Gregory, author of *A Father's Legacy to his Daughters* (*DNB*, I:186-87).

58. George William Frederick (1738-1820), George III, for whom Dr. Matthew Baillie was a court physician, died after several years of tormenting mental and physical illness on 29 January 1820 in his 82nd year.

59. William's eldest surviving son Charles Sotheby (d. 1854) and first wife Jane Hamilton had a son, Charles William, in 1820 (d. 1871) who later became high sheriff of Northamptonshire.

taking up that character, which I have known nearly these 3 months, had I put any very firm confidence in its really coming to pass. It is only within this last fortnight that I have put compleat faith in it, and I understood from some body or other that you had left the Forest for Brighton or some other place. I have been so often disappointed in proposals to bring forward my plays, that, when I received the present, in a letter from Elliston, I told no body, neither friend, relation, nor neighbour. — And now I will let you know what has been done about it. Kean was anxious to die upon the stage, but did not like the death which I had formerly provided for him, when Ld Byron wished him to act it, so after having had an interview with him which took place last saturday week, and hearing him explain his notions on the subject, I have written a new last scene, where he is made to die of a broken spirit after having the chains put upon his limbs.[60] In a note from Elliston some days ago, I am informed that he is now quite satisfied with his part, but that he had (as I gave him full leave to do) taken some liberties with [it]. Now all is arranged and John Bull have mercy on me!

I am desired by Mrs Baillie to say (for as I am writing at any rate I am to answer & thank you in her stead for the very kind note you sent to her) to say, that she has no box for tuesday but she, has bespoke a place for you in Lady Campbell's box,[61] who will be very glad to receive you, and when you will probably find my Sister. She also desires me to say that she hopes you will give us the pleasure of your company to dinner here on that same important day, at half past five. I think I shall be in Town, whether I go to the play or not, and it will be a great satisfaction & cheering to me to see you.

Give my kind regards to Mrs Sotheby & your Daughters. I was sorry to hear yesterday for the first time of her recent loss, in the death of her Brother. I shall be glad to know how she does. —— I have not said on Mrs Baillie's part all that she wished, for the kind interest expressed in your

---

60. Edmund Kean appeared in several productions at Drury Lane before his departure to America, some of them adaptations of Scott novels, and was in an "altered" production of *De Monfort* on 27 November 1821. Robert William Elliston (1774-1831), an actor who made his debut at Drury Lane in 1804, became lessee and manager of the theatre from 1819-26, retiring in debt in 1826 (*DNB*, X:1150).

61. Lady Campbell, Agnes Hunter, surviving daughter of Dr. John Hunter and Anne Home Hunter and cousin to Baillie, married Sir James Campbell first; after his death, she married Col. Benjamin Charlewood, retaining her title.

note gave as much pleasure to her as it gave to me.

    Many thanks

        affectionately yours

            J Baillie

Cavendish Square

Wednesday Novr 21st [1821]

HB.ix-25 (Address: William Sotheby Esqr / Post Office / Brighton--postmarked 1821)

                                    Hampstead Decr 4th 1821

My dear Friend,

    You were kind enough to express a wish to hear from me, after a week should be past from the bringing out of our Play, and a week has just past and with it the poor Play also. This I have learnt to day, by accidental report of those who have seen yesterday's Play bill, in which Hamlet was announced as the Play and no notice taken of De Monfort at all. You left us in the height of our apparent prosperity, and my Sister went with a party to see it next night, when there was a full house tho' not so full as the night before and a very good reception (probably some orders had helped to make it appear a better house than it really was) but the 3 night was not so good as Kean expected which (I was told by a friend of his) had made him very angry, and friday & saturday, I suppose, were still worse. Any farther particulars I have not to give you, for since I left Town which was last friday, neither Mrs Baillie or any of my friends have written me one line on the subject, and I have gathered up my information in a chance way, like a person no wise concerned in the matter. I am very sorry for this, as it is in some degree a mortification to myself and is a very great disappointment to Kean, who has bestowed great pains upon his character & performed it with great power. I dare say he wishes me & my Play at the bottom of the red sea; however, it is a comfort to me that the bringing of it forward was entirely his own doing and did not arise from the desire of myself or any of my friends. — I had the kindest letter from Lady Dacre a few days ago, congratulating me, as she thought, on my success, and saying she would come to London soon on purpose to see it,[62] — so kind that it did my heart & soul good to read it, tho' I began by that time to suspect that my success was rather of a tinsel kind, and as the old proverb says, "'tis not all gold that glitters."

    I hope you got well down to Brighton and found Mrs Sotheby & all your family well. What a magnificent sight you must have seen of stormy seas

---

62. Mrs. Wilmot became Lady Dacre on her marriage to Thomas Brand, baron Dacre, on 4 December 1819.

during this last week! The very walls of our house have been rocked by the storm on this hill, whilst the blasts have roared about us like immense billows of troubled air that threatened to overwhelm us. We had a call this morning from your old Tenant Mrs Achmaty,[63] who will become your neighbour soon, as she is going with her children to Brighton. —— Write to me by & by and let me have a word of comfort at your leisure, for I am a reasonable person on such occasions and easily set right again, so that such words will not be thrown away. — Pray give my kind regards to Mrs Sotheby & your Daughters, and believe me always,

My Dear Sir,
yours gratefully & sincerely
J Baillie

HB.ix-28 (Address: William Sotheby Esqr / Rock Garden / Brighton-- postmarked 1821)

Hampstead Decr 29th 1821

My dear Friend

You disclaimed all idea of giving me comfort, yet your kind and more than kind letter did comfort me; and since you have therein desired me to write to you again, I should be little better than one of the ungrateful were I not to obey. You will like to know all that has past since I wrote to you <u>anent</u> (as we say in Scotland)[64] this same play of ours. I say <u>ours</u> for kind interest you took in it entitles me to say so. I received a note from Elliston better than a fortnight since, to offer me his thanks for all I had done regarding the alterations of De Monfort, and expressing himself as perfectly satisfied with the effect &c; after which follows his apology for giving it up so soon, as not being sufficiently productive to the treasury, for says he "What John Bull does not partonize [*sic*] we cannot act" and then he adds, that he is not yet in despair but is determined to bring out the play again in Spring, when there shall be more company of the higher ranks in Town. In my answer to him I have very politely expressed <u>my</u> satisfaction at <u>his satisfaction</u>, laying all the blame for want of success in the Play itself, to the exonerating of John Bull & every body else; but on the subject of his determination to produce it again in spring, I have been altogether silent; meaning by this, that he should understand, I consider the matter entirely as his own affair & not mine. I learnt from Mrs Kean & other quarters that they had not had better houses for any other play, and this has perhaps made Elliston think of producing it again, however it

---

63. Spelling here is difficult to decipher and may be Achmecty, though I cannot identify.

64. anent: in the face of (*SND*).

appears to me a very doubtful thing whither he will do so or not. ––– Fare well to this subject! I have lately had other things to occupy my thoughts. We were in dreadful anxiety the beginning of last week about my Nieces little Girl & only child,[65] as dear an object to our family as your Babe can be to yours. She was taken with the Scarlet fever, very severely, at Windsor, where her Father is stationed with his regiment, and my Brother & M[rs] Baillie went there & remained till all danger was over. Thank God it is over! for it makes me tremble to think what misery would have ensued had it been otherwise. An only child swept away and the house left desolate! –– We spent after this a tolerably merry Xmas in Town, and are likely to spend a still merrier New year in Hampstead with our Neighbours the Carrs; for there is Miss Edgeworth & two of her Sisters as Inmates to say nothing of D[r] Lushington, who is like a School boy at holy days.[66] A happy new year to you & yours! well may you all be thro' the course of it and of many others! — What an eventful year it promises to be over the face of the earth. Will there be a Grand Turk in the world this day twelve month, or a King in Spain? every country seems more or less unsettled & ripening for change. I have become lately a great reader of the news paper and greatly interested for the Greeks. You who are a Traveller & a Scholar ought to be doubly so. –– My Sister unites with me in all kind wishes & regards to M[rs] Sotheby & your Daughters. What magnificent sea storms you must have had to gaze upon lately! –– Yours always my very kind tho' too flattering friend

    gratefully & sincerely

    J Baillie

HB.ix-35 (No address or postmark)

Hampstead Jan[y] 27th 1822

My dear Friend,

    I want you to lend me some assistance in an undertaking which I have just begun for the advantage of an old school-fellow of mine, who has

---

65. Elizabeth Margaret Baillie Milligan and husband Capt. Robert Milligan had one child, Sophia (1817-82).

66. Maria Edgeworth (1768-1849) first focused her writing on educational topics, translating Madame de Genlis's *Adèle et Théodore*. She experimented with various teaching methods, publishing a series including *The Parents Assistant* (1796) and *Early Lessons* (1801); but she became well known for her novels *Castle Rackrent* (1800), *Belinda* (1801), *Popular Tales* (1804), *The Modern Griselda* (1805), *Leonora* (1806), the six volume *Tales of Fashionable Life* (1809-12), *Ormond* (1817), *Helen* (1834), etc., many of which document Irish society. Edgeworth is one of the first women novelists "to apply an insight articulated by Wollstonecraft, that women have their own language" (Todd, 204-7). Baillie and Edgeworth met in 1813 (see Scott letter 3884 ff.184-187). Her sisters were Mrs. Beaufort and Mrs. L. Wilson.

suffered great reverse of fortune. I have not time at present to give you the particulars of her situation, but when I have the pleasure of meeting again, you shall know them, and I am sure both M<u>rs</u> Sotheby & yourself will be interested in the distress. What I have engaged to do, is to edit a volume of collected poems which will be published by subscription, and I wish to have the poetry chiefly manuscript or taken from printed works which have not been published. Will you send me something of yours or rather some <u>things</u> for insertion? or will you let me take what I like from your remembrances of Italy which stands in the last predicament. That upon Venice I particularly covet.[67] Be kind enough to help me out in any way you please and I shall be very thankful. I wish to make the collection as creditable as I can and therefore I shall write to Sir W. Scott & several other Brother poets to send me contributions.[68] ---

I hope you have all enjoyed this mild season at Brighton. Even on Hampstead hill we have had the birds singing to us and purple primroses bursting the bud as if it were April. -- With kind regards to M<u>rs</u> Sotheby & your Daughters in which my Sister begs to join me, I remain

 my dear Friend
  very truly yours
   J Baillie

HB.ix-58 (Address: William Sotheby Esqr / L: Grosvenor Street--no postmark, RCS dates 1822?)

        Hampstead Nov<u>r</u> 5<u>th</u> [1822?]

My dear Sir,

I have delayed thanking you for your last very kind letter till we should be returned home and now I do so very heartily. We arrived from Devonshire last Wednesday after having spent nearly four months there & in Gloucester sh<u>r</u> very agreeably. We did not travel about so much nor visit so many places as you have done in your summer excursion which seems to have been so pleasant a one to you, but we were happy in the few families where we were domesticated and had little inclination to rove which suited our purse as well as our humour. I am glad that you have had so much enjoyment; there is no good thing that I begrudge you. Indeed I should be very ungrateful if this were the case. ----

---

67. Sotheby contributed "Fair Mead Lodge" and "The Lay of the Bell" to Baillie's 1823 *A Collection of Poems, Chiefly Manuscript, and from Living Authors* for the benefit of her friend Mrs. James Stirling.

68. See Baillie's letters to Scott (NLS 3894-3896) about his contributing *MacDuff's Cross*. Other contributors included Campbell, Southey, Wordsworth, Barbauld, Hemans, etc.

I feel greatly indebted to you for offering me the use of your manuscript poems so liberaly and think I should like to have them all, Rome, Elements, Bell & everything; but this would be very unreasonable so we must consider the matter. I am quite of your opinion that speaking is better than writing upon the subject, so if you would have the goodness, next time you are in Town, to come to Hampstead & eat a quiet dinner with my Sister & I, we should talk over the matter without interruption. Will you have the kindness to let me know when this may be, that we may be sure not to go from home or make any other engagement on the day you shall fix upon, and say likewise at what hour you would wish to dine. If this may <u>not</u> be, I will go to Town and give you the meeting. Pray let me know your pleasure on these points as soon as may be. —— I have written to Miss C. Fanshaw, earnestly requesting to have something of hers,[69] but I have not received an answer; indeed there has not been time for me to receive it. I expected to have found a packet from Sir W. Scott lying on my table when I returned,[70] but I have been disappointed and have written to put him in mind & to hasten him. I am now anxious to close the subscription and put my book to press by the middle of the month, but I fear it will be some days later.

Give our kindest regards to M<u>rs</u> Sotheby & your Daughters. How much longer shall you remain in the Forest? I have many things to say to you, but hoping to see you soon, and being somewhat tired of writing, I will take my leave for the present, always remaining

most truly & gratefully

yours

J Baillie

The following letter is owned by the Huntington Library:

HL SY1 (Address: William Sotheby Esq<u>r</u> / L. Grosvenor Street / Grosvenor Square--postmarked 1825)

Hampstead Saturday May 28<u>th</u> [1825]

My dear Friend,

Old & out of fashion & laid on the shelf as I am, who is there who will praise me so liberally as your own friendly & generous self? Walter Scott & you have been my staunch supporters, but he has for a long time

---

69. Catharine Maria Fanshawe (1765-1834), who lived with her sisters at Hampstead for many years, contributed anonymously to Baillie's 1823 *Collection*.

70. After much pleading (see letters to Scott during this time period), Baillie finally received Scott's *Mac Duff's Cross* for her 1823 Collection.

seemed to forget me,[71] and its sweet to have my heart cheered at this late hour of the day by the voice of a friend — a highly gifted friend, whom I so much esteem. — I have read the three Cantos of your Rome which is full of lofty & affecting thoughts & admirable discription, yet I should not have written to you till I had deliberately read through the book, had not my Sister, late last night, stumbled upon those beautiful lines addressed to me of which I am right proud, and for which I beg leave to thank you right heartily,[72] It may become me to follow up these expressions with others of disqualifying consciousness on my own part in receiving such high commendations and of the strong sense I have of your too great partiality, but it is difficult to be both proud and humble in one breath and that must be reserved for after reflection. — And now let me return again to that point of the book which I have read, for my time has been for 3 days past so incroached upon by visitors & sordid necessary avocations, that I have not been able to read more with any due attention. The Rome is indeed rich in striking thoughts & discription and as discriptive poetry, from some pecutiarity [peculiarity] or defect in my own mind, has always taken greater hold of my memory & imagination than the poetry of sentiment, I must in the first place say how much I have been delighted with your discription of St. Peters; it presents a truly solemn, noble & varied picture to the imagination; and that part above all which discribes the pillars of the arcade by moon light is exquisite. I was much pleased at the opening of the Poem with the transition from lonely deserted nature to the sounds motions & interests of the great City; it is an opening worthy of the subject. The Coleseum [sic] is excellent, but I remember being struck with it before, so it had not the advantage of novelty, and even setting novelty aside, I think I prefer St: Peters. — But I may no longer go rambling on in this manner with many things abiding me which must be done, so accept my grateful thanks for all the honour and all the pleasure I owe to you, and believe me most truly

My dear Friend

  affectionately yours

   J Baillie

---

71. Following the great commercial crash of 1825, partly because of his own borrowing and partly through the mismanagement of his publishing partner James Ballantyne, Scott found himself with Ballantyne and Constable involved in financial ruin, personally responsible for £130,000. The stress of this period in his life is probably the reason for his not answering all letters; there seems to be no other explanation for his ignoring Baillie. See NLS letters to Scott 3901 ff.113-114 and 3902 ff.157-161.

72. Sotheby's impressions from his visit to the continent first appeared in *Farewell to Italy and occasional Poems* in 1818, reissued as *Poems* in 1825.

PS. My Sister desires me to tell Mrs Sotheby that she spoke to William Baillie about Tremain[73] and he says it is entirely at her service and so we shall send it to Grosvenor St: by the very first opportunity. —

HB.ix-65 (Address: William Sotheby Esqr / L: Grosvenor Street--no postmark)

Hampstead Novr 5th 1825

My dear Friend

What a brilliant temptation you have set before me with all the native buoyancy & of your kind heart & poetic fancy! And what answer am I to make? Three days — delightful days that will on the dull mists of November produce an oasis (I believe that is what you call the little green Islands of the sandy desert, tho' probably I spell the word wrong) —— an oasis of brightness surpassing all the splendour of June! I would fain enjoy them, though my contribution to the feast could be nothing, my matter of witchcraft having gone on slowly & vilely, no speed or progress to signify, my broom stick being a very broom-stick fit to be set behind the door instead of careering it on the clouds.[74] But though I be willing, I see or foresee many hindrances to my leaving home, subject as I am in winter to bad colds, and with other arrangements on hand which run entirely counter to such an enterprize. Many many thanks both on my own part & my Sisters for your very kind invitation! If I come at all, however, I will come alone, for Agnes says she cannot leave home at that time and has good reasons for saying so, tedious to mention at present. ——— Do I read your letter right where it is set down that your opera of Aladdin in five acts was written [in] one day?[75] This is a feat to me incomprehensible; for tho' I were not to pause one minute for idea or expression, I could not trace it with my pen in three days with all the diligence in my power. With such facility you might rival the not unknown himself. Surely the writers of the present day, like the steam-looms of the present day, have a power of production entirely unknown to their slow-paced, timirous [sic] predecessors. I have a curiosity to see this piece of yours, and whether I be an Inmate of the Fairmead Paradise on or about the 18th inst. or not, I shall hope from your Brotherly indulgence to be gratified soon. ——— The account Murray has given you of Sir Walter's affairs is cheering, and I am

---

73. This is probably Scott's *The Bridal of Triermain* (1813).
74. Baillie probably refers to her play *Witchcraft: a Tragedy, in Prose.*
75. I have not identified this possibly unpublished work.

very glad to hear it. A ruin so incurred & so repaired, never before took place since writing was writing and money was money.[76]

Give my kind & grateful regards to all your Ladies of the Lodge, all kind & good & agreeable to me. I am glad to learn that your Sister is still with you, and hope to meet her again, some time or other. In this my Sister joins me heartily.

ever truly yours

J Baillie

PS. I have just been committing a most absurd mistake in writing a postcript [*sic*] on the first page of this letter which was meant for another letter which I have written to the Aunt of this same J. Mylne[77] — pray excuse it, for I have no time to make a fair copy of this to you[78]

HB.ix-39 (No address or postmark)

Hampstead Sunday April 29th
1827

My dear Friend

We do indeed sympathize with you — sympathize deeply. I seemed to be stunned when I read your letter, so unlooked for and so afflicting is the event which it announced. In the prime of life & the strength of manhood, and under such hopeful & interesting circumstances to be taken away from so many dear & affectionate Relatives! this is one of the appointments of Providence which it requires the strong faith of a Christian to bear with becoming resignation; and, thank God! you & your excellent Wife & Daughters are blest with that powerful support.[79] It will not fail to cheer & elevate your minds in the darkest hour; and will, I hope, present the body also from sinking under the weight of grief. — And woe is me! for your poor bereft Daughter, in her present trying state, — bereft of a husband so amiable & estimable and congenial to the elevated character of her own mind & dispositions! Little did I think when I saw her with you, not a fortnight ago, and looked at her pleasing & happy face, what evil was abiding her! But it is presumptuous in me to call it evil, when we know that a wise & beneficent Creator orders every thing (even the most distressing) for the final good of his creatures. —— Alas,

---

76. See HL letter SY1 and notes above.

77. Anne Millar, a childhood friend of Joanna and Agnes, was the daughter of John Millar, a professor at the University of Glasgow and colleague of Joanna's father James. John Millar had three daughters; one married Professor James Mylne and the other, probably Helen, Dr. John Thomson (*DNB*, XIII:403).

78. Baillie has begun a postscript on the first leaf of this letter but crossed it out.

79. Sotheby's son Hans died on 27 April 1827 while in the service of the East India Company.

my dear friend! your portion of affliction within a few months has been very great, and this is the heaviest of them all. I grieve to think of it, and wish I could do or say any thing that might console you. But it may not be; there is nothing can be done; and "God's will be done" is the amount of all that can be said. ———

You & yours have been almost constantly in my mind since I received your letter by last night's Post, and I shall think of you very often for a great while to come. Both of us, Agnes & myself, will be very anxious till we hear of you again. It was most friendly in you to remember us and to write to me in your distress. But how many years have passed by in which I have never failed to receive proofs of your friendship & kindness on every needful occasion, and they have been a pleasing support to me under various circumstances. Accept my hearty thanks for all your goodness & partial indulgence to me. ——— My Sister unites with me in offering our sincere, heart-felt condolence to you & M<u>rs</u> Sotheby & family. We shall be in Town the beginning of next week, and your door will be one of the first places we shall go to, in hopes of hearing that your healths still continue to sustain, without much injury, the severe trial with which you have to wrestle. — In the mean time I remain with sympathy & affection,

    my dear friend
       very gratefully yours
        J Baillie

PS. Since I wrote the above, I have had a call from M<u>r</u> Morris, who, hearing at M<u>r</u> Carr's of your distress, came anxiously to me to enquire after you & M<u>rs</u> Sotheby, and expressed great sympathy & concern for your heavy loss. —— He is to enquire after you tomorrow, and is to let me know what he hears of you. ——

HB.ix-21 (Address: William Sotheby Esq<u>r</u> / Fairmead Lodge / Loughton / Essex--postmarked 1827)

                        Hampstead August 22<u>d</u> [1827]

My dear Friend

Before I say any thing of your sacred verses, let me express my sympathy with you & M<u>rs</u> Sotheby & your family on the loss of your near relation and also of your dear & valued friend. How heavy the sum of your losses by death in a very short time have been! That God enables you to bear it as Christians ought, I know well; and may such support & consolation always be your's [sic]. —— But woe's me for poor M<u>rs</u> Stables & her afflicted family! What will become of them, deprived of the one who was their pride & support; every thing Daughter friend & Sister could be?[80] If you know any thing of them, I should be glad to hear it from you. Mrs Baillie, as I passed thro' Town last friday on my way from Twickenham, sent to Brook St: to enquire, but the servant there could only give the usual answer as to the living tho' he related the striking circumstance of the suddeness [sic] of Miss Stables's death. —

You flatter us too much in sending your verses to us as you say for Castigation; such exercise on such writing is beyond our skill, but I shall tell you simply what I think of them and Agnes I believe will be of the same opinion. I like your two psalmes [sic] and what you call Nunc dimittes; but the passage from Job, noble as it is and expressed in your lines with great spirit, does not appear to me adapted to church psalmody, the language being to my ear not sufficiently smooth & harmonius [sic], and David's lamentation over Saul & Jonathen is made too long with the continued repetition of "How are the Mighty fallen!" There is a little alteration which I would make, if you agree to it, in the line of the 15 psalm. The passage runs thus

"Days of sweet peace & nights of blest reposing:
> While on his tearless lid,
> In midnight darkness hid,
The light that seraphs hail, rests on its hallow'd closing."

I would change it to

The light that seraph's hail dwells with its hallowed closing

This would prevent the too close repetition of the two ons and make the sense more perfectly clear, at least it so strikes me. In the seventh & eighth verses of the Nunc Dimittes there appears to me an imperfect expression,

"Twas he to whom the promise given
To see ere death the Christ of heaven
Twas he &c."

To make the sense perfect ought it not to be

"Twas he to whom the promise was given"

for without the was something more should follow to complete the sense.[81] Ask your Daughter Miss Sotheby if I am not right and what Maria says I will abide by, for I myself am a poor grammarian. But probably I am taking all this grave pains upon what is a mere oversight from your writing in hast[e]. — If you write any more pieces, as I hope you will, for

---

80. This is apparently on the death of Miss Stables, daughter of Mrs. Stables of London who was a friend of the Carrs. I have no further identification.

81. These appear to be new lines for the psalmody and not a revision or repetition of the lamentation scene from Sotheby's earlier poem *Saul* (see Reiman's 1978 Garland edition).

the Principal, I will give you a hint which he gave to me but has not repeated to you, namely, that the Committee for Church psalmody do not wish to have many of their additional pieces taken from the psalms, as they think themselves well provided from that source already.

Our Scotch friend left us yesterday for the North, and if Mrs Sotheby is disposed to receive a visit from Agnes & me and it should prove perfectly convenient for her to receive us, for a few days, we will come to you in the course of next month at the time you chuse to appoint, and about the middle of the month will suit us better than an earlier time. Mrs Hans I hope & her dear Babe continue well, I long to see them both. —

How generous your friend Mrs Andre[82] and her friends are! I shall speak to you on this subject when we meet. Adieu for the present.

Ever faithfully yours
J Baillie

HB.ix-14 (Address: William Sotheby Exq^{r} / Fairmead Lodge / Loughton / Essex--postmarked 1828)

Hampstead Jany 28th 1828

My dear Friend

Mrs Baillie told me on Saturday that you have been complaining of my not acknowledging the receipt of two notes from you and the Skeleton Drama, saying at the same time that it is not like my usual accuracy. I know not whether to be distressed at having on this occasion behaved so badly, or flattered by having accuracy attributed to me as my usual quality: it is a kind of mixed feeling that now possesses me. Indeed I fear I have behaved somewhat worse than usual, let my habits be as they may; but we have had an Invalid friend staying in the house, who took up my time & attention very much; and that poor Skeleton, having now a counterpart clothed with flesh & skin, seemed to me a thing of so little value that you ought not to have been at all anxious about my receiving it or not. — But I was bound to thank you for your agreeable notes and the pleasant accounts therein contained of your family; and I do thank you with all my heart, tho' my pen has been too long of expressing it. —

I have a great pleasure in expectation: I am invited to the Hod [?] Theatricals next saturday and mean to go, should no cross luck come in the way which I hope will not be the case. Lady Dacre tells me that you &

---

82. The only connection I can make here is to Major John Andre (1751-80) who was in charge of the secret negotiations with Benedict Arnold concerning the intended betrayal of West Point. He was captured and hanged as a spy, leaving three sisters (also mentioned in other Baillie letters): Mary Hannah, Anne Marguerite, and Louisa Catherine (see Robert McConnell Hatch, *Major Andre: a Gallant in Spy's Clothing* [Boston: Houghton Mifflin, 1986]).

your family are to be there on that day, and very kindly asks me at the same time, knowing how well I like to meet you & yours, and how few I am likely to know of the company besides your selves. My Sister (tho' also kindly invited) I must leave behind, as her rheumatism is still troubling her, and she dare not venture so far from home. – I make no doubt we shall have a high treat, and hoping to meet so soon & so agreeably, I remain with all kind wishes to Mrs Sotheby and the domestic circle at Fairmead,

affectionately yours

J Baillie

HB.ix-19 (Address: William Sotheby Esqr / Fairmead Lodge / High Beech / Essex--postmarked 1830)

Hampstead monday sept^r 20th [1830]

My dear Friend,

The Authoress in whose favour I spoke to you when we last met, is the Daughter of a very respectable Goldsmith in Colchester of the name of Hedge, who died a good many years ago, leaving her quite unprovided for with a very sickly constitution, after having been brought up in a very comfortable home with every reasonable indulgence. The delicacy of her health having made it impossible for her to support herself by any active employment, she endeavoured to live by writing books for young people, and I have now on my table a list of her works amounting to more than twenty volumes – "Memorials of early promise" — "Letters on history sacred & prophane" — "Memoirs of James 2^d" &c &c. — But she now finds (finds) it impossible to earn any thing by her writings.[83] All she has now to live upon is a very small weekly pension, given by a relation, but resting on no agreement or security for continuance. Her health is sinking fast under the anxiety & privations which she suffers, and the addition of a small yearly pension would relieve her from painful distress. --- I remember Miss Hedge in Colchester some thirty years ago, a very delicate looking Girl with a pretty face and a figure so slight that she had the appearance of a child rather than a young woman, and she had all that engaging modesty about her which suited her appearance and the very amiable character she received from every one who had the opportunity of knowing her. She was related to the Clergyman's wife of our Parish who frequently spoke of her to my Sister & me in terms of high praise, both as to abilities & disposition. --- From her having published so

---

83. Mary Anne Hedge has twelve volumes listed in the *British Museum General Catalogue of Printed Books* (Vol. 100), including several children's books published in Colchester between 1819 and 1824: *Samboe: or the African boy* (1823), *Juvenile Poems* (1823) and *The Orphan Sailor-Boy; or Young Arctic voyager* (1824).

many things, we may infer that some of them had sufficient merit to be in a degree successful, for she could not have afforded to continue publishing & losing money. That she should at length find this occupation perfectly unprofitable, when there are so many competitors in this branch of writing, is not at all wonderful, and need not imply any want of merit in her productions. —— The literary fund have not often, I believe, bestowed a small annuity on a more deserving person,[84] and if you can influence (can influence) the Members or Directors to grant the boon which through you I take the liberty most earnestly to solicit, they will relieve an amiable & worthy woman from great & mortifying distress. ——

I make no apology to you for this trouble, knowing that it is your pleasure to do every thing that is helpful & kind, but remain

very sincerely & faithfully yours

J Baillie

PS. M[r] Richardson called here yesterday and assures me that so far from being very busy (as his Wife reported him to me) he is quite idle and will have the greatest pleasure in meeting you here at dinner.[85] Not to hurry you as to time, I have named to him two days somewhat distant, friday or saturday se'nnight: the dinner to be at six o'clock and no company but your selves. Whatever day you chuse, you will I hope stay all night, for we have a good room to offer you, and if you chuse saturday I hope you will stay with us till monday and take such a sermon as Hampstead Church affords. —— Give my kindest remembrances & thanks to our late amiable Hostess & all the family Circle at Fairmead. ——— I mean to write to M[r] Rogers in favour of Miss Hedge, that he may back your application.[86] Will

84. The Royal Literary Fund was started in the late eighteenth century and still exists. Created to offer temporary relief to "persons of genius and learning, or their families, who shall be in want," its assistance was confidential. Those in need could apply for assistance and support their case through members' testimonials as well as with samples of their published work (R. H. Super, "Trollope at the Royal Literary Fund," *Nineteenth Century Literature* 37.3 [1982]: 316).

85. John Richardson (1780-1864) was a parliamentary solicitor and for 30 years discharged the duties of crown agent for Scotland, reputed as the most learned peerage lawyer of his time. He had literary tastes and in 1821 was introduced to George Crabbe in Joanna Baillie's house; he regularly corresponded with Walter Scott, whose deathbed he attended shortly before Scott's demise. He married Elizabeth Hill, a close friend of Thomas Campbell, in 1811 and had several children (*DNB*, XVI:1118-19). Richardson submitted "Song - Her features speak the warmest heart" for Baillie's 1823 collection; and in a letter dated 18 January 1842, he tells Baillie, "It is, as it has long been, a great pride and gratification to me to have enjoyed your friendship; a few circumstances of my life have afforded me more real pleasure" (NLS Ms 3990, f.41).

86. Samuel Rogers (1763-1855) was a banker and well-known art collector who became a highly successful poet in his lifetime. Between 1822-28 he published a

not this be right? — What Richardson will tell you of your friend a t Abbotsford is good but not quite so good as I hoped for.[87] — — —

HB.ix-30 (No address or postmark)

Many thanks, my dear Sir for the friendly service you have done me! It is indeed very pleasing to me to have got £20 for poor Miss Hedge and to owe it to your exertions. It is quite as much as I expected, and as much, I daresay, as present circumstances would admit. —

You will not, perhaps, be much surprised to receive from me soon a short pamphlet which I have put into Longman's hands for publication on a very serious subject which I think I have once or twice ventured to touch upon in your presence, and tho' I do not venture to hope that it will entirely meet with your approbation, yet I believe we shall not differ very widely in our opinions; and when you take into consideration that I am publishing for conscience sake, neither for fame nor for profit, you will at least be inclined to judge of me charitably. I entitle it "A view of the general tenor of the New Testament, regarding the nature & dignity of Christ, from the various passages relating to that subject."[88] It is not a work of argument or controversy, but will I trust be more useful than if it were. I shall say no more about it at present; after all this bustle about the reform bill is over, you will receive your copy and judge yourself. —

We received a visit from Mrs Walker day before yesterday and had an opportunity of enquiring after you all but did not get so good an account of your Daughter Harriet as I hoped for, tho' she said she is better. – I wish we could get to Town to see you but we expect two Ladies from Scotland next week to stay a little while with us, and this makes all our movements very uncertain. — — My Sister unites with me in kindest regards to Mrs Sotheby & family circle

Your grateful & affect.

J Baillie

Hampstead

friday evening March 11th [1831]

---

collection of verse tales entitled *Italy*. JB does ask Rogers to help; see UCL letter 14/31 to Rogers dated 6 October 1830.

87. Sir Walter Scott suffered a series of apoplectic strokes between 1829 and his death in 1832.

88. Baillie's *A View of the General Tenour of the New Testament Regarding the Nature and Dignity of Jesus Christ* (London, 1831), in which she analyzes the doctrines of the Trinitarians, the Arians, and the Socinians and argues the human nature of Christ, caused a great deal of controversy. Her pamphlet prompted a series of letters from the Bishop of Salisbury (Volume 2).

HB.ix-32 (No address or postmark)

[1831]

My dear M<u>rs</u> Sotheby

When your good & friendly husband told me on monday that the advice he came to offer me was also the wish & advice of yourself & Miss Sotheby, it went to my heart & doubled the pain I felt in not complying with it. My reasons which I stated to him, he has no doubt mentioned to you, so I shall say nothing further on that subject. — But allow me to thank you most heartily for your kind & friendly concern on my account; for I know it is your fears that I may by the intended publication provoke unpleasant attacks and injure my own peace which chiefly causes your anxiety. But do not my kind friends be uneasy on this score! I do not think I shall be severely attacked, and at my age such things are felt, or ought to be so, like the pattering of a hail shower on ones back (not face) when one has got to the last steps of a journey and is about to cross the threshold of ones own home. Be of good cheer therefore, and that (and that) you have been so kindly interested in me will always be a grateful thought to my heart whatever may betide. —

My Sister unites with me in kind regards to yourself & Daughters & to M<u>rs</u> Hans Sotheby who I understand is in Town. I hope M<u>r</u> Sotheby got well home on monday. He scarcely had time to rest from his fatigue with us, and we could not much press his remaining longer, as we were to dine with M<u>rs</u> Hoare[89] and her carriage was to call & fetch us at a certain hour. We expect two Ladies from Scotland on friday to stay with us for a short time and when they are gone we hope to be for a little while in Cavendish Sq<u>re</u> and one of the first houses we call at will be 13 L G St: ——

Believe me
My dear M<u>rs</u> Sotheby with much esteem & regard
very gratefully yours
J Baillie

Hampstead
Wednesday morning

---

89. Samuel Hoare, who married Louisa Gurney, was Lady Byron's banker, and Baillie was a close friend of his family. Children she mentions include Jane, Joseph and several others.

HB.ix-26 (Address: Miss Sotheby / Fair Mead Lodge / High Beech / Essex--postmarked 1832)

Hampstead saturday August 25 [1832]

My dear Miss Sotheby,

It is better than a fortnight since Mrs Baillie, my Sister & I returned from the Isle of Wight and I think our kind friends in Fair mead Lodge will not be ill pleased to hear something about us. I have the pleasure to tell you that we have all been better & felt ourselves stronger during our stay there, the good effects of which we still carry about with us, and that we enjoyed ourselves under the roof of our very kind Host & Hostess the Milligans, and had the satisfaction of leaving them & their Girl, who must no longer be called a <u>little Girl</u>, well. Their house is in a very private watering place called Bembrige, delightfully situated on a height, commanding a cheerful open sea view which was alway[s] calling on our attention to mark the progress & varying appearances of vessels moving with their white sails to & fro, from the stately men of war to the little graceful fishing boats; a pleasing & animating sight. We were five weeks on the Island; Mrs B. remained all that time with her Daughter, and I should gladly have remained in the same good quarters, but as my Sister had never been there before, I wished her to see the back of the Island with its famous Under Cliff & fairy cottages, so we set forth by ourselves, and took our first station at Shanklin, where we spent six days in a small country Inn very comfortably. I need not tell you of our daily visits to the Chine, walking on the cliffs, sitting on the beach &c &c. for I suppose you have been at the Place and can guess well enough what two single women with time enough on their hands & no one to control them would do there, even though the stifness of old age did somewhat hamper them. Our next station was a beautiful place called the Rock-spring Hotel at Niton, where we were two days and saw the whole of the under Cliff to its termination; and from a high point of land near it, the whole coast to the wester[n]most tongue of land, scalloped out & in with bright borders of amber coloured sand & green herbs or sea weed, like the edges of a Lady's petticoat. Having had enough of the sea cost, we struck into the interior, saw Carrisbrook [Carisbrooke] Castle, slept one night in Newport and the next morning returned to our friends at Bembridge, by a fine lofty road, lately made over Areton downs, which shewed us all the richest part of the country with its Towns, wood & village farms & the sea on either side like a panorama.

And what do you think of our good luck after all this to have the Miss Fanshaws here for our neighbours? Indeed we consider it as very lucky for us, and I hope it will prove so to them by improving the health of dear Cathrine. They have got an excellent house with which they seem quite satisfied. They took possession on thursday evening, and I have not yet seen their Invalid who was in bed yesterday, when I called with rheumatism. Mrs Baillie came to us yesterday to stay while her son is in Gloucester, and this makes our home at present all that we could wish. —— Now my story is told, and I have a right to ask some account of you & yours. Give my love to your Father & Mother; I hope they are both well. And how does your Sister do & Mrs Hans & little Willy? I hope you have, including yourself, a favorable report to give of all. I wish we could see some of you here, now that your friends the Fanshaws are of our community. If you can tell me any thing of the Dacres I should be glad to have it. Lady D. seemed in her last letter to me some time after Mr Ogle's death, very much disheartened. I hope the Cholera keeps aloof from your immediate neighbourhood. A Gentleman in the lower part of Hampstead died of it last week but there has been as yet no other instance of that dire desease, though every one taken ill with a common bilious attack thinks it is the Cholera, and we have alarms of that kind every day.[90] ———

My two companions unite with me in all kind wishes to your family Circle. May a kind providence watch over you! These are times to make one think of friends wherever they are. Hoping then to hear from you soon, I remain my dear Miss Sotheby

affectionately yours   J Baillie

PS This ought to have gone by to days post but visitors have prevented

J: Baillie

PS By missing saturday's post I have received Mrs Sotheby's very kind note before this was sealed. My Sister & I return many thanks for her invitation which we should gladly have accepted, but as we expected friends to come to us the end of this week & Mrs Baillie to return to us again when they go, it is out of our power. Pray tell her this, and say how we regret it. — The Fanshaws are well, Cathrine excepted who is however better and much pleased with their present home. ——

---

90. The first world-wide epidemic of cholera, with its vibrio attacking the intestines through contaminated food or water, began in 1817 in India and spread to Russia and western Europe. England was invaded in 1831, with approximately 50,000 deaths resulting throughout the British Isles. Four other pandemics during the 19th century showed similar characteristics (see Sir Macfarlane Burnet, *Natural History of Infectious Disease*, 3rd ed. [Cambridge: Cambridge University Press, 1962], 331-32).

HB.ix-33 (No address or postmark)

Hampstead July 3<u>d</u> [after 1835]

My dear Miss Sotheby

It was very kind in you to write a second note or letter, and I thank you too for your friendly enquiries after us. It is pleasant to find that we are not <u>out of sight out of mind</u> with you. Indeed I gratefully feel that you & your Sister continue to me as beseems your Father's daughters, and there is a soothing comfort in it. —— I have a very good account to give of myself, but my Sister is sadly teased with her stomach, and her strength seems considerably diminished this last half year. Thank God! her spirits are good and she does not repine. We have great comfort in William & his Wife &c being so near us, and meet them some way or other every day.[91] M<u>rs</u> Baillie will come to us next monday, and then we shall be a family of harmony altogether. ——— We congratulate you on your Cousin's marriage which promises so well and will, I trust, fulfil its promise. Such a wedding is a very pleasant remedy for your Sister's indisposition and will be, I hope, an effectual one. We are sorry to learn that she had beforehand suffered so much from fever & Influenza.

How kind you have been in calling upon M<u>rs</u> Ross! We thank you for it sincerely. We are glad to hear that her spirits appear good and that she is about changing her place of abode for a pleasanter situation. Though it may not be a fashionable place, if well aired & cheerful, a sober Inmate, a little past the heyday of her youth, may be very well pleased with it. I wish she could hear of such a one. I have taken the liberty of inclosing a letter for her; and I should be much obliged to your Aunt if she would allow her Servant to carry it when he is going to that part of Bath at any rate. ——— As to your enquiry about poor M<u>rs</u> H. Palmer's death & the bereft friends belonging to her, I have scarcely any answer to give, for we have not seen M<u>rs</u> Baillie nor M<u>rs</u> Cockerel for some time. If you do not already know it you will be grieved to hear that M<u>r</u> Palmer has also lost a Daughter. ——— I can tell you something of Lady Dacre, for we have seen her. She came here one morning about a fortnight since, and it was evidently a great effort for her to see us. Her face tells the sad story of her bereavement very sensible. We talked about serious things but not directly on the subject most interesting & present to our minds. Whether this was wise or not, I am very doubtful, but it was an implied agreement before we met that the deep core of her wound was not to be touched. Yet she is

---

91. William Hunter Baillie, (1797-1894) the only son of Matthew and Sophia Baillie, graduated from Oxford, married Henrietta Duff in 1835, lived many years in Hampstead, moved to Richmond and later back to Upper Harley Street in Joanna's last years. They were the parents of 8 children.

determined to exert herself to the utmost for her husband's sake and the children her Daughter has left, and I daresay she will do it nobly. May God grant her strength, and she will in time be cheered in doing her duty with the consciousness that she is doing (doing) it. She speaks of Mr Sullivan in the very highest terms & most affectionately. We have had with us to day a Lady who brought letters of introduction to her from America, but she was not able to see her and begged Lord Dacre to pay her some attention in her stead which of course he will do. This Lady is Miss Sedgwick who is reckoned at present their first female Author in America,[92] some of whose works you have probably read. She has been twice here, and I met her & her family at a very pleasant breakfast given last week at Mr Harness's[93] where there were many blues[94] most of them unknown to me. Mr Milman[95] was the only person there I could call an acquaintance, towards the end of the party, Miss Jane Porter[96] appeared

---

92. Catharine Maria Sedgwick (1789-1867) was one of the first authors to draw from American life for material for fiction. Many of her works possessed a strong moral purpose, endeavoring to render wholesome living and unaffected goodness attractive. *Redwood* (1824), while conventionally romantic in plot, relied on a simple home life for backdrop. One of the most popular writers of her time, Hawthorne called her "our most truthful novelist" (*DAB*, VIII:547-48).

93. William Harness (1790-1869), writer and Anglican minister, is best known for his eight-volume *The Dramatic Works of William Shakespeare* (1825), followed by *Literary Remains of Catharine Maria Fanshawe, Life of Mary Russell Mitford*, etc. Intimate friends included Baillie, Lord Byron, Crabbe, Southey, Wordsworth and others of the same circle (*DNB*, VIII:1300, and Lambertson).

94. bluestocking: The "acceptance of women into intellectual life was both manifested and promoted by the Bluestockings, a group of literary minded women-- and men--who formed around the wealthy Elizabeth Montague during the 1750s and 1760s." Their most specific aim was to bring men and women together socially for the purpose of conversation, which amounted to introducing them to each other as equals (Katharine M. Rogers and William McCarthy, eds. *The Meridian Anthology of Early Women Writers* [New York: Meridian, 1987], xviii). The society continued well into the 19th century.

95. Henry Hart Milman, (1796-1868) Dean of St. Paul's and Oxford Professor of Poetry, was the most distinguished ecclesiastical historian of his day and a close friend of Lockhart who said, however, that his friend "ought never to have been a poet." Scott praised his *The Fall of Jerusalem* (1820), but Byron attacked him in *Don Juan*. He married Mary Anne Cockell in 1824, with whom he had 4 sons. Milman contributed regularly to the *Quarterly Review* and produced many literary and historical works, including *The Martyr of Antioch* (1822), *Belshazzar* (1822), *History of the Jews* (1829), and translations of Horace (*DLB*, 96:236-42).

96. Author Jane Porter (1776-1850) was a childhood friend of Walter Scott in Edinburgh but moved to London in 1803 where she met Hannah More and Laetitia Barbauld. Her works include romance *Thaddeus of Warsaw* (4 vols., 1804), the very successful novel *The Scottish Chiefs* (5 vols., 1810), drama *Switzerland*, acted at Drury Lane in 1819, and *Sir Edward Seaward's Narrative of his Shipwreck and*

among us. Miss Sedgwick has come to England with her Brother, who is recovered but very imperfectly from a frightful stroke of Paralysis which seized him in the middle of a speech at the bar (for he is a Barrister and was practising his profession successfully), her Sister in law (his wife) and three young Ladies; a party of six. They brought letters to me from D[r] Channing & the Nortons.[97] She is or has been rather a good looking woman some what sunburnt though naturally fair with a quantity of fair ringlet[s] hanging about her face otherwise gravely dress'd and seems between forty & fifty. She is, I am told an excellent woman who never thinks of her own pleasure or convenience but is devoted to benevolent & friendly actions. She seems a woman too of good plain sense and that will make her benevolence turn to better account. Her late books have been written for the improvement of the lower & middling ranks in her own country, and have been successful. The Americans I am told think themselves much obliged to her. She & her large party leave England, I believe next week for the German Baths and proceed before winter to Italy. ――― I shall write to Lady Dacre and remember you to her as you desire and as she will have satisfaction in knowing.

My Sister sends you her love and accept of mine also. It is given with hearty & grateful good will, and should therefore be acceptable

Most truly yours
    J Baillie

---

consequent Discovery of certain Islands in the Caribbean Sea (3 vols., 1831) (*DNB*, XVI:182-84). Baillie acknowledged her indebtedness to Porter's *Scottish Chiefs* when writing her *Wallace* in *Metrical Legends*, and Scott, given credit for developing the historical novel, might surely be indebted to Porter as well.

97. William Ellery Channing (1780-1842) was ordained to the ministry in 1803, pastored the Federal Street Church in Boston from 1805-42, and became a leader in the Unitarian movement by his argument against Calvinism. He organized the Berry Street conference of liberal ministers in 1820 and the American Unitarian Association in 1825. Interested in Jeffersonian politics and in literature, he influenced Emerson and Thoreau, supported abolition, temperance and peace. He authored such works as *Remarks on the Character and Writings of John Milton* (1826), *Analysis of the Life and Character of Napoleon Bonaparte* (1828), *The Importance and Means of a National Literature*, and his *Works*, which went through 20 editions in England and America. Channing was an intimate friend of Baillie, who kept him up with literary happenings in Britain and reported on the success of his work there. She informed him of Byron's death and later questioned him about "that 'rake' Tom Moore." See Arthur R. Brown, *A Biography of William Ellery Channing: Always Young for Liberty* (Syracuse, N. Y.: Syracuse University Press, 1956), 161-62. Baillie was particularly impressed with Channing's Dudleian lecture of 1821 on "The Evidences of Christianity"; see David P. Edgell's *William Ellery Channing, An Intellectual Portrait* (Boston: Beacon Press, 1955), 202, and introduction and letters to Dr. Andrews Norton (Volume 2).

HB.ix-31 (No address or postmark--before 1824?)
My dear Sir,

I received on Sunday from the Author M<u>rs</u> Heman's new volume which is rich in high-toned beautiful poetry, and of the longer pieces I particularly admire that which she stiles "the last of the Constantines.["] Had it been in a dramatic form, she would as you said, have run me very hard and perhaps more than that. But fortunately for me she has shaped it into a poem in the Spencerian measure, and now it belongs to Lord Byron to be jealous of her not me. Her Dramatic poem, The Siege of Valencia, is finely written and the songs or old Spanish (supposed to be) ballads &c are excellent. But there is a short thing at the end of all called the voice of Spring which is my great favorite and is quite exquisite. I think there can be no doubt that this publication will be of great advantage to her worldly affairs as well as her reputation, high as that was already.[98] --
If the book is published you already possess it; but if the author's gift-copies be sent out a few days before, I have perhaps still the advantage of you. —

As you have no objection to a walk to Hampstead in fine weather, pray bend your walk that way next friday morning, and be with us as soon after one o'clock as may be convenient, you will find, I hope, a friend or two with us whom you may like to meet.

— Give my kindest regards to M<u>rs</u> Sotheby & your daughters. I suppose you now begin to think of the Forest.

ever truly yours
J Baillie
Hampstead tuesday June 24<u>th</u>

---

98. Felicia Hemans (1795-1835), poet, hymn writer and essayist, published many works, among them, Poems (1808), The Restoration of Works of Art in Italy (1816), Modern Greece (1817), Hymns for Childhood (1827), Records of Women (1828), National Lyrics and Songs for Music (1834), etc. Educated by her mother, her first book of poetry appeared when she was only 15. She married Captain Alfred Hemans, an Irishman serving in the Royal Welsh Fusiliers with her brother, and bore five sons. Her marriage ended after the birth of her fifth son (~1818), and her husband departed for Rome. Hemans continued to publish and tried playwrighting with Vespers of Palermo, performed with some success at Covent Garden and Edinburgh. After the death of her mother in 1827 she moved near Liverpool and then to Dublin in 1831. She was introduced to Sir Walter Scott in 1829. Hemans often contributed to the Edinburgh Monthly Magazine and Blackwood's and is said to owe more to the 18th century for her style than to her contemporaries (Todd, 327-28). Though Baillie writes to and about Felicia Hemans, they apparently never met (see her letter No. 12 dated 1835 to Dr. Andrews Norton); Hemans, however, contributed "Belshazzar's Feast" to Baillie's 1823 A Collection of Poems. Hemans' The Siege of Valencia; A Dramatic Poem and The Last Constantine: with Other Poems appeared in 1823.

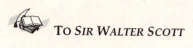

5

To *Sir Walter Scott*

(1808-1829)

Walter Scott was born 15 August 1771 to middle-class Scottish parents, his father a lawyer and his mother the daughter of a medical professor; but his line of ancestry reached back to Scott of Harden, a famous hero in the Border warfare.[1] His father, Walter Scott, was the first of his family to adopt a city life; he was a strict Calvinist, studied church history, and was staunch to Scottish prejudices. Walter married Anne Rutherford in April 1758, who bore twelve children, six dying in infancy. Surviving were Robert, John, Anne, Walter, Thomas and Daniel. Suffering an attack of infantile paralysis at the age of two, Walter was left permanently lame and spent his childhood at his grandfather's farm in the border region of Scotland, where he was immersed in romantic songs and tales of his clan. By the time he was well enough to attend high school, he had acquired a store of knowledge about Scottish history and developed a gift for storytelling. After Edinburgh High School (1779-83) he entered Edinburgh University (1783-86) and was apprenticed to his father's law office. Admitted to the bar in 1792, he was active in debating societies and a member of the Edinburgh volunteer cavalry, but he spent his holidays scouring the country for ballads and relics of antiquity seasoned with imaginative tales. Despite his literary interests, however, he never completely relinquished his legal profession.

Scott began his literary career with the anonymous publication of *The Chase* and *William and Helen* in 1796, translated from German. Falling in love with Williamina Belsches, he proposed marriage at this time, but she refused; and on Christmas Eve 1797 he married Charlotte Carpenter, the daughter of a French royalist refugee. They moved to Lasswade, about

---

1. For brevity's sake this information comes from general sources which include the *DNB*, XVII:1018-43, and Russell Noyes, ed., *English Romantic Poetry and Prose* (New York: Oxford University Press, 1956), 514-20. More specific information, however, comes from the following biographical sources: Edgar Johnson, *Sir Walter Scott: The Great Unknown*, 2 vols. (New York: Macmillan, 1970) and John Gibson Lockhart, *Memoirs of the Life of Sir Walter Scott, Bart.*, 7 vols. (Edinburgh: Cadell, 1838). In addition *The Letters of Sir Walter Scott*, ed. H. J. C. Grierson, 12 vols. (London: Constable, 1936) are invaluable, providing his letters to Joanna Baillie and some excerpts from her own responses.

six miles from Edinburgh, where he was appointed Sheriff of Selkirkshire, and in 1802 moved to 39 Castle Street, a home they maintained while they also owned Abbotsford. Their oldest daughter Charlotte Sophia (later Mrs. John Lockhart) was born in 1799 (d. 1837); their son Walter was born in 1801 (d. 1847); Anne, who remained unmarried, followed in 1803 (d. 1833); and their last son Charles was born in 1805 (d. 1841).

Between 1801 and 1805 Scott started to write seriously, entering into a secret business partnership with publisher James Ballantyne which eventually led to the financial ruin of all involved. In 1809 he promoted the founding of the Tory *Quarterly Review* and in 1812 moved to a cottage at Abbotsford on the Tweed, with plans to build a castle and revive the ways of a feudal laird. On the brink of financial disaster in 1813, Scott was rescued by publisher Constable who had read the opening chapters of *Waverley* begun earlier; well aware he was eclipsed by Byron as the poet of the age, Scott declined the offer of laureateship, recommending Southey to the position. But when "Scott gave up verse for prose and sat down to finish *Waverley* in 1814," explains Russell Noyes, "he had already proved himself a master of dramatic narrative, scenic painting, and the delineation of a wide variety of characters and situations."[2] By 1819 Scott had reached the height of his popularity as a novelist, admired both by his fellow countrymen and a universal audience. The first major writer to unite great historical events with the lives of ordinary people, Scott focused on the virtues of morality and self-sacrifice and was so popular that almost every writer of his time aspired to produce at least one work in this historical form. In 1820 he was made a baronet.

Following the great commercial crash of 1825, however, partly because of his own borrowing and partly through the mismanagement of his publishing partner James Ballantyne, Scott found himself with Ballantyne and Constable involved in financial ruin, personally responsible for £130,000. In an effort to save Abbotsford for his family, he tried desperately to clear this enormous debt by writing; and while successful, the stressful effort probably shortened his life. His wife died the following year (1826), and in 1830 Scott suffered a stroke of apoplexy. In failing health, he died 21 September 1832 at Abbotsford and was buried at Dryburgh Abbey. Commissioned in August 1846, Edinburgh's Scott memorial, designed by George Kemp with a statue designed by Sir John Steele, is itself a testament to his popularity and influence.

---

2. Noyes, 517.

Because Scott's literary achievements are so copious, only major contributions are listed below for reference. Baillie mentions many of his works in her letters.

1801　*Glenfinlas* and *The Eve of St. John* for John Lewis's *Tales of Wonder*

1802　*Minstrelsy of the Scottish Border*

1805　*The Lay of the Last Minstrel*

1806　*Ballads and Lyrical Pieces*

1808　*The Works of Dryden* and *Marmion*

1810　*The Lady of the Lake*

1813　*The Bridal of Triermain* and *Rokeby*

1814　*Waverley* and *Works of Swift*

1815　*Guy Mannering* and *The Lord of the Isles*

1816　*Paul's Letters to his Kinsfolk, The Antiquary, The Black Dwarf* and *Old Mortality*

1817　*Rob Roy* and *Harold the Dauntless*

1818　*The Heart of Midlothian*

1819　*The Bride of Lammermoor, The Legend of Montrose* and *Ivanhoe*

1820　*The Monastery* and *The Abbot*

1821　*Kenilworth* and *The Pirate*

1822　*The Fortunes of Nigel*

1823　*Peveril of the Peak, Quentin Durward* and *St. Ronan's Well*

1824　*Redgauntlet*

1825　*Tales of the Crusaders, The Betrothed, The Talisman* and began his *Journal*

1826　*Woodstock*

1827　*Chronicles of the Canongate* and *The Life of Napoleon Buonaparte*

1828　*The Fair Maid of Perth* and *Tales of a Grandfather*

1829　*Anne of Geierstein*

1831　*Count Robert of Paris* and *Castle Dangerous*

Joanna Baillie was introduced to Scott by William Sotheby in 1806 and first visited Scott in Edinburgh in 1808, after which Scott told Charles Kirkpatrick Sharpe, "Miss Baillie is the only *writing* lady with whose manners in society I have been very much delighted. But she is simplicity itself, and most of them whom I have seen were the very cream of affectation."[3] Scott admired her plays immensely, contributed *Mac Duff's Cross* to her 1823 collection of poetry, had a special brooch made for her, and provided unfailing encouragement to her literary endeavors, as she also inspired him.[4] She presented him with a lock of Charles I's hair, crafted a coin purse for him, and provided him with critical insight about his and others' works. To say that Baillie cherished Scott more than any other of her friends is to point out the obvious, for her letters to him are intimate, humorous, critical and sensitive, exhibiting a tone unlike any she takes with other correspondents. But her letters are not all praise, for not only does she tell him candidly what she finds lacking in his works, in one of the finest letters of the collection (3888 ff.37-39) she also attacks him vehemently for his praise of Lord Byron in the *Quarterly Review* after the poet's ill treatment of her close friend Lady Byron; so, while Baillie admired Scott exceedingly, her admiration was not blinding. Many of Scott's journal entries likewise reveal his admiration for her. And contrary to Margaret Carhart's analysis that Scott's last journal entry about his friend and her publication of *View of the General Tenour of the New Testament* (1831) shows his indignation toward her, Scott seems, instead, genuinely concerned that she might be ill-thought of by others; the two old friends met for the last time in the autumn of 1831.[5]

---

3. Johnson, 286.

4. See Scott's journal entry of 4 December 1827, for example, written as he contemplates his *Fair Maid of Perth*:

> Miss Baillie has made the Ethling [Ethwald] a coward by temperament and a heroe when touchd [*sic*] by filial affection. Suppose a man's nerves supported by feelings of honour or say by the spur of jealousy supporting him against constitutional timidity to a certain point then suddenly giving way — I think some thing tragic might be produced. James Ballantyne's criticism is too much moulded upon the general tast[e] of novels to admit (I fear) this species or reasoning. But what can one do? I am hard up as far as imagination is concerned yet the world calls for Novelty. Well — I'll try my brave coward or cowardly brave man.

See W. E. K. Anderson, ed., *The Journal of Sir Walter Scott* (Oxford: Clarendon, 1972), 390.

5. Scott writes on 17 May 1831:

> I wrote and rode as usual and had the pleasure of Miss Ferrier's company in my family hours which was a great satisfaction; she has certainly less affec[ta]tion than any female I have know [who] has stood so high, even Joanna Baillie hardly excepted. By the way She has entered on the Socinian controversy [for] which I am very sorry. She has published a number of texts on which she conceives the controversy to rest but it escapes her that she can only quote them through a translation. I am sorry this gifted woman is hardly doing herself justice and doing what is not required at her hands. Mr. Laidlaw of course thinks it the finest thing in the world. (Anderson, 655)

See postscript of letter 51 to Margaret Holford Hodson, 11 November 1831, Volume 2.

Unfortunately, not all can be known about their relationship, for in a letter to Anne Elliott dated 13 November 1832, Baillie reveals,

> We went one morning to see poor Mrs Lockhart, who was kind & confidential, and in a natural state of sorrow, mixed with great thankfulness that her Father was released from much suffering. The very end, however, thank God! was easy. Since we returned home, I have been employed in reading over all his letters to me; and they will all (except about 20 which I have reserved or burnt) be put into Mr Lockhart's hands to use as he thinks fit.

To do Baillie's letters to Scott justice, one should read them in conjunction with H. J. C. Grierson's twelve-volume edition which includes Scott's letters to Baillie. I have cited many of those letters herein and quoted from some, but, unfortunately, it is not feasible to provide in full the other side of the correspondence.

Except for one letter from Edinburgh University, the following letters to Sir Walter Scott, two to Lady Scott and one to Miss Scott, are transcribed herein by generous permission of the National Library of Scotland, Edinburgh:

3876 ff.48-49 (No address or postmark, NLS dates 1808)

[1808?]

Dear Sir,

We are very much obliged to you & Mrs Scott for offering to alter the day when we are to have the honour of dining with you; but we had no thoughts of seeing Mrs Siddons on Saturday and will therefore stick to our first agreement if equally agreeable to you.[6] Miss Maxwell is sorry she is engaged and cannot have the honour of waiting upon you & Mrs Scott. If however, <u>you</u> have any idea of going to see Mrs Siddons on Saturday, make no scruple at all in changing the day, and we will come to you on Sunday, tho' that is a day in which, generally speaking, we are not fond of visiting; for I have just been reading Marmion,[7] and I am quite in the humour to do every thing you desire me to do, short of a very great <u>fault</u>. Indeed you have made me a very proud woman! and I don't know how to express my thanks to you.— I have gone thro' the Poem with unabaiting [sic] delight. Inriched throughout with so much exquisite description of inanimate objects, and characteristic sketches of human beings, & natural & touching sentiments it will for ages to come be the common inmate of Palace & Cottage; and very long may you — even all the days of your life, enjoy unobliged the honours you have so fairly won! As for myself – I must get me back to Hampstead again, and try, both for your credit & my own, to do something better than I have yet done.

My Sister joins me in best respects to Mrs Scott, who, with all your <u>Imps</u> I hope to see soon and with much regard believe me dear Sir

your obliged & obedient

J Baillie

S: Castle St:

Tuesday morning

---

6. Sarah Siddons (1755-1831), actress and friend of Baillie, achieved celebrity under Garrick's management at Drury Lane, giving her farewell performance as Lady Macbeth at Covent Garden in 1812. Siddons had played the role of Jane in Baillie's *DeMonfort* in 1800 and after her retirement continued to give private readings.

7. The first 2,000 copies of Scott's *Marmion* appeared in February 1808; 6,000 more copies had been sold by the following May; two editions of 3,000 each followed in 1809 and 5,000 more in 1810. In 1811 9,000 more were issued, surpassing what the popular *Lay of the Last Minstrel* had sold in seven years (Johnson, 279).

PS. excuse my not answering your note last night. I was engaged with company rather ceremoniously.—

3876 ff.239-240 (Address: Walter Scott Esq[r] / N: Castle Street--no postmark, NLS dates 1808)

N: Castle St: Sunday
morning [1808?]

My dear Sir,

A small spark of praise from you has immediately set fire to a very worthy if not a great poet of our neighbourhood at Hampstead, who, upon learning from me that you had promised two of his sonnets (which I hope you remember I showed you on the way to Rosslyn [Roslin]) by return of post sent me the inclosed. The coppy [sic] of the sonnet, made, by desire, with my own <u>fair hands</u> I have kept to my own fair self, and you not only <u>may</u> but <u>must</u> keep the original. — The Poet who invites you to his humble Bower, gives that name to a very comfortable house upon Hampstead heath, where I am sure he would be proud & happy to see you.[8] — Forgive me for this intrusion and with best regards to M[rs] Scott, believe me, my dear Sir,

> your sincerely obliged
> J Baillie

3877 ff.3-4 (No address or postmark, NLS dates 1808)

Brown's Square April 4th [1808]

My dear Sir,

I am afraid before we leave Edin[r] I may have no opportunity of speaking to you, and therefore I write to you along with your manuscript, which I return with many thanks. I have read your Tragedy twice, and have been more pleased with it the second time than the first.[9] The story is very interesting, the writing forcible, and the characters of Rudiger &

---

8. Though Baillie does not identify this poet, I am inclined to believe it is her neighbor Edward Coxe, a topic of conversation for Scott and Baillie in many later letters.

9. Scott had for some time been working on his Gothic melodrama *The House of Aspen*, based on Weber's *Der Heilige Vehme*. Around 1801 it was rejected by Kemble for production at Drury Lane. Scott, too, realized its flaws and later wrote,

> At one time I certainly thought, with my friends, that it might have ranked well enough by the side of the Castle Spectre, Bluebeard, and the other drum and trumphet [sic] exhibitions of the day; but [Baillie's] *Plays of the Passions* have put me entirely out of conceit with my Germanized brat; and should I ever again attempt dramatic composition I would endeavor after the genuine old English model.

(qtd. in Johnson, 186)

George – the dignity of the one & the spirit of the other, well imagined & contrasted. The opening of the piece pleased me very much, and so did that scene, which is the most important one in the whole play, between the Mother & her son when he wants to discover whether she is really guilty or not, tho' perhaps it is rather under-written (if I may use the phrase) from a fear of being extravagant. The scene in the chapel I was also struck with, when the Lady is led off by the figure in black coming from behind her husband's tomb; and the last scene is finely imagined, particularly the first part of it, when George discovers himself, and the man of four score is appointed to be his executioner.— There is in the whole Play sufficient knowledge of Nature and force of expression to make your friends look forward with a very pleasing hope to (to) what may hereafter follow, when you shall write on a better dramatic plan, and allow your delightful imagination more liberally to enrich the work. The dry bare German way of writing suits a poor Poet, but not a rich one. — If you ever make any use of this piece, I would have you to disencumber your plot of some things that might easily be spared, and bring more into view the character of George, which you have so justly imagined, while he is in the terrible state of suspence in regard to his Mother's guilt. It is a pity that all this should be put over in one scene when the audience might be kept in a state of the most agitating suspense that would wonderfully heighten the effect of the whole Play. — But I hope some time or other to have an opportunity of speaking to you of these matters, so I shall only at present return you a great many thanks for the confidence you have put in me and for the high gratification I have had in reading the House of Aspen.

Do you know! I have a Tragedy at home in which a Wife discovers the guilt of her Husband, by the dying confession of a servant who was present at the crime, and I have scenes afterwards between her & the husband in which she tries to discover whether he is really guilty or not.[10] Don't after this think, if you should see it, that I have borrowed the idea from you; it has been long written and is now in the hands of Mrs Baillie; and if you should ever work up this part of your piece more fully, it may be an amusement to us some time or other to compare the two plays in this respect together. I will not let you beat me on my own ground if I can help it; but, if it must be so, I will less grudgingly yield the victory to you than any other Poet I know of. —

With kind wishes to Mrs Scott & the young Laird of Glenschee [Glenshee], & every living being that belongs to you, I remain, my dear sir, your sincere & obliged

     J Baillie

---

10. See Baillie's tragedy *The Separation*.

3877 ff.5-7 (Address: Walter Scott Esq[r] / N: Castle Street--no postmark)

[1808?]

I send you, my dear Sir, a letter which I received yesterday from Struthers.[11] I gave him, as you will perceive, an opinion different from yours, after having talked over the matter with a friend here, and taking into consideration the probability of his getting a considerable subscription amongst the Antiburghers[12] to which he belongs, but he prefers yours, and probably he is right. I hope you will be able to prevail on M[r] Constable to give him 30 or 40 copies for himself,[13] and then he will be compleatly satisfied, and both him & I will feel ourselves very much endebted to your goodness.——

I hope to see you before we leave Town, and should have liked to have gone over to Castle St: this morning to have had an early chance of finding you & M[rs] Scott at home, but a vile cold makes it prudent for me to keep the house as much as possible. On our return from Gladsmuir where we go to morrow, we shall hope to see you once more, and thank you before we go for all the kind attention we have received from M[rs] Scott & you since our stay in Edin[r][,] attentions which we shall long remember with pleasure as one of the most flattering & agreeable circumstances of our visit here. —— I

---

11. John Struthers (1776-1853), Scottish poet, was born in Lanarkshire while Baillie's family were residents of Long Calderwood, and they read to him and played with him while he was a child. Struthers became a shoemaker in Glasgow but reading widely and writing considerably began to earn some literary reputation. He gave up his trade to become an editor for two different publishing firms, finally becoming librarian of Stirling's public library in Glasgow. His most popular publication was *The Poor Man's Sabbath* (1804) which went into 4 editions, followed by *The Peasant's Death* (1806), *The Winter Day* (1811) and *Poems, Moral and Religious* (1814) (*DNB*, XIX:63).

12. Antiburghers were a section of the Session Church in Scotland which held it unscriptural to take the Burgess Oath and in 1747 separated on this question from the other, or "Burgher," section; the two reunited in 1820 (*OED*).

13. Archibald Constable (1774-1827), Scottish publisher, set up his own shop on the north side of High Street, Edinburgh, in 1795 after several years of apprenticeship. His tendency to take risks and accept varied publications enabled him to transform the business of publishing. In 1802 the start of the *Edinburgh Review* saw his connection with Walter Scott, and he had a share with Messrs. Longman & Co. in the publication of *Lay of the Last Minstrel* (1805). In 1814 the first chapters of *Waverley* were shown to Constable, who detected the author and arranged to publish it by dividing the profits with Scott. On the advice of John Ballantyne, Scott afterwards sometimes deserted Constable for other publishers, but they remained friends. On the failure in 1826 of Hurst, Robinson, & Co., the London agents for Constable & Co., the latter firm became insolvent along with James Ballantyne & Co., consuming the investments of Scott along with them (*DNB*, IV:957-58).

hope you have safely received your manuscript which I gave to your servant with my own hand, and my billet-doux along with it.

    Truly & sincerely
      your obliged
        J Baillie

3877 ff.39-40 (Address: To Walter Scott / North Castle Street-- postmarked Glasgow 1808)

Gairbraid May 1st [1808]

My dear Sir,

    I am always well pleased to have a pretence for holding some intercourse with you, and yet upon the present occasion I would as lief have been excused, because I am ashamed to be still troubling you about our Bard Mr Struthers, after all you have so kindly done for him. I sent for him yesterday when I was in Glasgow, to shew him a small list of people who would take copies of his book, taking it for granted he had concluded his bargain with Constable and had got 30 or 25 copies to dispose of, but to my surprise & disappointment he told me Constable had never written to him at all. He then went to his Bookseller in Glasgow, where, letters for him often lie for some time neglected but found no such thing. Will you have the goodness to enquire about this? I am unwilling to think that Constable who is getting rich upon your labor would entirely neglect to write to Struthers after having promised to you to do so, and yet letters by the post very seldom miscarry.

    And now that I have done my business & asked my favour of you, let me enquire kindly how you do, and how Mrs Scott & all the children have been since I had the pleasure of seeing you. I was sorry to leave Edin^r without meeting you once more, but I regret it the less because I hope before the summer is past to see both you & Mrs Scott in London & Hampstead. How much my Sister's visit & mine to Edin^r was sweeten'd, and I may say brighten'd, by your kind & flattering attentions we shall never forget. Pray continue to remember us some times, and believe that with true & cordial good will we will often think of you. Farewell, my dear Sir! With esteem & regard I remain

    Sincerely yours
      J Baillie

PS. Mr Constable probably does not know Mr Struthers's address, which is, John Struthers, Moffat's Land, Rutherglen Loan,[14] Gorbals, Glasgow. My Sister & I will not leave this part of the country for 10 days or a fortnight, and our address is at Miss Graham's Gairbraid near Glasgow.

---

14. Loan: dial., lane or by-road (*OED*).

3877 ff.59-60 (Address: Walter Scott / North Castle Street / Edin[r] --
postmarked Glasgow 1808)

Gairbraid Sunday May 15th [1808]

My dear Sir,

You are really very good both to my Bard and to me. When you pluck
your crow with Constable, the feathers will go to line our poet's nest for
him, which is the best poke they can be put into; and if he is a wise poet
(which is not perhaps so rare a thing as the world is willing to imagine)
they will line it & keep it warm for many a day to come. I think the best
way M[r] Constable can make his peace with us after this great subject, is to
add a few more copies to those he is to allow M[r] Struthers to dispose of;
and as he has offered 25 or 30, let him give 30 or 35 and we will forgive
him freely. I saw M[r] Struthers yesterday, and he will send you his book &
manuscripts as soon as he can find a safe conveyance for them which he
hopes to do very soon.

I am glad to hear you have enjoyed the spring so much on your pastoral
banks and hope M[rs] Scott & you enjoyed your pilgrimage to the bonny . . .
Traquair,[15] where I would have given one of my ears (as they say) to have
gone with you. My Sister & I are to leave the place to morrow, and on
friday next will set our focus determinedly southward, hoping to get to the
Lakes by monday se'nnight. We are to take Lanarick & Garthland Craigs
on our way, so you see we do not forget the places you have praised. —

With all kind wishes to you & yours, and hoping to see you again
before many months go by, I remain, my dear Sir,

your sincerely obliged

J Baillie

3877 ff.97-98 (No address or postmark, NLS dates 1808)

Hampstead June 20th [1808]

My dear Madam,

When we parted from you in Edin[r], you were kind enough to say you
should be glad to hear from us when we got to London; and after the many
kind & friendly attentions we received from you & M[r] Scott there, we
cannot but believe that you are really interested in our welfare wherever
we are. I obey you then with pleasure, and am happy to be allowed to put
you both in mind of us. — We arrived here better than a fortnight ago,
after a very agreeable journey by the Lakes of Cumberland, where we spent
8 days with as much enjoyment as very indifferent rainy weather would

---

15. This passage is almost totally illegible because of fading. The ellipsis here
indicates unreadable words.

allow us to have, and had the pleasure of finding my Brother & our other friends as well as when we left them. After all our wanderings, pleasure as they have been, and endeared to us by the kindness of so many friends & old acquaintances who did really seem glad to see us in our native land, we are pleased to find ourselves under our own roof again, and to be for a while stationary & settled. This at least we shall be as soon as we can; for at present we are chiefly in Grosvenor St: at my Brother's,[16] our house here being in great confusion with Blacksmiths & housepainters &c. &c. and by no means a desirable abode, even for weary wanderers. We shall put ourselves in order as soon as may be, and please ourselves, while [we] are doing it, with the hopes of seeing you & Mr Scott in our house before the summer is at an end. I hope it is still your intention to come to London this season. I have many enquiries made to me after Mr Scott, and when he is to come to this country; and being very proud that he should be enquired after at me, and willing to appear to know as much as they suppose I do, I boldly tell them all that he is to be in London as soon as the sessions are up. ——— I hope this will find you & Mr Scott and all the children well. Well may you all be! and long may you continue so! My Sister begs leave to join me in offering you our best regards. Pray when you are at leisure have the goodness to let us hear from you, for we must not be forgotten by you. Farewell, my dear Madam, and believe me most truly

    your obliged ser^t

    J Baillie

3877 ff.158-61 (Address: Walter Scott Esqr / North Castle Street / Edin^r -- no postmark)

                              Hampstead Octr 22th 1808

My dear Sir

    If Mrs Scott has such a substitute as you to answer her letters, she must keep it a secret, else she will have letters from all corners of the country poured upon her, from Ladies who will be glad to say, they have received a letter the other day from Walter Scott. —— Pardon me for calling you by the plain ungarnished name by which you are called by every man woman

---

16. Dr. Matthew Baillie (1761-1823) was the only brother of Joanna and Agnes Baillie. Dr. Baillie had been trained by and had taken over the medical school of his uncle Dr. William Hunter and was a respected physician to George III. He married Sophia Denman (1771-1845), daughter of Dr. Thomas Denman and sister of Lord chief-justice Denman, in 1791 who became one of Joanna's closest friends; their two children were William Hunter (1797-1894) and Elizabeth Margaret (1794-1876). Agnes Baillie (1760-1861), mentioned below, was Joanna Baillie's only sister and constant companion. See Franco Crainz, *The Life and Works of Matthew Baillie* (Santa Palomba, Italy: PelitiAssociati, 1995).

& child in the kingdom, and will continue to be called for ages to come, tho' the king were to make a Duke of you. Thanks to you then for your letter, whether it came to me from your own good will or Mrs Scott's; and thank Mrs Scott for me for having so kindly put you upon the service. I am glad to find you have been enjoying yourselves in the country -- your own pastoral, modest, unassuming country, which has quite attraction (attraction) enough, while it is your country, to bring abundance of visitors; where [*sic*] it besides beautiful as the Lakes of Westmoreland, you would be obliged as the old tales say, to take the door on your back and go to push your fortune. -- My Sister & I were delighted with the Lakes, tho' the weather was not favourable; and we did see two of the Poets you mention viz. Wordsworth[17] & Southey,[18] who were both very civil & attentive to us. Wordsworth came over to Ambleside which was our head quarters for a little time, and spent a compleat day with us there at our Inn, and took us to see many of his favourate [*sic*] spots in the neighbourhood. He is a man with good strong abilities and a great power of words, but I fear there is that soreness in regard to the world & severity in his notions of mankind growing upon him that will prevent him from being so happy as he deserves to be, for he is I understand a very worthy man. We saw his sister too, whom you have probably heard of, and were very much pleased indeed with the sweetness & modesty of her appearance, the shortness of our visit at his house not permitting us to become better acquainted with her.[19] -- We drunk tea with Southey & his wife at Keswick in a magnificent library with as many gold-lettered books glancing on us from the shelves as would have honoured the Library of a Peer. He is an animated agreeable man, with a certain degree of the Beau or fine Gentleman in his appearance that amused without displeasing us. --

---

17. William Wordsworth (1770-1850) is mentioned by Baillie several times in various letters. Margaret Carhart writes that Baillie probably did not meet him until around 1812 (Margaret Carhart, *The Life and Work of Joanna Baillie. Yale Studies in English*, Vol. 64 [New Haven: Yale University Press, 1923], 23); but, in fact, Baillie describes the meeting here. Wordsworth provided JB with two sonnets ("Not love nor War" and "A volant tribe of bards") for her 1823 *Collection of Poems chiefly Manuscript and from Living Authors* whose profits were for charitable purposes.

18. Robert Southey, (1774-1843) a college friend of Coleridge and one of the "Lake Poets," was Poet Laureate from 1813-43, having accepted a pension five years earlier. Given the pronounced Jacobinism of his youth, several of Southey's contemporaries, especially Byron and Hazlitt, felt he had betrayed the principles of his youth in such acceptance (*OCEL*, 923). Southey moved to Greta Hall, Keswick, in 1803 so that his wife Edith Fricker Southey could be near her sister Sara Fricker Coleridge. This is apparently the first time Baillie meets Wordsworth and Southey.

19. Dorothy Wordsworth (1771-1855) spent her life in the Wordsworth household, accompanying the poet on his walks while her health allowed.

I am glad to find your visit to this part of the World is to take place at farthest early in the spring; and if you & Mrs Scott, if she comes with you, will honour us & gladden us with as much of your Company at Hampstead as you can spare, you will find us in the humour to do every thing in our power to make it agreeable to you. You shall read the play you so kindly inquire after as much as you please; and I will tell to you, what I do not tell to many people, all that I am about & all I intend to do. The spirit of Laziness has done more than put her finger upon me, as you hint, she has clapt the whole of her great flat hand upon my – not very broad shoulders, and I cannot shake my self loose for the life of me. I have not been Lazy in all respects, however, I have been like your Gothic King training my Collar my dogs to hold &c. and that makes my indolence in higher matters last so much longer. —— I do not in return for your kind enquiries ask you what you have been about, for all the world can tell me that wherever I go. The last information, however of that kind that I received pleased me not, therefore I do not believe it, and will not believe it tho' a man were to swear it unto me. It said that you were about to publish a Poem on the Battle of Banockburn, which is to be dedicated to Jeffry [sic].[20] Pray write me a few lines giving me leave to contradict this whenever I shall hear it, for to use a word of your friend Pitscotie,[21] I have been greatly comoved there at. I am not comoved that you should dedicate a work to Jeffry as Mr Jeffry; but greatly so that it should be supposed you would dedicate a work to any Reviewer whatever. Tell me then, for my peace of mind, that this is not so. Pray forgive me speaking to you in this manner! it is the language of love, not of presumption. I admire your genius so much that I feel myself as it were related to the man who has given me so much ~~pleasure~~ delight; and, being many years older than yourself, I take in my own fancy the place of an Elder Sister or Mother in regard to you, and am jealous over you with something of what St: Paul calls a Godly jealousie. Would not that you should dedicate a work to any Reviewer under heaven for all the money (could I afford to pay it) that you received for Marmion. ——

---

20. Francis Jeffrey (1773-1850) was a critic-journalist for his generation, producing some 200 review articles on literature and public issues of the day. No journalist was so influential. He was notorious for injuries to Wordsworth and his contemporaries, but he is said to have invented the review article and to have made criticism a profession (see Philip Flynn's *Francis Jeffrey* [Newark, Delaware: University of Delaware Press, 1978]). Sharing a similar Glasgow background with Baillie, he attacked her writing severely in 1812. *Marmion* was not dedicated to Jeffrey; furthermore, Jeffrey's condescending analysis for the *Edinburgh Review* reported its success would "be less than brilliant" (Johnson, 281).

21. This is probably early chronicler Robert Lindesay of Pitscottie whose work Scott read avidly.

Speaking of Marmion, let me tell you how much I am pleased to find it gaining ground in this country every day. When we came from Scotland I was surprised to find a general disposition in this country to prefer the Lay[22] before it; but this is not now the case, as far as I have opportunity of knowing, and its warmest admirers now can scarcely distinguish themselves in any company by their particular opinion. -- I had a letter while ago from your friend M[r] Graham[e] Author of the Sabbath,[23] informing me that he is going to take orders in the Church. He is very well fitted indeed for the profession he has chosen, and I wish he may meet with the preferment in it that he so well deserves. I fear, however, that he has but few connections amongst those who have preferment to bestow. O! if you who are beloved & caressed amongst the Great, could but help this modest Brother-Poet to a living, what a feather that would be in your bonnet! Try to do it like a good man! You have bugs enough rustling upon your head: how gracefully would such a plume as this nod beside them! -- The Author of the other Sabbath, I mean Struthers, is I am sure greatly endebted to you, and so of course am I. I hope he thanked you as he ought; I am sure he spoke very gratefully of his obligations to you when I saw him at Glasgow. You are really most liberal in your views for him amongst these you call the Saints. It will be a good field for him if he can get into their favour. --

I must now conclude this long letter — (for me this is a very long letter) with noticing the postscript of yours, where you exalt over the glorious change of affairs in Spain & speak of William Wallace[24] & the Cid Rodrigo. Alas! it came to my hands just as we received the news of our

22. *The Lay of the Last Minstrel* had been published in 1805.

23. James Grahame (1765-1811) was a Scottish poet born in Glasgow. He studied for the church and was admitted to the Society of Writers to the Signet in 1791. In 1809 he was ordained by the Bishop of Norwich and appointed curate of Shipton Moyne, Gloucestershire, but left to attend to family matters in 1810. He was an unsuccessful candidate for St. George's Chapel, Edinburgh, but was later appointed sub-curate of St. Margaret's, Durham, transferring to the curacy of Sedgefield in the same diocese. His poems were admired by Scott and attacked by Byron; works include *The Sabbath* (1804), *Birds of Scotland* (1806), *British Georgics* (1808) and *Poems on the Abolition of the Slave Trade* (1810) (*DNB*, VIII:366).

24. William Wallace (1272?-1305), Scottish general and patriot famed for his skill and almost superhuman strength, led a successful Scottish uprising against Edward I for which he was executed in 1305. In both English and Scottish records, Wallace stands as the chief champion of the Scottish nation in its struggle for independence and the chief enemy of Edward in his premature attempt to unite Britain under one scepter. It has been said that Wallace's natural hatred of the English and their king was the measure of the natural affection of his own people. See *DNB*, XX:563-72, and James A. Mackay's *William Wallace: brave heart* (Edinburgh and London: Mainstream, 1995).

military convention and it gave my nerves a twitch as I read it. But in spite of our mismanagement in the good cause, I hope it will at last be triumphant, and that Cids & Wallaces, & good sturdy Military Priests will still rise amongst them to break off the intolerable yoke that enthrals so many lands; and let Kings learn a lesson from this, as people had a lesson given to them in the French revolution. — My Sister & I have been reading __thy's translation of the Chronicles . . . the Cid,[25] and have been greatly amused & pleased with it.— Pray let us both join in offering our respects & best wishes to you & Mrs Scott. I hope this will find you & your children all well. — Shall I say again, excuse & forgive the liberties I have taken in this letter? So, I will not do you the wrong to repeat that apology which would look as if I were less than I really am your sincere friend & admirer

    J Baillie

3878 ff.78-79 (No address or postmark)

                                    Hampstead June 23^d 1809

My dear Sir,

    I hope this will find you & Mrs Scott well after your journey; enjoying your home & your children, and all the other comforts your own native place – your "own romantic Town" so richly bestows upon you. —— I thank you very heartily for the kind, friendly note I received from you before you left London, and might easily have done so before you set off; but I know too well what it is to be hurried — or as they say in this country <u>worried</u> – on the eve of a journey, to pester any friend of mine with a letter at that time, if it be not absolutely necessary. — I need scarcely tell you – indeed I cannot tell you how sensibly I feel the friendly interest you take in the success of my Play.[26] Your zeal in getting so immediately the drawing of a highland Lady's dress from Mrs Maclean and the tartans of the two clans, is like the happy eagerness of a school-boy who works with his whole heart & soul to get up his holy-day Drama. You are a happy man to retain

---

    25. The dash for first few letters of this word and the following ellipsis indicate a hole in the paper, but this must be Robert Southey's *The Chronicle of the Cid*.

    26. Her play is identified in the following letter as *The Family Legend*, published in Edinburgh by Ballantyne in 1810. Biographer Margaret Carhart quotes from one long published letter dated 19 October 1805 from Joanna to Dr. Matthew Baillie in which JB politely explains why she is rejecting Sir John Sinclair's (1754-1835) advice on writing tragedies adapted for stage effect (he offers her *On the Fall of Darius* to consider). She does, however, accept Sinclair's suggestion to write a play for charitable reasons and later produces *The Family Legend* in Edinburgh for the aid of an unnamed family. See Carhart, 24-25, and *The Correspondence of the Right Honourable Sir John Sinclair, Bart.*, 2 vols. (London: Henry Colburn and Richard Bentley, 1831), 167-70.

so long, when all the applause & attention of the world to spoil you is possible, such youthful alacrity. — After this very pleasing trait of your good & brotherly disposition towards me, you might have transmitted to me a whole bushel of criticism, and I should have received it kindly. I thank you then for Lady Louisa Stuart's note as well as your own,[27] and shall take an early opportunity of looking over the Play in reference to what she says of the character of Sir Hubert. If I have made him appear insensible to the wrongs of his Mistress, it is very faulty indeed, and must be rectified. Perhaps, however, if this is attended to, that through out the play the Clans men & not Maclean himself are represented in wishing to get rid of Helen, that she in telling her story would naturally throw the whole blame upon them, and that Sir Hubert had not like John of Lorne any previous dislike or prejudice against him, it will not appear so very objectionable. In regard to his going away and leaving his friends to fight it out with their enemies themselves, the enemy were to come to the Castle as peaceable visitors, few in number, therefore staying to assist them would have been a post of no danger and altogether useless. But do not think I am defending myself from an unwillingness to alter what I have written. If the character of Sir Hubert makes any thing of the same impression on yourself when you shall have the goodness to read it a second time that it has done upon her Ladyship, it is not right, and must be set to rights; tho' we must avoid having two people vehemently loud upon the stage about the same thing. — I feel myself very much obliged to Lady L: Stuart for her remark which is certainly a very plausable one and deserves to be considered, and very much flattered by the praise she bestows upon the piece. I have been taught to value her taste & opinion on these subjects, and do not feel at present any disposition to underrate my lesson. — You asked leave to show the play to your Friend Mr W. Erskin which I granted willingly,[28] as I shall be glad to have the benefit of his remarks upon it; and there is another Gentleman to whom I wish to have it shewn, both from the opinion I have of his taste, and because I feel that I

---

27. Lady Louisa Stuart was daughter of Lord Vere Bertie and wife of Sir Charles Stuart (1753-1801) (*DNB*, XIX:74). See NLS letter 931 No. 51 to Lockhart.

28. William Erskine, Lord Kinneder (1769-1822), became an intimate friend of Scott when the two young men began to study German together in the 1790s. It was Erskine who negotiated for Scott's translation of Burger's ballad "Lenore" in 1796, helping launch Scott's literary career; and Scott dedicated the 3rd Canto of *Marmion* to Erskine in 1808. Erskine became sheriff deputy of Orkney in 1809, and in 1814 Scott accompanied him and other friends on a voyage to the Orkney Islands. Lockhart credits Erskine with the critical estimate of the Waverley novels. In 1822 Erskine was promoted to the bench as Lord Kinneder but died shortly afterward under the stress of having been unjustly accused of "improper liaisons" (*DNB*, VI:864-65, and Johnson).

owe him this attention, viz. Mr Mackenzie the Man of Feeling.[29] -- I will say no more to you on this subject. Do for me what you think right, and desire me freely at all times to do for myself what you think right, and you shall both find me thankful & docile. — That I may leave you at the conclusion of this letter with a good & reasonable impression of me, be it known to you that I expect no answer to it. Your time is too precious to be taken up writing letters unnecessarily, and I shall soon learn, I hope, by other means that you have got safe to Scotland. -- My Sister joins me in kind regard to Mrs Scott & yourself. Believe me always, my dear Sir,

your truly sincere & obliged

J Baillie

3878 ff.180-84 (Address: Walter Scott Esq / North Castle Street / Edinburgh--postmarked 1809)

Hampstead Octr 21st 1809

My dear Sir,

I have been wandering to & fro upon the face of the earth for these 3 months past, and did not receive either of your friendly & very kind letters one dated the 15$\underline{th}$ of August the other the 13th of Oct^r, till last night when I found them both lying on my table on my return to Hampstead. On going from home, my Sister & I desired the servants to forward to us to Devonshire only the general post letters, and as your first had some how or other come by the 3^d post, it was treated with no respect, but allowed to lie amongst the other London letters of no consequence, for which I am very sorry, and truly crave your pardon. -- I cannot express to you how much I am gratified & obliged by the warm-hearted, Brotherly interest you take in the success of my Family Legend. I entirely agree with you in the alterations you propose, and will set about making them forthwith, as far as I am able; tho' I shall have difficulty in doing it, from having no copy of the play by me to refer to, except the original rough copy, so blotted, & interlined, & different in many parts from the other, that I question whether I shall be able to unravel it. When I put the play into your hands, I thought I had another copy of it which Mrs Baillie was kind enough to write out for me; but drawers, & trunks, & even band-boxes have been searched in vain; it is no where to be found; I believe the Brownies or Fairies have taken it. What regards the Lover's character,

---

29. Henry Mackenzie (1745-1831), miscellaneous writer and novelist, was born in Edinburgh. His first sentimental novel entitled *The Man of Feeling* (1771), influenced by Sterne, appeared anonymously and was mistakenly attributed for a while to a Mr. Eccles, a clergyman of Bath. One of the earliest members of the Royal Society of Edinburgh, Mackenzie was a friend of Hume, Dr. Home, Davy and Scott (*DNB*, XII:594-96).

that he may have no blot, as you say, on his scutcheon,[30] I will contrive to alter myself, and I shall also try to shorten the Cavern Scene; but as for altering names & all the other improvements, I must beg that you, or Mr W. Erskin[e], (of whose approbation I am always very proud,) or any of your friends who may be willing to undertake the task, will have the goodness to make them for me. I shall be well pleased with all you may do or appoint to be done in this way, and shall thank you with all my heart.[31]

I feel myself very much obliged to Mr H. Siddons for his obliging readiness to receive the piece,[32] and make no doubt that he will do all, and perhaps more than I could wish to procure its success. Pray have the goodness to offer him my sincere acknowledgements. In regard to the unrighteous Mammon, we shall have no difficulties to overcome. You know for what purpose the play was originally written. The family it was meant to serve I am convinced never knew any thing of the matter, and probably do not now stand in need of it. I therefore think myself at liberty to dispose of it as I please. My pleasure then is, that Mr Siddons should, if the piece be successful, take to himself what you & he shall consider as a fair & reasonable profit, and if there be any overplus beyond this, that it should be laid out in purchasing any new scene or decoration for your little Theatre that you & he may wish to add to it. — I hope Mr S. will be at no great expense in getting it up, for that is a risk he ought not to run; and if it will not do without this, it is not worth bringing forward. Let no scenes be painted for it that will not do for other plays; nay I would even have the Laird of Maclean's philabegg[33] made up in such wise that it may afterwards serve, if need be, for Banquo or the Thane of Fife.[34] I recognized, some years ago, part of Rezenvelt's attire, in my poor De Monfort, on the Bastard Falconberg's back,[35] and it gave me great comfort to think that all the money laid out on that unfortunate play was not entirely lost. I am very prudent & economical myself, and I am always ready to recommend the same virtues to every body in whom I am at all interested. You will not suppose after this that I have any praise to bestow

---

30. scutcheon: obs., a shield or badge (*OED*).

31. See Edgar Johnson for alterations to the play (322-24).

32. Henry Siddons, who married actress Harriet Murray, was the eldest son of Sarah Siddons. He and Harriet managed the Edinburgh Theatre which suffered monetary losses early, but the turning point for the theatre came with its popular production in February 1819 of Scott's *Rob Roy*, with Mackay as the Bailie.

33. fillabeg: the kilt (*SND*).

34. Shakespeare's "Scottish" play, *Macbeth*.

35. This is probably Philip the Bastard, son of Sir Robert Faulconbridge, in Shakespeare's *The Life and Death of King John*.

on your magnificent proposal of building a Theatre that will cost £20,000. Large Theatres are a bane & pest to the Drama; and if the enlightened society of Edin^r has not good taste enouf to prevent itself from falling into this vulgarism, we are in a hopeless state indeed! As long as you are in this mind, I shall not be sorry at the poverty that confines you to your temporary house, like proud gentry who hamper themselves in a Cottage, because it is beneath their dignity to call any thing their house that is less than a Castle. --

You were very kind in wishing to see my Brother & Mrs Baillie when they were in Scotland, and I am sure it would have given them great pleasure. I fear, however their route did not lead them near Ashestiel, and they have not been thus gratified. They arrived in Town yesterday, and Agnes & I will hear the story of their travels to morrow. We have not yet seen them. I understand they return very much delighted with their visit to the Land of Lakes. My Brother has been very proud to shew his english Wife what kind people, & lofty mountains, & noble water falls there be in his native country. -- I have not yet seen our Friend Mr Coxe since our return,[36] but he wrote to me some time ago, being greatly delighted with two letters he had received from you, and above all with the beautiful little song you sent to Miss Coxe which I hope she will provide with music worthy of it. Indeed I make no doubt but she will, for she is a Girl of no common talents, writes verses elegantly herself, and withal an excellent Musician.

I must now answer that part of your first letter which regards Mr Balantine's [sic] selection of poetry. I am very easily persuaded to do any thing you desire me to do, and for the good song I heard Mr B. sing at your house I owe him a good turn. Stray verses, however, is a commodity very scarce with me: every thing of this kind that I possess would not furnish matter for a three penny book. I have looked over all I have this morning, and can find nothing but verses upon a Kitten, or rather a poem called the Kitten, that can be of any use to him.[37] Perhaps such a subject is not

---

36. Edward Coxe (1784-1814?), a minor poet and friend of Scott, contributed "The Last Leaf" and "On Reading Marmion" to Baillie's 1823 *Collection of Poems, Chiefly Manuscript.*

37. Baillie's "The Kitten" begins its second stanza as follows:
Backward coil'd and crouching low,
With glaring eyeballs watch thy foe,
The housewife's spindle whirling round,
Or thread or straw that on the ground
Its shadow throws, by urchin sly
Held out to lure thy roving eye. . . .
The Dramatic and Poetical Works of Joanna Baillie (London: Longman, Brown, Green, and Longmans, 1851), 805

admissable amongst what you call minstrelsy, but I shall write out a fair copy of it and send it to you very soon, and Mr B. will admit it or not as he pleases. If you please, I shall apply to Mrs Hunter for some verses for Mr B.; she is a much better person to apply to for this kind of poetry than me.[38]

I hope Mrs Scott & your young people are well, and that you have had as much enjoyment of your pastoral hills as this rainy cold season would allow you. I am glad to hear you have had some idle days of fishing & hunting to reproach yourself with. But you are very mis leart[39] to call them so; for they have furnished you with that which those call[ed] your busy days have only enabled you to communicate to others. — My Sister & I have been scrambling amongst the marble rocks of Torquay & coasting along the beautiful well wooded shores of Devon, and pacing thru' the solemn wiles of Exeter Cathedral by moonlight, with one candle carried before us which cast up its partial light upon the lofty pillars & arched roof, producing such striking & various effects, as made the Devon Dames who were with us call out with one accord "are we not near the grave of Michael Scott?"[40] I will pretend to give you no further account of our travels, only that we have been delighted with Devon; and if you have never seen that country, as I wish you all good things, I hope you will see it some [time] or other. — We did not see but we heard of your friend S. T. Ackland [sic][41] when we were there, who lives within 16 miles of Mr Elliott. He is very popular in that part of the country, and every body is charmed both with him & his young Lady. Since I wrote the inclosed part of this letter, I have seen my Brother & Mrs Baillie, and told them of your kind wish that they should have visited you while they were in

---

38. Anne Home Hunter (1742-1821), writer and oldest daughter of surgeon Everard Home, married Baillie's uncle Dr. John Hunter in 1771. Of her four children two survived her, son John and daughter Agnes who married Sir James Campbell. Anne Hunter published *Sports of the Genii* (1797) and miscellaneous poems throughout her life, several of which appear in Baillie's 1823 *A Collection of Poems, Chiefly Manuscript*.

39. misleart: misguided (*SND*).

40. *Lay of the Last Minstrel* presents a scene in which William of Deloraine wanders through darkness of night to Melrose Abbey and the tomb of the wizard Michael Scott. Walter Scott claimed a debt to Coleridge's *Christabel* for elements of this poem (Johnson, 338).

41. Sir Thomas Dyke Acland (1787-1871) was a politician and philanthropist who voted steadily with Sir Robert Peel through all the divisions forced by Lord George Bentinck and Disraeli. In 1807 he married Lydia Elizabeth Hoare, only daughter of banker Henry Hoare. Acland supported religious progress and is referred to in Scott's diary for 1828 as "the head of the religious party in the House of Commons" (qtd. in *DNB*, I:62).

Scotland. They both desire me to thank you, and to say that had they been at all near your part of the country, they would have gone to see you & Mrs Scott (who is by the bye a great favourite of my Brothers, I hope you will not be angry there at) without waiting for any formal invitation, and that they left a message for you to this effect, with Mr Alison when they were in Edin^r — My Sister joins me in all good wishes to you & Mrs Scott & your children. — My friend Miss Graham writes me a very pleasing account of the young Laird whom she saw frequently at Rillermount [?] this summer.[42] — Farewell! and well may you be till I see you again!

    Truly & sincerely yours
    J Baillie

3878 ff.189-90 Fragment (Address: Walter Scott Esqr--no postmark, NLS dates 4 November 1809)

[1809]

. . . in regard to it; and I hope, tho' it is a hope disturbed by fear, that your good Provost of Edin^r will not be the only person benefitted by the production of the piece. That story amazed me much; and since he is so grateful, I shall not, on Mr Siddons's account, so much begrudge the price of the hose, tho' they should not come to any luck upon the legs of either our Campbells or Clangillians. ——

You will see by the inclosed note from Mrs Hunter that your request as a Sandiknow [sic] Bairn was very reasonable,[43] and I hope Mr Balantyne will be pleased with the liberal supply she sends him, some of the pieces of which we think very pretty & tender. I send him what I promised, my Kitten, for I have no stores by me to be liberal with. It is a thing I wrote some years ago from a little circumstance. Hearing my Sister as she stroked her kitten one day by the fireside say, "your claws are like the prickles of a rose bud, kitty" I was pleased with the fancy, and took it up.[44] M^r B will not, I hope, think himself at all obliged to give it place in his selection if it should not please him or suit with the stile of poetry he wishes it to be composed of. I am glad you like my Welch Bard, and should make Mr Balantine very welcome to it, did I not consider it as entirely belonging to Mr Thomson.[45] All I can therefore say is that if Mr Thomson chuse to permit M^r B to print it, I have no objection. You see in what a docile frame I am regarding every thing you would have me to do. ——

---

42. This Miss Graham is possibly the daughter of Scottish poet James Grahame (1765-1811), much admired by Scott. I have not identified "Rillermount."
43. Scott's grandfather had been a prosperous farmer at Sandyknowe near Kelso.
44. See letter 3878 ff.180-84 above.
45. See introduction and letters to George Thomson herein.

I have reserved for myself in this last part of my letter the pleasure of noticing the last & kindest part of yours. Tho' an Aunt may not in these matters compare notes with a Father, I enter'd well into your feelings on hearing your Boy babble latin as a youth of the High School of Edin^r. May a good end come of what his babbling begins. I am not entirely a disbeliever in hereditary talents - general talents, tho' experience obliges me to do so regarding those that are peculiar. I may hope to see your son (alas! not to see for I am too old for this) honourably distinguished on the Bench, in the pulpit or the field, but never on Parnassus. No no! two great Poets never rise successfully in the same family, so encourage him in every thing but the writing of verses. Pardon this caution. I hope you will have comfort & honour in all your children, as their claims in the world will be great, and I trust readily acknowledged: very different from those which the Sandiknow Bairn set out withal. —— Offer my best regards with those of my Sister to Mrs Scott. – Farewell for the present, my good and affectionate friend; since you honour & gratify me so far as to subscribe yourself such; and believe me with all regard & good-liking,

truly & sincerely yours

J Baillie

PS. Will you have the goodness to send the inclosed letter to your neighbour Mrs Hamilton? Franks[46] are scarce here at present, and so I have made . . .[47] with Mr Freelings permission[48]

3879 ff.13-15 (Address: Walter Scott Esqr--no postmark)

Hampstead Feb^{ry} 4th
1810

My dear Sir,

You have indeed sent me a loud & hearty cheer from my native land, and I feel it at my heart sensibly & dearly. The applause of the most brilliant London Theatre I could not so feel, and I receive it as a gift from that great hand which has bestowed upon me many blessings for which I must endeavour to be as thankful as I can. And now, before I proceed one line further, what shall I say to you, my brave & burly champion, who have taken the field so zealously in my behalf, and thro' many difficulties gained for me this proud day? I have nothing to say but a great deal to think, and it will be matter of grateful & pleasant reflection to me

---

46. A frank was a letter or envelope bearing the super scribed signature of a member of Parliament entitled to send letters post free (*OED*).

47. This word is smeared and illegible.

48. Sir Frances Freeling (1764-1836) was a postal reformer and book collector, elected fellow of the Society of Antiquaries in 1801 (*DNB*, VII:679).

as long as I live. Consider yourself then as thank'd without more words; for I am withheld from saying all that I feel upon this subject, and I would not say (say) less. ――― And so you sat shaking last monday night lest any awkward blunder should bring disgrace upon us (for I will say us) and I sat by the fireside here with the most composed assurance that Mrs Siddons, according to my usual cross luck was still confined with her eyes, and that the play would be put off for some time, not withstanding you told me monday was the day.[49] Once or twice during the evening it came across me that my Legend might at that moment be in representation at Edin^r, but my Sister began reading Froisard [sic][50] and it went out of my head. This would not have been the case with me ten years ago when De Monfort was acted; but so many disappointments & cross fortunes have visited me since that time, that I have become now, as to hope, like a very aged person. Well; if hope with me has grown old, a sensibility to honourable notice & the partial kindness of kin & country has not, and I trust never will. ――――
Pray let me beg of you to offer my warmest thanks to all those Friends who have exerted themselves most in favour of my Legend; Mr W. Erskine I will take in my own hands, he has very kindly given me the opportunity of doing so. M^r & Mrs Siddons I learn from other accounts as well as yours, did their parts in the Play all the justice I could wish; their acting throughout being very good and many portions of it excellent. Have therefore the goodness to offer my best acknowledgments to them and to all the other actors, who exerted themselves so willingly and with such good effect in my favour. You are too fastidious on my account, I am persuaded the Play could not be so well acted at present in London. And now that I am dealing my thanks about as in duty bound (for I were worse than a Turk at present if I were not thankful) desire your good Lady, kind as she is, to take her share of them for all her care in mustering her large flock about her on that important night, like a Clucking hen (as you say) gathering her brood. She has with many other friends cluck'd well for me, and I am very sensible of it. ―― We have been greatly delighted with your Prologue; it is elegant & touching & sweet, and admirably fitted to give that tone of mind to the audience which suited our purpose. There were some lines in it which, had I been near you, would have been too presumptuous in a Prologue; but distance makes things pass well enough

49. Though only Scott's insistence put Baillie's *The Family Legend* on stage, on 29 January 1810 the curtain rose to a packed house, and the highland play scored a tremendous success for three weeks, followed by a revival of *De Monfort* (Johnson, 223-24).

50. This is probably the annotated edition of the Old English *Froissart*, edited by Henry Weber, that Scott suggested Murray publish as a reprint project around 1809 (Johnson, 307-8).

that would otherwise offend. I am glad to learn the Epilogue was well received; I was very much pleased with it and its Friendly writer for entering the list for me so handsomely.[51] ––– It now remains to be seen after this brilliant beginning what strength the piece really possesses to support itself for a length of time. I am glad you have altered it so as to act more lightly. I had a secret good will to that same Benlora,[52] but, since it must be, to the keep let him go with the rest. ––– I think it is entirely against the interest of the Piece as an acting Play to publish it at present. I shall therefore let that subject rest, and take your advice upon it another time. –– I received your second letter this morning for which I thank you heartily. I shall grow very proud under the praises of so many able & distinguish'd critics. My Friend Jeffry behaves handsomely to me; I suppose I must begin to love him now.[53]

Have you yet seen a Poem called Wallace or the Fight of Falkirk?[54] It is written in imitation of you, and seem'd to my Sister & I as we read it the other day a work of great merit. It is written, as I am told, by a Lady. She can set her lance at rest, hang her battle axe to her saddle bow, clasp her haberk & her habergeon,[55] raise her battle cry & ring her slogan with the best military antiquarian of you all; and she abounds in striking thoughts & spirited lines of your irregular measure, that carry one on eagerly; but her powers of discription, and of touching the heart are not equal to her other merits, and the character of Wallace is not the Wallace Wight that one would wish it to be. However, of all the Imitators & followers you are likely to have, and they will probably be a long train, you are not, I think, likely to meet with one that will do you more credit. It is but fair to confess, however, that I have read the Poem only once, and am giving my opinion of it rather rashly. Did you receive verses some years ago from a Lady of the name of Holford? This, I believe, is the writer of Falkirk Fight; and I am told she was very much hurt that you never took any notice

---

51. Scott checked the Highland costumes and wrote the prologue, while Henry Mackenzie wrote the epilogue; both men attended rehearsals (Johnson, 323).

52. Benlora is one of the kinsmen and chief vassals of Maclean in *The Family Legend*.

53. While Jeffrey did not always admire Baillie's work, he admired Baillie herself and after the success of her *Family Legend* wrote in 1811, "Southey, and Wordsworth, and Coleridge, and Miss Baillie have all of them copied the manner of our old poets; and, along with this indication of good taste, have given great proofs of original genius" (qtd. in James A Greig, *Francis Jeffrey of The Edinburgh Review* [Edinburgh: Oliver and Boyd, 1948], 194).

54. Margaret Holford Hodson's first work entitled *Wallace, or the Fight of Falkirk* appeared in 1809. See Baillie letters to Hodson, Volume 2.

55. habergeon: sleeveless coat of mail originally smaller and lighter than a hauberk but sometimes the same (*OED*).

of those verses. If this be so, it is a hole in your manners that will not easily be bouched up;[56] and I see she does not mention you in the Preface nor make any allusion to you in the course of the Poem.

You cannot imagine how highly gratified my Brother & Mrs Baillie are to say nothing of my Sister here with my Edin^r honours. As for Mrs Baillie, being a woman of few words & a warm heart, I believe she will find no other way of thanking you next time you meet than by giving you a good hearty hug. --- Give my kindest wishes with those of my Sister to Mrs Scott & the Children. The young Laird is a noble Fellow, and will do honour both to his blood & his breading [sic]. Fare well! and believe me very truly & gratefully & affectionately

    yours

    J Baillie

PS. Have I done enough in regard to thanking Mr Siddons? Tell me frankly, and dont let me be deficient in this matter, neither let me do too much. I am at this moment somewhat like the Manager himself, very docile, and will do whatever you bid me. —

3879 ff.17-18 (Address: Walter Scott Esqr--no postmark)

                        Hampstead Feb^{ry} 12th 1810

My dear Friend,

I think you are pushed more than enough about the honour of this Play of mine: let them critisize [sic] for a time our poor Laird of Maclean; and if you hear them, particularly the Ladies, bearing very hard against him, desire them to have a little patience with him for this bout, and I will endeavour by another winter to trim him up a little, and make him as good a Laird for them, as the circumstances of the story will admit. I say by another winter, because, tho' it is a thing that would not take a long time of doing, I am busy with something else at present, and, having been very unwell lately with a tedious feverish cold, I feel myself still quite spiritless & good-for-nothing, and very unfit for the task. Besides this I dont like to alter the piece so immediately till I shall be well assured of the general opinion. — As to publishing the Play I still think it against its interest as an acting play to do so; and, as I should wish it to be as profitable to the Edin^r Theatre as may be, I should wish if I could, not to publish it; however there is another consideration that may, perhaps, oblige me to it. Within this last fortnight we have got some information regarding the family for whose benefit it was originally written, which lead us to suppose they may really be in some want of its assistance. My Brother will soon enquire into this, by writing not to Sir J Sinclair but

---

56. bouched up: var. of botched up, repaired (*OED*).

directly to the family itself,[57] and if we find that this assistance is really wanted & acceptable, the whole profits arising from publishing the Play will go to for this purpose; and in this case I will keep no reserve for myself of inserting it afterwards amongst my other books but dispose of the copy right or published edition after edition as may be most advantageous. In regard to bringing it out in London, I have no thoughts of the kind. I shall never, as long as I live, offer any Play of mine to the Managers of either Covent Garden or Dury [Drury] Lane, but if they should ask it of me, I shant refuse it. This, however, I dont suppose they will be inclined to do, therefore my expectations of seeing it on a London stage amount to nothing.[58] —— You are very kind to say that when I bring out another Play in Edin^r I must come down and look after it myself. Indeed if I had been down with you now, you would not probably have gone on so well with me as you have done without me; I should, at best, only have been to you like the Child in Wordsworth's story of Old Michael "Something between a hindrance & a help,"[59] for the sight of all the Actors & Actresses about me at a rehearsal, repeating what I have almost never had face enough to hear the reading of, even in the most private way by my own intimate friends, would have cowed my better parts entirely. If ever I go to a rehearsal in which I am at all interested, it will be when you have a Piece coming out there; and if I could give them any useful hint, were it but in the cut of their doublets & hose, I should be a happy woman. When shall this be? and in the mean time, when shall we have your Lady of the Lake which every body here is so impatient to see, and continually asking me about? Did you think me very <u>misleart</u> in my last letter to say so much

---

57. Sir John Sinclair (1754-1835), first president of the board of agriculture and member of the privy council, was well known by Scott and Lockhart. He had been engaged in the literary controversy over the genuineness of James Macpherson's translation of the poems of Ossian and was himself a voluminous writer (*DNB*, XVIII:301-5). *The Family Legend* was apparently for the benefit of the Henderson family; see letter 3879 ff.67-68 following; I have not identified further.

58. See "Joanna Baillie Vs. The Termites Bellicosus" in Ellen Donkin's *Getting Into the Act: Women Playwrights in London, 1776-1829* (London and New York: Routledge, 1995) for a legitimate explanation of Baillie's unsuccessful attempts with Drury Lane. Donkin believes that because Baillie was outspoken, proprietor Sheridan became "unfriendly" to her cause and discouraged Kemble from staging her plays.

59. See William Wordsworth's *Michael*:

> He as a watchman oftentimes was placed
> At gate or gap, to stem or turn the flock;
> And, to his office prematurely called,
> There stood the urchin, as you will divine,
> Something between a hindrance and a help. . . . (185-89)

about Miss Holford & the verses she wrote to you? I hope you did not, for I thought it was right you should know it, and did it all for good.

I recollect nothing else I ought to say to you at present, and your time is too precious to be taken up with needlessly long letters. I learnt from my Friend Miss Millar that the alterations you & yours friends have made in the Legend are very judicious, and I (no thanks to me for it) am perfectly satisfied with it. She says you have turned off Dr Grey from his love scene altogether: e'en let him go if the Play does better without it. You did not tell me before that you had added a cracker to Argyle's squib[60] to please Mr Terry.[61] Mr Terry was very right to ask it from you, and it pleases me too, right well. ――― When I know about the real state of the Family I have mentioned I will trouble you with another letter to ask your advice about the best way of making the publication useful to them, and shall be glad if it should not be necessary to publish till next year. ― Remember me very kindly to Mrs Scott, and thank all your little folks for me for all the tears the[y] shed for the distress of Helen. You did not mean to say that little Charles wept for her. My Sister offers her best regards.

Truly & faithfully yours
  J Baillie
PS I thank you for the paper & the Playbill. I did like to see the bill. As for the paper, if the Critic had praised the Poetry less, and given a better & fairer account of the story, it would have been as well. ――

3879 ff.33-35 (Address: Walter Scott Esqr / North Castle Street / Edinburgh--no postmark)

Grosvenor St: March 13
1810

My dear Sir
  You set yourself & me above ordinances, and so be it; I need not therefore make any apology for having so long delayed to acknowledge your last letter in which there were so many things to give me pleasure; yet as I think I have good reasons for not having wrote to you sooner, you shall have them. As soon as I received your letter, I begged my Brother to write to the Gentleman for whose use we wish the Family Legend to be published, to know his mind upon the subject, and have for these last 8

---

60. squib: a short, satiric speech or lampoon (*OED*).
61. Daniel Terry (1780?-1829), actor and playwright born at Bath and respected in London and Edinburgh alike, idolized Scott and imitated him in manner and style. Terry, who performed dozens of roles opposite such greats as Mrs. Siddons and Kean, played Argyle in Baillie's 29 January 1810 production of *The Family Legend* and on 12 March 1816 produced a musical adaptation of Scott's *Guy Mannering* (*DNB*, XIX:563-66).

days expected an answer from him by every post, and I have been unwilling to write to you till we received it. No answer, however, has yet come, and as you think the Play should be publish'd without delay, I now write to say, that I should be glad to have a thousand copies printed off as soon as may be and this aforesaid Gentleman, may afterwards dispose of the copy right, or do what else in regard to it he may think most for his own advantage. Will you then have the goodness to settle this affair with your Bookseller in Edin^r as you see fit? for I am not afraid that you will on this occasion let one penny slip through your fingers that can reasonably & justly be made. When this Play was first given to Sir J. Sinclair, I promised to Mr Longman, my Bookseller here that whenever it should be published, he should have the first offer of it.[62] I spoke to him about it yesterday, and he is very well pleased that it should be publish'd at Edin^r but should be glad to have his name put along with the Edin^r Bookseller's as a joint publisher, and he will either go halfs with him in the business or take any smaller share in it or not share at all as the other may wish. If you think it had better be printed from the original copy I gave you, without any of the stage alterations, let it be so; leaving out, however, any thing you may think had better be left out. I shall write a few words of introduction to it, which I shall send to you in about 8 days hence; for I am at present in Town, and have no time to write. As to correcting the press, Mr Balantine must look after that himself: and I suppose his Compositor has wit enough, if he finds any ill spelt words in the manuscript, to set them to rights of his own accord. --- Having finished the important business of my letter, I will next speak of a pleasanter subject, the pride & pleasure I have had in hearing how handsomely De Monfort has been received on your stage; a thing so unexpected, that, tho' I heard a day or two before I received your letter that it was to be brought out, I did not believe it, but thought it was some blundering mistake. Pray give Mr Siddons my best thanks for this, which I must receive as a mark of his own good will to the interests of my romantic prosperity. I am very much satisfied with what I have heard of his exertions in the Character of De M:, and hope the public favour will continue so long to bear him up in it, that he shall have no reason to repent of having undertaken it. I hear he is going to bring out a Play of his own

---

62. Thomas Longman III (1771-1842) published such authors as Wordsworth, Coleridge, Scott and Baillie, carrying on in the publishing tradition of Thomas Longman (1699-1755), who founded the publishing firm which still exists today. After the collapse of Archibald Constable in 1826, the firm became the sole proprietors of the *Edinburgh Review*, of which they had previously owned one half; but by this time the firm had become Longman, Hurst, Rees, Orme, Brown, & Green. Thomas Longman died at Hampstead 29 August 1842. The elder Longman had helped publish Johnson's *Dictionary* (*OCEL*, 585).

soon;[63] I am sure I am in duty bound to wish for it success, and do so very sincerely. —

I will now say a word or two upon your business of Miss Holford, for those, who have got above ordinances, generally I believe, attend, as I have done, to their own business in the first place. I wrote without losing time after I got your letter, to my Friend Mrs Elliott, who is acquainted with a friend of Miss Holford, who is one of the learned Ladies of Bath, desiring her to convey your message to the said Friend for Miss H. and I daresay it has been, or will be done very handsomely. Your excuse for not writing to her formerly, is a very pretty excuse, but dont suppose it will pass with me: you had a better reason for not writing than not liking to write one letter about yourself & your poetry; you were afraid of having an unknown sentimental correspondent saddled upon your back, no very desirable thing I readily admit, and so on this score you will stand fully excused in my mind, whatever you may do in Miss Holford's. I dont think her character of Wallace will be popular; but not exactly for the reasons you give for it, and therefore I hope they will not prevent that Poet from undertaking a picture of our favourite Hero, to whom it of right belongs. I have been enquiring at Mr Longman about Sir Lancelot, and he says we shall have it the end of April or beginning of May. I have only one reason to fear for it, that no Poet since the world began ever brought out three great poems eminently successful. However, people who live in the days of Buonaparte, need not marvel at new things. —— I have been often interupted [sic] since I began this letter, and dont know if I have said every thing to you I ought to have said, but as I shall write to you soon again there is less matter whether I have or not. — Give my kindest wishes with those of my Sister & Mrs Baillie to Mrs Scott, and believe me, my dear Sir

    truly & faithfully yours
     J Baillie

3879 ff.40-41 (No address or postmark--NLS dates 1810)

              Hampstead March 20th [1810]

My dear Sir,

I herewith send you what I promised in my last, and trouble enough have I had, by staying so long in Town and other interruptions, to get it ready. My pen is not like yours: the very mechanical part of writing, with

---

63. Henry Siddons wrote several plays (*The Friend of the Family, Times a Tell-Tale* and *Tale of Terror, or a Castle without a Spectre*), some of which were performed at Covent Garden around 1803, but I find no reference to a performance in Edinburgh at this time.

this vile-looking, slovenly hand of mine, goes as slowly on with me as if it were painting out a message card for a hand-screen, so that when I write any thing that requires to have a fair copy taken from it afterwards, I am a dreary while about it. However it is done now; and if you think it will do after it is done, I shall be glad. I have been longer, in my address to the Reader on the Character of Duart than you will, perhaps, think I ought to have been,[64] but I could not be satisfied without trying to say something in its behalf as to design at least; and I have in so doing been speaking a word for you as well as myself, if you have wit enough to find it out; for by the common place rules by which they condemn Duart, they have also attacked your superb but nefarious Marmion. I have taken the liberty, you will see, of inscribing the Play to you. It pleases both my heart & my fancy to do so, therefore you must take it in good part and not gainsay me in this particular. The 2^d vol. of the series of Plays I inscribed somewhat in the same way to my Brother; and little thought I should ever again have done the like to any one; but a Brother & a very friendly Brother of the Muse has drawn from me once more this sisterly token, and I verily believe it will now be the last. Why are you not a good staunch Whig? and we should go on together very pleasantly. I know no good Tories are for but serving as a balance against wrong-headed republicans. ——

My Brother has not yet received any answer to the letter he wrote to the person I mentioned, for whose use the Legend is publish'd, which we think very odd, if the letter indeed has reached him, and we got the direction for him from Sir J. Sinclair. I forgot in my last to say that the money arising from this edition of the Play must be in the Booksellers hands till we know what to do with it. I saw a letter from Miss Douglas to Miss Berry the other day where she mentions having seen the Legend, and that neither the prologue nor Epilogue was spoken.[65] How comes this about? I hope you dont mean to leave them out when the Play is printed. This I could by no means admit of, for they do it great honour, and can by no means be spared.

---

64. In her "To The Reader" for *The Family Legend*, inscribed, as she states further on in the letter, to Walter Scott, Baillie explains that "In the 15th century, a feud had long subsisted between the Lord of Argyll and the Chieftain of Maclean; the latter was totally subdued by the Campbells, and Maclean* [*Called in the representation Duart] sued for peace, demanding, at the same time, in marriage, the young and beautiful daughter of Argyll" (*DPW*, 479).

65. Miss Mary Berry was a long-time friend of Baillie and one of the first to praise her *Plays on the Passions* in 1799. Berry was also a writer and asked Baillie to provide the prologue to her *Fashionable Friends* in 1801. See letters to Mary Berry herein.

Some little time ago I saw a set of engravings from drawings of Westalls from the Lay & Marmion, and I was told he is about to prepare a set for Sir Lancelot.[66] If he does so, I hope he will have the goodness to represent your stories as you tell them. His death of Marmion might be the death of any man with a coat of mail (coat of mail) on after any battle whatever, were it not for the Lady & the horse behind him. "On Chester on"! there is neither word in his mouth nor action in his body of any kind; and for the broken sword he ought to brandish, if it were taken to give the artist a good rap upon the scull, it would be well employed, and I should then forgive its not being in the picture. This Palmer too that strove so stately thro' the hall and fronted Marmion where he sate, he is tall enough it is true, but he slouches under his coat as if he were begging alms for St. Benedict. There are some good & beautiful figures I own in the course of those drawings, but faults like these in so good an Artist are not to be tolerated, and I have been grumbling about it exceedingly to M[r] Longman, who has, I believe, some concern in it. He told me you had seen the engravings and were pleased with them. I told him you might be civil enough to say so, but it was impossible you could be pleased with them. – Give my kindest wishes to M[rs] Scott & the young folks in which Agnes joins me heartily. Truly yours   J Baillie

3879 ff.47-49 (Address: Walter Scott Esq[r]--no postmark, NLS dates 1810)

Grosvenor St: March 28th [1810]

My dear Sir,

You say nothing in your (in your) letter to me of your probable visit to London, but in that to M[rs] Baillie I find there is some hopes of seeing you & M[rs] Scott in these parts soon, and right glad I am thereat. I should not have teased you with a letter so soon upon the heels of my last (for I am no sentimental correspondent) but to put you in mind of what you said last Spring, when I asked why you did not bring Miss Scott with you, viz. that you had had some thoughts of doing so but did not know what you should make of her when you got to London; and what I thereupon said again, that there were friendly quarters for her at Hampstead where she should be well taken care of while you & M[rs] Scott were engaged in Town with the gay world. I hope you have not forgot this, and, if you have any wish to bring her with you in this proposed journey, deposit her with my Sister & I on your way to London, you know we are but a mile & half out of your

---

66. Richard Westall (1765-1836), historical painter, illustrated several books, including Scott's *Marmion* in 1809, his *Lord of the Isles* in 1813, and Johnson's *Rasselas* in 1817 (*DNB*, XX:1258). The Sir Lancelot to which Baillie refers is actually Scott's *Lady of the Lake*.

way, turning off at Highgate, and we shall keep her safely while you remain in Town; and whenever you wish her to come to Town for any purpose, she shall always be forth coming. Pray prefer this suit to Mrs Scott; and I trust I need not say how much satisfaction it will give both Agnes & I to have a Bairn of yours under our roof. She may think our house without young people dull; but we shall take her to Grosvenor St: sometimes where my Niece who is merry enough will be delighted to see her. —— Mrs Baillie desires me to thank you for your kind & obliging note, and to say she would not write to you again, because she believes you are teased with too many letters and you ought to have no unnecessary ones that can be spared you. She is very glad the box came to hand safe, and that you & Mrs Scott are pleased with the inkstand. ——— I hope you have received my last packet. I did not say any thing in my letter about having any copies of the Legend sent to me; for I mean to give none away, and the one or two I may want for our own family I will get from Mr Longman.

I am glad to hear you have some cheering confidence in regard to the Lady of the Lake, (for I find I was wrong in calling it Sir Lancelot.) I am sure you do not feel so on light grounds, and owning to me that you do feel so, is the kindness of a friend. What a talking we shall have about it when it does appear! discussing the expedition to Walcheren will be nothing to it.[67] I was glad to learn from Mr Longman the other night that it is not Westall, but an Artist of a very promising genius, a Mr Cook, that is to make drawings for the Lady.[68] This was a comfort to me, for I had not yet done grumbling about Marmion. ——— We saw your old neighbour & Brother Poet Graham last week, who is now about to leave his Curacy in Gloucester sh: to settle for a time in Carlisle on account of his Father in law who wishes him to be near him. He preached here last Sunday in one of our churches in the west end of the Town, and a Lady who heard him told me his sermon was excellent, his manner good & impressive, and what he had of the Scotch accent (this Lady is an English woman) not at all offensive. He had been introduced to some of the most respectable clergy in this country, and from what I can learn they seem well disposed towards him. His thin, sentimental, care worn face is found to have effect in the pulpit and much shall I rejoice if he can preach himself into a comfortable living. He seems care worn indeed; but there is nothing like sourness nor envy in his character, and he seems to have become more cheerful than he

---

67. Walcheren is a Dutch island at the mouth of the Schelde, involved in Napoleon's campaigns.

68. Richard Cook (1784-1857), historical painter elected associate to the Royal Academy in 1816, sent five pictures for exhibition, including four from Scott's *Lady of the Lake* (*DNB*, IV:998).

was tho' he has been tormented with rheumatism all the winter, and has lately recovered from a dangerous attack of plurasy [sic]. ——— I had a letter from a Glasgow friend the other day, after seeing the family Legend acted there for the first time, and from what she says I can learn that it has been received handsomely, but not so warmly as at Edinburgh. ——

All your friends of this family join me very heartily in kind wishes to you & Mrs Scott, and hoping to see you soon, I remain, my dear Sir,

Truly yours,
J Baillie

PS. I am very glad Mr Siddons Play has been so well received. He deserves that it should be so.———

3879 ff.67-68 (Address: Walter Scott Esqr / North Castle Street / Edinburgh--postmarked 1810)

Hampstead May 7th 1810

My dear Sir,

My Sister & I have just now received a letter from your old neighbour, Graham the Poet, the Sabbath Graham I mean, telling us that he is a Candidate for the Lectureship of St: Georges Chapel Edin^r which Mr Alison has declined accepting,[69] and begging me to write to you intreating your good offices on his behalf. This I know you would of your accord most readily grant, as far as you find yourself at liberty to do so; therefore I do not intreat, but only inform you what this Brother Poet of yours, who is at the same time (so I am told) a very good preacher, desires. I own I do not think him wise in desiring such preferment, as he has been so much encouraged by many of the higher Clergymen in this country that I think he has a good chance of getting a living here, were he to remain with us, at the same time, he is old enough to judge for himself and I will do as I am bidden. The nomination, as he tells me, is in the vestry which consists of the following persons viz: Lord Elibank, Mr Erskine of Mar, Mr Ker of Blackshields, Mr Drummond of Stragouth, Admiral Sir Edward Neagle, Mr Scott of Seabank, Mr Dallas writer to the Signet, Mr Manderson Apothecary, Mr David George Extractor, Mr Charles Stewart writer to the Signet, Mr Hume of Carrolside, & Mr Laing Architect. Who of all this goodly list, if he has either ears, heart, or imagination belonging to him, will refuse the request of his Townsman Walter Scott? Try them then: and

---

69. Archibald Alison (1757-1839) was a writer on "taste" and became minister of the Episcopal chapel, Cowgate, Edinburgh, in 1800, where he remained the rest of his life. His sermons were much admired, and two volumes published in 1814-15 went through several editions. He was married to Dorothea Gregory, daughter of Dr. John Gregory, author of *A Father's Legacy to his Daughters* (DNB, I:186-87).

let us have as good an account of them as you can. Your friend Mr William Erskine will obtain Mr Drummonds vote for us, and I think we have a round-about way of getting to the Apothecary. It is my real honest opinion, from what I have heard that Graham is a good Preacher. But I will teaze you no more on this subject knowing that your inclinations are on our side & that it is needless.

What has become of your journey to London? I thought by this time – long before this, for the 12 of May is not far off, to have seen you. The Lady of the Lake also does not make her appearance, and hope delayed maketh the soul sick.[70] I am glad she is of Loch Cathrine: Sir Lancelot & all the round table would not have been so welcome to me. It cheers me to think you have confidence in her; and so have I too: and be not afraid that you have gained too much fame in your life time to flourish long with Posterity. You will both eat your cake (as you call it) now, and it will be like the bread of Life which nourishes for ever. — Have you received my letter by Mr Henderson yet, the Gentleman to whom I have given [my] Family Legend? I saw him but for an hour, and never had seen him before; and he appears to me like an indolent, heavy young man that would do any way he is bidden. Poor man! this is not a character for struggling with the world in behalf of seven Sisters & two Brothers, all unprovided for. —— But I must not close my letter without thanking you for the copy of the Lady of the Lake which you so kindly intend for me. I shall be a proud woman when I receive it; and I shall put it into such a binding by this day twelve mounth, as shall shame all the books in the house. – Give my kindest regards to Mrs Scott: Perhaps after all we may see you soon, and that will be a great pleasure to your sincere & obliged

J Baillie

3879 ff.88-90a (Address: Walter Scott Esqr.--no postmark)

Hampstead May 13th 1810

Bravo, my dear Friend! I am no longer in any pain about you: your young Babe is [a] comely, well-limbed, burly Brat, and will bring (no mean praise) no discredit on the family it belongs to. If my being, – not amused (for that is not the term that belongs to it) but greatly interested & delighted, can harden your sides any how against the Critics, you may make light of them indeed. How they will treat you I cannot tell; but a great host of Readers, whose hearts have been touched & whose fancies have been fired by the Poem, will rise up in your defense, and if they cannot fight for you with sword & shield in knight-like order according to

---

70. "Hope deferred maketh the heart sick; but *when* the desire cometh, *it is* a tree of life" (Prov. 13.12).

the stated rules of arms, they will nevertheless lay about them lustily with such weapons as they have, and do the work of valiant varlets, which never fails in the end to carry the day. The day before I received the book, I had dined with Mr Freeling at Mr Coxe['s] who was praising it enthusiastically; yet, notwithstanding this, I must confess I sat down to read it with considerable depression of spirits, which all the beauties of the first canto, and the first appearance of the Lady which is truly engaging & delightful, could not over come; but as soon as Clan Alpen appeared in their boats and the bag-pipes struck up, my spirits rose, and I felt after that, thro'out the whole as bold as a Lion.[71] It is certainly the most interesting story you have yet given us, and the Characters you have introduced into it more attractive & engaging. That of the Lady has a lightness, spirit & grace joined to its nobleness, so different from the serious . . .[72] of a common-place heroine which is particularly pleasing. That parting look of human vanity which she sent after the knight of Snowden, is contrary to all rules of romance, but he were a Loggerhead that would alter it. The parts of the Poem that struck me most are the Clan Alpen in their boats &c. The scene between Roderick Dhu, Douglas & Graeme in their contention about Ellen, (the agitation of Clan Alpen's chief is wonderfully grand) –– the Gathering with the fiery cross and funeral & wedding therein contained, (the funeral most truly pathetic), –– the rising of the ambushed Highlanders on the side of the hill, with the combat between Roderick & Snowden's knight, when they threw away their scabbards, and look'd round upon the earth & the sky as a thing they might never see again (a thought so finely imagined, so true to nature, and yet, as far as my learning goes, so new!) –– and, last of all, the conclusion of the story which came upon me with a pleasing surprise, not having had wit enough to find out before who the knight in Lincoln green might be. I dont know that there is any one descriptive passage in the Lady of the Lake so powerfully striking as some of those in Marmion, tho' there are many of them admirable; but as I have said already the story is more interesting the characters more pleasing and in these respects it excells both Marmion & the Lay, which is perhaps the only way in which it was possible to excell them. ––– But I will say no more upon this subject, for you will hear so much of it from so many different hands that tho' it does regard your own young Babe – your own comely quarto, you must be tired of it. Many of your other friends may give you an idea of what the learned may think of it, but I consider myself as not a bad representative of those

---

71. Scott sent splendid royal quartos of *The Lady of the Lake* to his special friends, Baillie, Southey and a few others (Johnson, 329).

72. This word is in the fold of the leaf and is smeared and illegible.

same sturdy varlets that are to do so much in your favour should their betters be inclined to deal hardly with you. — I was very proud of myself last thursday, for I received the Lady of the Lake from you with some thing written on the first leaf of it that went bubling [*sic*] into my noddle like a bumper of Champaign, in half an hour afterwards I received Mr Freeling's copy which he had the goodness to send me from Town, and by & by another copy from Mr Longman; so I sat with all those copies lying on my table, like some Queen or great person that receives offerings from every quarter of the earth. --- Along with your Lady there came a criticism on Grey's Country Church Yard[73] from the Editor which I have not yet had time to look into. Who is this Editor? the hand writing, on the first leaf is very like yours, but this is impossible.

I must now thank you for the letter I have received from you this morning along with the copy of the Legend. How good it was in you to send it! Yet I am sorry you did for I was no wise impatient to see it, and I have at last got some copies of it from Mr Longman. It is very handsomely printed, and is I dare say very correct: thanks to you for its so being!

I am sorry to hear you have had so much illness in your Nursery; and I hope for the sake of your Bairns that the weather in Edin^r may be milder than we have it here, for we are still sitting by the fireside and sometimes with a shawl about us. The chin-cough is a good thing to get over, but it is hard upon them poor Lambs! to have it so soon upon the back of another illness. Our experienced Mothers here, rub their children's backs, when they have this complaint severely, with what they call an <u>embarkation</u> (but probably I dont spell the word right) or infusion of garlic, which makes it much easier for them.[74] The young Laird perhaps may be too proud to have his back rubb'd with such stuff, but little Charles & your younger Girl may not be so lordly, and may be the better for it. — Pray forgive this if it is impertinent, for I am not commonly a giver of medical advice.

After May set in & no words of you, I began to despair of seeing you & Mrs Scott at this bout; but I hope by next winter or next spring at farthest we shall have this pleasure, and will be particularly gratified by your confidence in letting us have your Sophia with us as long as you remain in this part of the world. If she should be at all much better of being with us, as you obligingly say, we shall be no less so for having her with us; for old

---

73. Thomas Gray's "Elegy in a Country Churchyard" was published in February 1751. Two editions of Gray's works appeared in 1814, one by T. J. Mathias and one anthology including many of Gray's poems (*English and Latin Poems*) by John Mitford. I have not identified an edition appearing in 1810.

74. This is probably an adulteration of imbruement, or tincture (*OED*). See letter following.

people are as much benefited by being with the young, as young people are
by being with the old. I am sure I have reason to say so: for Children much
more than sages have been my school masters. ——

I am glad to hear you are doing what you can for Mr Graham, even tho'
the tide should set against him. He will have a satisfaction in thinking
you have served him, for I do believe he bears you a most unfeigned good
will, and begrudges not the wreath that circles your brow tho' his own
laurels are of a less vigorous & wroth. —— He was tormented last winter
with rheumatism, and found the duties of his curacy particularly the
funerals which obliged him to stand bare-headed in the church yard in
cold weather, too much for him. ——

My Sister joins me in every kind wish to you & Mrs Scott & your young
ones who will I hope soon be better; and so for the present fare well! I
suppose without any impropriety at my time of life (tho' pray consult M^{rs}
Scott upon this) subscribe myself,

your affectionate as well as obliged friend
        J Baillie

PS. I have just now received a letter from Mr Freeling, who besides his
former expressions of admiration regarding the Lady of the Lake says and
I think he is right "Snowden's knight & Scotland's king is enriched with
every high & princely grace & feeling. It is wonderful to see the nice
discrimination which Mr Scott has shewn in his delineation of that
character: it is perfect." ——

I have for my own liking a great fancy for Roderick Dhu.

3879 ff.38-39 (Address: Mrs Scott / North Castle Street / Edinburgh--
postmarked May 20)

                                        Hampstead March 16th [1810][75]

My dear Mrs Scott,

I have done a thing for which I deserve to be well whipt, and I
daresay you will think so too when I tell you what it is. I have told M^r
Scott in my last letter that our good experienced Mothers in this place rub
their children's backs when they have the hooping-cough with an
Embarkation (for so I call it) or infusion of garlic which they think does
them a great deal of good. I have been enquiring this morning more
particularly about it, at a very experienced Lady, and she tells me that it
is Roach's <u>Embrucation</u> for the hooping-cough they use, which has no
garlic at all in it, and is rubb'd upon the breast instead of the back. I hope
you will believe me when I mentioned it in my letter, I thought myself

---

75. The date here appears to be Baillie's error, for the postmark is May 20 and
the subject clearly follows ff.126-128 above.

perfectly correct; nevertheless such a mistake shews a degree of stupidity & heedlesness [*sic*] that would disgrace a Girl of fifteen, what then shall we say of it coming from a woman so far advanced on the wrong side of forty? Pray forgive me! and dont publish my great ignorance & presumption to the Apothecary. I comfort myself somewhat with thinking you have not, most probably, paid any attention to impertinent advice in such a questionable shape, and that no harm is done: but I must say again, pray forgive me! I hope the weather will soon be warm, and the Children get over their complaint as easily as you can expect.

I hope to be soon in Town where I suppose I shall hear every body talking of the Lady of the Lake. She is indeed a charming creature herself, and the Highlanders that belong to her are more attractive beings than the Border Thieves (if it be not treason to say so to a Scott) If those who read it are as much delighted with it as I have been, I shall hear nothing said of it but what will give me pleasure, and so I feel that I shall go amongst them boldly. —— My Sister sends her kind wishes with mine to yourself & Mr Scott & all the young folks; and I remain, my dear Mrs Scott,

your truly ob. . . [etc.]

J Baillie

3879 ff.126-128 (Address: Walter Scott Esqr / N. Castle St^r / Edinburgh-- no postmark)

Grosvenor St: June 5 1810

My dear Sir,

I fear you will think I am making a cat's paw of you to convey a letter to our friend Mr Graham, in whose service you have lately been so kindly engaged, for which, many thanks to you! Whatever may have been the result of the business. However, I could have you to know that were I not really inclined of my own good will & pleasure to write to you, I am not without other means & devices for conveying the said letter, tho' I do not at present know how to direct it, having lost, or burnt, or mislaid M^r G's last letter to my Sister & I in which his address was set down. — Indeed I am glad of a pretence to write to you; for I have been so greatly delighted in reading the Lady of the Lake a second time, and its beauties have so risen upon me every time I have look'd into the book, that I had a strong hankering to tell you so; and yet to write on purpose seemed to me foolish, since praise must be wafted to you from every quarter, so that you must be tired there with, if it is possible for a Poet or any body else to be so tired. I have the satisfaction to find my friends feel in regard to it pretty nearly as I do myself. Some of them have praised it on the first reading, less warmly than I expected, but there is not a soul of them that has not on the second reading expressed their delight in it with the greatest animation.

Mrs Hunter, speaking on this subject the other day, said if the opinion [of] any one so unimportant as herself could give you satisfaction, she should be glad that you knew how much she admired the Poem, which she has read with the greatest pleasure & delight. We regaled my honest Brother yesterday, who has no time to read books of any kind, and who deals as little in works of Poetry or imagination as most people, with reading to him the rising of the ambush, the combat between Fitz James & Roderick Dhu, and Roderick's death in Prison, as specimens of the work; and had you seen the expression on his face, it would have been worth more to you than pages of praise from a common place sentimental reader. ["]Faith!" says he "this is wonderfully fine: this must be poetry of the very highest order." In short from all these signs I perceive that what I feared would not come to pass, as being too extraordinary even for these days, will come to pass, and I shall not therefore regret any reproach it may bring upon my sagacity. I will not trouble myself about which of your three poems people may give the preference to, since there is not one of the three that would not on its own strength alone have raised the obscurest man in the country to the rank which you now hold. Your march has been a steady, bold, onward march, tho' perhaps some astonishing strides or bounds in Marmion have been greater than in any other part of the way. You established yourself by the Lay as our first discriptive Poet: to this, in Marmion you added strong dramatic discrimination of character; and to these, in the Lady, you add interesting story enriched with amiable & attractive Personages. Sweetness & interest I should think will be the leading traits of this last Poem, opposed to the brilliancy & power of the second. What you will arrive at in a fourth Poem, I wot not, but I will never again let my sympathy for you give me so much anxiety as it has done. —— But to return again, before my paper is finished, to our Friend Mr Graham; will you have the goodness to make out the direction of the inclosed for him, as I doubt not you know where he is at present, and afterwards let one of your servants take it to the post? and I shall be very much obliged to you. ——— I suppose you are now busy discussing this horrible story of the Duke of Cumberland: we are still engaged with it, tho' it is almost a week since it happen'd, and the more we think of it the more horrible & wonderful it seems.[76] We had not recovered from our surprise & wonderment regarding

---

76. George III's son Prince Ernest (1771-1851), later Duke of Cumberland and King of Hanover, lived as a bachelor in a suite of apartments in the palace until his marriage to Frederica, Princess of Solms-Braunfels (her 3rd marriage). On 31 May 1810 Ernest was found in his apartment with a terrible wound to the head; shortly after, his valet Sellis was found in bed with his throat cut. Public opinion was that the prince murdered Sellis, though the opinion was not confirmed by a jury (see Stanley Ayling, *George the Third* [New York: Knopf, 1972], 376, and *DNB*, VI:812).

the Chevalier Deon,[77] when this extraordinary event came upon us, and now one may safely call on the dullest person within the liberties of Westminster without danger of lacking conversations. — I hope your young folks go on favourably with their hooping cough, and that Mrs Scott has forgiven me for my stupid mistake about the embrackation of which I was sufficiently ashamed. Offer her my kind wishes and believe me always

Truly yours

J Baillie

PS. They have got your Coronach from the Lady of the Lake set to music already, and it is advertised as one of the attractions of a fashionable consert [sic] for next week.[78] I should like to be there but may not. —

3879 ff.156-158 (Address: To Walter Scott Esqr--no postmark)

Hampstead August 8th 1810

You are very <u>very</u> good, my dear Sir, in writing to me from the Isles where you have been surrounded with objects of so much interest and must have been so much occupied & so happy.[79] There is no body so good to me as you are; and were you beside me now, I verily think I should not be able to keep my hands off you, but should be tempted to pat & stroke you like a kitten, great man as you are both in mind & in stature. Great enjoyment you must have had amongst your friends & your chieftains & your Highland Boatmen. I would have given many a <u>plack</u>[80] out of my <u>pouch</u> to have been with you, were it not for a very mean weakness unworthy an admirer of Ossian & the Warriors of old, viz a marvellous fear of being drown'd. That you & yours have escaped after rowing twenty miles against an Atlantic tide and the winds gathering round you I am glad; and tho' I have not been at Staffa myself, I look (look) by & bye with the help of certain discriptive powers in the Bard whose store is consecrated on its shore, to have as vivid an impression of Fingals Cave, its lofty roof, pillar'd sides & pavement of ruddy marble carpetted by the waves, as if I had really

---

77. Chevalier Charles D'Éon de Beaumont (1728-1810), writer and captain of dragoons, was baptized as a boy, but congenital questions about his sex led to a public dedication at age three to the Virgin Mary under the feminine name Charlotte Geneviève Louise Augusta Timothea. Until the age of seven D'Éon was dressed as a girl, but afterward he was educated as a boy. He served France as a secret agent for many years in the guise of both male and female, but when he died 21 May 1810, it was finally revealed that he was a man (*DNB*, V:831-35).

78. The "Coronach" appears in Canto III of *Lady of the Lake*.

79. In July 1810 Scott and his family took a trip to the Hebrides as guests of Ranald Macdonald, the Laird of Staffa. From Oban, they passed close to the Lady's Rock in the Sound of Mull, the very rock Baillie mentions in her *Family Legend* (Johnson, 332).

80. plack: small coins (*SND*).

been so. I shall, with this great help, have in my imagination a perfect imagry [sic] of all those things, which shall there be laid up as a part of its most valuable furniture for life. In truth, if you were to turn out of my fancy, as far as scenery is concerned all that this same Bard has put into it, you would leave but an ill plennish'd house. Indeed the Hebrides, and I suppose also the North of Irland [sic] which you have in your thoughts, as you mentioned in your former letter, for the subject of your next poem, seems to be an excellent one, most happily suited to your genius: the scenery, the manner of the people & the characters of their Chiefs, will make a new world for our common world here to peep into, full of attractions. — I have been very much pleased with the character you give of your host the Laird of Staffa. The fair side of his picture is very pleasing, and the little darkening it receives from prejudice and the necessary effect, as you observe, of solitary power, do not greatly deminish [sic] our respect for the whole. Let him even beard the Lord Lieutenant & hate the whole race of Macleans who fought with his ancestors two hundred years ago: it is hating individuals not whole bodies of men that spoils the heart; and I could be sworn that no distressed single Maclean would ever go from your noble host without relief, nor have injustice put upon him even contending with a Macdonald. Would you had many more Lairds of his character both in the Highlands and in Ireland! they would do a great deal more good in their generation than a multitude of lazy philosophical Philanthropists. Since man cannot be perfect, give me Staffa and keep a great many learned & gentle, & unprejudiced characters, (if unprejudiced are to be found) to yourself. I am too much in love with Rhoderick [sic] Dhu at present, violent & tyranical as he was, to have any thing said against a highland Chief, provided he does not actually come and burn my house over my head.

My Sister & I are living here rather in a solitary state at present, having lost for the remainder of the summer some of our best Neighbours, and having taken leave of my Brother's family who are to set out for Gloucester Sh: day after to morrow. This will be a great relief to him, poor man! for he is to give himself 3 months of the country to recruit his tired mind & body after a campaign of very hard service, tho' his rural enjoyments will be greatly interrupted by stated journeys to Windsor, (nearly 80 miles from his own house) every fortnight. This poor Princess lingers on sadly.[81] We hear every now & then of her being a little better,

---

81. Princess Amelia (1783-1810) suffered greatly from 1806 to her death of erysipelas and consumption. Her sister Mary attended her at Augusta Lodge, Windsor, where George III could see her daily until her death on 2 November 1810 (Ayling, 445-47).

and yet her progress in amendment seems to be almost nothing. Yet having lived so long under the hands of a succession of Physicians, her thread of life must be of a good tough texture; and I believe her present Doctors have never despaired entirely of her <u>getting well</u> at last. This is my Brother's phrase for it, for he never pretends to cure any body. We shall live (I mean Agnes & I) in this solitary state till the middle of next month, when we shall likewise go to Gloucester to spend a couple of months, the first with a Friend we have on the Coteswold hills, afterwards with my Brother's family. We think to remain there some time after he is returned to Town to over look the planting of trees & some other improvements about his house. If I have opportunity I will send you a letter from thence in return for yours from Staffa. But wo[e] is me! you must be contented to receive in lieu of your Cave & your Castles an account of bare sheep walks & corn fields & teams laired [*sic*] in the deep ruts of a cross road pent between two hedges, and cheese chambers fill'd with yellow cheeses, and kitchens with their rafter'd roofs hung not with broad swords & targets but sides of fat bacon. I will write tho' in spite of these discouragements, and good will will be recepted by you instead of good matter. — We have had your Neighbour Mrs E. Hamilton staying with us for a short time lately, who seemed to be the better for our pure Hampstead air. We found her a very cheerful, sociable Inmate, and parted with her when she left us with regret. Her health is very indifferent, and she talks very doubtfully of ever being again in this country. —— Pray lay by my pebble for me; and bring it to me in your pocket when you come to London. Coming from St: Columbus & Walter Scott, I shant care a jot what the Lapidaries say about it. — I thank you for your account of Mull & the Lady's rock, and am proud to hear the Highlanders like my Legend. – Henderson has got his money Mr Longman tells me; but if he did not call upon you when he was in Edin^r he did wrong. —

I hope this will find you & Mrs Scott & your little Sophia, who must needs have been a very happy Girl, safely returned from your journey. Give my kind regards with my Sister to Mrs Scott; and with all kind wishes to yourself, I rest always, my dear sir,

truly yours

J Baillie

PS. Mr Coxe has been kind enough to send his letter for you open, so I shall put this into it without a seal. ——

PS. Mr Coxe has desired me to tell you that he feels himself much pleased & flatter'd with the very kind, friendly manner that dictates your occasional letters to him, but I like an ungrateful Jew, have forgot it, having been more occupied with my own saws than with his.

3879 ff.236-39 (Address: To Walter Scott Esqr / N. Castle Street / Edin^r-- no postmark)

Duntisbourne Abbots Octr 27th 1810

My dear Sir,

When I received your very pleasant letter from the western Isles, I thought it well worth two of the very best letters I could possibly send you from any part of this country, so, in answering it from Hampstead, I promised you another answer from Gloucester sh: Do not think, however, that I put even my <u>two</u> letters <u>fornent</u>[82] yours, and say to myself "now he is repaid." By no means: I shall still feel myself your debtor.

My Sister & I have now been nearly two months in the part of the world, dividing our time pretty equally between my Brother's house, from which I write at present, and the house of a Friend on the Cotiswold hills about 4 miles off;[83] and we are left at last by our friends of both families having gone to London for the winter, and entire Mistresses of this mansion and its domains. This divided dominion we have been sharing as amicably as we could; she within doors sole director & arranger of Parlours, bed rooms, & china closets; I without, ordering as I please the planting of fields, banks, & orchards. My part, you will allow, is the most noble of the two; I say to oaks that are to flourish centuries to come "grow ye here" and to beeches chessnuts [sic] & other noble trees "grow ye there" and I go up & down where I list with a load of young trees under my arm followed by a Gardener & two or three labourers, leaving marks of my taste & liberality behind me. I believe in the morning I laid as many oaks in to the holes destined for them as may some time or other build a first rate man of war. Indeed I have for this last week had a taste of dominion & activity which has been extremely agreeable to me; and when I censure the kings of the earth for tearing kingdoms from one another and making war for territory, I must henceforth do it with charity. I find likewise that in taking an active part in the improvements of the place, I am become attached to it & the country round it. I believe I gave you no very favourable idea of it in my last letter, when I mentioned flat fields & deep rutted roads between straight hedges &c. It is indeed a flat country, and somewhat bare; the Ladies of the last century not having been so fond of planting trees as they are now; but this flat, upland level, is ploughed or hollowed with innumerable narrow vallies, some of them deep, & winding, & beautifully varied with woody banks & green sheep-walks & bushy knolls seen between. I wish I could add a clear running brook in the middle, but there

---

82. fornent or forenent: in front of or before (*SND*).
83. The friend is probably Anne Elliott of Devon.

we have little to boast, and the poorest scotch burnie[84] would put us quite out of countenance. My Brother's house stands on the top of a bare <u>bray</u>[85] looking down one of those beautiful vallies; even our brook, which afterwards calls itself strood[86] water, does in some places pretend to make a noise over the pebbles and dance in the sun like a noreland[87] burn, and we have many pretty wild walks in which we can wander with endless variety. A part of our vallie farther down the stream called Superton which belongs to Lord Bathurst,[88] is so famed for its beauty that strangers come from Cheltenham to see it. Thus, you see, I am not in a very despicable country, and, after having planted so many trees in it, may be allow'd [to] have some affection for it. My Brother means to spend a good part of every summer here and hoped to have done so this season, but the Princess Amelia's illness called him to Windsor some weeks ago, where he has remained ever since, and greatly shortened his stay to our great regret: for much as I love dominion, I would have given it up to him to which it rightly belongs with all my heart. The last accounts we had from him, a few days ago, the Princess continued in the same sad lingring [sic] state with none or next to no hope of recovery, and the king who is the most tender & anxious parent that can possibly be cannot be easy unless both Sir. Halford & him are constantly with her; so they are both kept in thraldom tho' they can do her no good. — But I have said nothing to you of our neighbourhood here; for you must permit me to return to my old subject again. It consists of one or two country squires & some Clergymen, who, on account of bad roads & other difficulties, do not meet together very frequently. The Clergyman of this Parish is a comfortable middle aged Bachelor, who can order & arrange a dinner of two courses very handsomely. He is no great reader and is not fond of literary conversation: he read Don Quixotte [sic] a great many years ago, but cannot well converse even upon this book as he has forgotten all about Sancho Panca [sic]; he has read another book not very long ago; namely the Lady of the Lake, and on that he speaks with greater freedom; for the discription of the morning sun on Lock Katerin has pleased him very much. The Clergyman of the next parish, whom we see very often, is the Father of a large family; a bad poet (for he is one) but a very orthodox divine having publish'd in defence of the high church doctrines, and spends all the money he can spare in buying books; he is also a reader & great admirer of the Lady of the Lake.

---

84. burnie: little stream (*SND*).
85. bray: the *SND* actually defines the word as "bare."
86. strood: trickling water (*SND*).
87. noreland: from the northern part of Scotland (*SND*).
88. This is most likely Tory statesman Henry, 3rd Earl of Bathurst (1762-1834).

Thus you see you have admirers of all characters, tho' this according to the last Edin^r Review of your works, is no proof of the highest merit, which, from various philosophical causes, difficult to comprehend, is generally found but to please a select few. Pray who wrote that review? Tho' Jeffrie has neither feeling nor fancy enough to write a very good review of any poetical work, he surely could not make such a perplexed & laborious attempt at philosophical reasoning as is to be found there.[89]

Just before we left Hampstead, I received a letter from Mr Balantine inclosing a draft for, I believe, £70 as the copy money for the Family Legend. I told him in answer, as perhaps he has told you, that he must write to Mr Henderson upon the subject, for that I meant only to receive what you & he agreed on as right for two Editions, leaving Mr H. to make the best bargain for himself that he could for what remained of the entire copy right. This Mr H. is a strange man; I dont know what to make of him: I find he never called on either yourself or Mr Balantine last spring when he passed thro' Edin^r — But I have teased your good nature upon this subject too often. —

I hope this letter will find you & Mrs Scott & the Children well, whether you be in Edin^r or the country, tho' I guess by this time you should be in Edin^r. Perhaps I shall hear by & by that you intend coming to London some time in the winter or spring. I shall be right glad to hear it; tho' in our great City where every body is full of your name, and every body from admiration or vanity anxious to feast you at their houses, the share that I may expect to have of your company cannot be great. ——— I have not told a soul of your intention of making the Hebrides the scene of your next poem, never the less every body that hears you have been there expects it to be so. I daresay your host of Staffa bestowed his hospitalities upon you very disinterestedly:[90] but could the most sordid Laird of the north do a wiser thing? Your visit will double his rents. Tell me what place you intend to celebrate after that, and I'll (much as my means are) purchase lands there immediately. A Friend of mine writes me word that the concorse of people that have been to see Lock Katterin [sic] this season is inconceivable; more than all the Inns, cottages & haylofts in Callender could contain, and even Stirling crowded with them besides. Alac a day! When shall I be able to make any thing worth the counting for myself or any much? Having made this letter I perceive another more than a reasonable length, I will now conclude with many kind wishes to you & Mrs Scott in which my Sister joins me. We shall remain here only a few days; for an account of M^{rs}

---

89. Though *The Lady of the Lake* had shattered all records for the sale of poetry, critic Jeffrey disliked certain parts of the poem (Johnson, 342).

90. disinterestedly: impartially (*OED*).

Baillie leaving the place sooner than was intended & my Brother's anxiety & hers that the planting should be well looked after, we have stayed behind her so long; and our work being now nearly done, we shall return to our own home. Farewell! and believe me always truly yours

    J Baillie

3879 ff.266-269 (Address: Walter Scott Esqr / North Castle Street / Edinburgh--postmarked 1810)

                                     Hampstead Novr 28th 1810

My dear Friend,

    On returning yesterday from Town, I found a packet lying on my table with a great star upon the seal, and open'd it very ungraciously, saying to myself as I broke every different fastening of wax, plague take it! deuce take it! — I had almost said <u>De'el take</u> it! for I thought it came from Sir John Sinclair; but most agreeable was my disappointment when I found that it came from yourself, and with such a token in it too as shall make me a prouder women [sic] than I have ever yet been all the days of my life.[91]

    Your harp of the north is a most beautiful & elegant harp, not to mention the other virtues it possesses; and as soon as this mourning is over, I'll buy me a new gown to put respect upon it, and ware [sic] it in the stomacher of the same very gallantly. Many thanks to you for the kindly gift! and I will fancy I may thank Mrs Scott also for the very elegant taste of the thing; no impeachment to your skill in these matters neither. The green stones of St: Columbus do indeed possess the virtues ascribed to them; for I have already put it to the proof by wishing a wish over the smallest of them viz a fine day for a Friend of ours who left us this morning for Scotland to travel in, and behold a beautiful sunny morning after many days of gloom & rain. I am reserving the largest stone to wish my Brother back from Windsor to the comforts of his own fireside; and if that succeed also, I shall take my next largest stone to wish you up from Edin^r in the course of the winter or spring, with as much business to do as will make it perfectly prudent in you to indulge it. You must come & see how well I shall look with my broach & my new gown; were there no other thing for you to do but this, it were cause sufficient.

---

    91. On their highland visit, from Staffa Scott and family had rowed across the sea to Iona, where children on the beach offered some green pebbles for sale, each of which was said to have the virtue of granting a wish. Mrs. Scott bought a few for a necklace, and Scott bought several which he had set into a brooch for Baillie (Johnson, 333) (see letter 3879 ff.156-158 above).

I am greatly pleased to hear that our two priority Dramatists I call them are at work upon the Lady of the Lake; and my Sister & I have already made engagements with some of our neighbours here to go & see it as soon as it is produced on the Covent Garden stage, where I make no doubt it will be got up (as the phrase is) with all becoming splendour. Are you sincere when you say you wish them at the bottom of Lock Katrine for this? Popularity has become a drug with you; and I wish you could transfer all that you have over & above what pleases you to a certain friend of yours, who loves it with all her heart. I never was better pleased than upon hearing that De Monfort was acted at a county fair, in a great waggon along side of the wild beasts. But dont you despise popularity; else I may find a way, perhaps, of filching more of it away from you than you can spare. Mr Jeffry tells us you get a great proportion of your fine ideas out of certain books;[92] and as soon as I can learn the names of those books and where they are to be found (for this he does not tell us) I will go a gathering in the same field too, being as free to do so as yourself or any man. The Covent Garden Managers, however, with their two Dramatists have been already for stall'd; Mrs Baillie & my Niece went and saw the Lady of the Lake last week without letting me know (for which I owe them a grudge) at the Royal Circus.[93] I took my account of it from Elizabeth, my Niece, for critics of fifteen are very often as much to be depended upon as critics of fifty. She tells me that it is but badly managed thro' out; that Ellen is pert & impudent, and everything that your Ellen is not; and that King James at the end, mounted upon his throne (for it is necessary it seems to be so in order to shew that he is a king) lets her even kneel at the foot of the steps till she is weary; and to be sure with such an Ellen as this, we cannot greatly blame him for so doing. "tho not a moment could he brook – The gentle king, that suppliant look" is too great a nicity [sic] for the Circus, how much more refined they may be at Covent Garden I wot not. Mrs Baillie told me portions of the poem in the original words were repeated on the stage, and she was never more struck with the

---

92. Francis Jeffrey had attacked *Marmion* for various reasons in the *Edinburgh Review*, criticizing its "ostentation of historical and antiquarian lore," when Baillie visited the Scotts in spring 1808. She met Jeffrey at one of Scott's gatherings, where the critic "entertained them 'with the detection of faults, blunders, absurdities, or plagiarisms'" (qtd. in Johnson, 281, 295). His review of *Lady of the Lake* (1810), however, was mostly positive. Jeffrey's implication about Scott's "sources" may have arisen at a gathering with these literary figures.

93. The popular *Lady of the Lake* was published in May 1810, with 20,000 copies being sold in one year (*DNB*, XVII:1026). Biographer Johnson does not mention this performance, but H. Philip Bolton notes a performance at Surrey, London, during September, October and November 1810 (for complete stage history, see Bolton's *Scott Dramatized* [London: Mansell, 1992], 12-42).

beauty of the poetry than in hearing it so repeated in the midst of all that absurdity. They have added also verses of their own to it, but I hope they have the discretion to sing those or at least to snuffle them thro' their noses.

I thank you for comiserating my poor Brother in his present grievous Thraldom. I saw him two days ago at Cranford Bridge, the stage between Windsor & Town, where Mrs B. goes once a week to meet him and have an hour of his company. It was like meeting a banish'd man on the confines of siberia, and we parted from him again with heavy hearts. When this confinement is likely to come to an end or to be mitigated we cannot at present guess. To day the Physicians are to be examined by the Privy Council, and I hope there will be no kind of difference in their evidence to create any disagreeable discussion in Parliament. My Brother keeps the daily journal of every thing that takes place with the concurrence of the other Physicians, and I trust it will be found to be an accurat[e] & clear one. You will see by the daily bulletins that the poor king has been upon the whole rather worse for these 8 or 10 days past, and I receive, I do assure you most literally, no other information than what the bulletin gives. Some kind of Regency, I suppose must be settled for a time; and it may be done I should hope without creating such violent party contention either in Parliament or the nation as it would have done some years ago.[94] The Prince of Wales is in the probable course of nature so near the throne that neither the present ministry nor the opposition will venture to grapple so greedily for <u>present</u> power as they would otherwise do. The Prince himself has met of late years with many rubs & mortifications which it is to be hoped have improved his character; and certainly at this time he has had the good sense to keep quiet, to live in harmony with the rest of the family and not to shew any inclination at all to grasp at power. One instance of sense & delicacy I can tell you. When my Brother attended the Princess, he took tea every evening by himself in some room or other of the Castle or Lodge and the Prince of Wales very frequently came & drank tea with him and would stay an hour or hour & half chatting very pleasantly; but from the moment that the kings illness was discover'd he has never come near him, and I daresay has observed the same delicacy in regard to all the Physicians. Every body here feels great sympathy for the poor king, and great desire that he should get well; for the strong affection & tenderness of his character during his Daughters illness shew'd itself in a most amiable light and endeared him to every one about him. I'm sure if

---

94. See Franco Crainz for details on Dr. Baillie's attendance on George III. In February 1812 the Regency was made permanent and George Augustus Frederick, Prince of Wales, took control of the monarchy.

we thought my Brothers attendance on him could do him any real good, neither himself nor us would murmur at it, grievous as it is.

I will now tell you about my short Tragedy on Fear which you are kind enough to enquire after.[95] It is finish'd; at least I think so; and if I may be allowed to be my judge in this case, it is very well suited for the stage. It is written in prose and consists only of 3 acts, and has no poetical ornaments given to it but sticks closely to the delineation of the passion & the interest of the story. As to its coming out upon the stage, however, there is no chance of my ever being gratified in this respect: I shall never offer a play to our London Managers, and they are too proud to ask for one. I have now nearly finish'd materials for another volume of the series, and might bring it out, if I liked, by the beginning of summer, a very good time for publishing, but I feel more inclined to put it off to another year. This vol: will consist of a Tragedy on fear in 5 acts, chief character in which is a woman; the Tragedy mentioned above on the same passion; a comedy on fear in 5 acts the chief character a man, and a little serious musical piece in 2 acts on hope, which is all I shall write upon this passion, and being a little thing shall be made as finish'd & pleasing as I can. This volume is probably the last thing I shall ever publish; but I shall continue as earnestly as ever to write for the stage upon my own plan, for two of the passions best fitted for representation remain behind, jealousy & remorse. My reason for this is I think a good one, and you will probably agree with me. My great desire is that my plays should in this country become common acting plays; and I know well that when pieces are publish'd without being acted, it is supposed they are only fit for the closet. I therefore wish that the remainder of my works should remain in manuscript to be brought out upon the stage after my death, when other Managers, the circumstances of the stage, and the disposition of the public towards me shall be more favourable. If these manuscript plays should happily be successful, people may then think that the other plays that have been published may possibly be better fitted for representation than they were taught to believe. These are my present motives upon this subject, and I dont believe I shall have occasion to alter them. ---- I am very much surprised at what you tell me of Mr Balantine not having heard from Mr Henderson if Mr B. has written to Mr H. as I begged him to do Mr H.'s address is at Clyth Caithness. If Mr Balantine has not written, I beg he

---

95. *The Dream: A Tragedy, In Prose, In Three Acts*, would appear in volume 3 of *A Series of Plays: in which it is attempted to delineate the stronger passions*, etc., in 1812 along with *Orra* (tragedy in 5 acts), *The Siege* (comedy in 5 acts) and *The Beacon* (musical drama in 2 acts) which she mentions below.

will do so and let me know the result, and if Mr H. still does not answer, I will enquire into the reason of it.

December 1st

I have delayed finishing my letter till I could get a frank which makes the date at the beginning of it rather old, but no matter. I read last night the examination of the Physicians by the Privy Council and find the king is better, and that the bulletins two days before their examination, which I had not seen, were favouable. Does not this look as if my green stone were beginning to operate? for surely the best & most agreeable way of having our good man home is by the King's circumstance that has amased [sic] us. Sir J. Sinclair sent a short while ago to the king's Physicians a recipe for curing his Majesty by the vapour bath (having heard, what was not true, that they proposed using the warm bath) and the Physicians, obstinate men as they are! notwithstanding Mr Percival in his great wisdom sent a messenger express to Windsor to enforce it, refused to adopt it. What heavy charges will they have to answer if they do not cure his Majesty without it?

Give my kindest wishes to Mrs Scott, and tell her she was perfectly right to keep you away from Portugal: I would not (had I any control over you) let you come within ear shot, far less eye shot of a battle, as I should not, so circumstanced, have the least faith to put in your discretion. ―― I hope the Children are all well; my love to them; and my Sister who joins me in this & in kind regard to you, desires me particularly to enquire after the young Laird. ――― Fare well! I thank you again for your friendly & flattering gift. It shall be kept for your sake & my own sake and the honour of my family (who will value it when I am gone) most devoutly. Yours most sincerely

J Baillie

3880 ff.25-29 (Address: Walter Scott Esq / North Castle Street / Edinburgh--postmarked 1811)

Hampstead Feb^ry 7th 1811

My dear Sir,

I am going to write to you on a subject which I really believe you care very little about; nevertheless as you are made of flesh & blood like the rest of us, it must needs be that you have some little curiosity regarding it, and so I shall make no apology for troubling you. The day before yesterday, my Sister & I went with a large party to see the first representation of the Knight of Snowdoun at Covent Garden Theatre, and had the satisfaction of seeing it very handsomely received by a very crowded house which was filled throughout with most respectable looking people.[96] Our box was a side box in the lowest circle, so that we had an excellent view of what the pit contained; and I never saw so many well dressed Gentleman-like men there in my life. — And now I would fain give you some idea of this dish that has been hashed up from your provisions if I could, but I fear I shall scarcely be able. I cannot say that on this occasion any thing has been done to falsify the old proverb, that "God sends us meat and the Devil sends us Cooks." Let this however be between ourselves; for I have some goodwill to Morton the Master of the kitchen in this case, and I believe he has miscooked his dish as little as any body was likely to have done who might have been put in his place. The piece opens with a view of Lock Katarin with the boat seen; the Gallant Grey lying dead and his Master lamenting him. The story has been somewhat altered to make it (as they think) more dramatic. Graeme the lover is entirely left out; and Roderick Due, whisked up into a compleat stage Hero, is both the favoured Lover & champion of Helen. A young Douglas, a child, is introduced; Brother to Helen, whom Roderick delivers from the hands of the Earl of Marr; and he likewise delivers Old Douglas just as they are about to behead him, with the procession for the execution seen [sic] &c., from the hands of the said Earl, by giving up himself to procure his ransome. The king at the end, for all this generous heroism, rewards him with the hand of Helen. The Lady Margaret, Roderick's mother, is left out and an old Nurse put in her place, whose son, Mac Loon, a silly, conceited, cowardly Fellow, who presumes to be in Love with Helen [Ellen], is the Drole of the piece; and this character was acted by Liston,[97] one of our first comedians, but I dont think with much effect. The Drama, when one thinks of the work from which it is taken, has little chance of pleasing any body; but upon the whole, taken by itself, is a splendid, varied, tolerably amusing piece, and will, I doubt not, continue, for this winter at least, to be attractive. The most striking scenes which pleased the audience best, because in them they recognized most perfectly favourite passages of the original poem, were the first scene, Norman's

---

96. Fitz-James, who calls himself "the Knight of Snowdon" appears in Scott's *The Lady of the Lake*. Dramatic versions were presented in Edinburgh, Dublin and London between September 1810 and February 1811 (Bolton, 14).

97. Actor John Liston (1776?-1846) gained renown in the north as a comedian and was vainly recommended by Charles Kemble for the management of Covent Garden. Colman then engaged him for the Haymarket, where he played many roles and in October 1806 appeared at Covent Garden where he remained until 1822. In Scott adaptations he was the original Dominie Sampson, Bailie Nicol Jarvie, Jonathan Oldbuck and Wamba. In January 1823 he made his first appearance at Drury Lane as Tony Lumpkin and retired from the Olympic in 1837. I do not find an account of Liston's role in *Lady of the Lake*.

wedding interrupted by the fiery cross, and the rising of the ambush which was indeed exceedingly well managed. The court scene was splendid, but the knight of Snowdoun led in Helen with his hat off, and when she asked to see the king, he very cleverly, while she turned her head aside, sat himself down on a throne, put the robe on his shoulders & the crown on his head, and was a king in all his formalities in a trice. She then knelt in a very orderly manner at the foot of the throne, and made, in this posture, a long speech which he did not interrupt. This to be sure is not very like your knight of Snowdoun; but perhaps it might be necessary in so large a Theatre to make those at a distance understand the story. There were two things in the course of the play which raised a very hearty clap. The first is when a soldier asks Norman if he can write; the other says no, but he can comment on what other people write, the soldier then says something I did not distinctly hear about northern critics, which the audience did not fail to apply: the second is at the end of the last act when the king prophesies that some future Poet will in deathless rhime record the gallant feats of Snowdoun's knight. This last is all the notice taken of your worship from beginning to end, as the piece has neither prologue nor epilogue in which to introduce any thing of the kind. Charles Kemble[98] is the knight of Snowdoun & Young[99] is Roderick Due. — There are plenty of songs in it of M^r M's own composing, suited to the present taste in stage songs, the only one of yours he has introduced is the guard-room song. I have not sent you a book of the songs as I once thought of doing, because Mr Morton, I suppose, will send you a copy of the whole as soon as it is printed, and I dont care for sending this to Mr Freeling but would rather make a common frank do for it.

I suppose I have said as much as you would desire about the knight of Snowdoun, and now let me ask how you & Mrs Scott and the <u>Bairns</u> do; and when we may hope to see you both in this part of the world, with the good Girl that you are to drop with us at Hampstead in your passing to the great City. I hope I shall hear something agreeable upon this subject soon.

You will see by the papers that the King goes on favourably: and I believe his Physicians have now no doubt of his getting thro' the wood, tho' perhaps slowly. The Prince is to keep on the present ministry and to make every thing as soothing & easy for the king's return to power as may

---

98. Actor Charles Kemble was the brother of Sarah Siddons and John Kemble.

99. This is probably actor Charles Mayne Young (1777-1856) who made his debut at Covent Garden in 1808. Kemble was making few performances at this time, and Young was beginning to take over many of his roles (*DNB*, XXI:1280-83). Bolton notes only the name Young in this performance but in later performances cites a Braham Younge. Ellen was played in this London version by Miss S. Booth (Bolton, 14).

be this at least is confidently said, and there is every appearance of its being true. My Brother comes now to Town about twice a week, and I have sometimes the satisfaction of seeing him, tho' in a hurried uncomfortable manner. ――― How well we were amused with your account of Sir J. Sinclair's proposals to you! I would give a good deal for a sight of those rules he sent you for writing a heroic poem. Did he give you any particular directions how to make this same Lady of the sea trail along her scaly trail in a graceful & dignified manner? What you say is true enough that he must have a finger in every man's pie: he would teach you to write poems; and I should not be surprized to see him stop a Lamp-lighter on his way to shew him the best way of trimming lamps. This by the same association that introduces him in your letter, leads me to speak of Mr Henderson's affair. I wrote to him immediately after receiving yours, expressing my surprise at his not having answered Mr Balantine's letters, and begging him to do it immediately, for that I considered myself as having nothing to do in the business which rested with himself entirely. I receive[d] an answer to my letter about eight days ago, written in a different hand from his own but signed by himself, saying he had been very ill and was still very weak, and that he should give me an answer on the subject of my letter, fully, as soon as he should be able to write. There it must rest till he shall please to signify his pleasure. I am very sorry Mr Balantine has had so much trouble about it.

I will now finish this epistle (which is a much longer one than I generally write, or fully as long a one, I guess, as you generally wish to receive) with many kind wishes to yourself & Mrs Scott, and all that belong to you. My Sister joins heartily in the same, and so farewell for the present, saith your sincere friend

J Baillie

PS. Mrs Baillie gives you many thanks for your remembrance of her & her family, and always speaks & thinks of you with particular interest & good will from the friendship you have shewn to me, and the great delight she has received from your writings. – Indeed people here are perfect gluttons in regard to your poetry for they have no sooner feasted on the Lady of the Lake but they come teazing one to know whether you are not employed in writing another poem the Hero of which is the Pretender. I tell them I dont know, and then they tell me "O! but it is so" ――――

3880 ff.172-176 (Address: Walter Scott Esq / N. Castle Street / Edinburgh-
-postmarked 1811)

Hampstead July 9th 1811

My dear Sir,

I am indeed much disposed to like Don Roderick because it is yours,[100]
but it has also strong claims on its own account which I am sure I should
the more readily allow, had I not, for I dont know how many years past,
taken a most unaccountable aversion to visions. However, Vision as it is,
the beauty & spirit of many parts of it cheated me out of my prejudice; and
my fancy followed the <u>Kingly Likeness</u> on his horse Oralio as if it had
been the immediate fortunes of a real man, tho with a very different
feeling from that which drew my whole mind & attention into one point at
the real shriving of the King by the holy Prelate; a solemn striking
picture, that stands boldly on the foreground of the piece, having the
visionary part in proper subordination (or in the artist's phrase) in due
keeping, behind it. May the good cause for which it was so liberally
written be triumphant, and that will be a noble recompense for you and a
most joyful event for every creature who has any right & generous
principles within them. — Many thanks to you for thinking me worthy to
have one of your Author's copies sent to me, and I assure you I shall keep it
by me all the rest of my life right proudly.

So you have become the Laird of Abbotsford.[101] A respectable sounding
name this; and would become a large estate fully as well as a little farm;
and I hope it will be the name of a good estate with a good house upon it
too, in which your prosperous descendants, ages after this, will proudly
point out the picture of the first Laird. With all my ambition on your
behalf, however, I like the thoughts of your Cottage & your plantations &
your streams exceedingly; and should be happy indeed to plant some trees
round your doors, tho' you would find me I doubt a troublesome assistant in
your labours, having become very conceited of my taste & skill in these
matters since I studied them in Gloucester sh:, and much readier to give
advice than to follow it. Many happy days may you & Mrs Scott & the
children have in your new habitation! but dont let all the idle Travellers,
who come to visit the country & the ruins which you have made famous,
make an Inn of your house, for their own convenience and that they may
boast in their stupid Tours afterwards of the great attentions they

---

100. Scott published *The Vision of Don Roderick* in July 1811, whose profits he
dedicated to the Portuguese war sufferers (Johnson, 375).

101. Scott purchased an estate of 100 acres of rough land and a small farmhouse
in 1811, naming it Abbotsford, but the family was not to move there from Ashestiel
until the following spring.

received from their <u>Friend</u> Mr Scott.[102] I believe it would be fully as wise in you to follow my advice in regard to the number of your spare rooms as the planting of your grounds.

I have reserved this last side of my paper for answering a question you very kindly put to me, viz if it is true that I mean shortly to publish. It is true; and when you are sitting by your Christmas fire, you shall have my next vol. almost entirely occupied with the passion of Fear to amuse you. A good winter, fire-side subject, if it be well managed. I have been advised to bring it out at that season, as more likely to be read with attention than in spring; and should the winter readers give a good report of it to the spring <u>Literati</u>, they will buy it whether they read it or not.[103] Having done this, I shall consider myself as having finished my task, as far as publishing is concerned, for it is not my intention ever again to publish another vol. of Plays. I should have been contented to go on publishing could I have hoped, as I once did, that, after my death some of my Plays (I mean a fair proportion of them) might have made their way upon our Theatres here, and have been considered as works belonging to the Theatre as well as the closet. But I have the mortifcation to find that, as they are not acted in the London Theatres, they are considered as not adapted to representation; and how long this opinion may continue after I am gone, should it ever be changed, I know not. My scheme therefore is to go on writing, but to reserve all the rest of my plays in manuscript to be produced by my heirs upon the Theatre when we shall have, (as we doubtless some time or other shall have) Theatres better fitted & better disposed to receive them. The Public then, having them brought before them as new works, will have their curiosity gratified, and will shew them that favour, at least, which is commonly bestowed upon novelty. This change in my plan, which the more I consider it the more [r]easonable it appears to me, I should have adopted with some regret had I considered the Public as at all eager to receive the rest of my work, but as I have no reason to suppose this is the case, I shall do it with less concern.

I am sorry you are at such a distance, for you else have seen the whole contents of my forthcoming book in M^s and I should have profitted by your observations. I should particularly have liked to shew you the prose Tragedy on Fear, taken from the story I shew'd you when you were here, which I think well fitted for acting, and which you seemed to think had

---

102. In NLS letter 3902 ff.157-161 Baillie later writes that this very influx of "idle Travellers" was partly the cause of Scott's financial difficulties in 1827.

103. Volume 3 of *A Series of Plays: in which it is attempted to delineate the stronger passions* . . . would appear from Longman, Hurst, Rees, Orme, and Brown in 1812.

materials in it for an interesting plot.[104] Since this cannot be, if I live some years longer, and you come now & then to this part of the world, I shall shew you things that no body but yourself & a few Friends beside shall ever see in my life time; and if there be many faults in them you tell me how to mend them, and, if there be some beauties to commend, you will cheer me. ――――

My Brother is still attending at Windsor, but for many weeks past he has only been there two days in the week. How long this arrangement will continue I dont know, but he has given up all hopes of going to Gloucester sh: this year, excepting for one week, and has taken a house at Sunning hill, 4 or 5 miles from Windsor, for the summer. The King I understand is in very good bodily health. ――― I was like to have my bones broken & my sides squeezed together last week crowding with all the other curious people in London (a goodly host!) to see Carlton House. It is rich & superb beyond any thing I could have imagined, and for the tented supper rooms that we walked thro', besides those within doors, there seemed to have been accommodation enough to have feasted a whole army. The crowds who went to see the house have trodden all the new carpets there into shreds, and whether we shall be grateful enough to pay the Master of it back in popularity I wot not. A young Lady, Daughter of a rich Brewer was almost crushed to death, so that for some time it was thought she was dead; but the Prince sent every day after that to enquire for her, and I hear she considers this honour as an ample recompense for all she has suffered.

――

Farewell! My Sister joins me in kindest wishes to yourself & Mrs Scott and all your young folks. ――― I have now wrote you what me [may] be considered for me, who am no letter writer, as a good long letter. Do you at some convenient time, that is to say when you shall be visiting at some stupid house in the country, and want to retire an hour or so to write some <u>very important</u> dispatches, indite to me a good, long, handsome letter in return, and that will keep you in my good books for half a year there after and no longer. ―― Farewell again, and believe me always with sincere regard

      your truly obliged friend
       J Baillie

---

104. See *The Dream: A Tragedy, In Prose, In Three Acts.*

3881 ff.15-19 (Address: Walter Scott Esqr / Ashestiel / Selkirk--
postmarked 1811)

Hampstead August 15th 1811

My dear Friend,

I thank you with all my heart for your kind letter which was a
pleasure I scarcely expected to receive so soon; I therefore have no fault to
find with the goose berries & currants at Ashestiel, and wish that you &
your young folks may enjoy them for some weeks to come. It is a fleeting joy
which we, in these parts, look back upon; a half withered berry being now
only to be found in the middle of a prickly bush, for which we are
contented both to tear our gowns & scratch our fingers.

Indeed you are very good at the end of three weeks to write me such a
long & pleasing letter: and the ballad inclosed in it we have read with
great approbation. There are indications of strong vigorous fancy in it,
which is a much better thing to find in the works of a Poet of fifteen (or
indeed at any age) than elegant versification; tho' I dont mean to say that
the verses of the Robber Polydore are, for a work of the kind, at all amiss.
You have given him good wholesome advise [sic] and I hope he will profit
by it, and do credit to the great Master-Poet whose Disciple he is.[105]

"An't were not for the gibbet rope["]
"My voice were clear & free.["]

Gives me a twitch; and the story is really told with good effect. —— I need
scarcely tell you that I feel very much gratified by the interest you take in
what I am at present preparing for the press. If the Printer & his devil
together could fall upon any conjuring way of printing one copy of the book
a great deal sooner than all the rest, that copy should be sent to you; and
whether it were read by you at midnight or mid-day, I am confident it
would find you most favourably disposed at least to receive from it all the
impression I could desire. My mind is very seriously made up to publish no
more volumes, unless some unexpected thing should happen to alter it (for I
have made no vow) but you shall not wait till I am buried for the
gratification of your curiosity. No; you shall have a peep behind the
curtain, and see all that I keep in reserve, whenever you desire it, and are

---

105. See Scott letter of 4 August 1811: "I have lately found a young man whose
genius appears to me very uncommon considering he is but sixteen. He was with me a
few days ago and brought me a little goblin tale founded on fact which has many of
the faults attached to that slovenly composition, the German ballad, but I think has
also merits more than sufficient to redeem them. . . . I made use of the youths
application to me to direct his study towards what appears to me the most useful
and improving branches of learning assuring him he could not be a poet without a
general acquaintance with letters" (Grierson, 2:526). Grierson identifies the young
poet as W. Howison.

so situated that it can be done, that is to say a visitor in this part of the world. What am I to think of what you say at the end of your letter about walking in like a wraith, soon after your letter? that would be an apparition from which we should not invoke Ministers of grace to defend us:[106] but I have so little faith in any chance we have of this, that I would give it all up, most willingly, to be assured we should see you walk in so, or in any fashion, in the course of the next spring, greatly as I approve of the old proverb "A bird in hand &c.["][107] However, I will not believe that it is likely you may not visit London for several years: it is not in the nature of things that this can be. — A thousand thanks to you for thinking to have my short Tragedy on Fear brought out upon the Edin.ͬ Theatre! If I thought this would really be agreeable to your Manager & all parties concerned, I should be nothing loth; but I am afraid that your Brotherly zeal may tempt you to bring my things forward when they are not, perhaps, entirely wanted, and so make a bcre of me with those with whom I should particularly dislike to be so. Consider it well; and if you can then honestly say that you are well assured upon this point, I shall write or cause to be written out a manuscript copy of the piece which you may give them to bring out whenever it shall be most for the advantage of the Theatre. I am glad to hear you have such a promising Actor as Mͬ Jervy.[108] It is only in such a Theatre as Edin.ͬ at present possesses (thanks to their want of money perhaps) that good acting is of any value. In our great Theatres here it is lost. ――― And this leads me to think of the family Legend, and to thank you for your great goodness to Mͬ Henderson. I am glad he had activity enough at last to go & get his money: to have written to Mͬ Longman to be sure of having all that could be got, would have been too great an exertion. I received a letter from him about a week ago, telling me of this transaction, which is dated the 17ᵗʰ of May; and I suppose has been on a fishing voyage to the north seas since it was written in some of his smacks.[109]

My Brother is not likely soon to be released from his attendance at Windsor: and I am sorry to say it may still be of long or at least

---

106. See Hamlet's first reaction to the Ghost (1.4.39): *Ham.* "Angels and ministers of grace defend us!"

107. "A bird in the hand is worth two in the bush" is an English proverb borrowed from the Greek (H. L. Mencken, *A New Dictionary of Quotations on Historical Principles* [New York: Knopf, 1942], 104).

108. Baillie could be referring either to Henry Jarvis, who had played Osbaldistone in *Rob Roy*, or the actor Jervis who played Dougal in *Rob Roy* (see Bolton). I have not identified a Mr. Jervy.

109. smack: a single-masted sailing vessel or a fishing-vessel with a live well for fish (*OED*).

considerable continuance. I may without crime say <u>sorry</u>, since the hope of his Patient's recovery amounts, I should apprehend, to almost nothing, and the state he is in is so deplorable. You look forward with anxiety and so we must all do; yet, as far as manners are concerned, I hope the future Court will not be so bad as might have been feared. In that same grand fete that you mention, some regard to character in the Lady's was attended to; and divorced, or notoriously <u>papa</u> Dames,[110] were not invited. Let us take a little comfort from this in the midst of many distresses.

Mrs Baillie & the family are gone to the house they have taken at Sunning hill, where my Sister & I mean to visit them soon. Mrs B. talks or rather writes in raptures of a ride they have thro' the forest to Windsor where there are the most beautiful trees of all ages, and every old Oak they pass might be a study for a painter, and do honour, itself alone, to any mansion near which it might grow. I doubt not my Sister & I will enjoy & admire it very much; but we would exchange all this forest beauty very willingly for the bare sides of Ben Lomond. You do very handsomely to plant 70 acres of your new possession.[111] Let a good portion of that be together, in the fashion of a wood, that it may be knowing venerated for your wood, as long as Scotland shall know & her proud of herself.[112] You see I will always be giving you advice, whether it may be to my purpose or not. You make indeed a kind of fashion of following it as to the number of your spare rooms in your future cottage; but with such a warm heart as you have, hankering after every being of your kind, what does it signify whether you have many rooms or few, as long as a dormitory can be made of the barn or a great empty garret?[113] Ah! poor Mrs Scott! she has not got you into good training, and I fear you are now incorrigible. ——— I am very glad to hear of the popularity of Don Roderick; I should have guessed that its success must be great from [the] number of copies I have met with, even in the narrow circle of our acquaintance. They all praise it in a degree, but immediately throw the Lady of the Lake at your head, as a poem of superlative beauty. It is true and must be confessed, that in chusing such a subject, interesting as it is, when connected with present events, you have put it out of your power to make any considerable use of two admirable talents which you possess above all our other poets, namely the power of circumstantial individual discription and of delineating variety of

---

110. *papa dames*: rich or spoiled women (*Oxford French Dictionary*).

111. Scott began planting seedlings and acorns all around Abbotsford, hoping one day to surround it with noble English oaks (Johnson, 378, 384).

112. This sentence is awkward and seems to have some words missing.

113. Scott told Baillie that the farmhouse had "five tolerable rooms in it kitchen included and if all come to all, we can adopt your suggestion and make a bed in the barn" (Johnson, 375).

natural characters. General discription suitable to a vision has but a weak power over our imaginations compared to the other, and particularly when continued to any length. It is only the first grand unveiling of such scenes that affects us; and this I must do you the justice to say you have excuted [*sic*] with masterly hand. ––– My Friend Mr Coxe has had a little bickering lately at his own table with Rogers the Poet,[114] who is not the greatest admirer you have in the world, defending one of your lines in which you say, a person "tip toe stands" instead of <u>on</u> tip toe stands, as Mr R. maintains it should have been. Mr Coxe very triumphantly found authority for your expression in a verse of Shakespear which he repeated; but the other Poet in reply asserted, that Shakespear is no authority. ––– I would send you M^r C's verses on my Broach as he desired me to do, but dare not encrease the weight of this frank. You shall have it next packet I send, and then you shall judge whether the fine things you had thought of on this subject or his fine things are the best. —

With many kind wishes to Mrs Scott & the Children, believe me, my dear Sir,

truly & affectionately yours
J Baillie

3881 ff.122-126 (Address: For Walter Scott Esqr--no postmark)

Hampstead Decr 5th 1811

My dear Sir,

My book is now out of the printers hands and gone to Longman's to be bound; and 60 copies of it which I intend for my Friends, will be sent to their different destinations, I hope, very soon, some time at least before it is publicly disposed of.[115] But there is one of those 60 copies which I have coaxed Mr Longman to let me have before the rest; and this I shall send to you, by the aid of Mr Freeling, as soon as I get it; and hoping this may be in a day or two, or perhaps tomorrow, I think it best to say my <u>say</u> to you before hand, that it may be ready to go with the book when it does come, without losing time. Of the short Tragedy on Fear which you so kindly enquired after in your last,[116] I had written out a copy to have sent to you, lest, even after the hint I gave you not to push any thing of the kind where it might not be entirely welcome, you should still have wished me to send

---

114. Samuel Rogers (1763-1855), banker and well-known art collector, became a highly successful poet in his lifetime. Between 1822-28 he published a collection of verse tales entitled *Italy*. See introduction and letters to Rogers, Volume 2.

115. Volume 3 of Baillie's *A Series of Plays: in which it is attempted to delineate the stronger passions*, etc., appeared from Longman, Hurst, Rees, Orme, and Brown in 1812 and included *Orra*, *The Dream*, *The Siege* and *The Beacon*.

116. *The Dream*.

it. You have, however, done more wisely, I will venture to say, in not desiring me to send it: and now when all parties concerned shall have it in their hands in a printed book, they will not think themselves at all called upon to bring it forward, unless it be entirely agreeable. Mr Freeling is a good man to me, and long may he be at the head of the Post Office I pray sincerely! for I can scarcely tell you how much satisfaction I have in sending this book to you so cleverly for of all my country men I would wish you first to read it, persuading myself that such a beginning will bring it good luck. Being near Christmas time, such things have power. You will be to me on this occasion what a <u>first foot</u>[117] is to one of a New year's day morning, and will cast upon it at least the <u>blink</u> not of an ill, but of a good eye. Aye; were all my readers of the same spirit with you, I should be sure of getting all the credit I am entitled to & a good bit more bestowed upon me most ungrudgingly; and, being sure of this, I should take all the censure that is likewise my due very meekly. However, with no more favour than is likely to be found, we shall e'en try to behave ourselves as well as we can; having this comfort before our eyes that it is likely to be the last brunt we shall encounter. I shall henceforth, if I am spared, go on writing when I am in the humour and resting when I am not, which is certainly the case at present; for I have taken a rage for carpet work that is likely to hold out for some time, and then I shall betake myself to some thing else which a Lady wearing towards fifty may do by candle light without the aid of spectacles; and if this industrious humour continue, I shall net you a purse which you will fill with bank notes very soon & very richly, if all that the world whispers here be true.

I suppose this find you in Edin^r busy in your law court as usual. My Sister & I were very much pleased the other day with reading in the newspaper the promotion of Ld Craig to be your president.[118] I believe you could not well have one of greater integrity, and I hope he will be spared in such a state of health as to do the duties of his high office for <u>some</u> years — I dare not tho' I would gladly say, <u>many</u>. As to your other law promotion knowing nothing of the parties, I have not concerned myself at all about them; but I daresay they have occasioned conversation & wrangling enough with you. For promotion in general, whether Whigs or Tories are favoured, I should hope that Scotch men will have their share,

---

117. first foot: the first visitor on New Year's day (*SND*).

118. Baillie probably means Sir James Gibson Craig (1765-1850), Edinburgh politician and leader of the Scottish Whigs, though in a subsequent letter she admits she is misinformed. Craig and Scott were at odds on several issues, but after the passing of the Reform Bill, Craig's political activity abated (*DNB*, IV:167-68).

since the Regent has sprained his leg teaching his Daughter to dance the Highland fling.[119] — — —

I have been greatly concerned since I wrote you last at the death of our Brother Poet James Graham. Poor man! he had suffered a great deal, and with a heart craving sympathy which he was always ready to give, had received very little, from the notion entertained by every body about him that he had little real disease but was only hypochondriac. He was not much fitted for this world; but he had talents for the pulpit and a benevolent heart (had his health permitted) to make a good Parish Pastor, and might have done much good in it, and enjoyed himself more than he had hitherto done, and more than worldly men generally do. But he is better off now than any Bishop could have made him, and it is only for his family that we ought to grieve. I felt for him great respect, and a very sincere regard. There was great tenderness in his character & his writing, with warm but delicate & reserved piety which was beautiful in itself and calculated to make a useful impression on others, as I hope it has often done.

We have had, as far as weather is concerned as [sic] very cheerful November & up to the present time. No body I'm sure can have hanged himself in this part of the country that would not have done so in June: little rain, generally falling in the night too, and clear sunny mornings with none, or almost none of the dark fogs that we are accustomed to at this season. Yesterday we had frost & snow, and to day the children are sliding on the ice, the sight & sound of which always does me good; for having never rode after the hounds, nor swam in the water, nor flown along upon skirts[120] like a dutch woman, the remembrance of darting down a long slippery slide upon my <u>tricuppet</u> shoon,[121] with half a dozen children shouting behind me on the same track, as the keenest delight and most exalting situation I have ever experienced, is very pleasing to me still. Thus we have made a kind of lingring [sic] summer or autumn shake hands with Christmas. I am sorry to learn it has not been so in the north. A

---

119. In November 1811 George Augustus Frederick (later George IV) attended a ball in honor of his only daughter, Princess Charlotte. While giving her a lively demonstration of the Highland fling, he slipped and strained his ankle against the leg of a sofa. It was soon evident that he was not suffering merely from a twisted ankle, for he had violent pains stopped only by "a hundred drops of laudanum every three hours." This illness continued well into December, and it has since been suggested that the Prince Regent was suffering from porphyria, which in more severe form afflicted his father George III (Christopher Hibbert, *George IV, Regent and King, 1811-1830* [New York: Harper and Row, 1973], 13-15).

120. skirts: either a reference to the lower portions of a saddle, a saddle skirt, or the side or leach of a sail (*OED*).

121. shoon: dial., shoe (*OED*).

Scotch Lady who is in Hampstead at present is greatly pleased with what she considers as a specimen of an English Winter. By the bye this same Lady boasts of you as having been an old Bedfellow of hers. — Dont start: it is upwards of thirty years since this irregularity took place, and she describes her old Bedfellow as the drolest [*sic*] looking, odd, intertaining little Urchin that ever was seen. I have told her that you are a great strong man nearly 6 feet high, but she does not believe me.

I hope Mrs Scott & all your young folks are well, and beg to offer my regards & best wishes in which I am joined by my Sister. Mrs Baillie is pleased with your kind remembrance of her, and thinks of you always with great admiration & good will. Fare well! and believe me always, truly & faithfully yours

J Baillie

Decr 9th The book is come at last, but some days later than I expected. — — — I inclose my good Friend Mr Coxe's verses on my broach, which he desired me some time ago, but not then having any room in my frank I put off doing it till now. — He is well; but has not sent me any verses lately — J is always enquiring very warmly for you. — — — —

Farewell again!

3882 ff.7-11 (Address: Walter Scott Esqr / North Castle Street / Edinburgh--postmarked 1812)

Hampstead Jan^{ry} 2^d 1812

My very kind & dear Friend,

You never fail to cheer & encourage me with a most brotherly good-will, whatever the rest of the world may do; and whatever they may do, I will be cheered & encouraged. It gives me great pleasure to hear that you think my present volume will bring no disgrace upon me; and I shall go on with what remains of my task, if it should please God to spare me long enough, with good heart.[122] — I entirely agree with you in what you have said of the disadvantages & difficulties in acting such a play as the Dream with Actors such as we commonly find them; and entirely acquiese

---

122. In his letter of 17 December 1811, Scott praised Baillie's third volume of plays, replying that

> The whole character of Orra is exquisitely supported as well as imagined and the language distinguished by a rich variety of fancy which I know no instance of excepting Shakespeare. . . . I think the Dream extremely powerful indeed but I am rather glad we did not hazard the representation for the reasons mentioned in my last. . . . The latter half of the volume I have not perused with the same attention, though I have devoured both the comedy and the Beacon in a hasty manner.

(Grierson, 3:36)

[*sic*] in your opinion that it should not be brought out in the Edin.^r Theatre, under its present circumstances. The character of Osterloo,[123] would not suit many an Actor with good general talents for acting, while others, I am persuaded, may be found, not possessing general talents, who would do i t very ably. John Kemble here could do it powerfully,[124] but he will not do it, and I do not now expect or hope that it will ever be acted. ––– So you are going to have a new Play of Sir G. Mackenzies brought out in Edin.^r.[125] I hope it will succeed (so as it do not put the nose of my poor Family Legend out of joint), not for any regard I have to the Author, whom I dont know; but that it may encourage you to bring out new plays now & then, while our Theatres here are so ill suited for any such attempt. What you have said of your old military friend, I have shewn to no mortal, and to make all safe I have done, what it grieves me to do with a letter of yours, – put it into the fire. ––– It is a whimsical enough thing (talking of putting papers into the fire) that you should have found a song in Orra so like one of your own.[126] I am quite proud of this, tho' I put no faith at all in the inferiority which you so gallantly ascribe to yours. And why did you burn it? Is my curiosity to be raised in this manner without being gratified? Granting it were worse than mine: can you not bear to be mine inferior in so slight a matter, standing above me in so many of far greater importance. I am proud enough, yet I should not be ashamed to have written worse verses than the

---

123. Osterloo is the imperial general in her play *The Dream*.

124. John Philip Kemble (1757-1823), one of England's most famous actors, began playing parts in his father's company in early childhood. His sister, Sarah Kemble Siddons, first recommended him to the Chamberlain's company as Theodosius in Lee's tragedy in 1776, with dozens of parts to follow. Kemble was a scholar, a man of breeding and a fine actor with a larger range of characters in which he excelled than any English tragedian. He wrote prologues for charitable institutions in York and Leeds, where he appeared for the first time in *Hamlet*--he is said to have written out the part over 40 times. He managed the Edinburgh Theatre for a while in 1781, and his first appearance in London was at Drury Lane as Hamlet in 1783. He remained at Drury Lane for 19 years, presenting over 120 characters himself; and on 25 January 1800 Kemble played DeMonfort in Baillie's play. In 1802 he acquired a 6th share of Covent Garden, but in 1808 when the house burned, taking 20 lives, Kemble and other investors were nearly ruined for lack of insurance. A loan of £10,000 from Lord Percy helped him reopen the new Covent Garden Theatre. Portraits of John Kemble abound, several of which are by Lawrence, notably Kemble as Cato, as Hamlet and as Rolla (*DNB*, X:1260-66).

125. I have not identified Mackenzie's play, which is further discussed in the following letter 3882 ff.128-131.

126. She must have destroyed the letter, for I find no such reference. Scott had responded earlier: "I have a great quarrell with this beautiful drama [Orra] for you must know you have utterly destroyed a song of mine precisely in the turn of your outlaws ditty and sung by persons in somewhat the same position" (Grierson, 3:35).

<u>worst verses</u> you ever wrote in your life. Let it therefore, I pray you, be your good pleasure that I shall have a copy of this said song, which still exists in your tenacious memory tho' it has been cast in to the fire. ––– Every body here enquires at me about a new Poem which you are writing, for which you are to receive 3000 guineas[127] (money enough this to fill the purse I am to net for you) and I in return, to pressure some little consequence consistent with the truth, say that I am only in your confidence in regard to your building & your Farming & the planting of your woods. It was not me who sent you the bay of acorns from Windsor forest but Mr Ellis,[128] I suppose, tho' I may possibly have been the cause of their being sent. I had the pleasure of meeting him when we were at Sunning Hill, and liked the little I saw of him very much. His appearance at first is rather gawky than sensible, but there is an unaffected kindness in his manner that pleases you from the first; and when he sits down by you, he chats very agreeable with great freedom & variety. He is a very favourite writer with me & so I was disposed to like him. I liked his wife, as I have liked the wives of some other men, because she seemed good humoured & proud of her husband; and she shew'd us some Ms. book of his writing, or rather transcribing, which did more credit to his neatness of hand than I should have supposed he would have cared for. We only met him at the end of our visit to Sunning hill; I wish we had met him at the beginning of it. ––– I am glad to hear you have got Mr Stark for the Architect for your new house;[129] I know him very well; he is a very superior man in his profession. Let the walls of this same house be thick, for it will be a monument in the south of Scotland for many ages. –– There was a part of your last letter that made me feel most uncomfortably till I got to the end of it: I need not tell you what part it was. Little did I think when I last parted with you at Hampstead what a predicament you were to be in so shortly after. I know the place you discribe very well, and shall never walk by the side of that hedge again as carelessly as I have done.[130] It makes me shudder to

---

127. Scott was working on *The Bridal of Triermain* and *Rokeby* simultaneously, both appearing in 1813, and Baillie does not identify which poem she means.

128. This is probably George Ellis (1753-1815), author and friend of Scott, whose works include *Poetical Tales by Sir Gregory Gander* (1778), *Specimens of Early English Romances in Metre* (1805), some translations and contributions to the *Anti-Jacobin*. Scott often stayed with Ellis at his home at Sunninghill near Ascot (*DNB*, VI:694-95).

129. During the summer of 1811 William Stark, a brilliant Glasgow architect suggested to Scott by actor Daniel Terry, had looked over the proposed site for the home at Abbotsford and sketched a beautiful, fanciful, convenient plan with which Scott was delighted (Johnson, 375).

130. See Scott letter dated 17 December 1811. Discussing Baillie's use of "fear," he follows with:

think what might have befallen you. Thoughts of this kind come powerfully upon us poor Inhabitants of the environs of London at this time, after the dreadful murders that have been committed so near us. I assure you we do not sleep so sound as we were wont; and no body knocking at our door after dark is admitted till he has been questioned thro' the key hole as strictly as a stranger at the barriers of Paris in the reign of Terrour. ——— And I have been a great Goose it seems in supposing Ld Craig was made President because he opened the sessions. My Sister read me his speech upon the occasion from the news paper and called out with much satisfaction that he was made President and I believed her. I am generally too busy with my needle at the time the papers are read to be very hard of belive [sic], particularly when the news pleases me. In the list of names sent to Mr Ballantyne as those to whom I wished copies of my book to be sent, I have put down the Lord President but luckily I had wit enough to put Craig to the end of it to make sure, and so I hope Ballantyne will understand who I meant. I am very sorry to hear he is in such a melancholy state. His Father was a very intimate friend of my Fathers, and I have a great good will & respect for him. ——— You say in your first letter that you suppose my Brother is now released from his attendance at Windsor. Indeed <u>indeed</u> I wish this were the case. He still goes there every friday evening and remains till monday morning, and he might as well stay at home for any good he does or pretends to do. The poor King, I understand, is in very good bodily health, and as likely to live as if he were in every respect well. The Physicians will not now be released till the regency bill is up.[131] — What sad, perplexed uncertain & cross grained

---

The most dreadful fright I ever had in my life . . . was in returning from Hampstead the day which I spent so pleasantly with you. Although the evening was nearly closed I foolishly chose to take the short cut through the fields and in that enclosure where the path leads close by a high and thick hedge — with several gaps in it however — did I meet one of your thorough-paced London ruffians. . . . I had nothing to say to him if he had nothing to say to me but I could not help looking back to watch the movements of such a suspicious figure and to my great uneasiness saw him creep through the hedge on my left hand. . . . Immediately after, he came cowering back up the opposite side of the hedge as returning towards me under cover of it. I saw no weapons he had except a stick but as I moved on to gain the stile which was to let me into the free field with the idea of a wretch springing upon me from the cover at every step I took I assure you I would not wish the worst enemy I ever had to undergo such a feeling as I had for about five minutes.
(Grierson, 3:37)

131. The reign of George III effectively ended on 6 February 1811 when the Prince Regent took his oath of office; in February 1812 the Regency was made permanent. During this time Sir Henry Halford was put in control of the King's room, allowing the princesses to visit their father in pairs. The Queen saw him for a short time in June

times these are in the political world! While indeed the world with us in any other character is not very prosperous. I am glad, however, to hear that manufacturers in Scotland are going on better than they did.

What you said of James Graham has pleased me much; but I hope his Widow & children will be very well provided for, as I understand Mrs Graham's Father is a wealthy man, and is not likely to have any other heirs but her children. I have seen a poem on his death lately which has feeling in it and gives a true & amiable picture of the man, but there is a childish, too partial fondness in it that breaks in unpleasantly on the sentiments it would otherwise inspire; I have not yet heard who is the author. But I should not find fault with a childish stile of writing since I ha' my self (according to your Edin. Reviewer)[132] with Wordsworth & some others under . . .[133] same condemnation. — have . . . of thanks from your Friend [Ers]kine for the book I have sent him. . . . the goodness to convey to him my . . . for his obliging letter. I shant . . . to letters of civility on this occasion . . . should be some particular reason for it, . . . only be embarrassing both to myself & my. . . .

My Sister joins me in wishing . . . & yours many happy new years . . . I beg to be particularly remembered to Mrs Scott. She is one of those good-humoured women whom I like because she is proud of her husband, and besides this, she has graces of her own which I am sure I should have liked tho' she had not been the wife of Walter Scott. My Sister Mrs Baillie is always pleased & flattered by your remembrance and sends you most cordially her best wishes in return. — Farewell! I shall not expect to hear from you again for a good while; for I will not be unreasonable in my demands upon your friendly regard that it may hold out the . . . I trust indeed that it will hold . . . dying day, and be to me while I . . . pleasure & a great comfort.

Most truly yours

[J Baillie]

1812, and it is likely that she never saw him again for the remaining six and a half years of her life. In November the King's three physicians, Halford, Heberden and Baillie, signed a fruitless memorandum of protest to the Queen's Council that they were being made mute spectators of his condition without being given the power to contribute to his recovery or comfort (Ayling, 452).

132. On the publication of Baillie's 3rd volume of plays in 1812, Francis Jeffrey wrote in the *Edinburgh Review*: "Miss Baillie, we think, has set the example of plays as poor in incident and character, and as sluggish in their pace, as any that languish on the Continental stage, without their grandeur, their elegance, or their interest" (*Edinburgh Review*, February 1812, vol. 19:265-66).

133. The following ellipses indicate a large tear in the paper.

PS. The Lady who claims you as her old acquaintance is a good old Friend of ours Miss Wight sister of Dr Wight late Professor of divinity in Glasgow. She went to London by sea in the same ship with you & your family many years ago, and she says you were not a disagreeable child but very far from it & very amusing. —

3882 ff.99-103 (Address: To Walter Scott Esqr--no postmark)

[1812]

Here, my dear Friend is your purse and along with it (notwithstanding my great dislike to writing when I feel that I have nothing to say) a letter for Mr W. Erskine. Pray never desire me to do any thing that is not perfectly right, for you see I obey you in all things. This same letter too has cost me another of the same kind to Mr Mackenzie, for I could not omit writing to him if I sent any answers to complimentary letters on the present occasion. Be so obliging then as to take charge of them both. I'm sure if they were sent to them by the penny post they would be 3 farthings too dear. — But to return to my purse; I hope you will like it, and I have made it strong enough that your heavy gold coins may not break thro' it. If it should do you little good it has done me a great deal; for I have worked with pleasure at it for some time past when I could be pleased with no other employment. It put me in mind of an old woman in Hamilton, who was haunted by the <u>De'el</u>; and she got some flax to spin from my Mother which proved a great blessing to her; for she returned in a few days, telling my Mother with great delight, that as long as she was employed in spinning the Minister's yarn, the De'el had no power over her. Dont suppose, however, that working for you has charmed down on every evil spirit, tho' I confess it has had power over a dull and often a very cross one.

We have all admired the old mouthpiece, and long much to know the history of it if any there be besides its being old. I doubt the Laird of Abbotsford has not told me truly & honestly all the rooms that are to be in his new house and that the Museum room has been omitted. Rob Roy's answer (for I suppose you have got it; pray let me know if you have) this purse with its old coins, and many other things gathered & to be gathered, must require a place to be kept in, and we shall see there some years hence a collection like that at Strawberry hill: the collection of a poetical, sentimental Antiquarian, where such things as the gloves of Mrs Hamden have their value along with the armour of Francis the first.[134] But I hope this room will be filled with contributions from your numerous admirers

---

134. JB compares Scott's collection at Abbotsford to Horace Walpole's antiques kept in his Gothic home Strawberry Hill. Mrs. Hamden may be the Mrs. Hamblin who later played Ellen in American performances of *Lady of the Lake* (Bolton, 27).

rather than purchases from curiosity-Brokers; tho' your last very friendly letter has informed me of what gives me great pleasure, and I ought not now to be so much alarmed at the liberality & magnificence of your ideas. Well may you prosper! & fortunate may you be all your life long! and may those you leave behind you be so also! It was very kind in you to tell me of the happy change in what regards the salery [sic] of your office. And since it is told me in confidence I shall keep it for my own private satisfaction. To encourage you in your prospects as a country Laird I must tell you that the trees I planted in Gloucester sh: are doing well; and the land on which they are planted is nearly double in value since my Brother purchased it about 7 years ago. He then paid £30-000 for it, and he could sell it now for £55-000. I must say, however, he has spent and misspent nearly £10-000 upon it. But I must say no more on this subject lest you think me entirely worldly in my sympathy for my friends; now tho' I do wish those I love to be comfortably rich, it is not the first blessing I think of on their behalf. To see how your laurels flourish in this country, growing every year deeper in wood and sturdier in stem, gives me more pleasure than all the lands of Abbott's ford [sic] as they lie here & there.

So you think my Play of Orra is likely to have a good effect on the stage. I am glad you think so; for if this be the case it may some time or other, in some place or other be produced upon it. You will be glad to hear on the authority of my Bookseller that my new vol: sells better than any of those that preceded it; so that having made my curtesies [sic] to the Public with as good a grace as I could, they do not let me retire unhonoured. —— I suppose you know that your Brother Poet Campbell is going soon to give lectures on poetry at the British Institution.[135] Mr Sotheby has persuaded him into this,[136] and I hope he will do himself credit. His remuneration is to be, I understand, £200 for 6 lectures. I hope his Scotch tongue will not stand greatly in the way of his popularity; but in reading specimens of poetry to an English audience it must be a considerable disadvantage, for his is a bad kind of Scotch. — You tell me nothing of your Friend Sir G. Mackenzie's Play, but I have heard in a brief way with no detail of circumstances that it has not succeeded. An English Baronet is

---

135. Thomas Campbell, born in Glasgow in 1777, was a friend of Scott and Byron, a poet and editor of the *New Monthly Magazine*. Campbell contributed "To the Rainbow" to Baillie's *A Collection of Poems, Chiefly Manuscript* in 1823.

136. William Sotheby (1757-1833) was a prodigious poet, playwright, and translator and the consummate man of letters in the Romantic Era. Though Byron disliked him, satirizing him as Mr. Botherby in *Beppo* (1818), Sotheby provided a societal focal point for many of the brightest literary minds of his time. Scott, Wordsworth, Coleridge, Southey were his friends (*DLB*, XCIII:160-70). See introduction and letters to Sotheby herein.

now making a similar attempt at the small Theatre here in the Strand, viz Sir J. Bland Burges, with a kind of dubious success, for they still go on acting it & abusing it.[137] ___ My Sister & I are in Town with my Brother & family, where we shall stay some time longer to comfort & amuse ourselves. I was last night to see the Play of Julius Cesar [sic] in Covent Garden, and saw all that magnificence with good writing and a pretty fair portion of fine acting, will do for a Play naturally heavy & not very interesting. I found at the end, in my simple thinking, that all this cannot do a great deal. But I have spoken to [sic] freely in saying only good writing, for many of the speeches are wonderfully fine, and I never was more convinced of its merit than last night, having sat in a private box close to the stage where I heard every word perfectly. ___ Have you, M[r] Scott any thoughts of being in London this spring? I hope to hear that you have. It is a long time since you were here; and surely you must have some thing to do after so long an absence. I shall tremble for you however when you do come, unless you come incognito for you will else be oppressed & over-come strong as you are. I have already had an application from a young Cantab,[138] son to a great Philosopher of this country, made secretly & earnestly by a female friend of his, that he may be invited to see you when you come to Hampstead, and he will come from Cambridge on purpose. He is a deep mathematician this, and has nearly by heart all that you have written. ___ Farewell! and give my kindest remembrances with those of my Sister & all this Family to M[rs] Scott; our best regards also we send to yourself. It is good time I should end this letter, for I have been many times interrupted since I begun it, and am likely to be as much so if I should go on. — Farewell again! Your sincere Friend

    J Baillie

London March 1st

PS. March 4th

I have been prevented from sending off my packet by the tassel for the purse not having been made to my fancy & sent back to the silver smith for alterations. It is not just what I intended, but I hope you will not dislike it. Being made of frosted silver it must be cleaned with soap & water when tarnished. Within the purse you will find to bring it good luck a purse peny [sic], which my Niece Elizabeth hopes you will do her the honour to accept from her little store of old coins. She has picked out from them

---

137. Politician Sir James Bland Burges (1752-1824) devoted himself to literary pursuits in his later years, with two plays produced on stage: *Riches* and *Tricks upon Travellers* (*DNB*, III:306).

  138. Cantab: colloquial abbreviation of Cantabrigian, i.e., belonging to Cambridge (*OED*).

what she considered assisted by the skill of her Aunt Agnes (being the Antiquarian of the family) as the best.

You talk doubtfully to me of your writing another poem, saying "when I do write another" but the world here says you are writing one, and I have always found that its reports of this kind, regarding you, have always been true. May you not only have three but ten thousand pounds for it and I shall be most truly glad. In this new poem I hope & trust that you will give us a grand storm at sea, and if you please, a grand thunder storm on land. This is what no poet yet has given, to my mind, and no one but yourself can do it. Therefore (speaking like our old English monarchs, whose letters I have been reading last night at the chambers of M^r S Lyson, Keeper of the records of the Tower.) "I woll that it be done." ———
The very pleasing & uncommon character you give of your Friend Mr Ellis I believe to be a just one, and I am pleased to think I have a chance of meeting him again. My Brother speaks of taking his cottage at Sunning hill for another year, as his attendance at Windsor is still likely to prevent him from getting to Gloucester sh: for any considerable time. So you see what a turn politics have taken. Tho' wishing as well to the Whigs as you do to the other party, I cannot say that I am much troubled at it; for they ought to have had sense enough long ago to know that they should at all times stand upon their own legs without courting the support of a P. of W. or any part of the R. Family forgive this little serap[h] of politics: and little as it is I very seldom write as much to any body else.[139] You are my only political correspondent & you may guess I do not greatly exercise my mind upon these high matters. — Once more fare well! affectionately yours

J. B.

May I beg you will send the enclosed letter for Mr Macneal to your neighbour Mrs Fletcher who will send it to him?[140] ——

---

139. With the Regency came power struggles between Whigs and Tories. Thomas Creevy, a dedicated Whig, waited for some indication that the Regent would dismiss the Tory government he had inherited and cast out Tory Prime Minister Spencer Perceval. Whig support of peace talks with Napoleon, however, was absurd to the Prince Regent, and he left Perceval in power, outraging the Whigs (Hibbert, 9-18).

140. This is probably Elizabeth Fletcher (1770-1858), the wife of Archibald Fletcher and mother of sculptor Angus Fletcher of Edinburgh. Fletcher and Baillie had a great many friends in common, including Susan Ferrier, Sotheby, Barbauld and Scott (see the unpublished dissertation of Chester Lee Lambertson, "The Letters of Joanna Baillie [1801-1832]" [Ph.D. diss., Harvard University, 1956], cxxv-cc). I have not identified Mr. Macneal.

3882 ff.128-131 (Address: To Walter Scott Esqr / N: Castle Street / Edin^r-- no postmark)

Hampstead April 6th 1812

My dear Friend

I received your letter two days ago and did not think of keeping up so close a fire as to write to you immediately but for a circumstance which you shall hear. We have a most agreeable neighbour here, a great favourite of my Sisters & mine, and being a Borderer, tho' an English one, claiming (tho' unknown) some little favour from you: Mr Carr,[141] a learned Barrister, at the head of the excise office. Now being a Borderer, he is clannish; and has a great desire to trace the history of some other Border Families; and he remembers when he was a Boy of seeing an old folio book printed in small columns givin[g] an account of all the Border families both on the Scotch & English sides, but he neither remembers the title of it nor the name of its Author. Do you know of such a book? does your friend Mr Ballantine know? If you could get me any information on this point at your own leisure, I should be very much obliged to you. I am in this hurry writing to you about it because I promised to do so a great while ago and forgot, till Mr Carr came in the other evening as I was reading your letter & put me in mind of it; but you need be in no hurry answering me, unless you please, only have the goodness to keep it in mind. ——

I thank you for your letter, which notwithstanding your apologies came fully as soon as I expected, for knowing how your time is occupied, I ought to be and will be reasonable in my expectations. But there is one part of it that made me sad tho' I do not believe it, viz that you do not think of being in this country for a long time. I do not say <u>sorry</u> but <u>sad</u>; for when I parted with you here, in bidding me farewell you said, you should see me again if you could (meaning before you left London) but that, should we not meet again, it would be well "this parting had been made" repeating those solemn words in Julius Cesar [*sic*], and I never hear of its being a long time before you come here again but those words come across my mind as if we should never meet.[142] I readily agree with you that a short residence in London, oppressed as you are with the legions of people that you must see, is not a very desirable thing; yet I hope some temptation will ere long fall in your way to make you overlook its disadvantages. There is another part of your letter that makes me neither sad nor sorry but does in a little degree mortify me. You tell me that you are busy writing but give me no hint at all as to the subject. O fy! is not this treating me rather

---

141. This is Thomas William Carr of Frognal, Hampstead.
142. See Shakespeare's *Julius Caesar*: *Bru*. . . . "If we do meet again, why, we shall smile;/ If not, why then this parting was well made" (5.1.117-18).

shabbily after all the love & kindness that I bear you? I shall know nothing about it I suppose till some stray Scotchman, by & by, gives me an account of the whole story from some cousin or seward cousin of his to whom you have read every word of it. As for me I am not busy but mean very soon to write a Tragedy on remorse, the story of which I have scetched [sic] out in the form of an anecdote taken from an old chronicle, and when you are retired to the country in the summer vacation, if you have any inclination to see it, I will send you down a copy of it.[143] The sale of my new Vol: goes on moderately. Longman raised a great cry better than a month ago that a second edition was wanted, and I sat down without loss of time to prepare a few alterations much pleased with the idea that in point of popularity I was beginning to be as Burns says of Jenny in his Cotter's Saturday night "respecket like the love"[144] but there was no such thing: when he examined further into the matter at Paternoster row he found there were plenty of copies still on hand notwithstanding all the good poetry that is in it. ――― Ld Byron's poem is very much read here and I have heard it highly praised:[145] I shall read it when it falls in my way or rather when I can find somebody to lend it to me. There is another book very much read, I hear, & praised also, your friend Sir G. Mackenzies travels in Isceland [sic]. This may console him for the misfortune of having had his Tragedy condemned by the Wernerians.[146] I am reading it just now, and began very briskly to read what I considered as a very good amusing book, and so it did appear to me to be for some time at the outset: but the spirit of the Wernerians I fear is creeping into me, and whether I shall be able to hold on in the same good faith I know not. What a pity it is that Travellers will slightly record without discrimination every thing they see & meet with, instead of selecting good specimens to represent the whole and

---

143. She does send him a copy of her *Henriquez,* based on an "Old Chronicle"; see following letter 3883 ff.73-76.

144. See Robert Burns's "The Cotter's Saturday Night": "The Mother, wi' a woman's wiles, can spy/ What makes the *youth* sae bashfu' and sae grave;/ Weel-pleas'd to think her *bairn's* respected like the lave" (James Kinsley, ed., *The Poems and Songs of Robert Burns,* 2 vols. [Oxford: Clarendon, 1968], 148).

145. She probably refers to Byron's *Childe Harold's Pilgrimage;* see letter following.

146. See Scott's letter of 4 April 1812: "As for Sir Geo: Mackenzie's play it was damned to everlasting redemption as Elbow says and that after a tolerable fair hearing. The most mortifying part of the business was that at length even those who went as the authors friends caught the injection and laughed most heartily all the while they were applauding. The worthy Bart. has however discovered that the failure was entirely owing to a set of chemists calld Wernerians who it seems differ in their opinion concerning the cosmogony of the world from Sir Georges sect of philosophers the Huntonians" (Grierson, 3:101).

giving those very circumstantially. We should then have a short book containing many things that would rest in our memory, instead of a long book containing very few. There is nobody whose writings are so well adapted to my weak memory as your own, by continually presenting images so vivid & so true that they cannot be forgotten. When people speak of your works I can take my part in the conversation as handsomely as any of them; but when most other books are mentioned I am at a loss, and appear more ignorant & worse read than I really am which is a disgrace to me.

You say nothing to me of your children, but I trust they are all well. They are grown great creatures I daresay since I saw them. Well may they thrive, and happy may they be! —— I thank you for the list you give me of your curiosities, and Elizabeth will be very proud when she hears that her little tribute is put at the head of it. If any thing comes in my way here that I can boldly ask or wheedle from any body to add to it, I will send it to you. I congratulate you on getting the sword of the great Montrose amongst your grand matters: that is indeed a thing of value.[147] I have nothing of this kind to boast, but I have lately become possessed of a thing that gives me pleasure every day and of which I am mighty proud. It is a drawing of my Niece, by Lawrence the Painter,[148] which he has had the goodness to do for me and to present to me in the handsomest manner, having understood that I wished to have such a thing. It is considered by artest [sic] & connoisseurs who have seen it as a most exquisite piece, and indeed I cannot conceive any thing more beautifully done & more elegant while at the same time it is very like.

There are one or two things more that I have an itching to tell you, but it is an idle itching which ought not to be encouraged and I must not enlarge my letter. —— How sorry I am for the account you give me of the snow! I hope it will go off without ruin. I fear the poor will by & by be very ill off here. —— Give my kindest wishes to Mrs Scott.

yours very truly   J Baillie

147. In the same letter of 4 April 1812 noted above, Scott writes, "I have moreover a relique of a more heroic character - it is a sword which was given to the great Marquis of Montrose by Charles I and appears to have belonged to his father our gentle King Jamie. . . . It is independent of it's [sic] other merits a most beautiful blade. I think a dialogue between this same sword and Rob Roys gun might be composed with good effect" (Grierson, 3:100).

148. See Baillie's letter LAW/2/5 to Sir Thomas Lawrence herein.

3882 ff.169-172 (Address: For Walter Scott Esqr / N: Castle Street / Edinburgh--no postmark)

Hampstead May 27th 1812

Many thanks, my dear Mr Scott, for the trouble you have so kindly taken on Mr Carr's behalf! and he will thank you himself very soon (if he has not done it already) and tell you his own way what he further wishes on the subject, which is much better than my writing about things that I might not very clearly apprehend. If he writes half as pleasantly as he converses, you will not be ill pleased to receive a letter from him. He was very much gratified by your letter, the first part of which I gave him to read. — I thank you too very cordially for what you tell me of your present employment, and should be much delighted to see any part of the poem at your good time; but to send it to me is really too much, and too great a risk for the gratifying of my fancy & curiosity, so I shall not expect to see any part of it before it is published, unless you bring it to this country yourself, and may Mr Carpenter have a safe voyage from Indea very soon![149] As to the little story which I intend and were the ms. lost there would be no matter, so I shall send it to you as soon as I find time to write out a fair copy, without fee or reward of any kind but your own friendly good will in receiving it, and any remarks that you may make upon it as the ground work of such a Play. — But think you there is spirit at all in me now to write Plays of any kind, after all that our great Northern Critic hath said of the deplorable dullness & want of interest in those I have already written?[150] I must try what I can do, even under this great gloom of his <u>dis</u>countenance; and as I mean to try speedily too, you will not be very long of receiving a packet from me. Indeed this last review of Jeffry [sic] is more severe than I expected, but fortunately for me, it is of a kind which I greatly prefer to others that might have been given. One of more ability & discrimination, and somewhat less severe would have teased me a great deal more. However, I dont mean at all to dispise it; it will do me, I doubt not, considerable mischief as far as the present circulation of the work is concerned; if it do more than this, his criticism must be just; and, in that case, any credit it may have acquired, it would very soon have lost in the natural course of things, without his interference. — I see by the paper that your Friend Mr Terry has been performing in the Haymarket, and I hope during the summer to have an opportunity of seeing him there; in the mean time if he thinks it worth his while to come to Hampstead to see me,

---

149. Jean David, who later took the name of Charles Carpenter, was Scott's brother-in-law and part of the East India Company.

150. Baillie refers to Jeffrey's malicious attack in the *Edinburgh Review* on her 3rd volume of plays in February 1812. See note 132 above.

I shall be glad. Being your Friend & by your account worthy to be so, I cannot possibly have any objections to being acquainted with him. I hope his success in London will be equal to his merit. ——— Some time ago, after receiving your last but one, I read Child Harold, and thank you for recommending it to me.[151] I think like you that there is real genius in it, but unlike you I liked it better the first reading than the second. There are many striking thoughts in it very happily expressed; it contains often true sentiments & feeling, tho' they are too generally those of a diseased & degraded mind; and it gives one now & then some good discription, as the sailing of the fleet & passing the straits by moon light, the evening scene in the Turkish Basha's court, the dancing of the albanians round their night-fire &c. However, I think you go too far when you call it powerful discription. The Ball-feast which might have given occasion for this is I think but indifferently given, excepting at the end when the great dark carcase [sic] of the mighty beast drawn off upon the cart passes before one like part of a powerful & animated picture, and the view of Lisbon is rather a pleasing enumeration of what is to be seen than any scene that actually rises to the imagination: if it be meant for more than this, it is I think false, for it gives you in one point of view things which must be seen, if they are distinguished at all, from different points, — the minute & the general; while that awkward line "sunken glens whose sunless shrubs must weep" comes in the middle of it, and to my ear & taste discompose the whole considerably. I ought, however, to speak with diffidence, for this passage has been much admired. It is altogether a very able work for so young a man or indeed any man; but Lord Byron wants the generous spirit, and, I should apprehend, the lofty & inventive spirit of a great poet, tho' there is a great body of classical critics here, who would assign him the highest rank among British poets after Shakespear[e] & Milton. I think I may at least say that if such a place shall ever be his, he has it still to earn. ——— I fear by & bye we shall have things to think of far different from Poetry. These general commotions in our Manufacturing Town with the terrible oaths they are taking and the savage spirit that is beginning to appear in the country, are very alarming, and our Regent is I fear neither very firm nor conciliatory.[152] It is said indeed that his nerves have been put into a terrible state, but all this I have merely from common

---

151. Even after Byron's sneers in *English Bards and Scotch Reviewers*, Scott had praised Byron's *Childe Harold's Pilgrimage* to Baillie as a very clever poem "though one hardly speaking well for 'the writers heart or morals'" (Johnson, 386). Byron and Scott began corresponding in 1812, Byron apologizing for his "sneers," and the two remained on friendly terms thereafter.

152. This may be a reference to riots by the Luddites, frame-breakers named for weaver Ned Lud, occurring between 1811-13.

report. I hope people will associate & strengthen themselves against this disorder every where, and let the good sense & courage of, I trust, a very large majority of the people support & make amends for a feeble government, without giving up any of their views of moderate, wholesome reform. Who comes into power or who goes out I am not at all concerned about, but as it may affect the good of the country. I hope next harvest will prove abundant, and things perhaps may not get desperate till that comes in aid of subordination. — To talk of very different matters, I met the other day your relation Mrs Apriece [sic], now Lady Davy,[153] & her Bridegroom at Sotheby's, and they both seemed so happy I could not help liking them for it, tho' I had not before been particularly so disposed. She talks much of Sir Humphr[e]y & herself differing & wrangling upon a great many points of poetry & taste; and gives you to suppose, with a most delighted expression of countenance, that they lead a life of very <u>pretty</u> contention, and have a very spirited honey moon, free from all its tiresome sweetness. I do believe they will continue to be very happy tho' they may not by & bye be in such a state of what one may call <u>picturesque</u> happiness for an unconcerned spectator like me to enjoy — or rather I should say, admire.

This, I suppose will find you in Edin^r engaged in your official duties again after having accomplished your flitting from Ashesteel [Ashestiel] to Abbotsford. Yourself & Mrs Scott & the Children too would feel sorry on leaving the first which will long have a consequence & be an object of kindly feelings with many from having once been the place of your residence. If I should ever be happy enough to be at Abbotsford you must take me to see Ashesteel too. I have a kind of tenderness for it as one has for a man's first wife when one hears that he has married a second. ——— My Sister joins me in kindest wishes to you & Mrs Scott. The young folks, who must now be growing out of my knowledge, are I hope all well, and long may they be so! Farewell!

ever truly yours

J Baillie

May 29th

PS. This has been two days by me for an opportunity of sending it to Town to be franked, and as it contains nothing of any importance it does not signify; and now having time enough I will not send it off with one whole page of blank paper. — To return to Ld Byron again, I was much pleased with some of his smaller pieces (it is the quarto edition I have read) in

---

153. On 11 April 1812 Mrs. Apreece, the widow of Shuckburgh Ashby Apreece and daughter and heiress of Charles Kerr, married scientist and poet Sir Humphrey Davy, later president of the Royal Society (*DNB*, V:637-43). See letters to Lady Davy.

which there is tenderness & good & respectable feeling: the second piece particularly, a farewell to a Lady born in Constaninople [*sic*], is my greatest favourite of all.[154] — You are kind in being interested that I should sit to Lawrence, but this is a thing which for divers reasons cannot be done tho' there is no doubt we have no man of equal genius in his department of the art. I have sat, however, very lately to a very good painter & an old acquaintance of your[s] Masquerier.[155] It is a full length in small life in a sitting posture. Poor Masquerier, who is very docile & obliging has taken great pains with it, but in order to make my countenance very expressive & very <u>wise</u> he has (my friends say) made it melancholy & somewhat peevish. He has also given me a long body with short limbs, which being the reverse of my natural proportions, they say I look as if I were sitting upon a book. But strangers who dont know the original like the picture, and one good man was so pleased with it that he bespoke a picture just the fellow to it, posture, figure, dress & every thing, only the face is to be left out and the face of his own wife put in its place. I am to sit once more and then I hope my friends will be better pleased with it, for I believe it is like (the face I mean) and I am grieved to think of the trouble it has given to a very good & ingenious Artist. ——

Farewell again! JB

3883 ff.73-76 (No address or postmark)

Hampstead Sept.[r] 2.[d] 1812

My dear Friend

I send you inclosed the story I mentioned to you a great while ago; but pray be it understood that it is sent with no claims at all upon your present attention. Look over it at any time when you are at leisure & disposed, were it monday hence; and you need not even give me notice of having received it, unless you mean to gratify me with a letter at any rate; for I know it will go safe enough, and were it to be lost, there would be no great matter. When you do read it, I should like to know what you think of it as

---

154. This is probably Byron's "To Florence" (1809) about Mrs. Spencer Smith who was born in Constantinople where her father was Austrian ambassador; she later excited the vengeance of Buonaparte (see note in *The Complete Poetical and Dramatic Works of Lord Byron with a Comprehensive Outline of the Life of the Poet*, ed. John Nichols and J. C. Jeaffreson [Philadelphia: David McKay, 1883], 428).

155. John James Masquerier (1778-1855), the son of French parents and student of the Royal Academy, joined the studio of John Hoffner around 1796, painting his friends as well as the famous. Producing such paintings as *The Incredulity of St. Thomas* and *Napoleon Reviewing the Consular Guards in the Court of the Tuileries*, he retired to Brighton a wealthy man in 1823 (*DNB*, XIII:1-2). Masquerier's portrait of Joanna Baillie hangs in Special Collections at the University of Glasgow. See miscellaneous letters for 3 letters to Masquerier.

the ground work of a Tragedy on remorse; in the mean time like folks who marry first and ask advice about it afterwards, I have fairly begun my play and have nearly written the two first acts.[156] In going on I find it necessary to add some little circumstances, and a character or two, but I believe I shall keep pretty closely to my story. Do not think me, however, so entirely absurd as those same folks who marry first & ask advice afterwards, for I often alter my plays greatly after the first writing, while the poor Bridegroom must keep what he has got for better or for worse. ——

I suppose you have now got a great way on in your forth-coming poem which every body is ardently expecting.[157] My Poet of the Bower, Mr Coxe, writes me from Cheltenham that it is already advertised, and praying fervently that it may add to your reputation. As for me I look forward to it very assuredly, and will never be afraid on your account anymore; tho' how you are to add to your reputation I cannot well conceive, unless it be by the wonder that may be excited by continuing to soar on such a lofty wing so long. – Your cottage, I hope, goes on to your mind, and that you are in good health enjoying the progress of your improvements. Pray give my best remembrances to Mrs Scott, and receive my kindes[t] wishes for all your Children. Our Friend Miss Gra_[158] who is staying with us just now, and has had the pleasure of meeting you sometimes at the Ld Advocates, gives us a very favourable report of your young Laird. She says he is as fine a sensible well-behaved Boy as she ever met with. ——

Your Friend Terry delivered his credentials to us a great while ago, and I have to thank you for making us acquainted with him. He is a sensible & a modest man, and has given us a very favourable impression of himself which I doubt not further acquaintance will justify. I have not yet had so much talk with him upon Theatrical matters as I could wish; for the first visit was a short one with some degree of restraint in both sides, and the second & last was mightily interrupted by an Airshire Laird, who broke in upon us to dinner unexpectedly and usurped nearly the whole conversation. I had however a private parley with your Friend in a corner, and I trust we shall see him again before he returns to Edin^r if he does return. We took a box about a fortnight ago, on purpose to see him act at

---

156. Scott's reply to this sketch of *Henriquez* is dated 11 October 1812. He asks how Baillie is to prevent the audience from anticipating the conclusion with "that sort of certainty which banishes the interest excited by suspense" but is assured she will be able to revise satisfactorily. *Henriquez*, included in Vol. 3 of *Plays on the Passions*, was ultimately performed at Drury Lane with Vandenhoff in the leading role (Grierson, 3:175-77).

157. This would be Scott's *Rokeby*; see following letter.

158. The corner of this letter is missing, but this is probably Miss Grahame.

the Little Theatre, where I had not been for many years, and we were fortunate enough to see him in both Play & entertainment. The Play was a new Melo Drama taken from Dr Moore's Zeluco,[159] and he represented the jealous morose villain of a husband, with some power indeed, but with the heaviness & monotony that such an uninteresting, unmixed character is so apt to inspire. But he made us amends for this in the Farce (Who's the Dupe) by personating a pedantic, bashful oxonian,[160] who gets himself pawed (if I may so speak) into love by a fine, free, impudent City Miss, who undertakes to teach him modern behaviour; all the changes of this character he represented with great truth & effect to our great entertainment. I hear a very good account of his acting from many people, and I hope he will get a good engagement in one of our Winter Theatres if it is right to hope he should be put into the road to be spoilt. ――― Now that I as__[161] talking (as it is somewhat natural in me to do) of Theatrical matters, I must tell you that I have by me a Tragedy of great merit, written by a Lady very much admired in the world for many various talents & accomplishments as well as personal attractions. Her name is Mrs Wilmot; you have probably heard of her, the Daughter of Sir Callender Ogle and cousin to Mrs Sherriden.[162] I had heard a great deal of it, for it had been read to a great many of her friends, and hearing I had expressed a wish to see it, she very obligingly permitted me to have it. She has contrived a very interesting story, the scene of which is in America amongst Indeans & Spaniards, and there is a great deal of tenderness thro the whole with true & generous feelings, and with much poetic beauty. I should guess it to be well calculated for the stage, and I should not be surprised if it were produced upon it soon. ―――― My Sister & I are going next week to visit our old quarters again at Sunning hill, where I hope we shall have the luck to meet with your friend Mr Ellis. I'm sure if he knew how I longed to pull at his coat, as the children do to be noticed, when he passed me in a crowd at the royal institution last spring, not having courage to speak to

159. John Moore's novel *Zeluco* (1786) was also said to have been the inspiration for Byron's *Childe Harold* (*The New Century Cyclopedia of Names*, ed. Clarence L. Barnhart, 3 vols. [New York: Appleton-Century-Crofts, 1954], 2:2812).

160. Oxonian: belonging to Oxford (*OED*).

161. There is a tear in the leaf.

162. Lady Dacre, Barbarina Brand (1768-1854), was a poet, dramatist, translator and sculptor. The third daughter of Admiral Sir Chaloner Ogle, Bart., and Hester, she married Valentine Henry Wilmot in 1789, an officer in the Guards. After Wilmot's death Barbarina married Thomas Brand, 21st lord of Dacre, in 1819. Her published works include *Pedarias* (1811), *Ina* (1815), *Translations from the Italian* (1836), etc. (*DNB*, II:1120). Lady Dacre contributed "Stanzas suggested by a Canzone of Petrarch" to Baillie's 1823 *Collection of Poems, Chiefly Manuscript*, etc. Lord Dacre was appointed arbitrator for Lady Byron on the death of her mother in 1822.

him, he would not fail to pay me a visit. I hope, however, as he has something to do now & then with the quarterly review, it is not him who has handled my friend Mrs Barbauld so roughly.[163] If it be, I could almost feel inclined, agreeable as he is, to pull him by the beard rather than the coat. (I have not seen the review but only heard of it) – speaking of Mr Ellis puts me in mind of acorns, and these again of planting trees. Have you considered in your own mind what kinds of trees you are to plant close to your Cottage? for I presume you dont mean it to stand in the middle of a green lawn, as most new houses in Scotland do, quite aloof from the planting, and as unconnected with it as if it had been dropped from the clouds like a moonstone. We have in our garden here a common willow, not above eleven years old, and it is a fine spreading, beautiful tree, higher than the house tho' that is 3 stories; and the delicate, floating lightness of its branches come elegantly between the eye & a building without giving too much darkness or any appearance of damp. It grows upon a dry situation as well as a damp, and will become a pretty good sized tree in 5 or 6 years. I have the pleasure to tell you my Gloucester sh. trees are thriving delightfully. —— You are kind enough to say in your short note by Mr Terry that you would send me a packet soon and I rejoiced there at. It has not yet come tho', as I suppose you know. But do not think I mention this with any reproach: far from it: for I can honestly say to you I receive more letters from you than all things considered I could reasonably expect, and more than I deserve.

Septr 7th You see how long this letter has been laid by, but containing no very pressing matter it was of little consequence. As I intended to send it by one of Mr Freeling's franks and bethought me at the same time that Mr Terry might have some thing to send you, I wrote to him offering the

---

163. Anna Laetitia Barbauld (1743-1825) was the only daughter of classicist and Nonconformist minister John Aikin and became one of the teachers at the new Dissenting academy in Warrington. In 1774 she married Rochemont Barbauld, also a Nonconformist cleric, who took over a congregation in Plasgrave, Suffolk, where ALB took charge of a school for young boys. The Barbaulds traveled in Europe for a while and settled in Hampstead where Barbauld ministered to a congregation and ALB took a few pupils. Mr. Barbauld was never very stable and died insane in 1808. In 1782-86 ALB, in conjunction with her brother, wrote *Evenings at Home* for her adopted son and in 1804 edited *The Correspondence of Samuel Richardson* in six volumes and *The British Novelists*, in 50 volumes, in 1810, along with *The Female Speaker* (1811), selections of the best British prose and poetry long used in the education of girls (Janet Todd, ed., *British Women Writers* [New York: Continuum, 1989], 37-40). In 1811 Barbauld published her poem *Eighteen Hundred and Eleven* which prophesied that on a future day a traveler from the antipodes would contemplate the ruin of St. Paul's. The work provoked a coarse review in the *Quarterly* from John Murray which he later admitted he regretted (*DNB*, I:1065).

conveyance; and not to hurry him allowed him a few days, which he has taken to the utmost limits and only given me a simple letter after all, which he brought himself to Hampstead yesterday, making my words in the first part this letter good — that we should like him better when we should see more of him. —— I have forgot to say that, in reading over the story from the Old <u>Chronicle</u> (of my brains) I should be glad if you would, from your better knowledge, fill up the blanks that are left for the names of places, the time being supposed when the Christian & Moorish kings of Spain were both flourishing & contending with one another. —— I inclose a little poem of Mr Coxes sent to me the other day from Che[l]tenham. Every thing in praise of Lord Wellington, who is earning so much glory for himself & his country in Spain, must be acceptable to every body that has one particle of generous feeling in their composition, and particularly to yourself, so long his professed Admirer. — Farewell, with all kind & affectionate regard!

J Baillie

3883 ff.105-106 (Address: To Walter Scott / Abbotsford near Melrose / N.B.--postmarked 1812)

Hampstead October 13th 1812

My dear Friend,

Thou art indeed a Creature of strength and of fancy & generous inexhaustible! fortunate am I that I live in your days, both for the very great pleasure I receive from your poetry, and the better chance I shall have of being known & esteemed myself in after days as being your contemporary & honoured with your regard. I am sitting with the first printed sheet of your Rokeby on the table beside me which Mr Longman very kindly put into my hands last night and I cannot find terms to express how greatly I admire it.[164] No poem you ever wrote or that ever was written ever opened more finely. The scene without doors and the scene within illustrating one another, are most powerfully imagined & happily executed, and were we to receive it as a fragment of some great Poet whose works are lost, how we should admire it, and pant after the rest of the story as that which kings & Antiquarians might dig for; a treasure worth a kingdom! It has roused & animated me wonderfully: and I think you are going to give us a story more akin to my own labours, tho' far beyond these, than any thing that has yet been attempted in published verse. Is it not

---

164. *Rokeby*, with action focused on the hostilities between the Roundheads and Cavaliers, did not actually appear from Longman until 1813. Scott seems to have been annoyed that Longman gave this early proof copy to Baillie; see letter following and his letter dated 16 October 1812 to James Ballantyne (Grierson, 3:175-77).

so? I trust it is. Your picture of remorse will be a grand & powerful picture: and I will be proud enough to think, whether you allow me to do so or not, that I have been the means of turning your imagination to the contemplation of the stronger passions. Ah! how much you possess to make those pictures more attractive than I can do! But I do not repine: let all the favour of the world be heaped upon you twenty fold! I shall not be injured but on the contrary supported thereby. I trust that Longman will indulge me with the other sheets as they come out, and give me some thing to expect & long for from week to week which makes time pass with spirit. I shall not be afraid as I advance to find the remainder of all beneath its noble beginning: I feel quite confident, and therefore I shall read it without any drawbacks. I need scarcely say how eagerly it is now expected & enquired after by every body here. It will be a Christmas feast for Thousands (for Longman tells me it will be out by Xmas). ――― I know you are now very busy so dont think of writing to me: I have only written to you now because I could not help it. I want no . . .[165] from you for a long time . . . story from the Old Chronicle;[166] and should not be the least offended were I to know that you have not yet looked at it. I am sticking in the mire at present, and cant get on. Little domestic matters & things that you would despise occupy my time & my thoughts beyond their real worth — in short deplorably. I wonder when I shall become wise! I fear never, a fool of forty &c. the old proverb says, and I am far beyond forty. —— We returned about a week ago from Sunning hill where we spent 3 weeks, but had not the luck to meet Mr Ellis. He was in Devon. Things go on at Windsor as usual, and how long they may do so nobody can say. My Brother wishes to take a better house in that neighbourhood if he can find one.[167] Those who rule the roost at present are going to do a most horrible thing: viz inclose the greater part of Win[d]sor Forest. 10-000 acres will then become private property and lose by degrees the appearance of forest. – The Royal Forest – the noblest – almost the only remains of a forest in the kingdom –– Oh Oh!![168]

---

165. This and the following ellipses indicate holes in the leaf.

166. Baillie also writes to Sotheby about her "Old Chronicle" (Royal College of Surgeons, HB.ix-9 & 11); "An Old Story" follows the RCS letter in 8 leaves numbered 10a-b and begins: "The old chronicle or\ legend of the noble Family of Mondega. . . ." She has apparently not yet received Scott's letter of 11 October 1812 with advice for her *Henriquez*.

167. Dr. Matthew Baillie had become Physician Extraordinary to George III in October 1810 and was more and more frequently required to be close at hand (see Crainz, 175).

168. The Terrace in Windsor Forest had generally been used for a promenade for citizens and spectators, and George IV, seeking privacy, ordered it closed except for Sundays, causing a great deal of resentment. Local newspapers regarded the closure

Give my kindest wishes to Mrs Scott & the Children, in which my
Sister joins me: and believe me
     most truly & faithfully yours
          J Baillie

3883 ff.118-121 (No address or postmark)

                                        Hampstead Novr 7 1812
My dear Friend,
     This may rather be of an old date before you get it, for I mean to send it
by Mr Terry, who told me he should leave London on the 14th; but as I
shall be very much engaged next week, I think it wise to take time by the
fore lock and prepare my dispatch when I can. I must thank you again for
introducing us to your Friend Terry: we have found him very agreeable,
particularly the last time we saw him, when he shewd us a specimen of
his powers in reading the ancient Mariner with admirable effect.[169] My
Sister & Miss Graham were quite delighted; and I was as much so as bad
spirits, which from particular circumstances had seized upon me that day,
would allow me to be. Our people here are not wise to let him go back to
Scotland again if they have had it in their power to prevent it. ――― I am
really sorry you have been angry with poor Longman. I have not seen him
since, so I dont know how he has taken the letter you proposed to send him
which he must have received some time ago. When he gave the proof
sheet to me, I supposed it was a thing frequently done by Booksellers, and
truly I think your Friend Ballantyne more to blame than him; for he might
very well know that Longman does not care a jot for poetry be it ever so fine
for his own private reading; and if he was not to shew it to any body, of
what use was it to him? and if he was to shew to any body, I must really be
allowed to say, I think myself that <u>very body</u>. Your packet with the first
Canto is not yet arrived and I long for it mightily. I have not, however,
told a creature, Mrs Baillie excepted, so that no body shall tease me for
what they shant get – a sight of it when it does come. To my good Sister
and your warm admirer Mrs Baillie I suppose I may shew it, and indeed
will shew it whether you give me leave or not. ― You have no doubt seen
the rejected addresses which have been amusing all the world here. We
think them very clever and imitations very happy for such a light jeu
d'espirit. In the one done for yourself, notwithstanding all the burlesque,

---

of the Terrace as necessary for the king's privacy, but the Canons of Windsor were
outraged, claiming they had had legal right to walk upon the Terrace since the time of
Charles II (Hibbert, 169). This is the only explanation I have for Baillie's distress,
though there appears to be more to her concern.
     169. Surely a reference to S. T. Coleridge's *Rime of the Ancient Mariner.*

one could easily recognize the first poet of the times, tho' one had never read a line of the original, for it bears itself eminently above all the rest. That for Crabb[e][170] is exceedingly good, and so I think is Southey's. I am not very sure but if Ld Byron's real address, which was actually spoken at the opening of the Theatre, had been inserted amongst them, it might e'en have passed for a nonsense-thing along with the rest. --- Many thanks to you for the attention you have paid to my old story. I am sorry you took the trouble of returning it to me as I had another copy. Your remarks are very just and I hope to profit by them as I proceed. It never was my intention to declare the purpose of the Hero till the very end of the Play, but now I shall be particularly careful that it shall not be at all understood or divined till the very last. My greatest difficulty will be in making him, circumstanced as he is and shunning all confidence or communication with any body, sufficiently discover the dreadful picture of his own mind without loading the play with soliloquy which could be a great fault. I must try to get over it the best way I can. I wish I were better acquainted with the manners of Spain in those days. I have read Southey's chronicle of the Cid, and was delighted with it; but what signifies reading to one who has no memory?[171] I have all my life been quite discouraged from reading for this very reason, that when I had not read a book, I did not feel ashamed of knowing nothing about [it]; whereas to be in this same predicament after having read it, was rather humiliating. However I will get the Cid into my hands & some old history of Spain too, before I finish my piece, and it will go hard with me if I cannot with all this give it some smack or seasoning of older times. – As to what you say of the difference of our popularity – (remember it is you who have said our: I should not have been so presumptuous) – your metaphor is a very ingenious one; but it has one fault; it does not apply. No no! my shot may indeed hit a choice person here & there, but yours hit both the choice & the vulgar -- every thing falls before it; and I am not one of those who comfort myself for the want of general success by despising the vulgar. Some charm is wanting

---

170. George Crabbe (1754-1832) was a parish doctor before deciding to travel to London and pursue a career in writing. He took orders, becoming a curate in 1781, and established himself as a poet with *The Village* and its grim picture of rural poverty. Crabbe met and became friends with Sir Walter Scott. Throughout the Romantic era, Crabbe persisted in presenting a precise, realistic vision of rural life and landscape. Byron called him "Nature's sternest painter yet the best," while Scott referred to him as "the English Juvenal" (*OCEL*, 237).

171. In his letter of 11 October 1812, Scott suggests concerning *Henriquez*, "Should you want a subordinate retainer as an assistant assassin pray look at the account of the Almagarves or some such name in the notes to Southeys Cid" (Grierson, 3:172).

which I cannot give my works, else even with all their faults, or at least many of them, they would be more generally liked. ——

I greatly admire & approve your spirit in what you say regarding the struggle for national independence. But I think the meaning of Mrs Barbauld's poem is in some degree mistaken by you as it has been by many people.[172] Tho' she condemns the system that has prevailed for many years of being constantly at war, she looks forward to the unhappy change which she supposes will take place in this country as a thing that must happen in the natural course of events in the course of ages, as we learn from experience learning & arts have travelled over the globe from one country to another remaining permanently nowhere, and not as a misfortune soon or suddenly to befall us. Her poem has been greatly admired here by people not at all agreeing with her in politics and who have no greater love for GeNLS Hall or the American's [sic] than yourself. Her hopes of the Americans I believe arises from her having had no connection with them and knowing little about them. Have you ever seen her lines on the King's illness?[173] To sweeten your mind in regard to her, I will send them to you some day: they are full of respect & delicate comiseration [sic], and are perhaps the most touching verses ever written by any subject upon any Prince. ——— It would please me to see you a Whig tho' not such an outré one as would to [sic] for a Westminster election; but my chance of seeing you so from the present minister's disparking [disbarking?] Windsor forest, is not great, for I dont know that they have any thing to do with it. Many private individuals, it seems, have certain manorial rights upon the forest, so that the king cannot cut wood &c. without their consent. It has been proposed, I dont know by whom, that those rights shall be given up for so much of the ground in actual possession, by which means ten thousand acres out of 24-000 which the whole forest contains, becomes private property and must soon be disforested, and this by far the finest part of the forest. When this was proposed to the Regent, he felt properly on the occasion and would not consent to it; but what signify feelings without firmness. I had my information while at Sunning hill from a Gentleman belonging to the Court, who is one of the commissioners for settling this business; and I inveighed against it most bitterly, telling him I believed the country would rather submit to a tax for the preservation of the forest than see it

---

172. See Barbauld's "Eighteen Hundred and Eleven, A Poem" (1812).

173. Barbauld's "On the King's Illness" came after George III suffered a relapse of porphyria in July 1811 from which he never recovered. The regency had been declared in February 1811 (see *The Poems of Anna Laetitia Barbauld*, ed. William McCarthy and Elizabeth Kraft [Athens: University of Georgia Press, 1994], 307).

so destroyed. I had the satisfaction of speaking out my mind, and he smiled at me as Courtier's do. — Well; while one part of the country becomes less interesting another becomes more so; I was much pleased with your account of your spring with its bank & its mossed stones & its willows, to say nothing of the young oaks as high as my netting needle. I wonder much that birch seed cannot be got good in Scotland. If it can be got good in England, you shall have some, and perhaps I may be able to send you a parcel of it along with this. If this is not the case I shall find some opportunity of sending it before spring.

And now I should imagine it will be civil & proper & prudent in me to take my leave of you for the present. Farewell! --- Give my kind remembrances to Mrs Scott, my best wishes to your Children, and believe me always

    ever truly yours
    J Baillie

PS. Pray have the goodness to send the inclosed to Mrs Branton: I believe she lives in John St: but I am not sure so I could not send it by post. ——

3883 ff.152-153 (No address or postmark)

London Decr 8th 1812

My dear Friend,

I dont know how to thank you enough for the great delight & gratification we have received in reading the three first Cantos of Rokeby and your great goodness in sending them. The very striking opening of the poem which we had seen before, did indeed make it difficult for us not to be disappointed, yet the scene between Oswald & Bertram which follows it is so excellent and presents such a strong picture both to the eye & the mind that the interest increases upon you & your admiration gives not up one inch of the high ground it occupied at the beginning. Indeed the character of Bertram is conceaved [sic] & discribed [sic] & represented in a very masterly manner and has a highly dramatic effect besides that which the drama cannot give, a representation of great bodily energy along with that of the spirit. I think his starting away from Wilfred on their journey & scrambling up the steep rocky height after the supposed spectre is wonderfully fine. The superstition & seeds of generosity, when he would not let the man he had murdered be accused of having fraudfully earned his treasures, are well imagined. He is as wicked as any man ought to be made for either moral or poetical effect, and we fear & hate yet are interested for him too. Wilfred's character is beautiful. Oswald's I do not at present so well understand, but I make no doubt it will in the sequel clear upon me and perhaps turn out the most skillfully delineated of them all. The discription of scenery is very excellent but the country itself being less wild & romantic than that which you have formerly described, I dont think it will be so popular. In short, for having at present very little time I must be <u>short</u>, we are full of admiration and counting the time when we shall see the whole with all the impatience you could desire. ——— I must appear ungrateful in not thanking you sooner, but I received it at Hampstead the day before we went to Town, and have been so much occupied since we came to Town that I could not write. No mortal has seen Rokeby except my Sister & Mrs Baillie & my Niece, who all unite in grateful thanks, and it was despatched as you desired to Mr Morritt after it had been in our hand about 3 days.[174] He will be a proud man I am sure, at least I should be so in his place. ——— We are all greatly excited here with these good & wonderful news from Russia. To day it is actually believed that Buonapart is taken prisoner.[175] Heaven grant it may be so! and we shall then look with some confidence for the blessing of peace. How powerfully the tide has set against him when once turned! What a mighty structure is broken down in so short a space and how eagerly do we look forward like the king in your vision of Don Roderic for the change of scene that is to follow! —— I hope this will find you well: and a cheerful comfortable winter may you pass with your family round you & every thing you put your hand to prospering to your wish. I am glad to hear you mention a chance of your coming to Town next spring tho' it is but in a very

---

174. John Bacon Sawrey Morritt (1772?-1843), traveler and classical scholar, visited Scott in 1808, 1816 and 1829. Their friendship was never broken. Returning from London in 1809, Scott spent a fortnight at Rokeby, Morritt's estate, and described it as one of the most enviable places he had seen; in 1811 he discussed with Morritt his intention to make it the setting of his poem of the same name. Morritt was an occasional contributor to the *Quarterly Review* and produced such works as "The Curse of Moy, A Highland Tale" (poem), "History and Principles of Antient Sculpture" (essay), and *Miscellaneous Translations and Imitations of the Minor Greek Poets* (volume) (*DNB*, XIII:1009-10).

175. In September 1812, Napoleon entered Moscow with 95,000 men and found the city almost deserted. Installing himself and his staff in the Kremlin, he awaited czar Alexander's proposal for terms. Winter was too near for a march to the capital at St. Petersburg where the czar resided, and while Alexander waited him out, Napoleon's troops, finding riches of all sorts, were not finding the needed shoes or meat. The French army began to die from exposure, malnutrition and disease. Finally, opting for a withdrawal to Smolensk and its supplies, Napoleon left Moscow in October. As the French army marched north, Cossacks almost captured Napoleon, but he arrived in Smolensk on 13 November, having lost most of his horses and troops. Escaping the Russians again in December, Napoleon turned his *Grande Armée* over to Murat and departed for Paris; by 19 December 1812, he was back in the Tuileries. French records show that 210,000 Frenchmen were killed, captured or disappeared in Russia (see Owen Connelly, *Blundering to Glory: Napoleon's Military Campaigns* [Wilmington, Delaware: Scholarly Resources, 1984], 157-81).

doubtful way. — Fare_[176] my best remembrances to Mrs Scott, M^{rs} B & my
. . . send their kind regards. Affectionately yours
  J Baillie

3884 ff.26-29 (Address: Walter Scott Esqr / N: Castle Street / Edin^{r}--no
postmark)

Hampstead Jan^{ry} 14th 1813

A thousand thanks to you, my dear Friend! you are very good and
therefore, as is meet & right, very dear to me. Your lumbering 4to as you
call it — the noble poem of Rokeby as I call it, came to my hands two days
ago, and I have already read it twice. It came not under Mr Elder's but M^{r}
Freelings cover. Take my best thanks again for your valuable present,
before I begin to speak of it, lest I should forget to thank you afterwards. It
is a part of my treasure & worldly goods that will do me good all the days
of my life. I wish you could have seen me when it arrived. My Sister was
from home, so I stirred my fire, swept the hearth, chaced [sic] the cat out
of the room, lighted my candles and began upon it immediately. It is
written with wonderful power both as to natural objects & human
character, and your magnificent Bandit, Bertram, is well entitled to your
partiality; for it is a masterly picture, and true to nature in all its parts,
according to my conceptions of nature. Your Lady & both her lovers are
very pleasing & beautifully drawn. Her conduct & behaviour to them both
is so natural & delicate and so is their's [sic] to each other! How many
striking passages there are which take hold of the imagination that can
never be unloosed! The burning of the Castle in all its progress is very
~~grand~~ sublime: the final scene also when Bertram rides into the church is
grand & terrific: the scene between him & Edmund, when he weeps to find
that there is [not] any human being that will shed a tear for him is very
touching, and finely imagined, — I say nothing of what struck me so much
in the 3 first cantos — and besides those higher beauties there are those of
a softer kind that are wonderfully attractive; for instance, the account of
the poor Irish-mans death after he had deliver'd the child to the Lord of
Rokeby which made me weep freely, and the stealing of Edmund back to
the cave by night with all the indications of his silent path – the owlet
ceasing its crie, the other leaping into the stream &c. is delightful. Your
images or similies [sic] too, with which the work is not over-loaded –
(Like a Lady with few jewels but of the best water[177]) – are excellent. Your
songs are good, particularly those of Wilfrid, but they have struck me less,
some how other, than the rest of the Poem. As to the invention of your

---

176. This and the following ellipsis indicate a torn corner of the leaf.
177. water: first, second and third water were grades given to diamonds (*OED*).

story, I praise that more sparingly, for tho' the leading circumstances are well imagined, the conducting of it seems to me too dramatic for a Lyrical narative [sic], and there are too many complex contrivances [that] go to the bringing about the catastrophe. It seems to me that you are hankering after and veering to the Drama prodigiously. Take possession of it then fairly & manfully: you have ample powers and the favour of the public into the bargain; and if I must be eclipsed in my own domicile[178] I will take it from your hand rather than from any other. Send me a better Play than any I have to boast of, and if a shade of human infirmity should pass over my mind for a moment, by the setting of the sun I shall love you more than ever. ––– I am quite gratified to hear that the Family Legend is not neglected by my friends in Edn^r and pleased with your account of Mr Terry's Malvolio: I can easily imagine he would act it admirably well. –– You will perceive from this that I have received your letter as well as the book. I was just sitting down to write this, when the Post brought it to me most opportunely. I am pleased to think you have enjoyed yourself so much since your hand has been set free from your pen. May your trees & every thing you plant flourish to your wish. But praise this amiable trait of human nature, illustrated by the anecdote of Dr Robertson, with some allay when applied to yourself. Other men plant trees for succeeding men, who will possess them as if they had sprung out of the ground up themselves, but the Laird of Abbotsford has it not in his power to be so entirely disinterested. His name will be so closely & so long associated with every thing he does, that I might with a little perverse ingenuity resolve every stick he puts into the ground as an act of the selfish love of perpetuity. I mean when I can find an opportunity to send you the birch seed, like Sancho Pancho's [sic] wife sending the Duchess a bag of acorns in return for her rich gifts.[179] Kenedy & Lee — our first seeds men in this part of the world, have it very good, but they get it from Scotland: probably from the highlands.

---

178. The word is not clear here.

179. The encounter between the Duke's household and the household of Teresa and Sancho Panza in *Don Quixote* appears in chapter 50 of part 2 and accentuates the differences between common man and nobility. The Duchess sends Teresa a coral necklace with gold clasps, and Teresa sends (chapter 52) the following:

> I feel about as bad as I can feel that, this year, there haven't been any acorns in this town, in spite of which I'm sending your majesty almost half a bucketful that I went up on the mountain and picked for you, by hand, but I couldn't find any bigger ones: I wish they were regular ostrich eggs!

See Miguel de Cervantes Saavedra, *The History of That Ingenious Gentleman Don Quijote de la Mancha*, trans. Burton Raffel (New York and London: Norton, 1995), 626.

There is a thing I forgot to tell you a great while ago for which myself or my memory is much to blame: Mr Carr charged me to give you from him a great many thanks for the information you gave him respecting the different families of his name; but going to the Herrald's office, he found the whole account of his own branch of the Carrs, given very distinctly so would not trespass on your goodness any further. He has the true spirit of a Borderer in him, and is of course one of your warm admirers.

I can think of nothing to tell you from this that will at all interest you: the public news you have nearly as soon as ourselves.

All things go on at Windsor as usual. Mrs Siddons was at Frognalmore the other day and read plays to the Queen. She is returned from Southampton where she had bought a large house which she is now tired of, and on which she will lose (so a neighbour of hers told me) a thousand pounds. I am sorry for it: for money so fairly & honourably made should not take wings to itself. I met an acquaintance of hers at the Chief Baron's the other night, who told me she is to have public readings this winter but I scarcely believe it. I met there too your friend & relation Lady Davy who talked to me a great deal about you and was longing as every body else is for Rokeby. Sir Humphr[e]y has had an alarming return of the malady in his eye from the accident, and tho' better it is still very bad. A medical man who attends Sir H. told me that she has behaved thro' the whole of this affair with great good sense & feeling, tho' the Patient is very impatient & unmanageable. --- My Sister & I have kept well, but we have had in regard to weather a dismal winter. Sun moon & stars have become strangers to us; a thick damp mist, even on the heights of Hampstead, wrapping us round like . . .[180] from the shoulders of Ben lom. . . continually. --- I say _even on_ the heights of Hampstead, for our mists here are generally low and rest on the great City. --- Fare well! I have written you what I consider as a very long letter, and I fear you may consider it so too. — My Sister joins me in kindest wishes to Mrs Scott & to all your young folks. A happy winter (what of it is yet to come) may you have in Edin^r! and a happy year & many happy years! Yours most truly

    J Baillie

PS. So far I had written to you yesterday morning but I have been at a gay dance last night with your highland broach in my tartan, and am now much in the humour to write more would my paper allow me. I met some friends there who have by favour of some other friends already read Rokeby and they spoke of it with the highest -- I may say unbounded praise. What a buzz we shall hear about it by & bye! -- I must not be so ungrateful as to finish my paper without thanking you in addition to all

---

180. This and the following ellipsis indicate a hole in the leaf.

my other thanks for the very handsome notice you take of me in the notes to Rokeby.[181] You lose no occasion to stick a sprig in my cap when it offers and there are no honours which I wear more proudly

    JB

3884 ff.75-76 (Address: For Walter Scott Esqr / N: Castle Street / with a small parcel / Edin^r--no postmark)

London Feb^{ry} 20th 1813

My dear Friend

    After all my magnificent promises of sending you birch seed, like many other magnificent promises in these bad times they come to nothing. I went yesterday to our first seedsmen in this country, Kenedy & Lee, and had the mortification to learn that this last year has been so unfavourable for the seed of trees that they have got none from Scotland the place from which they get their Birch seed, and that there is none to be got. To shew you that I have gone to the first seedsmen, I must tell you that I found Mr Kenedy dressed in an old dusty coat & a blue apron before him, lamenting to a Lady, whom he was serving with shrubs &c., that his presents from the Empress which had been landed at Ramsgate, were seized upon by the custom house officers — a snuff-box – a ring – I think a watch — and some prints of the Emperor. This he did not regret for the value, which he supposed would not be above two hundred pounds, but the gratification of receiving such an honour. You have guessed, I suppose, that this is the Empress Josephine. You will own then that I have paid all due respect to Abbotsford in seeking birch seed for it from such a quarter; and indeed I was unwilling to leave it without getting the seed of some tree or other that would thrive in Scotland but that is not produced there, so on enquiring, Mr Kenedy recommended <u>Pine astres</u> as a most beautiful kind of pine, a great quantity of which he was sending to Ld Morton; but here again was another difficulty, for all he had of it was already packed up & sent to his Lordship. Having got this information I set off to another great seed shop whose master does not, I suppose, receive imperial presents and there, tho' I could find no birch, I got Pine astres, a small parcel of

---

181. Scott's *Rokeby* was dedicated to his friend John B. S. Morritt, Esq.; in the notes to Canto First, Scott credits Baillie as follows: "I have had occasion to remark in real life, the effect of keen and fervent anxiety in giving acuteness to the organs of sense. My gifted friend Miss Joanna Baillie, whose dramatic works display such intimate acquaintance with the operations of human passion, has not omitted this remarkable circumstance"; Scott quotes from *De Monfort* as example (see *The Poetical Works of Sir Walter Scott*, 3 vols. [Edinburgh: James Nichol, 1858], 3:163).

which you will receive with this.[182] ––– Much pleasure may you have when your vacation comes, in your country occupations! and well may your trees & your plants thrive! I like very much your idea of the hanging wooded bank with the weeping trees on the front ranks: it will have a beautiful effect. —— Rokeby is making its way here as its elder Brethern have done: great strength & splendour of genius acknowledged, with many small faults found with the conduct of the story & particular lines &c. Which are urged less confidently as time wears on and the multitude of readers take courage to speak from their feelings & genuine impressions. —— We have a new Tragedy here by Colridge [sic] called remorse which is going on prosperously under the disadvantage (I am told) of very bad acting.[183] I shall go to see it as soon as I can; in the mean time I have read it. There are some beautiful passages and the circumstances of the story are interesting, tho' it does not seem to me to be very affecting, and remorse is a title which does not seem to me more appropriate than any other would have been. I am very glad poor Colridge has had his success, for the public hitherto have not been much inclined to allow his merit. –– Farewell! Give my kindest regards to Mrs Scott. Mrs Baillie & My Sister send you their kindest remembrances with mine. — God bless you!

    J Baillie

3884 ff.184-187 (No address or postmark, NLS dates 1813)
My dear Friend,

    Since you heard from me I have been more in Town & more in company than I fairly like – that is to say more than suits my natural habits; but now that it is past I am pleased in looking back upon it, and the more so that I have done two things during the time which you wished or desired me to do. I have met with your friend Mr Morrit [sic] and begun, I hope, an acquaintance with him, for I should be sorry to think that what is past is all I shall ever have of his society. I had the good luck to find myself

---

182. On 13 March 1813 Scott replies, "The pinasters have arrived safely and I can hardly regret while I am so much flattered by the trouble you have had in collecting them. . . . I have got a little corner of ground laid out for a nursery where I shall rear them carefully until they are old enough to be set forth to push their fortune on the banks of Tweed" (Grierson, 3:235).

183. Samuel Taylor Coleridge's five-act *Remorse*, originally entitled *Osorio*, opened at Drury Lane on 23 January 1813 and closed 28 nights later. A five-hour performance, the play was found by the London *Times* to be "'singularly involved and laboured,' lacking in verisimilitude, and replete with flat, declamatory characters" (Virginia L. Radley, *Samuel Taylor Coleridge* [New York: Twayne, 1966], 97-8).

seated next to him at dinner at Sir R. Milbank's,[184] tho' we had not been
introduced to each other, and had the luck also, while I was struggling
with my own foolish reserve for something to say to him, to be spoken to by
him first. This made all easy: we talked about you & Rokeby & some other
agreeable subjects, and I found myself so much placed to my hearts content
that all the wit & learning of Dr Parr,[185] who sat smoking his pipe in
great glory at the other end of the long table, was entirely lost to me
without regret. Mrs Morrit too was very obliging & good to me, and invited
me to see her in Portland Place which I have promised to do; and tho' I
scarcely ever make use of such invitations, I will, for my own sake in the
first place & yours in the second, actually take courage & call upon her
next winter. This then is one of the two things; the other is getting
acquainted with Miss Edgeworth.[186] If you would give a silver sixpence as
you say, to see us together, each of us would I am sure have given a silver
crown – (no small part now of the rent cast contained in any body's purse)
to have seen you a third in our party. I have found her a frank, animated,
sensible & amusing woman, entirely free from affectation of any kind; and
of a confiding & affectionate & friendly disposition that has really
gained upon my heart. We met a good many times in large parties, &
thrice in a more familiar way; and when we parted she was in leave like
one who takes leave of an old friend. She has been received by every body
— the first in literature & the first in rank, with the most gratifying
eagerness & respect, and has pleased – I should rather say delighted them
all. She is cheerful, & talks easily & fluently; seems interested in every
subject that comes into play, and tells her little anecdote or story (when
her Father does not take it out of her mouth) very pleasantly. However, in
regard to her Father, tho' it is the fashion to call him a great Bore, she is

---

184. Sir Ralph and Judith Noel Milbanke, the parents of Anne Isabella Milbanke
(Lady Byron), took the surname Noel by royal license in accordance with terms of his
wife's inheritance from her brother, the 2nd Viscount Wentworth.

185. This is probably schoolmaster and writer Samuel Parr (1747-1825), who
was a friend of the Burneys, Moore and later Byron. Landor and Lord Lytton
acknowledged Parr's kindness to them, and he was befriended by a great many
members of the peerage (*DNB*, XV:356-64).

186. Maria Edgeworth (1768-1849) first focused her writing on educational
topics, translating Madame de Genlis's *Adèle et Théodore*. She experimented with
various teaching methods, publishing a series including *The Parents Assistant* (1796)
and *Early Lessons* (1801); but she became well known for her novels *Castle Rackrent*
(1800), *Belinda* (1801), *Popular Tales* (1804), *The Modern Griselda* (1805), *Leonora*
(1806), the six volume *Tales of Fashionable Life* (1809-12), *Ormond* (1817), *Helen*
(1834), etc., many of which document Irish society. Edgeworth is one of the first
women novelists "to apply an insight articulated by Wollstonecraft, that women have
their own language" (Todd, 204-7).

not so much hampered as she must have been when in Edin^r where I was told she could not get leave to speak to any body and therefore kept on the back ground wherever she went. When they take up the same thing now, they have a fair wrangle (tho' a good humoured one) for it, and she as often gets the better of him. He is to be sure a strange Mortal, with no great tact, as it is called, and some small matters of conceit, yet his Daughter is so strongly attached to him that I am sure he must have much real good in him, and, convinced of this, I have taken a good will to him in spite of fashion, and maintain that, if he would just speak one half of what he speaks, he would be a very agreeable man. You would have been amused if you had seen with what eagerness people crowded to get a sight of Miss Edgeworth, who is very short, peeping over shoulders & between curld tetes[187] to get but one look. She said very well herself at a party where I met her, that the crowd closed over her. She did indeed cause a strange commotion; and had Mad^m Stael come as she was expected at the same time I dont know what would have happened – the Town must have run mad altogether.[188] She, Mad^m Stael, is now arrived, and has the whole field to herself, but her reign for the season must be short as the company will so soon leave Town.

I have been almost a fortnight in Devon with my good friend Mrs Elliott,[189] in perfect quiet & contentment, walking & riding about this rich cheerful country, eating cream, and trying to get on a little in my learning, having a snug room appointed for me and the command of some good books of solid reading which I have not at home. I wish I may be the fatter & the wiser for all this; however, if I should get no good by it, I have some pleasure. The country is particularly pleasant just now, for the people are in the midst of hay harvest & the crops very abundant. My Niece & I & Mrs M. had a delightful journey from Town, passing thro' Bath & Wells, where we saw the fine old Cathedral & the fortified walls of the Bishop's Palace, in compleat repair tho' entirely covered with ivy & other green things, & the moat full of clear water reflecting the whole as in days of yore. We also passed thro' Glastonbury & saw the noble ruins of the old Abbey & had a twig – not of the famous thorn which

---

187. tête: obs., a woman's head of hair or wig, elaborately ornamented in the style of the late 18th century (*OED*).

188. Mme. de Staël (1766-1817), Anne Louise Germaine Necker, Baronne de Staël-Holstein, was a French writer and influential arbiter of aesthetic taste who admired Rousseau and dedicated her first serious essay to him in 1788. She met Goethe, Schiller and Weimar in Germany in 1803-04 and was much disliked by Napoleon. Her novel *Delphine* appeared in 1802, followed by *Corinne* in 1807 (*The New Century Cyclopedia of Names*, 3:3683).

189. See letters to Anne Elliott herein.

is now dead but one of its descendants, a very particular kind of thorn, having its leaves bend down from the stalk, contrary to the use of vulgar thorns, & flowering as our china roses do about Xmas. Apropos of this, I must tell you a superstition belonging to Devonshire. On a certain night of the year (Candlemas I believe)[190] they sing a song to their apple trees to make them fruitful. Their harvest-home song is always the old ballad of Lord Thomas & fair Anny, which is always the song first sung at the harvest supper, a kind of religious song of thanks for the good crops & wishes for the continuance of this blessing, following immediately after it, before the other songs begin.[191] How this unnatural arrangement in favour of fair Anny comes to be established I have not been able to learn, antiquarianism not being very common in Devon. Their midnight orgies have not, however, done much for their fruit-trees this season, and there will be very little cyder made in this part of the (the) country! which being the usual drink of the country people is a great loss. This place is about nine miles from Sidmouth where I went yesterday with my Niece −− my companion de voyage — & Mrs E. and had a most magnificent view of the sea from a high cliff which always soothes me & does me good. The coast here with its rich wooded valies [sic] running down to the sea is most beautiful. Elizabeth & I with our friend hope to make a little excursion to see the bold romantic coast of north Devon and then in the end of July or beginning of August return home. My Sister during my absence is staying with a friend at Sunning Hill. My Brother has got a good pretty house there in the same Lane and almost close to Mr G. Ellis' where he hopes to go in August. —— Mrs Baillie made a fair copy of what you wished Sir H. Halford to know concerning the burial of K. Charles 1st, and sent it to him long before I left Town, but had not when I came away received any answer from him, else I should have heard of it. Your observations on the character or rather conduct of Charles I like much: for a Tory born & bred, whose family have suffered so much for their attachment to the royal cause, I must say you are a very reasonable man. −−− I have been reading lately Ld Biron's [sic] new poem, The Giour [sic], which I suppose you have seen.[192] There are beautiful passages in it, the sinking of the body into the sea, the murder of Hassan, and the simile of the butterfly chaced [sic] by a child, compared to another vain pursuit, which is eminently beautiful &c.

---

190. Candlemas, the feast of the purification of the Virgin Mary (or presentation of Christ in the Temple), is celebrated with a great display of candles. The date of this feast, February 2, is one of the quarter-days in Scotland (*OED*).

191. There are numerous versions of the "Ballad of Fair Annie"; see *The English and Scottish Popular Ballads*, ed. Francis James Child, 5 vols. (N.Y.: Pageant, 1956), 2:63-83.

192. Byron published both *The Giaour* and *The Bride of Abydos* in 1813.

and on the first reading, notwithstanding the strange broken way of
<u>insinuating</u> the story, it pleased me exceedingly. However after being
open-mouthed in its praise for a day or two, when I came to read it a second
time, a great part of the charm, I know not how, had fled. He is satisfied
with giving the energy of passion without its nobleness & grace; and one
cannot be the least interested for either Leala [Leila] on her Giour but very
well satisfied that they should either be drowned or confined in a
monastery as the Poet may see fit. Hassan is the only person in the story
that I could sympathize with. L$\underline{d}$ B. has no mean portion of native genius
but he seems to me, notwithstanding the very different character of his
persons & stories, to have Walter Scott perpetually in his eye. I wonder i f
he is himself aware of this, and whether he would not be ready to break
my head for saying so. There were touches here & there at which I could
not help calling on your name – viz where he says on the ambushed foes
firing on the followers of Hassan, four or five –– I forget the number ––
["]came to the ground, and <u>three shall never mount again.</u> "[193] I say not thi s
to his discredit: I believe he has not <u>imitated</u> such graces from you but
caught them. Tho' passion, as he chuses to paint it, is revolting, yet it is
naturally & forcibly expressed; and if he thought more worthily of human
nature, he might, I should think, excell in Tragedy; and possibly he may
turn his thoughts this way. ––

How I have filled up my paper with I dont know what! Fare well! it
is time to have done. I hope this will find yourself & Mrs Scott & the
children well, and offer my kindest wishes most cordially.

    With all kind & Sisterly good will

      yours truly

        J Baillie

Egland Honiton
July 1st 1813

---

193. See *The Giaour*:
    Scarce had they time to check the rein
  Swift from their steeds the riders bound,
    But three shall never mount again;
  Unseen the foes that gave the wound,
    The dying ask revenge in vain.
(Jerome J. McGann, ed., *Lord Byron: The Complete Poetical Works* [Oxford: Clarendon,
1981], III:58)

3884 ff.189-191 (No address or postmark, NLS dates 1813)

Sunning Hill Nov^r [1813]

My dear Sir,

I hear [from] our neighbour Mr Richardson that you remember me with your usual kindness,[194] and that a token of it is safely arrived from Scotland, a good bottle of old Whiskey; which I accept with all thankfulness. I am afraid he got it from you in a begging kind of a way, and at some risk of my character; but I shall have my pleasure out of it without troubling myself much about these niceties; and I reckon I shall drink your health in the first glass thereof about Xmas time with true good will and as much glee as a respectable person of my years can decently indulge. Our said Neighbour pleased us with the good account he gave us of yourself & your young people & your new place with all its beauties natural & improved. Long may you prosper & enjoy yourself there! a good wish I have often repeated to you and cant help still repeating. But I was sorry to hear by him that you are likely to be troubled by the greedy Tax gatherers concerning your literary profits. Now if I were of an envious disposition making so little in this way myself, I might have some satisfaction in your troubles; like a beggar in a shower of rain, who sees better folks hurrying along to save their fine clothes, but I am not, and contrary wise feel my back bristling up as stiffly against the wrong as if I were to lose by it the ransom of a knight. I hope you will get the better of them with all my heart: it is well they begin with you who are powerful to contend with them.

My Sister & I came here about a fortnight ago, and find it very pleasant quarters indeed. My Brother has got a better house than he had, very near your Friend Mr G. Ellis, who is a very kind obliging neighbour, and so very agreeable that all the Ladies of the family from my Niece upwards are down rightly in love with him. I told him last night I meant to write to you and he charged me with his kind regards for you and to say that he longs much to see your hand writing. He is looking well & in good

194. John Richardson (1780-1864) was a parliamentary solicitor and for 30 years discharged the duties of crown agent for Scotland, reputed as the most learned peerage lawyer of his time. He had literary tastes and in 1821 was introduced to George Crabbe in Joanna Baillie's house, and he regularly corresponded with Walter Scott, whose deathbed he attended shortly before Scott's demise. He married Elizabeth Hill, a close friend of Thomas Campbell, in 1811 and had several children (*DNB*, XVI:1118-19). Richardson submitted "Song - Her features speak the warmest heart" for Baillie's 1823 collection; and in a letter dated 18 January 1842, Richardson tells Baillie, "It is, as it has long been, a great pride and gratification to me to have enjoyed your friendship; a few circumstances of my life have afforded me more real pleasure" (NLS Ms 3990 f.41).

spirits. But indeed who is not in good spirits at present? The news from Holand [sic], following all that has passed so lately, has animated the dullest. We may now look forward to a better order of things; and the lessons taught during these last twenty years to all ranks of mankind – kings & people, will I hope tend to make it lasting & steady.[195] ––– Some time before we left home we saw your Friend Terry, who seems in very good heart about his Theatrical prospects, and I am glad to learn by the news paper that he has been received with great applause in his new character in this revived Play of Drydens which I understand from him is a favourite Play of yours.[196] It is long since I read it, and I remember it very imperfectly, but I shall renew my acquaintance with it as soon as I can if not upon the stage which I should prefer at least in the closet. Talking of the stage puts me in mind that I met with Mr Whitbread when I was last in Town, and he told me that he himself or a friend of his (I forget which) saw in passing thro' a country Town not long ago written on a board, " a reading of Rokeby may be had here for a penny a piece." These are the honours I envy you for; to see one of my own Plays acted in a Burn[197] would make me a happy woman. I have since my return from Devon sh: been getting on a step in my long task which I have now the prospect before a long time shall pass over my head of bringing to a close, at least I shall, if I am spared, bestir myself to do so. –– Every body at present is reading Mad^m de Stael's new book and I hear so good an account of it that I long to begin.[198] I thought to have had some time both to read & write here; but I was mistaken, we have more visitors than in Town and are much too gay to take to our larning. ––– Farewell! Mrs Baillie & my Sister & all the family offer their respects & best regards to you & Mrs Scott, and pray

---

195. If, indeed, this letter is from November 1813, the reference is to Wellington's success in driving a wedge between Madrid and the French frontier in the spring of 1813. He defeated King Joseph's French army on 21 June, liberating Spain from French control and persuading Austrian Emperor Francis I to join the British coalition. By October 1813, Napoleon was being overwhelmed at the Battle of the Nations near Leipzig, and Wellington was invading southern France. After a disastrous Scheldt expedition, British forces had begun to concentrate on the Iberian peninsula (Gordon Bond, *The Grand Expedition: The British Invasion of Holland in 1809* [Athens, Georgia: University of Georgia Press, 1979], 164-65).

196. Daniel Terry made his appearance at the Haymarket in May 1813 and at Covent Garden in September 1813, taking on dozens of roles (*DNB*, XIX:19). I have not found a specific reference to a Dryden play.

197. burn: stream (SND).

198. de Staël's *De l'Allemagne* (*On Germany*) had appeared in 1810. It is possible, however, that Baillie is referring to one of her earlier novels (*Delphine* and *Corinne*), which makes the dating of this letter questionable.

accept my kindest wishes for your young folks, tho' they must now have nearly forgotten me. Believe me always

most truly yours

J Baillie

PS. I have forgot to tell you that I have taken a liberty with you for which I hope you will pardon me. When Miss Edgeworth was in Town last spring, I mention'd to her the very gratifying terms in which you had mention[ed] her in your letter to me which I had received a short time before; and thinking it was in my pocket, meant to read to her the passages but finding it was not there, and Mr Edgeworth wishing much to see it, because says he "it will shew you, Maria, that he is sincere in the professions he makes" I wishing to justify your sincerity & my own truth, said I would send it to her when I should return home. (I was then on my way to Devonshire) On returning to Hampstead I found your letter very safely lodged in my trunk, & the other day I wrote to her & inclosed that part of it which concerned her, defacing the name of Miss H. & of her Poem therein not so handsomely spoken of, and also defacing on the back part of the paper all the other writing which contained some thoughts on other matters which I thought I had no business to shew to them; and so completely that I would defy a post office Clerk or any one else to decypher it. I hope I have not done any thing very bad. ——

3885 ff.31-32 (Address: Walter Scott Esqr / N: Castle Street / Edinburgh-- postmarked 1814)

Hampstead Feb^{ry} 3$^{\underline{d}}$ 1814

Your last letter, my dear Friend gave me particular pleasure as I learnt by it that we may at last trust soon to see you here. I did verily sometimes think in my own gloomy fancy we should never meet again. Well; when is the time fixed? and does Mrs Scott & your young Sophia come with you? If this be the case, as I hope it is, do you remember my former proposal in regard to the last mentioned Lady. She is still too young to run the gauntlet with you thro' all the great parties in the west end of the Town, so she shall be safely housed with my Sister & I, and always forthcoming whenever you really wish to have her with you. I hope I need not say to you that this arrangement would give both my Sister & I great pleasure; and tho' she might find our very confined establishment & the company of two old people rather dull; yet we have my Niece & other young folks, who would be very glad to be often with her & make her time pass cheerfully. Pray let Mrs Scott & you think well of this.[199] I suppose you

---

199. Scott replied that "Sophia will be delighted to be your honored guest, and I will be charmed with the opportunity of making her acquainted with you," though he

will set out by the 12$\underline{^{th}}$ of March or as soon as you can, and this is not now far distant.

By the time you reach the continent, most likely the great battle will be fought that is to decide who shall be Master of France. And as far as I can judge from what we see in the news papers, this will be fought as fairly as it could be fought in the deserts of Tartary [?]; for the French seem not at all attached to either Buonaparte or the Bourbons & no wise inclined to disturb or assist the operations on either side. If they are inclined to have the Bourbons I shall be glad to see them there, not otherwise: and as for Buonaparte, the Muckle Deel[200] may take him, or he may teach a school in America for any thing that I care. But there is one point on which I am not at all indifferent; that we may have peace; and I hope you will reach the Allies in time to see all the pomp & circumstance of war in its brightest moment, just after it has conquered peace.[201] You would like I know to get there (for I "know the naughtiness of your heart") before the battle, but I think the grand vestiges or wreck of it may do for you, and your grand imagination will supply the rest. ––– Your bottle of whiskey had the cork drawn yesterday and right good whiskey it is: I drunk your health in as large a driblet of it as a respectable private Gentlewoman may venture upon: it is very potent as well as very good. Many thanks for so kindly offering to supply me with this precious beverage: but one bottle will last a long time; and I must not have it entirely at will, for plenty like familiarity breeds contempt. ––– As to what you say of your friend Miss Smith, I can have no objections to become acquainted with her, on the contrary it will give me pleasure. She is I know a very respectable woman, and a respectable woman in her situation is like well tried gold doubly precious. I have never heard her read nor seen her act, but I understand she is a very clever woman. I should be sorry that she should take the trouble of coming to Hampstead in winter weather to see me; she is well acquainted with Sotheby & his family; when I am in Town in spring I shall desire him to introduce me to her and that will be the handsomest way on my part. –––[202]

---

sent her only after she had been "noticed and caressed" for a month in society (qtd. in Johnson, 489, 493).

200. muckle deel: great devil (*SND*).

201. The Peace of Paris came in 1814 when the Allies defeated France, but Napoleon was not to see final defeat until the Battle of Waterloo in June 1815. See letter 3886 ff.162-165 following.

202. In his letter to Baillie dated 10 December 1813, Scott writes,

Sarah Smith who is a very excellent and well disposed young woman has been long very anxious to be known to you. I have always rather waved this request. . . . She is the leading tragic actress after Mrs. Siddons but the

We have not seen Play or any thing the whole winter: Mrs Agnes &
Mrs Joanna Baillie, for so (after a prevailing & I think very good fashion
of this country) we now call ourselves, have been shut up by the frost &
snow at their own fireside, reading their books with spectacles on nose,
since Xmas. Pray when you direct your next letter to me, remember this my
new dignity, for I hope you will not be ashamed of such an antiquated
correspondent as Mrs Joanna Baillie. This good fashion has long been in
disuse in Scotland, but I think it would not be much amiss were it revived
again. People it is true shrink naturally as passing a direct line of
demarkation to any thing that smacks of old age, but there are other
privileges attending it that would make amends for this mortification.
Well, as I have said, with spectacles on nose we have been reading our
books and amongst these Patronage.[203] There are some well drawn
characters in it & good lessons for many people, but I fear it is too much
loaded with discussions in dialogue & ordinary love matters to give it
every chance for being so popular as most of her other works are. She –
Miss Edgeworth, was so good as to send it to me with the kindest letter
imaginable – so kind – genuinely kind that it did my heart good to read it.
I see she has been greatly pleased with the extract I sent her from your
letter. ――― I think from what I hear of Mad^me de Stael that you would
probably have liked her had she gone to Edin^r better than you are aware
of. Be assured when you come to Town you will have enough of her
company whether it be to your taste or not; for she considers Poetic
imagination as the first of human gifts. She visits in some houses that I
know & I am in part engaged to meet her, but the weather has prevented
parties from taking place, and I have not yet had my curiosity gratified.
What a current of thought she seems to have continually passing thro' her
mind! and with what brilliancy & felicity she expresses herself! She is a
very extraordinary woman. — Have you heard that Sir H. & Lady Davy
are very unpleasantly situated in Paris, if they are not yet released? no
respect at all paid to them, & no liberty to go about & gratify their
curiosity! The <u>nouveaux Rich</u>, it seems, look down upon Philosopher & his

---

interval is more distant than I could wish for the sake of my little friend who
is nevertheless an excellent Actress.
(Grierson, 3:390)
    203. Maria Edgeworth's novel *Patronage* was published in 4 vols. in 1814. The
tale was, her stepmother said, "less studied, less criticized, less corrected and more
rapidly written than any other that Maria had produced" (qtd. in Marilyn Butler,
Maria Edgeworth: A Literary Biography [Oxford: Clarendon, 1972], 277).

Lady. ——— Farewell! My Sister sends her kind regards with mine to yourself & Mrs Scott. Hoping then to see you soon, I remain

   my dear Friend, ever truly yours
      J Baillie

3885 ff.37-39 (Address: Walter Scott Esqr / N: Castle Street / Edin^r - - postmarked 1814)

Hampstead Feb^ry 8th 1814

My dear Sir,
   Tho' I wrote to you last week, here I am set down to trouble you again, trusting that by the time you have read what I shall now endite [sic] you will pardon me. — When I returned from Sunning hill, I met in the house of a friend, your song of "Summer's eve is past & gone" from Rokeby, set to Music by Dr Clark[e] of Cambridge and inscribed to me.[204] I had had no notice of this, nor any copy sent to me, nevertheless my vanity & something better than vanity was pleased with the mark of respect & above all with the Idea that some natural association had made this same Mus. Doctor couple my name with verses of your writing. Not meeting with many honours, I thought it would not do for me to neglect any that did fall in my way, so I wrote a civil letter to Dr Clark upon the occasion & received his answer a day or two ago. By it I find that I owed this honour to no natural association as my foolish vanity had suggested, but to your particular kindness, my dear Friend, who wished some of my songs to be brought into notice & had recommended them to Dr C. some time before; an agreeable mortification to me – I say agreeable leaving you to find out how this may be. The good Doctor in his letter then proceeds to lament that a song of yours which he had set for an oratorio last winter was damned he supposes on account of certain words in it which were too loyal for the audience, and after this follows words that I must extract for your consideration. — "It is the last song I shall ever write for the public. –– After the performance of it, I wrote a letter of lamentations to Mr Scott, to which (with two former ones) he has returned no answer. – If Mr Scott knew how proud I was of his

---

204. The "Song" appears in Canto V of *Rokeby*; this portion follows after the wanderer is instructed that the king wants soldiers:

   'Bid not me, in battle-field,
   Buckler lift, or broadsword wield!
   All my strength and all my art
   Is to touch the gentle heart,
   With the wizard notes that ring
   From the peaceful minstrel string.' —

Dr. Clarke composed many of the musical scores for dramatic adaptations of Scott's works (see Bolton).

notice; and how bitterly I feel his silence, he would not suffer his faithful Minstrel (who would wish for no prouder title) "To sigh, to weep, to mourn"! —— If the feeling of gratitude to Mr Scott for his former kindness; having done nothing to forfiet it; and having exerted my feeble talent to the utmost to render my music in some degree not unworthy his Poetry, has merited neglect, then have I indeed merited it." ——

This is the language of a mind deeply hurt but not offended, and if you have not some good reason for your silence, you will send words of comfort to your Minstrel, else you are made of sterner stuff than I take you to be.

I have just been reading Ld Byron's Corsair, which I suppose you have seen some time ago.[205] It was highly praised to me before I read it by those whose judgment I greatly respect, but both my Sister & myself have been much disappointed. The Corsair appears to us an untrue, inconsistent, outré character; and that nicety of his about the killing of Seyd asleep, under his circumstances & with his principles appears to us perfectly absurd – I will write <u>absurd</u> twice lest you should not be able to read that scrawl'd word. There are fine passages in it, particularly that where Conrad hears the storm & the sea roaring so near him when he is in his dungeon, and that at the end where the corpse of Medora is described, but there are I think fewer good passages than in his former long poems and the versification seems laboured, and frequently to my fancy very bad. His dedication to Moore is a foolish thing, and yet I believe it is good nature & goodness of heart that has made him write it. I am glad that poor Moore is honoured & cheered, which he deserves better now than when he wrote his first reprehensible poem which his friends say he now thoroughly repents; but as the world dont know of this good change in him, and as there is a general impression against Ld B. as a man of licentious principles, I wish he had dedicated it for his own sake to some other body.[206] I am somewhat interested for Ld B. for I have lately learnt a great many things concerning him – things that have given me a very good impression of him and have made me look forward to his becoming a worthy & retrieved man. I cannot help thinking that this same Corsair

205. Byron's *The Corsair* had been published in 1814, selling 13,000 copies on the day of publication (Noyes, 782). The 2 January 1814 dedication to Thomas Moore, Esq., begins as follows: "I dedicate to you the last production with which I shall trespass on public patience, and your indulgence, for some years; and I own that I feel anxious to avail myself of this latest and only opportunity of adorning my pages with a name, consecrated by unshaken public principle, and the most undoubted and various talents" (McGann, III:148).

206. Baillie probably refers again to Thomas Moore's *Poems of Thomas Little, Esq.* (1801) which drew charges of immorality from Jeffrey.

has been lately manufactured out of some cast-off Tragedy that he has written when he was under twenty. What think you?

Fare well! I hope to hear soon that we are to meet soon, and in the mean time every good thing be with you & yours!

faithfully & sincerely yours

J Baillie

PS. This may be rather of old date before your receive it, but as Dr Clark has not desired me to write & perhaps does not expect it, this will reach you time enough before you leave Edin^r which makes me venture on an indirect conveyance by means of our good neighbour Richardson. —

3886 ff.22-25 (Address: Walter Scott Esqr / North Castle Street / Edinburgh--postmarked 1815)

Hampstead Jan^ry 15th 1814 [1815]

My dear Friend,

It did me good to see your hand writing again, and the reading of it did me still more good, as it informed me of the best news I could hear from you – your intention of coming to London so soon. I had begun to despair of seeing you again, and my heart had sometimes felt as if the <u>Bodach Glass</u>[207] had said we should never more meet in this world. I have now good courage on this point, and shall be looking out for you the end or middle of March and putting a room in order that your Sophia may be as much here as you & Mrs Scott may please to spare her to us. I trust that you still consider her as too young to go into all the hurry of company that you must encounter. But you know what I have said on this subject in a former letter, and I will not tease you by repeating it again. I almost tremble for you when I think how you will be beset by your innumerable admirers in this country, all your perils on the northern seas are nothing to this. ––– And this brings me naturally to speak of your Lord of the Isles. A book calling itself so & a new publication was sent to us by a friend a week ago, but so bethumbed & used that it looked as if it had been the drudge of a circulating Library for a year past; and therein I read such things as will ensure its being still well bethumbed for many <u>many</u> years to come. Indeed we have been greatly delighted with it. The beginning of the story is very interesting & the marriage festivity interrupted by the noble strangers with the Priest & his excommunications irrestibly [*sic*] turn'd into an inspired blessing "I bless him & he shall be blessed" is highly dramatic and touches every

---

207. bodach glass: specter or enchanted glass (*OED*).

generous feeling of the heart.[208] The characters of Bruce & his Brothers are finely marked & so noble & engaging while all the events connected with Bruce are important & interesting, that one cannot help wishing that the Poem had taken its name from him. Indeed I fear your fictitious herd & his love affairs in company with such a personage & Robert Bruce & the deliverance of Scotland & the battle of Banockburn [sic] will have less respect paid to them than might be desirable; however as we give to your king what we take from your Lord <u>you</u> are not greatly defrauded. The whole is a succession of beautiful pictures which struck me still more in the second reading than the first; and of those the vessels on the sea in the first canto, the journey thro' the bare desolation of the Island (I forget its name) where the cave & the ruffians are, those most beautiful lines on the cave of Staffa, the effects of the supernatural light on the shore of Carrick and above all the assembled armies on the field of battle struck me most forcibly. I must give you my best thanks for furnishing my imagination with a new idea which it had often endeavoured to call up to itself but without success, viz a great army drawn up & covering a great extent of country. This you have affected by your skillful succession of <u>armed distances</u> if I may use such an expression, and when the last of those amongst the farther hills & verge of the horizon glanced upon my fancy, I call'd out with admiration. Mrs Baillie in Grosvenor St: has been greatly pleased & <u>comoved</u>[209] as Pitscottie says in the reading of it & our neighbours here also. So from what I can learn you will lose no Laurels at this bout; as for gaining any, that is impossible unless you were to take up some other department of poetry. —— How much respect you put upon me & my pines yet I doubt they will prove but scrubby trees after all, and that I should be as well off to have my seat put under a good native birch. This important matter with other important matters we can settle when we meet. —— I shall tell you nothing at present about our Welch [sic] journey, but only that not having been caught up & married by the way we had no interruption given to our curiosity, and saw many grand & beautiful & desolate & wild scenes which we shall always recollect with pleasure. It was well for you that you were caught & married before you got to Wales

---

208. Scott's verse romance *The Lord of the Isles*, published in 1815, deals with King Robert Bruce's struggle against England and his ultimate victory at Bannockburn. See Canto II:

> 'De Bruce, thy sacrilegious blow
> Hath at God's altar slain thy foe:
> O'er-master'd yet by high behest,
> I bless thee, and thou shalt be bless'd.! — (*Poetical Works*, 3:254)

209. probably commoved: brought into a state of commotion, offended, disturbed or displeased (*SND*).

rather than after, for I assure you the Welch [*sic*] women rule the roost, and consider their good husbands but as secondary beings. You may now go safely.

We consider ourselves as being very lucky in having your Friend Richardson & his Quiet, simple, modest wife as our neighbour, we like them more & more as we get better acquainted; and I am glad thro him to hear tidings of you much oftener than I should otherwise do. --- How glad I was in your notes to the Lord of the Isles to find you have paid such a handsome compliment to Miss Holford![210] She is now in Town and will enjoy it perfectly. — We are going to lose Mr Sotheby & his Family for a year or two; they are going abroad, and will have left London I fear before you arrive. I have done what I believe not many people can boast of, read nearly the whole of Charlemagne.[211] It is totally without interest, but some passages of discription here & there appear to me good and towards the end he improves so much in this respect that I think he must have caught fire (a feeble fire however) from reading our modern poets of England. There are a few passages near the end that, were I French woman enough, I daresay I should think really very good. What a vilanous [*sic*] maker of speeches he is! I am some what proud of having got thro' this great book. I once began to get the 119th psalm by heart but s[t]opt short at the middle of the 2^d devision [*sic*]; I really think if I were to set to it now I should have better luck. —— I have heard Mr Hog's poem of the Queen's wake much admired & will read it soon; you have credit of your former protégé.[212]

My Sister joins me in kindest remembrances to Mrs Scott & kind wishes to all your young folks. It will delight us to hear Sophia sing a Scotch air tho' she should but croon; and I am well inclined to believe she sings very sweetly. — Being such a person as Mrs Joanna Baillie, you very properly

---

210. Note "C" to Canto First states that the castles "of Dunolly and Dunstaffnage are first passed, then that of Duart, formerly belonging to the Chief of the warlike and powerful sept of Macleans, and the scene of Miss Baillie's beautiful tragedy, entitled the *Family Legend*" (*Poetical Works*, 3:362). Note "L" to Canto Fifth on the battle of Falkirk cites 14 lines of Holford's *Wallace, or the Fight of Falkirk*, and Scott explains that "The English historians have commemorated the tall and stately persons, as well as the unswerving faith of these foresters. Nor has their interesting fall escaped the notice of an elegant modern poetess, whose subject led her to treat of that calamitous engagement" (3:412).

211. Lambertson identifies this as *Charlemagne, ou l'Eglise Delivrée* (1814) by Lucien Bonaparte (1775-1840).

212. James Hogg (1770-1835), the Ettrick Shepherd and poet, sent a copy of his poem "The Queen's Wake" to Byron, who recommended it to publisher John Murray. Murray undertook the publication with some other poems and corresponded with Hogg from 1813 on (*DNB*, IX:993).

subscribe yourself in your letter to me yours respectfully: I hope there will be nothing improper in my saying in return

yours affectionately

    J Baillie

3886 ff.39 (No address or postmark--this is a fragment)

Hampstead Jan^{ry} 22$^{\underline{d}}$ 1815

My dear Sir,

Very soon after I had sent my letter for you to the post, I received your very valuable gift, the Lord of the Isles. Nothing could be more grateful to me, and besides the proud distinction of being one of those to whom you send such a token, I may now repeat as often as I will the great delight I have already had in reading its grand & beautiful discriptions of nature & interesting traces of character. It now lies upon my table with two of its elder Brethren marks of your goodness to me, and shall soon be put into the same livery after the first fatigue of use shall have prepared it for the book-binder. Many, <u>many</u> thanks! I feel your kindness very sensibly. ––– I frequently now think of your coming to Town, and think that I see you in our little parlour drinking perhaps a little of your own whiskey after dinner, which is still <u>to the fore</u>, and cannot be produced, being kept for great occasions, upon a greater. Nothing, I hope, will come in the way to prevent these pleasant prospects, and much pleasure & enjoyment of every kind may you & Mrs Scott & your young Damsel have in this country where you will be run after & stared at just a little less than the Emperor Alexander or old Bucephalas.[213] And pray, have you any intention of being made a Baronet? this you may certainly have if you think it worth the taking, only you must consider that if you do not leave the young Laird of Abbotsford fortune enough to support his title, you must bring him up by times with the prudent idea of marrying an heiress. I'll be bound for it, if he grow up the tall comely creature he promised to be, he will find heiress[es] enough glad to have. . . .[214]

3886 ff.162-165 (Address: For Walter Scott Esq$^{\underline{r}}$ / N: Castle Street / Edin$^{\underline{r}}$ -no postmark, NLS dates 1815)

London June 22$^{\underline{d}}$ [1815]

My dear Sir,

You will receive this by a Gentleman who is very ambitious of being introduced to you, Sir John Nichol[l], Kings Advocate whose name,

---

213. Bucephalas was the magnificent stallion of Alexander the Great.
214. The remaining words are missing.

perhaps, is not entirely unknown to you.[215] He wishes to see all the Scotch courts of law with the advocate's library, and would be particularly gratified in being introduced to them by you. I have not the honour of knowing him myself, but he & his Family (most worthy people) are intimate acquaintances of Mrs Baillie & the family in this house; and Mrs B. would have made a bold push to write to you herself on this occasion, had not I like a good convenient Sister, stepped in to relieve her from doing what she naturally shrinks from. Sir John & his family who mean to visit a great part of Scotland will only be in Edin^{r} for a few days. I make no apology for giving you this trouble, for I know you will consider it as none.

——

So now you are in our own land again, and many <u>and many</u> a mile o'gate lies between us: thus every thing passes away in this world, and your visit to London which I had so long looked forward to with so much desire now lies behind me to be recollect[ed] with pleasure & some regret. But how could I expect to see you oftener than I did as you were situated? it was foolish to do so, and I feel that you were good & kind in letting us see you so often. I begrudged very much my not getting to Town to see you & Mrs Scott & my young friend Sophia before you left it as I fully intended to do, but an old friend of ours from Glasgow, who came to us at that time was taken ill, and it would have been both unkind & ungrateful in me to leave her. I hope you had a pleasant voyage and find yourselves all well after it. What a happy meeting it would be for your young people who had been left at home! and how many stories their Sister will have to tell them! happy may you all be & long be together! I say this with a deeper feeling at present, while every body round me is anxiously waiting for news of their friends in Belgium after this great but I fear bloody victory. Mrs Baillie whose Nephew is in the guards is by me just now, pacing up & down in a most anxious & restless state, and our good friends & neighbour Mrs Milligan has her eldest Son there also. In short we are all less or more in misery till the return of killed & wounded are received. Oh! may all this blood purchase what we are striving for! and our brave 42^{d} our noble hilanders [sic] how they have suffered! I grieve for them: They generously devote themselves in every field.[216] ———

---

215. Sir John Nicholl (1759-1838) succeeded Sir William Scott in 1798 as king's advocate, spoke strongly against Roman catholic emancipation in 1812 and afterwards, and became judge of the high court of admiralty in 1833 (*DNB*, XIV:435).

216. On 15 June 1815 Napoleon crossed the Sambre River and marched into Belgium. Wellington reached the battlefield at Quatre Bras on 16 June, where he found the Prince of Orange and 8,000 men holding the French force at bay. He began reinforcing Orange as fast as possible and by the day's end had increased the Allied Force to 36,000 men. On 18 June the Scots Greys and Household Cavalry cut through

Since you left town I have seen your friend & admirer Lord Byron oftener than once: he has very kindly sent me a very handsome copy of all his works, and invites me in the most gratifying way to give some of my plays to Drury Lane as he & his colleagues wish to begin their management by producing something of mine.[217] For this I feel myself mostly indebted to Lady Byron & partly to yourself. You have always been in the way like my good Genius to do me a good turn when it could be done: and I can only say in return that it delights my heart to be obliged to you. I have told Lord B. that I do not intend to offer any new plays to a London Theatre but shall be very proud to have any of those already published produced upon their boards, and shall be at all times ready to alter & arrange any of them for the stage in any way they may desire. Whether this will really come to any good I know not, but it is at least something not disagreeable to think of in the mean time. L$^{\underline{d}}$ B. has his eye upon De Monfort which he thinks will suit Kean. He thinks to please the generality of the audience I must give some stronger reason for De Monforts hatred and I think to please all ~~parts~~ classes of the audience I must alter the ending of the piece which does not produce good stage effect in its present state. Mrs Wilmot tells me that our friend Sotheby has left Town in great glee to prepare his Ivan (a character that Kean has taken a fancy for) for the Drury boards, and should not be surprised to see Kean make a great deal of it;[218] —— I can say no more about plays for the return of the killed & wounded has just been brought in and tho' our two young men we have good reason to believe are safe, I can think of little else and such things —— plays I mean —— are but shadows. The 42$^{\underline{d}}$ I hope is not so dreadfully cut off as was at first reported, the 44$^{\underline{th}}$ seems to be the greatest sufferer. I hope no one in whom you are much interested is amongst the killed: and let us be thankful that our brave British blood, since it must be shed has purchased so great a victory, which I would fain hope will now utterly destroy all the resources of our fell enemy. ———— I received a letter two days ago from Miss Edgeworth who tells me she has

---

the French line and were joined by the infantry of the 92nd Highland regiment, who faced the bayonets while their pipe major played "Hey, Johnny Cope, Are Ye Waulkin' Yet"; while Scots Greys took a toll on French gun crews, they were annihilated by French lancers. Also part of the Allied Force were the 42nd (Royal Highland/Black Watch) and the 44 (East Essex) regiments. On 18 June 1815, outnumbered 2 to 1, Napoleon was defeated for the last time at the Battle of Waterloo (Connelly, 207-17).

217. Byron tried unsuccessfully for some time to get Baillie's work on stage at Drury Lane. See Donkin's *Getting into the Act*.

218. Byron for a while attempted to convince the management to produce Sotheby's *Ivan* in 1816, which was withdrawn after only a few rehearsals; Byron later attacked Sotheby in *Beppo*. See introduction and letters to Sotheby.

had two delightful letters from Walter Scott, and truly she does seem delighted therewith. She desires me to write her all about your visit to London and makes particular enquiries about Miss Scott. Sophia may be assured I shall tell no bad tales of her, and as you did not indulge me with any details of the great homage paid to you here by Prince Peer & Commoner, I am at liberty to make use of common report which I shall do to the full. She seems to me to be a very friendly warm-hearted affectionate character. — But I must have done for I have been many times interrupted in writing this letter, and am likely to [be] so again every moment. Mrs Baillie & all the members of this Family beg to offer you & Mrs Scott their best regard & kind wishes and we all make bold to send our love to your Daughter. Our young Oxonian my Nephew[219] has been making many enquiries after her. Farewell; and let Sophia write me a few lines soon to say how it goes with you all, for I dont desire your time to be spent in writing to me.

God bless you!

J Baillie

Sir Nichol is a great friend of our neighbour Mr Carr of Hampstead.

PS. Mrs Baillie's Nephew is wounded but we hope not very severely: he has a ball in his foot.

3886 ff.188-90 (Address: To W. Scott Esqr / Abbotsford--postmarked 1815)

Hampstead Octr 2^{d} 1815

My dear Friend,

Many many thanks to you for your interesting letter! When I received it and considered how many things of the first importance & greatest difficulty you have to write & how little time to spare, I could scarcely keep from lifting up my hands with amazement. I would fain think that your love & good will for me must be great when you could think of writing me so long a letter so situated; but the rapidity & facility with which you do every thing, however difficult, curbs my pride and I must even be contented to say to myself, "my Friend is very good to me & to every body, yet some what better to me than to many bodies and I must allow somewhat better than I deserve." I found it on my table on our return from Surrey where we had been for some days, and wrote to you a little grateful billet which I hoped you would receive when you call'd in Grosvenor St: but tho' the house keeper ran to your hotel with it as soon as she received it, you were gone. And I know what took you along in such a hurry (for a Traveller to stay but one day in London is a thing that does not happen

---

219. Dr. Matthew Baillie's son William was educated at Westminster School and Oxford and then called to the Bar, though he apparently never practiced law.

over in a hundred years) and who you travelled to Scotland with also. You had need to behave yourself well, for we take account of your motions here, what company you keep and every thing you do. —

Nothing in your letter — not even the voracious appetite of your Pru pines astonished me so much as the small number of French amongst the spectators of that grand review. That any circumstances, however humiliating or distressing, should keep them from a grand spectacle was quite a new idea in my mind. I am glad they have such natural feelings, but let them take their mortifications with all my heart; I hope it will do them good. A year or two of civil war (if the allies would have sense enough to let them fight it out themselves) ending in a reasonable limited monarchy would be well for them & all their neighbours. For they will prize a constitution they have fairly struggled for; and will not be tempted for many years to disturb other nations. This seems a hard-hearted wish of mine in the first instance, but it is founded on humanity. I am pleased with the spirit of moderation in your letter & the degree of sympathy you express for the French notwithstanding all their demerits; and now that you like them a little more and I a little less than we used to do, I think we should agree on certain points better than we might have done a twelve month ago.[220] — The whole world is looking intently forward to the Grand Poem of the battle of Waterloo.[221] And that such a battle should befall in these days, almost under the eye of such a Bard, is one of the many wonders of these days. I am exceedingly glad that you have visited the memorable spot. You will thus preserve many anecdotes of the individual feats of that day which might otherwise be lost; and many brave men (in your notes I mean) be remembered, who have earned such distinction dearly tho' neither graced with high rank or command. I wish a memorial to be preserved of every very valiant deed even of the common soldiers. Every body must have been willing & proud to bring in their anecdotes to you as the Israelites did their gold to Moses for the building of the ark, and what is over & above for the decoration of the sacred Edifice may be laid up in the treasury. — Go on and prosper to the utmost of your hearts desire!

My Sister learnt from Lady Byron last week that you had been there. But as your time with Lord B. was so short, I can scarcely think you would occupy it with speaking of De Monfort. If you did, you will find that

---

220. Scott had little sympathy for Napoleon I; setting out for Paris with news of Waterloo in the air, Scott met the Duke of Wellington, certainly the epitome of a Scott hero, finding him "the most downright man he had ever met, utterly devoid of humbug" (Johnson, 499).

221. *Paul's Letters to his Kinsfolk* would follow in 1816.

difficulties have arisen to bringing it forward. I shall therefore be scarcely at all disappointed if it should not be represented. Lord B. is my staunch friend, but I do not wish him to get into any contention with his colleagues on my account. What these same difficulties are I know but imperfectly, but I fear Kean does not like the character and in this case i t would be madness to press it. I'm sure you will be pleased to hear that h e has taken a fancy to the character of Sotheby's Ivan which is I find to be produced in February. Poor Sotheby wants some object to interest & occupy him at present after the severe affliction he has had in the death of his eldest son,[222] and I believe nothing else could do it so effectually as this. I shall get him to carry me to one of his rehearsals, and this is all I expect to have to do with the Theatre this winter. ––

I have been busy of late putting my house – that is to say my chest of papers in order, not expecting to die the sooner for having done so, but being better prepared (in this respect at least) for that event if it should please God to bring it suddenly upon me. I have altered Rayner so as to make it an acting play if _any_ manager of _any_ Theatre should hereafter wish to produce it; and I have done or think I have done the same good turn for the 2^d part of Ethwald. O how I wish you were my next door neighbour that I might run in to you with my papers in my hand! ––– Our good Neighbour & your friend Richardson was here yesterday and I let him read your letter. I suppose I have not done wrong. If I have, you are in bad plight, for the penny post brought it to me with no seal on it and how many people may have read it before me I wot not. But tho I have only shewn it to Richardson, I have turned it to good account elsewhere in quotations, and I hope all the good people who have fallen in my way these last 10 days have had some toleration for a little vain-glory & self-importance.

Farewell! I send all my kind wishes in another letter that shall go under this cover.

Ever truly yours   J Baillie

3886 ff.208-209 (Address: To W: Scott Esqr / Melrose--postmarked 1815)
Sunning hill Novr 3^d 1815

My dear Friend,

The night before yesterday your most kind & welcome present of the Field of Waterloo came to my hands.[223] If I had been at home it would have reached me sooner. The whole family forthwith put down by our winter fire to hear it and my Brother to the best of his abilities (which

---

222. William Sotheby's son William was killed in the foot-guards in 1815; see introduction to Sotheby letters.
223. See previous letter.

are not great in such matters) read it aloud to us, and I read it yesterday to myself. It is written with much feeling and the reflexions are manly just & natural. I have however, perhaps foolishly, felt some degree of disappointment in the discriptive part in which you seem to me to have reigned in your strength – strength belonging to yourself alone and that of a Giant. But I know my fancy is always going after <u>great sights,</u> and since you have edified & touched our hearts in this poem as you have truly done, why should I not be content? My two favorite stanzas (and they are excellent) are the 14<u>th</u> & the 20<u>th</u> the simile of the mountain stream when deprived of all its winter torrents as applied to Bounaparte [*sic*] struck us all as just & original & finely poetic, and I liked it still better on the second reading. The reflexions on so many human ties sever'd by the battle is beautiful & tender and go directly to every heart. Many thanks then for the great pleasure I have received and for this gratifying mark of your regard. I marvel you could write at all when you were abroad. I thought you would have done so from your recollections in the quiet of your own house. What has become of all the anecdotes of the battle? I hope you have a great treasure of them which will be a treasure to the world after (after)wards. You are very bountiful in this publication; I am sure it will bring in a very princely sum to the subscription. ——

Pray offer my best regards to Mrs Scott and my love to my own little friend. I had a letter from Miss Edgeworth a few days ago making particular enquiries after her; she has become a Lady of renoun [*sic*].

Lord Byron is my staunch friend here, but I fear he will get into trouble by it, for the rulers of old Drury in regard to certain plays are very restive. — All this family desire to be most kindly remembered to yourself & Mrs Scott. Fare well! for being oppressed with a heavy cold I <u>dow</u> write <u>na mare</u>.

kindly & truly yours
    J Baillie

3886 ff.266-268 (No address or postmark)

Hampstead Decr 1815

How proud you make me, my dear Friend, in calling your little fairy dell with all its ever greens after me![224] I should have been gratified & honoured by having my name given to the turf or carousel summer seat in your garden. Many thanks to you & all to plant & decorate Joanna's bower, and if fate has it in reserve for me that I shall sit with you and bless you all there, I shall think myself one of the favoured & happy beings of this world. May Sophia for her share in it, continue to please and to gain the

---

224. The Scotts named one of the gardens at Abbotsford "Joanna's Bower."

good will of every body as she did here last spring! and many black Guells may her brother shoot on the up-lands (I suppose it must be on the upland) of Abbotsford! As for yourself, may your new purchase –– your large lump of Land turn out both a pleasant & profitable domain, and this is no light wish in these days of low rents & grumbling Landlords. Indeed I am very happy that your estate is doubled and your first purchase encreased so much in value. You shall be rich beyond all reason in Warld's gear before "I cry hold enough!" ––[225]

I am much gratified by your Friendly interest about my Dramas. When I wrote to you last I had some hopes that Lord Byron's powerful interest would have produced some of them on the Drury stage but now my hopes, as we say in the West country, are dung a' wither shins.[226] Lord B. has done for them, I thoroughly believe all in his power but from the beginning he met with strong opposition. Learning that this was the case some time ago, I wrote to Lady Byron to beg that his Lordship would not push the matter, nor let my Plays be the subject of any contention between him & his colleagues, as I had foreseen difficulties and the disappointment would scarcely be one to me. In answer to this she wrote that Lord B. would not give up the point, that it was on public grounds he wished to bring these Plays forward and not favour to me; and that as soon as Mr Lamb returned from the circuit it would be decided whether they should produce De Monfort, the Dream or the Beacon.[227] Of course I remained quiet; and a short while ago called on Lady B. when she told me that Lord B. had at last been obliged to give up the point altogether. Thus my expectation of ever having any of my plays in my life time brought out on a London Theatre, is for the present extinguished. Your kind & friendly advice to offer them a MS. Play by Lord B's means, concealing my name, for many reasons, too tedious to mention here, I cannot follow. Did I not tell you in a former letter that I have altered De Monfort and made the (the) ending more dramatic by killing De Mon^t on the stage? and I really think it is a great improvement, and Mr Lamb & Lord Byron I am told think so too. Should they ever think of acting this play again in Edin^r pray send to me

---

225. See *Macbeth*: *Macb.* "And damn'd be him that first cries, 'Hold, enough!'" (5.8.34).

226. withershins: gone in a direction opposite the usual (*OED*).

227. George Lamb (1784-1834), politician, amateur actor and writer, was an early contributor to the *Edinburgh Review* and, as a result, was satirized by Byron in "English Bards and Scotch Reviewers." Byron later admitted he had been unjust, and he, Lamb and Douglas Kinnaird became members of the Drury Lane management committee in 1815. Lamb's adaptation of *Timon of Athens* was produced and published in 1816; 1819 he was elected as a Whig member of Parliament. In 1830 he became under-secretary of state to his brother Lord Melbourne (*DNB*, XI:430-31).

for this new alteration and dont let it be acted the old way. Having had the hope of my plays being acted here, I have likewise altered Rayner & turned the 2^d part of Ethwald into an acting play which it certainly was not before. It is well then that I have had this little hope to bestir me tho' it has proved deceitful, for the above mentioned plays if they should ever be brought on the stage when I am no more, will be found greatly improved for the purposes of representation by what I have done.

Our Friend Sotheby's Ivan is to be produced in Drury Lane very soon. Mr Kean has taken a fancy to that character and I hope it will have good success. It will do my heart good to see how happy it will make him; and when it does, I shall pay him back but one half of the friendly interest he would take in my success on a similar occasion. — Fare well! My Sister unites with me in kind regards to Mrs Scott & the young folk, may you all hold a merry Christmas together! Most truly yours   J Baillie

The following single Baillie letter to Sir Walter Scott is included by permission of Edinburgh University's Special Collections. Other Baillie letters owned by Edinburgh University appear in "Miscellaneous Letters," Volume 2.

La.III.584/28 (No address or postmark)

Hampstead Feb^ry 3^d 1816

"The kind advice Jock ga'd his Dad
    you'll ken whan ye these lines ha' read"[228]
Saith an old Scotch poem, and proceeds to tell how the Dad complained to Jock that his back & his sides & his head ached and he could neither sit nor stand nor lie; upon which Jock kindly advises him to hang a while. A bad cold has put me nearly in the state of Jock's Dad, but instead of hanging a while I will write a while to my good Friend which will be the best way of making me forget my ailments. — I received from Edin^r per favour of Mr Freeling about 10 days ago Paul's letters to his kinsfolk and know right well the kind hand that sent it — even that which has sent me so many valuable & delightful things and whose liberality & kindness to me I delight to think of and acknowledge. Verily I think this same Paul does consider me as one of his kinsfolk and I would not possibly belong to a more honourable stock. But no more of this! — I have then had the honour & glory of reading this new book before any of my friends here could get

228. After exhausting sources in Edinburgh, I have not been able to identify this poem.

their bespoke copies from the Booksellers, and besides this have had the pleasure of being greatly interested & instructed. The order of the battle & our manner of receiving the enemy in hollow squares, I never before understood from any other account of Waterloo; and it has left noble images in my mind to help out both my understanding & my memory. I wonder much that such a striking & terrific circumstance as the Cuirasiers [sic] being thrown headlong in to the gravel-pit men & horse &c. should have been mentioned in no other account of the battle but your own.[229] I have been much pleased with your account of the great energy & skill of Bonaparte [sic] before & during the battle till the last push. It is speaking w/ an enemy as one ought. He who could organize & put such power into action and attach the hearts of so many brave men to himself was great tho' he was unworthy of them. It was satanic greatness, tho' deprived of personal dignity, and gives the mind a strange mingled unhappy disjointed feeling in contemplating it. His character is like nothing that ever was presented to it before. Your political views & conjectures regarding the present & future state of France appeared to me very just & plausible, but this is small praise from me who have no head for such matters tho' I cannot help sometimes entering into them as warmly as if I had. --- I have at last got the monthly magazine which contains the verses to Miss Scott on her return to Scotland, and my sister has copied them. You will find them inclosed for Sophia's perusal. On reading them again I think I have spoken too slightingly of them; they are better than I supposed. --- Some good Friend sent me a news paper from Edin^r the other day containing an account [of] the celebration of Burn's [sic] birthday[230] with a list of toasts drunk in the occasion, in which I find my name mentioned most honourably. I thank you very cordially for putting this feather in my cap, for I know to whom I owe it. I am sure if I am not very popular it is no fault of yours; you have done all you could (and who could have done so much?) to make me so. I am glad that Mr Maule in the warmth of his enthusiasm has committed himself regarding the exertions he will make

---

229. Baillie refers to the following passage from Scott's Letter VIII, "Battle of Waterloo":

> John Ellery . . . obtained permission to bring up the heavy brigade . . . the effect of which was tremendous. Not withstanding the weight and armour of the cuirassiers, and the power of their horses, they proved altogether unable to withstand the shock of the heavy brigade. . . . Several hundreds of French were forced headlong over a sort of quarry of gravel pit, where they rolled a confused and undistinguishable mass of men and horses, exposed to a fire which . . . soon put a period to their struggles.

See *The Miscellaneous Prose Works of Sir Walter Scott, Bart.*, 3 vols. (Edinburgh: Cadell, 1847), 1:467.

230. Robert Burns was born on 25 January 1759.

for Burn's family. He is a man (is he not?) of great wealth & interest, so the cause is in good hands.[231] ——— I have no news that you would care about to send you from thence, and I am now tired of writing. - Give my kind regards to Mrs Scott & my love to my own young Friend. I hope this will find all well round your fireside, and a happy fireside may it be for many years to come!

  Yours affectionately
   J Baillie

866 ff.68-72 (Address: Walter Scott Esqr / Castle Street / Edinburgh-- postmarked 1816)

London Feb^r 26th 1816

My dear Friend,

  I have some things to say to you which you may be interested to hear and am at present in the land of franks, so I send you this volonteer [*sic*] letter, that will not require of you one line in return, nor a letter written to me one day sooner than you would have done it at any rate. You are therefore all the gainer, if I am not mistaken in the interest & curiosity I suppose you may feel in regard to some of the things I am going to mention. —— You must have heard a good while ago reports of Lord & Lady Byron's separation, and it was generally said that this was occasioned by his improper connection with a beautiful Actress of Drury Lane.[232] It is not however believed, by those who have the best opportunity of knowing, that gallantries as they are called of any kind had any thing to do with it. Your kind & manly heart will be grieved when I tell you, from authority that cannot be doubted, that he has used her brutally, and that no excuse can be pleaded in his behalf but <u>insanity</u>. For the credit of human nature, proofs of this are so strong that in any court of justice they would procure a separation, and I believe a legal separation will soon be

---

231. This philanthropist may be Sir William Henry Maule (1788-1858), Trinity College fellow and judge.

 232. Lady Byron returned home to her parents in January 1816 after only a year with Lord Byron. For details, see introduction and letters to Lady Byron (Volume 2). Marchand writes that Lady Byron had not been happy with Byron's "absorption in Drury Lane affairs . . . and his familiarity with actors and actresses in the greenroom" (Leslie A. Marchand, *Byron, A Biography*, 3 vols. [New York: Knopf, 1957], 2:539). Apparently, a climax occurred on 3 January "when Byron came to [Lady Byron's] room and talked with 'considerable violence' on the subject of his affairs with women of the theater" (Marchand, 2:557).

settled.[233] When I say <u>brutally</u> I use the word that was made use of to me, not knowing any particulars as to the manner of it, tho' I fear it has been very bad. Symptoms of this mental disorder began to shew itself the first week after their marriage. His nearest relations declare that Lady Byron behaved throughout in this most trying situation like an Angel; and from what I know myself of the sweetness & kindness of her nature, & the good sense calmness & self-possession of her character, I can easily believe that every thing was done on her part to conciliate –– not irritate him. I had good cause to know that her motives for marrying him were of a very generous nature bordering on romantic, and there is scarcely a man in England who would not have thought himself blessed & honoured in being the husband of such a woman. Her happiness now, at the age of 24 is wrecked for life. There are some who will not allow the excuse of insanity, for he still continues to do business at the Theatre; but I thoroughly believe there can be no doubt of it. He was very impatient, counting days & hours till she was confined; and when the child was born seemed delighted with it as a child is with a new toy, but very soon it ceased to be an object of any interest.[234] Our friend Sotheby sat with him the other day half an hour and observed nothing like insanity, except a degree of restlessness. ––

An extraordinary thing has happened to me; I sat down to write this letter with no other idea but to give you the information I had on this sad affair which I thought you would wish to know, when I was called away to see one most deeply interested in the whole and who has informed me of a very unhappy circumstance which I think it is possible you may have some influence in aleviating [sic]. According to the marriage settlements, the whole of Lady Byron's large fortune will go to him after her Mother's death, except three hundred a year which is her pin money, she wishes without bringing any thing into public court, to have a regular separation settled between them; and to have wherewith her own fortune to live upon respectably, for she is moderate in all her desires. Lord B. wishes most ungenerously to keep every thing to himself. Now there is no body whose good opinion he is more anxious to preserve than your own, and he at the same time prizes himself upon his generosity in money matters. Could you not write to him, introducing the subject in any way you please, and stir up his pride by telling him that the only way he can justify his character from the suspected meaness [sic] of having married from sordid motives

---

233. Byron later stated that "Wherever the wrong lies, it does not lie in her: she is perfect in thought, word, & deed" (qtd. in Johnson, 515). Byron agreed to the terms of the separation on 17 March 1816 and left England forever; Dr. Matthew Baillie had been consulted on Byron's sanity earlier (see Marchand).

234. Augusta Ada was born in December 1815.

will be by settling of his own free accord a liberal income on his wife: that if they should ever come together again at any future time, they would both have the credit of doing so from inclination; that without this Lady B. could never consent to return to him when it might be supposed that necessity was her reason for so doing, and that even if her spirit could submit to do this, it would be a very humiliating thing for his Lordship to have it supposed that his wife returned to him again only from such motives. That it would be very painful to those who admire his genius and have interested themselves in his fate to see him so poorly degraded, with what else your shrewd head & good heart may please to say. Pray my good Friend if you have any regard for your old Friend Joanna Baillie do not cast this service from you and say "how can I meddle in such matters?"[235] You can & may with powerful effect, and punctilios are not to be regarded when so much good may be done. As sworn Brother-Poet, his good name must be dear to you and if you knew her as I do, you would go thro' fire & flood for her sake. I am persuaded Lord B. will shrink more from being thought meanly of by you than any other motive. Manage this matter as you please, but let it be done and done soon. He has a perfect Friend of an attorney at his ear to advise him to all manner of iniquity.[236] ——— I will now have done with this subject which truly distresses me & weighs upon my heart. —— Paul's letters take mightily in this part of the world.[237] Their good sense, their right feelings, their impartiality, their animated clear descriptions, their agreeable stile please almost every body I have met. My Brother is delighted with the book. There is only one fault found with it viz. that it would have been better to have given them not as the letters of a fictitious person, altho' the introductory letter is a very good one of its kind. —— We had a visit from Mr Terry and his wife some days ago, and he brought with him an Opera written by himself on the story of Guy Mannering.[238] The first & a part of the 2^d Act are very

---

235. As Baillie feared, Scott did reply that he could not possibly meddle in such matters, declining to intervene; while Byron and Scott were not intimate, they had carried on a friendly correspondence for some time (Johnson, 391, 515).

236. Byron's lawyers for the separation were John Hanson and James Farquhar (Marchand, 577), but Baillie may actually be referring to his friend and confidant John Cam Hobhouse.

237. See Scott letter La.III.584/28 from the Edinburgh University collection herein.

238. Baillie probably refers to Terry's second wife Elizabeth Nasmyth, who was known for her taste in design and reportedly shared in decorating Abbotsford. After Terry's death she married lexicographer Charles Richardson (*DNB*, XIX:563-66). *Guy Mannering* was the first of Scott's novels to be popularized on the stage, and Terry's musical *Guy Mannering; or, The Gipsy's Prophecy*, which debuted at Covent Garden on 12 March 1816, was one of the great hits of the nineteenth century (Bolton, 56).

good indeed, and I hope the rest may be born out with bustle and stage effect. — And now that I am speaking of plays, I have to tell you that Sotheby has withdrawn his Tragedy of Ivan from Drury-Lane, having I think been unfairly & hardly treated. He had altered it on purpose for Kean, who either had or pretended to have a great desire to act that character: He had been called upon about 6 weeks ago to read it in the green room which he did, the result being so favourable that they gave him notice they should have it in rehearsal in a fortnight; there was public notice given that a new Tragedy was in preparation, and Sotheby of course thought himself sure, enjoyed his prospect and was no wise reserved in talking of it to his friends. But presently they (they) found out that the public liked old Plays revived better than new ones, that the treasury of the Theatre was too poor to run the risk of losing any thing, and therefore let him know, upon his going to the Theatre to enquire after it, that they had set it aside for an indefinat [sic] time & should bring out Massinger's Duke of Milan in its stead.[239] How much better they have behaved to me in setting their faces against me from the first! I feel myself comparatively obliged to them. Sotheby behaves with great good-sense & temper upon the occasion. He is going abroad with his family by & by, and will spend I believe a considerable time in Italy. Sir Humphry [sic] & Lady Davy too, who are just settled in a very handsome house in Grosvenor St: talk confidently of spending the next winter in Rome, and many others are going abroad. Will poor England not be thought good enough by & by for cultivated people to live in? The sheriff of Ettrick forest or some such simple souls may still prove constant to their <u>ain Countrie</u> but who will mind them? — My brother & his family & ourselves have got thro' this winter better than most people. Do you know that the medical people say, more people have died in London this winter than have died in the same space of time since the time of the plague. They have not died of any prevailing disease but of all kinds, not having the usual strength to rally from any illness. — How did my friend Sophia like the fair long poem of Vich Jon Hay? Has she been searching amongst all the odd Bodies or all the handsome men of the country for the author, or very wisely troubling her head little about the matter? Give my love to her, & remember me kindly to M<u>rs</u> Scott. Yours most truly

    J Baillie

PS. Lady Noel, Lady Byron's Mother is not expected to live many months & her Father Sir Ralph is very infirm and not likely to live long. When they are gone she will have no near relation to protect her. — I perceive in looking over this letter I seem to be dictating to you what you should

---

239. Philip Massinger (1583-1640) wrote *The Duke of Milan* in 1620.

urge with Lord B. Do not believe me such a fool as to mean so. I have told you the point so necessary to be obtained and that he will shrink more from your bad opinion than that of any body else; this is all I ought to have said. You will move his proud – I should rather say vain mind in a more effectual way than I could possibly suggest. I am sorry I must add on better information, that tho' irregularities of a certain kind are not the foundation of Lady B's conduct in leaving him, he has been miserably corrupted in this way. —

866 ff.81-82 (No address or postmark, 1816)
My dear Friend,
　　Situated as you are with Lord Byron, I confess I do not think you could have written to him on the subject I mentioned, but had you been with him on the footing I imagined I should not so easily have acquiesced with your reasons for thinking your writing would have been of no use. He thinks so ill of the world and, has so long associated with the base & the worthless, that he is scarcely aware of the execration & contempt he would expose himself to by his conduct to his wife; and it is only from a burst of honest indignation from some superior mind which he stands in awe of, that he could be made sensible of it.[240] I must own that after I had written to you under great excitement from a particular circumstance, I feared that I had asked of you an unreasonable thing and was therefore not disappointed by your answer. However, I am not sorry that I put you to the trouble of considering & writing upon the subject since your letter which I sent to Lady Byron has been a great satisfaction to her, as the mode of conducting the business pointed out by you is exactly that which she had pursued tho' without success. Sir Ralph Noel made the demand of Lord B. himself in the least irritating terms that could be devised. I had a letter from her a few days ago saying that she fears it must at last come into court, a measure very painful to her. I was told by a Lady from Town yesterday that a separation has been signed in which Ld B. consents to give up the child to her & a part of her fortune, but this I fear can only be an idle report, as so few days before Lady B. herself had no hopes of it. — [241] But

---

240. Ironically, Scott had declared to Morritt that it was Byron's misanthropy that gave "an odd poignancy to his descriptions and reflections" (qtd. in Johnson, 387). Byron later sent Scott an inscribed copy of *The Giaour* (461).

241. Lady Byron had feared that Byron would try to take Ada from her; her lawyer, Stephen Lushington, fearing he could not prove the charge of incest in court with Lady Byron's evidence legally excluded, sought a separation based on Byron's "brutally indecent conduct and language" (Marchand, 2:583). Byron had proposed to resign Lady Byron's present fortune (£1,000/year), but she wished only to receive £500 and leave the other half to Byron. Lady Byron proposed that Byron should

I will tease you no more upon this disagreeable subject. Many thanks to you for the consideration you have given it: but pray try to be a little more indignant at bad men who ill-treat their wives, for I do not entirely love you for the tone you take upon this occasion. If you can do us no good, you might at least be angry with us and that would be some sympathy. You would have been amused some time ago when, after talking of Lord B. my good Sister in law, tho' she delights in poetry, began to abuse all the men of genius of the present day for selfishness excentricity & affectation, yourself only excepted. I put in a good word for your friend Campbell, but she unfortunately had heard of his wife sitting up sometimes to prevent his sleep from being disturbed by the barking of their neighbour's dog, so she would give him no quarter any more than the rest. Speaking of Campbell, I must tell you that I was delighted to see him here 10 days ago looking fat & comely & contented; so I should think the barking of his neighbour's dog does not disturb him so much now as it did before the receipt of that happy legacy which he well deserved, and will I hope live long to enjoy.[242] There was another circumstance about him too that pleased me much which I learnt after he was gone — he had a mighty handsome, new fashionable great coat on, and he was seen walking up the street of Hampstead with the skirts of it turned over his arms to save it from the dirt & the rain. Could any thing be more prudent or orderly than this? It is a perfect example as far as it goes to all poets. ——

I have not yet been to see Terry's play but hope to go soon. In the mean time I am pleased to hear a good account of its reseption [sic]. — I hope Mrs Scott, Sophia & all the family are well and beg to be kindly remembered to them. When I sat down to write to you last I little thought to write a letter that should give you the trouble of an answer. Tho' I am always delighted to hear from you, never suppose that I expect a letter in return for such a thing as this. Farewell!

    ever most truly yours
      J Baillie
Hampstead
March 17th 1816

---

legally stipulate that when her parents died the Kirkby property would be divided "on fair terms of arbitration" (Marchand, 2:588).

    242. In 1815 Thomas Campbell's Highland cousin, MacArthur Stewart of Ascog, died, leaving him a legacy of almost £5,000 (Mary Ruth Miller, *Thomas Campbell* [Boston: Twayne, 1978], 29).

3887 ff.36-38 (Walter Scott Esqʳ--no postmark, NLS dates 1816)

[1816]

My dear Friend,

My Sister is going to send a little packet of roots for your Daughter's garden at Abbotsford, and I will not let it go without slipping into it a few lines to you, tho' I have little to say & still less time to say it in. — I thank you for your last friend[ly] letter, and have been somewhat amused at your taking up so seriously the defence of the whole Brotherhood & Sisterhood of poets against the charge of excentricity & selfish (selfish)ness. —— Mʳˢ B.s' remark was made in an untoward hour and we will not maintain it in all points. — That most extraordinary Poet who gave occasion for it is now gone abroad and will I hope return no more. The separation was signed before he went, after drawing back & refusing to sign it in various pretences, fear, that powerful agent! was supposed to prevail upon him at last. Lady B. poor thing! will now I hope have some peace. She has the advantage of having now no contrary or devided affection to contend with for she can feel nothing for him now but unmixed aversion & disgust. —— I have just received an invitation to see our friend Sotheby's Play of Ellen or the Confession acted by Gentlemen & Ladies at Mʳ W. Spencer's at Petersham.[243] This was altered for the London Stage, and Sotheby has a good buoy and spirit which if it miss one object very readily takes up with another. It is truly amusing to me and very happy for him. H will go abroad with his family soon, I suppose, but I hear nothing of it at present. — Mʳˢ Baillie's Brother[244] is just returned from the sessions full of admiration of Paul's letters to his Kinsfolk which was his book of amusement there, but constantly taken out of his hands by his Brother Barresters [*sic*] who were all very eager to read it and as fond of it as himself. —— We have just got Miss Holford's new poem Margaret of Anjou, and have read 3 cantos;[245] we think there are many sweet & beautiful passages in it: what the general interest of the story may be, we

---

243. William Sotheby's *Ellen, or the Confession*, was published in 1816. Though Sotheby wrote several dramas and offered them to the London Theaters, it appears that only his *Julian and Agnes* was ever accepted at Drury Lane, with Mrs. Siddons and Kemble in the leading roles in 1800. See introduction and letters to Sotheby herein.

244. Lord Chief Justice Thomas Denman (1779-1854), Sophia Denman Baillie's only brother, came to London to study law in 1800 and began his own practice in 1803. He married Theodosia Vevers in 1804, moving to Russell Square, the most fashionable region for leading lawyers. He was an advocate of legal reform, abolition of slavery and was connected with several important trials. Thomas and Theodosia had 5 sons and 6 daughters (*DNB*, V:809).

245. Margaret Holford Hodson published *Margaret of Anjou* in 10 cantos in 1816.

cannot yet say. ––– Farewell! for truly I must have done. With all good wishes to you & yours,

I remain ever truly yours

J Baillie

Hampstead

April 4th

3887 ff.83-85 (Address: Walter Scott Esq[r] / Castle Street / Edinburgh-- postmarked 1816)

Hampstead July 2[d] 1816

My dear Friend,

I know you are truly interested in what concerns my happiness, and I am going to tell you of an event in our family which deeply concerns us all and has one way or another agitated our minds very much for these some months past. My Niece is going to be married; and tho' she has chosen a very worthy young man, whose family we have long known & highly respect, yet our anxiety for her happiness has been very great, perhaps unreasonably so, and I would not live the last April & May over again for a great hire.[246] She is a very clever woman, fond of books and with a mind & taste well cultivated; he is a plain honest Soldier, whose education has been quite neglected and who, dogs & horses & military matter excepted, has little information on any subject. This being the case, you may believe we had all of us many discouraging thoughts in regard to her future happiness, and her poor Mother above all has been very anxious; but the young man himself has behaved under some very trying circumstances and throughout the whole of the affair, with so much sense & delicacy & sweetness of temper & forbearance, that we now, thank God! begin to hope with some confidence that she will really be happy. You will wish them all good I know, when I tell you that he was one of our brave Dragoons at Waterloo, where he was what was called severely wounded. He is to remain in the army, and hopes soon to get into the guards which are never ordered abroad but on actual service. He has a good moderate fortune, and being admirably fitted both in mind & body for a Soldier, it is the best plan. His name is Milligan, and it was a Sister of his, who sat next you when you last dined with us at Hampstead. You may have forgotten her indeed, but she will never forget having sat by you. I believe this same wedding will take place next week. And a thing is to follow this marriage

---

246. Elizabeth Margaret Baillie (1794-1876), the only daughter of Matthew and Sophia Denman Baillie, married Capt. Robert Milligan (1781-1875) on 11 July 1816; the couple, with one daughter, Sophia (1817-82), lived at Ryde on the Isle of Wight for most of Joanna's life.

(at least is intended to do so) which I think you will rather be pleased with; a most unlooked for thing I am sure to me. I am going abroad with the new married pair and my Nephew William to spend some weeks & see part of Switzerland & Geneva. They all pretend that I will be of use to them, and do not shrink from having an old Aunt to over-look them; and, as they are all thoroughly good natured & I believe truly attached to me, I do not shrink from the undertaking. Our first step is to visit the field of Waterloo; and I shall think much of you, and of those, who on <u>that spot</u> must be thought of before you, when I am there. I have had a kind of passion all my life for the mountains of Switzerland; but it was love cherished without hope, for I never expected to see them. We shall set out on our journey I believe the beginning of next month, and must return at the end of six weeks on account of William's keeping his terms at Oxford. But I must tell you that our Soldier, tho' scantily provided with book learning, observes accurately & well the face of nature, and he shall make his debut in poetry with your works which I think he is fitted to enjoy truly. If he does not, however, I will <u>truly know,</u> for he is quite honest & affects nothing.

I had a letter from Miss Edgeworth about a fortnight ago, full of praises of the Antiquary which she rather prefers to Guy Mannering.[247] She thinks there is but one person in the world able to write such works and therefore they must be his. It is indeed rich in characters & in original pictures of human nature; but I know not how to give it a preference to the other, my admiration of Meg Merrilies & my love for Dandy Dinmount being great; besides that the story of Guy Mannering is more uniformly animated & entertaining. I had a letter likewise a very short time ago from poor Lady Byron. She says that when she returned to her Fathers she found her health more injured by her last residence in Town & the great anxiety she had suffered than she expected and had therefore gone to the seaside at Lostoff [Lowestoff] with her Child. Poor thing! she comforts herself with thinking that, had she not married L<u>d</u> B and he become ruined & abandoned afterwards as he would certainly have done, she would have upbraided herself for not endeavouring to save him and would probably have been more miserable than she is. It is a good thing that she views it in this light. — I suppose you have read Lady C. Lamb's book.[248]

---

247. Scott's 2nd novel, *Guy Mannering*, the account of an Englishman wandering into Scotland, had been published in 1815; *The Antiquary* followed in 1816.

248. Lady Caroline Lamb (1785-1828), the daughter of Viscount Duncannon, was married to the Hon. William Lamb in 1805. She had a brief affair with Lord Byron in 1812 which she made the most of publicly with her novel *Glenarvon* in 1816. She separated from her husband in 1825 (see Doris Langley Moore, *The Late Lord Byron* [Philadelphia and New York: J. B. Lippincott, 1961], 522).

It is not without some ability, yet I doubt whether I should have had patience to read it if my curiosity had not been excited by believing the characters to be taken from real life. Her outré fantastical loves & sentiments are like the ravings of a crazy person. She insinuates that Lord Byron took great pains to win her love; but I have always been informed that it was quite the reverse and that he always shunned her and repressed her advances. — I have seen Mrs Siddons act again in the character of Queen Catherine.[249] Her expression of face & dignity of action seemed to me as great as ever. Time has spared her wonderfully. I have not yet seen the New Tragedy Bertram which I regret; but as it is so well received, it will no doubt be acted next [year?] and if I live I shall have my opportunity still. I have read it and think it very finely written, but neither like the characters nor the story. It was said, when it first came out, that the author had sent the MS. to you and you had recommended it to Drury Lane but this I suppose is false.[250] — I hope you & yours are well. Give my kind regard to Mrs Scott and my love to my young friend Sophia. I would give something to look upon her happy face now & then; it would keep anxiety a little at bay. My Niece Elizabeth has desired me [to] say some kind thing to her on her part. Let her take the will for the deed. Elizth often remembers & speaks of her with pleasure. Fare well!

    affectionately yours

     J Baillie

PS. May I beg you will let your servant take the inclosed to your next door neighbour?

3887 ff.98-100 (No address or postmark, NLS dates 1816)

Hampstead July 24th [1816]

    I thank you for your kind & encouraging letter, my dear friend; and I will be encouraged. Indeed the more I see of our young man the more I am inclined to believe that Elizabeth will be happy and the good you predict realized. The marriage took place on the 11th of the month and Mrs Baillie's spirits kept up on the occasion much better than we could have hoped; but it was a great trial to her & my Brother, and in some degree to all of us. The young Pair are returned to Grosvenor St: again after having spent some time at Tunbridge, and we are to set out on our travels next tuesday. I dare say (for at my age one only says <u>dare say</u>) I shall

---

249. After her retirement from the stage, Mrs. Siddons continued to give private readings, one of which was Queen Catherine.

250. Through Scott's influence Charles Robert Maturin's tragedy *Bertram* was accepted for production at Drury Lane by Lord Byron, who was on the management committee (Johnson, 514).

have much enjoyment & amusement; but were this not the case; were all the time of my journeying to be a state in some degree of actual suffering, I would take the sight of those great objects of nature which have so long been shadowed in my fancy, even upon these terms. I would snatch at the time at least a "fearful joy" and retain a most noble recollection which may be called a mental patrimony, afterwards. So away to the mountain, whatever betide! I shall see your field of battle and yet, I know not how it is, I can think of nothing but Mont Blanc. Pray do not despise me for this. —— I take the opportunity of sending this letter by our good neighbour Mr Richardson, who will I hope find you safely returned from your highland tour, enjoying yourself at Abbotsford. Walter Scott is a great man, but the Laird of Abbotsford is a happy one. Pray look after my bower, and give the trees as much encouragement to grow as watering & a little good manure will afford. I had a pretty good account of my Gloucester plantations the other day from Mrs Baillie, who has just returned from thence and this makes me somewhat <u>crouse</u>[251] upon the subject. I hope your London Ladies liked the Highlands more than you expected; but I fear they had not much cause to do so, for our bad weather I hear has been general. —— And you think of going next year to Rome & Naples & perhaps as far as Athens! Go to Rome & Naples with all my heart; but do not risk your life on those dangerous <u>Islandy</u> seas to behold Athens, where there is so little remains of what was great and your association must supply nearly all that interests or delights you. Let Scholars who have been flogged into a certain portion of greek run after those old stones and then write a dull quarto about them afterwards, but I would not have <u>you</u> to follow such people's tract. I am quite sick of modern Greece and all its worshipers. ——

We saw your friend Terry & his pretty wife the other day. He repeated to us a Ms. song of yours to be put to highland music soon to be published.[252] The subject was a martial gathering of the clans and it was admirable. If this music be the old highland airs, many of which were published many years since by Macdonald, and if you write <u>many</u> such songs to it, we shall have quite a new character of melody introduced to the fashionable world. This would be a happy thing if it would rid us for a while of those stupid Italian airs which every young Lady sings now a days whether she has a voice or not. I think my young Friend at Abbotsford will sing some of them with very pleasing effect. Tell her that her congratulations shall be particularly given to the Bride, and I am sure they will be most welcome. ——

---

251. crouse: bold, confident (*OED*).

252. These songs are probably from Terry's recent stage adaptation of *Guy Mannering*, which included many Scottish folk songs (see Bolton, 57).

I have mentioned your kind congratulations to Mrs Baillie who sends you many thanks. Tell Sophia that had she been in this country she would have had a bit of bride's cake drawn thro the ring, which was only given to great favorites.[253] — I must make an end of this, for I have many letters to write & many visits to make before I go and little time for it all. —

Fare well then my dear & kind friend! Give my kindest regards to Mrs Scott.

 yours affectionately
  J Baillie

3887 ff.112-113 (Address: Walter Scott Esqr / Abbotsford / Melrose-- postmarked 1816)[254]

Fontenbleau [*sic*] Septr 13th 1816

My dear Friend

You were kind enough to express a wish that I should write to you while on my travels, and I should be very ungrateful if I were not ready to do what you wish at all times. I have been thinking of this for several days past, ever since I left Chamoune [Chamouni] and had got my sight of the great mountain, but we have been travelling since [by] post, and I have been glad when we reached our . . . to get to bed instead of writing. Now an opportunity casts up which I am glad of, since the mishap which gives it was that the axle of our carriage is broken and we must stay here till it is mended. We are in high luck that it has broken at such a place where there is so much that is interesting to see and not near some poor village on the road. Indeed we have no reason to complain of fortune in any respect since we left England, excepting that Mont blanc was ungracious to us while we were on his skirts & at his foot humbly & wistfully looking up for one sight of the lofty summit, but he has in some degree made us amends for this by unveiling his lordly head when we were at a distance and shewing himself in all his superior dignity amongst the loftiest peaks of the snowy Alps which from one point of view were stretched before our eyes for a

---

253. The connection between the bride-cake and the wedding is strongly marked in an English custom where the cake is cut into small square pieces, thrown over the bride's and groom's heads, and then put through the wedding ring. The cake is sometimes broken over the bride's head and then thrown among the crowd to be scrambled for; young people who put pieces of the cake under their pillow that night will, according to superstition, dream of their lover (W. Carew Hazlitt, *Faiths and Folklore: A Dictionary of National Beliefs, Superstitions and Popular Customs*, 2 vols. [London: Reeves and Turner, 1905], 1:73-74).

254. This entire long letter, sent from abroad, is very faded and almost unreadable; I have had to guess as best I could at some words, and there are several words simply torn away, thus the ellipses.

prodigious extent, and a most wonderful & noble vision it was. This was my last look of Switzerland which above all the rest will remain (I think unfadingly) on my mind. We beheld the view in question from a very high hill or mountain, about 10 miles distant from Geneva, winding our way up a part of the grand road which Bounaparte [*sic*] made to convey himself to his Italian dominions; a great & admirable work when difficulty is considered. Great part is terraces cut in the solid rock and we passed under an arch or tunnel cut thro' it. But to return to our view which I suppose cannot be equalled in Europe; besides the Alps we saw the lake of Geneva and its city smoking at its western extremity, the course of the rhone and a vast extent of rich country along the sides of the lake and bearing along to the westward to a great distance. If you ever see this view (as I trust you will) I hope you will see it on as bright a morning as we did: its image will then rest with one worthy to possess it and able to transmit it to others. –

We left London at the time we proposed and made our first halt at Brussels, visiting the field of battle. A Gentleman of the place who had been friendly to Capt. Milligan when he was confined there with his wound, and who had been on the field the day after the battle & many succeeding days recovering the wounded, accompanied us and told us many sad things. We were in the garden of Hugamount [*sic*][255] and in other places which had a peculiar interest for the party. We went to a cottage and looked at a little earthen-floored chamber where Milligan had lain several hours on the ground surrounded with wounded & dying men. It was now quiet & set in order after the country fashion with some broken caps ornamenting the chimney and a leaden crucifix while the cottager himself stood by the door, caressing a baby which from its appearance must have been born very soon after the battle. We were after this much delighted in travelling up the banks of the rhine which by no means disappointed our expectations, and the falls of Schaufhausen even exceeded them.[256] Not in height, however, for they are not above 50 or 60 feet, but in power. That noble river was full of water, more so than it has been for several years past, and the force with which this water was cast or rather seemed to be exploded from the rocks was truly astonishing. The longer we gazed at it the fiercer & more tremendous it seemed to become; and the spring rose from the gulph below as if it had been the blowing up of a magazine of gun powder (so at least our Soldier said). We have seen several pictures of it but they give no more idea of it (nor could they do it were they ever so

---

255. The Chateau of Hougoumont was an Allied stronghold during the Battle of Waterloo, held by Colonel James Macdonnell against French commander Reille on 18 June 1815 (Connell, 213-14).

256. This must be a reference to the Rhine Falls at Schaffhausen.

well done) than a marble Gladiator in the act of striking could give you of the energy, strength of the. . . . From Schaufhausen we went to Zurich, then to Eused [Uster?] but were not greatly struck with the beauty & grandeur of Switzerland till we came to Schwyz & the Lake of Lucerne. We went in a boat for 18 miles along the Lake which with the scenery on it was enchanting. The beautiful, desirable & sublime are there most happily combined; and if I were to fix my abode in Switzerland it would be on the shores of that Lake. We were much pleased with the Swiss themselves, that is to say the Peasantry; we had no opportunity of seeing the higher ranks. Their varied whimsical, picturesque costume is amazing & some times agreeable, and there is a frank, cheerful, honest familiarity with which they accost you that I liked – that became a free people in such a country. But one never finds things altogether as one wishes & expects: who would have thought of being mollested with beggars there as much, aye more, than in the ruinous Towns of Germany? It really mortified us exceedingly to see decent dressed people, young & healthy, holding out their hand for money as you passed, and troops of children following the carriage for a great way with a sing song petition that was most tiresome & distressing. Most of these children evidently did not beg from necessity but for money to play with. There was less of this begging in the protestant . . . but even there it was too. . . . Excepting the human kind we were surprised to see so few living creatures either wild or tame. A very few goats, scarcely any sheep, not many cattle & a very few starved pigs were all that we saw, yet there is much pasture land . . . you may suppose comparatively. . . . A wild bird about of any kind we scarcely ever saw. No vulture, no Eagles, no chamois, scarcely even a crow, and no small birds. —— At Lucerne we met Mr Sotheby & his family, and afterward again at Geneva. He is in high spirit and going very soon to Italy. I learnt from him & from Mr Pictet a Savant of that city,[257] that Lord Byron has shut himself up in a small house on the border of the Lake & sees no body. Mr Pictet said that he had been at his (M^r P) house at a large party soon after he arrived, but that the other English who were there received him very coldly so that he could not go into company as the Town is full of English. Sotheby says he hears he is busy writing and has nearly finished the 2^d part of Childe Harrold [sic]. I suppose in this 2^d part he will try to justify himself to the world. He is living in a respectable Swiss family, where he boards, and I believe Hobhouse is with him but I could not learn for

257. This is probably the Marc Auguste Pictet-Turretini referred to in Holford letters 7 and 8, Volume 2.

certain.[258] I tell you this more minutely because it was said in England that he was keeping house near Geneva in a very dissipated, disorderly manner. Our visit to Charmouni & the neighbourhood took us so much time that we had but two days & a half to spend there which I regretted; for we had letters of introduction that would have given us an entrie to the best company of the place which I should have liked, tho' my imperfect knowledge of the french language would have prevented me from profiting greatly by it. — On our way from Lausanne to Geneva we visited Ferney, the Chateau of Voltaire, more from curiosity than respect for its former Master, and were a good deal amused with some things we saw there and with its present Master, who is somewhat of a french petit maitre full of taste & sentiment & very polite. He met us in the garden and took us to see the spot which he had dedicated to the memory of the great poet. There, in a little scruby [sic] grove, was erected a monument of wood, painted to represent black marble, in the form of a small pyramid with tablets of white (white) paper framed & glazed, stuck on its sides, inscribed with verses in praise of the deceased; and at the top of all was fixed a gilded trumpet, such as one would buy at a fair for a child, representing the trumpet of fame with one of Voltaire's pens twined into the handle of it. He very modestly said it was not magnificent <u>mais ca le sentiment</u>.[259] I was thankful to get away from this place of woe with a grave countenance. You have probably heard this place described by some Tourist or other, so I shall say no more about it. – We have travelled from Geneva to Fountainbleau over better than 300 miles of French ground. The country is dull & ugly and, excepting in vines, not productive. The soil seems generally poor and the Farmers ignorant of our british improvements. They seem to run out the ground with constant crops of corn, they have very few potatoes & no turnips. In the south maize [?] is cultivated to a considerable degree; perhaps that may be of the nature of a green crop, yet I should think not. The country however is plenteous, the people are tolerably well clothed and seem tolerably fed also. Since I sat down to write I have been interrupted by a call to see the Palace & gardens of this celebrated place. The apartments are very rich & splendid; I have been in the room and

---

258. John Cam Hobhouse (1786-1869) was a statesman, writer and intimate friend of Lord Byron. His works include *Essay on the Origin and Intention of Sacrifices* (1809), *Imitations and Translations from the Ancient and Modern Classics* (1809), *A Journey through Albania, and other Provinces of Turkey in Europe and Asia* (1813), *A Defence of the People, in reply to Lord Erskine's "Two Defences of the Whigs"* (1819) and *Italy: remarks made in several visits from the year 1816 to 1854* (1859), in which the notes to the 4th canto of *Childe Harold* are "recast and greatly enlarged" (*DNB*, IX:941-42).

259. *mais ca [c'est] le sentiment*: that seems to be the consensus.

have laid my hand on the table on which Bounaparte [sic] signed his abdication. We go to morrow to Paris, where we shall stay but a few days, and then for our own countrie! where I shall sleep in my bed and begin my daily habits again. — I hope you & all your Family are well. I send my kindest wishes for your welfare. Believe me always, my dear Friend

most truly yours

J Baillie

PS. Having brought this with me to Paris and not having sent it immediately to post I will say a few words to you more, and inclose it to Mr Freeling. We have been here four days which have been fully occupied all the morning seeing the Town and the evenings at the Theatre. How this celebrated City has struck me generally I need scarcely say; just as I believe it does every one who comes from London where there are fine streets & squares but few Palaces or public gardens. We went last Sunday to the fair at St. Cloud which was very amusing & characteristic of the french. All ranks of people were there. Old women of the lowest rank with clean caps on their heads were enjoying themselves simply amongst the young & gay, and at night the lower ranks some dressed like Ladies & some like servant-maids were dancing cotillions together with the young men under the trees which were hung with lamps something like Vauxhall. Then there were men frolicking along with Lady's bonnets & shawls on which the Lady to whom they belonged was hanging on his arm & in return figuring along with his hat on her head. But the thing that struck me most of all and I must own with some disgust was great numbers of people fully come to mans estate 4 or 5 & twenty at least who went about every where with two-penny trumpets at their mouths making a noise that was annoying. Nobody however pushed or did any thing uncivil to another. In this respect they certainly have the advantage of John Bull. Night before last we went to see Talma act Hamlet.[260] I was much disappointed. His expression of feeling appeared to me exaggerated & harsh, and tho' the action of his arms is often very good yet he is upon the whole neither dignified nor graceful. He is not Hamlet Prince of Denmarc to my fancy but a good Bourgeois of Paris thro'out. I ought not however to judge so severely from one character only, and my imperfect knowledge of the french language – or I should rather say my not being accustomed to hear it spoken prevents me from being sensible of many

---

260. Francois Joseph Talma (1763-1826) was a French tragic actor educated in England. A friend of Napoleon, he made his debut in Paris in 1787 in Voltaire's *Brutus* and first introduced on the French stage the custom of wearing costumes of the period represented in the play. His dramatic roles were numerous (*The New Century Cyclopedia of Names*, 3:3788).

excellencies in speaking his part which others might be sensible of. I was too far distant to see the expressions of his face, for my eyes begin now to wax dim, and unless I am very near I see nothing well. I suppose you know this French Play of Hamlet. It is an old Play I find & quite after the French School. There has been so much pains taken to make poor Hamlet well-bred that the whole character & spirit is extracted from it. That Goth Shakespear has no notion how a Prince & a Lover ought to speak. —

Farewell again! and sometimes remember me.

JB.

August 18th

I shall be at Hampstead I hope in 10 days or so.

3888 ff.37-39 (Address: Walter Scott Esqr / Castle Street / Edinburgh-- postmarked 1817)

London February 21st 1817

My dear Sir,

I inclose to you a letter which I received from Lady Byron yesterday, and regret that any thing I have to communicate to you, or any thing I have to say immediately from myself (which may be the case before I finish this letter) should give you pain, as I know such things must do to a heart like your own. — The amiable & candid view she takes of your motives in reviewing, as you have done in the Quarterly, Lord Byron's late works, is not the effect of prudence & deliberation, but was the immediate fruit of her own sweet & forbearing nature.[261] I saw her, just after she had read the review, not knowing who was the writer, and she well perceived the use that will be made of it against herself. The next time we met, a few day[s] afterwards, she told me she was informed the article was written by you (which I was not willing to believe) but added that tho' it was calculated to give an unfavourable impression of her to the world, she believed it was written from a generous desire to befriend Ld Byron and honoured you for your motives. She soon returned to the country and has, I suppose, met with friends, who have viewed the publication in a very mischievous light which has induced her to send you this message, for when she left me she hinted at no such intention.

There is nothing which the world can pretend to censure in Lady Byron but that she is supposed to be of a very cold & unforgiving nature. That she is a woman of great self-command I know; and where this is the case we

---

261. In this *Quarterly Review* article, Scott had given Canto III of Byron's *Childe Harold's Pilgrimage* a just and generous review, though many of Lady Byron's friends resented it. Byron was deeply moved, and told Murray that Scott "must be a gallant as well as a good man" (qtd. in Johnson, 562).

cannot well judge of the degree of feeling; but I never in the whole course of my life met with any person of a more candid & forgiving disposition. She has borne treatment & wrongs exceeding any thing I have ever heard of in married life; and could she [have] hoped for any amendment in his character, or even with this hope, could she have continued to live with him without becoming herself worthless & debased, she would I am confident never have left him. You may perhaps suspect my testimony as being partial to her & coming from her, and I know not well how to remove the difficulty. I can only say that I am most thoroughly convinced of the truth of it, and that I hope you will receive what I say with some degree of confidence till you shall find from better authority that it is false. Why should I be too ready to think or believe ill of Lord Byron? After the great friendship, I have on all occasions experienced from yourself, I have not from any of the modern Poets received stronger proofs of a disposition to serve me than from him. You will remember too that when I returned from Switzerland, having heard here that he was living with a Gentleman & his Wife on the banks of the lake, how ready I was to suppose he was in a respectable house and to interpret this in his favour. But I wish I had been less ready, for I have innocently misled you, perhaps, to think better of him & of his present state than he deserves. Not long after I sent you my last letter, I learnt that this same Gentleman & his Wife were a married man who has run away from this country and a Girl whom he has seduced and that their house was any thing but a respectable one.[262] This information did not come from Lady B. —— O! why have you endeavoured to reconcile the world in some degree with that unhappy man at the expence of having yourself, perhaps, considered as regarding want of all principle and the vilest corruption with an indulgent eye? indeed my good, my kind, my unwearied friend, this goes to my heart! I truly believe that you have done it to cheer in some degree the despair of a perishing mind and rouse it to make some effort to save itself; but this will not be: you cannot save him tho' by that effort you may depress, a most worthy character who has been already so sinned against, and who bears the deepest part of her distress in silence. And now that I am taking the privilege of a Friend I had almost said of a Mother to rate you thus, let me ask why you have reviewed Lord Bs poetry in a strain of praise which in my simple opinion is far beyond its real merit? I may not think you

262. Though Baillie does not seem to know who these people are, it is apparently the company of Percy Shelley, Mary Godwin, their child, and Mary's stepsister Clair Clairmont. Claire had been writing intimate letters to Byron for several months and decided to visit Switzerland about this time, staying at the same hotel with Shelley's party. See Margot Strickland, *The Byron Women* (New York: St. Martin's, 1974), 123.

insincere and therefore I must even believe that your wits have been a wool gathering. I shall give but one instance of it as I would not prolong my letter: the thunder storm on the Lake which you praise as the most sublime discription

"Far along — From peak to peak the rattling crags among,
Leaps the live thunder! Not from one cloud alone
But every mountain now hath found a tongue
And Jura answers thro' her misty shroud
Back to the joyous Alps who call to her aloud."

"And the big rain comes dancing to the earth
And now again 'tis black – and now the glee
Of the loud hills shakes with its mountain mirth."[263]

These familiar personifications give meanness instead of sublimity to the discription (if discription it may be called) besides being far-fetched & fantastical. I have transcribed these lines from the Edin[r] review which also greatly praises this passage, but nonetheless my opinion is the same in spite of two such high authorities. What I should consider as bad in Wordsworth I can never believe is good in Lord Byron. ––– I have many things which I wished to ask your advice, notwithstanding your bad taste in poets but I cannot speak of any other subject at present. I hope this will find you all well in N. Castle street and send my kind wishes to M[rs] Scott & my young Friend Sophia.

Believe me always; my dear Friend
truly & affectionately yours
J Baillie

ff.45-47 is the letter from Lady Byron that Baillie encloses in the above. On it Baillie writes the following note:

Since I sat down to write to M[r] Erskine I have received this letter, and shall put it into your cover instead of my epistle to him. — Had I received it sooner I should not have troubled you with many things which I have mentioned in my letter. —

---

263. See XCII and XCIII in Canto III of *Childe Harold's Pilgrimage*.

3888 ff.40-42 (Address: Walter Scott Esqr / Advocate / Edinburgh--
postmarked 1817)

Hampstead March 3$^{\underline{d}}$ 1817

My dear Friend,

I have this evening received a note from M$^{\underline{rs}}$ Baillie, telling me that
her husband has sent you an answer to your letter by to day's post; and that
he thinks your complaint, tho' it may for a time occasionally return, is not
likely to be attended with any dangerous consequences.[264] This is a great
ease to my mind; and I hope he has put you upon some way to mitigate the
pain when it does return, that you may not to the disgrace of poetical
dignity be constrained to bellow like a Bull-Calf any more. The only very
violent pain I ever felt was, I take it, some thing of the same nature. It was
called a cramp in the stomach, and seized me many years ago so violently,
that when my Mother left me to fetch something from the ajoining [sic]
room, I looked after her in my agony, doubting if I should ever see her
again. This is a discipline which the great Father of us all sees fit to
exercise us with, and we learn (for I hope & trust you have done so) to bless
him in our sufferings. I hope you had a good sleep the night after you wrote
to me: and how delightful it would be to fall into it on your own bed, free
from pain!

I thought I could not do better than send your previous letter to Lady
Byron that you might immediately speak for yourself; and I am sure her
mind will not harbour a doubt as to the honesty & innocence of your
intentions. It appears to me that you have somewhat mistaken the
meaning of her letter which was not to complain of what you have done,
but to prevent you, should expressions of strong complaint from her friends
reach you[r] ears, from supposing they expressed her sentiments. I entirely
agree with you in your postcript [sic], that it is unwise in her friends to be
vehement in their outcry against Lord Byron; and I am sure they receive no
encouragement in so doing from her: but you will readily grant, that it is
not easy for those nearly concerned, who see such an excellent young
creature with all her large fortune & fair prospects, fall a sacrifice to the
deliberate, calculating selfishness of a man, who only feigned an
attachment to her for his own worldly interest, to refrain from the
bitterest expressions of indignation. In his poem of the dream he says, he
pronounced his marriage vows scarcely knowing what he said, his mind

---

264. In January and February Scott had seizures so severe that he fainted,
passing many sleepless nights in pain. He wrote Baillie that "Truly I thought the grim
skeleton was about to take my harp out of the Minstrel's Hands" (qtd. in Johnson,
565-66). Dr. Matthew Baillie found the problem to be gallstones.

fitted with another object.[265] However, who those vehement friends are I dont know, for tho' I am intimate with Lady Byron herself I am not acquainted with any of her relations Sir Ralph & Lady Noel excepted. -- The firearms & daggers, kept at night on the table of Lord B's bed room, Lady B. herself made light of, and said that she never supposed they were intended against her tho' he once pointed a pistol at her with threats. I must not tell you the darkest part of L^d B's character, and if I did, you would most likely not believe it. But I will give you one trait of him which I may tell and must be believed. In those verses upon the poor Governess, he represents her as sowing all the mischief between Lady B & himself.[266] This person never entered his house or had any thing to do between them till Lady B was confined of her child, and she was then sent for at his sister Mrs Leigh's desire to take care of Lady B. Now Lady B. was resolved to separate from him before her confinement and had taken advice of counsel upon it at least a month before it, and was advised by her counsel to stay in his house if possible till after her child was born. But the real reason for Lord B.'s writing those verses was to wound the character of Lady Noel Lady B's Mother: a most manly revenge for any displeasure she might have given him! -- As for the other matter in your postcript regarding pecuniary affairs it <u>was</u> settled before he left England.[267] I thought I had informed you of this: it was very wrong in me not to do so.

---

265. Byron had written "The Dream" in July 1816; lines 145-46 & 156-58 follow:
. . . - I saw him stand
Before an Altar - with a gentle bride; . . .
And he stood calm and quiet, and he spoke
The fitting vows, but heard not his own words,
And all things reel'd around him; . . .
(McGann, IV:27)

266. See lines 9-12 of Byron's "A Sketch from Private Life":
Quick with the tale, and ready with the lie -
The genial confidante, and general spy -
Who could, ye gods! her next employment guess -
An only infant's earliest governess!

The object of the satire was Mary Jane Clermont, Annabella's maid who had also been her nurse and governess; Byron believed her responsible for the separation (McGann, III:495).

267. This is in response to Scott's brief letter to Baillie of 1 March 1817 in which he discusses his acute illness (gallstones). There is not, however, a postscript printed with this letter which discusses Byron's "pecuniary affairs." Scott's next letter to Baillie, a long one dated 17 March 1817, thanks her for Dr. Baillie's help and determines that he "will not trust myself to say anything on the subject of Lady Byrons letter but I feel a great deal. I must say I never heard anyone say any thing to her disparagement though several have endeavoured to palliate and apologize for Lord B's conduct - all the Whigs by the way" (Grierson, 4:409).

After refusing for a long time to give up a reasonable part of her fortune for the maintenance of herself & child, he was induced to do it from <u>fear</u> on finding that she was possessed of stronger evidence of such matters as he wished to conceal than he had been aware of. This is a vantage ground which she will always keep for great occasions, tho' trusting to her repugnance to all exposure, he will still venture to use the language of a man who has been hardly used. As to his feelings, were they genuine he could not expose them to the world in the manner he does. That alone would be to me the mark of a hypocritical & vulgar mind. Yes; I say <u>vulgar</u>, gifted tho' he be with poetical talents of no ordinary kind. ――― I am but little in company and hear little of what is said in the world; but last week, in a small assembly of literary people, I heard this review mentioned by several people, not connected with Lady B. nor knowing that I was even acquainted with her, and they blamed it as an attempt to cast a lustre over vice which did not become the writer, tho' some allowance might be made for one Poet wishing to help out another. I will say but one thing more on this subject and then drop it for ever. – You have not told me all your reasons for writing this review. It is said in Scotland, there is "na ganging thro' the warl without a wee tate o' fancet." Now your wee tate o' fancet on this occasion I take to be, that the world & reviewer, rating Lord Byron's works above their real merits (tho' that merit is great) you were afraid by talking of him & them in reasonable terms to be supposed capable of feeling a degree of envious rivalship. Had you done this justice to your own genius, you would not have fallen into this snare: your modesty pleads your excuse. Walter Scott has no rival; and he is little better than a <u>Goose-Gibie</u>[268] not to feel it more assuredly. —— But I have forgot to say, adverting again to your postscript. What comes from those who may be supposed to be Lady Byron's friends will often make against her, for some of her near relations who are worthless people of the world – Lady Melbourne for instance,[269] have always been her worst enemies: while on the other hand two of her staunch friends are Lord Byron's nearest

---

268. gebbie: tuft of a fowl or mouth of a fowl (*SND*).

269. This is apparently a reference to Lady Caroline Lamb, who married the Hon. William Lamb, Lord Melbourne, in 1805, separating from him once in 1813 after an infatuation with Lord Byron (it is in her diary that the poet is described as "mad, bad, and dangerous to know") and finally in 1825 (*DNB*, XI:421-23). Baillie refers to William La b as a cousin to Lady Byron in Ms. 93, ff.159-160 (letters to Mary Montgomery, Volume 2).

relations, Capt: Byron, Mr Wilmot, while his daughter Mrs Byron always speaks of her in the highest terms.[270]

As I mean under this cover to write to your friend Mr Erskine, I must be brief on the other subject which I wish to mention to you. — I have by me 3 poems if I dare venture so to call them, upon a plan which I believe has never been thought of before: I call them Metrical Legends, taking this last word not in the common sense but as a chronicle.[271] My idea is a poem, short enough to be read at one sitting, containing the chief events in the life of a great character, free from fiction, reflections & discriptions only allow, what in short may be left as a memorial of the mighty dead. This I have executed in irregular verse, some what in imitation of your own, and my 3 characters are Columbus, William Wallace and Lady Grizell Baillie. Which last I fell in love with from the account given of her in Mr Rose's answer to Fox's historical work.[272] My Brother & some of my friends here think I ought to publish them, but as I am so very unpopular, I am unwilling to publish and receive nothing or next to nothing now for what might probably produce a considerable sum to my heirs when I shall be no more. If a Bookseller were to give me a sum for the work he would for his own sake then promote the sale in every way, but without this I do not think it advisable to venture, particularly as publishing is to me at all times a painful thing. If you are to be in Town this spring or summer, as I hope you are, I will shew you my manuscript, tho' the last is not yet in a finished state. If you are not to be in Town, I will by some safe conveyance send you Columbus & Wallace to give you a distinct idea of them; and, if

---

270. Mr. Valentine Henry Wilmot was Byron's cousin and husband of writer Barbarina Brand (the Mrs. Wilmot mentioned in letters 3883 ff.73-76 & 3889 ff.182-184), later Lady Dacre.

271. Baillie's *Metrical Legends of Exalted Characters* were actually published in 1821 by Longman, Rees, Orme, and Brown.

272. Lady Grisell Baillie (1665-1746) was the daughter of Sir Patrick Hume of Polworth and Grisell Kerr. She reportedly saved her father's life (under suspicion for participating in the Rye House Plot) by hiding him in the family vault near Redbraes Castle, her father's friend Robert Baillie hanged, drawn and quartered on the same charge in 1685. The family fled to Utrecht, exiled with other Scottish Presbyterians, and Grisell made a secret voyage back to Scotland to rescue her sister and the family's fortune. At the 1688 revolution she and her mother returned to Britain in the company of the Princess of Orange. She married George Baillie, son of the executed Robert, in 1692, and helped manage both his and her father's estates. Her works include *Orpheus Caledonius or a Collection of the Best Scotch Songs set to Music by W. Thomson* (1726) and *The Household Book of Lady Griselle Baillie* (1692-1733) (Todd, 28-29). Statesman Charles James Fox's (1749-1806) *History of the Early Part of the Reign of James II* was published by Lord Holland in 1808, to which statesman George Rose (1744-1818) responded with *Observations on the Historical Work of the late C. J. Fox* in 1809.

after seeing them you think I ought to publish, you must then advise me what to do as to disposing of the copy right. The three Legends together with their notes will make the best part of a small volume and I have two [or] three ballads which will make up the rest. There is no disposition in the public at large or in any of the reviewers to favour me, so I must not venture but upon some good grounds to suppose that on their own account, aided by an able Bookseller, they may meet with some degree of success. — I shall long soon to hear how you do and whether the enemy has again attacked your stomach. My Sister unites with me in kindest regards to you & Mrs Scott, not forgetting our young friend Sophia. Much enjoyment may you all have at Abbotsford. Our friends in Grosvenor St: are pretty well, and the young married folks who are now gone to their own house, very happy. Farewell! and believe me always, whether angry or pleased, yours affectionately

    J Baillie

3888 ff.73-75 (Address: Walter Scott Esqr--no postmark)

Hampstead May 19th 1817

My dear Friend,

    I have heard pretty good accounts of you from time to time by our Friend Richardson, who having to do with all the Scotch Lawyers that come to London has good opportunity of learning. This has kept me easy, and prevented me from writing till I should have a packet to send, and I hope by & by, in return for this, to hear from your own hand that you are continuing free from violent attacks, and by minding the Doctor's orders, getting your stomach into good conditions so that it may cease ere long to give you any trouble. As my information goes, you have had but one slight attack attended with a little inflamation since the violent one you wrote me of; and I most heartily hope & pray that you may never have such another bout of it as long as you live. The circumstance of your great Dog howling round your bed during your agony is very striking. Not long ago a Servant of ours had a Brother who died of a decline, and his dog who had been a great favorite & was old, watched by his bed and would not be put away; and afterwards, being seized with a kind of paralitic fit, crawled to the side of the coffin where its master was laid and stretched itself out & died. Mary our Servant was present. ——

    You are very kind to take so much interest in my attempts of poetry, and I send you the first of my pieces, mentioned in my last, for your friendly perusal & criticism. Your heart will teach you to be a gentle critic; but your real friendship for me must teach you to do violence to your heart if need be. I am no wise anxious to publish soon or even at all; and were it not that my Brother has expressed a strong wish that I should publish a small vol: of poetry, I should have very little pleasure in the thought. I could not send you this piece sooner because having only [my] own copy, I was afraid it might be lost, and I could not find time to make another. M<u>rs</u> Baillie in her goodness has taken this task off my hands and so much the better for you, for it is a pleasure to read her beautiful writing. The measure is irregular, in imitation of that which you have used with such eminent success, but you will find the lines not always properly set down to give notice of the intended variety: had I copied it out myself I should have rectified this. I have told you already my ideas in writing these Metrical Legends; and do you tell me whether I have done as I ought according to those ideas. After I had written Columbus, in examing [sic] the history I found he had taken four voyages to the western world, and I have mentioned but three. Do you think this of any consequence? In his story the boldness of the attempt and persevering intrepidity in pursuing it, finding land & afterwards the great Continent, his return to Europe & the ingratitude of Spain, are the only things that can be laid hold of in a chronicle, for the history itself is full of small & often repeated tho' curious detail which, unembellished by fiction, would be flat & tedious. The story of William Wallace therefore is a much better subject and when I can get it copied out (it is considerably longer than Columbus) I will send it to you also. Lady Grizeld [sic] is but lately written, so I should like to let it lie by that I may forget it before I write it out again. --- I have not seen your Friend M<u>r</u> Erskin[e] but I suppose he received my letter from Richardson. We have had Lady Byron here for our Neighbour, who has had a house in Hampstead since the beginning of April and will remain to the end of this month. She has business with Lawyers concerning her child and finds this a convenient retirement where her friends & men of business can reach her and from whence she can occasionally go to London without being plagued with too much company. She gave a small dinner to a few friends last week and the Landlord was Capt: Byron, L<u>d</u> B's nearest male relation.[273] He is a very pleasing man & very worthy; lately married & the Father of one little girl. He is much interested in poor Lady B. and will I hope be her steady friend thro' life. She was in better looks & spirits when she came to us than she is now. I fear her health begins to give way, and she has some thoughts of taking a little journey to the Lakes for change of air; I should not be surprised if she were to prolong it to the mountains of Scotland, if she can make up her mind to leave her little Girl so long who is one of the comeliest rosy Brats I ever saw. ——

I have nothing more to tell you of in which you can take the least interest unless it be that every body is reading Miss Edgeworth's Comic

---

273. See prior NLS letter 3888 ff.40-42.

Dramas. I like the two Irish ones much, particularly the first tho' it is too long for the plot. It finishes with a scene before the Justice, which if well acted would have an admirable effect on the Stage. There is an Irish Scold in it quite characteristic & original that has hit my fancy wonderfully. The English one in higher life, tho' the characters are well imagined & supported, wanting the charm of Irish manners is comparatively flat and will not please so generally, tho' Mr Edgeworth considers it, so he wrote to me some time ago, as much superior to the others. The Tragedy of the Apostate is I hear a piece of real merit, but I have not yet been lucky enough to see it nor to read it.[274] The last gratification I hope soon to have but the other poor Miss Oneal's illness puts I fear out of the question. — But I am ungrateful not (not) to have thanked you all this while for what you have told me concerning Booksellers.[275] I do thank you kindly and shall be faithful to your secret; my nearest of kin has not nor shall not see that part of your letter. I have never put a question to you upon a certain subject which all the world dies to know; and were you now seated by my side with the secret ready upon your lips I would forbid you to tell it to me, that I might still be able to say "I dont know it."[276]

My regard for you exceeds my female curiosity – how great that must be! — Farewell! – Give my kindest wishes to all your Family my young Friend Sophia in particular.

Affectionately yours

J Baillie

3888 ff.108-109 (No address or postmark)

Hampstead July 2^d 1817

My dear Friend,

It is a great while since I heard of you from any immediate authority and I long to know how you do. But besides this (as truth will out) I have another reason for writing. I sent you, I believe about 6 weeks ago, by a frank from Mr Freeling (at least I inclosed it to him to be franked) a small parcel containing a letter and one of the Metrical Legends which I had

---

274. Maria Edgeworth's *Comic Dramas, in three acts* appeared in 1817 and included *Love and Law, The Two Guardians* and *The Rose, the Thistle and the Shamrock*. Ulick, an apostate Anglo-Irishman, appears in her *Ormond* (1817).

275. Scott's letter of 17 March 1817 attributes low sales of Baillie's works not to her reputation, but to the unpopularity of dramas for reading rather than for acting. He provides statistics on his own sales with various publishers (Constable, Longman and Murray) and suggests she might, like he, sell editions but not their copyrights and suffer some temporary loss in order to keep rights (Grierson, 4:407-13).

276. See letter 3888 ff.235-237 following.

mentioned to you before and which you so kindly expressed a wish to see. Supposing you were then in Edin.ͬ I desired it to be directed to Castle St: but I learnt very soon afterwards that you were at Abbotsford. Perhaps you have never received it and it is still lying in Castle St: If this be the case, have the goodness to ascertain whether it has arrived, and at any rate do not suppose that I have been so negligent as to omit sending it. If this letter, however should reach you when you are occupied do not think yourself bound to answer it immediately; for if I should not hear from you for some time longer, I shall not be uneasy but take it for granted every thing is right till I know the contrary. ––– I have just been reading Miss Edgeworth's new tales.[277] The first holds out a good lesson given with ability, but being less animated than many of her best tales, and too obviously perhaps in the form of a lesson it will not probably be very popular. The second is full of picturesque Irish characters Sir Ulick, King Corny, black Connal etc. as far as I know original & drawn with great skill, and it will I should think be a favourite. It might however be shortened with some advantage. She has been hurrying on with those tales to have them published before her Father's death, he all the while struggling with mortal disease: what unfavourable circumstances for invention! Her Dramas are full of nature, good Irish nature, but they have not enough of plot, and this last falt [*sic*] makes them not so well received here as they deserve. I think the last scene of Love & law with Cutty Rhooney & the Macbrides &c before the Justice, is quite excellent. And talking of Dramas, who can forget to mention Lord Byron's? You have no doubt read it long ere now. Is it not a most extraordinary production? The principal (I should say only character[)] is just such a dark blasted Being as one might expect him to delineate, but the homely meanness of his incantations & spirit songs &c the scene too amongst the lofty alps w[h]ere nature is so majestic & sublime is what one could not have expected. Surely his head is going fast now, and it would be a relief to the minds of his best friends to hear that he is mad. There are striking lines here & there, however, as there always are even in the worst of his poems; the last scene between Manfred & the Abbot of St: Maurice is very good;[278] and that is a beautiful passage where he describes the Coleseum [*sic*] at Rome by moon light. — Lady Byron left Hampstead about a fortnight ago and returned to her Father's, I should rather say her Mother's house. She is in bad health, very much occasioned I believe by the state of her mind, and she means very soon for change of air to take a short tour to the Lakes of

---

277. See Edgeworth's new tales appearing in 1817: *Harrington, a tale* and *Ormond, a tale.*

278. Byron's *Manfred, A Dramatic Poem*, was published in 1817.

Cumberland. ––– I hope you have been well enough to enjoy Abbotsford since you came to it and found every thing there in a flourishing state. How does my Friend Sophia do? has she grown much taller since we saw her here? I wonder why I never asked this question before. Pray give my love to her & kindest regards to M<u>rs</u> Scott.

    yours affectionately
      J Baillie

3888 ff.134-135 (Address: Walter Scott Esq<u>r</u> / Abbotsford / Melrose--postmarked 1817)

                  Hampstead August 9<u>th</u> 1817

My dear Friend,

    I have just learned that Lady Byron <u>does</u> intend to extend her journey to Scotland, and I hope you will have the opportunity of being as kind & as useful to her as I know you desire to be and will have pleasure in being. I am doing what I can, at least, that you should meet. If she goes to Edin<u>r</u> by Melrose or returns that way, she will surely see you, and I have written to beg she will give you some intimation of it. I know not whether she has any Friends in Edin<u>r</u>, but if she has not, I should be glad if you would put her under the guidence [sic] of some Friend of yours, that she may see every thing worth seeing in your "own Romantic Town." ––– I need say no more on a subject when your own heart is so prompt. —

    I have received your kind letter, and thank you <u>kindly</u> for the account you give me of yourself and the attention you have paid to my Legend of Columbus. — I am sorry you are still distressed with your stomach attacks.[279] I wish you had been better rewarded for being a <u>good Boy</u>. I doubt however (notwithstanding this favourable account of yourself) that you are only good by halves. Pray make your virtue perfect and try what that will do for you. Your observations on Columbus have good plain sense in them, and I will follow them as far as I can do so, consistently with my own notions of the species of writing which I have attempted. The whole family of <u>haths</u> & <u>do's</u> shall be sent a packing, one or two of the most favorite members excepted; and I will tell you when I have more leisure, why there is such a numerous family of them to expell. — The Ms. & your

---

279. Though he had been placed on a strict meatless diet, Scott was still suffering gall bladder attacks (Johnson, 571).

promised letter is not yet arrived, but I am not in the least hurry about it.

　　With kind regards to Mrs Scott & love to Sophia,

　　I remain, my dear Friend

　　　　yours affectionately

　　　　　　J Baillie[280]

3888 ff.203-206 (Address: Walter Scott Esqr / Melrose--postmarked 1817)

Wentworths Octr 22^{d} 1817

My dear Friend,

　　I received your letter with my Ms. by Mr Freeling's frank a short time since and I thank you for all the pains you have taken with it. The general faults & disadvantages you mention in the poem & its plan cannot I fear be removed, but the few slight alterations of particular passages & lines I shall make most gladly as well as I can, one excepted.[281] This is naming the particular countries & ports which Columbus leaves behind when he makes his way cross the Atlantic, instead of mentioning it generally. <u>You</u> would name particular places with grace & dignity but I feel that <u>I</u> could not, so it will be wiser in me to forbear. Indeed the faults you find in the detail are so few, that could I suppose you have mentioned all that you perceived, I should be very proud of having done so well in this new business of writing rhymes; but I am not confident enough to take it so, but rather fear that what the poem <u>wants</u> has made you more lenient to what it <u>has</u>. My thoughts of publishing any poems would be willingly set aside if it were not that I have particular reasons for wishing to get possession of a thousand pounds for a particular purpose which I will not at present explain. If by & by I can find any Bookseller willing to give me as much for a vol: of Poems, I will publish & take my chance of praise, or abuse, or neglect; but if I cannot do this which most likely may be the case, I will not publish. My Brother's wish that I should publish was at first my <u>first</u> motive, but if I cannot get the money I will talk him over to my own

---

280. Written at the end of this letter is a brief note from Lady Byron to Scott thanking Baillie for the introduction and saying that she will travel by Melrose and visit the Scotts.

281. On 26 September 1817 Scott replied that the story of Baillie's Columbus is "admirably told" and that he has penciled in a few observations offered "rather as subjects of consideration than with any confidence that they are just" (Grierson, 4:524). He does not specify what these are in the letter but suggests that "We also seek a sort of individual interest arising from the collision of character and the detail of incident . . . so far you quit some of the most powerful claims you possess on the attention of interest. But on a second perusal these objections are not so powerful" (4:523).

opinion & be quiet. Many thanks again for the kind interest & attention you have shewn me on this subject.

I am glad you were so much pleased with Lady Byron.[282] That trait which struck you of decidedness of character I have often observed, but I believe that while she lived with Lord B. she was most compliant to his will in every thing excepting when she was required to mingle & become an associate of the profligate & debased. I do not believe that she ever for the sake of argument or consequence opposed him; but nothing would satisfy him but the grovling [sic] devotedness of a ~~Gulnere~~ gulnair.[283] She wrote to me a few short lines just after she had been at Abbotsford, chiefly to inform me of the state of your health, and in it she told me of your kind reception of her. There seems to have been but one thing in the day she spent with you which she could have wished otherwise, viz. your having asked company to meet her; she was in hopes to have found you in famille but she nevertheless took your asking company in very good part as wishing to pay her respect. I have had a letter from her since, but that regarded a little cross occurrence that distressed her and so I had no more particulars of the visit to Abbotsford. I should have liked to have seen your young sportsman that day come in with his . . .[284] & brace of birds, a handsome young man as you report & I believe of six feet one inch for, so tall he must be if he is taller than his Dad. Much pride & comfort may you have in him! I wish I had another Niece to marry, some years younger than himself; I should be much tempted to do what Aunts are so often accused of, – try to make a match. I am much pleased to think you are to be in London next spring & him along with you; I hope I shall live to see you both. Give my kind regards to M⸍ˢ Scott and Sophia, are they not to be of your party as far as London? We have got a little Sophia in this house whom I would gladly shew you, and you would pat her round cheeks very kindly, and think perhaps of what your own has been some sixteen years ago. It is my little Grand Niece, who is staying with her Grand mother for country air, and it is truly as pretty a little fat puss as one could wish to look upon.[285] I have nothing else to tell you of from this place where my

---

282. Lady Byron had visited Abbotsford one day in the last part of August, and the family took her on an excursion to the banks of Yarrow. Scott thought her young, beautiful and admirably sensible, every quality likely to bring happiness to Lord Byron; and he said his heart ached for her the whole time she visited (Johnson, 577).

283. This word is a puzzle, and even Baillie is unsure of the spelling since she marks through it the first time. I find no such word in the OED or the SND. A possibility according to context is "gullion," a worthless wretch (OED).

284. There seems to be a word left out here.

285. Little Sophy (Sophia, 1817-82) was Elizabeth and Robert Milligan's only daughter.

Sister & I are staying for a few weeks to prevent my Brother & M<u>rs</u> Baillie from feeling lonely now that their son is gone to Oxford & the dark season coming in. It is very retired; a modern Gothic Castle on a small scale, built by the Regent's Architect for M<u>r</u> Cullen Smith about seven miles from Windsor, and enriched with plantations such as the Laird of Abbotsford may boast of possessing 15 or 20 years hence.[286] It is, however, a pretty place and must be cheerful when the sun shines, a circumstance which has scarcely taken place since we arrived, full 8 days ago. -- My Brother is in daily & hourly expectations of being summoned to Claremont to the confinement of the Princess Charlotte,[287] tho' his attendance like that of the Chancelor & other great people will only be a matter of State. This state of expectation is great annoyance to all concerned; I hope it will soon be well over. —— M<u>rs</u> Baillie desires me particularly to remember her to you & M<u>rs</u> Scott & Sophia to whom she send her kind wishes; my Sister also send hers.

Farewell! Yours with all true regard
J Baillie

3888 ff.235-237 (No address or postmark)

Hampstead Dec<u>r</u> 3<u>d</u> 1817

My dear Friend,

Most people begin their letters by making apologies for not writing but in writing to you I feel always an inclination to do the reverse, for your time is so precious, and you must be so oppressed with letters that it is not reasonable to send you any that might be spared, especially as I have written to you not long ago. But a few days since I received a letter from Miss Edgeworth part of which I thing [sic] you ought to see, and the substance of which she must have wished me to communicate to you, tho' she has a bad impression which she thinks some late very injudicious publications may have made. I shall send you more of the letter than I

---

286. During Dr. Baillie's stay in Gloucestershire, convenient to Windsor for his attendance upon the king, the Baillies had purchased Duntisbourne House in 1806, first as a country retreat but later as an estate which William Baillie inherited. See Anne Carver, *The Story of Duntisbourne Abbots* (Gloucester: Albert E. Smith, 1966), 27.

287. Princess Charlotte Augusta was the only daughter of the Prince of Wales, later George IV, estranged from her father for many years and, many agree, sorely mistreated because of the Prince's estrangement from her mother. In 1816 she married Prince Leopold of Saxe-Coburg; living with him in Claremont, she gave birth to a still-born son on 5 November 1817, herself dying a few hours after (see *DNB* and Rose Weigall's 1874 *Brief Memoir* about the princess). While Dr. Matthew Baillie was called to attend the birth, he reportedly spent the day in the library and was not a party to the delivery. See following Scott letter 3888 ff.235-237.

strictly need to do, as it may amuse you and can do no harm; but pray do not think that I have done so to provoke you to tell me in return any part of a secret which you have no doubt good reasons for keeping. You know I do not desire it; and am better pleased to be able honestly to say that tho' I believe you to be the author of all the best parts of those celebrated novels, I am ignorant of it as a fact. — The first part of Miss Edgeworth's letter is about herself & her family, informing me that she has been busy transcribing for the press a life of her Father, written up to the year 82 by himself, and that she is to fill up what remains. All this she does to fulfill a promise she has made to him; and she is very anxious to do justice to the Dead without disgusting the living as too many Biographers do. — I shall transcribe what I wish you to see, as far as it is joined to this first part, and then refer you to the inclosed, written by herself. ——

Alas! What a sad event has taken place since I wrote to you last! I think I mentioned in my letter that my Brother was in hourly expectation of being summoned to Clermont [sic], and considering his attendance, as he is quite unaquainted [sic] with that part of the medical profession particularly applicable to the occasion, as a formality, because he was the Princess's official Physician, so little were we or any body apprehensive of danger. My Brother returned to us again the friday after she expired, deeply grieved for the dismal loss; and his heart so full of sympathy for Prince Leopold & admiration of his behaviour thro' the dreadful trial, that what concerned the public & all other considerations were comparatively forgotten. Their union was a most happy one; her character which was at bottom a very good one, was improving under his influence every day; and had the child lived it would have probably had the advantage of being brought up under an excellent Father whose interest could never have interfered with his own. All this enhances the misfortune. The medical attendants as you must have seen by the papers, have been grately [sic] blamed, particularly poor Sir Richard Croft; and nothing can be more amiable & considerate than Prince Leopold has been to him in expressing by letters, in the kindest manner, his entire conviction that every thing was done to save the Princess that could be done.[288] The Regent has also been very kind & gracious in this respect, and poor man, I

---

288. Dr. Matthew Baillie later wrote, "I can never forget the most afflicting Scene which I witness'd at Claremont in November 1817, which not only cover'd this Country with mourning, but filled it with real sorrow of Heart– In looking back very often upon this most distressing event, I am convinced Sir Richd Croft did all that the Melancholy Case admitted of " (qtd. in Crainz, 38). The labor lasted two days and nights; the princess gave birth to a still-born son on 5 November and died 5 hours later. Though the labor had been in accordance with the best contemporary practice, Dr. Sir Richard Croft shot himself three months after (Crainz, 39).

mean Sir R., he requires it all, for he has been sadly shook & distressed. It is a satisfaction to know that she did not suffer a great deal – not more than most women do, and that she was never aware of her danger. Nothing could exceed the gloom cast over every body here; the news paper does not go beyond the truth. One met with no creature who was not moved and common people were in tears in the streets. ––– My Sister & I left Wentworths last friday. The day before we left it, we had our curiosity gratified by seeing the Duke & Duchess of Gloucester,[289] who called there on their way to pay their first visit of condolence at Claremont. She spoke of Prince Leopold in the highest terms. They were both very condescending to us and this is the nearest approach to royalty I have ever made or am ever likely to make. –– I hope you continue to have fewer & gentler attacks of spasm. Give my kind regards to M‾r‾s Scott & Sophia! My Sister joins me in all kind wishes. Farewell! affectionately yours

　　J Baillie

PS. I have forgot a little message in Lady Byron's last letter to which. After saying that she felt most grateful for your kindness to her at Abbotsford which nothing could exceed & other handsome things which I do not repeat, she desires to be remembered to you and adds "Will you tell him that tho' I keep the heather flowers which he put into my hand, they are not necessary to remind me of his hospitable roof – and kind circle" She is pretty well but oppressed with many cares. ––––

Extract from Miss E's letter

Ardbroacean Palace Nov‾r 14‾t‾h

We have come here to spend a few days with one of my Father's oldest friends, the Bishop of Meath. He & his family are some of your Friend Walter Scotts most enthusiastic admirers and on this as on many other subjects we heartily agree. The questions whether Scott did or did not write the 3 celebrated novels – whether he wrote parts or the whole, & why he or their author does not acknowledge them, are at this moment subjects of as eager conversational discussion in Dublin and in all literary companies in Ireland as they have been in London & all over England – If the Author's object by this mystery was to keep alive public curiosity & interest, (in his case a very unnecessary object) he has perfectly succeeded. . . .[290]

---

289. William Frederick (1776-1834).
290. Edgeworth refers to Scott's anonymously published Waverley novels, the authorship not publicly revealed until February 1827 (Johnson, 1009).

3889 ff.135-136 (No address or postmark)

Hampstead July 6th 1818

My dear Friend,

Next to my Brother I begrudge giving you trouble of all people in the world, because I know how much you have to do and how much you must be teased with all manner of intrusions; yet there are things which you may grumble at as you please but cannot avoid, and that which occasions my present writing is one of them. I have received a letter from an old acquaintance & once a very kind neighbour of ours, inclosing a letter to you from her Brother, containing some questions, (I suppose) regarding Scotch antiquarianism, and earnestly requesting me to transmit it to you with some notice that I am acquainted with the writer; fearing that otherwise sent from a perfect stranger, you might not give it such immediate attention as he wishes and as perhaps some urgent business of his may require. If you will have the goodness to answer his questions for him, as soon as may be convenient for you, you will do me a great favour. ––– It is long since any letter has "passed between us twain" and I had a mind to write you a long letter soon, when you should be retired to Abbotsford & at leisure & in the humour to attend to a long rigmarole about my own affairs & designs against the Booksellers. I have done a good deal (at least I think I have) to improve Columbus since you saw it, and have applied your remarks on it to the other Metrical Legends for their improvement also. –– But I will reserve all this for another time, and probably your Friend Richardson may be the Bearer of my next dispatch. ––– I saw – I will not say I had the pleasure of seeing the portraits of yourself & the family at Abbotsford some time ago at the exhibition, and I have often been amused since, at the earnestness with which almost every body abuses it, & poor Wilkie for placing it there.[291] Tell Mrs Scott & Sophia, for their comfort, that no body thinks either of them at all like. Mrs Scott is certainly represented as a shepherds wife of a most reverend appearance; and if it has any resemblance to her present mien, you must

---

291. Sir David Wilkie (1785-1841) began drawing before he could read. He entered the Trustees' Academy and made some progress in portrait painting but in 1804 left Edinburgh and returned to his home of Cults to paint on his own. In 1805 he left for London, carrying a small picture entitled *Bounty Money; or, the Village Recruit*, and established himself at Portland Road, shortly after beginning attendance at the Academy and finally earning true fame in 1810 with *The Village Festival* (now in the National Gallery). He became ill around this time and was attended by Dr. Matthew Baillie, migrating for his convalescence to the house of Joanna Baillie. By 1830 Wilkie was made painter in ordinary at the death of Sir Thomas Lawrence, retaining this office under William IV and Victoria. In 1836 he was knighted. Scott invited him to Abbotsford in 1817, and while there he painted the Scott family in the garb of south-country peasants, put on exhibit in 1818 (*DNB*, XXI:253-58).

have been treating her very ill during the last four years past since I saw her, to make age come on so rapidly before its time. As for Sophia, poor Wilkie had been sounding her praises in such a high strain to Mrs Baillie, that I expected to find her altogether charming; but love with him is blinded after a most extraordinary fashion; he must have got one of the good-wife's thread-bare <u>cheese cloats</u> put before his eyes to cast over them such homely shadows. But to make some amends to the public for his failure in this, he is painting a picture – the subject a Scotch penny wedding, which it is said, by every body who has seen it, will be one of the finest things he has ever done.[292] It has been of late sadly interrupted by a bad fever from which he is just recovering. ––– How do you like Lord Byron's last canto of Child Harold?[293] But I know you are a great hypocrite and will not tell me truly what you think of it. I am none, at least upon this occasion, and say with all freedom that I think it very dull & obscure: he seems constantly straining after original thoughts & original expressions, yet every thing that he says passes away from the mind of the Reader (such readers at least as myself) as soon as he lays down the book. With very few exceptions at least I have found this to be the case. He dismisses his hero as quietly as may be; I was in hopes that the Devil would have run off with him like Dr Faustus or at least that he would have gratified us with some horrific uncertainty regarding it to have created some excitement & employment for conjecture, but I only guess that the Child grew very fat & prefered his easy chair to any further travelling or adventure. ––

What a summer we have got! All the flowers are of a brighter colour & more luxurient than I remember them for at least twenty years past, and the fruit is abundant. Farther than this no Hampstead person can testify from ocular proof, for there is not a field of corn to be seen within miles of us; a thing I regret much, for this variety – the cheerful variety it produces both in summer & harvest is very pleasing both to the eye & the heart. I'm sure the people at large have need of the sociable influence of the harvest field to bind them together again after all the rioting & quarrelling of the elections. We are become a filthy commonality here: our mobs disgrace us now more than they ever did. I, being a sober-minded Whig, am mortified & grieved at this & should have given my vote for Sir M: Maxwell with

---

292. A penny wedding is one for which guests contribute money for the entertainment, customary in poorer classes of Scotland, Wales, etc. (*OED*). Wilkie's "The Scotch, or Penny Wedding" was finished in 1818 after recent travels in Scotland.

293. On reading the last canto of *Childe Harold's Pilgrimage*, Scott was assured that Byron was a poet of great merit and that at least his misanthropy was now more moderate (Johnson, 627).

all my heart.[294] — My Sister unites with me in all kind wishes to yourself & Mrs Scott & our young Friend Sophia. I hope you will have much enjoyment with all your family in the country soon; for I suppose you are in Edin^r at present. – I make no enquiries after your health, having heard so repeatedly from different quarters that you are quite well. Long may you remain so! every good thing that can befall you will always give some additional satisfaction to

    your affectionate friend
     J Baillie

3889 ff.182-184 (Address: For The Laird of Abbotsford–-no postmark)
Hampstead Septr 1st 1818

My dear & kind Friend,

    My Neighbour Richardson, must not go to Abbotsford withou: some token in his pocket of my grateful remembrance of the good & happy Laird thereof, tho' it were but a few lines. Had I known of his going sooner, I might have had my poor matters in greater forwardness & I should have had more to say to you; but this subject I put aside for the present, only that I must just tell you how kindly I take your <u>kind</u> cheering in regard to my labours, and that I <u>am</u> cheered. — I thank you also for complying with my request regarding Mr Halls with such a handsome grace; it were enough to tempt one to covet occasions of giving you trouble, but be not alarmed: I have not reached these years without having learnt some little discretion.

    But what gave me most pleasure of all from your last letter was, that it is so evidently the letter of a happy man. You are surrounded with blessings & you are sensible of them & enjoy them with the light cheer-(cheer)fulness of a man unspoiled by the world & a full tide of prosperity [sic] such as the world seldom bestows. I hear there is a very good comparison drawn in the last Edin^r review between the Character of Rousseau & Ld Byron;[295] I am sure an excellent comparison of contrast might be made between Ld Byron & yourself; and such a comparison will often be drawn in after times, when we are all in our graves. – For poor Lady Byron, I heard of her the other day. The accounts are pretty good at

---

294. Sir Murray Maxwell (1775-1831), naval captain, was knighted in May 1818 for humanitarian aid to his men after having been acquitted in court marshal hearings on the loss of the British ship the *Alceste* (*DNB*, XIII:131-32).

295. This particular *Edinburgh Review*'s commentary on *Childe Harold's Pilgrimage, Canto the Fourth*, began, "There are two writers, in modern literature, whose extraordinary power over the minds of men, it may be truly said, has existed less in their works than in themselves, - Rousseau and Lord Byron" (see *The Edinburgh Review*, vol. XXX [Edinburgh: Constable, 1818], 87-8).

present but she has suffered a great deal from bad health, probably very much occasioned by anxiety, and I doubt she is not yet essencially recovered. A intimate friend of hers, Miss Montgomery,[296] saw Ld Byron not very long ago at Venice and says, he has become very fat, his face being round as a cheese & his body somewhat of the form of a large china jar that we have in our drawing room. He spoke to her very courteously, tho' he had not previously been acquainted with her, and she received it with distant civility. But perhaps I have told you this already in my last – I have a wretched memory.

My Brother & Mrs Baillie have been in the country at the same place they had last summer, for this month & more; they are all well, and the last particular account I had of the good Doctor was, that he had been reading aloud to the Family the last tale of my Landlord, and weeping like a child over the misfortunes of Effy & Jenny Deans & their pious Father donce David.[297] The author of these works whoever he may be, has the blessing of many a tired man of business in vacation time, Invalid in the dreary sick-room, and all manner of listless & retired folks, resting on his head; much good may it do him! — I suppose the character of Argyle is drawn from the real man. It is truly a most delightful picture of a noble, popular chieftain. ——

My Sister has been from home for some time on a visit to a Friend at Brighton, and in her absence I went <u>short sin</u>[298] to visit Mrs Wilmot at Hampton Court. I found your Friend Wilkie with her the first day, very animated & crammed full of poetry to the teeth. When I asked him in the evening how long he had been returned from the garden where we had all gone to stroll in separate parties in the moon light, he answered with solemn & measured cadence "While one with moderate haste might count a hundred." Has he got this spark kindled within him at Abbotsford? He has been very ill but is now quite recovered. Mrs Wilmot is a person you would both like & admire. She is cheerful, kind, open, confiding & guileless; without conceit & full of talents. Her house is full of her own works, drawings & models, the first very good, the last excellent. They consist of all kinds of animals, horses, cattle, deer & dogs &c &c and some of them in interesting situations to whom she has given expression that is

---

296. Mary Millicent Montgomery grew up under the guardianship of Lady Gosford, a friend of Judith Milbanke, and later became Annabella's closest friend, spending a great deal of time at Seaham. Though she spent much of her life as an invalid, Montgomery outlived Annabella. See Baillie's letters to Miss Montgomery in Volume 2 for more detail.

297. Scott's 4-volume *Tales of My Landlord* began with *The Black Dwarf*, followed by *Old Mortality* (1816).

298. sin: while, time since (*SND*).

quite pathetic. She has from her childhood been very much acquainted with animals and she tells me the Ass has a great deal of sense – she thinks, in proportion to his wants, more than a horse. Now she is the first horse woman in this country & very fond of horses. —

Return my best thanks to Mrs Scott & Sophia & my other young Friends of your Family, Charles in particular since he does me so much honour, for their kind remembrance of me. There is no love lost; I think of them with all kind sentiments, and remain,

    my dear Friend
        ever affectionately yours
           J Baillie

PS. Since your health is so perfectly recovered which I rejoice to hear, do you not think of being in London next spring. But Mr Richardson will inform me when he returns of all your motions. –– We have now got some refressing [sic] showers for which we are very thankful, but the drought has been so great that our grass fields are like stubble land & our trees nearly half stripped of their leaves. I had a letter from Mr Sotheby the other day who is at his house at Epping forest and seems to be in a very comfortable reasonable state of mind after the sad loss which he & all his family felt so severely the beginning of summer.[299] ––

3889 ff.279-280 (Address: Walter Sott [sic] Esqr / N: Castle Street / Edin^r -- postmarked 1818)

               Grosvenor St: Decr 14th 1818

My dear Friend,

I have this morning received your very kind letter, for being from home it came to me later than it would otherwise have done. The event it announces with the consequences of it are of a mixed nature to you, as you justly observe, but to me it gives unalloyed pleasure. I ought indeed to sympathize with the feelings of Mrs Scott & your own derived from hers, but I cannot do it, not having her grief under my eye. I can think of nothing but of your family being established in the country as prosperous & distinguished, gracing the honourable root they <u>immediately</u> spring from, and it pleases my fancy well. As to your for [sic] father, tho' every body who speaks honestly is proud of having a gentle or honourable descent, yet in your particular case, no body but yourself will ever consider that

---

299. Sotheby's son William was killed in the foot-guards in 1815 and son George had been killed defending the residency of the East India Company at Nagpoore during the Mahratta war some time in 1817, but I have not identified a tragedy occurring in the summer of 1818. Because William Sotheby had been on the continent for most of 1817, it is possible the news of George's death did not reach him immediately (see introduction to Sotheby letters herein).

circumstance. The Regent will do himself great credit by bestowing a Baronetcy on such a subject as very few Kings or Regents have it in their power to honour; and I think you are very right to accept of it.[300] The descendants of a great man when unmarked by fortune or title soon mix with the common mass & are forgotten, but a title marks whose son the chief of the family is for ever; and may the Baronets of Abbotsford be a distinguished & prosperous race for many <u>many</u> generations. But I need scarcely assure you of my approbation upon this point; for, if you have not entirely forgot the circumstance, you may call to mind that a good many years ago you almost snubbed for suggesting that such a distinction might be a desirable thing for the young Laird. I honour this same young Laird for his spirit in chusing the profession of a Soldier; and I like his choice most of all on another account.[301] Unless he had distinguished himself more at the bar or as a literary man than one is warranted before hand to expect of any young person, every one who feels for you as I do, would be in some degree mortified; but a good brave Soldier is son enough for any man. Your friend Richardson gives a most pleasing report of his fine handsome Soldierly appearance; and if he should be lucky enough to fall in love with an heiress, he will not be refused, tho' this last speculation I know you will never put into his head. This promotion will also be of use to your Daughters & will do a second son no harm. --- I hope the only part of your letter which did not give me pleasure, arose from the humour of the moment rather than any serious determination. Not after this undertake any work of consequence! a strong healthy man under fifty & the darling of the public to take such a notion into his head![302] <u>hoot awa'</u>![303]

I am here in my Brother's for a few days, and Mrs Baillie & all the members of the family are gratified by your kind remembrances. I am sorry to tell you the game you so kindly intended for Dr B. has not arrived, but he will be much pleased with your kind intentions towards him. I know that the passage from Inverness is but 4 or 5 days in favourable weather, but adverse winds may soon make all your Ptarmegan[304] & Black Grouse only fit to feed the fishes. --- We all unite in kind regards to yourself &

---

300. On 30 March 1820 the Prince Regent signed papers granting Scott and his male heirs the dignity of baronet.

301. Son Walter received his army commission on 4 July 1819. Scott sent letters of introduction for him to Ireland where he would be stationed, including one to Maria Edgeworth. Counting Walter's two horses, the cost of starting him in the cavalry was over £1,300 (Johnson, 680-82).

302. Scott actually very quickly started work on *The Monastery* (Johnson, 682).

303. hoot awa: nonsense (*SND*).

304. ptarmigan: a bird of the grouse family found in the highlands of Scotland (*OED*).

M<u>rs</u> Scott & my sweet young Friend Sophia. I hope soon to see you in London & hope, however unwilling you may be to come to this part of the world, that business will compell you. – I send you this single scrubby letter, because my heart is too full to wait several days for a cover; but I will write you by & by & express to you in a better manner, if I can, how truly I am gratified you do hold me amongst those who will rejoice at every thing that can add to the prosperity of your family. Believe me
    always affectionately yours
      J Baillie

3890 ff.3-5 (Address: Walter Scott Esq<u>r</u>--no postmark)
                            Hampstead Jan<u>ry</u> 7<u>th</u> 1819
My dear Friend,
    We went to Town yesterday to see Twelvth [*sic*] Night acted in Covent Garden, and dined at my Brother's where the most honoured & favorite dish was a brace of your Ptarmegan. They have arrived at last in most excellent condition; and I am charged by my Brother & more particularly by his good Wife to thank you heartily for such a dainty, bountiful & rare present. They likewise wish me to express to you how much they are gratified by your kind remembrance of them, and the interest they take in your wellfare which makes them feel great pleasure in hearing of any thing that can add to the happiness & prosperity of you & your family. I have had no occasion to keep prudently as I proposed a part of the information contained in your last letter but one, for I have been told by I dont know how many people that you are already made a Baronet which by the direction of this letter you will perceive I do not yet believe. –– But I have not done with the Ptarmegan; Agnes & I must thank you for our share. M<u>rs</u> B. gave us a brace home with us and we have been admiring them in their feathers. I suppose you call them white grouse: they are like Muir-fowl that have become white amongst the snow of a Norwegian winter. –– I like much what you tell me of your hogmanae[305] party particularly the young men who work for their Widow mothers & Brothers & sisters. I am pleased & proud of my native land when I think how much she excells this country in filial duty. A man very seldom works for any body here but his own wife & children; and this I believe is the consequence of our poor's laws. There is a trait of Cuddy in the tales of my Landlord that delighted me,[306] viz. that necessary union with his old Mother (even while he speaks to her with little reverence) which could

---

305. hogmanae: the 31st of December, New Year's Eve (*SND*).
306. Cuddie is the laborer who appears in Scott's *The Black Dwarf*, the first series of *Tales of my Landlord* (1816).

not in imagination be broken; for "how can I gang to be a Soldier (says he) ye're o'er old to sit cocking on the tap o' a baggage waggon we' the corporal's wife &c.["] It is a generous, excellent feeling and many good consequences arise from it. But I was pleased & surprised the other day to learn from a Clergyman settled in Northampton shire, that in his parish there is not a public house in which spirits of any kind can be bought: they are only licenced to sell beer. This for the credit of England must be set opposite to the virtue of your Hogmanae guests. Did you meet with Mrs Fry when she was in Edin^r?[307] She seems to act under the commission of an almighty Master & moves & persuades all who listen to her. We really hope to see great things effected by her means for bettering the morals of the corrupted & miserable culprits of our wicked metropolis. –– To return to a very different subject, the play we saw yesterday; I went to it expecting to be greatly entertained, for it is perhaps of all Shakespear's comedies the one that is best fitted for the stage: but excepting Sir Andrew Aguecheek by Farren,[308] the characters were indifferently acted, the dialogue ill heard & the witty scenes of the clown with the conceat [sic] of Malvolio producing little effect. After this came a pantomime so splendid & so full of fancy that I could not help saying the fabricator of all this must verily be a man of Genius. The house is lighted with gas from one grand chandelier in the ceiling and it gives a simple distinctness & unity of effect to the whole Theatre & its audience which is striking, – I may say grand. They go on, however after their old fashion with the stage and still depend for light almost entirely on foot-lamps, by which means the actors look like fools & the audience like wise people. But there is no help for it; they will sacrifice the head to the tail; the human countenance to red buskins & foil petticoats. ––

I was much pleased to day, before I left Grosvenor St. in reading a translation of Mrs Hunter's from the Italian of Pindemonti; verses addressed by him many years ago to her Daughter.[309] She is no[w] 73 and

---

307. Elizabeth Gurney Fry (1780-1845), early feminist and prison reformer, was the sister of Louisa Gurney, who was married to Sir Samuel Hoare. See June Rose, *Elizabeth Fry* (New York: St. Martin's P, 1980).

308. Actor William Farren (1786-1861) made his acting debut in 1806. He came from Dublin to Covent Garden in 1818, acting the roles of Sir Peter Teazle, Sir Anthony Absolute, Sir Andrew Augecheeck and others.

309. Anne Home Hunter (1742-1821), writer and oldest daughter of surgeon Everard Home, married Baillie's uncle Dr. John Hunter in 1771. Of her four children two survived her, son John and daughter Agnes. Anne Hunter published *Sports of the Genii* (1797) and miscellaneous poems throughout her life, some of which were included in Baillie's 1823 *Collection*. Ippolito Pindemonte (1753-1823), Italian traveler and writer, published *Poesie* (1785), *Prose campestri* (1795) and a translation of the *Odyssey* on which he worked for 15 years; he was influenced by

writes with as much elegance & ease as she ever did & is awake to every affection & innocent amusement like a young person. Perhaps you have read Mr Hobhouse's notes to Lord Byron's last Canto of Child Harold. The Lady mentioned there, to whom the Marquis de Pindemonte was so much attached while in England, is her Daughter, now Lady Campbell & still very handsome.[310] I remember seeing Pindamonte at Mrs Hunter's evening parties frequently; a great Beau of those days with a striped coat & cut steel buttons & every thing about him so delicate & trim that he looked as if he had come out of a bandbox. I little thought to read of him afterwards in a printed book as one of the first writers in Italy. -- Lady Byron, whom you enquire after, is I believe at present not in very good health but by no means ill. I heard from her about a month ago when she did not mention her health, and I have heard of her very lately. She is happy at present in the company of an old & dear Friend Miss Montgomery from whom she had been separated for a good many years but I fear her spirits are often depressed & that affects her health. -- We spent our Hogmanae with your Friend Richardson, and in his house there is always hearty kindness & good cheer & honourable mention of you. -- My spirits received a damp at that time from the death of your excellent Towns woman Mrs Brampton. She must be much lamented for the useful worth of her character, her distinguished abilities & the melancholy circumstances of her death. ---
Fare well! I can think of nothing more to say, even to fill up the end of this page. My Sister desires me to give her kind remembrances to you & Mrs Scott. Many happy Hogmanaes may you spend at Abbotsford with your happy family & virtuous Labourers about you! -- Believe me always, my dear Friend,

    gratefully & affectionately yours
      J Baillie

3890 ff.132-135 (Address: Walter Scott Esq / Melrose--postmarked 1819)
                  Hampstead June 18th 1819

My dear Friend,
    Your kind letter of the 7th of April is before me in which you cheered me greatly by reporting yourself to be really a convalescent, but alas I know that you have had a severe attack from the enemy since that

---

Thomas Gray and James Macpherson, and his *Abaritte* is an imitation of Johnson's *Rasselas* (*Dictionary of Catholic Biography*, ed. John Delaney and James Edward Tobin [New York: Doubleday, 1961], 936).

    310. Lady Campbell, Agnes Hunter, surviving daughter of Dr. John Hunter and Anne Home Hunter, married Sir James Campbell; after his death, she married Col. Benjamin Charlewood, retaining her title. She had no children.

time.[311] I hear that you are again a convalescent, and I wish & pray you may remain a longer time in that state and have much less pain to endure from the next attack, for to expect that you will be relieved from it entirely for a good while to come, would I fear be vain. Does what you say in this letter of the pain giving way more readily in that same warm bath where you lie like a <u>haulded</u>[312] salmon than it used to do, still continue to hold good? if it does it is indeed a very hopefull circumstance, tho' the fits were to be both frequent & severe. People here say that you are coming to Cheltenham, and if this be so, you will no doubt proceed afterwards to London, where my spent eyes (for I can do nothing now without spectacles) will be gladen'd with the sight of you, tho' I must not look to see the same healthy vigorous countenance that I parted with some years gone by. You will then come to Town when there will be few people in it to plague you, and my Brother has got a country house very near London for the season, so you will be very near your Doctor if he should be wanted. —

All the world, since Sunday se'nnight, have been busy reading the new tales of my Landlord, and I feel myself covered with honour & glory in being therein mentioned in terms so very exalted.[313] I dont pretend to dive into mysteries, but I'm sure that Walter Scott his own self wrote the passage I allude to, tho' the Grand Cham of Tartary should have written all the rest; for there is no body but him who takes any pleasure in praising me. I am, as we say in Clyde'sdale, very <u>vogay</u>[314] of it, tho' I try to behave myself as modestly as may be. The Bride of Lamer Muir [*sic*] is exceedingly & almost painfully interesting: the Lovers there are the most engaging & interesting of all Jedediah Clieshbottom's [*sic*] lovers, and the tone of the whole notwithstanding the lightning up of Caleb, who would make a most notable character in a farce, is so melancholy that it left a gloom upon my mind for a long time after I had finished the story.[315] Tho' I do not wish to dwell upon this subject there is one scene between the old Hags, as they are preparing to <u>staught</u>[316] the corpse, which struck me as fearfully natural & original; and before Mͬ Clieshbottom or Pattieson give

---

311. Scott was very ill for most of the early part of 1819; see Johnson for detailed accounts.

312. hauld or haud: kept, confined (*SND*).

313. I have not identified the passage to which Baillie refers in *The Bride of Lammermoor*.

314. vogey or vogie: proud (*SND*).

315. There was considerable controversy over the new edition of *Tales of My Landlord*, containing *The Bride of Lammermoor*, because Scott changed publishers (see Johnson for details). *The Bride of Lammermoor*, which Johnson calls the "most perfectly constructed of all Scott's novels," appeared in 1819 (670). Jedediah Cleishbotham was Scott's pseudonym.

316. straught or straucht: lay out [the corpse] (*SND*).

up writing tales as has been so seriously threaten'd to the great dismay of thousands & ten of thousands of grateful & admiring readers, I would fain have him to give us a tale to be called the Witch. It would be connected with much curious history of human nature & of the times, when so many people were executed for witch craft, confessing the crime. I can see in the scene just mentioned a metaphysical view of the subject glimmering through the infernal dialogue of those hags, their own malevolence & envy associating them in their own imaginations with the Devil; and this pursued in the powerful & masterly manner in which it would be pursued by the Author that you wot of, would be a most valuable & striking work. The author of <u>Marriage</u> or any other author whatever, cannot take this up, tho' they may pursue with some success the peculiar manners of the Scotch Highlanders.[317] Pray let this matter be taken into consideration, for these said Hags have created in me a prodigious hankering after it. The bewitching of Lord Torphichen's son caused the death of many reputed witches both young & old, so the story need not be confined to old women.[318] I can imagine a malevolent mind in those days by degrees actually believing that it acted by power from the devil, and to trace those steps would be very curious & subtle & give much insight into human nature.

I sent my play by some <u>safe hand</u> which our friend Richardson found out a great while ago, but I have heard no tidings of its arrival. I hope it has proved a safe hand: a diffidence approaching perhaps to foolishness prevented me from applying to Mr Freeling. I have some time ago corrected & altered & copied out fair all my 3 Metrical Legends viz of William Wallace, Lady G. Baillie & Columbus. To this last in the way of reflection or imagery I have added nearly a third, besides altering all that you

---

317. Susan Ferrier's (1782-1854) first work, *Marriage: a Novel*, appeared in two volumes in 1818, the theme of which is virtue rewarded and pride abased, describing the happy and unhappy consequences of marrying for love. Ferrier's father's friendship with Scott gained her easy access into Edinburgh literary society (Todd, 242-43).

318. James Sandilands (d. 1579), first Lord Torphichen, Lanarkshire, had a son (d. 1579) who was in 1543 appointed preceptor of Torphichen and head of the order in Scotland, supporting the Reformation and approving the privy council's *Book of Discipline* in 1561. Baillie takes up the subject of witchcraft in her play *Witchcraft: A Tragedy in Prose, In Five Acts*, in whose preface she credits a scene in Scott's *Bride of Lammermoor* for inspiration and explains that "Soon after the publication of that powerful and pathetic novel, I mentioned my thoughts upon the subject to Sir W. Scott, and urged him to pursue the new path he had just entered into. That I was unsuccessful in my suit, and failed to persuade him to undertake the subject, all his warm admirers - and who are not? - must regret, - a regret that will not be diminished by the perusal of the Tragedy on Witchcraft" (*DPW*, 613).

directly found fault with; for tho' you did not for fear of discouraging me too much, absolutely tell me that the poem was dry & bare, I had gumption enough to guess at your thoughts, and I hope I have profited by your opinion as much as if you had really set it down in black & white. I want to know from you how I should proceed in offering this small volume of poetry to the Booksellers. Unless I get a thousand guineas for it I will not publish at all. I mean to give Mr Longman the first offer, and should he decline it, as probably he will, I would offer it next to Constable or Murray or any body you would advise me to.[319] This same immortal Joanna Baillie should be held in some estimation even amongst the Booksellers, and after being so yclepted[320] by such high authority, perhaps – perhaps a thousand guineas is too little for her. –– Give this important point a turn or two in your sagacious brain and write to me concerning it entirely at your own leisure, for a month hence will do just as well as at present. If you do not come to London this summer I will send you the Legend of Lady Grizeld to read, as I think you expressed a wish to see it. ––– I wish my play, should Mrs H. Siddons bring it out, may have a fourth part of the success of Rob Roy and I shall be quite satisfied. Jeany [*sic*] Deans, who is a very popular personage in this country, charmed & moved the audience much more at the little surry Theatre than she did at Covent Garden, for there they kept to the original story & Jeany procures her Sister's pardon by Argyle from the Queen; but your friend Terry to conform more to what are called the rules of the drama, has ground down this most striking & pleasing feature of the story to mere common place – the Judge turning out the young man's Father &c! But I heard a scandalous story whispered the other day, that you yourself was in some degree art & part with Terry in this nefarious improvement. O fye shame, if this be so. How could you treat your great author Mr Pattieson with so little respect. –– I think you are hard upon the elder & great Mrs Siddons. Her manner is too solemn & her voice too deep for familiar society, and having her mind little stored except with what is connected with her profession, and thinking at the same that every one who spoke to her expected to hear her mouth utter some striking thing, she uttered many things not very well suited to the occasion; but I think she has a mind which has been occupied in observing what past within itself, and has therefore drawn her acting from a deeper source than actors generally do, besides her native talent for expressing emotions; and I think she has a quick perception of humour & character in other's, at least she tells a humorous anecdote, not withstanding her deep toned voice, very droly. She was received in Lady Randolf as you would

319. Longman did, in fact, take Baillie's *Metrical Legends*.
320. yclept: called (*OED*).

read in the papers,[321] with the greatest warmth & respect, and I have heard from those who sat near enough the stage to hear & see well that she acted with all her wonted power & still look'd noble & beautiful. I heartily agree with you that we shall never see her like again or one approaching within many degrees of her excellence.

I suppose you are now in your own romantic Town which, however, romantic as it is will not make amends for leaving the fields & braes, and woods (that are to be) of Abbotsford. Give my kindest wishes to Mrs Scott & Sophia. We shall get acquainted with your young Laird by & by if it be true, as I hear, that he is going to enter into the Guards. In all kind regard to you & yours Agnes joins me heartily. Believe me always, my dear Friend,

most gratefully & affectionately yours
J Baillie

3890 ff.216-217 (No address or postmark)

Hampstead Novr 12th 1819

My dear Friend,

A great while ago in your last letter to me, you kindly desired me to send you my Legend of Lady Griseld Baillie, hinting at the same time that I might do so by means of Mr Freeling. Now, from a slight circumstance, yet too tedious to mention and perhaps from an over-strained delicacy, I am not very fond of making use of this mode of conveyance; I therefore put off doing so in hopes our friend Richardson who then spoke of going to Scotland, would carry it; but being disappointed of this view, I bethought myself of what I had rejected and should have sent it to you (as I now do) by Mr Freeling a good while since, had I not, on consulting our said friend, learnt that you were more likely to be at leisure to read it on returning to Edin^r than during your abode at Abbotsford, where, as Poet, Host, country Laird & Sheriff, you are like to be torn to pieces by clients & neighbours & travellers from all parts of the earth & of all degrees. I hope I have judged right, and that it will reach you at a time when you may look over it without such inconvenience to yourself. I told you in my last that with the three Legends of Wallace, Columbus, Lady Griseld & four Ballads (one of which is the story of Fadon's Ghost which I did not chuse to put into the Legends)[322] and with a slight preface & notes, I have matter by me for a

---

321. Sarah Siddons still gave private performances after her retirement from the stage; Lady Randolph was one of her greatest roles, along with Lady Macbeth, Belvidera and Queen Catherine.

322. Baillie's mysterious *The Ghost of Fadon* is taken, she explains in her introduction to her 1851 collected edition, "from the story of Fadon in the Blind Minstrel's Life of Wallace" (*DPW*, 710).

small volume which I would willingly publish, provided I receive for it my price, viz a thousand guineas, and begged to receive your advice as to how I should set about this momentous traffic. I wish first to offer it to my neighbour Mr Longman, but if he should decline it, you must tell me who to offer it to next. If I dont receive my price, I dont publish for two good reasons, first that my chief object at present is the money, & secondly that a volume of poetry for which a Bookseller will not give a thousand pounds in these times ought not to be published. I received a letter from Mrs H. Siddons some time ago simply acknowledging the receipt of the Play which I sent her and informing me that she had sent it to you & should make no alterations to fit it for the stage without your approbation. Thus you see I make no scruple in teasing you with all my matters. You have allowed me as a kind of Sister Poet, Friend & Country Woman to take a strong hold of you, to make a kind of property of your good will & good nature, and so in truth I do.

Tho' I have not heard from you for a long time, I have lost no opportunity of hearing of you and am glad that none of those reports make any mention of your having had any severe attack; I therefore hope that you have gained ground considerably and that I shall have the pleasure of hearing this confirmed by yourself by & by. I regretted very much not having seen your young soldier when he passed thro' London; and had I received notice in time, I should have gone to Town to see him and satisfied my interest & curiosity without giving him much trouble. I hope he is a steady young man, for with all his advantages of figure, parentage & prospects he is in danger of being spoilt. If his change of quarters in Ireland should take him any where near the county of Longford, he will have a host of Ladies to seize upon him from Edgeworthtown. I never receive a letter from the celebrated Lady of that place in which there is not honourable mention made of you with generally some sly hankerings expressed after information which I cannot give – "What will he do next? – He'll write Dramas, yes yes! Old Play will come out at last" I dont know how it is, but this Old Play quoted so frequently in the notes (I believe) of the Antiquary has run in her imagination wonderfully. She talks of going abroad next spring to get out of the way of the critics when the memoirs of her Father are to be published. ––– My Sister has been at Paris since I wrote to you last. She has seen the Gay city with its palaces, some religious processions & peasantry dancing of a Sunday, bought a cheap gown or two & taken a great fancy to the politics of the Parisian Grisettes; and now she is by her own fireside again ready to join the conversation with a good grace when travell'd people come into the house, a thing now of no rare occurrence. She has got all this satisfaction at a cheap rate and I am glad she has been in France (indeed I advised her to go) but O! how I grumble & grieve at the numbers of our countrymen who go abroad to reside for a considerable time – some for years with their families! This is most unpatriotic & unjust. There is a set of goers to France too for whom I have neither sympathy nor charity; The English Gourmand, who go almost every holy day time to Paris to drink champagne & eat ragouts at a cheap rate. I could almost wish that the Radicals had the clapper-clawing of such people for a short time, just as Madge says in the Gentle shepherd "to shake their harrigles a wee."[323] –– I went with my Brother into Gloucester Sh in the end of the summer to look at the trees Agnes & I had helped to plant so many summers ago. The birch & firs of all kinds are doing well, but our oaks & ashes & even beeches make very little progress indeed. There is something generous in people past middle age who delight in planting. However, even a young fir growing from the green sward[324] is better than an orange tree in a tub. ––-

Give my kindest regards to Mrs Scott & my love to Sophia, – give my kindest wishes to all that belong to you. I hope I shall see you all once more in our own dear north country. God bless you & restore you to perfect health!

your affectionate friend
J Baillie

3891 ff.3-4 (Address: Walter Scott Esqr / to the care of Mr Richardson--no postmark)

Hampstead Jan^ry 9th 1820

My dear Friend

I truly sympathize with you in your present sorrow for the great breach which it has pleased God to make amongst those who are most dear to you. It is indeed a fatal sweep & very extraordinary, and makes a solemn — I might almost say awful impression on the mind. When Death leads away from us a group of friends at once, we may well stand aghast. But you have much to sooth[e] your grief particularly in all that concerns her whom I believe you justly call your excellent Mother.[325] She has

---

323. See Act IV of Allan Ramsay's pastoral comedy *The Gentle Shepherd*:
   Madge: I think I have towzled his harigalds a wee!
   He'll no soon greiv to tell his love to me.
See *The Poems of Allan Ramsay*, 2 vols. (London: Cadell and Davies, 1800), 2:104.
   324. sward: tangled mess (*SND*).
   325. Scott's mother, Anne Scott, died on 24 December 1819. She had continued to live comfortably at her small home on George Street to her 87th year, refusing monetary help from her son and annually devoting £300 of her income to charity. Her granddaughters had been to drink tea with her on 12 December, finding her vivacious and telling them the differences in the real story of the Bride of Lammermoor and her

enjoyed life to the last; and being a person of the character you describe, you must be conscious that you yourself, in your course of prosperity & honour, have made a great part of that enjoyment, & a healing balm for misfortunes which the Mother of a family is liable to meet in this trying world: and at her advanced age, you must have looked forward to the near approach of her end, not knowing what bodily sufferings lay before her. She has now had an easy end, and that great anxiety is removed from your mind; and being well prepared to die, by having lived a pious life, we call it a happy end. I speak the more feelingly upon this subject, because my poor Mother (a person also of spirit & of worth) died at the age of 85, after having been four years blind & two of those years confined entirely to bed, with many infirmities, & still mind enough left to be sensible of them. ——

I need not tell you how glad I shall be to see you in March. There are many times since I saw you last when I would have been very thankful to be well assured that I should ever see you again. I must make the most of the little time you will have to bestow upon me, for you will be torn to pieces here amongst contending friends & those who are no friends but vain admirers who would make themselves a little consequence at your expence.[326] May you be able for your health's sake to stear your way wisely amidst all this hurly-burly! You say nothing of your health & report says you are weak, so I trust it is so. ——— I am glad you have been pleased with Lady Griseld [sic], and I thank you for your advice regarding the bookselling matters. Nevertheless, tho' it is good advice for a popular author, I take it to be bad advice for me. I have experience how those fare who publish with an agreement to receive half the fair profits, and it is of a most discouraging kind. When Booksellers give a price for a work, they bestir themselves to promote the sale of it; when this is not the case they are careless; and it is only a very popular writer who may be deemed independent of their care. I shall therfore [sic] offer it for a Thousand pounds to Longman & should he decline it, to some other of the Trade, & should they all refuse it (which may likely enough be the case) I shall e'en let it remain amongst my other Mss. for the advantage of my heirs.[327]

---

son's handling of the tale. The following day she suffered a sudden stroke; Scott also lost an uncle and aunt (Rutherford) in the space of a few days (Johnson, 692-93).

326. When Scott did arrive in March to receive his baronetcy, he spent a quiet Sunday in Hampstead with Baillie and John Richardson and was then plunged into a round of entertainment (Johnson, 702-3).

327. Scott suggested to Baillie (1 January 1820) that Longman or any other bookseller would make money by giving her the sum she was asking but explains further that he had

> ... found great comfort in making my returns from a work contingent by selling only one edition at a time the bookseller paying all expences and

— I am quite sorry that my Tragedy cannot be of any use to Mrs H. Siddons. It would have been a great pleasure to me had it been otherwise; and if I had any other Play amongst my Mss that I thought more likely to succeed on her Theatre, I would send it to her frankly. Pray if you have opportunity, tell her so. I would write to her now myself, but this is to go in a frank of Richardsons and there is no room for more. I am much obliged to you for the trouble you have taken in reading the play & considering of it, and am convinced that your decision has not been lightly grounded. I hope, however, that as Mrs Siddons has made so much this last year by the unprecedented run of Rob Roy, that this little disappointment will be of no consequence to her. If she were really in difficulties I would endeavour to write some lighter domestic drama for her, but you will readily allow that to write for a particular set of actors who are unknown to me, would be rather puzzling. — What a pleasing picture you give of your Mountain Shepherds with their Grey plaid & Jackets of their own forest green. Would all the cloth & wearing apparel in Europe were made in the same simple manner as those grey plaids! We should have no starving weavers or turbulent cotton spinners for wicked people to practise upon. We are all now even in this part of the world beginning to believe that the danger is over.[328] I hope your duty with your gallant Mountaineers will prove an easy one, and how gratifying it must have been to be chosen by such men for their Leader! Every body here is reading or has read I venture, and almost worship, the beautiful character of Rebecca.[329]

I beg to be kindly remembered to Mrs Scott & Sophia, and my Sister prays also to be so remembered. Many happy new years may you all see!

ever truly & gratefully yours

J Baillie

---

ensuring me half of the free profits by granting bills for that amount at publication. . . . But as to your right to ask £1000 if you prefer that plan to mine I think it cannot be doubted. A first edition in 4to would clear the booksellers. . . .
(Grierson, 6:96)

328. Given the date of this letter, Baillie is almost certainly referring to the dangerous unrest incited by the "Peterloo Massacre" in Manchester in August 1819 (see Elie Halevy, *The Liberal Awakening*, vol. 2 of *A History of the English People*, trans. E. I. Watkin [1926; London: Ark, 1987]).

329. *Ivanhoe* was published in 1819.

3891 ff.136-137 (Address: Sir Walter Scott Bart / Abbotsford / near
Melrose--postmarked 1820)

The Hill Creetown 12th Oct^r [1820]

My dear Sir Walter,

Nothing can be kinder than your welcome letter which I received
yesterday, and I was about to write an answer this morning and accept
thankfully of the proposed Beau whom you offered for our companion to
London, when your second letter arrived. I hope, however, we shall see
this same young man at Abbotsford before he set out on his journey, tho' it
should make us (as I doubt not it will) regret still more that we cannot
have the pleasure of travelling in his company.[330] I was just thinking that
him & I would have some games by the road of Travellers picquet, if you
know what that is, a cat looking out of a window being the highest-card of
the pack, and an amusement by no means to be despised on a flat dull road
which one as [has?] often travelled before. — You are very kind in
wishing us to make a longer visit but we have reasons against this which
ought to enable us even to withstand so great a temptation, but I will not
enter into particulars till I see you. You say there is room enough to lodge us
tho' Lord & Lady Compton are to be your guests at the same time. Tell
Lady Scott that one room will serve my Sister & I; we frequently lodge so
and have no objection to it.[331] I mention this because I know that great
people with their servants take up much room. — I have also to thank you
for offering to send your carriage to meet us, and if it be perfectly
convenient, we should be glad to have it for the last stage, as it would then
carry us to Abbotsford without fear of taking a wrong road. The way we
mean to go is by Annon, where we mean to stay a night with Mrs Dirom at
Mount Annon,[332] and the stages between that & Melrose we marked down,
but the list is left at Dumfries & I have forgot them. We hope to set out
from Mount Annon to Abbotsford on thursday the 26 or 27th, but this
depends upon our answer from Mrs Dirom to whom we have not yet written;

---

330. Scott's son Charles, now 15, was enroute to London and on to Wales to
study with the Reverend Mr. Williams (Johnson, 716).

331. Joanna and Agnes visited Abbotsford in November 1820 at the same time
that Lady Compton was there. Anne Scott, then 17, was charmed with Joanna and
declared, "No one would ever guess by her behaviour that she was an authoress" (qtd.
in Johnson, 718).

332. This was the wife of Alexander Dirom (d. 1830) of Dumfriesshire. He was
author of *A Narrative of the Campaign in India Which Terminated the War with Tipoo
Sultan* (1793) and minor works such as *An Inquiry into the Corn Laws and Corn Trade
of Great Britain* (1796) and *Account of the Improvement on the Estate of Mount Annan*
(1811) (Lambertson, cxxv-cc, and *DNB*, V:1001). Lieut. Dirom also contributed
"Annan Water" to Baillie's 1823 *A Collection of Poems, Chiefly Manuscript.*

should she not receive our visit, we will gladly come to you a day sooner.

We have got here a bright day at last to enjoy the shores of Wigton bay which have wood & hills & cultivation to beautify them, while the sea when the tide is in appears like a fine lake. One enjoys a bright day at this season doubly, because dull days are before us; not sentimentally, but in the good homely way of "Lets be merry while we may." I am more at my ease and more cheerful here, being with friends whom we shall leave with the hope of meeting very soon again.

Agnes is much pleased with your kind remembrance of her, and joins me heartily in thanks & kindest wishes to you & Lady Scott & Miss Scott, not forgetting our young Beau that might have been. I will trouble you again with a few lines from Dumfries to which we return saturday 21st to our friend Miss Wight in Waterloo Place, in the mean time believe me my dear friend

most truly & gratefully yours
J Baillie

867 ff.80-82 (Address: Sir Walter Scott B$^\text{t}$--no postmark)

Hampstead Nov$^\text{r}$ 27th 1820

My dear Sir Walter,

Knowing that you have heard from our Neighbour Richardson of our safe arrival at Hampstead, I have delayed writing to you till now. I have had several letters to write with grateful acknowledgements to make for much kindness received in our native land, but none which I have written with more grateful & gratified feelings than the present, tho' it is the last. Both my Sister & myself beg that you & Lady Scott & Miss Scott will accept our very hearty thanks for all your daily & hourly kindness shewn to us at Abbotsford; a pleasure to us which passed hastily away in one sense, but will in another last with us thro' life. -- The friendly face of your Coachman John, as he came in to the parlour to take leave of us at Selkirk, was the last <u>kent</u>[333] face that smiled on us in Scotland, and then was felt ourselve[s] set loose amongst entire strangers to pursue our Southward journey as we might. We travelled on with our fellow passengers in the Mail in darkness & silence (or nearly so) till we got to Carlile [*sic*], and there we took in a broad, open (open)-faced, talkative, middle aged man, who was very entertaining company for us till we got within two stages of Manchester. He had a self-satisfied look & an air of consequence about him, yet his notions both on religious & political subjects seemed to me enlightened & reasonable; and had it not been for

---

333. kent: dial. and p.p. of ken, understanding, knowing (*OED*).

certain misgivings in my own mind, when he began to talk of 17 thousand acres of property in Wales & other great matters, I should have been much pleased with our Companion. The other Passenger, whom we had likewise taken in at Carlile where the Selkirk people left us, was a sleek, rosy, good natured Englishman, who did not seem quite so liberal in his notions, and appeared as if he would have gainsaid him now & then had it not been for the fear of getting himself into trouble. -- an easy Poke pudding, who declared to us, that he was no epicure for he would eat anything if it were good of its kind & well cooked. In going out of Bolton a stage short of Manchester, the night was so foggy that the coachman took the wrong road, and the weel [sic] going somewhat to our side, he got off the box and took one of the lights from the carriage with which he looked close along the ground as if he had been in search of something he had dropped, when he discovered that we were close upon the edge of a marl-pit. This was the only danger we were in during our journey, from which, thank God! we escaped not only unhurt but unfrightened, not knowing of the peril till it was over. – We stayed, as you advised, all night at Manchester & next day pursued our journey, not in the Mail, but a post coach, holding only four passengers, and fully more convenient every way. Our Fellow travellers there were, I believe, two Barresters, for they talked in an under voice to one another a great deal about cases & evidence & circuits & sessions &c and seemed to have mighty little desire to enter into conversation with two elderly Gentlewomen. A stage short of London, they humanely, (as night was coming on) gave up their places to a decent dressed woman who was an outside Traveller with three children. This change at first pleased us much, but they were spoilt children & exceedingly restless, and set up such a crying & murmuring & skirling,[334] for perfect waywardness, that we seemed to be packed up for the rest of the way with a nest of little fiends. It was in vain that we took them on our laps to soothe them & their poor silly Mother kept coaxing and calling them good children; there was no peace for us till we came to the Peacock in Islington, when we were transferred with all our baggage to a hackney coach which carried us to my Brother's in Cavendish Sq^r about 10 o'clock on the monday evening. There we had the pleasure of finding all the family in good health & receiving a very hearty welcome; for indeed nothing but such a welcome would have gone well down with us after all the kindness we had been accustomed to from the friends we had left in our ain countrie.

Thus I have given you a slight detail of our journey and I make no apology for doing so, tho' savouring somewhat of egoism, as I know their [sic] is nothing I could write you which you would be better pleased to

---

334. skirling: dial., screaming, whining (*OED*).

hear. — We have just dined out once since we returned here, at Mr Hoare the Bankers, where we met Mr Wordsworth, his wife & sister, just returned from a tour thro Switzerland. I sat next him and it would have done you good to have seen with how much pleasure he listened to my account of Abbotsford and the Bard with all his Inmates dwelling there. He is thin but has got rid of a complaint in his eyes which some months ago threatened him with the loss of sight. He is going home with a mind full stored with Lake, clouds, & Mountains for the benefit of the next poem he writes, which from what I learnt afterward from Mrs Hoare, will probably be the continuation of the Wanderer.[335] — My good housewifry [sic] was sorely taxed some ten days ago with paying sixteen pence for clay candlesticks to illuminate for the Queen. We were not very zealous here, but we did not like to have great scores to pay to the Glaziers.[336] However, the Boys had a famous bonfire on the heath in which were burnt a very fat & a very thin figure, called Majocchi & Sacci, after having their heads well soaced [socked] with a great green bag that was afterwards thrown into the fire also. ——— I am now busy preparing the notes for my Legends, a business which I detest; and you would laugh well in your sleeve if you saw how I am perplexed & bewildered for a whole day copying & arranging what would scarcely take you a whole hour. The craft of pen & Ink certainly does not come to me by nature any more than the craft of rhiming.

I hope this will find you all comfortably settled in Castle street. Pray give our kindest regards to Lady & Miss Scott & also to Mrs Lockhart, who I hope is well. We beg likewise to be remembered to Mr Lockhart. ——

---

335. 1820 brought a 4-volume edition entitled *The Miscellaneous Poems of William Wordsworth* which included bibliographical material and edited poems that Wordsworth now regarded as his canon of miscellaneous work. By 11 July 1820 he was again traveling to Calais with Mary, Dorothy and Thomas Monkhouse and party. The tour was a "reenactment of formative experience," writes Stephen Gill, but Wordsworth was 50 now (338). Determined to return to the Alps at the end of the journey, he and his party went first to Belgium to the battlefield of Waterloo, moving on to the Cologne Cathedral, the Rhine Gorge, and Falls at Schaffhausen and into the mountains. While Mary and Dorothy wrote accounts of the journey, Wordsworth produced only a series of unimaginative poems, published in 1822 as *Memorials of A Tour on the Continent, 1820*. The tour ended in Paris, where Mary met Annette Vallon for the first time; they returned to England in November 1820 (see Stephen Gill, *William Wordsworth: A Life* [Oxford: Clarendon, 1989], 336-40).

336. The reign of George IV was just beginning, and though he and his wife Caroline of Brunswick openly loathed each other, she assumed the title of queen. George IV had spent months, if not years, in prolonged scandal and had been long unpopular with the nation.

Farewell! my dear friend, and believe me always
gratefully & affectionately yours
J Baillie
PS. Mrs Hunter is considerably better and may likely enough last thro' the
winter. She suffers no pain but is always in bed.[337] – –

3653 ff.26-27 (No address or postmark)
My dear Sir Walter
This is to certify that the writer of the inclosed letter is a Gentleman
who has been known to myself & to all the members of our family for many
years, and a person whose account of the matters detailed in it may be
depended upon. –– He begged that I would send you a line or two to this
effect, supposing that you may be teased with many letters on similar
subjects from designing & interested people and therefore pay little
attention to such information from a mere stranger. ——

As I have heard nothing from good authority to the contrary, I would
fain hope that you are coming to London by & by to sit again to Sir T.
Lawrence &c &c but general report now says that you are not coming. ———
Well & happy may you be wherever you are! but I would rather behold i t
with mine own eyes than hear of it from any body. —— With all kind
regards to Lady Scott and both your Daughters, in which my Sister joins me
with right good will, I remain
affectionately yours
J Baillie
Hampstead
May 29th [1821][338]

---

337. Baillie's aunt Anne Home Hunter died in 1821.

338. Edgar Johnson writes that Scott sat for a painting for Lawrence in 1821
(728). Lawrence's biographer dates the Scott portrait's completion as 1827, when it
was displayed in the Royal Academy (Douglas Goldring, *Regency Portrait Painter:
The life of Sir Thomas Lawrence, P.R.A.* [London: Macdonald, 1951], 312). And in a
letter to Scott dated 18 November 1829 the Hon. Robert Peel, for supplying the writer
with some letters from the Duke of Montrose regarding Rob Roy, information
pertinent to Scott's novel, asks that Scott sit to Sir Thomas Lawrence so that the
portrait might be added to his collection of "Illustrious Men of the Age" (see Grierson).
In keeping with other letters about the painting, I would date this 1821. Biographers
Johnson and Goldring are probably correct, for the portrait is still in progress in
1825 (see letter 3900 ff.93-94 below).

3893 ff.21-24 (Address: Sir Walter Scott Bar$^{\underline{t}}$ / Abbotsford / Melrose-- postmarked 1821)

Hampstead August 3$^{\underline{d}}$ 1821

My dear Friend,

One of the gratifying sights which I expected to enjoy from the coronation,[339] was a sight of your face but this as well as every other pleasure connected with it has been denied me, and the brightness of the rockets cast up from primrose hill, and as much light as we could produce from our own windows by the means of 4 doz$^{\underline{n}}$ of clay candlesticks, has been all the satisfaction which this grand event has afforded me, by my immediate eye sight, for I say nothing of discriptions from others. However, I do not complain; for as for not seeing your face, when I learnt how short a time you remained in Town and how you were engaged I considered it as a thing altogether out of the question; and the short call you made in Cavendish Sq$^{\underline{r}}$, and your great kindness in going up stairs to see the Old Lady, when you learnt M$^{\underline{rs}}$ Baillie was out, has put you in the greatest favour with the whole family; and the same Old Lady is so elevated therewith, that I doubt if a call from the King himself with the crown upon his head could have made her prouder.[340] As for the solemn & splendid shew in the Abbey & the hall, it was neither want of interest in the occasion nor want of curiosity that kept me away, but simply this, that no body offered me a ticket; and it was too great a favour to ask of those, who had them to give, having all relations & connections of their own to oblige. Good D$^{\underline{r}}$ Bell,[341] one of the Prebendaries, offered indeed the only ticket he had to dispose of to my Sister or I, but it was too late then for either of us to get to Town & be properly prepared. Your having been there, under such favourable circumstances, we all consider as a public benefit and hope to profit by it in good time. — Had I not expected to see you, I should have written to you some time ago in answer to your letter concerning Mackie. As far as was in my power, I did your bidding. M$^{\underline{rs}}$ Baillie, after taking every pains to learn the night of his acting could not find it out in time, and was therefore unluckily engaged with a formal dinner party a t

---

339. The coronation of George IV took place on 19 July 1821 for which Scott came briefly to London.

340. This is probably a mention of the dying Anne Hunter.

341. It is likely this is Sir Charles Bell (1774-1842), who was elected a fellow of the College of Surgeons of Edinburgh in 1799 and moved to London in 1804 where he met Dr. Matthew Baillie. Bell's *Anatomy of Expression* appeared in 1806, *The Nervous System of the Human Body* in 1830, in addition to many other works on the nervous system. He received the medal of the Royal Society in 1829 for his discoveries and returned to Scotland in 1836 as chair of surgery at the University of Edinburgh (*DNB*, II:154-57).

home on that day, but Lady Campbell took her place and we mustered a pretty strong party, who were all highly delighted with Mackie's Baillie Jervy, and also I think, better than Macready tho Macready acts it very well.[342] Our neighbours the Carrs also took a box & filled it well & your friend Richardson was not behind hand in all friendly zeal. But I need say no more on this subject as you must be perfectly informed regarding the compleat success of your favorite actor. The postcript [*sic*] of your letter was not thrown away upon me neither. M̲ṟ̲ṣ̲ Baillie got the anals [*sic*] of the parish forthwith, and I read with much satisfaction about one half of it, when by cross luck the book was sent out of the house to be lent to some good friend of hers, and I have been plaguing our Hampstead circulating Library man about it ever since. For I am obliged to go to work in this wimbling[343] way for my learning, my purse being always at so low an ebe [*sic*] that I have difficulty enough to get a gown to my back & shoes to my feet, letting alone books of either prose or poetry. I have had better luck, however, regarding the other work you mentioned, — Valerius.[344] I have got it from the Hampstead Library for 2^d a night and read it out stoup & roup,[345] as we say in the west of Scotland. I was the more interested in this because I know it is written by a friend of yours and from having written a Drama on a similar subject (as I told you at Abbotsford) myself.[346] There is great power of discription in the work, and the delineation of roman manners is animated & pleasing. I was very much pleased with the scenes at the roman villa, at the amphitheatre & the execution of the Traitor in the court of the prison, and in short the whole of the first volume interested me much; but the second pleased me less and the ending was not satisfactory. I disliked the mixture of humorous characters in the work, such as Drom & the other drole whose name I forget, because they did not seem to me good of their kind, and unbecomingly introduced into such a serious subject, as if the author had not himself a very deep feeling or respect for religion or else was afraid of being thought to have it. However, I except from this censure the humours of the amphitheatre with the monkey dancing &c which are so characteristic of the roman

---

342. Baillie must refer to actor Mackay here, who had first taken the role of the Bailie in Scott's 1819 Edinburgh production of *Rob Roy*. William Macready regularly acted at Drury Lane and Covent Garden and was in a renewed 5-year term at the date of this letter, though I find no mention of the role to which Baillie alludes. In a letter dated 11 June 1821, Scott asks Baillie to attend Mackay's one-night performance as Baillie Nicol Jarvie at Covent Garden (Grierson, 6:464).

343. Baillie must mean wimpling here, i.e., meandering (*SND*).

344. Lockhart's Roman Briton novel *Valerius* was published in 1821.

345. stoup and roup: every bit, "lock, stock and barrel" (*SND*).

346. Baillie refers to her *Constantine Paleologus; or the Last of the Caesars* (1804).

populas that I could scarcely wish them removed. Another part of your postcript I must not forget to thank you for, viz. the cheering you give me in saying the Metrical Legends are approved of in Edin^r. I have need of this cheering, for it does not appear to me that they are very much approved of here. After having very early been desired by Mess^r Longman & Co. to prepare my corrections for a new edition in a <u>day or two</u> which looked like some hurry, it is now above a month since it was actually published.

And now let me turn my thoughts from all books & bookselling to the pleasures of Abbotsford. You are now at your pleasant home, telling your travel's story as no other creature can tell it, to your own family & friends, and this is delightful weather for the banks of the tweed & all out o'door recreations. Your young Mama with the Bairnie and the fournishing of the cottage & all are passing thro' my fancy and a cheerful moving picture it makes. Well may you all enjoy it! and remember me very kindly to Lady Scott & Miss Scott, your neighbours at the cottage,[347] not forgetting my young friend Charles, who is at home, I understand, and with him an old <u>young</u> acquaintance of mine, who I darsay [sic] has forgot me, Mr Villars Surtees.[348] Amongst the last sights I got of him he was in a state of deep humiliation, having wet his trowsers in the brook at Cotswold, and being set to the dinner table in a Girl's petticoat. It was a serious matter then and we durst not look at him for fear of adding to his distress. ––– And to add to the animation of Abbotsford have you not got a buxom Bridegroom in the neighbourhood? who may now sing Johny Cope with greater glee than ever and follow it up also with "woo'd & married & a'[.]"[349] If he <u>is</u> in your neighbourhood I beg to offer my congratulations to him & my compliments to the Miss Ferguson. ——

I have done a thing which I am always very loth to do but I could not well avoid it, — I have given a letter of introduction to you in behalf of a Major Douglas son to General Douglas of Woolwich,[350] who is to be a hasty passage thro your part of the country and had a craving desire to see you. I never saw him but it was requested as the greatest favour by connections of his who have been most kind & obliging Neighbours to my Brother & his family at Hanger's Hill near Acton, and I could not refuse it. I know that you take all these matters with the greatest good humour yet that does not make me the less unwilling to plague you with those starers who like to

347. John Gibson Lockhart had married Sophia Scott on 29 April 1820, and they resided in a cottage close by Abbotsford. See letters to Lockhart.

348. Charles was home for a visit in August with school fellow Villiers Surtees, nephew of Lord Chancellor Eldon, who would visit later for the holidays (Johnson, 769).

349. See Baillie's "Song, Woo'd and Married and A'."

350. This may be the son of General James Dawes Douglas (1785-1862).

tell all the world that they have been at Abbotsford. —— I will now have done for I have plagued you long enough in another way and written for me an extraordinary long letter. I think I write longer letters to you than I do to any body, you may therefore guess how far you are in the good graces & affection of

yours &c

J Baillie

3894 ff.37-39 (Address: Sr Walter Scott Bart / Edinburgh--postmarked 1822)

Hampstead Feb^ry 2^d 1822

My dear Friend

You have been always so kind to me, that I apply to you with a degree of confidence, whenever I want your good offices on any occasion, which you must not blame me for, being the natural consequence of your own friendly & open disposition. You can now do me a very great favour. There is a friend & old school fellow of mine, whose Husband is insolvent and dying, I believe, of a broken heart; and she will be left without a sixpence (a very small annuity promised by some friends excepted) and with a family of daughters, who have, till very lately, been brought up in affluence. I have offered to edit for her benefit a volume of collected poems, to be published by subscription; and being anxious to have as much good Ms. poetry in the book as may be, I am soliciting my literary friends to contribute. Pray send me something of yours, let it be ever so small! and if you can procure me any thing from other quarters send it to me also.[351] All will be thankfully received. I have by me a copy of Polydore the Robber, written by a young friend of yours which you sent me a great while ago.[352] I should like much to have it in my collection: for it is good strong stuff (I mean <u>stuff</u> in the best sense of the word) such as school Boys & country Lairds will like to read as well as fine Ladies, and I must not have my vol. too much filled with what is called <u>pretty</u> poetry. Perhaps you can prevail on [the] Author to let me have it. Tell him I request it of him earnestly and shall consider his consent [*sic*] as a very great favour. ---
Now some thoughts will pass across your mind (I should guess) to this purpose "What puts it into her head to come forward in this manner, putting her hand into every bodies portfolio or pocket because a friend of

351. Scott eventually provided *Mac Duff's Cross* for Baillie's *A Collection of Poems, Chiefly Manuscript, and from Living Authors* (London: Longman, Hurst, Rees, Orme, and Brown, 1823), a subscription collection for the benefit of her friend Mrs. James Stirling.

352. "The Robber Polydore" did appear in Baillie's *Collection*, the author listed only as "F."

hers is distressed?" In answer to this I have to say that my Friend, M‹rs› James Stirling, the person in question, has so many people, who respect her & wish her well, in this country & in Scotland, that I am doing this only to give her an opportunity of profitting by her own good character, and her friends an opportunity of assisting her in an easy way and without embarrassment. The collection is to consist only of one vol. and the subscription will be a guinea, and I am in hopes it will produce a considerable sum. ——

And how are you all in Castle Street? Lady Scott & Miss Scott & M‹rs› Lockhart tho' not actually resident there? All well I hope! I heard how happy you all were in holy-day time when Charles & his friend Surtees were at Abbotsford. This last was made very happy & very proud by your kindness and has lost his heart, I understand, to M‹rs› Lockhart, who is the first of human beings, in a female form, and full of all perfections. Had the heart been lost to the unmarried Sister, we should not, belike, have heard so much about it. If he is happy with <u>having been</u> at Abbotsford, a friend of ours, who spent some days with us lately, seems no less so with the prospect of going there, — Miss Edgeworth.[353] She is in very great request here, as she ought to be, and has been visiting at one friend's or admirer's house after another since the beginning of Winter. I was surprised to hear her say she has never yet seen you <u>bodily</u>. You will find her an entertaining, merry hearted Inmate with a good flow of easy, natural conversation, stores of information gained by quick observation at home & abroad to feed that flow. Her Sisters are clever Girls with great store of knowledge, and the eldest of the two very pretty. They have a good deal of the Irish brogue, and are in other respects neither english nor scotch; but by no means offensively so. Miss Edgeworth herself is most amiable regarding these young Sisters, whom she loves & attends like the fondest Mother, and indeed regarding her strong devoted affection to all her Father's family & her step Mother. The love powders which her Father certainly gave her, have not lost their effect after his death. ——— I went yesterday by invitation from Sir T. Lawrence to see your picture & the King's. This last is a very admirable, splendid gallery piece: and yours is the best likeness of you that I have ever seen. Indeed I don't think it could be better. That bust by Chantry [*sic*] represents you as a humourist,[354] this

---

353. Maria Edgeworth, accompanied by her sisters, first met Scott in June 1822, being struck that he was so "delightfully natural - as if he did not know that he was WALTER SCOTT or the great unknown of the north" (qtd. in Johnson, 811-12).

354. Sculptor Sir Francis Legatt Chantrey (1781-1841) began earning his reputation with a bust of Dr. John Brown and a statue of George III for Guildhall. He received commissions at once and began to rise steadily to the head of his profession. A long list of credits includes busts of Scott, Wordsworth, James Watt, etc. He

picture as a Poet; both excellent of their kind but the last the most noble.
— —

Since my poor Play of De Monfort was brought out & left so pitifully sticking in the mire, after such a creditable outset,[355] I have been once at the Theatre to see the Gentlemen of Verona & Mother Bunch.[356] The first we could not hear at all, tho' we sat in a side box in the dress circle, but the scenery & pageantry were very beautiful, and we had a good hearty laugh at the Pantomime. This is the most memorable thing that has varied my quiet life for this six weeks past. —— With all kind wishes to you & yours, I remain, my dear Sir Walter, affectionately yours

    J Baillie

PS I have just learnt from our Neighbour Richardson that your friend Mr W. Erskine has got a Judges gown. I am very glad of it, and pray offer him my hearty congratulations & my Sister's also. I have been told that he writes elegant verses, if I could procure one of his poems I should be glad.[357] — Sir T. Lawrence told me he should not venture to touch your picture again till he saw you, so I hope you are to be up ere long that it may be finished. It would scarcely be respectful to royalty that it should continue long in its present state. It is very honourable for the King himself that he has desired to have such a picture. I shall think the better of him for it as long as I live. —— Pray have the goodness to send your servant to hill street with the inclosed; I shall be much obliged.[358]

---

actually executed two of Scott, one in 1820 and one in 1828; the earlier one was made a present to Scott with a copy sent to the National Gallery (*DNB*, IV:44-7).

355. According to Jeffrey N. Cox, after its initial run at Drury Lane in April 1800, Kean revived *De Monfort* for five nights in 1821 at Drury Lane (*Seven Gothic Dramas, 1789-1825* [Athens: Ohio University Press, 1992], 231).

356. See Shakespeare's *The Two Gentlemen of Verona*. Scott replies (10 February 1822) that "I wish the London audience great joy in Mother Bunch. They deserve no better nor half so good as they do not know what they possess in Joanna Baillie (Grierson, 7:61). Bunch's fairy tales can be found in *Pasquil's Jests, with the Merriments of Mother Bunch* (1653) (my thanks to Ed Williams of The Literary Arts Allied Collective for this information).

357. In 1822 William Erskine was promoted to the bench as Lord Kinneder but died shortly afterward under the stress of having been unjustly accused of "improper liaisons" (*DNB*, VI:864-65 and Johnson), thus never having the opportunity to contribute to Baillie's *Collection*.

358. Enclosed herein is a brief note from Richardson to Scott dated 4 Feb. 1822 concerning a bank draft.

3894 ff.83-84 (No address or postmark)

Hampstead Feb^{ry} 24 1822

My dear Sir Walter,

Like your own William of Deloraine, "good at need," you never fail me, and many thanks to you! I like your fine generous story of the Laird of Swinton very much indeed:[359] it will in your hands make a noble & pathetic scene or _act_ as you please, and any thing of a direct Drama from you, will be such a novelty to the public that had my Collection no more legs to stand upon than this, it would not be left in the mire. It will be drole enough to have _you_ writing in blank verse for it and _me_ writing in rhyme, like changing sides in a country dance. We shall stand opposed to one another, but I must not presume to say on the equal footing of partners. But give me good blank verse, and dont go like Lord Byron to cut prose into junks, calling _that_ blank verse; for the blind courtisy [_sic_] which the British public shew to their mysterious Idol, great as you are, will not be shewn to you. If I durst tell what you propose writing for me, I should have little trouble in procuring subscriptions; but this would not be fair, so I only let people know that you have promised me _something_. I thank you also for giving me leave to add your name & Lady Scott's to the list, but I have not done it, because I wish all the subscribers I can gain in Edin^r to pay their money into some branch of the Scottish Bank & their names set down there. From that Banking house it will be transmitted to Mess^r Coutts in the Strand, who very kindly take charge of the whole and this will save confusion.[360] I shall request Mrs Thomson of No 5 George St: to send you a subscription paper with the name of the Edin^r Bank fixed upon for this purpose written upon it, and you can then set down your name when it is convenient for you. — I excuse you from doing more, as I have others to go about plaguing people for subscriptions, who can neither write blank verse nor rhyme.

I am truly glad to hear that Charles is to stay in his own country and take his chance (a very good one I trow) at the Scotch bar. I used to grieve for you when I thought of his going to Indea. My friend Miss Milligan read a letter to me the other day from Mrs Surtees in which she speaks of him with the affection of a Mother, praising him for his head & his heart & his beauty also, tho' she admits at the end that he stoops more than is

---

359. Scott's drama _Halidon Hill_, begun for Baillie's _Collection_ but growing too long, centered around the legend of the Knight of Swinton, who at the battle of Bannockburn befriended the young heir of the Gordons, his feudal enemies (Johnson, 786).

360. Thomas Coutts (1735-1822), along with his brother James, operated one of the most successful banking houses (Coutts & Company) in the Strand (_DNB_, IV:1279). Baillie mentions in various letters doing business at Coutts.

perfectly graceful and would be the better of a drill sergeant. This letter was somewhat amusing, for tho' the main purport of it was to request Miss M. to set every engine to work to rescue a poor Boy taken up for house breaking, from the penalties of the law, & remitting money to promote that tender-hearted purpose, yet she returns upon the theme of Charles Scott three different times, as if she were loth to have done with it. — My Nephew is now about to make one step towards making <u>his way</u> at the English bar, I wish it may lead to a prosperous journey. He is going to occupy chambers in the Temple at Lady day and be no longer a compleat Inmate of his Father's house[.][361] He is also becoming very argumentative & tinged with metaphysics which is also, I take it, another step. He tries his niceties of distinction & his arguments upon me as Molliere [*sic*] did his Plays on the old woman,[362] and you would be well amused to hear us wrangling together. His mind at present seems to be making a stride and new thoughts, new views & greater power of attention seem to be breaking upon him every day.

I am much obliged to M<u>rs</u> Lockhart for her kind remembrance, and the very pleasant information she tells me of her little nurseling.[363] Ma ma & bow wow are very good progress for his years (or rather <u>months</u>) and may he go on encreasing in words & stature to her heart's desire with many kind friends to sympathise in her delight! What a pretty scene that is in Pizaro,[364] where Cora speaks to her husband of a Mother's three (or four I dont know how many) holy days, — when the Infant cuts his first tooth, speaks his first word &c.! It is to me the prettiest thing in the whole play, tho' critics I understand despise it. Give my thanks & kind remembrances to both herself & her husband, tory tho' he be. I will only say on this subject as Froisart [*sic*] does when he tells of a brave man dying in his bed, "the more the pity"![365] ––– Remember me with all respect & kindness to Lady Scott, our very kind hostess of Abbotsford. Give my love to Miss

---

361. William Baillie had been educated at Westminster School and at Oxford and called to the Bar. He was present at the trial of Queen Caroline, whom his uncle Lord Chief Justice Denman was defending and later acted as Judge's Marshal to him when he became a Judge; but apparently William never practiced law, mostly traveling and managing his estates.

362. Jean Baptiste Molière (1622-73).

363. Sophia Scott Lockhart had given birth to her first son, John, on 14 February 1821, the Scotts' first grandchild.

364. Produced in England in 1799, *Pizarro* is generally attributed to Richard Brinsley Sheridan, though its translation from an early play is not his own.

365. Baillie attributes this saying to historian Jean Froissart (1337?-1410?), but it may appear as early as Phaedrus' *Fables*, i.e., "more to be pitied than censured" (see *The Macmillan Book of Proverbs, Maxims, and Famous Phrases*, ed. Burton Stevenson [New York: Macmillan, 1948], 1802).

Scott, and with all friendly affection to yourself, I remain

your truly obliged & grateful & gratified

J Baillie

PS. I am obliged to send the inclosed to Miss Millar instead of Mrs Thomson, and have therefore no opportunity of telling her to fix on a Banker for receiving the subscription. But you will receive from her a subscription paper when you wish it, and I should be glad if you would chuse a Banker for me. It must be a branch of the Bank of Scotland. Coutts has dealings with them all, so it does not signify what Bank you chuse. —— Have the goodness to allow your servant to take the inclosed letter to George Street.

3894 ff.195-196 (No address or postmark)

Hampstead May 28th 1822

My dear Sir Walter,

I received your kind letter yesterday, and considering where it was written, had no right to complain of its shortness.[366] Neither have I any right to complain of its contents. I had some misgivings in my own mind that you would not get your Drama brought within proper bounds, and to curtail & hamper the course of your imagination would have been a sin: – like cutting a pine elm (as is some times done near London) into shape of a Lady's fan. I thank you with all my heart for what I am to have in its place and am sure that I shall like it; and, what is more to the purpose, that my Readers will like it also. But I must return again to the subject of Haldan [sic] Hill. A hundred pages is a prodigious length for two acts and will give a heaviness, even in the reading, if any thing of yours can be so; I suppose this arrangement is for the sake of making the same scene continue thro' each act. But two pauses at least or great divisions in so long a piece, even for reading, is very desirable; and if they should without your leave produce it on the stage, and nothing is more probable, it will either suffer for want of those divisions or the Managers will divide it at their own hand, and do it unjudiciously. Think of this: fifty pages to an act!![367] ___ And what shall I say in return to this part of your letter? "I hope you will permit me to inscribe Haledon Hill to you, as without you most assuredly it would never have had an existence." The people of England might as well have asked Charles the 2^d to permit them to set the crown on his

---

366. This letter does not appear to be in Grierson's collection.

367. Scott wrote *Halidon Hill* quickly, but once begun it swelled into a 2-act drama, too long for Baillie's *Collection*; he was then pressed to come up with something shorter for her. In the meantime, he was finishing *The Fortunes of Nigel* and beginning *Peveril of the Peak* (Johnson, 786).

head and might have been as sure of the answer. If I could set up this honour to sale, instead of receiving it my self, I should have no need to trouble my friends for subscriptions in behalf of my Old School-fellow. A goodly sum I should make of it; and yet I think I would rather strip myself to my last gown than part with it to any body. – How clearly you can assist those for whom you are interested! Your young friend will be handsomely fitted out for Indea and no trouble given to any body. This is heavily said, but not grudgingly. I am happy to tell you that we have now of subscription money paid into Coutts house nearly 13 hundred pounds and are still receiving and will, I hope receive till the end of Octr. The beginning Novr we put to press. I have received a beautiful poem from Mrs Hemans & one from Crabbe & one from Milman and I hope for one from your friend B. Heber and other poetical worthies, that will do credit to the work, so I come on well every way.[368]

Our Neighbour Richardson has had a dismal spring of it, but the sun is breaking thro upon him again and his day will be bright (I hope) very soon. He was within an ace of Losing his Wife, who has been long ill after her confinement, but is so far recovered as to be in the drawing room; and he is going to Scotland with all his family in July, and means to take a house for some months in Edin^r. Fear & anxiety & business together have shook him a good deal. —

All this family are pleased with your remembrance and send thanks & kind wishes in return. ––– I send this to Abbotsford, where I presume you will be ere it can reach you. Much enjoyment may you & Lady Scott & all the members of your family have there in this delightful weather! for I presume it extends much farther north than the Tweed.

With many <u>many</u> thanks which I cannot sufficiently express, I remain, my dear Sir Walter

    ever truly yours

      J Baillie

PS. Will you have the goodness to send the inclosed to Dr Gardiner when any of your servants are going that way? I should be much obliged. —

3894 ff.226-227 (No address or postmark)

My dear Sir Walter

When people are both proud & pleased, they are generally very ready to take up their pen, and by this rule I ought to have written to you immediately after having read Haledon hill which I received last

---

368. Baillie received "Belshazzar's Feast" from Felicia Hemans, "Hope and Memory" from George Crabbe, and "The Loss of Royal George" from Henry Milman for her *Collection*; but unless submitted anonymously, there is no selection from Heber.

tuesday late at night; but I was greatly hurried next day preparing to pay a visit to our friend Sotheby at his Manor in Epping Forest, and during my stay there with walking about to view his improvements & other weighty affairs, I could find no quiet time to do it in; and after waiting so long for this quiet time, I am now fain to sit down in the midst of all confusion, carpet lifting, beds screwing, chimney sweeper's calling, and fifty other annoyances, for I will not suffer another day to pass without making my grateful acknowledgements for the great pleasure I have had in reading your very interesting & tender Drama, and the very great honour you have done me. My feelings have not been so much affected by any dramatic work for many a day, and the harmony & simplicity of the blank verse with the felicity & manliness of the language, charmed me throughout. If the thousands of readers who will have it in their hands in a day or two like it as well as me, your Laurels will not be one whit faded for the new ground on which they are planted. — Good fortune attend your Nephew Walter & his out-fit! It will indeed be like that of a Thane and to do it credit he can do no less than return from Indea, in due time, a generous & magnificent Nabob.[369] ––– You have certainly in the arrangement of your Drama plainly shewed that you wish it not to be produced on the stage with your two long acts & no female characters at all, but I could take you a good bet that they will put in an Elizabeth into it with her mouth full of all manner of common place sentiments and bring it out at the Surry or Coborgh very soon. In this foresaid Elizabeth I think I recognize Lady Compton, but I am not very positive.[370]

The cause of all the present hurly burly in this house is that we are going from home for four months and have just let it to a Tenant who is to take possession in a week, and we are just in the beginning of our preparations for this movement. We go first to my Brother's in Gloucester Sh^r and afterwards to Devonshire. I shall return home by the end of Octr to put my book to press, and, if not before I leave London which will be 3 weeks from this date, I shall expect on my arrival from Devon to find the poem you have promised me lying on my Table; but you had better direct it for me at 25 Cavendish Square, where I shall be first of all after our return, and last of all before our setting out. —— All my Family send you their best regards, and I ought to say thanks, for they are all as vogey of your having inscribed Halidon hill to me as if it has been done to them at large, and my

---

369. Scott was planning for his upcoming book profits to enable him to outfit nephew Walter for the East Indies (Johnson, 786).

370. *Halidon Hill* (1822), an historical drama set in 1402 around the Battle of Bannockburn, has, as Baillie says, no women characters; I find no record of the play's performance. Scott explains in his introductory notes that the piece was written at the request of his esteemed friend Joanna Baillie.

Brother above all as if it had been done to himself. — My kind wishes & best respects to Lady Scott: remember me also very kindly to Mrs Lockhart & Miss Scott. The thoughts of Abbotsford and all the kindness received there rises fresh in my mind. —— Farewell, my dear & generous Friend!

　　J Baillie
Hampstead Monday
June 22^d 1822

3895 ff.57-58 (Address: Sir Walter Scott Bart / Melrose--postmarked 1822)
　　　　　　　　　　　　　　　　Cottiswold House August 29th 1822
My dear Friend,

　　I received your letter yesterday and read it with deep concern. The death of a man so estimable & amiable in himself, whose life was of such importance to his family and likely to be useful to the public, who had just attained that rank in his profession which he had long looked for and became him so well, and who was so beloved & valued by yourself & no doubt many other friends, would under any circumstances have been very distressing, but under those which you mention doubly — O much more than doubly so! To fall a prey to detraction and the extreme delicacy & sensibility of his own mind is a death that calls for the deepest sympathy. Innocence does not support such a mind, for a shock is given to the imagination which makes it read suspicion in the eyes of all men, and tho' you can make it as plain to common reason as the noonday sun that no body can sincerely suspect it, you do nothing towards removing its misiry [sic]. A guilty man has the advantage of an innocent in this respect that the injustice of accusation does not torment him, and if he has any remorse & any good in him, the religious act of repentance is a wholesome exercise to his mind, he works for relief & gains it; but your poor Ermine who cannot bear the spot, what can he do, and what can be done with him? Indeed I sympathize with you very much. In the midst of all that hurly burly of the king's visit to have such an affliction sent to your heart, while every thing round you was at varience with your feelings, was a heavy trial. ——
I am here so much out of the way of news of any kind, the most public excepted, that I had never heard of Lord Keneder's [sic] death, nor the story connected with it.[371] You may be sure that both my Sister & myself with hearty zeal defend his character should we ever hear it attacked in

---

　　371. Scott was just recovering from preparations for George IV's visit to Edinburgh when his closest friend William Erskine, Lord Kinneder, died. Kinneder had not long enjoyed his elevation to the Bench until vicious rumors accused him of a liaison with a tradesman's wife; though the rumors were false, the stress injured Erskine beyond repair (Johnson, 796).

any degree. To think what he must have suffered from the delicate sensitiveness of his mind, and the helpless defencelessness of such a mind, gives him a right to the zeal of every heart, and I should be peculiarly ungrateful could I withhold it. --- I hope his Daughters are bearing up under their heavy affliction as well as may be expected, and if you see fit, offer them the sincere condolence & best wishes of my Sister & myself when you have an opportunity. Alas! this is a dreadful blow for them.! —

We have now ended our visit to my Brother, and are here in the neighbourhood with M<u>rs</u> Hughan where we shall remain to the 11<u>th</u> of Sept<u>r</u> and then go to Devonshire. Our stay at Duntisbourne was a very cheerful one; we were a great deal out in the fields & the woods, doing as <u>we thought</u> a <u>great deal</u> of useful work, and my Brother & William were sure to be near us with hedge bills & pruning knives in their hand, cutting off all the low branches of the young trees which obstructed their growth; a pleasant employment which they have taken to this summer for the first time and it does them both good. William begins to be attached to the place & the country, a very happy change. He is in other respects a very affectionate cheerful Inmate, with no lack of abilities, but somewhat too fond of argument. However, take the good & bad of him together he gets a stronger hold of my heart every day. God guide him thro' this evil world! Your young friend Villiars Surtees is our near neighbour here and I saw him yesterday. He longs to hear that your son Charles is in Wales, for then he will go & be with him as long as he can before his time for going to Oxford. He is an excellent young man and tho' very shy likes to speak of Abbotsford. — My Sister unites with me in all kind wishes to you. Have you not M<u>r</u> Crabbe with you in Edin<u>r</u> or have had? The news paper mentions not his name amongst the courtiers of Holy rood. — Farewell my Dear Sir Walter with affectionate regard!

  J Baillie

3895 ff.207-208 (No address or postmark)

Hampstead Nov<u>r</u> 4<u>th</u> 1822

My dear Sir Walter

I made myself quite sure that our friend Richardson, would bring me a packet from you containing the Vigil which you kindly promised me or any other poem or poems that you may please to bestow upon me for my forth-coming pick-nick volume. But no such thing! he comes empty handed and I am much disappointed. I am now anxious to get my book to press as soon as may be, and if you will have the kindness to send me your much desired contribution with all convenient speed, I shall be very much obliged to you. I likewise wish to close the subscription by the middle of this month, and any money that may have been deposited for it in any of the Royal Banks in Edin.ʳ which have all transactions in the way of business with Messʳ Coutts, would do well to remit it to Coutts as soon as may be and a list of the subscriber's [sic] names along with it. You would do me a very great piece of service if you (if you) would take the trouble or desire somebody else to take the trouble of enquiring after this, and requesting it to be done, if it be not done already.

I learn from Richardson that the grief & anxiety you suffered on the death of your poor Friend & the bustle of the royal visit has cost you an illness which was relieved by a rash breaking out upon your body: let me know something about your health when you write your answer to this, which is always a subject of deep interest to me.[372] Some time before we left Devon (we have been returned but a few days) I saw your friend Mʳ Mariet[373] at Mʳˢ Elliott's[374] who enquired very much after you and begged to be particularly remembered to you when I should write. I read to him your letter on Lᵈ K's death in which he appeared to sympathize. He has had afflictions of his own poor man! very recently and was with his Sister in law who accompanied him, (a very engaging looking person) in deep mourning for his wife. He looked to me in very delicate health, but I was told he looked rather better than usual. His Sister in law lives with him & takes care of his children. – We came to the Vale of Honiton where Mʳˢ E. lives just when the orchards were loaded with beautiful apples of all shades & colours from the brightest coral-red to the palest yellow, and we left the Cyder casks full of the richest juice they have contained for many years. We saw the process of making Cyder too which is cheerful work to all but the poor blind Horse who generally turns the apple-mill, and very simple. It is the more cheerful that the makers of it are the drinkers of it, tho' I dont know that this is entirely for their good: they export little & consume much. The blind Horse employed, as I have said, in the Farm that we inspected, was often urged to his worked [sic] and called to by the name of Blossom.

The Richardsons have had a very rough passage in the steam vessel, after which Mʳˢ R. was very ill, but she is now got the better of it. They arrived on friday. I was glad to hear so good an account from them of Lady Scott & all the family at Abbotsford. And they tell me the house is now assuming the look of a Palace. Rooms of 40 & 50 feet long and a handsome stair case! –– Our friend Crabbe has, I learn by Mʳˢ Hoare, been much

---

372. Scott was so exhausted by George IV's visit that long afterward his arms and legs were still "spotted like a leopard's" (qtd. in Johnson, 796).

373. Mr. Mariet may be a misspelling for John Morritt; I have not identified otherwise.

374. This is probably Anne Elliott's sister-in-law.

pleased & gratified by his visit to you, and talks much of the kindness of Lady Scott. If she was as kind to him as she was to us, he has good reason to do so. —— Farewell! for I have many letters to write & must not be long winded or rather <u>penned</u>. —— Do what I desire you, like a good friend as you have always been to

your grateful & affectionate

J Baillie

3895 ff.241-242 (Address: Sir Walter Scott Bart / Edinburgh--postmarked 1822)

Hampstead Decr 3$^{\underline{d}}$ 1822

My dear Sir Walter,

I presume you received a letter from me, written soon after our arrival from Devonshire, viz nearly a month ago, putting you in mind of your kind promise and requesting that you would have the goodness to send me your poetical contribution to my forth coming book so as I might have it by the 27 or 28th of Novr at the latest, being anxious to put it to press as soon as possible. This is the 3$^{\underline{d}}$ of Decr and I have not yet received it. If you were a forgetful friend or a lazy man, I should not much wonder at this; but you are neither, therefore I say with some degree of anxiety, "what has become of my promised poem the Vigil"?^{375} I fear you have sent it in some Bookseller's packet or by some private hand, where privately enough it may remain for 3 weeks to come whilst I am all impatient & <u>out of sorts,</u> because I cannot proceed one step further in my business till I have it. Pray write to me without loss of time where it may be enquired after, and I shall use all diligence to recover it. I am loth to dun you so, knowing how much you have to do and to think of; but I cant help it; I am dunned on my side, and therefore very naturally transfer a little <u>pat</u> to you, after my own back has felt the buffet. ——

You will be pleased to hear, that we have been very prosperous in gathering money; our subscription now is about two thousand pounds. I have got several new poems too since I wrote you last, some of them very good, but were I to give my subscribers 4 hundred pages of it without your contribution, they would cast my book at my head and hoot at me as a deceiver. ——— I suppose by this time you have read both Lord Byron's Werner & Lord John Russel's [sic] Don Carlos.^{376} I have been greatly pleased with the last: the sentiments & observations are excellent, the

---

375. Apparently, Scott never sends Baillie the poem entitled "The Vigil."

376. Byron's *Werner, A Tragedy*, was published in 1822. Statesman Lord John Russell's (1792-1878) works included *The Nun of Arrouca* (1822), *Don Carlos* (1822) and a translation of the Fifth Book of the *Odyssey* (1827) (DNB, XVII:456).

dialogue spirited & easy, the poetical imagery beautiful & often original, and the language & verse harmonious & elegant. As to Werner, the blanc verse is blanc enough, for it is no verse at all to the ear — only to the eye, being what Old B . . .[377] Painter used to call prose cut into junks . . . first scene is good and the last act very . . . and there are a few fine passages of the . . . kind here & there, all the middle part . . . however is uninteresting & tedious to a. . . .

I shall send this directly by post . . . where I take it for granted you are. . . . I hope it will find you well. I had . . . account the other day from . . . Somerville of the merry dinner she had at Abbotsford, . . . you all crossed hands round . . . table and sang jovial song . . . so many Bridal guests at an Infare[378] . . . tells me your Piper is discharged which . . . sorry to hear. However, he will perhaps . . . you again, if stealing away to Edin^r to see the King was all his fault, tho' it must be owned it was an act of great insubordination. —— With kind regards to Lady Scott & your Daughters, I remain,

my dear Sir Walter, affectionately yours
J Baillie

3896 ff.9-10 (No address or postmark)

Hampstead Jan^{ry} 13$\underline{th}$ 1823

My dear Sir Walter,

In spite of all you say against MacDuff's Cross, I am right well satisfied therewith. It is a very interesting scene, heroic & true to nature & comprised in small room so as to suit my collection perfectly; and as for the blanc verse it will sound well either in the hall or by the leaping-on-stone.[379] Many thanks to you for employing any part of your precious time, an[d] when your mind was so anxious about things that touch you nearly, in writing for me: it was the act of a kind friend and as such I feel & consider it. Tho' not very competent to the task, I have prepared it, by pointing it & adding an evidently forgotten word, for the press; and I have had the boldness in addition to all this to draw my pen across a few lines of the introductory part, as I cannot possibly let my <u>own</u> praise stand forth so

---

377. The entire edge of this leaf is torn away, and the following ellipses indicate missing words.

378. infare: a feast in celebration of the coming of the bride to her new home, usually given by the bridegroom on the day after the wedding (*SND*).

379. Scott apologized to Baillie for the delayed *MacDuff's Cross*, explaining that "I have tried my subject out of doors and in doors . . . in the kitchen and in the hall and in the garret and at length took it out to the Leaping-on stone. Really I am ashamed of what I have written and it is with much difficulty I muster courage enough to transcribe it" (qtd. in Johnson, 801).

conspicuously [sic] in the first page of a book I edit my <u>ownself</u>. So your beautiful lines about the Lady's rock & the Traveller runing [sic] in his steed &c go, as far as the public are concerned to disanull. Not so, however, as far as I am myself concerned, for no word of cheering or praise that you bestow upon me can ever fall to the ground. You have set yourself for many years to make amends to me for the general indifference of my country and you have made me great amends. To let you know that I feel it is all I have to give in return and you will receive it as your reward. — Yet my heart even now somewhat upbraids me for speaking thus on the present occasion, when so many poets have assisted me readily & cheerfully. I have a mixed feeling on this subject which I will not attempt to explain. — Let me thank you in the next place for the money you have sent me which is a very handsome addition to our subscription, and shall be paid into the sum total when I go to Town, day after to morrow. To morrow I shall put my Mss into Longman's hand, who promises me that the book shall be printed off immediately. I shall not forget to send you a copy in the way you desire before the general delivery of the book and am pleased to think you have so much curiosity on the subject. You will [find] a good variety of things in it, some good & some indifferent. Some of my friends in their zeal served me somewhat as yours did in the arrangement of your library and were more a hindrance than a help. For they begged poems for me where I did not want them, and put me into such situations as obliged me to accept not what is absolutely bad, but what I should rather have been without. This, however, is <u>a secret</u>.

I am pleased to hear you mention the improvements of Abbotsford as if you were satisfied with them and they had answered your expectation which is not always the case after much money spent in building and still seldomer the case after much money spent in <u>Planners</u>. Long may you & yours enjoy it! and I will not absolutely give up the hopes of seeing it tho' they are but weak. If you were only to be seen in Scotland, I would go to see you, but you must come to England every spring now and I will trust to that. Sir Thomas Lawrence will not put pencil to that fine portrait begun more than a year ago till you sit again in person, and that were errand enough if you had no other. — Mr Lockhart's Spanish translations will,[380] I doubt not be very acceptable to the Public, both from his own reputation as a writer and our knowing so little of Spanish poetry, some of their plays excepted. We all have an early prejudice in favour of Spanish poetry without knowing it; romantic adventures & serenades come into our heads

---

380. John Gibson Lockhart's *Ancient Spanish Ballads, Historical and Romantic, translated, with Notes* appeared in 1823. *Valerius, a Roman Story* was published in 1821.

at the very mention of it. —— Farewell for the present! — My Sister sends her kind regards to you & Lady Scott & Miss Scott & I join her most heartily.

    Your grateful & affectionate friend
      J Baillie

3896 ff.104-105 (No address or postmark)

                                    Hampstead April 2$\underline{d}$ 1823
My dear Sir Walter,

    I have this moment received a vol – I should say <u>copy</u> of my book and lose no time in forwarding it to you by the conveyance you have pointed out. It will reach you at a time when your spirits are some what shaded with grief, and if it keep you for a short while from dwelling on sad thoughts, I shall be glad. I sincerely sympathize with you on the loss of your Brother which tho' not unlooked for is one human tie broken for ever, and your heart is, I believe, particularly sensible to such trials.[381] I hope you are pretty well and shall be glad to hear how you do when you have leisure to write to me; not till then. ––– My book which you have so honoured is a very decent looking vol inside & out, tho' this last is scarcely so smart as I expected and there is good variety of things in it tho' it is, perhaps upon the whole rather grave & sentimental. I am particularly pleased that there is a line of praise contained in it, and from your pen, for poor John Kemble. If the lines I have addressed to Mrs Siddons had not been printed before the account of his death reached us here, I would have contrived to weave in a line to his honour in that little poem, tho' during his life I always considered him as being rather unfriendly to me. Perhaps it was my own fault: he was proud and I may have done something to offend him — I think I once unwittingly did so.[382] ––– But to return again to my book. You shall have your other 9 copies sent to you when the great package of them is sent to Edin^{r} which I suppose, will be about a week hence. I hope it will give satisfaction —— I think it will, for it will fall into the hands of friends & generous friends who will not be disposed to find fault. There is one thing, however, against it; many people take it into their heads that it contains pieces written with great care, like trials of skill amongst our modern Poets, whereas they have kindly sent me what

---

    381. The *DNB* reports that Thomas Scott died in Canada in April 1823, but it must have been earlier for the news to have reached Baillie by the date of this letter.

    382. John Philip Kemble died in 1823; Baillie's "To Mrs. Siddons" appeared in her 1823 *Collection of Poems.* In *Getting into the Act, Women Playwrights in London 1776-1829* (London and New York: Routledge, 1995), Ellen Donkin speculates that it was proprietor Sheridan instead who would not support Baillie's plays at Drury Lane (159-83).

came to hand at the time with no thought whatever of rivalry. ——— We have now something like spring about us & invalids who have been confined all this ruffian Winter (for so I must call it) are creeping abroad again. My Brother says the sickness of London for this last month has been more like a plague than any thing he remembers: whole families ill at once & many deaths particularly old people & children. I made my first visit to London the other day after an absence of two months, the greater part of which I did not even cross our own threshold; spring is therefore doubly welcome to me. —

Give my kind regards to Lady Scott & your Daughters; Mrs Lockharts friendly present to me has been a great amusement to me & to many of my friends & visitors. I suppose there cannot be a translation truer to the character of the original Ballads and this is just what one desires to have.

Farewell for the present! With many many thanks for your friendly assistance and for more kindly acts than I can number, I remain

my dear Sir Walter
yours very gratefully
J Baillie

3897 ff.3-4 (No address or postmark)

Hampstead July 1st 1823

My dear Sir Walter,

I wrote you a short & hurried letter at the time I sent you the first copy of my Collected Poems, and did not thank you half enough for the very powerful & friendly assistenc [sic] which I received from you in that troublesome business. Pray believe that I did not feel the less grateful on that account, and accept now of my most hearty acknowledgements. Your name helped me beforehand, and Mac Duff's cross which has been very much admired by a great proportion of my readers, helped me well afterwards. In short I took hold of your strong arm at the very beginning and, leaning upon that, put forth my [hand?] and & caught at all the rest of the Poetical Brotherhood likely to do me any good. And great good has come of it, for after paying all expences of printing &c. which came to £313 or 330 – I forget which, we have realized for my friend Mrs Stirling two thousand two hundred four percent stock, and when we have sold all the copies intended for Indean subscribers, we shall add better than two hundred more. This is much more than I at first expected and I have good cause to be satisfied. I believe of all my Friendly Poets none have been more gratified on this occasion than Gally Knight,[383] for his portrait of his Mother has been extremely noticed & liked, and as the public have not hitherto been very favourable to his Muse it must have been the more flattering to him, setting aside all the better feelings which belong to him as an affectionate son. Miss Catharine Fanshaw's pieces have been exceedingly admired and so has M[rs] Heman's [sic] Belshazzar's feast.[384] The admiration this last has received will now, I hope, be of use to her, and make her volume of Poems, just come out, be more eagerly sought for at first, tho' its own merit afterwards could not have failed to procure it a very honourable reception. She is a woman of high genius and respectable in every way, and the Public I hope will do themselves honour by supporting her as she deserves. There are many striking passages of the highest toned poetry in her Constantine, and there is a short poem at the end of the book called "The voice of Spring" which is to my fancy quite exquisite.[385] There is a great deal of character too in her Spanish Songs & ballads and M[r] Lockhart I think will be pleased with them. ――― I congratulate you on Miss Edgeworth's visit to Edin[r] and take the liberty of inclosing a letter for her which you will have the goodness to forward, if she should not be in your neighbourhood; for she is to go far into the highlands, I understand and shew her young people every thing. Her spirit, & ardour, & curiosity, & ready resource & happy temper, fit her admirable [sic] for a Traveller. A long list of requisites! I wish I had had the half of them. Tho' I have called it her visit to Scotland, I believe I ought rather to have said her visit to you, and the time to be spent at Abbotsford was the bright spot in her imagination. ――― But I have almost forgotten to say what I ought not to omit. Where is the Author of Polidor the Robber? I think you told me his name is Howison and that he is or has been in America.[386] I wish to send him a copy of our Pic Nic book which he

---

383. Henry Gally Knight (1786-1846) was primarily a writer on architecture. Some of his oriental verses, however, were praised by Byron (*DNB*, XI:254). He contributed "A Portrait" to the 1823 *Collection*.

384. Catharine Maria Fanshawe (1765-1834), who lived with her sisters at Hampstead for many years, contributed anonymously to Baillie's *Collection of Poems, Chiefly Manuscript, and from Living Authors* in 1823. Felicia Hemans contributed "Belshazzar's Feast."

385. Felicia Hemans' *The Siege of Valencia; A Dramatic Poem and The Last Constantine: with Other Poems* appeared in 1823; "The Voice of Spring," originally published in *The New Monthly Magazine*, ends the collection (see Felicia Dorothea Hemans, *The Siege of Valencia*, ed. Donald H. Reiman [New York: Garland, 1978], 315-60).

386. William Howison (*fl.* 1823) was a poet and philosopher who lived in Edinburgh and was a friend of Scott. Publications include *The Robber Polydore, Europe's Likeness to the Human Spirit*, etc. (*DNB*, X:122).

is well entitled to and I dont know how to manage it. ---- I hope this will find you & all your family well. I wish I could say as much for ourselves. My Brother is very unwell with one of those tedious obstinate coughs with inflamation on the wind pipe, and so exhausted with the fatigue of business, that he is gone to Tunbridge with Mrs Baillie, who is also very unwell, for change of air, looking very ill and in bad spirits. This makes us very anxious; and many are anxious on the same account who are neither kith nor kin to him. ----

Give my regards to Lady Scott & to both your Daughters

Farewell my good Friend!

always yours most truly

J Baillie

PS. Mr Crabbe has been in Town to consult Dr Baillie about the pain in his face which distresses him much. It is a kind of tick douloureax[387] but we hope if it cannot be entirely cured that it will never become exceedingly bad. He left Town in tolerable spirits. ----

3897 ff.84-86 (Address: Sir Walter Scott Bart / Abbotsford / Melrose--no postmark, NLS dates 1823)

Duntisbourne Sep^t 28th [1823]

My dear friend,

I doubt not you are already informed of the heavy affliction it has pleased God to visit us with, tho' in the notices sent to Scotland of the sad event, as is the custom there, your name was, I know not how omitted; and I feel well assured that you symathize [sic] with us truly.[388] I feel as if my Sister & myself stood now alone in the world, belonging to no body, and that what remains of our life which in the course of nature cannot now be very long, can be but a gloomy portion, — No more cheerful sunshine for us! But it is wrong to think of ourselves when there is the poor Widow by our side & those who are nearest of all, to say nothing of the many who will miss a kind & skillful friend, for they are spread broad & wide and are not

---

387. *Tic douloureux*: literally, painful twitching or grievous bad habit; more loosely, habitual pain.

388. Dr. Matthew Baillie died 23 September 1823. A few days later his brother-in-law Thomas Denman wrote that

> . . . it is now quite evident that from the time of their leaving London at the end of June there was no reasonable chance of recovery. His dreadful depression of spirits, which they endeavoured to ascribe to some disorder of the nerves, was only one of the symptoms of an exhausted constitution, attending a gradual decay of all vital power. . . . He appears to have gone on rapidly losing strength till a very few days before his death, when he became delirious, but he expired at length with the most perfect tranquillity.

(qtd. in Crainz, 56)

all clothed in black who will mourn for him whom we have lost. — I have been here nearly three months nursing him with Mrs Baillie and with her in a continued state of anxiety between hope & fear; but better than a fortnight ago, after a degree of amendment which seemed to promise better than any that had deceived us before, an encreased fever returned upon him, which his wasted frame could not contend with, and after keeping his bed for more than a week, he expired. Sir H. Halford & Dr Warren were with him at the last, and his friend Dr Baron of Gloucester had been unremitting in his attendance, so we had no reason to regret our being so far from London.[389] Poor Mrs Baillie who has thro' the whole of her very severe trial has [*sic*] done her duty with all the tenderness natural to her character & a strength of body & of mind which seemed to be lent to her by a divine power for the time, is as well as we could expect tho' deeply afflicted. When the funeral is over which takes place here next tuesday, we shall all go together to London. It will be a sad journey to us! When we travelled that road last how little did we think we should so soon return bereft of him who was then the sole object of our care! — But God's will be done! We have had the blessing and should be thankful that we had it so long.

I tell you all this, my dear Sir Walter because I know that you feel for us and will like to hear something about us in our present distress. ——— I hope you & your family are well: long may it be before any breach shall be made amongst you! — Farewell, my dear Friend. I thank you for your last kind letter, but will say nothing more of it now.

yours affectionately

J Baillie

PS. One of the books which we read out to my Brother, soon after we came here and which interested him more than any of the rest was the life of Adam Blair; perhaps Mr Lockhart may like to know this.[390]

---

389. Sir Henry Halford, MD (1766-1844), changed his surname from Vaughan to Halford by Act of Parliament in 1809; he was Physician to the Middlesex Hospital from 1793 to 1844, Physician Extraordinary to George III in 1793, Physician in Ordinary in 1812, and Physician in Ordinary to George IV, William IV and to Victoria. John Baron, MD (1786-1851), was Physician to the General Infirmary and Consulting Physician to the Lunatic Asylum at Gloucester until his retirement in 1832. Pelham Warren, BM & MD (1778-1835), was Physician to St. George's Hospital from 1803-16 (Crainz, 27, 30 & 66).

390. Lockhart published *The Life of Mr. Adam Blair* in 1822.

3898 ff.56-57 (No address or postmark)

Hampstead Feby 6th 1824

My dear Sir Walter,

Bad news travel fast, and no new[s] are it [is] said good news, yet I would fain hear from yourself or one of your family, that Mrs Lockhart is recovering favourably, after the loss of her Infant and all that she must have suffered besides.[391] I regret the disappointment to herself & her relatives, but I hope amends will be made to you all some other time in the possession of a bud that will not be nipt but swell & blossom & bring fruit to perfection. Nor must you think despondingly of your little man because he is not robust & because he is wise.[392] The thread of life tho' apparently very slender is yet very tough in some of those delicate creatures: I have frequently known them pass thro' diseases which prove fatal to stronger children, as if they had a charmed life and would not [be] kill'd; and as for his being wise, all clever children who are much with grown people & dont run about with other children seem to have minds too forward for their age. It is an evil that will subside. We hear of many wise children & few wise men. I have a little grand niece some what in his predicament, yet I expect her to grow on to Woman's estate, and just be a good, honest, clear headed lass after all.[393] --

You are very kind in your enquiries after us all. Our dismal blank cannot be filled up and every day some thing reminds us of it painfully, but we are perhaps nearly as well in this respect [as we] can reasonably expect to be. The young rise with new vigour from affliction, but it is not so with the old; and it is wisely ordered that it should be so, that we may disengage ourselves from the world before we are called away from it. Poor Mrs Baillie is better than when I wrote last, and begins again to speak somewhat in her natural voice. — I suppose you received about a week ago my letter concerning Mrs Heman's Tragedy, and I hope you are according to the nature of your own kind, friendly heart, inclined to smooth its way to the Edin^r boards, where the beauty of the writing will be more attended to, and the Actors, perhaps more suited to their characters than at Covent Garden.[394] --

---

391. On 31 January 1824 Sophia Scott Lockhart was delivered of a little girl who lived only two days. Sophia suffered severe cramps afterwards, alarming the family and her doctors for several days (Johnson, 857-58).

392. This is a reference to the Lockharts' eldest son, John Hugh, who became the Hugh Little John of Scott's *Tales of a Grandfather*. Always sickly as a child, he died in 1831.

393. This would be Sophia Milligan (1817-82).

394. I have not located the letter mentioned here in any library collection. Scott replies (9 February 1824) that the Siddons agree to act Felicia Hemans' drama *The*

We have been much pleased with the story of your gallant Murtherer of Jedburgh, if so he may be called, I should say that he was only a culpable homicide. Our Hertford hero was a vulgar Ruffian compared to him. But our newspaper writers are Anti Popes, who canonize for the Devils Calendar. The modification of the Lord's prayer was a strong instance of sense & self-possession in your namesake, whom I should not be ashamed to call cousin were he a namesake of mine. ――― I received some time since an application which amused me a good deal, from Montgomery the Poet in behalf of a committee at Sheffield for suppressing the use of Climbing Boys for sweeping chimneys, that I might send them a Poem on that subject to be added to a collection of similar poems, to engage the Public (that is to say the honest pot-boilers all over the country) to <u>sympathize</u> with their miseries. Instead of poetry I have sent to the committee in plain simple prose an account of the old Scotch way of cleaning chimneys with a rope & a lead & a parcel of brooms & brushes tied to it, as a far better thing. For all the verses on earth will never make them give up the old mode of sweeping till they get one in its place nearly as easy to themselves and as cheap. Is this old way still in use with you or do climbing chimney sweepers universally prevail?[395]

Our neighbour Richardson has had his wife very ill, but she is getting better again: she is an excellent but a delicate creature who keeps one always afraid. ―― Fare well! my Sister joins me in all kind wishes to you & all your family circle; who are by this time I hope entirely relieved from anxiety [for] her who is so dear to you and so great a favorite with every body, being after yourself the most popular person I know.

Yours my dear Sir Walter
truly & kindly
J Baillie

3898 ff.81-83 (Address: Sir Walter Scott Bart / Edinburgh--postmarked 1824)

Cavendish Sq^r Feby 27th

My dear Sir Walter,

I was very glad to receive your last letter with such satisfactory accounts of Mrs Lockhart, and I trust that her face is even by this time of the dimensions you assign, and trust further that when the Brown Nurse &

Vespers of Palermo but that Baillie should in no way infer that he has "interfered in theatrical matters," for "Everybody thinks they can write blank verse" (Grierson, 8:173-84).

395. See Wellcome Institute MS 5608/41 & 44 addressed to James Montgomery of Sheffield, postmarked 1824, in Miscellaneous Letters (Volume 2).

Black Doctor have done their offices to her, no size of coin in the realm will be compared to it.[396] I thank you for letting me know; it was very kind. —— And I am sure you are well worthy of thanks on another score. Truly I am grateful for it; and you will see by the inclosed letter that she whom it immediately concerned is also vey [sic] grateful. I hope the result will be favourable; and even if the success should not be very great, some degree of it will temper the disappointment of not having the Piece produced again at Covent Garden. They must be of a very sanguine temper who write Tragedies for the stage now. –– I had a call from Campbell yesterday, and he is going to publish a vol: of Poetry which I doubt not [will] sustain his reputation. I wish you would do so too, for those Scotch novels have put poetry out of fashion and I know no body that can set that matter to rights again but yourself. I was pleased with Campbell saying so frankly to me that the publication was kept back a little because his friends did not like some of the poems meant for this volume, and he was writing others to supply their place. He seemed altogether in a good, happy disposition of mind and his book will profit by it. I hate sad, bewailing misanthropic poetry, be it ever so good of its kind. Indeed he has hitherto written with a fine spirit and I trust he will continue to do so to the end. Yet he has many things to cast a gloom over him, and above all the unhappy situation of his Son. The young man is now at home with him and in a more manageable, docile state. So far well; but the Father's hope of his entire recovery amounts, I believe to nothing.[397] ––– Our friends here thank you for your kind remembrance of them. Mrs Baillie is much better and has almost recovered the natural tone of her voice. I am glad also to give a good report of Mrs Richardson who is now nearly as well as her tall, slender, delicate form will allow her to be. Women of her size do not often thrive well as in-door plants. If fortune cast their lot amongst Gypsies & Tinklers those wandering outlyers, they become stout, stately, efficient creatures; but pleasing as the Individual is we are speaking of, she is not of a true household measurement. – Is it not a curious circumstance that short men always marry tall women when they can get them? — an evident direction of Providence; for if the old saying – "like

---

396. Scott reported that after the death of her infant on 31 January 1824, Sophia's "face which was last week the size of sixpence has in three or four days attained the diameter of a shilling and will soon attain its natural and most extensive circumference of half a crown" (qtd. in Johnson, 858).

397. Thomas Campbell published *Specimens of the British Poets* in 1819, wrote "The Last Man" in 1823 and *Theodric and Other Poems* in 1824. After Campbell became editor of *The New Monthly Magazine* in 1821, he discovered that his son Thomas Telford (b. 1804) was mentally ill and, after becoming unmanageable, had to be admitted to an asylum near Salisbury (Miller, 33).

draws to like" held good in this matter, what an unseemly division we should have in the human race. This very <u>deep</u> observation you will probably assent to, and conclude from it besides what is also very true, that I have at this moment very little to say only that the pleasure of saying any thing to you draws me on. ––– With kind regards to you & Lady Scott & all the family. I remain my dear Friend yours affectionately
    J Baillie

PS. What a goose I am not to recollect that you asked me a question, namely how Crabbe liked his visit to Edin.ʳ With your kindness & Lady Scott's he was more than satisfied; highly gratified; but what he thought of your Highlandmen &c lies in his own breast along with many other odd enough matters I daresay I, but may, hereafter, perhaps, see the light. Have you heard that the youngest of Miss Edgeworth's two Sisters who were with you last summer, Miss Sophia, is going to be married to an Irish country gentleman of good fortune in their own neighbourhood? His name is Fox, and he is a man every way acceptable to the family. This will make up very well for having let all the Scotch Lairds escape unfettered. ––

3898 ff.163-166 (Address: Sir Walter Scott Bart / Edinburgh--postmarked 1824)

Hampstead May 10ᵗʰ 1824

My dear Sir Walter,

    Mʳ Lockhart kindly offered to take letters for me to Scotland, but for these few days past I have been too much engaged to write and I hope you will receive this nearly as soon as if I had sent it by him. We have been much pleased with his visit; and he has been less reserved than when we met him in Edin.ʳ and has shewn himself sufficiently to convince us that a further acquaintance would have made his company still more agreeable. We had my Nephew here to share in the pleasure of receiving him and the two young men seemed to take to one another, at least William has been very much pleased with him. We had Ladies with us too, who thought themselves very much obliged to us for giving them an opportunity of meeting him as one of the great geniuses of the north, and have expressed themselves warmly as Ladies are wont to do in praise both of his conversation & his <u>beauty</u>; and we remain greatly his debtor & yours for the (the) pleasure he has given us, hoping that when he returns to London again, he will not forget to bestow some small portion of his time on those who will prize this mark of his attention very sincerely. ––– I ought long ere this to have thanked you a second time for your friendly exertions in favour of Mʳˢ Heman's Tragedy, now that they have happily led to complete success,[398] but I put off doing so till I had seen your Son in Law, that I might not tease you with too many letters. The only account I received of its reception, for some time, was from the Edin[r] news paper which some friend or other sent me by post, and it seems to have been quite triumphant – every thing in short that her friends could desire; graced also with a prologue from the pen of a celebrated Baronet, so that both she & I have good cause to make you our grateful courtesies to the very ground. I have had a very well-expressed pretty letter on the occasion in which she mentions having written to you, so I shall say no more to you on the subject, but that I thank you again with all my heart. ––– Since I wrote you last I have been trying to do a little and looking over some of my manuscripts &c but it gows [sic] on badly with me and I have no heart to exert myself. I look at my papers as one who is called upon to set her house in order before she shall quit it for ever, and this sentiment is more deeply impressed upon me at this time by the illness of a friend at the side cf whose bed I sat yesterday where she has been lying many months and from which she will in all human probability never rise again. Do you remember Miss Holford, the Author of Wallace & whom you met in this House a few years since, when she sat by your side, more proud & delighted to find herself there, than if she had received notice & favour of the first Monarch in Europe? She is this poor friend: all her earthly hopes & flights of fancy are now at an end, while yet but in what <u>might have been</u> the best years of her life.[399] Yet I ought not to call her poor friend. She is rich in hopes tho' aware of the utter hopelessness of her disease, and so cheerful & contented & endearing that she is altogether an object of admiration and it is beautiful if I may so say to behold her. She has not had all the success which her genius & abilities entitled her to, but all is well with her now. If you write me soon, send her some kind remembrance in your letter, tho' you have met but once; if she be still alive it will cheer her. –––

We have now bright summer weather and people are putting on their lighter clothes & their lighter looks together. I hope you & Lady Scott & your Daughter are enjoying the same pleasure in Edin[r]. Remember me to them both very kindly. M[rs] Lockhart, I know is in the west country. Pray tell her when she returns how much the Ladies here admire her husband unless you be afraid of making her jealous. He will deliver a book to you

---

398. Felicia Hemans tried her hand at playwrighting with *Vespers of Palermo*, performed with some success at Covent Garden and Edinburgh, but two other plays were never performed.

399. Ironically, Margaret Holford went on to marry Rev. Septimus Hodson in 1826 and lived until 1852.

which I have sent to replace that which you were kind enough to give on my account to the Author of Polidore. I am sorry to hear he has become a philosopher.

Farewell for the present, my dear friend!

your grateful & affectionate

J Baillie

PS. While writing the above, a packet was put into my hands which remained unopened till I had finished. What do you think it proves to be? a letter containing a request from a man who proposes publishing pocket books to rival (so it is expressed) the pretty German pocket books so much admired on the continent, and requesting me on my own terms to write little poems for it, a copy-pocket book being sent with it to show me what a handsome work it will be. Whether is this a proof of the sinking or rising of my reputation? Who would have sent such a proposal to me twenty years ago? ——— Your friend John Richardson is fagging very hard indeed, we cannot get sight of him now but on great occasions. He ought to make rich and I hope will do so, if he be spared long enough which all his friends wish & hope very ardently may be the case.

3899 ff.298, fragment (Address: To Sir Walter Scott Bart. / Castle Street-- no postmark, NLS dates 1824)

[1824]

. . . cured Lord Carlile, taking an emense quantity of bark in every way that he can possibly swallow it, and he is so much better that he hopes to be cured also by & by, and has returned to his living in the country cheered with the prospect.[400] Whilst he stayed here, in Mr Hoare's family, he wrote in one day (so Miss Hoare told me) five hundred lines. In my best days I could not have undertaken to write as many with my pen, tho' they had been ready composed to my hand. But this is a mystery which you fully understand and will not therefore be hard of belief. Tho' I should not say so neither, for if he were to tell me so himself I should believe him, and Miss H. is perfectly to be trusted, barring (as the Irish say) mistakes. — Fare well! and I take my leave with good hopes that you will grant the above mentioned request of your grateful & affectionate friend

J Baillie

---

400. This is evidently a reference to Crabbe, for in NLS letter 3897 ff.3-4 (1823) Baillie writes of his "bark" remedy for the pain in his face.

3900 ff.93-95 (Address: Sir Walter Scott Bart: / Edinburgh--postmarked 1825)

Hampstead Feby 14th 1825

My dear Sir Walter

I have learnt by a friend who is a more diligent reader of the newspapers than myself, that the happy event, lately announced to us by your friend Richardson, as soon expected, has taken place, and both my Sister & I congratulate you & Lady Scott thereupon with a right hearty good will and satisfaction. From what I understand to have been the purport of your letter to Richardson, and from other reports, your son has a good prospect of happiness before him in the choice he has made; and as for the Young Lady, it is agreed on all hands that the honour of being your Daughter in law is a full equivalent for all the beauty, goodness & wealth which she or any body could bring into the family of Abbotsford. To have your eldest son married entirely to your satisfaction, is so important a point, that I must rejoice in it; and the more so that a young Dragoon Officer, quartered in the Land of potatoes, (let his good-sense be what it will) runs a considerable risk of bringing home such a wife as will not be very acceptable in the land of cakes.[401] But now, as it were, the key stone is fixed in the main arch of your Castle and it is secure. Whether I call you a Castle or a Forest-tree spreading out its branches in the land, (for one should be a little poetical on such an occasion) may you prosper & endure for many generations in the Land which you have honoured and which will never cease in your descendants to honour your name! --- I should have written soon after receiving your kind message by Richardson, but as there was a promise of a letter contained therein, I waited <u>but in vain</u> to receive it. However, I thank you for your kind intention of writing to me, tho' not fulfilled and as I daresay you have a hundred & fifty letters to write on this occasion, I desire you <u>not</u> to write to me, for I'll take the will for the deed, till you are entirely at leisure. I do this the more readily as I understand you are to be in London by & by; and then perhaps I may fare the better as to claims on your bodily presence for my moderation & consideration in this respect. I shall be happy also to see your young couple if they return to Ireland by this Metropolis; and there is another young person whom I hope to see, for she has never been here at all, and that is Miss Scott. Give my kindest wishes to her & to Mrs Lockhart and say that I wish them joy of their new Sister.

In writing to a friend who has been so kind to me, I ought to say something of myself. But what can I say? This winter is passing away as

---

401. Scott's son Walter married Jane Jobson, daughter of a wealthy London merchant, on 3 February 1825.

dully & uninterestingly as my years now must naturally pass. I have great reason to be thankful for good regural [*sic*] health, and spirits which though not good are never painfully depressed, and I am thankful, and often try to be more so to that Divine Goodness which has so far conducted me through this mortal state, spared from many evils & distresses with which so many others are afflicted. I have even plucked up courage to write a little; but it is only a little, and has been done more from the desire of compleating what I had intended and of <u>setting my house in order</u>, than from taking any pleasure in it. I forbear to ask you what <u>you</u> have been doing; but if we are to have no more poetry from you, the more's the pity! you wrong us and yourself both. --- M<u>rs</u> Baillie has got through the winter rather better than we could expect as to health, but her spirits are often depressed, as if our great misfortune had happened but a month ago. — We are going next wednesday to be with her for 3 weeks; perhaps you may be in London before that time is expired. Sir T. Lawrence has been long wishing to have you, and I hope you intend to give him as many patient sittings as will enable him to finish the best likeness of you that has ever been taken, and one of the best pictures probably that he ever painted; no mean praise! for Vandyke has left no paintings superior to some of those which Sir T. has painted of late years.[402] --- And now farewell! may we meet soon! and may I find that favour in your sight when we do meet which you have always so partially & kindly bestowed on

    your grateful & affectionate friend

      J Baillie

PS. I had a letter from Miss Milligan not long ago full of the praises of your son Charles, who was neighbour to her & M<u>rs</u> Hughan at Cernie Parsonage during the late Oxford vacation[.]

Cavendish Sq<u>r</u> Feb<u>y</u> 17

    Waiting for a frank will make the inclosed of an older date, but it gives no[t] the opportunity of conveying to you & Lady Scott M<u>rs</u> Baillie's kind congratulations on your son's marriage which she sends from a heart truly interested in the welfare of every one belonging to you[.]

---

402. Sir Anthony Van Dyck (1599-1641), though born in Antwerp, spent much of his career in England, painting several portraits of Charles I and the royal family.

3910 ff.7-9 (Address: Sir Walter Scott Bart.--no postmark)

Hampstead August 6$\underline{th}$ [1825-1826][403]

My dear Sir Walter,

Our friend Richardson is going to Scotland and offers to take whatever we wish to send, and so I gladly charge him with a few lines for you. I would not write to you by the Sotheby's, for they were to stop at so many places on their way to Abbotsford, that my note or letter must have been much more interesting or important than I could possibly make it to excuse the staleness of its date. I hope the good Man & his companions have had or will have a pleasant meeting with you & your domestic circle there; and I do believe he carries back to Scotland as young a heart as he brought from it when an Officer of Dragoons some fifty years ago. I did not desire him to write to me, but if he should yet come in your way, just hint to him that a letter with his signature from the <u>North Countrie</u> would be very acceptable. I say nothing of receiving any other letter from a <u>worthie</u> in the North Countrie, for I am a reasonable woman, and <u>that</u> I do not expect, as you very well understand. How it fares with you and those most dear to you, I shall learn by our friend when he returns to Hampstead. —

We have been living on our friends lately while our house was painting and part of that time was spent in Town where I had the great pleasure of hearing M$\underline{rs}$ Siddons one evening read the principal scenes of King John with as much expression of voice & countenance as ever. Her power is still wonderful. I met at her house a young Lady who promises to be very distinguished by & by, Mr C. Kemble's Daughter who at 16 has written a Tragedy which, read in company by her Father, has struck every body as wonderfully forcible & Shakespearian.[404] I liked her countenance much; there is strong sense in it with some portion of beauty and she has escaped the very high strong features of the Kembles which I am not very fond of. I am sorry to learn both by M$\underline{rs}$ Siddons & Lady Byron that M$\underline{rs}$ Henry Siddons has not yet received any benefit from Mr Whitelaw's baths & decoctions which I believe was her principal view in coming to London.

---

403. References herein to George Crabbe's illness, mentioned in much earlier letters, and to Fanny Kemble's *Francis I*, written when she was about 17, would date this letter earlier than the NLS estimate of 1829.

404. Frances Anne Kemble (1809-93), daughter of actor Charles Kemble and niece of Sarah Siddons and John Kemble, debuted as Juliet in *Romeo and Juliet* in Covent Garden in 1829, an immediate success. She later toured both England and America and is known as a writer of *Journal of a Residence on a Georgian Plantation, 1838-39*; her first work, mentioned in this letter, was *Francis I*. See both Margaret Armstrong, *Fanny Kemble, A Passionate Victorian* (New York: Macmillan, 1938) and *Fanny Kemble, Journal of a Young Actress*, ed. Monica Gough (New York: Columbia University Press, 1990).

What a loss she will be to your Theatre if she do not recover! to say nothing of her private worth and the value of her life to her family & friends. ——— Before going to Town we passed a fortnight under the same roof with Mr Crabbe, who still talks of his visit to you & to Edin^r as one of the brightest portions of his life. He is still troubled with the tick in his face, but it is not so bad as it was some years ago, and of late he has found great relief from taking Bark mixed with a certain proportion of snuff. He is very feeble-looking, and walks with his legs so crooked that he seems almost in a sitting posture, yet he gets on at a tolerable rate and can stand for a long time without being tired, and eats every day a very good dinner. Long may he last! the world will be a less wicked world by a considerable proportion, as long as he remains in it. I am told by Miss Hoare that his kindness in visiting the sick is beautiful. ——— I am reading just now a translation of Goethe's Wilhelm Meister which gives a very strange picture of German manner amongst Stroling Players, some what, if I remember right, after the Fashion of Scaron.[405] I ought to admire it, for as the Translator informs us there have been but 3 men of genius in the world since the world began, Goethe is one of those 3 (Homer & Shakespear being the others) and this same Wilhelm Meister is in Germany his most esteemed work; but whether I do what I ought is a secret which I will not tell you. ——— Give my kindest wishes to Mrs Lockhart & Miss Scott, and tell Mr Lockhart that I sent him a note & a Ms for his friends annual before he left Town which I hope he received. ———

Believe me always my dear & kind friend
most truly yours
J Baillie

3901 ff.113-114 (No address or postmark)

Hampstead Octr 3^d 1825

My dear Sir Walter

Are you aware of how the matter of friendly correspondence stands between you & me? I think you are not, and shall therefore take the liberty of telling you. — The last letter I received from you (about a year & half ago) I had from the hands of your son in law Mr Lockhart and I wrote a letter to you not long after, in which I requested that you would, when you wrote to me again, send some kind message of remembrance to my friend Miss Holford, then in a very dangerous state of health and not

---

405. Johann Wolfgang Von Goethe published *Wilhelm Meisters Lehrjahre* from 1777-96, followed by *Wilhelm Meisters Wanderjahre* from 1807-28.

expected to live many weeks.[406] She was then receiving the sympathy of many friends which her fortitude & cheerful resignation so well deserved, and I knew that the slightest token of yours would be particularly gratifying to her feelings. I made myself almost certain that that letter would not remain unanswered; but it has; at least I have never received an answer. Upon the marriage of your Son I wrote to you again to congratulate yourself & Lady Scott on the happy event; but as there was a rumour at that time of your coming soon to London, and I thought you would have so many similar letters to answer, I desired you <u>not</u> to write to me and said that this forbearance on my part would give me a stronger claim upon you for an early visit when you should arrive here. But neither answer nor visit — not one line of your writing nor one moment of your bodily presence has fallen to my lot. You could not possibly suppose that I would desire you not to write but from the expectation of seeing you very soon, and I cannot suppose that a friend who has always been so kind, so encouraging, so useful, so indulgent to me has dismissed me from his consideration. What then can be supposed but that you have not received the letter which I wrote to you on Capt: Scott's marriage? If this be so, you may well think that <u>I</u> have been neglected, and so it is the more necessary that I should trouble you with this information. I put it into Richardson's hands that he might get it franked, and he has always been very exact; but he has many things to mind, and it may have been mislaid & never sent.

I have heard with much pleasure of your progress & reception in Ireland & thought of you often.[407] I have traced you likewise in your excurtion to the Lakes of Westmoreland, and now I hope you are enjoying your own home & family with your health no wise the worse for the fatigue you have undergone. ――― With best regards to Lady Scott & your Family, and all kind & affectionate wishes to yourself, I remain

my dear Sir Walter
most truly yours
J Baillie

---

406. Following the great commercial crash of 1825, partly because of his own borrowing and partly through the mismanagement of his publishing partner James Ballantyne, Scott found himself with Ballantyne and Constable involved in financial ruin, personally responsible for £130,000. The stress of this period in his life is probably the reason for his not answering all letters; there seems to be no other explanation for his ignoring Baillie. See Baillie's following letter and his reply to this one dated 12 October 1825: "It did not require your kind token of undeserved remembrance my dear friend to remind me that I was guilty of very criminal negligence in our epistolary correspondence" (Grierson, 9:236).

407. On July 9 Scott, daughter Anne and Lockhart had left Edinburgh for an excursion to Belfast and other parts (Johnson, 906).

PS. After writing the above, I learnt from our Neighbour Miss Hoare that Mr Crabbe was at their house where she & Mrs Hoare have been nursing him during a severe return of his complaint, (the tic douloureux) and would not send it off till I had seen him which I did last night, when he was well enough to drink tea with us & the family, but looks sadly changed since I saw him last, some months ago. He had been so much the better of Dr Kerrison's bark remedy, that he & his friends were in hopes he would not again be tormented; but this sudden & severe return which seized him in Church, Sunday se'nnight puts an end to this hope. This first attack, however, was the worst and he may not have another so bad; but it is an awful enemy to have as it were standing by one's side, tho' not in a state of activity. — I told him I was going to send you a letter, and he begged me to offer you his kindest remembrances, adding other warm expressions of regard & admiration which were not intended for your ear, tho' you must have been gratified by them so bestowed. — I fear he will not long be a creature of this world. —

3902 ff.157-161 (Address: S Walter Scott / Abbotsford / Melrose-- postmarked 1826)

Hampstead March 27th 1826

My dear Sir Walter

I sent you a kind message thro' Mrs Lockhart some time ago, I hope it has been received, for I would not then trouble you with a letter, knowing well that my not writing would not be considered as a mark of indifference. Not to be interested in every thing that materially concerns you & yours would be stupidity in the most ordinary person in the kingdom and in me it would be heartless ingratitude. You may guess then how pleased I am at the good report I have had from various quarters of your health & spirits. It makes me both pleased & proud. For though this commercial hurricane which has been felt over the whole country so generally & severely has bent upon your brow unsparingly, you are all in all such a one as almost any man in the country would change places with gladly; and you have more than this to cheer you, for I believe that you receive the change which has taken place as part of your fortune, appointed for you by that hand from whom cometh every good thing in whatever form it may be clothed. Many years ago in a letter to me, after mentioning gratefully the many happy circumstances that had attended your progress in life you added "I stand in awe of my own good fortune[.]" That awe may now be removed and having felt reverses like other men, you will afterwards be the happier for it. All this is well, and I think of it on your behalf with pleasure and as I said before with pride, but there is another view of the subject or rather part of the subject which gives me no satisfaction but on the contrary makes me whenever I think of it grumble & growl like an evil spirit; and that is the multitude of impudent Travellers with letters of introduction from their as impudent friends who have abused your hospitable nature & made Abbotsford for so many summers an Inn & a Tavern for way faring Idlers of all sexs [sic] & ages. I have no charity for such people. Travellers are the most selfish & the most impudent of human beings; and that you should have been their prey to such a degree provokes me, so that I must per force give some vent to my humour. It is a curious coincidence that we should learn a few weeks since that the ex-president of Congress, the celebrated Jefferson has applied to that Council for (for) leave to dispose of all that remains of his once great property by lottery, and one of the principle [sic] reasons given for this is the great concourse of Travellers who went to visit him &c &c.[408] So it is not without good reason –––– But I will not suffer myself to speak upon this subject any more; you are a good humoured, open handed, open hearted Dandy Dinmount [Dinmont] kind of a man, and I am a prudent, reserved, grave, ungracious kind of a woman, so we shall never come even now, perhaps, to a right agreement with one (one) another. –––– I need scarcely say how glad I was to see the Lockharts, particularly the Lady who wins every body's good will. I am sorry she has occasion to go to Brighton with her delicate child. I wish my Niece, who has also a very delicate child, had been there for they would have been good neighbours to one another. Perhaps Elizabeth may return before Mrs Lockhart leaves it, and then I am sure they will draw well together. I was very much obliged to Mr Lockhart some time since for procuring literary employment for a young man for whom I am interested, and the kind & ready manner in which he offered to serve him, even before I had time to make any request, added value to the obligation. You may be sure I wish him all success in

---

408. All over Virginia, in the aftermath of the panic of 1819, farms of cash-poor, land-rich planters were being auctioned. In January 1826 Jefferson himself was $107,000 in debt and suddenly responsible for two $10,000 loans for which he had co-signed. On 19 January he called for his grandson Jeff to propose a lottery that would sell off his nail-making mills and about 1,000 acres of land to clear the debts, but because lotteries were illegal, he had to obtain approval from the General Assembly. Jefferson's lottery bill passed by only a few votes, but in its final form the bill required that Jefferson sell everything--Monticello, its contents, slaves, horses, land, etc. He could only plead with his creditors to be generous and grant his deathbed request to free five of his closest servants, asking the University of Virginia to employ them. Monticello, like Scott's Abbotsford, had been a constant stop for dignitaries and travelers. Jefferson had no presidential pension and had gone $30,000 deeper in debt while in office. See Willard Sterne Randall, *Thomas Jefferson, A Life* (New York: Henry Holt, 1993), 585-91.

his arduous undertaking and I trust he will be very successful. Every body is looking with impatience for the next number of the Quarterly.[409] --

I have been very anxious of late for the success of a Translation of Klopstock's Messiah.[410] It is put into very elegant good blank verse, an honour which that poem, celebrated as it is, has never received before, and I am told it is also a very faithful translation. It is done by a very accomplished friend of mine, who publishes it (by Longman & Co.) in one vol: containing the seven first Cantos, to be followed by another vol. containing the remainder of the poem, provided this first vol: can be made [to] pay its own expences. Pray speak a good word for it in the north when you have opportunity. --- I am now in the press again myself, most probably for the last time, and with a very short, tho' I hope not uninteresting work, at least I am sure it is not an uninteresting subject. It has been written some years, and I mentioned it to you when we were last in Scotland. But I shall say no more about it now; you will receive a copy of it soon, and will not, I know, be inclined to judge of it severely. There are reasons why I wished to publish this in my own life time, be sides those which I have mentioned in the short preface; perhaps when you read it you will divine them. My popularity is so small that I expect but a very limited circulation for it, but to publish in my own lifetime at all events appeared to me to by [sic] my duty. I have this morning corrected the first proof sheet.[411] ---- My Sister unites with me in kindest regards to your Daughter & Lady Scott, & hope they are both well. I wish I had seen your youngest son when he was in Town, but I trust there are opportunities for this abiding me. It was a greater disappointment not to see your Nephew Walter before he sailed for Indea, for in his case & mine future opportunities are not to be expected. May he prosper in the last! his abilities & his name will serve him every where. --- Letters between me & Miss Edgeworth are few & far between; for tho' she writes night & day sleeping & waking as you say in your last, a small part of the Mss fall to my share. However, I know that a very reasonable portion of her good will

409. In 1825 Murray offered John Gibson Lockhart the editorship of the *Quarterly Review*, and he settled in London's Regent's Park for the remainder of his life. While editing the *Review*, Lockhart wrote his life of Burns, a life of Napoleon, and *The Life of Scott*, a biography surpassed only by Boswell's *Life of Johnson*, in seven volumes (*DNB*, XI:47-49).

410. Miss Fanny Head, Baillie explains in the following letter, translated poet Friedrich Gottlieb Klopstock's (1724-1803) *Messiah*.

411. In 1826 Baillie published *The Martyr* (London: Longman, Rees, Orme, Brown, and Green). Her preface explains that of all human actions, religion is the strongest and the Christian martyr only to be found in the first ages of Christianity. The preface is a statement of her own faith and philosophy.

falls to my share, and for me to complain of correspondents is really like the pot calling the kettle black —— From my good friend Miss Holford to whose Italian Marquis you were so kind, I hear frequently, and in her last she tells me that this same Marquis has been sent for by his own King and has left England full of fair prospects. He was a sanguine enthusiastic person, but appeared manly & good humoured; I hope he will not be disappointed. She herself is at her own home in Chester, still an Invalid and never expecting to be well, but not as formerly looking for death at the end of a few weeks or months. She has had a great deal of anxiety on her Sister's account, who is married to Mr J. Walker,[412] one of the many London Bankers who have suffered in the late confusion & alarm, and there is a large family of children to whom their good Aunt is strongly attached.

——— My Sister & I have had but a gloomy winter of it. She was long confined with a very painful tho' not dangerous illness called the Shingles, and I tho' comparatively spared have had some touts[413] (as we used to say in the parish of Kilbride)[.] At our age we must no longer expect a continued course of health, and it behoves [sic] us to be very thankful for the freedom from sickness & pain which we have in the course of many years enjoyed. But I cannot now welcome in the winter as I did in my younger days, almost preferring it to any other season of the year. At first in my opening fancy it was the time for sliding on the ice, scampering over the snow or striving against wind & rain with my frock over my head, a thing I delighted in; then it became the time when there were dances to go to & plays to be seen or at least a good chance for such happy excitements; and then it became the season for sociable fireside meetings and the various cheering gratifications which we call comforts: the dull long evening & the sick-chambers were not taken into the account. But I am thankful for the blessings which still remain in every stage of our existence, and will endeavour to be more so; for in this state of passage & of trial every thing that is appointed for us is for our good, and far better than aught we could appoint for ourselves, had we the power. This is a common reflection because all reflecting minds have a natural consciousness besides what they are taught by revelation, that it must be so. ——— If you have time & inclination to write me a short – or a long letter by [&] by I shall receive it gladly; if not, send me a friendly message by Mrs Lockhart, and it shall be to me as precious as a letter from any one else: it shall serve as a token of your remembrance & friendship, always gratifying to

your affectionate old friend

J Baillie

---

412. Mrs. Joshua Walker of Hendon, Middlesex, was Margaret's sister.
413. tout: as a more uncommon meaning, bout of crying (SND).

3903 ff.131-133 (Address: Sir Walter Scott Bart / Abbotsford / Melrose--
postmarked 1826)

Hampstead Octr 13$^{\underline{th}}$ 1826

Indeed, my dear Friend, I have not considered you as treating me
unkindly, and had I received no letter from you at all, either short or long,
you would have remained in my mind acquitted of all unfriendly neglect. I
wrote to you a letter which, perhaps, I had better not have written, at a
time when every one was interested in those events which so much
concerned you & the public, but when that misfortune which goes nearest to
the heart came upon you, I did not, knowing well that I could not console
you and that my silence would not be misinterpreted. And yet I should
have written with true sympathy, for I never yet lodged under the roof of
a kinder, more considerate Hostess than her whom it has pleased God to
take away from you to a better world.[414] That week spent at Abbotsford
was a sunny spot in our existence, and my Sister & I speak of it & look back
upon it often. Alas! as we grow old those remembered spots become the
brighter from the surrounding gloom that intervenes.[415] ––– You say not a
word in your letter of coming to London, tho' Mrs Baillie not long ago
learnt from Mrs Lockhart that you & Miss Scott intended to come in the
course of October. I hope you have not given up that intention, or at least
that it is only deferred for a short time. The beginning of winter is an
unfavourable time for a young person to come to London for the first visit,
but you would not object to the Town being quiet and not very full of what is
called company. We out-of-the-way people here would gain by the
circumstance, for we might hope thereby to have a little more of your
society. Dark nights have come upon us here before we can well bear the
comfort of a fire which should attend them. What contrivance will be
devised amongst so many modern improvements for a bright-burning demi-
season fire which sociable people may gather round in mild weather – I
mean the long dark evenings of mild weather? Sir H. Davy must see to
this. I frequently feel the evening now hang on hand: working with my
fingers (a woman's great advantage over man) goes on badly when ones
eyes can scarcely direct them, I tire of reading for I never was by nature a

---

414. Lady Scott, Mary Charlotte Carpenter, died 14 May 1826. Scott had gone to
Edinburgh, and a day later Charlotte became very ill as her body grew cold and her
speech and breathing became labored. Daughter Anne frantically nursed her to no
avail. When Scott returned on 15 May, Charlotte was dead (Johnson, 985).

415. This calls to mind Wordsworth's *Prelude, Book Twelfth*: "There are in our
existence spots of time,/ That with distinct pre-eminence retain/ A renovating
virtue/ . . . . Such moments/ Are scattered everywhere, taking their date/ From our
first childhood."

reader, and I have no heart to write. I believe I must betake me to a spinning wheel for the sake of the motion & the noise, or go out to tea parties, or coax my neighbours to come in to me & play at Back gammon, –– poor expedients all of them! My Sister reads a news paper, six columns of a side, every after (after)noon and fills up what is lacking for the night with processions & points of history from Holinshed, but I am a sorry wiglet, and must learn to adapt myself better to my circumstances. But what a vile letter I am writing! wearying you forsooth because I am weary myself. I had better have done with it, tho' there is so much white paper still at command. Farewell then, and give my kindest remembrances to your Daughter. (my Sister joins me in this very heartily) and whether you write or forbear, think, my dear Sir Walter, now & then of your

    old & grateful friend

    J Baillie

PS. Did not I mention to you some months since a translation of the first seven cantos of Klopstock's Messiah by a friend of mine? Perhaps I did not; but allow me to announce to you now that the whole of the poem is completed in another volume just published, making two middle sized volumes. The language & verse are excellent, and German Scholars say it is a faithful Translation; pray speak a good word for it when you have opportunity. And you will be inclined to do so on the Translator's own account, for she is nearly connected with Lord Somerville's family, and a pretty, clever, agreeable woman. She has been in your house; Miss Fanny Head by name. She would fain have kept her name & sex unknown, if her friends would have allowed it, and they were not very wise friends who thwarted her on this point. I speak feelingly on this subject like a burnt child. John any-body would have stood higher with the critics than Joanna Baillie. I too was unwisely thwarted on this point.[416]

3905 ff.260-261 fragment (Address: Sir Walter Scott B^t--no postmark, NLS dates 1827)

                                                   [1827?]

. . . Mr Carr's eldst Son, Morton Carr, who has just left his Father's pleasant house & family to be a lonely resident in the good Town of Edin^r as Solicitor for the Excess-of Scotland. Richardson will tell you of him, and you must not consider this as a letter of introduction, but as he is a young man of most amiable manners & character & one of my young favorites, I know you will be inclined to speak kindly to him & shew him countenance wherever you may meet him. He is with all his other good

---

416. Baillie's first volume of plays was published anonymously. See Donkin's "Joanna Baillie Vs. The Termites Bellicosus" on this point.

qualities a modest man, and will not presume upon it. ——— I congratulate you with all my heart on having completed & given to the public your life of Napoleon.[417] A great undertaking accomplished with less time & labour, I suppose, than ever was given before to a work of such magnitude & importance. This very circumstance while it raises people's astonishment at the readiness & ability of the author will make them somewhat suspicious of what they will term the solidity of the work; but saying nothing of that extraordinary man but what is true or what you believe to be so, and tracing the character from those many detailed facts with the spirit & <u>picturesqueness</u> (if I may use this word) with which you have drawn from a few hints the historical characters of your novels, the world will receive its impression of him from you & from no other, let the learned cavil at such predilection as they please. I shall read it as soon as I possibly can; and I have good confidence that you will not let your bias as a Cavalier prevent you from doing justice to the Ceaser [*sic*] of modern times. ———

My Sister unites with me in kind regards to yourself & Miss Scott, and also to your pleasant Sophia, Mrs Lockhart. I hope you are all enjoying one another's company in good health. —— When Richardson returns, you may send me some half dozen of lines or so, as kind & gracious as you please, just to say that you take this letter of mine in good part, and this is all (all) I expect in return. I should not else have written it; for every year that you live the number of your correspondents & the demands on your time must encrease, and it becomes a true friend to give place willingly & cheerfully, being proud & pleased that she had her share when it was reasonable that such shares should be had. ——— We went to the exhibition some time ago, and were very much satisfied with your portrait by Lawrence. It is the likest face that ever was given of you, besides being by far the best picture. — I have nothing left to say but that I finished my prose Tragedy on Witchcraft which I mentioned to you a great while ago, and after having let it lye by & reading it again at a considerable distance of time, I am inclined [to] think favourably of it.[418]

---

417. Scott's *The Life of Napoleon Buonaparte* was published in 1827.

418. Baillie's *Witchcraft: A Tragedy in Prose, In Five Acts* was suggested to her, she explains, by reading that very curious and original scene in the "Bride of Lammermuir." In a journal entry dated 22 July 1827, Scott writes,

> Rose a little later than usual and wrote a letter to Mrs. Joanna Baillie. She is writing a tragedy on witch craft. I shall be curious to see it — Will it be real Witch craft — the *Ipsissimus Diabolus* [the very devil himself] — or an impostor — or the half crazed being who believes herself an ally of condemnd [*sic*] spirits and desires to be so? That last is a sublime subject.

(Anderson, 331)

Renfrew Witches upon a polite stage! will such a thing ever be endorsed! And this naturally leads me to mention a visit which we had last week from Mrs Siddons when she very kindly read to us in the evening a part of Othello with as much power & truth of expression as ever. Her & I take to one another very kindly now. The world is past with us both; and on my part at least I look back upon what she was with undiminished admiration. How handsomely you spoke of her at the aforesaid Theatrical dinner ! I believe I must on this account forgive your misdemeanor regarding Allen Ramsey [sic].[419] And now I have really & truly no more to say (so much the better for you) but that I remain

    very faithfully yours
    J Baillie

3908 ff.78-79 (Address: Sir Walter Scott Bart. / Edinburgh--no postmark)
                                  Hampstead Feby 13th 1829

My dear Sir Walter,

    I have just been writing a note to your Daughter which I inclose in this, and I hope she will not be very much <u>fashed</u>[420] with the contents of it, for I could not do otherwise in the matter than I have done, without being very unkind to excellent friends to whom we owe many obligations. You were very gracious to Mr Morton Carr, the Brother of the young Ladies in question, and all his friends here as well as myself felt it gratefully. --- We were glad to learn an excellent account of your health not long ago when we called upon Mrs Lockhart, just before her husband's return from Scotland. You are a young person compared to me, yet upon the whole, like my own poor self, you are somewhat the worse for the were [sic], therefore it gives me particular pleasure to hear of your being in good bodily condition.[421] As to your mind it is an existence standing apart by itself, and

---

419. Allan Ramsay (1684-1758) was born in Lanarkshire, Scotland, to John Ramsay, a supervisor of lead mines. At the age of 20 Allan was apprenticed to an Edinburgh wigmaker, establishing his own shop in 1712 and that same year producing several poems in Scots and English. In 1718 he began to shift from his profession of wigmaking to bookselling and publishing. His collected volume *Poems by Allan Ramsay* appeared in 1721, followed by *Fables and Tales* in 1722 and volume 1 of *Tea-Table Miscellany* in 1723. *The Gentle Shepherd* appeared in 1725, the same year Ramsay established the first "circulating library" in Great Britain, and volumes 2 and 3 of *Tea-Table Miscellany* appeared in 1726 and 1727. In 1736 he opened a theatre in Edinburgh but was forced to close it in 1739. He died at the age of 74 (Bertram H. Davies, ed., *Allan Ramsay* [Boston: Twayne, 1985], "Preface"). See earlier letter 3890 ff.216-217 to Scott.

420. fashed: angered (*SND*).

421. Johnson says that 1828 was the Indian summer in Scott's career, for his health was relatively good and he labored steadily. He visited Joanna Baillie in April

as to its unchanging career, we have no rules to judge by. I hope you keep the thumbs of Craneoligists [*sic*] away from your head to save the sapient world a great rigmarole of philosophy. They found you out for a might[y] Mathematician at Chantrey's; let them stick to that; it will do <u>weel</u> <u>eneugh</u>. We found Mrs Lockhart with her children about her whom I had never seen before, one little thing excepted which I had formerly just peeped at in its cradle. Johny's face is handsome and looks sensible & refined; but Walter is a thing that one would like to steal and keep in one's own house for ones own companion & play-fellow. I would part with all the kittens that ever gamboled upon a carpet for such a thing as him. He is a very handsome likeness of yourself; but mark me, I say very handsome likeness, therefore Grandpapa need not be too conceated. ――― Your friend John Richardson has had much distress lately in his house amongst his children, who have been dangerously ill; and one little Girl cannot yet rise from bed and continues in a very precarious state. Our merry-making there, the last day of the old year (Mrs Lockhart was one of our company) ended with Nursery calamity, and the Apothecary became the <u>firstfoot</u> [422] (woe worth him with his leeches & his draughts!) in the new year's morning. ―― My Sister & I were the other morning in Town to visit a young Bride whom you know something about. ―― Miss Fanny Edgeworth, now Mrs Lestock Wilson. A courtship of seven years seems in this case to have turned out happily at last. I wish Irish women in general were as difficult to win; it would relieve us considerably from the living deluge which pours upon us from that quarter to our great <u>Contentation</u> and that of Mr Malthus.[423] But I must not enlarge on this subject, for what does not the word <u>Irish</u> bring into ones mind at this moment? I wish the country & his

---

1828, finding her well but looking more aged (Johnson, 1049); Scott writes to her shortly after (26 May 1826) that "business and domestic calamity" prevented his returning to Hampstead (Grierson, 10:424). But they clearly met again shortly before his death, for on 11 November 1831 Baillie writes to Margaret Holford Hodson that "I saw Sir W. Scott twice while he was in Town, and thought him looking remarkably well & in good spirits. I hope he is now safely over the bay of Biscay" (postscript to Hodson letter 51, Volume 2).

422. first-fit: the first person one meets on new-year's morning (*SND*).

423. Economist Thomas Robert Malthus (1766-1834) argued in *An Essay on the Principle of Population, As It Affects the Future Improvements of Society; With Remarks on the Speculations of Mr. Godwin, M. Condorcet, and Other Writers* (1798) that the population could be checked by "moral restraint," meaning postponement of the age of marriage accompanied by strict sexual continence before marriage. He remained profoundly pessimistic, however, about mankind's ability to regulate population by moral restraint, though he opposed birth control "devices" (Mark Blaug, *Thomas Robert Malthus (1766-1834) and John Stuart Mill (1806-1873)* [Hants, England: Edward Elgar, 1991], ix-x).

Majesty's Ministers well thro' their difficulties; and hope that in emancipating Irish Catholics which is just & right as well as expedient, they will take care not to make Catholics eligible to sit in Parliament for Scotch or English Boroughs or Counties. It is a reasonable line to draw and will enable them to calculate pretty exactly how many Catholic members they will have to cope with. Dont laugh at my scrap of politic, it is very sound, and is not the less so that it would probably not satisfy any of the contending parties.[424] — My Sister begs to be very kindly remembered to you. We have both weathered the severe part of the winter very well for one who is naturally subject to bad colds & one who has lately become subject to rheumatism. — I have at last got Mrs Heman's Captive knight with its music dedicated to you and find my copy to be one of a fourth edition.[425] This is going on sweetly. I have got "My earings" [sic] also which I am told is very pretty. What a got [good?] match such a composer must prove for a Welsh Clergiman! — Farewell, wish you are to be in Town in spring, and that I am to see you there; aye and here also — Yours always my dear friend, affectionately

    J Baillie

20437 ff.106-107 (Address: Miss Scott--no postmark)[426]

                         Hampstead Feby 13th [1829]

My dear Miss Scott,

    There are two young friends of mine at present on a visit to their Brother in Edin^{r} who are ambitious of your acquaintance. I know you have a large perhaps too large an acquaintance, yet I the more readily make the request I am about to mention, because I know that you will find them cheerful & agreeable and every way worthy of being known to you. Their

---

424. Throughout the late summer and fall of 1828, the Duke of Wellington sought to soften George IV's views on Catholic emancipation and by January 1829 announced that a Catholic Relief Bill would be forthcoming. The Duke of Cumberland immediately headed for Windsor and succeeded in fueling the king's anti-Catholic sentiments, but Wellington, believing Cumberland to be plotting to overthrow the government, went to Windsor on 26 February to relay to the king that Cumberland planned to bring together a mob of 20,000 Protestants to march on Windsor. By March 1829 George IV realized he must listen to Wellington and accept Catholic emancipation, and by April the king had given his consent to the Roman Catholic Relief Act (Hibbert, 304-10).

425. Felicia Hemans' "The Captive Knight" appeared in 1820 in *Records of Women*, a volume dedicated to Joanna Baillie. "Knight" opens with lines from Scott's *Lady of the Lake*: "The prisoned thrush may brook the cage,/ The captive eagle dies for rage" (Felicia Hemans, *Records of Women*, ed. Donald H. Reiman [New York: Garland, 1978], 213).

426. This letter is to Anne Scott (1803-1833), Scott's youngest daughter.

names are Miss Carr & Miss Isabella Carr, Daughters of my excellent friends & neighbours M^r & Mrs Carr of Frognel, and if you will have the goodness to call upon them and permit them now & then to call up on you of a morning, I shall truly consider it as a favour done to myself and think you a very <u>very</u> good Girl. — If your cousin Miss Anne Scott is with you, I beg to be remembered to her; and if she will also bestow a little of her time on my young friends, I shall feel myself very much obliged to her. My Sister also begs to offer her kind remembrances to yourself & Miss A. Scott. —— I saw your Sister not long ago with her little family about her, and fell much in love with your second Nephew Walter, who is a pleasant, lively, intelligent Urchin as I ever saw.[427] — Believe me

　　My dear Miss Scott,
　　　　very truly yours
　　　　　　J Baillie

---

427. Scott's oldest daughter Sophia Scott Lockhart (1799-1837) had two sons, John Hugh (d.1831) and Walter (d. 1853), and two daughters, one who died an infant in 1824 and Charlotte, a close companion of her father.

 To *Anne Elliott*

(1809-1833)

There is virtually no information available on Joanna Baillie's close friend Anne Elliott, for she apparently never published or married, making her life difficult to trace. In the early nineteenth century, Egland House, in the parish of Awliscombe, was the home of Anne's brother the Rev. Luther Graves Elliott (d. 1846) and his wife, whose eldest son was barrister George Percy Elliott (1800-1874). The family was not originally from Devon, so Anne Elliott's baptismal records would be housed in another location.[1] A collection of papers at the Devon Record Office includes an agreement entered into by Thomasine Elliot [*sic*] (described as a spinster of Honiton) for the building of Egland House in 1804, and the collection also includes leases of the house after 1835 by George Percy Elliott of the Temple, London.[2]

Along with different spellings of Elliott (Elliot), the date of Anne Elliott's death is also unclear. Devon county records show that Thomasine Anne Elliott of Egland House, Awliscombe, age 76, was buried at Dunkswell church on 7 April 1835; and a memorial inscription in the church records that she died on 1 April 1835, the daughter of Rear Admiral George Elliott, late of Copford, Essex.[3] Letter 65 (dated and postmarked December 1835) to Margaret Holford Hodson also mentions Elliott's death; but in a letter to Mary Montgomery postmarked 1834, Baillie writes,

> I am sure you will be sorry to learn, if you have not heard of it already, that we have lost our dear & excellent & pleasant friend Mrs Anne Elliott. She died in her own house in Devon about a fortnight ago, after an Illness from which it was expected she would recover till within a week of her end. We had expected her here the middle of this month on her usual visit every second spring to us & her friends in Essex. Such a friend, under any

---

1. I thank archivists John Brunton and S. M. Laithwaite, Devon County Council, Devon Record Office, for what little biographical information we could find on Anne Elliott. Mrs. Thomasin Anne Elliott, Egland, also appears in the "Index Indicators" of *The Gentleman's Magazine*, 1817 (page 194 of part 2).

2. Devon Records 5333M/E1.

3. See indexes of the Devon County Council, Devon Record Office, Exeter.

circumstances, would have been a grievous loss, at our age it is irreparable. How playful & pleasant & kind & generous she was! You have met her here, have you not, and I think you suited one another.[4]

Unless the postmark is unclear and the Bodleian has also numbered Baillie's letter to Montgomery out of sequence, I cannot account for the discrepancy.

---

4. See Bodleian letter 93, ff.184-186 to Mary Montgomery, Volume 2.

Most of the following letters to Mrs. Anne Elliott are owned by the National Library of Scotland, identified as **Acc 9467**, and transcribed by their permission; the individual numbers are mine:

1 (No address or postmark)

Hampstead Oct.ʳ 26ᵗʰ 1809

My dear & kind Hostess of Egland,

You never fed & cherished any body by whom you have got more credit than you have by me. Every body here says I am fat and looking well; I would fain have them to add comely to it, tho' on this point they do not express themselves so heartily as I could wish. However, your kindness has done all for my good looks and good condition that can be done; and so take, in return for all the good you have done us, and all the pleasure you have given us, my warm & hearty thanks: you have not spent your kindness on those who regard it not. The only bad thing I have got by being so long your inmate, is a disposition to quarrel with my breakfast, and to think my tea with the thin Hampstead milk in it much worse than it used to be, and I fear some of our good neighbours here may not appear quite so agreeable after the daily company we have had, but this I hope will wear off by degrees, and leave all the benefit of our Devon visit clear gain. ——

Agnes is to write to you under this same cover and will tell you of our journey to Town and our happy meeting with our friends in Grosvenor Street,[5] so on this subject I shall say nothing: I think I had better leave her the jubilee too, for she has a knack at putting more into her paper than with this scrambling hand of mine (tho' I am on my good behaviour just now and writing very close) I can possibly manage. But it belongs to me fairly, I think, to tell you of our poetical neighbour & your great admirer Mʳ Coxe,[6] in whose favour you hold as high a place as ever. We saw him for the first time day before yesterday, in very low spirits, being troubled with head aches for which he was going to be capped; but as we sat and talked about you, and the pleasure above all which his last verses had given to you & our selves, he revived wonderfully, and we left him like one who thought he might spend some years longer in this world very comfortably. Yesterday we received from him the cover which incloses

---

5. Agnes Baillie (1760-1861) was Baillie's only sister and constant companion. Their brother Dr. Matthew Baillie writes that Agnes Baillie, born in the Manse of Shotts on 24 September 1760, had "a quick ready Understanding, with a good deal of various knowle[d]ge, so as to be much beyond the common level of Women in these respects" (qtd. in Franco Crainz, *The Life and Works of Matthew Baillie* [Santa Polomba: PelitiAssociati, 1995], 10). Dr. and Mrs. Baillie were living at Grosvenor.

6. Edward Coxe, also a friend of Scott, contributed "The Last Leaf" and "On Reading Marmion" to Baillie's 1823 *A Collection of Poems*.

this, all written over with verses for you, and on a detached piece of paper, a fifth stanza to the last verses on his Wife's grey hairs, which is very pretty, and makes a good addition to it; but as it would, perhaps, make this packet heavier than a frank ought to be,[7] I shall send it to you in the leaves of M[r] Moor's book, where you may search for it.

Perhaps you will not be ill pleased to hear that my friends in Edin[r] are really intent on bringing out my Family Legend upon their little temporary Theatre;[8] for their new Theatre, as it is to cost according to their present plan £20,000, may probably be 20 years of being built. I found upon the table on our arrival here, two long letters upon this subject from Walter Scott, and he is very friendly & very zealous about it indeed. He has recommended to me a few alterations to suit it to the Edin[r] Stage which I shall adopt; and I have recommended to him & his Manager M[r] H. Siddons,[9] to be at as little expence with it as possible. I have even desired that the Laird of Macklean's philabegg[10] may be of such tartan as will do for Banquo or the Thane of Fife afterwards,[11] if the piece should not succeed, and that no new scenes may be painted for it that will not be commonly useful for other plays. If it should perfectly succeed, I own I shall be very much pleased there at, but I feel from so many former disappointments an impression as if some cross luck or other would befall it and am not very sanguine on the subject. ——— I now intend to be very busy with my pen during the winter months to make up for a long track of idleness, and when I look over the play I had with me at Egland, I shall remember the few improvements in the language which you were so kind as to point out to me. —— Pray offer my best regards to M[rs] Burgess & Miss Somerville, and remember me kindly to your Brother & M[rs] Luther, and also to your good neighbour M[rs] Watts & the Miss Simcoes: all of them so good to us! Farewell!

your truly affectionate   J Baillie

7. A frank was a letter or envelope bearing the superscribed signature of a member of Parliament entitled to send letters post free (*OED*).

8. Though Scott's insistence put Baillie's *The Family Legend* on stage, on 29 January 1810 the curtain rose to a packed house, and the highland play scored a tremendous success for three weeks, followed by a revival of *De Monfort* (Edgar Johnson, *Sir Walter Scott: The Great Unknown*, 2 vols. [New York: Macmillan, 1970], 223-24).

9. Henry Siddons, the eldest son of actress Sarah Siddons, had moved to Edinburgh to manage the Edinburgh Theatre. Usually suffering monetary losses, the turning point for the theatre came with its popular production in February 1819 of Scott's *Rob Roy*.

10. fillabeg: kilt (*SND*).

11. See Shakespeare's *Macbeth*.

2 (Address: Mrs Elliott / Egland / Honiton, Devon--no postmark)

Hampstead Feby 26th 1810

You profess, my dear Lady Egland, to love me dearly, and I have no good reason to believe it entirely a <u>hum</u>;[12] so I shall treat you as I do all those who make such professions, give you something to do for my sake. This present something will cost you the trouble of writing a letter to your agreeable friend Miss Maltby at Bath; but I think you will not begrudge it when I tell you that, besides your love for me, your love for Walter Scott is likewise concerned. Writing lately to him after having read Wallace, I mentioned the work to him lest he should not have read it, and said it was written by a Miss Holford who had sent him some verses a great while ago.[13] In return, he wrote to me, that he remember'd a long time since receiving a copy of very beautiful verses address'd to him, but that having no clue given him by which to find out the ingenious Authoress, to whose name & residence he was a perfect stranger; and being glad to excuse himself from doing what is always embarassing [*sic*] to him, viz writing a letter about himself & his poetry to a Lady he had never seen, he had committed a great incivility & neglect. After praising the work very highly he says "If you have any opportunity of sending to Miss Holford my earnest wishes for her attaining her deserved rank among the Authors of the day, and think it will please her to know them, you will oblige me greatly by conveying them to her[.]" I have no means of doing this but thro' you by the way of Miss Maltby, and I dare say she will have no objection to oblige us, as she woteth[14] not of the very merry dinner we ate together at Egland the day of her departure from thence, when we sat down at the table by the window as usual, emancipated from our three days good behaviour. No; she knows not a tittle of all this; and if we send our best comp^ts & remembrances to her, which I hope you will do for Agnes & I as well as yourself, she will be very glad to oblige such <u>civil</u> & <u>agreeable</u> people. — I trust then my kind Hostess, you will do this for me handsomely as it ought to be done, and I in return will give you the pleasure, (for you do take a friend's pleasure in it) to know that your old favourite the Family Legend still holds up its head handsomely at Edin^r and they have brought out, as a rival piece to it, De Monfort, which has also been very favourably received. This intelligence came upon me last week quite unexpectedly, for I had not had the slightest hint given me of

---

12. hum: murmuring, noise (*OED*).

13. Margaret Holford Hodson followed her mother's example and developed an interest in literature at an early age, her first work being an 1809 poem entitled *Wallace, or the Fight of Falkirk*. See letters to Hodson (Volume 2) and to Scott herein.

14. woteth: knoweth (*OED*).

their intention. I am told Mr Henry Siddons acts De Monfort wonderfully well, Mr Scott says ten thousand times better than he ever did any other character in his life; and tho' the noble Jane is represented by a Mrs Young[15] who is neither dignified, nor elegant, nor feeling, so great is the disposition of my friends there to be pleased, that it goes down with them mar-(mar)vellously. — Sir John Sinclair[16] has been playing me (but this you will not mention) a terrible trick by offering, unknown to me, after I had expressly forbid it, the Family Legend to the Manager of Covent Garden "in case" he says to Kemble[17] "Miss B. can be prevail'd upon to let them have a copy of it." This obliged me to write to Kemble immediately to put a stop to all further negociation, and at the same time to give Sir John a rap over the knuckles that will, I hope, keep him quiet for some time to come. —— I was in Town for a few hours about a fortnight ago, and saw Mrs Hunter who is in very indifferent spirits at present on having parted with her son, who, by the advice of his Physicians is gone to a warmer climate:[18] he sailed for Lisbon about a week ago. She is, however,

---

15. Bolton cites several Scott adaptations for the stage casting a Mrs. Young about this same time in Edinburgh, but there is no further identification (see Philip Bolton, *Scott Dramatized* [London: Mansell, 1992]).

16. Sir John Sinclair (1754-1835), lawyer and M.P. for Caithness, Scotland, often took up lost causes. He tried to form a third political party after the impeachment of Hastings in order to overthrow Pitt, presided over the Gaelic versions of *Ossian* which Macpherson refused to produce and attempted to advise both Baillie and Scott in literary endeavors (see the unpublished dissertation of Chester Lee Lambertson, "The Letters of Joanna Baillie [1801-1832]" [Ph.D. diss., Harvard University, 1956], cxxv-cc). Also see note 1 in letters "To Family" herein.

17. John Philip Kemble (1757-1823), one of England's most famous actors, began playing parts in his father's company in early childhood. His sister, Sarah Kemble Siddons, first recommended him to the Chamberlain's company as Theodosius in Lee's tragedy in 1776, with dozens of parts to follow. Kemble was a scholar, a man of breeding and a fine actor with a larger range of characters in which he excelled than any English tragedian. He wrote prologues for charitable institutions in York and Leeds, where he appeared for the first time in *Hamlet*--he is said to have written out the part over 40 times. He managed the Edinburgh Theatre for a while in 1781, and his first appearance in London was at Drury Lane as Hamlet in 1783. He remained at Drury Lane for 19 years, representing over 120 characters himself; and on 25 January 1800 Kemble played De Monfort in Baillie's play. In 1802 he acquired a share of Covent Garden, but in 1808 when the house burned, taking 20 lives, Kemble and other investors were nearly ruined for lack of insurance. A loan of £10,000 from Lord Percy helped him reopen the new Covent Garden Theatre. Portraits of John Kemble abound, several of which are by Lawrence, notably Kemble as Cato, as Hamlet and as Rolla (*DNB*, X:1260-66).

18. Anne Home Hunter (1742-1821), writer and oldest daughter of surgeon Everard Home, married Baillie's uncle Dr. John Hunter in 1771. Of her four children two survived her, son John and daughter Agnes who married Sir James Campbell. Anne Hunter published *Sports of the Genii* (1797) and miscellaneous poems

amusing herself with touching up some of her little pieces, and I hope she will by & by be in better spirits. -- Our Friends at No 72 are all well,[19] a bad cold excepted which Mrs B. has had for a short time. -- Agnes sends you her love with mine, and will write to you before it be long. Give our compliments to Mrs Watts: her Sister, our neighbour, I saw yesterday pretty well. She certainly stands this winter better than she did the last. Pray remember us to your Friends at Salviston; we are very glad to hear Mrs Luther's eyes are better. Fare well! in all hearty love & good-liking

    yours ever

     J Baillie

PS. On further thought, you had better in your preamble to our Bard's message to Miss Holford say nothing about my having written to him upon the subject: but only that Mr Scott having read & admired Wallace, and being informed it was the work of Miss Holford from whom he had received a very beautiful copy of verses which his great reluctance to write about himself & his poetry to a Lady entirely unknown to him; had prevented him from acknowledging as he ought, felt him self anxious to convey to her &c &c. —— I think they had better receive you & me into the corps diplomatique[.][20]

3 (Address: M^rs A: Elliott / Egland / near Honiton / Devonshire-- postmarked 1818)

                      Hampstead August 29th [1818]

My dear Friend,

    The accounts we received of you some time since from your Sister Mrs Elliott, and since she left Town from the Blands, thro' the medium of Mrs Hoare,[21] are favourable, so I hope you are now in such good conditions that I may enquire immediately of yourself, without doing any thing troublesome or improper. At any rate, if you do not care for writing yet, you have those near you, I am sure, who will willingly send me a few lines of answer as your Deputy. Indeed if I did not care a straw about you & were as hard hearted in regard to all your illness & suffering as any Turk, I must for my own credit know how you do; for there are so many enquiries made to

---

throughout her life. Extremely little is known of the son John; and the Hunterian Museum of the Royal College of Surgeons, London, have been unable to find evidence to shed light on his career and whereabouts.

    19. JB's brother Dr. Matthew, his wife Sophia and their children William and Elizabeth were at No. 72 Cavendish Square at this time.

    20. See NLS letter 3879 ff.13-15 to Scott.

    21. Louisa Gurney Hoare was married to Samuel Hoare, Lady Byron's banker; Baillie was a close friend of the whole family. Children included Jane, Joseph and several others.

me upon this interesting subject from M̲ṟ̲s̲ Baillie from Windsor[22] M̲ṟ̲s̲ Hunter now our Neighbour in Hampstead & others of your admirers & well wishers, that not to know any thing of the matter would by & by materially lower me in the estimation of them all. Do let me know faithfully & circumstancially how far you are recovered from your late illness, and I shall not only be a Turk but an ungrateful [ingrate?] into the bargain if I do not heartily rejoice in receiving the best possible accounts of you. —— I have been keeping house by myself here for nearly this month past while Agnes has been on a visit to Miss Wilson at Brighton. She is enjoying the sea view & the bathing there and also the crowds of dressed people & the painted brick houses which she, in her abundant happiness, calls picturesque. I trust she will return soon to me, but she has not yet named her day. M̲ṟ̲s̲ Hunter has got a small house here in Frognal, near M̲ṟ̲s̲ Watt, where you remember we took shelter with Miss Edgeworth from the rain.[23] I see her some part of every day, and were it not for this her days would pass with no variety at all, for her feet are so swelled & tender that she cant walk out. She is well otherwise & looks well and is always contented & cheerful. She wished to have had a small cottage near my Brother, at Wentworth and passed a week there with M̲ṟ̲s̲ Baillie, endeavouring to find one without success[.] M̲ṟ̲s̲ Campbell[24] & M̲ṟ̲s̲ Walker[25] went a good while ago to Bath & are now in the Isle of Wight. M̲ṟ̲s̲ C. suffers a great deal with rheumatism in her limbs, being very lame; and as she thought herself somewhat better for the Bath waters, I think it is not improbable she may spend the next winter there. Poor thing! she has but a melancholy prospect before her. She has a naturally cheerful temper

---

22. Dr. Matthew Baillie and his family had taken a house near Windsor Castle where Dr. Baillie could be near George III as one of the court physicians. Mrs. Baillie is Matthew's wife Sophia Denman Baillie.

23. Maria Edgeworth (1768-1849) first focused her writing on educational topics, translating Madame de Genlis's *Adèle et Théodore*. She experimented with various teaching methods, publishing a series including *The Parents Assistant* (1796) and *Early Lessons* (1801); but she became well known for her novels *Castle Rackrent* (1800), *Belinda* (1801), *Popular Tales* (1804), *The Modern Griselda* (1805), *Leonora* (1806), the six volume *Tales of Fashionable Life* (1809-12), *Ormond* (1817), *Helen* (1834), etc., many of which document Irish society. Edgeworth is one of the first women novelists "to apply an insight articulated by Wollstonecraft, that women have their own language" (see Janet Todd, ed., *British Women Writers* [New York: Continuum, 1989], 204-7). Baillie and Edgeworth met in 1813 (see Scott letter 3884 ff.184-187). Her sisters are Mrs. Beaufort and Mrs L. Wilson.

24. This does not seem to be Lady Campbell but may be the poet Thomas Campbell's wife, Matilda Sinclair Campbell, who was not well for many years before her death (see Mary Ruth Miller, *Thomas Campbell* [Boston: Twayne, 1978], 33).

25. This may be Mrs. Joshua Walker of Hendon, Middlesex, Margaret Holford Hodson's sister.

& an inexhaustible pleasure in reading for her greatest supports. – But there are other worthies of our family that you would fully as lief hear about. – Sophia is busy nursing her Grand child the young Sophia at Wentworths.[26] The poor little thing was brought almost to death's door with some bowel complaint before they left Town, but is now I hear thriving finely under the watchful eye of Grand Mama, and has got two teeth which had been very long of coming & anxiously expected. William, is with them at present, but returns to Oxford the beginning of October.[27] Elizabeth & her Husband have, I believe, ere this set off for the Lakes of Cumberland where they will spend some time; he having leave of absence for 3 months. — I have now given you an account of us all. —— Every body here has read the last volume of the tale of my Landlord; and Jeany Deans is allowed by <u>every body</u> to be the perfection of female virtue.[28] It is indeed a character of great simplicity & strong rectitude & not over-strained in any of its virtues. Her lover not Ruben Butler but Dumbie dykes, is a great favourite of mine. Having had in the former tales so much of the stiff borrowed phrasiology of the Covenanters & allusions to Scotch law, some of the other characters appear less new than they are in reality. —— Give my best respects & kind wishes to the friends that are round you if you are still at Woolford. I hope M<u>rs</u> Simcoe & all her family are well. Emember [sic] me kindly to M<u>r</u> & M<u>rs</u> Luther Elliott & your Niece, and should you see your neigbour M<u>rs</u> Watts soon, have the goodness also to remember me to her. Fare well! and believe me always, my dear Friend

    very affectionately yours

     J Baillie

4 (Address: M<u>rs</u> Elliott / Polste[a]d / near Nayland / Suffolk--postmarked 1819)

Hampstead August 9<u>th</u> 1819

My dear Lady Egland,

    I have news to tell you that will make your ears tingle. My Sister M<u>rs</u> Agnes Baillie is going to take a trip to Paris, and if this letter should

---

26. Elizabeth Margaret Baillie (1794-1876), the only daughter of Matthew and Sophia Denman Baillie, married Capt. Robert Milligan (1781-1875) on 11 July 1816, and the couple, with only daughter Sophia (1817-1882), lived at Ryde on the Isle of Wight for most of Joanna's life.

27. William Hunter Baillie (1797-1894), the only son of Matthew and Sophia Baillie, graduated from Oxford, married Henrietta Duff in 1835, lived many years in Hampstead, moved to Richmond and later back to Upper Harley Street in Joanna's last years. They were the parents of 8 children.

28. See Scott's 4-volume *Tales of My Landlord* which begins with *The Black Dwarf*, later followed by *Old Mortality* (1816).

reach you before thursday, you may think of her on that day as sailing upon the salt sea towards her high destination, somewhat sick perhaps, but nothing sorry. She is going with an old friend of hers, a widow Lady – Mrs Lamb, whom you may perhaps have seen in Grosvenor St: This expedition has been in prospect for some time, but as this same friend of hers, tho' professing many good qualities, has a certain infirmity of indecision about her, Agnes did not care for mentioning it to any body lest she should be disappointed. She is to leave Hampstead to morrow & London early on Wednesday morning, and has been busy for some days past preparing & packing her clothes and looking into the vocabulary now & then for some convenient french phrases useful to Travellers which are likewise put up for the journey. You know pretty well what kind of french scholar she is. She will turn a french book into English, after her fashion, as expeditiously as most people, and gallop thro' twenty volumes (I dont know how many) of Amedas de Gaul in old french with extraordinary expedition & perseverance;[29] but all this I fear will be of little avail, for the pronouncing of the language is as strange to her tongue as any highland Gilly,[30] and the sound of it to her ear, pronounced by others, nearly as much so. However, she goes with this friend who has been abroad before & a young Lady, Daughter of this friend who speaks french well, and she will not find herself at any very great loss, tho' now & then dashed with mortification. A young Oxonian, the son of Mrs Lamb goes also and perhaps another Gentleman, a party not too large to be inconvenient. She expects to be gone about 6 weeks. I am very glad of this movement; for she has had a great desire a long time to see Paris and I wished her to be gratified.

My Brother & his family have been at their Country Quarters near Acton for these 3 weeks, and we were to see them for a day last week, when we found them well & looking well and much contented with their situation tho' the house is a much worse one than they have been accustomed to. After my Brother had taken me over the house & pointed out the views from the window &c &c, he opened the door of a small chamber off the green house & said with great satisfaction on his countenance "and there is a sight for you!" This sight was his son William busy taking extracts from Blackstone.[31] The young man has taken to this regular daily employment of his own accord and his Father tells me his extracts are exceedingly well chosen. I really hope William will not be a

29. The chivalric romance *Amadis de Gaule* is attributed to Herberay des Essarts (1540).

30. gilly: dial., clove or pink wallflower (*OED*).

31. Sir William Blackstone (1723-80), judge, provided some of the most comprehensive legal writing of the day, including *Analysis of the Law* (1754) and *Commentaries on the Laws of England*, 4 vols. (1765-69) (*DNB*, II:595-602).

silly idle man in the world. — The greatest man in their immediate neighbourhood is Mr Willen the Cow-keeper, who lives in a very handsome Gothic mansion of his own building, in very good taste which would make a very handsome abode for any of our royal Dukes. There is one very singular circumstance belonging to it; M^r W's house is the only one in the parish, and the church is in his grounds in which service is performed every sunday by a clergyman paid of course by Mr Willen. He & his wife Mrs Baillie told us, are cultivated well-bred people with no vulgarity either of language or manners or stile of living. I must say, however that the business of cow-keeping has been somewhat assisted by contracts for supplying Government with horse to prevent you from risking your money on an uncertain speculation. — Mrs Hunter & Lady Campbell[32] have gone to Brighton together & I hope they will both be the better for it. — How have you been since we heard from you? and when do you move westward? Give my best respects to the friends you are with. Agnes sends you her kind love, and with all kind wishes & affection, I remain, my dear Friend most truly yours

   J Baillie

5 (Address: Mrs Elliott at Mrs Canning's / Abberton near Colchester / Essex--postmarked 1819)

                    Hampstead Septr 2^d [1819]

Alac alac, my dear Friend! your kind letter only tantalizes me for I am bound to leave home on the 12th to set out with my Brother & Mrs B. for Gloucester Sh: and we shall not be returned till after the 19th for we shall be gone a fortnight. This is very cross luck for me. — I thank you for the very beautiful lines you have sent me which I like much. The Imagination of the Poet & feelings of the Christian are finely blended. In return for them I will give you what farther accounts I have to give of our Traveller. After arriving at Calais, their first day's journey was to Bullogne [sic] where they found themselves at the close of day upon the streets not knowing where to find shelter, for the Hotels were all full. An English Lady, understanding their distress, very kindly directed them to one in the low Town, where Agnes was fortunate to meet with your favorite Mr Bonney, so far on his way to Paris in company with Dr Kay head of Christ Col: Cambridge; and these two reverend Gentlemen joined company with Agnes & her party, and not only took all the trouble of travelling off their hands for the remainder of the way, but took Lodgings for them when they

---

32. Agnes Hunter, surviving daughter of Dr. John Hunter and Anne Home Hunter and cousin to Baillie, married Sir James Campbell ; after his death, she married Col. Benjamin Charlewood, retaining her title. She had no children.

got to Paris.[33] The last letter I received from her was written a few days after their arrival and she had not then been to any public place or seen any of the great sights, so I have but little to report to you again. The most remarkable thing that had befallen her was going into the great fruit market with her friends to get a bargain of fruit, and losing their way home, from having given a wrong direction to the person who was to carry home the fruit, she & Miss Lamb being bold enough to separate themselves from the rest, under the conduct of this market Worthy, who took them thro' many odious places which appeared to be the St: Giles's of Paris and alarmed them not a little before they found out the mistake & could get back to the right St: Fortune does not always favour the bold. — I am going to my Brother's to day for a few days to meet Lady Byron, who takes them on her way from [*sic*] to South hampton, where she is going on a visit [to] Capt: Byron & his Lady.[34] I am rather hurried having not yet pack'd up my baggage & having other momentous affairs on hand. So fare well & God bless you!

your affectionate

J Baillie

PS. Where do you sleep when you come to Town? If you please you can have a bed in Grosvenor St: by giving Mrs Foster the housekeeper notice before hand; and you will find Mrs Hunter returned from Brighton who will be very glad to see you. – I beg you will offer my best respects to Mrs Canning.

6 (Address: Mrs Elliott / Egland near Honiton / Devon shire--postmarked 1819)

Hampstead Septr 25th 1819

My dear Friend,

You will not be ill pleased to hear of our Traveller, now that you are your self (as I suppose) settled again in your own quiet & pleasant abode after your wanderings. She is safe at Hampstead again, having arrived yesterday, and tho' I have been listening with greedy ears ever since, I have not yet heard half of her travel's story. She is well & glad to be home again; and I shall say no more about her till I have dispatched a little piece of secret business which is the reason of my writing to you at

---

33. Writer and divine Henry Kaye Bonney, DD (1780-1862), was presented to the rectory of King's Cliffe to succeed his father in 1810 and appointed examining chaplain to Dr. Pelham, bishop of Lincoln in 1821. He was an intimate friend of Dr. John Kaye (1783-1853), fellow of Christ's College and later bishop of Lincoln (*DNB*, II:822-23).

34. The Capt. Byron mentioned here (and in NLS letters 3888 ff.40-42 & 73-75 to Scott) is probably Mr. Valentine Henry Wilmot, Byron's cousin and husband of writer Barbarina Brand, later Lady Dacre.

this present. -- There is a Mr Warren, a Gentleman of considerable fortune, his place is called Bromely hall or Bromely Park (I forget which) and the Revd Mr Vernon, Clergyman of Bromely, is his Brother in law.[35] It is of great importance that a friend of mine should know what kind of character he bears in that part of the country, and I think that by writing to Mr Whitmore, you may be able to do us this service. He has (I mean Mr Warren) not lived at his own place but with his Mother in law at a house called Bromely Cottage which is not far from Mr Rigley's fine Place beyond Colchester, and he is intimate with Col: Rebow's family. By these marks I think Mr Whitmore will find out the man and be able, if he is not acquainted with him, to find out what character he has amongst his neighbours. Probably Mr Harrold may know some thing of him. In short get me information (information) in any way you please but by all means get it; for it is connected with a matter of grave consideration. --- Agnes was better than 3 weeks in Paris, and tho' she has seen fewer public places than I & my party did, [she] has seen more of the people, having been in a few private houses of English people resident there, where she met with some french. Her time would have been very agreeably spent if her Travelling Companion, Mrs Lamb, had not been of a very indecided & over careful disposition, so that in constantly balancing between two good things to do the very best, they lost much time & often did then very worst. It is well she wears peticoats [sic] & is not at the bar, lest she should be chosen as successor to the Chancellor. They returned by Normandy which gave them a view of one of the finest parts of France, and had a short but rough passage from Diepe to Brighton as sick as Toads all the way. She will herself, I hope, write or tell you more of these matters some time or other. -- I returned from Gloucester sh: day before yesterday, after having made with my good friends, a very satisfactory visit of 10 days to Dunsboum [sic].[36] I found the greater part of the trees which Agnes & I planted there 5 years ago thriving well and beginning to give some what of a clothed look to the barer side of the house so that it no longer looks like an Inn but like a strange ill-constructed Gentleman's house, – a great improvement this! The wild wood land walks upon the high banks of the brook near them are delightful; and every thing about us had the simplicity of the golden age while the daily papers were

---

35. This must be George Charles Vernon (1779-1835) who married Frances Maria Borlase-Warren in 1803. The *DNB* records that Frances Maria's brother was killed in Egypt but does not provide his name or date of death (XX:869-71).

36. During his stay in Gloucestershire, convenient to Windsor, the Baillies purchased Duntisbourne House in 1806, first as a country retreat but later as an estate which William Baillie inherited. See Anne Carver, *The Story of Duntisbourne Abbots* (Gloucester: Albert E. Smith, 1966), 27.

telling us of the triumphs of Mr Hunt & the bloodshed at Ma[n]chester.[37] I hope you are well. Remember me kindly & respectfully to Mrs Simcoe & all her family & to your friends at Salviston, like wise to Mrs Watts. I hope Miss F. Head will allow me to offer my remembrances to her.[38]   ever affectionately yours   J Baillie

PS. In looking over my letter I find I have made no apology for the trouble I am giving you regarding the information to be asked of Mr Whitmore; I hope you will not think me very ill-manner'd.

7 (Address: Mrs A. Elliott / Egland near Honiton--postmarked 1826)
                                        Hampstead July 11th 1826
My dear Friend,
    I shall make this letter serve both for you & your Neighbour of Ashfield; and as she has nobly come to the determination to sacrifice probably a considerable sum for the good of the literary public, I will spare her the 9 or 10 pence which this may cost, and take it out of your income. Give her my kind regards and say that I have written to Miss Hawkins, but if that save her from correspondence with this Lady, I shall be out in my reckoning. Say that I am very glad indeed she has come to a resolution to publish the remainder of the Messiah which will continue to do her credit when we shall be all in our narrow homes; and say also that I believe she (she) can more perfectly explain to him all that she wishes on the business, tho' I should consider it as no trouble whatever to correct the press for the 2^d vol: I will do it most readily and think it a pleasure rather than a toil. The only part of her letter which I dislike is her taking up so seriously, the little defence which I had made on Mr Sotheby's behalf,[39] regarding the mysterious passage: that, tell her, is naught & foolish, and not like a woman who has brains enough to Translate Klopstock as she has

---

37. Politician Henry Hunt (1773-1835) presided at the Smithfield reform meeting in July 1819 and at the meeting in St. Peter's Fields, Manchester, in August, which was broken up by the yeomanry and became known as the Peterloo Massacre. Hunt, a revolutionary and contentious man, was imprisoned for two years for his involvement (*DNB*, X:264-66).

38. Miss Fanny Head, Baillie explains in NLS letters 3902 & 3903 to Scott, translated poet Friedrich Gottlieb Klopstock's (1724-1803) *Messiah*. See letter following.

39. William Sotheby (1757-1833) was a prodigious poet, playwright, and translator and the consummate man of letters in the Romantic Era. Though Byron disliked him, satirizing him as Mr. Botherby in *Beppo* (1818), Sotheby provided a societal focal point for many of the brightest literary minds of his time. Scott, Wordsworth, Coleridge, Southey were his friends (*DLB*, XCIII:160-170). See introduction and letters to Sotheby herein.

done. I am much gratified by Miss Head's kind remembrance and her approbation of the Martyr;[40] and so ends for the present all that relates to Ashfield. ---

Now for the communication which I hinted at in my letter to F. Head. — The Mercantile house of Milligan & Robinson [*sic*] has stopped payment, and what it will be able to do for its creditors, we cannot as yet tell; that must depend on the sale of West Indea Estates which are a most unsaleable property. David Milligan at his death (about 8 or 9 years ago) left the business in a most free, flourishing state; what imprudence or misfortune has brought about the present state of things, I cannot pretend to say. This besides being a great mortification, is a considerable worldly loss to the different members of the M. family, and we are all depressed by it in sympathy with them, particularly our dear & good Sophia, who never-the-less bears it better than might have been expected, feeling thankful that it will not so injure Robert & Eliz[th] & the Ladies of the family as to make any necessity for altering their manner of living. Robert will or may lose £20,000 but as it is chiefly money which was left to him by his Brother David, the interest of which during his Mother's life & from different occurrences since he (I believe) never enjoyed, he may be said to lose what he never had, but only in prospect. At David's death, the business was considered as so advantageous, that the family wished Robert to return to it and fill his Brother's place; his Father in law set his face so strongly against it that the idea was entirely given up, most fortunately or providentially for himself & our poor Elizabeth. Willy Milligan will lose the half of his fortune, but with a Troop in the Life Guards & the other half, will not be very ill off. Poor M[rs] Henry Milligan will lose the half of her income and it is the harder upon her because of the recent misfortune of her own family. Mary Milligan will lose £5000 and Justina (I believe) £7000, M[rs] Hughan of course is not involved unless it be for some small sum.[41] This is all that I know, and we wished you should

---

40. Baillie's drama *The Martyr* appeared in 1826 from Longman, Rees, Orme, Brown, and Green.

41. Dr. Ruth Paley, Public Record Office at Kew, uncovered the following concerning financial difficulties of the mercantile house of Milligan and Robertson (not Robinson as Baillie records). Several bankruptcy cases are recorded under the name of Milligan, but the one most closely matching the time of this letter and the reference to West India Merchants is the 1828 bankruptcy file for Colin Robertson, Duncan Davidson Milligan, and Robert Milligan Dalzell of Milligan Robertson & Co., West India Merchants, 32 Fenchurch Street (PRO ref. B3/4340). Creditors included John Baillie (£2458) and Margaret Baillie (£1079) both of Devonshire Place, the estate of Robert Milligan deceased, late of Hampstead (£2836), Mrs. H. D. Milligan of Hertford Street (£145), J. Hughan and M. Milligan of Cotswold (£1189) and James Baillie, deceased, late of Bedford Square (£4861). The bankrupts' balance

be made acquainted with it by ourselves, both because it is due to your friendship which we have so long experienced, and because you might learn it suddenly & in some exaggerated manner, which would give your kind heart more pain than we could wish. Mrs Denman has returned to Welbeck St:[42] and Mrs Baillie has promised to come to us for a few days next Sunday, and we shall turn those few days into as many more as we can, and keep her with us till she goes to visit her Daughter at Rottendean [Rottingdean], near Brighton. William is now absent with his Uncle on the Circuit.[43] Whether this will induce him to pursue the profession we know not, but it is entirely from his own inclination that he goes. Your Nephew, I suppose is a busy man just now, and we do not pretend to disturb him. — We have suffered great listlessness & discomfort from the heat even on the top of our breezy hill; how has it fared with your old body (as you call it) in Devon? All the air that can possibly be made to pass through the open doors & windows of your dining parlour will be nothing to its demands. As ill luck would have it, our poor Agnes has entered upon her month of office as stewardess of the Friendly Society,[44] and she has notices given her every morning to visit this & that sick member thro' all the dusty lanes of the village with her face as red as the moon & her steps urged unnecessarily by an over-anxiety. I must take as much of the trouble off her as I can, but I have not yet had the satisfaction of sparing her at all, as we have two young Ladies staying in the house & other hindrances. — She sends you her kind love with mine. Fare well, dear friend!

J Baillie

---

sheet indicates debts and liabilities of £337,536, with a plus balance of £119,965; the apparent surplus arises from stating the sums due on mortgage of West India property at the full amount of principal and interest. Though the actual bankruptcy is recorded in 1828, it would not have been unusual to have a space of time between ceasing to trade and formal bankruptcy proceedings.

42. Sophia Baillie's brother, Chief Justice Thomas Denman, married Theodosia Vevers in 1804, moving to Russell Square, the most fashionable region for leading lawyers. He was an advocate of legal reform, abolition of slavery and was connected with several important trials. Thomas and Theodosia had 5 sons and 6 daughters (*DNB*, V:809).

43. For a while William Baillie acted as Judge's Marshal to his uncle Lord Chief Justice Thomas Denman (1779-1854) when he became a Judge; but apparently William never practiced law, mostly traveling and managing his own estates.

44. This must be a reference to the Society of Friends founded by Quaker George Fox (1624-1691). By the mid-1820s, "under the influence of the 'fire and vision' ministry of Joseph John Gurney (1788-1847), the Society had moved a considerable way toward mainstream evangelical Protestantism" (Sally Mitchell, ed., *Victorian Britain: An Encyclopedia* [New York and London: Garland, 1988], 314-15).

8 (No address or postmark)

Hampstead Octr 12th [1826]

My dear Friend,

I hope to get a frank or two at the Hoo,[45] where Agnes & I are going next Saturday to spend a few days, and I am glad of this opportunity to inclose my note of thanks for Ashfield to you and so make good the elegant proverb of killing two birds with one stone. Franks are now scarce articles with us and we must husband them. — I begin my writing with that which I know to be most interesting to you. We were in Town yesterday to see Mrs Baillie, after her journey from Brighton which she had accomplished with less fatigue than was expected, the day before. She was not strong enough, however, to sit upright in the carriage, but had some contrivance prepared to enable her to lie along in it. She is a little thinner, but in pretty good spirits, and seems altogether better than we could have supposed after such a tedious confinement. But I fear our plan of having her here for a little to brace her up before winter begin[s], will fall to the ground; she has got into her own home again and will not easily be induced to leave it. William has returned to Town with her, after having been some time at Dunsbourn [sic],[46] looking after the thinning of his woods; and truly he must have fared well there, for he has brought a pair of broad cheeks with him that might credit any country squire in the kingdom. I dont think your young man from Salviston returned with that advantage; we thought him very thin when he presented himself here, and town air & hard work has not probably fattened him much since. However, his complexion is healthy, he says he is well, and I trust that he speaks the truth. —— How much you would be concerned for Lord Gifford's Death! it comes upon poor Mrs Drew[e] after such a series of similar afflictions that it must I fear overcome her very sensitive mind altogether.[47] We have as yet had no direct way of knowing how she & Lady G. sustain their great loss, but we hope in a few days to hear by means of our neighbour Mrs Richardson[48] who has written to Mrs Alderson. ——— I was very agreeably

---

45. Hoo: from the Old English *hoh*, a place at the spur of land, i.e., Hoo Kent, Hoo Green Suffolk, etc.

46. William Baillie (1797-1894) became the Squire of Duntisbourne Abbots in 1823 on the death of his father Matthew.

47. Robert Gifford (1779-1826) was a judge appointed attorney-general in 1819. In 1824 he took the degree of sergeant-at-law and was then appointed lord chief justice of the common pleas and raised to the peerage as Baron Gifford of St. Leonard, Devonshire. His death on 4 September 1826 was probably a result of cholera. Gifford had married Harriet Maria Drewe, daughter of Rev. Edward Drewe, in 1816, with whom he had 7 children (*DNB*, VII:1185). Gifford's death would date this letter 1826.

48. This is probably John Richardson's wife Elizabeth Hill. John Richardson (1780-1864) was a parliamentary solicitor and for 30 years discharged the duties of

surprised by receiving the second vol: of the Messiah sooner that [*sic*] I expected. Fanny has worked hard, and her Printer has not been lazy. As a translation it has every merit; but shall I own to you that this 2^d vol: makes me less in love with the original than ever. I durst not tell Miss Hawkins or any German Worthy what I think of it for the life in my body. Do you know if Fanny has sent the second vol: to Miss Hawkins? It is a piece of attention she well deserves, and has not, I hope, been forgotten. It is a thing she would not omit if she thought of it, but our friend has more wit than consideration, and this makes me venture such a hint. Agnes is still keeping company with her friend Holinshed,[49] and when she takes up with him I think of no one with whom I would fain keep company as heretofore at the Back gammon table. The long evenings begin now and make one think of absent friends. I am old enough now to feel somewhat melancholy in the beginning of winter which used to be my favorite season, having more sociability in my original composition (composition) than romance and fearing neither illness nor aches. —— I have just been glancing at the contents of your last letter which reminds me of an omission. The kind interest you take in the affairs of the Milligans for our sake will make you glad to learn that they now wear a more favourable aspect. West Indea trade is less depressed than it was and the Estates which are to be sold to satisfy the Creditors will consequently fetch a better price, so that their losses at last may not be very great. I understand no misconduct attaches to Mʳ Robertson who [is] the Partner that managed every thing, but rashness & imprudence to a great degree. Mʳˢ & Miss Hoare have been staying at Cotiswold [Cotswolds?] lately with Mʳˢ Hughan & Justina and have gone from thence to the neighbourhood of Bristol; they return home the end of this month, and tho' Mʳˢ H. has not been much cheered by her changes of scene &c, I trust she has gained something. ——— I can think of little more to say to you which would not be a bad reason for concluding my letter tho' my paper were more ample. Adieu then with all kind affection in which Agnes joins me most heartily!

   J Baillie

Pray mention us as you ought to our friends at Salviston & Mʳˢ Watts. ———
I hope Mʳˢ Bannister is well & Mʳˢ Graves[.]

---

crown agent for Scotland, reputed as the most learned peerage lawyer of his time. He had literary tastes and in 1821 was introduced to George Crabbe in Joanna Baillie's house; he regularly corresponded with Walter Scott, whose deathbed he attended shortly before Scott's demise.

   49. Agnes Baillie, the antiquarian, is often mentioned in JB's letters as reading *Holinshed's Chronicles*.

The following single letter is part of Special Collections at Edinburgh University, transcribed by their permission:

AAF/B/23, Gen. 1730 (Address: Mrs Elliot--no address or postmark; letter mentioned is no longer enclosed. EU dates 1827?)[50]
My dear Madam,

If you know of any body going to Darnistadt [?][51] who would be kind enough to take charge of the inclosed, I should be very much obliged to you to put it into their hands which will spare our friend some expense. If you dont know of such an opportunity, be so good as [to] inclose the letter to me directed to 33 Cavendish Square, where my sister & I will be next saturday & remain for some days on our way to the Isle of Wight, and I must then send it by post; for by a letter received from Mrs Stirling the other day,[52] I find that she thinks I have neglected her. -- She gives a good account of her own health & of her family. --

My sister unites with me in best remembrances to yourself, Mr Elliot & the family. I fear our time in Town will not admit of calling in Gloucester Place which we regret. -- Pray excuse the trouble I am now giving you, and believe me
            Dear Madam
        yours sincerely
            J Baillie
Hampstead tuesday June 19th [1827?]

9 (Address: Mrs A. Elliott / Egland--no postmark)
                                            Hampstead Feby 14th [1827]
My dear Friend

I take the opportunity of a cover for Miss F. Head to send you a few lines to thank you for your last kind letter. Agnes has written to you since, and would say how sorry we were to learn that your Nephew George had

---

50. This letter is probably to Anne Elliott's sister-in-law.

51. This name is illegible but looks something like Darnistadt, though I can identify no such place in England. There is a German city named Darmstadt, but there is no indication Elliott is traveling to the continent.

52. This may be Mrs. James Stirling, the long-time friend for whose benefit Baillie's *A Collection of Poems, Chiefly Manuscript, and from Living Authors* (London: Longman, Hurst, Rees, Orme, and Brown, 1823) was produced. The successful volume earned over £2,000 for her friend.

been so ill. As he was able when you wrote to mount his horse again, we hope soon to hear from you of his perfect recovery. Young people soon regain strength. Our young man, William, who begins now to think himself an old man, set off yesterday for Rome to get the benediction of the Pope in holy week and witness all the religious pageantry of that solemn season. It was rather a sudden thought, but his Mother encouraged him in it, and he means afterwards to see all the remarkable places in Italy and return home again in four or five months. He travels by himself with a well recommended Swiss servant, but has several friends in Rome, at present, who will be useful & agreeable to him when he gets there. We hope it will be much for his advantage, and one rather wonders that he did not do so before. His Mother, to say nothing of ourselves, will miss him sadly, yet we are glad that he is gone.

Sophia is to dine with us to morrow and meet Mrs Hughan & Justina, just come to be our neighbours on the Heath, and we will try to cheer her as well as we can. Elizabeth & the little body do not come to her till the end of March, and in the mean time she must be looked after by all her sympathising friends in this her first long absence from her only son & constant companion. – The latter part of this winter has been a gloomy one to us from the death of many friends in whom we were more or less interested. The last shock I received was the loss of my kind & amiable friend of more than twenty years standing, Sir G. Beaumont.[53] He was a short while ill and it came upon us suddenly. This is the tax we pay for living long ourselves.

I have read Capt. Heads book with great interest & amusement and have just been writing to his Sister on the subject.[54] He is certainly a very clever creature, and somewhat of a fool-hardy one; and must have a frame of iron, like the wild Gauchos & Indeans he admires so much, to survive all the fatigue & dangers he encountered. It was well that his poor wife did not possess one of those fairy glasses through which a Lady or Princess

---

53. Sir George Howland Beaumont (1753-1827), patron of art and a landscape painter himself, married Margaret Willes with whom he cultivated the society of poets and painters. Sir George entered Parliament in 1790 and in 1800 began to rebuild Coleorton Hall where, according to Wordsworth's dedication to his 1815 edition, several of Wordsworth's best pieces were composed. Beaumont knew Dr. Johnson, was a close friend of Sir Joshua Reynolds and helped Coleridge procure his pension. He also befriended Sir Humphrey Davy, Samuel Rogers, Lord Byron and Sir Walter Scott (*DNB*, II:56). See Felicity Owen and David Blayney Brown, *Collector of Genius: A Life of Sir George Beaumont* (New Haven: Yale University Press, 1988). Beaumont's death would date this letter 1827.

54. This is either Sir Francis Bond Head (1793-1875) or Sir George Head (1782-1855), probably brothers of Fanny Head. Both men were involved with the military and with travel, and both were authors.

might at any time peep and behold what her love was a doing. ――― Pray remember us kindly to all your friendly neighbours who may enquire for us. Agnes has been but indifferent lately with slight rheumatisms & other little ailments, but nothing material. I hope your cold is gone and your nose soundly skinned again, after all its hard duty. — And have you got Mrs Smith's visit well over? It would not be a dull one to her, I guess, though you had not your elder Brother & his wife to help you in the civilities. You are as independent of assistance as any single woman in the county of Devon, perhaps I might say Middlesex. —— I must have done for it is late & time to go to bed.

    affectionately yours   J Baillie

10 (Address: Mrs A. Elliott / Egland--no postmark)

                                 Hampstead Novr 12th 1827

My dear Friend,

    We have heard of your safe arrival from the north and the pleasure you have had with your friends there, and we bid you welcome home again to dear Egland with all our hearts. I am glad of this opportunity of doing so, and telling you somewhat of ourselves, a subject you are kind enough to take some interest in, for I am sending a Cover to Ashfield and shall reserve room enough for this purpose. ――― Agnes & I have been in Gloucester lately passing a short time with Mrs Hughan & her Sisters, a visit both pleasant & melancholy. We went one day to see Dunsbourne [*sic*] and I need not tell you what sad recollections that recalled. We had on our way to it visited the Village of Dunsbourn & the church. It was a day of painful trial to us, but we were satisfied after we had been there, and have been the better for it ever since. – Justina Milligan has done a great deal to improve their Place which is now a beautiful commodius [*sic*] residence, and as it is surrounded by fine beechwoods, it still retained great richness & beauty even in the end of October. The good these Ladies do in that neighbourhood, by helping & teaching the poor to help themselves and giving work to the men at reasonable wages, is scarcely to be imagined but by those who are upon the spot: it gave us great satisfaction to witness it. And we were much pleased too by finding young Hughan so decidedly improved in body & mind – a docile intelligent, sociable Lad and promising fairly to be a real comfort to his Mother & his Aunts. Poor Mary is so much better since she followed Dr Granville's advice in her diet that there are considerable hopes now of her entire recovery. When we returned to London, we found our dear Sophia in Cavendish Square but still suffering from the effects of her visit to Brighton. She had recovered from the severe bilious attack she had had there, but the journey to Town brought on a return of the complaint and she was under good Dr Maton's care when we got to her.[55] Thank God she is now pretty well again, and looking forward to the pleasure of having Robert & Elizabeth & the little Sophy with her for the month of Decr. This I hope will be a pleasure to all parties concerned. Little Sophy I am told is now improving much in every way. — I have just been telling your friend Fanny that I am busy writing a Play which if it be acted at all will be somewhat in the Bartholomew-fair fashion;[56] but besides that I am busy assisting Mrs Baillie & Agnes in a canvass to get Miss Napier on the pension list of Herve's Institution, a task of no small trouble the voters being so very numerous. ――― I know not if I have any thing more I ought to say, and I have no time to consider wether [*sic*] there is or not. – So take what I have written as it is with my hearty love & Agnes's into the bargain. ever affectionately yours

   J Baillie

PS. Our letters from Glasgow give us a sad account of the depressed state of spirits of our friends the Millars since poor Helen's death, and there is another Sister – Mrs Mylne dangerously ill:[57] affliction presses heavily on them at present.

11 (Address: Mrs A. Elliott / Egland near Honiton--postmarked 1829)[58]

Hampstead Decr 25th 1829

My dear Friend

   Coldness & its constant companion (with me at least) lazyness, has kept me for some days past from writing to you, for we have not yet greeted you since your return to your own dear Egland after your long absence in the north, though both Agnes & I have thought of you & talked of you often. The account received of you from yourself & also from your Neighbour of Ashfield is favorable as to health & looks and I hope you continue well & are now enjoying the society of your friends about you, both your own domestic Circle, including M^r & Mrs Elliott, & that of your sociable neighbours; a merry Xmas to you all! In looking over your letter of Novr 18 to my Sister, in which you make such kind & anxious enquiries after our dear Sister in Cavendish Sq^r I cannot conceive how it is that we have sent

---

55. William George Maton (1776-1835), BM and MD, was Physician Extraordinary to Queen Charlotte in 1816 and Physician in Ordinary to the Duchess of Kent and her daughter (later Queen Victoria) in 1820 (Crainz, 57).

56. Possibly *The Bride* (1828).

57. University of Glasgow Professor John Millar had three daughters; Anne was Baillie's childhood friend, one married Professor James Mylne, and the other, probably Helen, married Dr. John Thomson (*DNB*, XIII:403).

58. The last leaf of this letter is *very* difficult to read, for Baillie has cross written on it, a customary practice for many writers (but usually not for Baillie) to save paper.

you no answer. I believe I prevented her from doing it by saying I would do it myself; and indeed <u>indeed</u> we have, to say the best of it, behaved ill and you must forgive us, and so I will say no more on an untoward subject. —— This same dear Sister has had no other bad attack since that alluded to by F. Head, and did not go to Cheltenham at all but to Brighton in its stead, from circumstances tedious to mention which made Robert Milligan & Eliz<u>th</u> leave Gloucester suddenly which took away her chief enducement for going to Cheltenham. She has been generally pretty well this winter, but had you seen her last monday when she dined here to meet M<u>rs</u> & Miss Hoare and eat nothing and had not a word to say to any of us though we tried to cheer her as well as we could, you would have felt for her a painful degree of sympathy. She had a cold coming on and the fear of being in two days called into court to give evidence in the Croft divorce case before her eyes; and you who know so well the shrinking delicacy of her character will be sufficiently aware of the pain which the thoughts of it must have given her. Probably by this time you have read an account of it in the paper; and truly it has passed over as well as one could possibly expect.[59] Her mind must now be relieved on that score and her cold I hope is better and that we shall find her much more comfortable next tuesday, when we are to dine with her at M<u>rs</u> Hoares & return with her to Town in the evening. Our stay in Town will be short, for our chief reason for going

---

59. Two cases actually arose concerning the Crofts. First, Sir Thomas Croft (the son of Sir Richard Croft, thus Sophia Baillie's nephew) brought an action for criminal conversation (adultery) in the Common Pleas against William Lyster (see 25 December 1829 *Times*). Essentially, Sir Thomas met Miss Lateward, an heiress worth £3,000/year, when she was 16. As she was a ward in Chancery, the couple had to secure the permission of the Lord Chancellor to marry, which was withheld for a year because of her youth; but they married in 1824 when he was 25 or 26 and she was 17. Sir Thomas then fell ill and moved to Bromley for treatment, but Lady Croft did not go with him, remaining with her mother-in-law the Dowager Lady Croft. The couple had had a daughter (Grace), who also went to Bromley. Young Lady Croft then went to live with her mother and stepfather (the *Times* account suggests she was *sent* away by Lady Croft for bad conduct), moving with them to Boulogne, where she committed adultery with Colonel William Lyster. Sir Thomas sued and ultimately received £2,000 in damages and kept the £700/year of her money which had been settled on him at their marriage.

Second, was the Croft case in Consistory Court (an ecclesiastical court), requesting a legal separation between Sir Thomas Elmsley Croft and Sophia Jane Lateward (married 9 September 1824). Records of 21 May 1830 indicate that Lady Croft did not dispute the facts alleged against her and that a separation was therefore pronounced, though neither party could remarry. After Sir Thomas Croft's death, however, the December 1835 *Gentleman's Magazine* carries the notice of the marriage of Colonel William Lyster and Sophia Jane Lateward Croft at Brussels on 7 November 1835. (Again, I thank Dr. Ruth Paley, Public Record Office at Kew, for providing this information.)

there at present is to see Miss F Kemble in the Character of Belvidera on wednesday evening,[60] after which we shall return to our own fireside & the easy chair in which you <u>are</u> to take your ease by & by. This cold weather [makes?] one very unwilling to move, and my love for the stage & the genius of Miss Kemble & the whole generation of Kembles would scarcely have tempted me to such an undertaking could I have foreseen 10 days ago that such biting frost was abiding us. But Sir Thomas Lawrence,[61] who is an enthusiastic admirer of Miss K. has procured an excellent box for me and he would reckon me no better than Goth or Hun were I to draw back from my engagement. I have seen this young Lady as Juliet and admired many passages of her acting very much, particularly in the first scene with her Mother & the Nurse and in the garden scene. She has saved Covent Garden from ruin & above a hundred Actors from being turned adrift to starvation and must feel a proud satisfaction in the success of her powers, and long may she enjoy it! — We have just lost our neighbour M[rs] Greaves who is gone to her Nieces for the winter & shall miss her much. She was pleased with your remembrance of her and your approbation of her friend M[r] Staneford and desired me to thank you for it a great while ago. — I went with a friend last saturday to see M[rs] Carr & her Daughters in their new house in Spring Gardens which is very pleasantly situated, looking into St James Park and not far from the Lushingtons.[62] She looked very sad, yet I hope she will cheer up by & by with so many good & dutiful children to support her, who conform so pleasantly to the change in their establishment & prospects. Of this we had not long since a good opportunity of judging when they passed a week with us (I mean 3 of them)

---

60. Fanny Kemble (1809-93) was the daughter of actor Charles Kemble and niece of Sarah Siddons and John Kemble. She debuted as Juliet in *Romeo and Juliet* in Covent Garden in 1829, an immediate success. She later toured both England and America and is known as a writer of *Journal of a Residence on a Georgian Plantation, 1838-39.* See both Margaret Armstrong, *Fanny Kemble, A Passionate Victorian* (New York: Macmillan, 1938) and *Fanny Kemble, Journal of a Young Actress*, ed. Monica Gough (New York: Columbia University Press, 1990). She played Belvidera in Otway's *Venice Preserved* at Covent Garden in December 1829 (Leota S. Driver, *Fanny Kemble* [Chapel Hill: University of North Carolina Press, 1933], 38).

61. In his last years painter Sir Thomas Lawrence (1769-1830) took a special interest in the career of Fanny Kemble, for he had supposedly once been in love with her sister Sally Kemble. See introduction and chapter of letters to Lawrence herein.

62. Sarah Grace Carr, the daughter of Mr. and Mrs. Thomas William Carr, married Stephen Lushington in 1821. Stephen Lushington (1782-1873) was one of the attorneys involved in the Byron separation settlement. He was also retained as counsel for Queen Caroline before the House of Lords and made a masterly speech in her defense in October 1820. He was an ardent reformer, supporting the abolition of capital punishment, and an able advocate (*DNB*, XII:291-93). Stephen and Sarah had five children.

at the time they were employed in removing all the furniture from Frognal, ere they left that delightful home for ever. Our former kind Neighbour Mrs Coxe who was as I suppose you know couched some months ago can now see to read & do many things to amuse herself; a degree of sight which has been recovered by degree & continues to improve. I have not yet seen her since this has been the case. I have received to day a letter from Mrs Hudson [sic] ex. Miss Holford full of delight from a weeks abode of the Poet Laureate under her roof,[63] a person possessing all the charming qualities that man or poet can possess. This smacks a little of the enthusiasm which you no doubt discovered in her when she was the guest of your neighbour Mrs Shouldham at Deer Park. — Agnes sends you her love. She keeps free from rheumatism not withstanding the severe weather but has just recovered from a bad & hideous cold. We have scarcely seen your Nephew at all for a long time; ourselves from some untoward circumstances being at fault. — Remember us to your friends at Salviston and give our kind regards to your Brother & his Lady now your inmates. — I give you joy of your twenty hogs heads of cyder. — Tell Miss Head & dear Fanny that I was delighted with what her last letter contained regarding their new chaise hose [house?] which I hope they will enjoy for many years. Farewell! for I will torment you with no more cross writing.

    yours very affectionately
      J Baillie
PS. I hope the Ladies at Woolford are well also Mrs Graves, Mrs Bannister & the Prings

---

12 (Address: Mrs A. Elliott--no postmark)

[1830]

My dear Friend,
    Having some copies of Lady Byron's "Remarks &c" which are printed not published,[64] to dispose of, I send one for your acceptance, and another to

---

63. Robert Southey (1774-1843) a college friend of Coleridge and one of the "Lake Poets," was Poet Laureate from 1813-43, having accepted a pension five years earlier. He was a friend of Margaret Holford Hodson.

64. Referring to Moore's account of her desertion of Byron, Lady Byron explained as follows:

The facts are: - I left London for Kirkby Mallory, the residence of my father and mother, on the 15th of January, 1816. Lord Byron had signified to me in writing (Jan. 6th) his absolute desire that I should leave London on the earliest day that I could conveniently fix. It was not safe for me to undertake the fatigue of a journey sooner than the 15th. Previously to my departure, it had been strongly impressed on my mind, that Lord Byron was under the influence of insanity. This opinion was derived, in a great measure, from the

your care which you will have the goodness to give to our Friend Fanny when it suits you. — I hope you will be satisfied with this Statement of facts, which has been wrung from poor Lady B. by what she decidedly considered as her duty, and I think she was right in so considering it. ——

When are you coming to us Deary? this is your Spring for being new-rigged, and you surely dont intend to go about in your old gowns any longer. —— Mrs Baillie has Eliz^th &c from Brighton with her at present who will remain, I hope, some weeks longer. Sophy is growing tall and is much improved in her appearance. I am sorry I have not a very good account to give you of our dear Sister there. She is not very well, but makes the best she can of it. ——— Remember me kindly to M^r & Mrs Elliott, who are, I suppose, still with you

affectionately yours

J Baillie

Hampstead March 22^d

13 (Address: Mrs A. Elliott--no postmark)

Hampstead March 7th 1831

My dear Friend,

There is a servant of our late good Mrs Merivale[65] who is going to Exeter and has offered to take any parcel &c so we are glad of the opportunity of enclosing to you two Tracts regarding the Temperance

---

communications made to me by his nearest relatives and personal attendant, who had more opportunities than myself of observing him during the latter part of my stay in town. It was even represented to me that he was in danger of destroying himself. *With the concurrence of his family,* I had consulted Dr. Baillie, as a friend (Jan. 8th), respecting his supposed malady. On acquainting him with the state of the case, and with Lord Byron's desire that I should leave London, Dr. Baillie thought that my absence might be advisable as an experiment, *assuming* the fact of mental derangement; for Dr. Baillie, not having had access to Lord Byron, could not pronounce a positive opinion on that point. . . . When I arrived Kirkby Mallory, my parents were unacquainted with the existence of any causes likely to destroy my prospects of happiness; and when I communicated to them the opinion which had been formed concerning Lord Byron's state of mind, they were most anxious to promote his restoration by every means in their power.

This lengthy argument appears as an appendix in Moore's later edition of *The Life of Lord Byron* (London: John Murray, 1844), 662. This would probably date the letter about 1830.

65. This is probably Louisa Heath Drury, the wife of John Herman Merivale (1779-1844), a scholar and minor poet accomplished in classical and romantic literature. He was a friend of Byron, who praised his translations and poetry; he published such works as *Orlando in Roncesvalles* (1814), a 2-volume collection of poems in 1838, and translations of the minor poems of Schiller (*DNB*, XIII:281-2).

Society of Glasgow & those in the neighbourhood which I think you & some of the Ladies near you may like to see. You can return them to us by any chance opportunity; we are in no hurry. The Mr Dunlop mentioned in the larger Publication as the Father of Temperance Societies in that part of the country is Nephew to our old friend Miss Graham, and the smaller Tract is written by him.[66] I dont know that with you there is much need of such societies, yet you may like to know something further of the progress of sobriety in the north, though it would be an affront to Cyder drinkers in the south to compare them to Whiskey drinkers on the other side of the Tweed. ——— Some time hence I hope to send you a pamphlet of my own writing which I hope at least will not offend you though it may differ from your own opinions on the subject of which it treats;[67] and yet I flatter myself we shall be as sincere & as accepted Christians as if we did more entirely agree. If you look sharply into some of your newspapers some time hence, you may read the following Advertisement "speedily will be published &c a view of the general tenor of the New Testament regarding the nature & dignity of Christ, by Joanna Baillie author of the Martyr & the Bride." ——— I shall neither earn fame nor money by this publication, but I shall do better, I shall earn peace. For something of this kind has appeared to me to be very much wanted, and not likely to be produced in a form sufficiently simple to be useful, so it is with me a matter of conscience. ——— We have very lately read Mrs H. Bowdler's posthumous work which shews the pure worth of her own mind and is in parts an interesting story very well told.[68] But as for the moral of lesson intended by it, I do not think _that_ very well made out. What do we Old Maids gain by having it related that a beautiful woman, with whom every man was in love, had from peculiar circumstances remained unmarried and was of course free from all bad & disagreeable dispositions which are generally imparted to the Sisterhood? The commonest novelist who introduces an amiable, old,

---

66. NLS 9261 f.113 is catalogued as a note to John Dunlop of Gairbraid concerning his work in the temperance movement, but the note, as follows, is not in Baillie's hand: "You have given in this work a strong and salutary lesson, and the characters of Caldon, Rugby and Jenny Rintoul [?] are cleverly drawn & effective. May you go on & prosper in your noble undertaking".

67. This would be Baillie's _A View of the General Tenour of the New Testament Regarding the Nature and Dignity of Jesus Christ_ (London, 1831) in which she analyzes the doctrines of the Trinitarians, the Arians, and the Socinians and argues the human nature of Christ, causing a great deal of controversy. See her letters to the Bishop of Salisbury.

68. Mrs. Henrietta Maria Bowdler (1754-1830) was author of _Poems and Essays_ (1786), _Sermons on the Doctrines and Duties of Christianity_, which appeared anonymously, and _Pen Tamar, or the History of an Old Maid_ (posthumously, 1830) (see Lambertson, cxxv-cc).

single woman as one of the persons of her story, without commenting at all on the subject, does us much better service. — I need not say much about ourselves, Agnes having written to you lately by your Nephew. We are all nearly as when she wrote, only the hopes of having Robert & Elizabeth settle in our neighbourhood is taken away, as Mr Broadie thinks it will be good for Sophy's general health to be the greater part of the year on the sea coast.[69] We were in hopes this would not have been necessary, and it is a disappointment to us all, Mrs Baillie particularly on whose account they chiefly wished to have a settled residence near London. There is a marriage going on in the Milligan family, but one which you will not care about. The youngest son with a very small income is going to quit the life Guards to marry a young Lady with a much smaller income, to be happy wedded folks in the country. She is the Daughter of Sir Charles Deveux, an old Irish Baronet who is married to a York shire wife, & the young Lady has been brought up in York Sh. His own family would rather that he had continued in the army as a Bachelor, but they are doing every thing that is proper & kind on the occasion. – We were very much pleased the other day to see Capt: Pring set his comely face within the door of our parlor, but of his short & agreeable visit I need say nothing as you have no doubt seen him since. — (the 8th) I left off here yesterday at the call of our daily newspaper which comes to us every day for an hour only; for who in these unsettled & interesting times can be indifferent to the daily occurences [*sic*] & What do you say to these reforms in Honiton? The pot-Wallopers there will not be quite at their ease, I suppose. — Our neighbour Mrs Greaves came home from her London abode last night and is to dine with us to day; looking well & cheerful and tells us that Mrs Mulso is in Town at the house of a friend, but so so in health and indetermined as to her plans for the summer, though her next move (about 3 weeks hence) will be to Lady Rivers's at Winchester — Fare well! for I must deliver my Packet to the conveyor thereof in good time, and have a note to write to Fanny Head ere I close it up. — Agnes sends her kindest love

always, dear Friend, yours affectionately

J Baillie

---

69. Elizabeth Margaret Milligan and her husband Robert, with their only child Sophia, appear to have continued at Ryde on the Isle of Wight almost all their married life.

14 (No address or postmark)

Hampstead Decr 19th 1831

My dear Friend,

I hope before this reaches you, your troublesome cold will have relinquished its hold and left you with a clear voice & easy bones to enjoy the society of your friends round your Xmas fires and to contribute your wonted share to the animation & merry making; you grow old no doubt like myself & must grow older, but I cannot possibly imagine you at any time too old for this. A merry exmas to you then and to all the good friends around you! ––– But, much as I love you, my chief reason for writing to you now (for I must be honest) is to draw two crowns, making 10^s from your pocket, and engage your friend Mrs Bawtree to extract as many crowns as she can from the good gentry in & round Colchester. The person in whose behalf I make this request is Miss Hedge,[70] whose Father you must remember as the first gold smith of the place, and a very respectable man. Some how or other, he died in bad circumstances, and left this one Daughter without any provision. She was always a poor little delicate creature, & quite unable to earn her bread by any active employment, so in these days of readers & printers, she betook herself to the writing of books which afforded her a very scanty subsistence with a small addition of 10 pounds a year allowed her by a relation. But now this resource is cut off, her books do not sell and her health is so bad that she requires help & indulgences which she cannot get. By indulgences I only mean the usual comforts of a sick-room, fire &c. By means of Mr Sotheby I procured for her twenty pounds from the Literary fund which then relieved her from distress,[71] about a year ago, but it was a donation which can never be repeated, and she has had long & severe illness since and is distressed'd [sic]. The little book which she proposes to publish by subscription, is a serious work entitlled [sic] "Self retirement or the joys of devotion,["] in one small volume price 5^s. It is to be published by a Mr Swinborne a Cholchester [sic] Bookseller. Very likely Mrs Bawtree may know all about this already, but it will not be amiss that she should be pricked on a little

---

70. Mary Ann Hedge has twelve volumes listed in the *British Museum General Catalogue of Printed Books* (Vol. 100), including several children's books published in Colchester between 1819 and 1824: *Samboe: or the African boy* (1823), *Juvenile Poems* (1823) and *The Orphan Sailor-Boy; or Young Arctic voyager* (1824).

71. The Royal Literary Fund was started in the late eighteenth century and still exists. Created to offer temporary relief to "persons of genius and learning, or their families, who shall be in want," its assistance was confidential. Those in need could apply for assistance and support their case through members' testimonials as well as with samples of their published work. (R. H. Super, "Trollope at the Royal Literary Fund," *Nineteenth Century Literature* 37.3 [1982]: 316).

by such a friend as yourself. ––– I make no apology for requesting you to put your hand in your pocket for a Colchester person of excellent character so circumstanced, that would be foolish. ––

We had the pleasure of seeing your Nephew here last Saturday when Mrs Baillie & William brought him out to dine with us. We had our opportunity of enquiring for the different members of his family & you & your neighbourhood besides, and he gave us a pretty satisfactory account. We hope to learn by & by that you are looking forward to your usual spring visit to us & your friends in Essex. We at least look forward to it with great pleasure, and I beg you will take good care of yourself and come to us in as good condition as you can. –– I am happy to tell you that Agnes has got back her strength again & promises to pass the winter as comfortably as usual. But who does not at present think of the great uncertainty of human life, particularly the old who cannot strive with any severe disease? But we are not alarmed as some of our neighbours are about the Cholera,[72] who are securing to themselves a present illness from fretting at the prospect of it. – We had a little party last night in honour of Young Sam^1 Hoare & his bride to which your Nephew kindly promised to come, but was prevented by a very stormy evening. The Richardsons & some other neighbours were with us, and they chatted & the wind roared, and there was no want of sound, I assure you. The Bride is not [h]andsome & has no great fortune, but she has great store of good qualities, so his family think as well as himself, and the connection promises well for reasonable happiness. –– Our good Sister Sophia continues in better health than usual. She & her friends in Welbeck St: were surprized nearly a fortnight ago with a visit of Madame de Chanteau, Lady Croft's daughter, bringing a step son with her, who is an artist, has been brought up in Italy and is come to establish himself in London as a painter.[73] Now Madame C. & none of the family knew that Monsr de Chanteau her husband had been married before or had any Son, so there is a mystery about it, and the whole business, as you may suppose, is neither gratifying not [sic] agreeable. Sophia with her usual kindness made a dinner & party

---

72. The first world-wide epidemic of cholera, with its vibrio attacking the intestines through contaminated food or water, began in 1817 in India and spread to Russia and western Europe. England was invaded in 1831, with approximately 50,000 deaths resulting throughout the British Isles. Four other pandemics during the 19th century showed similar characteristics (see Sir Macfarlane Burnet, *Natural History of Infectious Disease*, 3rd ed. [Cambridge: Cambridge University Press, 1962], 331-32).

73. Lady Croft, Sophia Denman Baillie's twin sister Margaret, married Sir Richard Croft in 1789, and the couple had several children. I find no evidence of de Chanteau's success as a London painter.

for them the other day to introduce the young man to Sir Martin Shee[74] & Wilkie.[75] --- Our friend Mrs Greaves who often enquires after you is absent at present & likely to be so for some time & we miss her much. -- Agnes sends her kind love & all the good wishes of the season, which always go hand in hand, in all that concerns you, with
  those of your affectionate J Baillie

15 (Address: Mrs A. Elliott / Egland near Honiton--postmarked 1832)
           Hampstead Novr 13th 1832
My dear Friend,
  You have heard from Agnes & heard of us in various ways since the date of your last letter to me. This is all very true, yet I might have had the grace & gratitude, long ere this, to have written, had it only been to have thanked you for your generosity regarding poor Miss Hedge of Colchester, on whose behalf I asked of you a crown & received a Sovereign. Indeed I have not behaved well, and moreover have not sent you the book for which you subscribed so handsomely, but have let it lie in my room wrapped up in paper to upbraid me, every time I look into that corner, for a lazy, inefficient creature, for it always says to me, as plainly as the outside of a book can speak, "you might have sent me to Egland free of expence some way or other." You have by this means lost in the mean time much good serious reflection and some amiable tracts of the Author's mind which are still I hope abiding you; for [if] I have no earlier opportunity, I trust if God spare us both, to put it into your own hand in spring. You will surely come to us then, and make up for our

---

74. Sir Martin Archer Shee (1769-1850), born in Dublin, was a portrait painter. The first half of his career was overshadowed by the fame of his rival Sir Thomas Lawrence, but his portraits are estimable works. On the death of Lawrence in 1830 the post of painter-in-ordinary was given to Sir David Wilkie instead of Shee, but Shee was at the same time elected president of the Royal Academy. In addition to painting, Shee wrote some poetry, namely, *Commemoration of Reynolds, and other Poems* (1814), and two novels, *Oldcourt* (1829) and *Cecil Hyde* (1834) (*DNB*, XVIII:4-5).

75. Sir David Wilkie (1785-1841) says he began drawing before he could read. He entered the Trustees' Academy and made some progress in portrait painting but in 1804 left Edinburgh and returned to his home of Cults to paint on his own. In 1805 he left for London, carrying a small picture entitled *Bounty Money; or, the Village Recruit*, and established himself at Portland Road, shortly after beginning attendance at the Academy and finally earning true fame in 1810 with *The Village Festival* now in the National Gallery. He became ill around this time and was attended by Dr. Matthew Baillie, migrating for his convalescence to the house of Joanna Baillie. By 1830 Wilkie was made painter in ordinary at the death of Sir Thomas Lawrence, retaining this office under William IV and Victoria. In 1836 he was knighted (*DNB*, XXI:253-58).

disappointment (disappointment) last spring. Both Agnes & my self & your dear friend in Cavendish Square look forward to it with great pleasure and long to hear under your own hand that you intend coming to us to cheer us again. — I wrote to Fanny Head some time ago to enquire after her Sister, who has had a short term of married life. I hope, being a free woman again with some additional advantages, she will pass the rest of her life in comfort with her Sister. – But I must not speak to you of things concerning your own neighbours; I must rather speak of ourselves & your friends here which will be more acceptable to you. Agnes & I are pretty well and have passed nearly a fortnight with Sophia lately, who was looking well and in very good spirits with her Mother seated by her, her constant object of attention who is to remain with her the whole winter, till the Crofts return from Hastings. They are much pleased, as you may well suppose, with Denman's being made Chief Justice.[76] Indeed they [may] well be so, and I sympathize with them heartily, for continuing Attorney General under a Whig Ministry which may not be very durable, was to a man with a large family a perilous situation. He has now steered his vessel into port, and will live long, I hope, to make provision for his Children & do faithful service to the public. ——— While we were in Town we went to see the Masque (as it was called) in honour of Sir Walter Scott. It was a melancholy gratification, mixed with many cross feelings. The scenery was beautiful & decorations magnificient; but when we saw a representation of his tomb & Dryburgh with all the simple solemnity of the scene disturbed by aligorical figures dressed out in pink & white gauze & crown & chaplets of flowers, gliding & dancing about & spreading out their arms in opera fashion, I was hurt & provoked.[77] Our friend Bartley,[78] the stage manager of Covent Garden, was kind enough to give us

---

76. Lord Chief Justice Thomas Denman (1779-1854) was Sophia Denman Baillie's brother.

77. Sir Walter Scott was buried in Dryburgh Abbey after his death on 21 September 1832.

78. George Bartley (1782?-1858) was a comedian born in Bath whose father was box-keeper at the Bath theatre. George acquired stage experience as a youth, appearing at Cheltenham in 1800 as Orlando in *As You Like It*. His London debut was in 1802, though for some time he was apparently employed as an understudy. In 1809-11 he unsuccessfully managed the Glasgow theatre, subsequently acting with increasing reputation as a comedian in Manchester, Liverpool and other locations. In 1814 he married his second wife, Sarah Smith, a successful tragic actress who appeared that same year as Ophelia at Drury Lane while George appeared as Falstaff, thereafter his favorite character. In 1818 the Bartleys made a successful trip to America, and on their return Bartley accepted a winter engagement at Covent Garden. In 1829 when Covent Garden's management collapsed, Bartley headed the actors who came forward with a proposal to furnish funds and recommence

a good private box, so we saw it to the best advantage. We went one morning to see poor Mrs Lockhart,[79] who was kind & confidential, and in a natural state of sorrow, mixed with great thankfulness that her Father was released from much suffering. The very end, however, thank God! was easy. Since we returned home, I have been employed in reading over all his letters to me; and they will all (except about 20 which I have reserved or burnt) be put into Mr Lockhart's hands to use as he thinks fit. To no other person could I entrust them. He is writing a life of Sir Walter which he is well qualified to do, and is thankful to have his letters to look over. The expressions of his friendly kindness to me in reading over these Mss have gone often to my heart as you may well suppose. Little did I think when I received them, that he would have gone before me; that I, so much older than him, should have been the survivor. ――― I know you take an interest in our good friend Mrs Carr; her Daughter Isabella – L^y Smith, is in Town expecting to be confined in the course of the month, and her youngest son William is appointed Attorney General for the Isle of Ceylon; an advantageous & honorable appointment for a young man, but it will take him far away and he was a great comfort to his Mother & Sisters at home. Her other two sons are married men. ―― Rember [sic] us kindly to your Brother & Mrs Elliott who are, I suppose, with you for the winter. Tell F. Head that I thank her much for her kind letter. Give our best regards to the Ladies Mrs Simcoe &c Mrs Graves & Mrs Banister, and remember us very kindly to our friends at Salviston. –

always affectionately yours   J Baillie

16 (Address: Mrs Elliott / Egland, H--no postmark)[80]

Hampstead Feb^ry the 9th -33

My dear Friend,

We were much concerned to learn by your Niece's kind letter how much you had suffered from inflamation on your chest, a bad way of taking a cold, though you have been long liable to it, and used to recover pretty quickly. I hope, though, we are both much older than when I have cut a blister for you on Red Lion hill, and not quite so merry, this present attack has imitated its predecessors, and that you are now in a comfortable convalescent state and thinking now & then of your promised visit to us in

---

performances. The death of his son at Oxford led Bartley to retire early from the stage (*DNB*, I:1255-56).

79. Sophia Scott Lockhart married John Gibson Lockhart (1794-1854), satirist, editor of the *Quarterly* and Tory biographer of Sir Walter Scott. See letters to the Lockharts, Volume 2.

80. The first half of this letter is written by Agnes Baillie, and I am transcribing only that portion written by Joanna Baillie.

spring, and when you are to set out. It will do us all much good, our dear friend in Cavendish Square included, to see your face again. Three years (the period since your last visit) is a long time! — Agnes no doubt has told you of Mrs Baillie's present state, so I say nothing to you upon that subject. — I believe I told you some time ago that I had written lines to the memory of my great & good friend, — they are now printed and distributed to those of my friends who will be interested in the subject, and you I know are most truly so.[81] You will find inclosed one copy for yourself, and one for Miss Hunt, and one also for Mrs Mulso, which you will be so good as to send to them when you have a convenient opportunity. ——— The Abbotsford subscription is still open, and I wish I could give you a good account of its progress. One might have thought that all hearts & hands would have been open to it, and that it would soon have filled up & overflowed, from general donations of small sums; but this as yet has not been the case, perhaps from some false notion of its not being wanted; the present man may from his Wife's fortune be tolerably well off, but when he dies without Children, his younger Brother will be the Baronet of Abbotsford with scarcely £700 a year to keep state in his Castle.[82] ———
Pray remember me kindly to Mrs Simcoe & the Ladies of Woolford, to Mrs Graves & to Mrs Bannister. Tell this last that her cousins in Garzon St: are both looking particularly well this winter. Fare well!

    affectionately yours
     J Baillie

17 (Address: Mrs A. Elliott--no postmark)[83]

                 Hampstead June 21st [1831-32?]

My dear Friend,

    I wrote yesterday to Fanny Head, and sent a kind message to you thinking the letter must go by post, but to day I have the prospect of a

---

81. This is probably Baillie's "Lines on the Death of Sir Walter Scott" (Hampstead: n.p., 1832).

82. As a result of his financial difficulties, Scott surrendered his collections at Abbotsford to his creditors, but they requested that he retain the furniture, plate, paintings, library and museum as a mark of their sympathy and respect. Valuing the collection at £10,000, Scott left it in his will (burdened to the extent of £5,000) to his eldest son for division among the younger children. This would have required son Walter to sell the collection except for a subscription raised among Scott's admirers to purchase the Abbotsford Collection and hold it in trust for the public and family (see William Smith and W. S. Crockett, *Abbotsford* [London: Adam and Charles Black, 1905], n120).

83. John Merivale married Louisa Heath Drury mentioned in letter of 7 March 1831 above. Being unable to find a death date for her makes dating this letter difficult. It would have to be, of course, after 1831 but before George Crabbe dies in 1832.

frank and hope to put this for you under her cover. I suppose it will still find you at Egland and Mrs Bawtree with you, in which case remember us kindly to her. I trust you are enjoying your pretty home together; and may the weather & other happy circumstances turn out in your favour when you take your journey to the Lakes. In my letter to Fanny I had mentioned the melancholy fate which attends us all as we advance in life of losing friends which fall off from us one after another, and that this last winter had been marked in Hampstead by the death of our dear Friend Mr Carr & the removal of his family from Frognal, little thinking that we had the loss of our nearest and very agreeable neighbour Mrs Merivale so close at hand. She had been unwell for 8 days but not supposed to be in the least danger and was yesterday in her drawing room, laid on the sopha, and thought by her medical attendants to be getting better slowly; but about ten o'clock she was taken very ill, then became easy & slept soundly, then became faint & went to sleep again, after that waked in the morning comfortable & easy but still faint, and expired to day about half past twelve. We are very sorry to lose her, for she was a kind, sociable intelligent companion and she will be much regretted by her own family; but for herself she leaves a very cheerless home on earth, for we trust a far better place. Her poor husband, who has been in his bed almost insensible to every thing for two years, has felt this blow much more than was expected & has wept & beat his forehead in great distress. It may be the means of rousing & clearing his ideas just at the time when one could most wish them to be blunted.

But I must not spend my paper & my little corner of time (for we expect friends to dinner) all on a sad subject, so we will say a few words upon Rybrent de Cruce which of course you have read.[84] I knew it pretty well before, but Agnes was quite ignorant, and I have been much gratified by seeing her so entirely interested with the story. She could not leave it till she had finished it, and then declared she had not been so much interested with any story for many a day. I have spoken & written to several literary friends about it as an interesting work, without letting it be known that I am at all interested in the author, and I hope this little piece of cunning will not be set down against me as a very Yorkshire or Scotch trick. — The language reads admirably; I am more sensible of this in the printed copy than I was in the Ms. —

Agnes & I are just on the eve of having our house turned upside down. It is not very pleasant to think of; but we must pay for what I hope will be a comfort to us hereafter, if it should please God that we live to enjoy it together. We hope too that you will be pleased with it when [you] come to

---

84. I am unable to identify this work.

us in spring. — Mrs Baillie is very well and William is still in Town; the future motions of either the one or the other, as summer advances, I dont know. Robert & Eliz^th & their Girl are out on a jaunt along the coast and were to be at Exeter, I believe last week, on their way to Plymouth; but of their plans at present I have no distinct notion. — Miss Hoare has been here this morning with Mr Crabb[e],[85] whose company, I hope will help to revive her. She has not been well, as I suppose you have heard, for several months. Nothing, however to cause any alarm, and she is somewhat better. — Agnes sends you her love combined with mine. Remember us to our friends at Salviston. —

yours very affectionately   J Baillie

The following letter is the property of Edinburgh University Library, Special Collections, and is listed by its acquisition date.

13 May 1938 (No address or postmark)[86]
Dear Miss Elliott,

As my Sister is from home I opened your note, and send you in consequence Mrs Baillie's polling paper which we have had in charge for you several days, but delayed sending it till we could inclose our own along with it. — Some how or other my Sister's polling-paper & my own have not been sent to us though all our neighbours here have received theirs. I went yesterday to the post office to enquire about it and found they had not been seen there, so I am this morning going to write to the Committee of the Institution to let them know of this omission. As soon as we receive them, we shall fill them up and send them to you. ——— I beg to be kindly remembered to Mrs Elliot and thank her for offering to convey any message to Mrs Stirling.[87] Will she then, when she writes, have the goodness to

---

85. George Crabbe (1754-1832) was a parish doctor before deciding to travel to London and pursue a career in writing. He took orders, becoming a curate in 1781, and established himself as a poet with *The Village* and its grim picture of rural poverty. Crabbe met and became friends with Sir Walter Scott. Throughout the Romantic movement, Crabbe persisted in presenting a precise, realistic vision of rural life and landscape. Byron called him "Nature's sternest painter yet the best," while Scott referred to him as "the English Juvenal" (*OCEL*, 237).

86. This EU letter has enclosed with it an anthologized copy of Baillie's poem "The Kitten," along with her obituary from the *London News*. The letter is probably to Anne Elliott's niece.

87. This is probably Mrs. James Stirling, the long-time friend for whose benefit Baillie's *A Collection of Poems, Chiefly Manuscript, and from Living Authors* (1823) was produced. The successful volume earned over £2,000 for her friend.

give my kind love to my old friend, and say that I have received her kind note, and hope to write to her some time hence when I have another opportunity.

    I remain, dear Miss Elliot
        most truly yours
           J Baillie
Hampstead
Saturday morning

    The following letter is the property of the University of Glasgow, Special Collections. Though this letter is probably to Anne Elliott's niece, like the one above, I am including it in this chapter.

MS Gen 542/15 (No address or postmark)
                    Hampstead wednesday Decr 20th
My dear Miss Elliot,
    I thank you gratefully for your kind compliance with my request, made of double value by the frank & liberal manner of doing it. Your assistance will be very acceptable, whatever success it may have; and we are now really beginning to have strong hopes. ——
    You are very kind too in mentioning your Father & Mother, and we are glad that, at their advanced age; you have such an agreeable account to give. I who remember Mrs Elliott conversing with so much animation & cleverness when we have visited her with our mutual friend Miss Graham of Gairbraid in days gone by, am still pleased to know that, though much ganged [changed] she can employ herself and enjoy a contented state of mind. Pray have the goodness to remember us (my Sister & myself) to her very kindly; we were talking of her not long ago, and it carried us back to old scenes & friends both pleasing & painful, when Glasgow was a very different place to what it is now. We are, like your Mother, much changed and go very little out, partly from feebleness and partly from laziness that so frequently attends old age. —— We beg to offer our best regards & the wishes of the season to Mr Elliott & yourself.
    Believe me, my dear Miss Elliott,
        very gratefully yours
           J Baillie
P.S. Mrs Baillie in Cavendish Sq^r will thankfully receive any notes you may send to her[.]

The following letter appears in the Bodleian Library's Miscellaneous English Letters, Department of Western Manuscripts, transcribed by their permission.

Ms. Autogr. c. 24, ff.183-184 (Address: Mrs Elliot / Upper Gloster Place / Dorset Square--postmark unclear, possibly 1834)[88]

Hampstead Novr 27th Monday

My dear Madam,

I thank you very much for your kind letter & notice of an opportunity of communication with our friend at Da. . . [?].[89] I have only received it this evening, owing to our having been from home for some time; I am afraid it may now be too late for your packet, but I inclose a letter for Mrs Stirling which you will kindly take charge of or return to me again should it be too late for your opportunity. ——

My Sister unites with me in kind regards to yourself & your family, and believe me

My dear Madam,

your obliged & faithful &c

J Baillie

---

88. Since Anne Elliott died in the spring of 1834 (see letter 93 to Mary Montgomery, Volume 2), this could be to her sister-in-law.

89. This is the same place name mentioned in letter AAF/B/23, Gen. 1730, and is unreadable here also; see note 51.

To Sir Thomas Lawrence

(1812-1829)

Thomas Lawrence (1769-1830) was born to innkeepers Thomas and Lucy Lawrence at 6 Redcross Street, Bristol, on 4 May, the youngest of sixteen children.[1] Thomas's father, however, had been well educated, and both parents were the children of ministers. As a young child the talented son Thomas entertained guests at his parents' Black Bear Inn, and later the White Lion, with poetry recitations and sketches. Thomas had minimal lessons in French and Latin from a dissenting minister in Devizes named Jervis, the only regular education he received. On at least one occasion, however, he was taken to Lord Pembroke's at Wilton and to Corsham House, the seat of Methuens, where he was permitted to study copies of old masters' paintings, of which he made copies from memory. When he was ten, the family moved to Bath; by this time his sketches were beginning to support the family, for he had already been noticed by Garrick, Foote, Sheridan, Johnson, Mrs. Siddons, and other influential people in London. He was soon recognized as a prodigy and as an artist of taste and elegance, and he began to draw eminent people at Oxford and small ovals of Mrs. Siddons, Admiral Barrington, and others. Thomas had his own studio in Bath by the time he was twelve and received acclaim from the Society of Arts in London soon after.

In his seventeenth year, Thomas began to paint in oils, an early effort being *Christ bearing the Cross*, some eight feet high, and a portrait of himself. Shortly after, he moved from Bath to Leicester Square in London and in 1786 submitted to the Royal Academy exhibition *A Mad Girl, A Vestal Virgin* and five portraits; in September 1787 he entered the schools of the Royal Academy, where he began a long professional friendship with Sir Joshua Reynolds. By 1792 Lawrence was living in Old Bond Street, and in 1792 a portrait of George III marked his progress in royal favor as Painter in Ordinary to the King. Literally dozens of paintings followed, and after the death of Hoppner in 1810, Lawrence had no rival, becoming the most fashionable portrait painter not only in London, but also

---

1. This and the following biographical information is taken from Douglas Goldring's *Regency Portrait Painter: The life of Sir Thomas Lawrence, P.R.A.* (London: Macdonald, 1951), the *DNB*, XI:719-27, and notes from the Royal Academy's collection of letters.

in Vienna, Italy, and Paris, painting statesmen and royalty alike. He was knighted in 1815 by the prince regent.

After spending some time on the continent, Lawrence returned to London in March 1820 to receive new honors as president of the Royal Academy, D.C.L. of Oxford, trustee of the British Museum, and portrait-painter in ordinary to George IV. In the catalogue of the Royal Academy for that year, he also added to his honors membership in the Royal Academy of St. Luke's, the Academy of Fine Arts in Florence, and the Fine Arts at New York. At this peak of his career Lawrence had attained a fame that never diminished; he went on to add to his works portraits of Sir Walter Scott, the Duke of Wellington, Canning, Southey, Cowper, Charles X and the dauphin of France, Thomas Moore, Mrs. Peel and her daughter, the Countess Gower and her son, and many more. Sir Thomas Lawrence died, probably of heart problems, on 7 January 1830 and is buried in St. Paul's. Today most of his paintings hang in the National Gallery and in Windsor Castle.

Lawrence's love of art was genuine and strong; and though shining in society, he was not a particularly sociable man. Most of his intimate friends were men, and he reserved his friendships with women, mostly to those married; but he was said to be flirtatious throughout his life, fancying himself in love with many women, Fanny Kemble being one of his last objects of affection (the painting he intended last was to be of Fanny Kemble). Mrs. Siddons and the Kembles remained his very closest friends. Joanna Baillie could have been introduced to Lawrence through a number of mutual friends at any time in the early nineteenth century; and though their relationship appears to be one of mutual professional admiration, he is often invited to her house for dinner and asked for advice on her manuscript plays. Her first letter to him in the following collection is dated 18 January 1812.

The Royal Academy of Art's letters to Sir Thomas Lawrence (1769-1830) comprise about 2,000 from various American and British statesmen and from others such as William Godwin, Sarah Siddons, and Dr. Matthew Baillie. Joanna Baillie's letters appear in LAW/2/5, 95, 122, 124-5, 179 and LAW/4/95 and LAW/5/409, transcribed by permission.

LAW/2/5 (No address or postmark)

[1812]

Dear Sir,

Of all the circumstances that have honoured & cheered me since I first attempted dramatic writing, there is none that has given me equal pleasure, one only excepted, to this of receiving from you the valuable present which you had the goodness to send to me yesterday. It indeed gratifies me to think that I have received a reward for my labours from the pen of Walter Scott & the pencil of Lawrence. I return you a thousand thanks with all my heart for the exquisite drawing. The manner in which it has been bestowed upon me gives it its chief value; yet it is in itself so delicately beautiful & elegant, and at the same time so like my Niece,[2] that to have been possessed of it in any way, (were not the misery of a guilty conscience before my eyes I should say, even by theft or robbery) had been desirable. I feel that I possess a treasure which will soothe & please me all the days of my life, and when these are at an end, I will leave it to the Friend in the world whom I prize the most. This Friend is almost as much gratified by it (for I will not allow that she can be entirely so) as I am myself;[3] her Daughter is delighted & surprised to find that any thing so beautiful can be a resemblance of herself.

It gives me great pleasure to learn, that my 3d volume of the Series has afforded you any amusement:[4] and I feel more regret at the prospect of never publishing another, when I think how much satisfaction it would

---

2. This is obviously a sketch, and possibly a verse from Scott, of Matthew Baillie's daughter Elizabeth Margaret (later Mrs. Milligan), Joanna's only niece, though I have found no reference in Lawrence papers to such a drawing. See Scott letter 3882 ff. 128-131, however, which would also confirm the date as 1812.

3. Sophia Denman Baillie (1771-1845), daughter of Dr. Thomas Denman (1733-1815) and Elizabeth Brodie Denman (1746-1833) and sister of Lord chief-justice Thomas Denman (1779-1854) and Margaret Denman Croft (1771-1838), married Joanna's only brother Dr. Matthew Baillie in 1791 and became one of Joanna's closest friends; Sophia's two children were William Hunter Baillie (1797-1894) and Elizabeth Margaret Baillie Milligan (1794-1876) (see Franco Crainz, *The Life and Works of Matthew Baillie* [Santa Polomba: PelitiAssociati, 1995]).

4. The 3rd volume of *A Series of Plays: in which it is attempted to delineate the stronger passions*, etc., appeared from Longman, et al., in 1812 and contained *Orra*, *The Dream*, *The Siege*, and *The Beacon*.

have given me to have had it hereafter in my power to send you a mark of the grateful sense I must ever retain of the great pleasure & honour you have done me. —— Believe me,

Dear Sir

your very <u>very</u> obliged & obedient ser^t

J Baillie

Grosvenor St:

Jan^{ry} 18th 1812

/2/95 (Address: To Thomas Lawrence Esqr / Russell Square--postmarked 1815)

Hampstead
sunday April 19th [1815]

My Dear Sir,

Mr Scott - (I mean Walter Scott) is to dine with us next friday, and my Sister & I will be happy if you will do us the favour to meet him.[5] Our dinner hour is half past five. Your friend Mr Sotheby I hope will be of the party,[6] and you can perhaps come together. I have given him a hint of this.

your truly obliged

J Baillie

---

5. Biographer Edgar Johnson writes that Scott sat for a painting for Lawrence in 1821 (*Sir Walter Scott*, 2 vols. [New York: Macmillan, 1970], 728). Lawrence's biographer dates the Scott portrait's completion as 1827, when it was displayed in the Royal Academy (Goldring, 312). But in a letter to Scott dated 18 November 1829 the Hon. Robert Peel, in return for supplying the writer with some letters from the Duke of Montrose regarding Rob Roy (information pertinent to Scott's novel), asks that Scott sit to Sir Thomas Lawrence so that the portrait might be added to his collection of "Illustrious Men of the Age" (see *The Letters of Sir Walter Scott*, ed. H. J. C. Grierson, 12 vols. [London: Constable, 1936], XI::266). Biographers Johnson and Goldring are probably correct, for the portrait is still in progress in 1825 (see Scott letter 3900 ff.93-94).

6. William Sotheby (1757-1833) was a prodigious poet, playwright, and translator and the consummate man of letters in the Romantic Era. Though Byron disliked him, satirizing him as Mr. Botherby in *Beppo* (1818), Sotheby provided a societal focal point for many of the brightest literary minds of his time. Scott, Wordsworth, Coleridge and Southey were his friends (*DLB*, XCIII:160-70). Sotheby's *Italy and Other Poems* was published in 1828. According to biographer Edgar Johnson, Scott originally met Baillie through William Sotheby (253). See letters to Sotheby herein.

/2/122 (No address or year postmark, RA dates 1815)

My Dear Sir,

I am always glad of any circumstance which gives me a fair pretence for asking you to see us here, and our Friend Mr Sotheby by a note which I have just received from him, furnishes me with such at present. He is to dine with us next thursday, that we may sit in council on a certain play of his, and wishes that your taste & judgment should be added [to] it;[7] will you then have the goodness to come with him? You will truly oblige us by so doing. —— He also says that a Ms. play of mine is to be critically read, but in this he deceives himself. To be present at the reading of a play of my own, would be torment to me. I have never yet endured it, and feel no greater courage now than formerly. If you have any inclination to read this same play, you shall have the Ms. whenever you please; and tho' I have no intention of offering <u>it</u> or any of my Ms. plays to the Theatre, I shall be happy to have your opinion of it as an act[ing][8] Play and of benefitting by your judgment in other respects also. ——— My Sister begs to offer her best compliments. We shall dine on thursday at 5 or half past five oclock. Believe me

My dear Sir,

      your truly obliged &c.

        J Baillie

Hampstead

saturday Decr 16th [1815?]

/2/124 (No address or year postmark, RA dates 1815)

My dear Sir,

My Sister, I hope will have an opportunity of leaving this with the Ms. Play at your house to day, so you see I lose no time in sending it.[9] When you have read it (do not hurry yourself) have the goodness to send it to 72 Grosvenor St: and desire your servant to tell the servant there to give the parcel immediately into Mrs Baillie's own hand, who will take care of it for me. I am particular in this because there are parts of the Ms. which were it to be lost I could never recover, having no compleat copy of the whole. I ask advice and like many people in this world seldom follow it;

---

7. If the Royal Academy's 1815 date for this letter is accurate, this play could have been one of Sotheby's five-act historical tragedies in blank verse, namely, *Ellen, or the Confession* (1816).

8. Letter is torn here. The ms. play is probably *Henriquez* discussed in following.

9. See note 11 below. The editor of *Sir Thomas Lawrence's Letter-Bag* (London: George Allen, 1906) dates this letter around 1796, assuming the manuscript to be *DeMonfort*, but the following letter (2/125), postmarked 1816, appears to be a continuation of this topic. *DeMonfort* was produced in 1800.

but let not this discourage you (if you be so kind) how it strikes you as a play intended for representation. Tho' I never expect to have any of my Plays produced upon the stage in my life time, yet I should like to leave them behind me in a state to be so produced when circumstances may be more favourable for it.

I see by the direction of your letter to <u>Miss</u> J Baillie that you have no mind the servant, who takes your letter to post, should know it is <u>not</u> a young Lady you correspond with. Pray give us this vanity. If he should read on the back of your letters to Mrs Joanna Baillie, he will only guess that you have an Aunt or God Mother of that name and it will not bring you any discredit.[10]

Believe me, my dear Sir, with regret that we cannot have the pleasure of seeing you to morrow & hoping to be more fortunate another time.

> your greatly obliged
>> J Baillie

Hampstead
wednesday Decr 20th [1815?]

/2/179 (No address or year)

> Hampstead
> Monday Jany 8th [1816]

My dear Sir,

I told you truth when I said I was in no hurry to have my Ms. again; it is as safe with you as with myself. I hope then you have not taken the trouble to send it to Grosvenor Street. If you are entirely done with it, Mrs Baillie will call for it at your door on thursday or friday next. I feel my self very much obliged by your having bestowed your time upon it and highly gratified with what you say of its dramatic effect; this part of my art being the only one in which, at my age, I can possibly expect to improve. Skill must now make amends for the want of power. ——— I fear between bad writing and bad spelling & other mistakes you have had more trouble than enough in making out the sense of it. But I have always thought one of the charms of Greek poetry is the difficulty of making out the meaning, so perhaps these same defects have stood me in some stead. —— With many thanks for all your friendly attention, I remain,

> My dear Sir,
>> your truly obliged
>>> J Baillie

---

10. In 1814 Baillie "officially" took the name of Mrs. Joanna Baillie. See Folger letter dated February 7, 1814, to her close friend Mary Berry herein.

/2/125 (Address: To Sir Thomas Lawrence / Russell Square--postmarked 1816)

Hampstead Jan^ry 15th 1816

My dear Sir,

I am very much obliged to you for your very friendly & gratifying note which I have received along with my Ms. You are very goodnatured it [in] setting forth all the defects of our present Actors in regard to the character of Henriquez,[11] to reconcile me to my fate; but indeed it is not their defects, but certain untoward circumstances connected with our present large Theatres, and my own want of favour with the public in general, that would prevent me from being very glad to see it presented by either of the 3 Actors you have named; tho' did his health admit of such exertion, I should greatly prefer your Friend Mr Kemble.[12] Offering it to either of our large Theatres for representation is entirely out of the question; and publishing it as far as I am able to judge of the final interest of the work, as much so. The approbation & good will of a few Friends, whose taste & judgment may be of use to me and to whom I should from gratitude & esteem be glad in the humblest way to give pleasure, is all that I now expect from the present generation in my own life time; and I am gratified that amongst these few I am permitted to include yourself, whose taste and judgment I value very highly. I do not mean by this, however, to insinuate that I am indifferent to general applause; if I were foolish enough to assume it on any occasion it would not be upon you I should venture to pass such affectation. I am as fond of it as the weakest person that ever wrote; but as I cannot get it, I contrive to make myself tolerably happy without it.

---

11. *Henriquez, A Tragedy in Five Acts*, appeared in 1836 in *Dramas*. The first of the three volumes contained *Romiero, The Alienated Manor*, and *Henriquez*.

12. John Philip Kemble (1757-1823), one of England's most famous actors, began playing parts in his father's company in early childhood. His sister, Sarah Kemble Siddons, first recommended him to the Chamberlain's company as Theodosius in Lee's tragedy in 1776, with dozens of parts to follow. Kemble was a scholar, a man of breeding and a fine actor with a larger range of characters in which he excelled than any English tragedian. He wrote prologues for charitable institutions in York and Leeds, where he appeared for the first time in *Hamlet*--he is said to have written out the part over 40 times. He managed the Edinburgh Theatre for a while in 1781, and his first appearance in London was at Drury Lane as Hamlet in 1783. He remained at Drury Lane for 19 years, representing over 120 characters himself; and on 25 January 1800 Kemble played DeMonfort in Baillie's play. In 1802 he acquired a 6th share of Covent Garden, but in 1808 when the house burned, taking 20 lives, Kemble and other investors were nearly ruined for lack of insurance. A loan of £10,000 from Lord Percy helped him reopen the new Covent Garden Theatre. Portraits of John Kemble abound, several of which are by Lawrence, notably Kemble as Cato, as Hamlet and as Rolla (*DNB*, X:1260-66).

I am very much pleased that you have noticed my line of "Juan dear dear Friend &c" which, simple as it is, is the line I like best of the whole Play, and the only one in it which I can repeat, and which nevertheless has not been noticed by any creature but yourself.[13] This is being in my mind the best critic of the whole world. What you say of curtailing the scene which follows the scene of confession to the King I feel is perfectly just, and I shall take your advice; tho' I believe I should have been somewhat obstinate on this point if you had not produced so . . . [good a reason][14] for it, not founded on pedantic rules of criticism but on human nature. — — Accept my very best thanks for the kind attention you have paid to this piece, and Believe me,

> My dear Sir,
>   your very grateful & obliged,
>   J Baillie

LAW/4/95 (No address or year, but probably 1822-1823)
Dear Sir Thomas,

I am very much obliged to you for honouring me with your name to my subscription list, and I beg you to accept my best thanks; but there is a far greater favour which I am bold enough to request of you, and I hope you will not refuse it, if it is not very uncomfortable to your own feelings. Perhaps Miss Croft,[15] who is always doing good and always kind to me, has already hinted it to you. I know, that besides your extraordinary power in your own delightful & difficult art, the gift of poesy has been bestowed upon you. Let me have one of your poems to put into my Collection,[16] and I shall be very thankful & very glad and very proud. It would be of real service to me & my distressed friend. Sir Humphrey Davy has been kind enough to give me one of his,[17] and to have poems from two

---

13. The line appears in scene 3 of Act 4 as follows: *Hen.* . . . . "My Juan, dear, dear friend! Juan de Torva!/ Thy name is on my lips, as it was wont;/ Thine image in my heart like stirring life;/ Thy form upon my fancy like that form/ Which bless'd my happy days" (*Henriquez. The Dramatic and Poetical Works of Joanna Baillie* [London: Longman, Brown, Green and Longmans, 1851], 372).

14. I have enclosed my supposition at these words in brackets because there is a hole in the letter, making the complete line illegible.

15. This is probably Miss Elizabeth Croft, sister of Sir Richard Croft and close friend to Lawrence.

16. Though this letter is not dated, her request is surely for *A Collection of Poems, Chiefly Manuscript, and from Living Authors* (London: Longman, et al., 1823), a subscription collection for the benefit of her friend Mrs. James Stirling. If Lawrence submitted poems for the collection, they are listed in the contents anonymously.

17. Sir Humphrey Davy (1778-1829) was a natural philosopher and poet who became president of the Royal Society in 1820 (*DNB*, V:637-43), which would also

distinguished Presidents would be very flattering to my vanity were there
no better purpose to serve by it. To the President of the College of
Physicians I dont mean to apply. —— Pray consider this, and send me if
possible, a favourable answer which will add greatly to the many
obligations which you have already bestowed on
     your very grateful
         Friend & servant
            J Baillie
Cavendish Sq^r
tuesday Feb^r 19th [1822?]

LAW/5/38 (No address or postmark)

                          Hampstead saturday
                        evening [after 1820]
My dear Miss Croft,
    I return many thanks for the President's address which I restore to you
again after having read it twice with great interest.[18] It possesses all of
the refinement, good feeling & good sense which one naturally expected
from any thing of his writing; and I have been particularly pleased with
the high & just praise so delicately bestowed on Mrs Siddons;[19] it will
fall like a cheering sunbeam on the evening of her life. —— That I should
be proud to possess a copy of the address I readily confess, and you are very
kind to encourage me to request one; but such a request would, I am afraid,
prove an annoyance to that delicacy which has prevented him from
distributing it to his friends, and I shall be satisfied with having it in my
power at any future time to borrow Mrs Baillie's copy; for surely the Person
to whom she has at present lent it, cannot be unreasonable enough to keep
it much longer.
    I am sorry to learn that you have had occasion to be capped and hope
it will be a long time before headache or any other cause shall oblige you
to repeat the operation. I am sorry also to learn that Mr W. Ryder has had

----

date this letter after that time. See chapter of letters to Lady Davy for information on
the family. If Davy submitted poems for the collection, they are listed in the contents
anonymously.
    18. This is most likely a copy of Lawrence's President's address to the Royal
Academy (dating this letter after 1820) sent from Lawrence by Elizabeth Croft.
    19. Foremost tragic actress Sarah Siddons (1755-1831), a friend of Baillie,
achieved celebrity under Garrick's management at Drury Lane, giving her farewell
performance as Lady Macbeth at Covent Garden in 1812. Siddons had played the role
of Jane in Baillie's DeMonfort in 1800 and after her retirement continued to give
private readings (DNB, VIII:195-202; many biographies are available). There were
many honorable notes on her after her retirement, this one probably from the Royal
Academy.

a relapse.[20] –– The good . . . .[21] we were last in Town, and found her looking every way, in good spirits, moving about easily and persuaded from her own improved feelings that she should recover.

My Sister unites with me in kind regards to you; and with repeated thanks for your obliging readiness in sending me what I longed so much to see,[22]

/5/409 (No address or year)

Hampstead wednesday
Decr 23^d [1829]

My dear Sir Thomas

I felt very much your kind remembrance of me regarding a box in Covent Garden to see Miss F. Kemble,[23] and I begged Miss C.[roft] to convey to you my best thanks which I trust she has done. I afterwards, viz. last saturday, wrote to her to say that if you could procure for me a box in the lower circle, as near the stage as may be for wednesday the 30th (next wednesday) to see her in the character of Belvidera,[24] I should be greatly obliged to you and that our party would consist of 7 or 8 (I believe I must now say 6 or 7 for some of the party have fallen off). I likewise added that we preferred a public box. The same note was sent to Miss Croft by last saturday's mid-day post, and though I knew afterwards that she was to go to Hendon on monday morning, I still trusted that she would receive it in good time to communicate its contents to you. Have you heard from her on the subject? and is there any chance of our getting a box for next Wednesday? Perhaps next week being holiday week, she may not act at

---

20. Though difficult to read, this name appears to be W. Ryder. I find no mention of a Ryder in works on Lawrence. A Thomas Ryder (1746-1810), however, was an engraver and one of the first students of the Royal Academy, engraving a portrait of Henry Bunbury after Lawrence. Ryder's son was also an engraver, and together they executed a full-length portrait of Queen Charlotte (*DNB*, XVII:539).

21. A portion of the letter is missing here.

22. End of the letter has been cut off.

23. Fanny Kemble (1809-93) was the daughter of actor Charles Kemble and niece of Sarah Siddons and John Kemble. She debuted as Juliet in *Romeo and Juliet* in Covent Garden in 1829, an immediate success. She later toured both England and America and is known as a writer of *Journal of a Residence on a Georgian Plantation, 1838-39.* See both Margaret Armstrong, *Fanny Kemble, A Passionate Victorian* (New York: Macmillan, 1938), and *Fanny Kemble, Journal of a Young Actress,* ed. Monica Gough (New York: Columbia University Press, 1990). In his last years Lawrence took a special interest in the career of Fanny Kemble, for he had supposedly once been in love with her sister Sally Kemble (Goldring, 321).

24. Fanny Kemble played Belvidera in Otway's *Venice Preserved* at Covent Garden in December 1829 (Leota S. Driver, *Fanny Kemble* [Chapel Hill: University of North Carolina Press, 1933], 38).

all. Pray have the goodness to let me know whether you have heard or done any thing on my behalf in this interesting business. It is truly so to me for I have admired your young friend already so much in the character of Juliet that I long mightily to see her in that of Belvidera which I should think will suit her particularly well; one of the few faults she has - (in my opinion at least) - a little over-acting, will not be so observed in that character. —— Besides thanking you very gratefully for your obliging offer of procuring a box, I must likewise say that I have been much flattered by your wishing that I should see Miss Kemble, and to be flattered by you must be a very agreed thing to both old & young Ladies.

I remain,

My dear Sir Thomas

your obliged & faithful

J Baillie

PS. If you have not heard from Miss Croft pray take no trouble about the box at all for in that case we will put off our party to the week after next which will give you more time to apply[.]

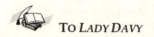 To LADY DAVY

(1813-1850?)

Lady Jane Davy (1780-1855) was the only daughter and heiress of Charles Kerr of Kelso and Jane Tweedie. She was married at Marylebone Church on 3 October 1799 to Shuckburgh Ashby Apreece, baronet of Washingley, Huntingdonshire, but he died in 1807 without children. Jane then retired to Edinburgh, opening her doors to the intellectuals of the city. She was a continental traveler and reportedly a remarkable beauty with grace and manners, and in April 1812 she married scientist Sir Humphrey Davy (1778-1829). Two months later he dedicated to her his *Elements of Chemical Philosophy*, and in 1813 the couple went on a lengthy foreign tour, accompanied by Sir Humphrey's friend the scientist Faraday. Apparently, the trip was not free from strain, for Jane was sometimes demanding and not particularly comfortable around "simple students of science." She did not join her husband on his last journey to the continent, where he died from a series of strokes in May 1829.

Sir Humphrey Davy had been apprenticed to John Bingham, a surgeon with a large practice in Penzance, in 1794; and in the apothecary's dispensary he became a chemist, his research full of striking and rich novel facts. In 1801 he was engaged in the service of the Royal Institution as assistant lecturer in chemistry, and his first communication to the Royal Society, "Account of some Galvanic Combinations," was read that same year. Several papers followed, and he was proposed a fellow in 1803. In 1807 Davy presented his experiments and discoveries in electricity before the Royal Society, making himself famous both in England and on the continent. At the end of 1807 he became very ill, probably from exposure to the unhealthy atmosphere of his work, and was not able to work again until April 1809, subsequently taking up the study of oxymuriatic gas and oxygen. Trinity College conferred upon him the honorary degree of LL.D. in 1810, and he was knighted in 1812 by the prince regent. Davy continued his experiments and lectures in Italy in 1813 and returned to England to deliver his experiments on the colors used by the ancients and other matters of interest to the Royal Society. Davy was a poet of some merit, publishing a volume entitled *The Sons of Genius* in 1795 and some miscellaneous poems thereafter, but he abandoned poetry for science early in his life.[1]

---

1. See *DNB*, V:637-44.

Baillie apparently knew Sir Humphrey and Lady Davy well, communicating with both, though only one letter in the following collection is addressed to Sir Humphrey.

Unless otherwise noted, the following letters and notes to Lady Davy are in the Cowie Collection of the Mitchell Library, Glasgow (Nos. 204c-232c), transcribed by their permission:

204c (Address: For Lady Davy / Berkley Square--no postmark, ML dates 1813)

Dear Madam,

I said the other night at M[r] Carr's[2] when you so kindly remembered your very obliging promise, that any morning till the end of next week that should be most convenient for your Ladyship & Sir Humphry [sic], we should be happy to have the honour of seeing you to breakfast. I reckoned however without my host, for I find I am obliged to go to Town preparatory to my going into Devonshire next wednesday, of course there are only next monday & tuesday when we can hope for it. My Sister & I will be very sorry if neither of those mornings should suit you. I hope one of them will, and that the weather will be favourable. We shall breakfast at half past ten o'clock or any hour most agreeable to you. My Sister offers her best respects[3]

  I remain
   Dear Madam
  Your Ladyship's
   very obliged
    J Baillie
Hampstead
thursday June 3 [1813]

---

  2. Mr. and Mrs. Thomas William Carr of Frognal, Hampstead, were the parents of Thomas, William, Frances, Isabella (Lady Smith), Anna, Laura and of Sarah Grace (Mrs. Stephen Lushington). Thomas, solicitor to the excise, later acquired Sir Samuel Bentham's portion of the Oak Hill Farm estate. Baillie was apparently a very close friend, for she talks of the family often.

  3. Agnes Baillie (1760-1861) was Joanna Baillie's only sister and constant companion. Dr. Matthew Baillie writes that Agnes Baillie, born in the Manse of Shotts on 24 September 1760, had "a quick ready Understanding, with a good deal of various knowle[d]ge, so as to be much beyond the common level of Women in these respects" (qtd. in Franco Crainz, *The Life and Works of Matthew Baillie* [Santa Polomba: PelitiAssociati, 1995], 10).

205c (Address: Lady Davy / Grosvenor Street--no postmark, ML dates 1816)

My dear Lady Davy

When I had the pleasure of seeing you last, to all your kindness you added that of offering me letters of introduction to some of your Friends at Geneva; and had Sir Humphry & you made good your kind intention of driving over the country to see us some morning the beginning of the week, I should have put you in mind of it. But the weather has forbid all such hopes on our part and still continues rainy. Permit me then to say, that I am to set off from Grosvenor St: with my young married folks & my Nephew for the continent next Tuesday,[4] and if your Ladyship can without inconvenience send the letter for me there by monday evening, I shall be glad & very much obliged. --- My Brother, who does not read much poetry, has been delighted with Sir Humphry's verses; and Mrs Baillie says if they were generally known they would do good to all the young men of the kingdom. Most certainly pious sentiments so finely introduced & expressed, and coming from such a quarter, would not be considered as allied to weakness. ---

My Sister sends her best respects with mine to Sir Humphry & your Ladyship.

Believe me Dear Lady Davy
          your truly obliged
                J Baillie
Hampstead
thursday July 25th [1816]

232c (No address or postmark)[5]

Hampstead Octr 12th [1816]

Dear Lady Davy,

Not knowing where you are at present I shall send this to Grosvenor Street 23 to take its chance of coming into your hands some how or other. I returned from my travels better than a week ago, and will not be longer of thanking you for the pleasure & advantage which my friends & I received from your kind letter of introduction to Mr Pictet.[6] We changed our plan of staying a week at Geneva, being tempted to go else where, and were there

---

4. Elizabeth Margaret Baillie, Joanna's only niece, married Capt. Robert Milligan on 11 July 1816; Baillie traveled with them and her nephew William to Switzerland, etc., afterwards. See NLS letter 3887 ff.98-99 to Scott.

5. This trip to Switzerland took place in summer 1816. See NLS letter 3887 ff.98-99 to Scott.

6. This is probably the Marc Auguste Pictet-Turretini referred to in Hodson letter 8, Volume 2.

only a day & half when we first went and as long on our return from Chamouny [Chamouni] & Martigny. We had therefore only time to see Mr Pictet for a very short time, and tho' he had just lost a favorite Nephew a few hours before we saw him (I was sorry when I learnt this that I had sent your letter) he was very obliging – truly kind, and insisted on our going to his house that we might see his models of Mount Blanc to give us a clearer view of the tour we were going to take. He said many handsome things of Lady Davy, really spoken with warmth & hearty good will. These I shall not now repeat. This letter to Mr Pictet was the only one I meant to deliver, my time being so short, but finding from its being so closely written that your letter to Mad^{me} Coustant was not merely a letter of introduction, I went to her house the evening before we left Geneva and put it into her hands, spending with her about half an hour, when she was obliging enough to shew me & my friends her beautiful grounds. She was sitting (the beginning of Sept^r) wrapt in a shawl by the fire, having slight cold. ———

I wish Mont Blanc had been as gracious to me as he was to Sir Humpry [*sic*], tho' I do not pretend to be so worthy of his favours. When we come to compare notes on this score I shall make but a poor figure. Yet I have seen some glimpses & faint visions which faint & short as they were repaid one for many miles of travelling

I hope your Ladyship & Sir Humphry have been well & enjoyed the country as much as the weather would permit since I had the pleasure of seeing you. My Sister begs to offer her best respects. Believe me dear Lady Davy

　　　your truly obliged　　　　J Baillie

The following letter to Humphrey Davy is the property of the British Library, catalogued in Additional Manuscripts, and included by their permission:

Add. Ms. 18,204, f. 49: Letter to Sir H. Davy (No address or postmark)
　　　　　　　　　　　　　　　　　　　　Cavendish Sq^{re}
　　　　　　　　　　　　　　　　　　Wednesday morning [1823]
Dear Sir Humphrey

I am going to ask a very great favour of you in behalf of Mrs Baillie which I know you will not refuse. She with all the family have been exceedingly gratified by the notice you have taken, in your speech at the opening of the Royal Society, of him who was so dear to her & to us; it was a soothing — a cordial to her sorrow to have such testimony given to his worth.[7] M[r] Sotheby[8] was so kind as to send me better than a week ago, a copy of that part of your speech which we had longed to see; but now she has taken it into her fancy that she should like to be possessed of a copy of those much-prized words written by your own hand, that she may treasure them as amongst her previous things. Her whole mind is now occupied with what regards his memory, and you will, I know, sympathize with it & indulge her. Any time when you have a little leisure & can do it without inconvenience, I trust you will be kind enough to grant our request, and you need not send me any immediate answer to this; your time is too valuable for writing notes which may be spared. — M[rs] Baillie is now and has been for some time fast confined to her room with a very bad cold & inflammation of the windpipe, but is rather better.

I was glad to learn yesterday that Lady Davy is come to Town in good health. I beg to send her my best respects & wishes

Believe me

Dear Sir Humphrey

gratefully & truly yours

J Baillie

206c (Address: Lady Davy / Park Street--no postmark, ML dates 1828)

Hampstead Wednesday

June 18th [1828]

My dear Lady Davy

We were in hopes of having the pleasure of seeing you here to spend a rambling day with us on the heath, and it would have been a real gratification both to Agnes & myself; but our friend M[rs] Elliott[9] is going to run off with us to Devonshire and sets out on her journey sooner than was at first expected which puts an end to our hopes for the early part, at least, of the summer. We are very sorry not to have it in our power to call

---

7. This appears to be a reference to Dr. Matthew Baillie, who died 23 September 1823. Mrs. Baillie mentioned above is his wife Sophia Denman Baillie (1771-1845).

8. William Sotheby (1757-1833) was a prodigious poet, playwright, and translator and the consummate man of letters in the Romantic Era. Though Byron disliked him, satirizing him as Mr. Botherby in *Beppo* (1818), Sotheby provided a societal focal point for many of the brightest literary minds of his time. Scott, Wordsworth, Coleridge, Southey were his friends (*DLB*, XCIII:160-70). See letters to Sotheby herein.

9. Anne Elliott and her sister-in-law Mrs. Elliott were both friends of Baillie. See letters to Elliott herein.

in Park St: before we go, as we shant be in Town at all but for a few hours to morrow, crouded [sic] with business, so in this way you must give us leave to wish you a pleasant summer wherever you may spend it, and improved health from variety of scene & air. My Sister sends with mine her best respects & all kind wishes. If you should be in Town in Oct.ʳ I hope we shall see you, but this is not very likely.

Believe me, my dear Lady Davy
most truly yours
J Baillie

231c (No address or postmark)

Hampstead Sunday evening [1829?]

Your note, my dear Lady Davy, is quite satisfactory, and I am sorry that the mistake of some ignorant guesser, has made us for a moment give credit to what did so much injustice to your friend. It will now be a great pleasure to the friends of the late excellent M.ʳˢ Barbauld, who have heard the surmise, to know that so able & distinguished a Critic as Lord Dudley & ward did <u>not</u> write the very offensive review in question and I shall take care that they be very soon relieved from that disagreeable impression.[10] — I can easily imagine the dispute about the comparative numbers of the French & English armies which formerly took place between M.ʳˢ B & Lord D. and that she was all the while admiring the spirit & acuteness of the Boy while she seemed to be provoking in good earnest his national ardour.

---

10. Anna Laetitia Barbauld (1743-1825) was the only daughter of classicist and Nonconformist minister John Aikin and became one of the teachers at the new Dissenting academy in Warrington. In 1774 she married Rochemont Barbauld, also a Nonconformist cleric, who took over a congregation in Plasgrave, Suffolk, where ALB took charge of a school for young boys. The Barbaulds traveled in Europe for a while and settled in Hampstead where Barbauld ministered to a congregation and ALB took a few pupils. Mr. Barbauld was never very stable and died insane in 1808. In 1782-6 ALB, in conjunction with her brother, wrote *Evenings at Home* for her adopted son and in 1804 edited *The Correspondence of Samuel Richardson* in six volumes and *The British Novelists*, in 50 volumes, in 1810, along with *The Female Speaker* (1811), selections of the best British prose and poetry long used in the education of girls (Todd, 37-40). In 1811 Barbauld published a poem entitled *Eighteen Hundred and Eleven* which prophesied that on a future day a traveler from the antipodes would contemplate the ruin of St. Paul's; the poem provoked a coarse review in the *Quarterly* from Murray which he later admitted he regretted (*DNB*, I:1065). But "the late excellent Mrs Barbauld" would date this letter after 1825, which is too late for the review suggested here.

I shall take the first opportunity also of reading the review of Horne Tooke in the 7th vol. of the quarterly which I shall read with perfect composure be it ever so severe.[11] ---

And now let me thank your Ladyship for the kind things you say on our behalf and for the great pleasure you gave us -- gave us too with so good a grace on thursday. That the world hath not spoiled you for a quiet fireside is evident. My Sister was much better for your chearful society. She is however, still suffering from the cold, and will I fear be confined to the house for another week which will probably be all the time that our tolerably fine weather lasts. She begs you to accept her kindest wishes & thanks along with those of your
    truly obliged & faithful &
    J Baillie

207c (Address: Lady Davy / Park Street / Grosvenor Square--postmarked 1834)

Hampstead monday
March 3 [1834]

My dear Lady Davy,

You kindly expressed a wish to know when we should come to Town, and I have the pleasure to say that we shall go next wednesday to Cavendish Sq[r] to spend a short time with M[rs] Baillie. Will you have the kindness to receive us either on thursday or friday morning and allow us to pass a couple of hours with you? We shall come half past 12 if this is not too early, and you will spare us a sandwich at your own natural luncheon time. We have declined dining with any of our friends in Town, so we hope you will permit us in this way to enjoy your company in the morning. -- I name thursday or friday because I may probably go to Acton on saturday to stay a few days with a friend. — My Sister begs her best regards.

    Yours, my dear Lady Davy very truly
    J Baillie
PS. The answer had better be sent to Cavendish Sq[r]

---

11. John Horne Tooke (1736-1812), radical politician and philologist, established his literary reputation with *Epea Pteroenta: or, the Diversions of Purley* (1786-1805), an extensive grammar. A second edition was published by Richard Taylor in 1829 (2 volumes) with revisions from the author's copy; it was both attacked and acclaimed. Tooke was among the first to see languages as historical developments rather than fixed structures, stressing the importance of Gothic and Anglo-Saxon. The work was praised by exponents of Utilitarianism, and Tooke's friends included Mill, Bentham, Coleridge, Godwin and Paine (*DNB*, XIX:967-74).

208c (Address: Lady Davy--no postmark, ML dates 1836)

Hampstead Jan.ʸ 2ᵈ [1836]

My dear Lady Davy,

It gave us both sincere pleasure to see your hand-writing again and to learn that you are safely in your own country again, where I hope the stock of Italian climate, as you call it, will last & keep you in good health through the winter and much longer. Many years & happy ones we trust lie before you; as far as our hearty good wishes may avail, they will be so. Many thanks for your friendly & affectionate remembrance of us. We have been generally well since you left us in May 1834, but you will find your old friends a good deal older for the time that has passed over their heads. But we have great cause to thank God that he has spared us to our advanced age so free from disease or suffering. ——

We shall be truly glad, my dear Lady Davy to look upon your face again and I hope when <u>you</u> return to Town & <u>spring</u> returns, we shall be so gratified. —— We made enquiries after you while abroad, as we had opportunity, and were generally answered by a favorable report though not very circumstantial or much to be depended upon. We were not even aware that you had arrived in England. This made your kind note received by yesterday's post, doubly acceptable.

With all kind regards from my Sister & myself, believe me, my dear Lady Davy

your obliged & affectionate
J Baillie

209c (Address: Lady Davy / Park Street / Grosvenor Square--postmarked 1838)

Hampstead Janʸ 3ᵈ [1838]

Many thanks, my dear Lady Davy, for your kind wishes of the season! they are returned to you on our part with right hearty good will. A very few years now can Agnes & I look forward to now, but we have great cause for thankfulness that we have passed so many years in this world of change & vicissitude with comparatively so little discomfort or pain. As to you, many years may still lie before you, and may they be years of happiness!

We shall be delighted to see you here and to hear the story of your 8 absent weeks, when your own convenience & weather are favorable for giving us this pleasure. ——

We have both been confined to the house for more than a fortnight with bad colds which seem very unwilling to leave us though the weather is very mild.

Hoping then to see you ere long, I remain, my dear Lady Davy
affectionately yours
    J Baillie

210c (Address: Lady Davy / Park Street--no postmark, ML dates 1839)
                                    Hampstead friday morning [1839?]
My dear Lady Davy
    My Sister & I were not at all easy about you when you left us last
saturday to walk so far to your carriage, the air so sharp and so much of a
heavy cold about you. — We hope you have not suffered from it and
should be very thankful to know that such is the case. A few lines by the 2⁻
post would be very acceptable (particularly if they give a good account) to
your two old friends here. Yours, my dear Lady Davy,
    gratefully & affectionately
    J Baillie
PS. Lockharts Ballentyne's pamphlet has been sent to me either by your
Ladyship or himself and we think he makes out his defence very clearly.
As to the <u>manner</u> of doing it there may be doubts.[12] – – –

211c (Address: Lady Davy / Palazzo Valdobrundini / Rome, Italy--
postmarked 1840)
                                    Hampstead March 31st 1840
My dear Lady Davy,
    Your friendly animated letter was most welcome to my Sister & me, for
we were longing to hear of you very much. It gave us great pleasure to learn
that your health was so good in your exalted Palazzo and that you so
perfectly enjoyed the objects of antiquity & celebraty [sic] around you
which you know so well how to appreciate. I hope since the beginning of
the year (the date of the letter) you have continued to enjoy these
pleasures, above all good health, that gives every pleasure its true zest. I
wonder what real admiration poor, sick, languid beholders bestow upon

---

12. Though it was Cadell who kept Scott unaware of the instability of their
publishing firm, Lockhart blamed Constable more. He saw James and John Ballantyne
as upright men, but it was impossible for him to write about the financial disaster
objectively, and he was caught up in the controversy between the Constable and
Ballantyne families. When the Ballantynes issued a pamphlet refuting Lockhart's
charges, he responded with *The Ballantyne Humbug Handled*. Maria Edgeworth
counseled,

> Only make a clear, general statement, and let there be an end of all that.
> Posterity will care nothing about the Ballantynes or Constable or any of
> them but Scott himself - and let me hear no more of the Ballantyne Humbug -
> what a vulgar word - unworthy of you!

See Marion Lochhead's *John Gibson Lockhart* (London: John Murray, 1954), 211-13.

the Apollo Belvidere &c; I suspect <u>not</u> a great deal, if they would speak the truth honestly. It will give us much satisfaction to hear some time hence that this is the case and in the mean time, perhaps, I may hear tidings of you through my friend Miss Montgomery, who is with her sister in law passing the winter at Rome and is I hope among those who are fortunate enough to enjoy your Society.[13] She is a very clever and a very excellent person with whom my Sister & I have been intimate for many years; and as she is well-acquainted with your friends the Somervilles,[14] now in Rome, I hope you have met frequently. Trusting to this indeed I ventured to send through her a message to your Ladyship some time ago. Though you live privately, you have no doubt friends about you of many different nations, but of them all I should best like to know Miss Fashill [Farhill?] the Lady who lives in that celebrated villa and does so much good among the Peasantry. That she should have continued to live constantly there for so many years has, one must suppose, some story connected with it which gives additional interest to her benevolence. I wish she had taken a fancy to some Estate in our poor Ireland where she might have done much good and where such kind hearts are much wanted. But this is a Churlish remark: wherever she does good, she is God's servant and ought to be honoured.

I know you will kindly desire to know something particular of ourselves, and I am thankful to say I have a pretty good report to give. We have passed through the early, dark, rainy part of the winter, followed by a severely cold dry spring, without being much injured by either of them. My Sister has had occasional ailments of rheumatism & stomach, and I scarcely any ailments at all. This is saying a great deal for people at our age and shews that we have been very mercifully dealt with. We have been very little in Town <u>to stay</u> for a long time, but to make amends for that we have made several short visits to Cavendish Sq^r to see Mrs Baillie & our friends from the Isle of Wight & Richmond, and they have

---

13. Mary Millicent Montgomery grew up under the guardianship of Lady Gosford, a friend of Judith Milbanke, and later became Lady Byron's closest friend, spending a great deal of time at Seaham. Though she spent much of her life as an invalid, Montgomery outlived Annabella. Her sister-in-law was Mrs. Hugh Montgomery. See letters to Montgomery, Volume 2, for more detail.

14. Dr. William and Mary Somerville resided for some years in the Chelsea section of London. Mary Somerville was a prominent scientist, whose *Connection of the Physical Sciences* was published in the 1830s and who became a friend and "tutor" to Ada Byron. The couple had two daughters, Martha and Mary, and a son from Mrs. Somerville's first marriage, Woronzow Greig (see Betty A. Toole, *Ada, The Enchantress of Numbers* [Mill Valley, California: Strawberry Press, 1992], 55).

made kind visits to us.[15] Last week our Nephew William Baillie came
from Richmond and staid two nights with us which was a bright spot in
our Calendar. As we never go out in the evening, Agnes has been busy of
late with some books of antiquity, looking out references for a friend, and I,
who have little turn for antiquity, have been occupied much to my own
satisfaction with Professor Smyth's lectures on Modern History, lately
publish'd.[16] It is very much read, and if it have not yet reached you, I
hope it will soon. His account of the reformation strikes me as particularly
enlighten'd, liberal & candid, as it affects all parties; and when our ultra
zealous Divines are making such learned coil at Oxford, it comes at a good
time and is judiciously instructive.[17] I think you know Smyth; I am almost
sure of it. He is a most excellent man and has gone through some trials in
early life that do him the greatest honour. Before this work came in play,
we were both of us much interested with Mrs Jameson's translation of the
Princess Amelia of Saxony's Plays,[18] Comedies which give one an insight
into German life, as regards the Middling Classes of society, that one
would have little expected from the pen of a Royal Author. Perhaps by &
by as the Queen & Prince Albert both like the Theatre and no doubt both
have a favorable leaning toward Germany, we may have some of them
produced upon the stage, where if well acted they would be exceedingly
interesting & entertaining. — The Sothebys who have been very much at

15. Niece Elizabeth Margaret Milligan lived at Ryde with her husband Robert
and only daughter Sophia. At the time of this letter nephew William Baillie lived at
Richmond with wife Henrietta Duff Baillie and 3 children.

16. Professor William Smyth (1765-1849) was a modern history professor at
Cambridge. Smyth tutored the elder son of Richard Brinsley Sheridan (1751-1816) for
13 years. But his relationship with Sheridan was hardly smooth, as his pay was
often in arrears and Sheridan himself less than sympathetic. Appointed regius
professor of modern history in 1807, he held the position till his death (*DNB*,
XVIII:599-600).

17. Baillie is probably referring to the Oxford Movement, or Tractarian
Movement, aimed to defend the Church of England as a divine institution while
reviving the High Church traditions of the 1600s. Such figures as John Henry
Newman, R. H. Froude and Edward Pusey were prominent in the movement (see
Richard D. Altick, *Victorian People and Ideas* [New York: Norton, 1973], 208-19).

18. Anna Jameson (1794-1860) was an essayist, travel writer and art historian
who married lawyer Robert Jameson in 1825 but separated from him in 1837. Seldom
living with her husband during the marriage, Anna accompanied her father and
friends on many tours through Canada, the Low Countries and Germany. Her circle of
friends included Baillie, Lady Byron, Fanny Kemble, Elizabeth Gaskell, and the
Brownings; and her many published works include *The Diary of an Ennuyée* (1826),
Memoirs of the Beauties of the Court of Charles II (1831), *Memoirs of Early Italian
Painters* (1845), and the voluminous *Sacred and Legendary Art* (1848-52) (Todd, 351-
53). Baillie refers to Jameson's translation of Amelia of Saxony's plays entitled *Social
Life in Germany* (1840). See introduction and letters to Jameson, Volume 2.

Bath and elsewhere are now (indeed some time since) come to south Audley St: I had a note from them this morning. All well with them & their belongings! Our young friend Sarah Bentham (M^rs le Blanc) returned from her visit to her Mother in the south of France a good while ago,[19] and has had the Countess Ladolf [Ludolf?] staying with her ever since. She has now furnish'd her house in Chapel St: and made it a little Palace, and now it is threatening to come down about her ears and will cost her a good sum of money to repair. Poor Sarah! she is well meaning but very rash, and puts me in mind of Mrs Siddons who very hastily purchased a house in South hampton, and when she was told it was a great deal too large, she said that it could be easily remedied for she could take off the roof and put down a story and put the roof on again.[20] She would have found no difficulty in dealing with your lofty Palazzo in the same manner.

My Sister sends you her kind love with mine, and we both live in hopes of seeing you again in the course of the summer. Pray do not let Rome tempt you to stay another winter! To hear of your well-being will always give pleasure to Agnes & to your affectionate friend

J Baillie

The Carrs & Lushingtons are well and the little deaf Girl really beginning to hear.

212c (Address: Lady Davy / Palazzo Valdobrundini di Respetta / Rome, Italy--postmarked 1840)

Hampstead Novr 26th 1840

My Dear Lady Davy

Your very kind and agreeable letter, of June last, was most welcome, and much we were gratified by your affectionate remembrance of us. I assure you your old friends at Hampstead think frequently of your pleasant visits when you drove up our hill and sat so cheerfully by our fireside or in the brightness of a summer day and told us all the amusing news of the gay world of London of which we were often as ignorant as if we had lived at

---

19. Sarah Bentham (1804-64) was the youngest daughter of Lady Bentham and Sir Samuel Bentham (1757-1831). Sir Samuel was a naval architect, engineer and inventor of mechanical contrivances. He was knighted and died in 1831, a year before the death of his brother Jeremy Bentham (*DNB*, II:281-84). As early as 1810, Jeremy Bentham writes about visits with Baillie (see his published correspondence).

20. Sarah Siddons (1755-1831), foremost tragic actress and friend of Baillie and the Milbankes, achieved celebrity under Garrick's management at Drury Lane, giving her farewell performance as Lady Macbeth at Covent Garden in 1812. Siddons had played Jane in Baillie's *DeMonfort* in 1800 and after her retirement continued to give private readings (*DNB*, VIII). Stories of her extravagance abound.

John 'o Groat's house.[21] Indeed we feel that while you are absent we have lost a friend and at our age, since your abode in Italy is to be prolonged, the chance of our seeing you again seems to be very doubtful. However, we must not repine; you have thoroughly enjoyed Rome and all the attractions of that happy climate & country, it has done good to your health, and therefore we should be satisfied and thankful that we <u>have</u> (have) enjoyed so much of your society. We heard of you after going to Naples and as having been ill with, I believe, influenza, but the effects of that, I hope is quite passed away. — Though I have wished for some time past to write to you I was oblig'd to be silent from not knowing your present address, I therefore wrote the other day to Mr Lockart [sic], thinking he could inform me and he has been kind enough to give it to me as he <u>believes</u> it to be, and on this his belief I venture to send my letter which I hope will find you out, and find you also well and enjoying the winter in Rome as much as the winter of last year. — I seldom have any news of public interest to communicate, but I shall speak of ourselves, knowing that your friendship will make that subject very acceptable. We have passed the summer as usual in our own home without an excursion of any kind, having little variety of employment but looking after our work people now & then, who were papering & beautifying our Drawing room, and looking over & transcribing or rather assorting my scattered rhymes as a preparation for my last dealings with the press. Our friends & neighbours were fled here & there on the sea coast & distant visits but we remained at home contentedly. Indeed we need not make any merit of this, for we are thankful that we have such a home and old folks so inert & easily tired as we are, are always best at home, even when indifferently housed. So far as the Winter is advanced we have been in pretty good health, though my Sister has frequently suffered from rheumatism and with weakness in her eyes. I was very much afraid of this last ailment, my poor Mother having been quite blind for three years before her death, but thanks God! it has very much decreased though she still wears a shade to screen them from any strong light. I have mentioned my scattered rhymes as in preparation

---

21. John o'Groats is proverbially and literally the extreme north-east corner of mainland Scotland, the opposite of Land's End. The story is that John o'Groat and his two brothers came from Holland during the reign of James IV of Scotland and purchased lands on the extreme north-eastern coast. In time there came to be eight families of the name who met every year in a house built by the founder. When there arose a question of precedence, John o'Groat built an eight-sided room with a door to each side and placed an octagonal table therein. The building thereafter was called John o'Groat's House. (My thanks go to Professor Malcolm Allen, University of Wisconsin; John Dellinger, Tucson, Arizona; and Edward Burns for concurrently providing this annotation. Also see *Brewer's Dictionary of Phrase and Fable*.)

for the press, that matter is now completed, and last week I went to Cavendish Sq^r to put up & disperse the copies of my book intended for my own friends and divers Authors from whom I have received particular civilities. The title of it is "Fugitive verses by J. Baillie" and I hope you will give it a place on your shelves when it can conveniently reach you.[22] I have put by a copy for you, and know that you will not be a fastidious Critic but read all my Ballads & Songs &c &c as though you had never known any thing about Viril [Virgil] or set (nor ever sat) foot upon Classical ground. Little of the volume is entirely new but composed of pieces that had been in various publications and were likely enough to be forgotten or lost. What reception it will receive from the public remains to be seen, though there is little encouragement for hope, as Booksellers universally declare that poetry is a <u>drug</u> in the <u>Market</u>. —— Some time ago we had a cloud cast over us by the death of our very dear friend Miss Milligan: her character was beautiful & excellent, and though she died of an illness that had lasted many months, we could not divest ourselves of hope till almost the end. Perhaps you may remember her, she once lived at Roslin in this neighbour hood and was frequently among us. She was the sister of Mr M. who married my Niece —— Since I began to write we have had a visit from Mrs Baillie who begs to be very kindly remembered to your Ladyship. She says she can never forget the ready and most important service you did her on the subscription publication of poor Mr Sumer's Poem.[23] That business turned out well and has been profitable in a considerable degree. She brought us the welcome tidings that Maria Edgeworth will be in London next week to pass the rest of the winter with Mrs Beaufort and her other Sister M^{rs} L Wilson.[24] I had had a sad misgiving that we should never meet again. She will now, perhaps enjoy her visit in Town more than she formerly did, when she was hurrying about from place to place, from sight to sight and from one gay party to

---

22. The first edition of Baillie's *Fugitive Verses* appeared in London from Moxon in 1840, followed by a second edition in 1842.

23. Unless this could be writer Charles Richard Sumner (1790-1874), praised by Macaulay in 1825, I cannot identify this writer also mentioned in the following letter.

24. Maria Edgeworth (1768-1849) first focused her writing on educational topics, translating Madame de Genlis's *Adèle et Théodore*. She experimented with various teaching methods, publishing a series including *The Parents Assistant* (1796) and *Early Lessons* (1801); but she became well known for her novels *Castle Rackrent* (1800), *Belinda* (1801), *Popular Tales* (1804), *The Modern Griselda* (1805), *Leonora* (1806), the six volume *Tales of Fashionable Life* (1809-12), *Ormond* (1817), *Helen* (1834), etc., many of which document Irish society. Edgeworth is one of the first women novelists "to apply an insight articulated by Wollstonecraft, that women have their own language" (see Todd, 204-7). Baillie and Edgeworth met in 1813 (see Scott letter 3884 ff.184-187). Her sisters are Mrs. Beaufort and Mrs. Lestock Wilson.

another with her Sisters. This remark shews how old I am, placing so much of human satisfaction on <u>rest</u>. ——— I know not that I have more to say, but that my Sister sends you her kind love & best wishes with those of your

      sincere & affectionate friend   J. Baillie

I received a letter yesterday from Miss Montgomery who is now in Paris with her sister & Lady Byron[25] where they will remain for some time. They go some times to the Play and are quite delighted with this young Jewess Actrice [sic] who is now the Queen of Tragedy in that gay metropolis.[26]

213c (Address: Lady Davy / Palazzo Valdobrundini / via di Respetta / Rome, Italy--postmarked 1841)

                         Hampstead May 3ᵈ 1841

My dear Lady Davy

    I received your kind message by Miss Coutts a good while since and requested her, when [she] should be writing to you, to say something grateful & affectionate on our part.[27] We feel, and it soothes us, that we are never entirely forgotten by you let the distance that separates us be what it may. I had intended to send my thanks & acknowledgements for your friendly and entertaining letter of the twenty first of last Decʳ the date of which gave me some compuctions [sic] of conscience, but this opportunity of sending a message through your friend made me again inactive & dilatory. Yet I know you will believe that, though my pen has not expressed it, your kind Xmas & New year wishes were heartily returned by your two old friends, and I hope this will find you in good health and with no remains of the illness we heard you had suffered early in spring. I knew you would be pleased to hear of Mʳ Sumer's promotion which you made a part of my message through Miss Coutts. I did not add to it that he was going to be married, for I hope it is not true. And yet why should one <u>hope</u> so? for no body will marry a poor, blind man

---

25. Lady Byron (Anne Isabella Milbanke, 1792-1860) married Lord Byron in 1815 and held a long correspondence with Baillie. See separate introductions and letters to Lady Byron and M. Montgomery, Volume 2.

26. This is most likely a reference to actress Elisa Felix, who became famous under the assumed name of Rachel. Born in 1821 to French Jewish parents, Rachel proved her talent as a tragic actress at the age of 17. She died of consumption at the early age of 38 (see H. Sutherland Edwards, *Idols of the French Stage*, 2 vols. [London: Remington, 1889], 2:248-72).

27. Miss Coutts is probably a granddaughter or other relative of Thomas Coutts (1735-1822) who, along with his brother James, operated one of the most successful banking houses (Coutts & Company) in the Strand (*DNB*, IV:1279). Baillie mentions in various letters doing business at Coutts.

unless one who has some affection for him and who means to make him a good Wife? —— My Sister has not been so active as usual this spring, and has done no work in the garden at all; but we have enjoyed the progress of spring, have seen our trees putting on their summer clothing by degrees, and felt the happy change in the air from cold to comfort, from gloom to sunshine with thankfulness. We went some time ago to Richmond to attend the Christening of a new grand Nephew, called James after my Father,[28] and afterwards we passed eight or ten days with Mrs Baillie in Town. We did as much there in the way of making forenoon visits to our friends –– more we could not do — and returned well pleased with ourselves & others to our quiet home again. I sat a good while with Miss Berry one day who was in very low spirits expecting daily the death of her favorite Cousin Fergusson of Raitten [Rainton?], and since then she has not only lost him but her other Cousin Genl Fergusson.[29] However, she has many friends who will help to comfort & divert her mind, and she feels that she has had enough of this world and is resigned to the will of God, humbly looking foreward to a better. We saw your friend Maria Edgeworth twice. She was then and has continued ever since in close attendance on her Sister Mrs L. Wilson, who has had another still-born child and has been dangerously ill after it. Mrs Edgeworth was to have come over from Ireland to take her place by poor Mrs Wilson, but she has been so ill after a severe, prolonged influenza, that Maria is much alarmed on her account. What a different life she has led from what she did during her former visit to London when she went about to every thing gay to introduce her young sister to the world! She has gone no where of an evening, but has been entirely devoted to her duty & affection. She can however, cry & laugh at nearly the same time and is as agreeable — perhaps more so than ever. —— We understand little about politics though we have been accustomed to think and call ourselves Whigs. What a perplexing & interesting state things are in at this moment! and who can tell what the events of this week will produce? The corn laws that were professedly held up by both Whigs & Tories to be given up to conciliate the manufacturing interest![30] What will our landed proprietors, both great & small, say to this? However, I suppose things will right themselves (as they say) some way or other and we shall still

---

28. This would have to be William and Henrietta Baillie's 4th child, actually named John Baron Baillie (1841-68). I cannot account for the name discrepancy here.

29. Mary Berry (1763-1852) was a long-time friend of Baillie and one of the first to praise her *Plays on the Passions* in 1799. Berry was also a writer and asked Baillie to write the prologue to her *Fashionable Friends* in 1801. See introduction and letters to Berry for notes on Ferguson.

30. Sir Robert Peel (1788-1850) supported free trade, and his ministry eventually pushed through the repeal of the Corn Law on 26 June 1846.

continue under a good Providence and have place & bread. Ones own Country is ones own Country, otherwise one should be almost tempted, were one young enough, to be with you in that delightful Italy which you enjoy so much and describe so well. Your Palazzo is I trust still the charming home you at first found it; and I suppose you will by & by be preparing to quit it for the warm season and take to the sea side or the mountains. Wherever you go, may you find health & happiness, but when shall we hear of your returning to England? I would fain hear something upon that subject. Your letter to Miss Coutts spoke much of the delightful society of your country men & country-women then in Rome, and more expected. This is not very encouraging for us who wish to see you here.

Our Exibition [sic] is just opened and I believe we shall go to see it, little as we are given to move about after sights, and fatiguing as the general Exhibition always is, for there is a picture of Landseer's in it, and subject taken from de Monfort, which we have naturally a curiosity to see. It is not by the first painter of that name but his Brother who is also an excellent and much admired artist.[31] When we go there, we shall miss Calcot's [sic] usual contributions that were so pleasing to look at. We saw him & his clever & excellent wife when we were in Town, she much as we had seen her last year a prisoner to her weary couch, and he feeble & delicate – but he has since been very ill. He painted nothing last year and it is feared he will never paint again.[32] –– Sarah le Blanc is in good health & good looks and is happy at the prospect of having her Mother & Sister &c. to settle for good in their own country, after a time not far distant. Her Brother with his Lady have left London entirely and become count & gentry, where he may follow his botanical pursuits as he has a mind. They have bought or taken a lease of a manor house & grounds I believe in Hereford sh[r] (near the Scademore's). The Carrs & Lushingtons are well – Laura returned from Scotland lately to attend the marriage of her cousin Miss Alison now Lady James. — My news & my paper are at an

31. Charles Landseer (1799-1879), historical painter, sent his first picture to the Royal Academy, *Dorothea* from *Don Quixote*, in 1828. In 1833 he exhibited *Clarissa Harlowe in the Spunging House*, now in the National Gallery, and was elected an associate of the Royal Academy in 1837 and keeper of the Royal Academy in 1851 (*DNB*, XI:504-5). His painting of Baillie's De Monfort was commissioned by Lady Byron ca. 1841. Sir Edwin Henry Landseer (1802-73) was a well-known animal painter.

32. Sir Augustus Wall Callcott (1779-1844) exhibited nothing but landscape paintings for many years. In 1810 he became a full member of the Royal Academy, exhibiting several paintings there every year. From 1822 until his death, however, he exhibited only 7 works, among these his best (*The Mouth of the Tyne*, *A Dead Calm on the Medway* and *Rochester*). He was knighted in 1837 by Queen Victoria (*DNB*, III:708).

end, and I must also give over. My Sister unites, for your acceptance, her (her) love & good wishes with those of your faithful & affec^t J Baillie

214c (Address: Lady Davy / Palazzo Valdobrundini via di Respetta / Rome, Italy--postmarked 1841)

[1841]

My dear Lady Davy

I suppose you have long been returned from your summer residence or rambles among the hilly regions of your delightful Italy, and are now enjoying your Winter home in Rome, where there is always so much to charm & interest you. I am ashamed of having been so long of acknowledging your very entertaining & kind letter of May 18th. I would fain persuade my self that I did write a short letter to acknowledge the receipt of your pretty present, the wooden staves &c for a basket; but my memory is so treacherous that I can put no faith in it, and it is generally safest for me to believe that what makes for my credit is less likely to be true than what makes against it. Receive then my best thanks for both. You would have been much pleased could you have seen me about 3 week[s] ago busy, with the help of Anna Carr, in setting up the divisions & fastening them with the ribbons according to our fancy; and our great admiration when we had accomplished it, and saw the elegant little Toy set upon the drawing room table, ready to receive any friendly card or other slight matter we might please to put into it. Agnes was a looker on, and you may be sure we both thought & talked of you the while. Anna was then staying with us for a few days, and Sir Culling & Lady Smith with Laura Carr, were on their way to Edin^r to pay a visit to Morton after his late marriage.[33] Probably you have heard of it. It is a match that pleases his family, though the Lady has no fortune. She is the Daughter of Lady Robert Carr, and has been very prudently brought up, though she is so highly connected. She is pretty too & accomplished. Anna herself, who used rather to stand on the back ground, has become a very agreeable, intelligent companion, tho' changes of time and the variety of scenes she has seen in Italy & in Ceylon have not been lost on her observing mind, and her ready talent for drawing whatever she sees, country, plants, beast or body, provides her with good illustrations for her story. Soon after she left us, we spent a short time with Mrs Baillie and found her or rather her Brother's family much occupied in preparation for a wedding which took

---

33. Mr. and Mrs. Thomas William Carr of Frognal, Hampstead, were the parents of Thomas, William, Frances, Isabella (Lady Smith), Anna, Laura (Lady Cranworth) and of Sarah Grace (Mrs. Stephen Lushington). Thomas Carr was solicitor to the excise and a close friend of the Benthams.

place the other day. We went one evening to Portland Place and saw all the near connections of both parties assembled to become known to one another, like meetings of that kind more ceremonious than gay. The Bride groom is Mr Henry Macaulay whose elder Brother has probably the honour of being known to your Ladyship, and Margaret Denman, the fourth Daughter of the Chief Justice, is the Bride.[34] She is very pretty & amiable and he clever & agreeable and we hope they will be happy though their worldly means is small. However, being by no means a romantic person, I must own I begrudge having our pretty Margaret (so we used to call her) pass through the difficulties of being a poor man's wife. Her Father & Mother seem to be quite satisfied with it. They are not so ambitious as I should have [been] in their place, and are perhaps the wiser for it. Among the few friends we saw while in Town were Miss Sotheby & Harriet who passed an evening with us both looking well and in good spirits.[35] They brought Capt Thurston the Widower of their Cousin, who seems now in some degree to have regained his spirits which were miserably low when we first met him after the death of his Wife. They gave us a good account of all their friends about Loughton and the Manor house. Before we left Cavendish Sq^r we had the satisfaction of seeing the walls of the drawing room enriched with a painting by Chas. Landseer, taken from my Play of de Monfort, the moment of time is when the officers of Justice come with the irons to fetter de Mon and Jane kneels to them to spare him that degradation. The story is in many respects well told, though Jane is much too young, and the colouring is beautiful. It was painted for my partial friend Lady Byron, as a present to me, and our rooms here being too small for such a picture, I begged it might be hung up in Cavendish Square. I hope you'll see it when you return to London. Ah! when will that be? I long much to hear about it. I & my Sister are both too old to look forward to any distant pleasure in this world.

I know you will not be pleased if I do not say something on the subject of health, and I am thankful to say we are both pretty well. She has frequently rhuematism [sic] & stomach ailments as usual, but upon the whole she has passed this first part of the winter comfortably; the great trial for old folks – the frost & snow of Dec^r & January ly[e] still before us. Agnes as a cure for her cramps has been advised to take a roll of Brimston [brimstone] to bed to clutch in her hand when she feels the pain beginning,

---

34. Henry Macaulay was the brother of Thomas Babington Macaulay (1800-59), historian and essayist. Henry married Sophia Denman Baillie's niece Margaret, daughter of Lord Chief Justice Thomas Denman.

35. See introduction to the letters to William Sotheby for details on family members.

and she really thinks there is virtue in it. She has tried it however only 3 nights. I am occupied at present in correcting my fugitive verses for a cheap edition to be printed in colums [sic] like those that Moxon has published for Rogers & Campbell, he was very earnest I should allow him to do so, a t his own risk, and though I am not like them a very popular writer, I hope he will not be a loser by it.[36] It will make a convenient travelling or fireside book, as it will be so light that it may be held up in the hand with ease. ——— I wish I had something to say of your friend Mr Lockhart but him I have not seen since last spring. I have heard much lately of the beauty of his new illustrated edition of the Spanish Ballads, published by Murray: from hearing of it so much I hope they are making money of it, notwithstanding the great expense of the drawings & engravings.[37] ———

I hope your summer was spent happily in whatever directions your wanderings lay and that you have returned in improved health to enjoy your Palazzo & friends & antiquities in Rome. You were kind enough to mention the Somervilles and her occupation in preparing a new work for the press. I wish Mrs Somerville success in every thing she undertakes, and health & happiness to her good husband and all that belong to her. She does us so much honour in those matters in which we are most supposed to be incapable & deficient that all her sex are in duty bound to bid her God speed! in whatever she writes. If she is in Rome and you should meet soon, pray tell her of Lady Byron's present to me of Landseer's picture! it will give her pleasure. ——— With every kind & affectionate wish in which my Sister joins me most sincerely, I remain, my dear Lady Davey [sic], very truly yours

J Baillie

215c (Address: Lady Davy / Palazzo Valdobrundini via di Respetta / Rome, Italy--postmarked 1842)

Hampstead May 6th 1842

My Dear Lady Davy,

Your affectionate greeting on Xmas day would have done our hearts good could we have been aware that you were then thinking of us, and it did us good afterwards when we received it in due course. Your letters are always interesting & amusing from the beautiful varied country you pass through in your summer excurtions and discribe so well, and when a tremendous thunderstorm makes one of the events of your journey, what can the imagination possibly desire more. I should gladly, however, have

---

36. This is probably Moxon's 1842 2nd edition of *Fugitive Verses*.

37. John Gibson Lockhart's *Ancient Spanish Ballads, Historical and Romantic, translated, with Notes* originally appeared in 1823.

exchanged all that part of your letter for a few lines containing a better account of your health, and adding you were now so well as to think of turning your face northward when you next leave Rome for the summer. I long to hear something to this amount, but neither letter nor rumour of it reaches me any way. But perhaps I may soon, and it is not wise to lose hope be one ever so old. ——— We are now enjoying on our hill all the bright freshness of spring, its light green foliage and garden trees covered with blossoms. This is gratifying after the long disagreeable winter we have passed, and the almost impossibility, by any means, of keeping ourselves warm, either by fires, cloaks, shawls, boas or any other appliances. This is one of the infirmities (infirmities) of old age, the great difficulty of being kept warm; but we should not murmur, for we have had pretty good health throughout and have been mercifully spared. Agnes at present receives great compliments upon her good looks with some reason, but I have of late received none, and indeed when I look at my shrunk, <u>quilted</u> face in the glass I cannot wonder at it. Thank God! Mrs Baillie and our other <u>belongings</u> at Richmond & the Isle of Wight are all well. ——— Your old acquaintance M^{rs} Le Blanc (Sarah Bentham) has been a busy & anxious woman for some time past with a business in which I know your Ladyship will sincerely simpathize, striving to vindicate her Father's right to be considered as the inventor of the floating Break-water about to be considered at Plymouth and for which a patent is to be granted to some young Engineer claiming it for <u>his</u> invention. Sir Samuel Bentham published naval Essays many years ago, in the fifth No of which (for they were published in numbers) this contrivance of a floating Break-water is proposed & explained, but wonderful to say and very provoking also, this 5 No. can be found no where. She wrote me about it and I applied to Longman, who published it, to make every possible search in his premises for this particular number which he has done; she has also applied to all her Father's friends to whom he had sent the work, yet, though all the other numbers have been recovered, this is no where to be found.[38] I am

---

38. I have been unable to verify this intriguing story. The National Maritime Museum in Greenwich own a work by John White entitled *An Essay on the Formation of Harbours of Refuge, and the Improvements of the Navigation of Rivers and Sea Ports, by the Adoption of Moored Floating Constructions as Breakwaters* (London: J. Weale, 1840) which states that

David Gordon, Esq., of Edinburgh, in January, 1822, took out a patent for improvements in steamboats and packets, and, as part of his patent he embraces a plan for making a *chevaux de frise*, or an arrangement of spikes to be affixed to a floating frame, which he contemplates being anchored at a sufficient distance from the bow of a ship as a breakwater. Whether this contrivance can be employed upon a considerable scale may be questioned; as, however it bears upon the subject, it may be properly noticed here, and

sure you will enter into the feelings of poor Sarah & her Mother on this occasion. The circumstance altogether seems to me very unaccountable. Lady Bentham with Mad^{me} de Chesnel & her two Grand Children are coming to England the end of this summer (so she confidently says) to settle again in Hampstead,[39] and I am sure we shall be glad to have her again as our near Neighbour; for with many peculiarities of character there are few people whose conversation is more agreeable. -- Every body at present is busy reading Mad^{me} Daurbley's [sic] Diary glad to get some insight into the literary society of Dr Johnson's & Mrs Montague's days and into the daily small occurrences of Queen Charlotte's court at Windsor.[40] In portions it is clever & amusing, and in other <u>pretty considerable</u> portions dull & wearisome; yet no body can refrain from reading it. Court Gossip even more than village gossip is an attractive thing. -- For my Sister she has been most occupied with Stephen's account of the lately discovered ruins in Central America[41] and referring very diligently to Herrera's account of the large cities still flourishing in that country when Cortes conquered the Kingdom of Mexico,[42] being by nature more of an antiquarian than a gossip. But, no doubt, both those works have found their way to Rome and you are already acquainted with them. --- I know how much you must have grieved for the affliction of your excellent friends at Loughton on the death of their only & beloved Daughter. She has also been very much lamented by her Husband's family. I had a Note from Miss Sotheby some time ago, full of warm praises of her whom she still calls their dear Jane Hamilton, and pitying much her parents and the poor young widower she has left behind. Soon after Xmas, when we were about a fortnight in Cavendish Sq^r, we saw her & Harriet with their friend Capt. (Capt) Thurston who came to pass an evening with us there; they

---

also, that the late Mr. Bentham was of the opinion that a system of buoys could be so moored as to produce the effect of the breakwater at Plymouth. (9)

39. Mary Sophia (1797-1865), the oldest daughter of Lady and Sir Samuel Bentham, married Louis-Pierre-François-Adolphe, marquis de Chesnel de la Charbonnelaye in 1819; he deserted her and their daughter in 1820.

40. Francis Burney D'Arblay (1752-1840), daughter of author and musician Charles Burney, married Alexandre D'Arblay in 1793. Following her earlier novels, *Evelina* (1778) and *Cecilia* (1782) and others, was her *Diary and Letters*, published posthumously in 1842.

41. In letter 62, ff.123-124, to Lady Byron, Baillie refers to American lawyer and travel writer John Lloyd Stephens's (1805-52) *Incidents of travel in Yucatan* published by Murray in London. This appears to be the same book, though the publication date is actually 1843.

42. This is probably a reference to Spanish historian Antonio de Herrera y Tordesillas (d. 1625). See letter 24 to Dr. Andrews Norton, Volume 2.

were both well and looking well. We have not met since, for our visits to Town have been too short to admit of it.

I suppose Mrs Somerville & Family are still in Rome and I hope the Doctor's health is now in an improved state. Pray give my very kindest rembrances [sic]. To hear her name mentioned here as I often do, gives me always a feeling of pride & gratification. She would be sorry to hear of poor Mrs Montgomery's death. I had a letter from your friend Miss Doyle the other day,[43] informing me of it: and poor Miss Doyle herself is very anxious on her Sister Mrs Davidson's account who is in Paris, and, at the date of her letter, dangerously ill. —— They are told that Miss Coutts has taken a long lease of Holly Lodge from the Duke of St: Albins; if this be true we shall have a better chance of seeing her now & then when she takes a morning drive. I hope it is true; for we find her very agreeable when we do meet. My Sister sends her love & best wishes which you will please to accept, my dear Lady Davy, along with those of your faithful & affectionate

J Baillie

216c (Address: Lady Davy--no postmark))

Hampstead Feby 6th 1843

My Dear Lady Davy,

I have thought of you often and have enquired after you at our friend Mr Lockhart, but it is long, and from my own fault too, since words – written words have passed between us. Allow me now to enquire how you do and how you have passed the winter, after all the excitement & exertions of the previous summer. Well, I hope, and fraught with many new ideas from the country you have visited that will prove a lasting amusement to your own mind, and, through you, to others. I believe no body with such advantages and so capable of profiting by them has visited the Turks & their sultanas since the days of Lady Mary Wortley.[44] Your diary or book of recollections & observations (for no doubt you have made one) will be a most desirable thing to peep into, and many will long for that privilege. Though turkish society is pretty stationary in its customs & opinions, many changes to a close observer must have taken place since

---

43. Selina Doyle was a friend to both Judith and Annabella Milbanke; she consulted with Annabella on and strongly supported her separation from Byron. The reference is to the death of Mary Montgomery's sister-in-law; see letter 93, ff.227-228 to Montgomery, 8 May 1842.

44. Lady Mary Wortley Montagu (1689-1762) wrote descriptive and astute letters while accompanying her ambassador husband to Turkey in 1716. From the letters composed at the time, she later composed a brilliant travel book, leaving it to be published after her death.

Lady Mary's time. ——— Though I have written Lockhart to enquire after you, I have not met him for a long time, but I saw your God Daughter Charlotte, not very long ago, and was very much pleased with the improvement that appears in her countenance & manners. I think she will turn out a pretty and very pleasing young woman. Her Brother I have not seen for a year or more, but I am told he has become a handsome Lad very agreeable & sociable and his company in great request. They seem both grand children such as our dear Sir Walter would have liked, and I hope through life they will do him credit.[45] — Your friend Miss Edgeworth was to have passed part of the winter & spring in London with her Sisters, but she was taken with a dangerous illness just before she was to have left home and is now recovering slowly[.] I received a short note from her, but not written by her own hand, to inform me of it, about a fortnight ago. There is her native cheerfulness in it, mixed with a serious impression of the precarious state she is in and great resignation. The Southeby's [*sic*] have been staying with Mrs Andre at Bath;[46] and have been made very happy by the honours their Brother has gained in Indea, where he has done good service and come off with a whole skin. Lady Bentham & the french part of her family are living in her son's house in 2. Sq^r Place Westminster. They are now to become entirely English. — You will be glad to hear that Agnes & I have got pretty well through the winter which has been generally mild. We both unite, my dear Lady Davy, in love & kind wishes to you. Affectionately yours

J Baillie

PS I believe your Ladyship is acquainted with Miss Montgomery now residing in Rome and often with the Somervilles. I inclose this to her, not knowing your present address.

---

45. Sir Walter Scott's daughter Sophia married John Gibson Lockhart in 1820; their daughter Charlotte later married James Robert Hope. Son Hugh Lockhart died in 1831, so this must be a reference to son Walter Scott Lockhart.

46. Baillie mentions the Andre sisters in several letters; but the only identification I have made is of Major John Andre (1751-80), in charge of the secret negotiations with Benedict Arnold concerning the intended betrayal of West Point. He was captured and hanged as a spy (1780), leaving three sisters: Mary Hannah, Anne Marguerite, and Louisa Catherine (see Robert McConnell Hatch, *Major Andre: a Gallant in Spy's Clothing* [Boston: Houghton Mifflin, 1986]).

217c (Address: Lady Davy / Park Street / Grosvenor Square--postmarked 1843)

Hampstead tuesday evening
August 1$\underline{st}$ [1843]

My dear Lady Davy,

It is full time that we should thank you for the elegant paper knife received by Mrs Baillie last saturday. It is a useful & acceptable present, and will put us often in mind of your Ladyship as it lies upon our table. Many thanks! —— Your kindness in coming to see us after so long an absence we felt very gratefully: and did not some gracious words fall from your lips, as you went away —— that you would perhaps see us again, before leaving Town, and in the evening as the time most convenient for you? Pray make good those words, if it may be, and come any evening, after next friday, when a friend may possibly be with us who has bargained that we shall be alone! To hope for this, I know, considering how much your time must be occupied, is some what presumptuous, but we trust to your indulgence. ——

Mrs Baillie has been with us since Saturday and left us to day. She has been very anxious and so have we, about her little Grandaughter [*sic*] who has been taken ill at Ryde, where she went to visit her Aunt, with scarlet fever.[47] The accounts, however, to day are very favourable and our minds easier.

My Sister unites with me in love & best wishes and we both beg to be remembered to Miss Stuart.

Yours, my dear Lady Davy, truly & affectionately
J Baillie

219c (Address: Lady Davy / Grosvenor Hotel / Park Street / Grosvenor Square--postmarked 1843)

[1843]

My dear Lady Davy,

We were very <u>very</u> sorry to learn by your kind letter of yesterday, that while we had been thinking of you as enjoying in the country the society of your friends, you were confined in London with illness. Unceasing sickness and severe spasms are most distressing while they last, and God grant, as they have been relieved by the hot vapour Bath, they will soon, under the care of your able Physician be sent off altogether! Had we known that you were still in Town, we should have contrived some how or other to have got to the Grosvenor Hotel, and will now, I hope, have the satisfaction ere

---

47. This could be Sophy Milligan, then about 26 and not so "little," but is likely William Baillie's daughter Sophia Joanna Baillie, then about 7, visiting her aunt.

long of hearing there that you are making progress to a perfect restoration.
——

You will be pleased to hear, kind & considerate as you have always been to us, that we have been in pretty good [health?], and have not as yet [been] much affected by the many changes of weather on our cold hill. We shall feast on the pheasants with good appetite, I dare say, and I am sure will like them all the better for coming from so kind a friend. Many thanks! — My Sister begs to offer her love.

I rest, my dear Lady Davy,
affectionately yours
J Baillie
Hampstead
thursday morning
PS. Your Ladyship has been too bountiful in sending <u>two</u> birds; one of them, nearly as large as a Turkey[.]

220c (Address: Lady Davy / Park Street / Grosvenor Square--postmarked 1845)

Hampstead
Decr 23 [1845]

My dear Lady Davy,
we were sorry to learn from your kind note that instead of going to enjoy yourself with friends in the country, the day after you parted with us, you have been kept in Town by illness and under medical care; happily so skilful. I hope it will soon be entirely passed away!

Ma[n]y thanks for rembering [sic] us so kindly! all your friendly wishes of the season are returned by my Sister & myself most heartily. May you live many years to give pleasure to your friends! a wish that may still be desired for <u>you</u>, though to the old it could not fail to be a very sad one. Our united good wishes, also, we beg to offer to your amiable Niece.

Poor Agnes has been suffering a good deal from her usual maladies but nothing to make us anxious. We were in Town last saturday having business to do both in Cavendish Sqr. and elsewhere, but unless to look at the Children in Cavendish Sq^r, she never got out of the carriage. We came home tired enough, and sat all the evening by the fire talking over the events of the day like two weary Travellers. Hoping ere long that one of your morning drives will be in this direction, I rest, dear Lady Davy

your most truly   J Baillie
I have mislaid your kind note and if I have omitted to say any thing I ought to have said pardon it[.]

221c (Address: Lady Davy / Park Street / Grosvenor Square--postmarked 1845)

Hampstead Decr 26th 1845

My Dear Lady Davy,

Your Cricket on the hearth has cheered us and how could it do otherwise when it reminded us of your kindness — of your kind consideration of two old friends who have not much to enliven or amuse them on Xmas eve or any eve of the whole year. Truly we feel that you think of us and care for us and we both thank your Ladyship very truly. —— It's great value is being your gift, but it is really a most beautiful thing to look at, both inside & out and will do much credit to our parlor table and help us to amuse some of our morning visitors when conversation begins to flag. ——

I hope all remains of your cold has past away. I trust you received a note from me some days ago, and that it was understood, though it was so written that I could scarcely make it out myself. I should have written it over again, if I had not been pretty sure the second would be no better than the first. Since then, my chief occupation has been wiping my nose: one of those stuffy head colds has made me very stupid, but is, I think wearing away. —— Agnes would, I know charge me with some especial kind words of thanks, but she is at present so busy with The Cricket that I dont like to disturb her.

May a happy new year — may many happy new years lie before you, my very kind friend!

yours affect^y   J Baillie

223c (Address: Lady Davy / Park Street / Grosvenor Square--postmarked 1846)

My dear Lady Davy

Your nice Pheasant has come to hand this afternoon by the way of Harley St: You are very kind & very mindful of us and pray receive our best thanks. It shall be our Sunday's dinner, and will taste all the better for having come from so kind a friend. Agnes continues getting better, but she is ordered to keep the house entirely not even to go out for a short airing in a close carriage. ——— We have been very anxious about our very dear Mrs Hoare[48] but are some what relieved to day by a favourable report from Mr Evans.

---

48. Mrs. Hoare, Louisa Gurney, married Samuel Hoare, Lady Byron's banker, and Baillie was a close friend of his family. Children she mentions include Jane, Joseph and several others.

We most heartily wish you all the good wishes of the season, and I hope the little worries hinted at will very soon be got over and your own sociable spirit be left free for enjoyment —

Do not think of coming to see us till it may be done with perfect safety.

Yours, my dear Lady Davy
     with affectionate regard
          J: Baillie
Hampstead Decr 24th [1846]

224c (Address: Lady Davy / Park Street / Grosvenor Square--postmarked 1847)

[1847]

And many thanks to your Ladyship for your kind present of a Pheasant & hare which we shall certainly eat with the better relish in thinking of the friend who sent it – a friend who has for many years always been mindful of us though having so many connections with the gay world as naturally to draw her attention away.

But this is a sad account you give us of yourself — still so bound by the cramp! but thaw is now come and warmer weather which we hope will last long enough to allow our Invalids to recover. My Sister joins me in offering her kind love & thanks. She is but for heart-burn & cramps pretty well. We are however both confined to the house. ——

Yours, dear Lady Davy, affectionately
     J Baillie

225c (Address: Lady Davy / The Right Honb^{le} Lord Polworths / Mertoun House / St: Boswells--postmarked 1848)

Hampstead friday Sepr 29th [1848]

I thank you, my Dear Lady Davy, for your letter from Abbotsford, and am glad to hear that you found every thing improved around the house and every thing within it, books, pictures & curiosities in such good preservation. I am indeed glad to hear it, though I heartily wish there had never been better than a Country Squire's house upon that bend of the Tweed. All the kindness —— the affectionate kindness I & my Sister have received there, and all the ultra abused hospitality that took place afterwards, come into my mind at once and create a strange mixture of feelings. Abbotsford was the last house in Scotland I & my Sister rested in and I left it with a heavy heart, though little could I foresee the changes that were to follow. The Hopes being there is a return of brightness, and may prosperity rest with all that remains of his family. ———[49]

We are glad also to hear the journey that took you to the Tweed was so agreeable; I know a little of the country round Dumfries though I am sorry to say nothing of Drumlaness [Drumlasie?]; yet I believe we saw a distant view of a part of the Castle and some of the fine spreading forest trees, beneath which we could easily imagine there were old Caledonian Cattle with their white skins & black ears grazing at the moment. ——— May all that remains of your summer excursion prove prosperous! and may we see you restored to us again in good health, prepared to go through the coming winter bravely. ——

Your poor friends Agnes & myself do as well as we can and try to be grateful as we ought, for the mercies that remain to us. Pain from cramps &c &c and much debility are in her portion – no pain & somewhat less debility are in mine. We hope to be well enough to get to Church next Sunday, and we do not look very far before us in this world. Our Harley Street friends are not yet returned from the North, and in the mean time we take care of their little girl, who is rosy & merry and delights & tires us by turns, particularly in rainy days. This I am sorry to say is the case at present, and we are anxious to get the Bricklayers to stop up cracks on our tiles, and cannot get it done. —— Mʳˢ Hoare & some of our kindest neighbours are still absent.

If this should find you still at Abbotsford, Give my kind love to the present Lady of the place, and should you meet Miss Pringle again, have the goodness to mention how pleased we are with her remembering us. —— In looking over what I have written, I find that I have not said all that I naturally should regarding the woods & improvements belonging to Abbotsford, yet there is not a slope or a nook, wild or dressed, about his house — that wonderful man's house, that has not an interest for me. You describe the Tweed beautifully as to the general Character of the river and truthfully, yet being seen through the trees is better than being more seen at Abbotsford for there is no silvery margin for the water to ripple upon just at that spot, and this, I think could not be remedied. I have heard of the neighbours at Kirklands. Richardson good man set himself down there just to be near Sir Walter.[50] ——

---

49. Charlotte Harriet Jane Lockhart married James Robert Hope on 19 August 1847 and later inherited Abbotsford. Abbotsford had fallen into disrepair after the death of Scott, and Hope did wonders to restore it, building a new wing in 1855 (see William Smith and W. S. Crockett, *Abbotsford* [London: Adam and Charles Black, 1905], 158).

50. John Richardson (1780-1864) was a parliamentary solicitor and for 30 years discharged the duties of crown agent for Scotland, reputed as the most learned peerage

And now, my dear Lady Davy, receive the love & thanks of both your poor old friends here, and
believe me always
truly & affectionately yours
J Baillie

229c (No address or postmark)

Hampstead monday Nov.ʳ 16ᵗʰ [1848]
My Dear Lady Davy,

It has given us great pleasure to learn from your kind letter that you have had so much enjoyment in Scotland. It has cheered us here sitting at our quiet fire side to fancy your happenings & activity among those beautiful romantic scenes of our native country that we shall never see again. To take the homliest [*sic*] way of estimating it we may say "it is not lost that a friend gets[.]" The country round Lord Bredalbain: Castle we are somewhat acquainted with; Agnes & I with a friend once past two or three days at Fay Mouth and visited from thence the Falls of Moness; the most sublime sight of rocks & water I ever beheld, though I have since stood at foot of the great fall of Chafhausen.[51] To be sure the Scotch burn – for it is little better – was then swelled with several preceding thunder showers. But no more of this till we meet which is a pleasure at no great distance now, I trust, since your Ladyship is not on your way home.

Indeed you have been very kind in thinking of us, and we both feel it. What I have to say in reply to your friendly enquiries is as favorable as could reasonably be expected, though we have heavy colds hanging about us for a month. We have been living very much in a damp fogg all that time, and many of our young neighbours have been worse off. We have had our Gᵈ Niece Sophy Milligan with us for a few days, and William with his kindly wife see us as often as they can. They are in the uneasy state of being about to leave their house in Cavendish Sq.ʳ for a larger one in Upper Harley St. and they wish to dispose of their long lease of the old house but have not yet found a purchaser or Tenant.

---

lawyer of his time. He had literary tastes and in 1821 was introduced to George Crabbe in Joanna Baillie's house; he regularly corresponded with Walter Scott, whose deathbed he attended shortly before Scott's demise. He married Elizabeth Hill, a close friend of Thomas Campbell, in 1811 and had several children (*DNB*, XVI:1118-19). Richardson submitted "Song - Her features speak the warmest heart" for Baillie's 1823 collection and in a letter dated 18 January 1842 tells Baillie, "It is, as it has long been, a great pride and gratification to me to have enjoyed your friendship; a few circumstances of my life have afforded me more real pleasure" (NLS Ms 3990, f.41).

51. This must be a reference to the Rhine Falls at Schaffhausen.

Accept my Sister's love & thanks along with mine, my dear Lady Davy, my eyes are weak with the effects of the cold, and I have little more to say, but that I always am very truly & gratefully yours

J Baillie

228c (No address or postmark)

Hampstead wednesday morning [1848?]

My Dear Lady Davy,

We receive your kind wishes of the season and all your other friendly expressions as proofs of your affectionate regard for us which we have long enjoyed and know will steadily remain with us to the end – We receive them all very gratefully. Accept in return our kindest love & Xmas wishes; would they could really avail & their influenza & every evil thing would keep aloof from your dwelling. We are sorry to hear that while we were thinking of you as still enjoying yourself with different friends in the country, after your return from that delightful excurtion to Scotland, you have been a poor Invalid, confined to your own dressing room and tormented with cough & spasm. We hope your amendment, now begun, will proceed prosperously, and that you will still continue to be prudent. I need not say that we shall be most happy to see you when it shall be perfectly agreeable & safe to go so far up our cold hill, but not one hour sooner. Agnes & I have hitherto fared better than could have been expected, though she has suffered considerably. She makes her day very short by getting up late & going to bed early, and I believe she is very right. We are both like Pilgrims near the end of a long journey, and hope that we shall be mercifully received into a better home & country when we get there. We have no future that we can reasonably look forward to here, yet we sit by the fire & read the newspaper and conjecture & take interest in what is to come like younger folks.

William & his Wife were here to [sic] days ago and are to dine (dine) with us to morrow; they are both pretty well & the Children all flourishing. They are now beginning to move from Cavendish Sq^r to a larger house in upper Harley Street: a most dismal time for such work! I mention them & their motions because I know your Ladyship kindly takes an interest in them.[52] —— We have heard some time since that your young friend & God Daughter Charlotte Lockhart is going soon to be married to a very rich Scotch Squire; if he be good also, I hope it is true. She is a

---

52. Because of the reference to Davy's visit to Scotland, this letter should probably be dated 1848 and follow letter 225c. At this time William and Henrietta would have had six children, moving to Upper Harley Street in Baillie's later years.

pretty, engaging creature; and all blessing be upon her head for her Grand Father's sake! — Yours my dear friend, affectionately

    J Baillie

227c (Address: Lady Davy / Park Street / Grosvenor Square--postmarked 1849)

My dear Lady Davy,

    I am glad that you have had so much pleasure in such a charming abode. We (my Sister & I) ought to rejoice in every thing that gives you pleasure and does you good, for you are always most kind & mindful of us. —— The Brace of Grouse was (was) duly received and the name was on the card but my head was so confused at the time that I wrote not a line to any body. — Indeed I can scarcely do it now, though much better than I was in this respect. — It will be a comfort to us to see you again on your return to Town and to mark the good effects of the country air upon your countenance.

    My Sister send[s] her love & thanks along with mine and believe me my dear & kind friend affectionately yours

    J Baillie

Your Ladiship's kind gifts are now coming into my thought many fold but I must send this to post without further delay

Hampstead tuesday Septr 11th [1849]

226c (No address or postmark, ML dates 1850)

                                         [1850?]

My dear Lady Davy

    Your very animated cheering letter from Bourne mouth has done us good and I intended to thank you for it by my Niece Sophy Milligan's pen but she has been prevented and you will not mind my slow pen & confused head[.]

230c (No address or postmark)

My dear Lady Davy

    We shall, I hope, be in Town to morrow to stop for a week or ten days with Mrs Baillie; when you are taking your morning drive pray remember us and take Cavendish Sq^r on your way. We shall call in Park St: as soon as we can, but Agnes is not at her best just now, though her late troublesome ailment is entirely gone.

    Your obligd & affec^t

        J Baillie

Hampstead Monday Jany 21st

The following undated letter is owned by the National Library of Scotland, transcribed by their permission:

2524 ff.74-75 (No address or postmark)

Hampstead thursday
morning [before November 1832]

My dear Lady Davy,

I am writing to trouble you with a note yet I cannot refrain from expressing my mortification & regret that you should have driven away from our door on tuesday without our having had the pleasure of seeing you. And it provokes me to think that I should have been sitting at the window all the time, for not knowing you at that distance and being quite ignorant that my Sister had given directions to the Maid to let no body in as we were dressing, on seeing your servant return from our door to the carriage and the carriage & Ladies then drive off, I naturally concluded that it was some of our neighbours who had merely stopped to give in some note or message. — When your cards were brought to me, I desired our damsel to run after the carriage & stop it, but it was then too late. I must henceforth make an agreement with my Sister that when she goes to dress she must not include me in her arrangements of exclusion. Indeed we are both vexed at this circumstance, but hope that you will not punish us for it. This is delightful weather for driving out, and excepting next tuesday I dont know a day when we are likely to be from home for a good while. But if it would not be giving you too much trouble, might I beg that you would give us notice by a note by the penny post, and then come early & put up your horses and make a long visit & ramble on the heath as much as you pleased. I need scarcely say any friend who might be with you we should also be happy to see. — My Sister unites with me in all kind wishes & regards

Yours, my dear Lady Davy
truly & affectionately
J Baillie

PS. I have this moment received by post a letter from Abbotsford with very cheering accounts of Sir Walter. ——

---

* This index is based on the most
common occurrences of names and
titles in Baillie's letters. Because
relatives like Agnes Baillie, Sophia
Baillie, William Baillie, etc., are
mentioned in almost every letter, not
every occurrence is indexed.